Nonverbal Communication:
The Unspoken Dialogue

Judee K. Burgoon
University of Arizona

David B. Buller
University of Arizona

W. Gill Woodall
University of New Mexico

1817

HARPER & ROW, PUBLISHERS, New York
Grand Rapids, Philadelphia, St. Louis, San Francisco,
London, Singapore, Sydney, Tokyo

Sponsoring Editor: Barbara Cinquegrani
Project Editor: Lenore Bonnie Biller
Text Design: Caliber Design Planning, Inc.
Cover Design: Delgado Design
Text Art: Fineline Illustrations, Inc.
Photo Research: Mira Schachne
Production Manager: Jeanie Berke
Production Assistant: Paula Roppolo
Compositor: ComCom Division of Haddon Craftsmen, Inc.
Printer and Binder: R. R. Donnelley & Sons Company
Cover Printer: Lehigh Press

NONVERBAL COMMUNICATION: The Unspoken Dialogue

Library of Congress Cataloging in Publication Data

Burgoon, Judee K.
    Nonverbal communication : the unspoken dialogue / Judee K.
Burgoon, W. Gill Woodall, David B. Buller.
        p.   cm.
    Includes index.
    ISBN 0-06-041044-2
    1. Nonverbal communication (Psychology)   I. Buller, David B.
II. Woodall, William Gill.   III. Title.
BF637.N66B87 1989
153.6—dc19   88-16591
                                                    CIP

89 90 91 92 9 8 7 6 5 4 3 2 1

To Michael, for making the unspoken dialogue lively,
To Erin, for keeping it joyful,
To Mary, for lending it spirit,
To Caitlin, for giving it wisdom, and
To Patricia, for making it lasting;
To Bradley, for teaching us about obverses, and
To Captain Communication, for putting it all in perspective.

CONTENTS

**5   Relationships Between Verbal and Nonverbal
     Communication   153**

PART II   Nonverbal Communication Functions   183

**6   Identification of Culture, Race, Gender, and
     Personality   185**

PREFACE

Humans are social creatures. We spend most of our waking hours in contact with other people—learning, working, playing, courting, parenting, negotiating, buying and selling, and just plain talking. We supplement this interpersonal contact by reading about people, watching them on television or in movies, listening to them on the radio, or interacting with them via telephones and computers. With so much of our day-to-day existence spent in sending and consuming communication, it is not surprising that people have become increasingly aware of nonverbal communication. One purpose of this text is to point up what a profound effect nonverbal communication has on our personal lives.

Nonverbal communication also plays a significant role in our professional lives. Surveys among business leaders, major employers, and employment counselors emphasize the importance of communication skills in acquiring jobs and performing effectively on the job. A study by the Administrative Management Society, for example, found that 80% of the managers rated communication skills as among the most important qualifications of prospective employees; 65% also cited interpersonal and leadership skills. A survey among women managers on strategies or techniques they credited with helping them reach their current positions further endorsed the importance of communication abilities. Rated as very or extremely important were communication skills (89%), personal power (78%), and charisma, charm, and social skills (53%). In another study by a college placement service, several hundred alumni reported that communication abilities were more important to their job success than the major subject they studied. And a local conciliation court reports that for the 14th year in a row, the number one reported problem among troubled marriages is the lack of good communication.

Although communication competence is not determined solely by nonverbal skills, they constitute a major component of the communication process. Yet for a long time the study of nonverbal communication was dismissed as trivial or suspicious. In a more sardonic moment, Aldous Huxley (1954) wrote:

> When it comes to any form of non-verbal education more fundamental (and more likely of some practical use) than Swedish drill, no really respectable person in any really respectable university or church will do anything about it. . . . Intellectuals feel that "what we perceive by the eye (or in any other way) is foreign to us as such and need not impress us deeply." Besides, this matter of education in the non-verbal humanities will not fit into any of the established pigeonholes. It is not religion, not neurology, not gymnastics, not morality or civics, not even experimental psychology. This being so, the subject is, for academic and ecclesiastical purposes, non-existent and may be safely ignored altogether or left, with a patronizing smile, to those whom the Pharisees of verbal orthodoxy call cranks, quacks, charlatans and unqualified amateurs. (pp. 76–77)

Much to our relief, this scorn for the subject has abated. In fact, the respectability of studying nonverbal behavior and communication is evident in the increase in writings on the subject. As one of us noted in 1980:

> If nonverbal communication in the 1950s and 1960s was regarded as the foundling child of the social sciences—disdained, neglected, even nameless—the 1970s marked a transition toward a legitimate and identifiable area of scholarship. An increasing consciousness and conscientiousness regarding nonverbal communication was reflected in the publication of literally thousands of articles related to it, in its emergence as a topic for courses and textbooks, and in its skyrocketing popularity with the lay public. (Burgoon, 1980, p. 179)

Interest in nonverbal communication has been unceasing ever since, to the point that the amount of information has become overwhelming. Our mission in writing this textbook has therefore been to sift through the voluminous literature on nonverbal communication and, while attempting to be comprehensive and current, to select the most valid and valuable information and distill it into useful, understandable principles. In contrast to Huxley's gloomy assessment, knowledge about nonverbal communication now springs from such fountainheads as psychology, psychiatry, sociology, anthropology, linguistics, semiotics, and biology, in addition to the field of communication itself. Trying to make sense of this diverse body of information is no small task, especially given that scholars from different fields approach nonverbal behavior with differing perspectives, assumptions, and methodologies. It is our hope that in taking the eclectic approach of drawing on all of these fields, we have escaped the plight of the three blind men trying to describe an elephant, each with only a limited experience of one part of the elephant's anatomy.

This does not mean, however, that there is no underlying perspective that unifies our orientation to nonverbal behavior. We believe that nonverbal *communication* can best be understood according to the functions or purposes it performs. This approach has been increasingly embraced by scholars and guided the precursor to this text, *The Unspoken Dialogue* (Burgoon & Saine, 1978). We discuss the primary features of this approach in Chapter 1. Its main significance is that it integrates various elements of nonverbal communication into the way people intuitively understand it. It makes it easier to answer the question, "What can nonverbal communication do for me or to me?" We believe that people are far more interested in knowing how to use nonverbal communication to make a good impression on an employer, influence a group, keep a conversation going, interpret a friend's emotional expressions, or woo a mate than to know how many different ways people use eye contact or how frequently they touch. Consequently, most of this textbook is organized around the communication functions in which nonverbal behavior plays a central role. The opening chapters supply some necessary background before the functions themselves can be explored fully. Our intent in taking this approach is to make the material as practical and comprehensible as possible.

Many popular books on nonverbal communication promise to divulge how you can "read a person like a book" or "how to win friends and influence people." We wish the state of our knowledge were that certain, but the truth is, there are as many questions about nonverbal communication as there are answers. Much of what we write about in this textbook is tentative because new research is daily challenging or disconfirming old beliefs while creating new ones. We make special mention of research because we are strongly committed to basing knowledge claims on solid scientific evidence that is supplemented rather than replaced by anecdote and personal experience. Though the absence of abundant clear-cut prescriptions about how to behave nonverbally may be unsatisfying to some readers, we are comforted by Voltaire's statement that "doubt is a not very agreeable status but certainty is a ridiculous one."

The process of producing this book has involved the labors and contributions of many people whom we wish to acknowledge most gratefully. Deborah Newton, besides producing the instructor's manual, provided valuable insights and editing suggestions throughout several readings of chapters. She was joined by Mary Buller, who assisted with the instructor's manual, and Joe Walther, Doug Kelley, Jim Baesler, Denise Perry, Kelly Aune, and Warren Pease, all doctoral students at the time, who amid numerous other demands made time to offer us their candid appraisals of drafts of the manuscript. We have learned so much from these people and the other graduate and undergraduate students who through their classroom curiosity and commentary helped us sharpen our thinking, approaches, and organization.

We are likewise indebted to the following individuals for their thoughtful and helpful reviews of the book: H. Britt Beasley, Florida State University; Rosley D. Rhine, University of Colorado; Rex Baskill, Normandale Community College; Ross Buck, University of Connecticut; Laura Stafford, Ohio State University; Stan Jones, University of Colorado; Timothy Edgar,

University of Maryland, and John Powers, Texas A & M University. We are convinced that the end result is far better for their contributions. We also wish to thank Barbara Cinquegrani and her assistants at Harper & Row for their enthusiastic support of this project.

Throughout this project, our life was made much easier by the very skillful word processing assistance we received from our administrative assistants, Nancy Finch and Merillee Jesseph. No department ever had better. Finally, those of us at the University of Arizona wish to express our sincere appreciation to Michael Burgoon, department head, for providing the resources and creating the intellectual climate that makes the pursuit of knowledge a pleasure and a compulsion.

Judee K. Burgoon
David B. Buller
W. Gill Woodall

PART I

Nonverbal Codes: Structures, Usage, and Interrelationships

CHAPTER 1

Nonverbal Communication

The word not spoken
goes not quite unheard.
It lingers in the eye,
in the semi-arch of brow.
A gesture of the hand
speaks pages more than words,
The echo rests in the heart
as driftwood does in sand,
To be rubbed by time
until it rots or shines.
The word not spoken
touches us as music
does the mind.

Sen. William S. Cohen (R., Maine), "Silent Meaning," *New York Times,* July 23, 1985.

This text is about the "unspoken dialogue," all those messages that people exchange beyond the words themselves. Nonverbal communication pervades every human transaction, from mundane requests at the grocery store to workplace discussions of job performance to delicate international negotiations. As the poem by Senator Cohen attests, the nonverbal side of communication is crucial and often overshadows the verbal communication that is going on. Successful human relations hinge on the ability to express oneself nonverbally and to understand the nonverbal communication of others.

In this text we will explore the many facets of nonverbal communication—the various "codes" that comprise it, the many kinds of messages it can send, the purposes or functions it can serve, and the processes whereby people generate, exchange, and interpret such messages.

The Importance of Nonverbal Communication

Intuition tells us, and research confirms, that nonverbal communication is a major force in our lives. In fact, it has been estimated that nearly two-thirds of the meaning in any social situation is derived from nonverbal cues (Birdwhistell, 1955). A more extreme estimate is that 93% of all meaning is nonverbal (Mehrabian & Ferris, 1967). This estimate, which has found its way into the popular literature, is faulty, however (as will be discussed in Chapter 5). Regardless of the actual percentage of meaning that can be attributed to nonverbal cues, there is abundant research evidence that people rely heavily on nonverbal cues to express themselves and to interpret the communicative activity of others. In a wide range of circumstances, the nonverbal cues actually carry more weight than the verbal ones. Some of this evidence will be reviewed in Chapter 5, where nonverbal communication is compared to verbal communication.

A convincing illustration of the power of nonverbal communication is the unparalleled political popularity experienced by Ronald Reagan, who very early in his presidency was dubbed the "Great Communicator." Despite numerous controversies, embarrassments, and defeats associated with his administration, he earned persistently high ratings in the public opinion polls. Many analysts attributed his success to his effective communication style. As the "Man of the Year" excerpt from *Time* magazine indicates, a key to that style has been his nonverbal behavior.

Although the significant role of nonverbal communication in daily transactions is indisputable, just why it has such influence is less well understood. There appear to be several reasons for its importance.

1. **Nonverbal communication is omnipresent.** Every communicative act carries with it nonverbal components. In face-to-face conversations, in public addresses, and in televised or videotaped presentations, all the nonverbal channels come into play. Bodily actions such as gestures, facial expressions, posture and eye contact; vocal behaviors such as pitch, loudness, and tempo; proximity and potential for touch; physical appearance cues such as attractiveness, dress, and grooming; time messages such as pacing and giving undivided attention; and surrounding furnishings and objects that may add to one's identity all play a part in creating the total communication. In telephone conversations or audiotaped presentations, fewer nonverbal channels are available, but vocal and time-based messages are still present. For example, the decision to talk to someone on the telephone rather than in person nonverbally expresses a desire for a less involving conversation. Even written communications such as letters potentially entail nonverbal features. The type of stationery one uses can be a message. The decision to write someone a nasty letter rather than confronting him personally can be a delaying tactic. Some theorists have argued that one "cannot not communi-

Man of the Year

The man at the center of this idea appears smaller than he is. At 6 ft. 1 in., 185 lbs., his body is tight, as tight as it can be on a large frame, though there is no sign of pulling or strain. It is the body of an actor, of someone used to being scrutinized from all angles, so it has all but willed as tidy and organized an appearance as possible. His size also seems an emblem of his modesty. Lyndon Johnson used to enter a room and rape it. Reagan seems to be in a continual state of receding, a posture that makes strangers lean toward him. In a contest for the same audience, he would draw better than Johnson.

The voice goes perfectly with the body. No President since Kennedy has had a voice at once so distinctive and beguiling. It too recedes at the right moments, turning mellow at points of intensity. When it wishes to be most persuasive, it hovers barely above a whisper so as to win you over by intimacy, if not by substance. This is style, but not sham. Reagan believes everything he says, no matter how often he has said it, or if he has said it in the same words every time. He likes his voice, treats it like a guest. He makes you part of the hospitality.

Source: "Man of the Year" by F. Trippett, January 5, 1981, *Time,* pp. 13–14.

cate" (Watzlawick, Beavin, & Jackson, 1967). According to this view, all behavior is communicative. Choosing not to interact with someone, for instance, carries a message in itself, and the absence of a greeting is as meaningful as the presence of one. Although we do not subscribe to this liberal view, it does underscore the ever present possibilities of nonverbal communication, for it indicates that any behavior can be interpreted by someone as a nonverbal message. Even when people are not talking to each other, it is possible to read nonverbal meaning in their actions. This makes every encounter between two or more people a potential nonverbal exchange, regardless of whether any verbal exchange takes place.

Nonverbal behaviors are omnipresent in another way: They are multifunctional. That is, they are part of almost every communication purpose one can imagine. For example, they may be used to create a favorable first impression, to persuade someone, to control whose turn it is to talk in a conversation, to express one's current emotional state, to signal attraction toward someone, or to clarify the meaning of the verbal message. In fact, they may do several of these things at once. Because many different nonverbal channels can be used to send simultaneous messages, they are often pressed into service to do just that—handle multiple responsibilities in conjunction with, or as a replacement for, verbal communication.

2. **Nonverbal behaviors may form a universal language system.** Many scholars believe that nonverbal signals are part of a universally recognized and understood code. This view is evident in an oft quoted statement by Edward Sapir (1928):

> We respond to gestures with an extreme alertness and, one might almost say, in accordance with an elaborate and secret code that is written nowhere, known to none and understood by all. (p. 556)

Behaviors such as smiling, crying, pointing, caressing touches, and threatening stares are examples of nonverbal signals that appear to be used and understood the world over. They allow people to communicate with one another at the most basic level regardless of their familiarity with the prevailing verbal language system. Such nonverbal actions thus transcend cultural differences, forming a kind of universal language.

This capacity of nonverbal communication to cross geographic boundaries was brought home when a former student sent a postcard describing her visit to relatives in Italy. She wrote:

> As a non-Italian traveller, it is amazing how much understanding can be grasped by carefully listening to other cues one hears and sees. When sitting at the dinner table with 25 relatives, it struck me how much I relied on the nonverbals.

Clearly, not all meaning can be gleaned from nonverbal cues alone, and there are differences between and within cultures. But the fact that exclusive reliance on nonverbal cues can produce a sense of commonality and understanding in a foreign situation is testimony to their universal character. When words fail us, we can always fall back on our nonverbal communication system to achieve some minimal level of mutual exchange.

3. **Nonverbal communication can lead to misunderstanding as well as understanding.** Although nonverbal signals can aid us greatly in making sense out of the world, they are equally important to us because of the misunderstandings they can cause. These can sometimes be tragic, as the following true anecdote illustrates.

A young photographer, accustomed to working alone, was flown into a remote part of Alaska for the summer. He so prized his solitude that on a previous survival retreat, he had chastised his father for sending a search party after him. On this trip, he failed to make clear arrangements for being flown back out of the wilderness. When the weather began turning cool, his father reluctantly sent a plane looking for him. The pilot soon located the camp. As he neared it, the young man waved a red jacket liner, which to pilots is a signal to wave someone away. The young man then gave a thumbs-up gesture and walked casually to his campsite. The pilot concluded that everything was OK and flew away.

A diary the young man kept revealed a very different interpretation of the encounter. He was thrilled to see the plane, and to ensure being seen, he waved his jacket in the air. He gave the thumbs-up gesture as a sign of his elation and his victory over his growing fears. He then jaunted to his campsite, expecting the plane to land, and was totally disbelieving when it flew on. Weeks later, when the weather turned bitter cold and he ran out of firewood, the young photographer used his last bullet to take his own life. The diary was found with his frozen body.

Not all nonverbal misunderstandings have fatal or even serious consequences. But the potential for nonverbal cues to mislead and be misread is there, and such misreadings can often have a more profound impact than the accurately exchanged cues. This is especially true when people believe they can "read another person like a book" and draw inferences from a person's unintentional behavior. Many mistakenly believe that nonverbal behaviors all have obvious meanings and that everyone interprets nonverbal cues the same way. Recognition of the potential for misunderstanding is a prerequisite to successful communication.

4. **Nonverbal communication has phylogenetic primacy.** This is a fancy way of saying that in our development as a species, nonverbal communication predated language. Although there are numerous theories about whether vocalizations preceded gestural communication or vice versa, there is no question that nonverbal forms of expression preceded verbal ones (Dew & Jensen, 1977; McBride, 1975; McNeill, 1970). In that nonverbal communication came first to the species, it can be argued that we are inherently programmed to attend first and foremost to nonverbal signals. This primacy of nonverbal cues should cause us to give them more weight in interpreting communicative events, especially in times of stress, when we are more likely to revert to more primitive (phylogenetically older) response patterns. If we as humans rely more heavily on nonverbal than verbal messages, it may be because we are innately predisposed to do so (see Figure 1.1).

5. **Nonverbal communication has ontogenetic primacy.** Just as members of the species first turned to nonverbal forms to communicate with one another, so, too, do individuals rely first on nonverbal means to interact with their caretakers and environment. Even before birth, the fetus in utero is already developing an awareness of its mother through the senses of touch and hearing. At birth, the infant's primary interactions with other humans continue to center around auditory and tactile sensation. Nursing, grasping, rocking, holding, crying, cooing, singing—all these experiences contribute to the infant's awakening recognition that humans communicate with one another. As the infant's vision improves, visual cues are

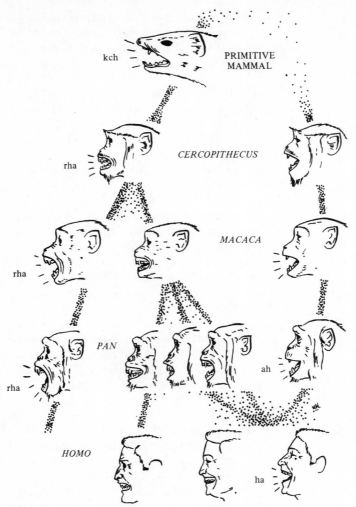

FIGURE 1.1 Smiling and laughing are universally recognized signals whose origins appear to predate language by millennia.

added to the nonverbal mix; sequences of separations and contact and other routines likewise add rudimentary understandings of spatial and temporal messages. Long before a child has begun to grasp the concept of verbal language, it has already acquired a rich communication system that is strictly nonverbal. The importance of nonverbal modes of expression at this critical and vulnerable stage of life may contribute to our continued dependence on them even though we acquire more sophisticated means of expression. For we do not abandon the nonverbal system; rather, as we mature, we broaden our communicative repertoire to include more complex verbal and nonverbal forms.

6. **Nonverbal communication has interaction primacy.** Besides being the first form of communication in the history of the species and in the life span of the individual, nonverbal behavior has primacy in the opening minutes of interpersonal and mediated communication events. Before people even open their mouths, their nonverbal behaviors are supplying a wealth of information to onlookers. Everything from posture to gait to hairstyle to voice quality paints a picture for the observer and provides a frame of reference for interpreting what is said verbally. Especially important are the visual nonverbal cues, such as physical appearance and gestures, that are available at a distance. These begin working before a communicator is within speaking range. Environmental nonverbal cues may also set the stage. For instance, when the president holds a news conference, the American flag, the red carpet, and all the other symbols of the White House create an image of power; they evoke respect from the gathered press prior to the president's opening remarks. This ability of nonverbal cues to "get in the first word," so to speak, gives them a temporal primacy that may also cause their meanings to take precedence over verbal ones.

7. **Nonverbal communication can express what verbal can't or shouldn't.** There are many occasions when to verbalize our thoughts and feelings would be risky, rude, or inappropriate, so we use nonverbal channels instead. In the early, faltering stages of a romance, people are hesitant to commit themselves too quickly for fear of being rejected. Rather than say how they feel, people usually rely on nonverbal approaches to determine if the relationship is going to escalate. If a prolonged gaze or lingering touch is not reciprocated, one can retreat to a less intimate level without embarrassment. Similarly, nonverbal cues can be used to satirize, criticize, or leak information without the communicator being held accountable for his or her acts. (See Applications, p. 10.)

8. **Nonverbal communication is trusted.** Either because of the preceding reasons or in addition to them, nonverbal behaviors are assumed to be more truthful and therefore more trusted. The naive belief exists that nonverbal behaviors are spontaneous and uncontrolled; that they are "windows to the soul." As we shall see later, this is a fallacious belief. Many nonverbal behaviors are intentionally manipulated, some for deceptive purposes, and people who are image-conscious work scrupulously to suppress expression of behaviors that make a bad impression. Nevertheless, there is a prevailing faith in the honesty and candor of nonverbal behaviors. Consequently, people believe them over the verbal behaviors. In fact, research shows that when verbal messages contradict nonverbal ones, adults usually believe the nonverbal message (e.g., Argyle,

APPLICATIONS

The Courtroom and the Military

Lawyers and soldiers share something in common: an ability to use nonverbal signals to send illicit information. Birdwhistell offers two illustrations:

> Take courtroom procedure, for example. The present system of restricting admissible evidence to exhibits and words still leaves the way open for the introduction of nonadmissible ideas and attitudes. The trial lawyer often is a master of the raised eyebrow, the disapproving headshake and the knowing nod. In many cases, these gestures if translated into words, would be inadmissible as evidence. Yet, as presented, they have a definite effect on the judge and jury. (Birdwhistell, cited in Rosekrans, 1955, p. 56)

> The salute, a conventionalized movement of the right hand to the vicinity of the anterior portion of the cap or hat, could, without occasioning a court martial, be performed in a manner which could satisfy, please or enrage the demanding officer. By shifts in stance, facial expression, the velocity or duration of the movement of salutation, and even in the selection of inappropriate contexts for the act, the soldier could dignify, ridicule, demean, seduce, insult, or promote the recipient of the salute. By often imperceptible variations in the performance of the act, he could comment upon the bravery or cowardice of his enemy or ally, could signal his attitude toward army life or give a brief history of the virtuosity of a lady from whom he had recently arisen. (Birdwhistell, 1970, pp. 79–80)

Alkema, & Gilmour, 1971; Argyle, Salter, Nicholson, Williams, & Burgess, 1970; Mehrabian & Wiener, 1967).

These eight reasons for the significant impact of nonverbal communication, though not exhaustive, highlight the need to understand how nonverbal communication works together with verbal communication and independently of it. Unfortunately, few of us receive formal training in this subject. Despite the emphasis placed on communication skills in elementary school, attention is devoted almost exclusively to reading and writing—in other words, to verbal communication. Ideally, nonverbal communication should be interwoven into all communication study from preschool forward as an integral part of the communication system. But since it is not, an introductory course in nonverbal communication becomes a necessity to remediate "nonverbal illiteracy." Although this text is about nonverbal communication, because we are committed to a more integrated approach to verbal and nonverbal communication, you will find a variety of general

The Unspoken Dialogue

In infancy, our first and only means of communicating needs and receiving reassurances is through nonverbal signals; even after we have mastered verbal language, nonverbal messages continue to permeate all our interpersonal transactions. We actively employ such messages to add color to what we say. They are the fine print and the hidden meaning where words are inadequate. We use them to carry sympathy, advice, innuendo, and punishment where words are inappropriate and to display feelings, attitudes, and reactions where words are unnecessary. With caressing touches, tender voices, and smiling faces, we speak love and are loved. With body movements, we tell a stranger that we would like to get acquainted. We signal disbelief merely by raising an eyebrow. We can encourage someone to talk longer or like us more simply by moving closer. We can command obedience by wearing a uniform.

We are also constantly receiving nonverbal messages from every direction. Family life is infused with them—they form a fundamental part of each family's unique communication system. The classroom bombards us with them—the actions of teachers, the reactions of other students, and the physical environment itself all tell us what is expected of us. Social relationships begin, grow, and end with the help of nonverbal messages, and conversations are regulated by them. Even in our leisure time, we are dogged by Madison Avenue's barrage of appeals. Vance Packard's book *The Hidden Persuaders* is rife with examples of the clever tactics used to manipulate our behavior as consumers. Even something so trivial as the color of a soap wrapper can be used to elicit a response.

Source: From *The Unspoken Dialogue* (p. 4) by J. K. Burgoon & T. J. Saine, 1978, Boston: Houghton Mifflin.

communication principles and some specific findings about verbal communication interspersed throughout the book.

Definitional Issues

So far we have been referring to nonverbal communication as if you and we shared a common definition for it. In reality, there may be as many definitions of it as there are readers of this text. Before we proceed any further, it is important that we come to a common understanding of the terminology being used. How you define nonverbal communication can make quite a difference in who you consider responsible for communicative acts. Take the following scenario:

Wife: Our marriage is falling apart. You have become totally detached from me.
Husband: How can you say that? Give me just one example.
Wife: I'll give you several. You sit silently at the dinner table. You don't spend any time with me anymore. You don't look at me when we do talk, and you never hug or kiss me anymore.
Husband: You're just imagining things. I've had a lot of problems at work to think about, but I haven't changed how I behave toward you.

The wife interprets the husband's actions as nonverbal messages of distance and lack of affection. He claims his behaviors are unchanged or merely indicative of being preoccupied with his work; any "messages" are her imagination. If the husband's actions are defined as nonverbal communication, regardless of his awareness or acknowledgement of them, he can be faulted for communicating detachment. Under a different definition, however, the wife could be seen as reading too much into unintentional and noncommunicative activity. In this very practical way, then, definitions can make a difference.

Communication

A starting point for arriving at a sound definition is the concept of communication itself. This term is a slippery one because people use it to refer to everything from communing with nature to talking with oneself to computer linkages to satellite transmissions.

However, if we limit it to *human* communication, that narrows the range substantially. By "human" we mean exchanges between two or more people. This eliminates a lot of things, including "intrapersonal" communication, human-machine communication, and animal or animal-human communication. Apart from philosophical justifications for such exclusions, this restriction has pragmatic value. It makes it far more likely that we will uncover general principles if the kinds of communication phenomena to be explained have some commonality. It is difficult to find principles that explain such things as signals between dolphins and interactions between computers in the same way that we account for nonverbal exchanges between humans. Nevertheless, we may learn some things about human communication processes by studying nonhuman interactions, and we will not hesitate to draw on these observations where they serve as useful illustrations or analogues.

Within the domain of human communication, most scholars agree that communication refers to a *dynamic and ongoing process* whereby people *create shared meaning* through the *sending and receiving of messages* via *commonly understood codes.* Verbal languages are one sort of code; American Sign Language and Morse code are others. In this text, we will examine the seven most commonly used nonverbal codes based on bodily movement, vocal activity, physical appearance, touch, manipulation of distance and space, manipulation of time, and manipulation of artifacts and features of the environment.

At this stage, it might seem that defining nonverbal communication is easy. But consider the following possibilities and determine for each whether you think it is a nonverbal message or not:

Wearing one red and one blue tennis shoe
Sneezing
Squinting in bright sunlight and having someone read it as disapproval
Unconsciously signaling depression through slumped posture
Crying
Breaking out in a rash
Standing close to others because of a hearing impairment

Most or all of these may seem obvious instances of communication to you. To others, none qualify. Additional criteria are necessary to resolve the issue.

Information, Behavior, and Communication

One way to clarify the matter is to distinguish among the concepts of information, behavior, and communication. *Information* can be conceived of as *all stimuli in the environment that reduce uncertainty for the organism.* That is, information is anything that individuals use to gain predictability about the environment and to guide their own behavior. The position of the sun in the sky is information about the time of day, but one would normally not call it a "message." After all, the sun did not establish its position for the purpose of signaling to observers what hour of the day it is on earth. It is simply there as an environmental stimulus from which observers can draw inferences and adjust their own behavior. Similarly, a botanist can examine blotches on a leaf and diagnose leaf blight.

Unfortunately, when the source of the information becomes a human, people are inclined to label the inference-making process as communication. For example, a red rash on a child becomes a "nonverbal message" to the doctor that the child has measles, even though the information being gleaned is no different from the leaf blight example. The child does not "will" the measles into being, nor can the child choose to suppress their appearance. Similarly, a sneeze may be symptomatic of an allergy, and a close conversational distance may be indicative of a hearing problem. In the absence of other knowledge about the situation, these behaviors should be regarded only as information and not as communication. In short, the passive or involuntary displaying of cues that an observer might wish to interpret should be treated only as information and not specifically as communication.

This is not to say that communication is not informative, for it is. In fact, all communication is potentially information. But all information is not communication. Communication should be treated as a *subset* of information rather than as synonymous with it. The relationship is shown graphically in Figure 1.2.

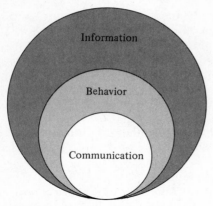

FIGURE 1.2 The relationship among information, behavior, and communication.

In the same vein, many forms of behavior are informative, but only some of them qualify as communication. Here confusion is even more likely, partly because of the perspective that regards any and all nonverbal activity as messages. If one subscribes to this view, there is no need for a separate concept of communication because it coincides entirely with behavior.

It seems more useful to distinguish between the broad category of *behavior,* which encompasses *any actions or reactions performed by an organism,* and the more specific category of communication. The difference is that behavior can take place without others witnessing it, responding to it, or understanding it. Typically, routine activities such as sleeping and eating would be classified as *informative behaviors* rather than as communication, unless there is some apparent attempt to make a statement through the manner in which they are done or the context in which they occur. As with verbal communication, there should be some notion of a sender encoding and transmitting a message to a receiver before an action is labeled communication. It is doubtful that a person taking a nap in the privacy of her own home intends to communicate something to an accidental observer; however, if she chooses to do it in the middle of a political science lecture, the publicness and inappropriateness of the act may suggest that it is a statement. The important point is that not every behavior should be regarded as communication; as with information, *communication is a subset of behavior, which is itself a subset of information.* This perspective reduces to a manageable level the number of things that qualify as nonverbal communication.

Source, Receiver, and Message Orientations

Another helpful distinction in defining nonverbal communication is the general perspective one takes on defining communication. This distinction revolves around issues of *intent, consciousness,* and *awareness.* Those who hold a *source orientation* believe that communication includes only messages that the source intends to send. Unintended or unconscious messages do not count.

A major difficulty with this perspective is discerning what is or is not intentional behavior. With verbal communication, one can at least assume an intent to communicate if a person vocalizes or writes something, even if the purpose or meaning of the message itself is unclear. With nonverbal communication, determining intent is much more difficult. As Knapp, Wiemann, and Daly (1978) note:

> Some messages, for instance, are planned and sent with a high degree of conscious awareness; others seem more casually prepared; some messages are designed to look casual or unintentional; still others are more reflexive, habitual, or expressive responses; and some are "given off" rather than "given." (p. 273)

Take the example of the employer who frowns whenever an employee gives him negative feedback. If he denies frowning, has he communicated nonverbally or not? And who decides whether he intended to frown or not—the source, the receiver, or some impartial observer? As this example illustrates, it is easy to disavow intent for much of what goes on nonverbally. Even taking a Freudian approach that says that a person's subconsciousness may intentionally send messages of which the source is unaware, what if the source says, "I didn't mean to do that"? Does the behavior qualify as communication? The frowning employer would probably say no; the disgruntled employee would probably say yes.

A related problem is that most nonverbal expressions and patterns are well-learned habits that require little forethought or conscious awareness. Just as we apply the car's brake automatically when approaching a red light, so too do we perform numerous nonverbal behaviors without thinking about them. For example, we do not have to remind ourselves consciously to smile and make eye contact when greeting a friend. A label that has been applied to this low level of awareness of routine communication activity is *mindlessness.* It does not imply that the brain is not engaged but merely that heavy cognitive involvement is no longer required to perform these habitual communicative acts. This raises the question of whether such activity is intentional communication or not. Intent can be claimed when the behavior is first learned, as when a child learns not to bump into people. But whether an adult's avoidance of contact with strangers can then be regarded as a deliberate message or just an ingrained, unconscious habit is unclear.

There are additional problems with trying to identify intent (Knapp et al., 1978). One is timing. During an encounter we may not be fully aware of our actions but in retrospect may admit that we purposely committed a particular behavior, such as snubbing someone. If questioned at the time of the act, we might deny intent but at a later time concede it. This suggests that a person's own self-report of intent is of questionable value and can vary greatly, depending on the timing of it. Another problem is that circumstances may alter whether the same behavior is seen as intentional or not. For example, you are probably more likely to see a "hard sell" in the glad-handing of a used-car salesman than in the same warm handshake from your friend. But if you meet the salesman at a social event, you are less likely to attribute ulterior motives to his handshake than if you met him on the car lot. Some situations and some people cause us to be more sensitive to intent than others, and we may recognize intent when the communicator does not.

These issues demonstrate that if all behaviors for which a source disclaims responsibility or professes lack of awareness are ruled out as communication, the nonverbal domain may become overly narrow, especially considering how poorly many people monitor their own nonverbal behavior. For this reason, important scholars of nonverbal communication find the source orientation unsatisfying. For instance, Knapp (1983b) argues that expressive behaviors—actions that produce similar interpretations in observers but are not intentional—are as important a part of nonverbal communication as are purposive (intentional) behaviors. The case of someone unconsciously slumping as a signal of depression would be an example of expressive behavior. Ekman and Friesen (1969b) likewise distinguish between informative (unintentional) and communicative (intentional) messages, both of which they regard as necessary to understanding nonverbal communication. Finally, Nolan (1975) notes that verbal as well as nonverbal behaviors can be placed along a continuum from highly intentional, deliberate, and conscious to highly unaware and nondeliberate; that is, they cannot be dichotomized as either intentional or unintentional. Nolan refers to this as the degree of *propositionality.* The more propositional the behavior (consciously and deliberately encoded and expressing a falsifiable statement), the more communicative.

At the opposite extreme of the source orientation is the *receiver orientation,* which holds that anything a receiver interprets as a message is communication, regardless of source intent or awareness. Accidental and unintended behaviors are included as long as a receiver chooses to read something into them. For example, if a hypersensitive classmate mistakes a squint for a frown and interprets it as personal rejection, the receiver orientation would say that communication has taken place. The main objection to this perspective is that it is too broad and verges on the "all behavior is communication" approach. It permits treating as communication such involuntary and idiosyncratic behaviors as allergic sneezing and frequent blinking. It also allows physical traits over which a person has little or no control—such as buckteeth, short stature, or a bow-legged walk—to be treated as messages so long as someone draws some inference from them. It should be clear from the discussion of the information versus communication distinction that we prefer to treat many of these latter examples as cases of information rather than communication.

The third perspective is the one we advocate. Called the *message orientation* (Burgoon, 1980a), it defines as communication only behaviors that *are typically sent with intent, are used with regularity among members of a social community, are typically interpreted as intentional, and have consensually recognizable interpretations.* In short, they form a widely shared coding system. This approach is similar to one favored by some psychologists (Wiener, Devoe, Rubinow, & Geller, 1972), who contend that better understanding of nonverbal communication is gained by focusing attention on behaviors with socially shared meaning and ignoring idiosyncratic ones.

According to this view, if the busboy at the local pizza place wears unmatched tennis shoes, this may be merely idiosyncratic behavior and is unlikely to produce consistent meaning among observers. It may be informative—we may infer from it that he is disorganized or socially inept—but we would probably not regard this single behavior as communication. However, if it is coupled with other behaviors such as wearing spiked blue hair and one earring, it becomes more apparent that the busboy is attempting to make a statement. The totality of his appearance is likely to produce consistent recognition of him as a would-be punker. Thus a key criterion for deciding if something is communication is whether or not a behavior or collection of behaviors generates consensually agreed-on meaning within a culture or subculture.

The concept of choice implies volition and deliberate action, which brings us back to the issues of awareness and intent. In the message orientation, the crucial consideration is whether the behavior is *typically* encoded intentionally and *typically* decoded as intentional. This means that on any specific occasion, the sender need not be consciously aware of committing the behavior; that is, the sender may do it "mindlessly." The key to a behavior being part of a recognized communication system is that people regularly use it in such circumstances to express a particular meaning and that it is usually regarded as an intentional message. Thus an unconscious frown qualifies because people often use a frown to express displeasure and people generally interpret a frown as carrying that meaning. Similarly, the routine and automatic looking at another as one finishes speaking is communication because it is a well-understood, deliberate signal that one wishes to relinquish a turn and the floor is now available for someone else's turn at talk.

The message orientation centers on the behaviors and sets of behaviors that form the "vocabulary" of nonverbal communication in a particular "language" community. This sidesteps the trap of trying to discern communicator intent for every action. It also avoids the problem of the relative skill, self-monitoring, and perceptiveness of communicators determining whether their behavior qualifies as nonverbal communication or not. The focus instead is on the message itself and what possible meanings might be entailed by a system of behaviors (although individual differences will certainly play a role in the meanings people select as possible alternatives).

This approach recognizes habitual behavior as part of communication. But it also stipulates that to qualify as communication, a behavior must be selected frequently by communicators to convey a particular meaning and must be interpreted frequently by recipients or observers as a purposive and meaningful expression. This is what makes it part of a socially shared coding system.

Symbols and Signs

A final issue is the distinction between signs and symbols. *Signs* are anything that stand for something else and produce at least some of the responses that the referent produces (Anttila, 1972). Used in this general sense, signs include language (linguistic signs). However, for our purposes, it is more useful to limit signs to referents that are *natural and intrinsic representations* of what they signify, as in smoke being a sign of fire. Signs may *index* a relationship between meaning and form. They may be an attribute of a larger substance or process and signal its presence. For example, nonverbal emotional expressions like crying and smiling are outward manifestations of internally experienced feelings or actional tendencies (Buck, 1982). Or they may have an *iconic* relationship with the referent, in which case there is a physical resemblance between the sign and the referent. For example, a sculpture is a highly iconic sign of the person represented; a photograph is a somewhat less iconic version (because it is only two-dimensional). Another term that Cronkhite (1986) prefers to use for these kinds of completely nonarbitrary representations is *symptoms*.

By contrast, *symbols* are *arbitrarily assigned representations* that stand for something else. The word *fire* is an arbitrarily selected label or symbol for the substance of fire (unlike the iconic visual representation on campground billboards). Nonverbal symbols include such things as the hitchhiker's thumbing gesture requesting a ride, the cleric's white collar signifying a religious occupation, and the "give me five" handshake used as a friendly greeting among many young people. A more precise definition of symbolic communication comes from Wiener et al. (1972): "(a) a socially shared signal system, that is, a code, (b) an encoder who makes something public via that code, and (c) a decoder who responds systematically to that code" (p. 186).

Some people have attempted to minimize the communicative value of nonverbal behaviors by claiming that they are not symbolic. Certainly, many nonverbal behaviors are nonarbitrary and better qualify as signs than symbols. Spontaneous emotional expressions and specieswide displays such as threat stares are naturally occurring behaviors, among others, that the individual need not learn to produce or interpret. Liska (1986) would call some of these behaviors *rituals*—"sign behaviors that are neither totally arbitrary nor totally symbolic" (p. 174). Such things as stylized fear expressions fall somewhere in the middle of the continuum from sign to symbol. What Knapp (1983b) refers to as expressive behaviors and Ekman and Friesen (1969b) refer to as behaviors with intrinsic meaning generally qualify as signs.

Buck (1982) makes a useful distinction between our *biologically shared signal system* and our *socially shared signal system*. Biologically based displays (e.g., territorial defense, anger displays, play behavior) fall into the sign category. What sets them apart from symbolic communication is that they are involuntary, spontaneous, and indicative of emotional and motivational content. Conversely, symbolic communication (a) is voluntary and intentional, (b) has an arbitrary relationship between the reference (symbol) and the referent (the thing itself), (c) is part of a socially shared coding system, (d) has propositional content, which means that it is capable of logical analysis and can be declared true or false, and (e) is processed primarily by the left hemisphere of the brain.

Is this gesture a sign or a symbol? Is it a biological or a social signal? Can it be both?

While this distinction is helpful in clarifying that some nonverbal behaviors are symbolic and others are not, it does not address adequately the question of posed or controlled emotional expressions. Such expressions as feigned sadness at the death of a despised coworker are deliberate and voluntary, have socially shared meaning, and are propositional in that they can be judged true (honest) or false (deceptive), but they are not arbitrarily concocted expressions. Similarly, the smile originated as a natural expression of pleasure or affection, but the smiling face is also used symbolically to express such nonspontaneous sentiments as approval and congratulations and it appears as a visual symbol on bumper stickers inscribed "Have a Nice Day." Moreover, one can take an essentially spontaneous expression and intentionally overintensify it (e.g., the person who gushes over a gift) or deintensify it (e.g., masking one's pleasure at besting an opponent). Viewing signs and symbols as representing a continuum, a position also advanced by Cronkhite (1986), is especially useful when we consider larger combinations of cues. Individual behaviors may have originated as natural cues, but together they may be symbolic. For example, greeting rituals usually include spontaneous or posed shows of liking, semiautomatic displays of mutual gaze as a show of attentiveness, and socially prescribed forms of handshakes or hugs. The larger pattern is symbolic but comprised of a combination of symbolic and nonsymbolic behaviors. Inasmuch as we typically respond to larger patterns rather than single cues, the nonarbitrary origins of individual signs may be irrelevant.

In short, the sign-symbol distinction is not a very useful one unless it is viewed as a continuum rather than two separate categories. What seems to be more important is that both biologically based signals and socially based signals—whether they are signs, rituals, or symbols and have species-wide or culturewide recognition—are major vehicles for communication. In fact, it is possible that the biologically based cues, because of their universal use and recognition, may be the more significant in the process of exchanging meaning between humans.

Structures, Functions, and Processes

The foregoing discussion should clarify somewhat that what we intend to cover as nonverbal communication includes signs and symbols that qualify as potential messages by virtue of regular and consistent use and interpretation. This becomes much more concrete if we consider the specific codes, patterns, and purposes involved.

Codes

A code is a set of signals that is usually transmitted via one particular medium or channel. Nonverbal communication codes are often defined by the human sense or senses they stimulate (e.g., the visual sense) and/or the carrier of the signal (e.g., the human body or artifacts). The various codes in combination form the structure of nonverbal communication.

A number of systems have been advanced for classifying nonverbal

Greeting rituals, at the pattern level, are symbolic but usually comprised of both socially based signals (e.g., bowing) and biologically based signals (e.g., touching).

codes and channels. One of the earliest approaches, proposed by Ruesch and Kees (1956), grouped nonverbal cues into three categories. *Sign language* included any type of gesture that replaces specific words, numbers, or punctuation marks—for example, a head tilt signaling the end of a question, the peace sign, and holding up five fingers to say "five." *Action language* included all other body movements not used as signs. Running and eating fit this category. *Object language* incorporated the intentional or unintentional display of objects that could act as statements about their user. Everything from the personal appearance, architecture, implements, and organization of space to traces of human activity such as footprints fell under this heading. This classification system has since been discarded, in part because its categories were too gross, grouping together dissimilar types of cues; in part because it omitted important facets of nonverbal communication such as vocal behavior and use of time; and in part because it cast the net too broadly in encompassing all manner of unintentional and noncommunicative behavior.

A second approach, offered by Harrison (1974), groups nonverbal communication into four categories. *Performance codes* include all nonverbal behaviors that are executed by the human body—body movement, facial expression, eye gaze, touch, and vocal activity. *Spatiotemporal codes* combine messages based on manipulation of space, distance, and time. *Artifactual codes* include any use of materials and objects to communicate. Clothing and adornment as well as architecture and arrangements of objects fit this category. A final, unique category, *mediatory codes,* is designed to account for the special effects of media when interposed between sender and receiver. For example, the camera angle used in a television commercial adds an extra nonverbal message.

A more common approach to classifying codes (e.g., Burgoon & Saine, 1978; Harper, Wiens, & Matarazzo, 1978; Knapp, 1978; Leathers, 1976; Malandro & Barker, 1983; Rosenfeld & Civikly, 1976) further differentiates them according to the transmission medium and channel used. Typically, body movement, facial activity, and gaze are combined into *kinesics,* or what is known in the popular vernacular as body language. (Some people use a separate category of *oculesics* for eye behavior.) Vocal activity forms another category known as *paralanguage* or *vocalics.* Likewise, touch is treated as a separate code called *haptics.* The use of space, called *proxemics,* and the use of time, called *chronemics,* are also usually given independent status. Finally, *physical appearance* is often separated from the use of *artifacts* (sometimes called *objectics*), and occasionally olfactory-related cues are treated as a separate category.

The first seven are the ones we will study in this text. Because of their commonalities in appealing to the visual and auditory senses, kinesics, physical appearance, and vocalics will be covered in one chapter. Proxemics and haptics, which are highly interrelated in signaling approach and avoidance, will be covered in a second chapter, and chronemics and artifacts, with their strong influence on context, will be covered in a third.

Although it is necessary temporarily to decompose nonverbal communication into its component structural features, ultimately we must look at the interrelationships among codes if any understanding of nonverbal communication is to be achieved. As Cherry (1957), a communication theorist, has rightly observed, "The human organism is one integrated whole, stimulated into responses by physical signals; it is not to be thought of as a box, carrying independent pairs of terminals labeled 'ears,' 'eyes,' 'nose,' et cetera" (pp. 127–128). Katz and Katz (1983) likewise note that each of the nonverbal channels simultaneously sends forth a stream of information, and it is the totality of all the channels, their juxtaposition, and their degree of congruence or incongruence that produces the meaningful pattern. Like many other writers on nonverbal communication, Katz and Katz call for an integrated approach. One way to take an integrated view is to look at how the codes work together to achieve specific communication functions.

Functions

Functions are the purposes, motives, or outcomes of communication. Early analyses of nonverbal communication focused on its subsidiary role to verbal communication. Ekman and Friesen (1969b) proposed five functions that became the popular view of the primary functions of nonverbal behavior. Discussed more fully in Chapter 5, they are *redundancy* (duplicating the verbal message), *substitution* (replacing the verbal message), *complementation* (amplifying or elaborating on the verbal message), *emphasis* (highlighting the verbal message), and *contradiction* (sending signals opposite to the literal meaning of the verbal message). Except for substitution, this list of functions tends to deny an independent and powerful role for nonverbal messages. Nonverbal scholars, however, have come to realize that nonverbal behavior can play a much more central role and can accomplish a number of functions with or without the help of verbal behavior. This is what most students of nonverbal communication are interested in learning—what does nonverbal communication *do?*

One of its most important functions, alluded to already, is *emotional communication.* We rely heavily on nonverbal cues to express our feelings and emotional states. However, contrary to the claims of some, this is not all that nonverbal communication can do. A very significant function is the process of *impression formation and management*—how receivers develop first impressions of communicators and how communicators manipulate their image. The whole area of communicator credibility falls under this function. Part of this process is the manner in which communicators supply *identification of culture, race, gender, and personality.* In projecting their personal identity and in conforming to the norms of their ethnic group, sex, and race, people frequently reveal much about themselves. One's stereotypic identity—for example, as a white Anglo-Saxon female or an Arab male—sets expectations that greatly influence how people communicate with one another.

Although people's communication is typically designed to be consistent and straightforward, occasionally it includes *mixed messages and deception.* Mixed or contradictory signals may be due to inadequate communication skill, poor self-monitoring, intentional ambiguity, or outright deception. This aspect of communication clearly impinges on impression formation and management. It also affects another function, *relational communication.* Relational communication encompasses all the ways in which people define their interpersonal relationships, including how much they like each other, how much they trust one another, who is dominant and who is submissive, how comfortable they are with each other, and how involved they are in the relationship.

Additional communication functions relate to the interaction process itself. Nonverbal behaviors play a major role in *structuring interaction.* They dictate what behavioral programs are expected, what roles people are playing, how formal the interaction is to be, what topics are proscribed, and so forth. Once the stage is set, nonverbal behaviors also *coordinate the ongoing interaction* by regulating turn taking and establishing interaction rhythms. They signal who has the floor and who wants it, and they are largely responsible for producing a smooth interaction or an awkward one.

Finally, nonverbal cues affect the outcomes of communication. They are part of the *social influence and facilitation process;* that is, they aid or inhibit persuasion and behavioral change. At the most fundamental level, they also significantly affect *information processing and comprehension.* The absence of nonverbal cues or the use of inappropriate ones can seriously impair learning and understanding.

In sum, nonverbal communication accomplishes a multiplicity of functions. The nine that are covered in Part II of this text are neither mutually exclusive nor exhaustive but together demonstrate the robustness of nonverbal behavior in achieving communication goals. For some alternative analyses of functions, see Argyle (1972), Eisenberg and Smith (1971), Harrison (1974), Higginbotham and Yoder (1982), Patterson (1983), Scheflen (1967) and Scheflen and Scheflen (1972).

Process Perspective

Equally important to taking an integrated approach to nonverbal communication is taking a processual one; that is, we need to understand nonverbal communication as an ongoing, dynamic process rather than just a static snapshot of cues or final outcomes at one moment in time. Unfortunately, even though most scholars pay lip service to looking at interaction sequences and longitudinal patterns of nonverbal behavior, little of the research has actually done so. Exceptions include developmental research, which looks at the acquisition of nonverbal behaviors in childhood and changes in communication ability over the life span; research on interpersonal interaction sequences, especially turn-taking patterns; and writing on stages in relationship development. Where a processual perspective has not yet been taken, we will suggest some questions that still need answering. Inasmuch as nonverbal communication study is still in its infancy, one objective of this text is to raise questions in addition to supplying tentative answers.

How many of the following communication functions do the nonverbal behaviors of the pictured people serve—identification, emotional communication, impression management, deception, relational communication, structuring of interaction, conversational management, message processing and comprehension?

Issues in Studying Nonverbal Communication

Before closing this introductory chapter, we need to consider a few final issues that affect how we study nonverbal communication. One concerns the various disciplinary perspectives that can inform us. A second one is the role of context and circumstance in altering nonverbal patterns. The issue is whether cultural differences and the wide variability of situations in which people find themselves make generalizations impossible. A third issue is the nature of individual differences in the use and interpretation of nonverbal behavior and the extent to which such differences also undermine the ability to generate universal principles. A final related issue is the distinction between what is designated ideal or competent behavior and the behaviors people actually perform. In the age of increasing emphasis on communicator competence, we need to be clear on the use of these terms and their importance in studying nonverbal communication.

Approaches to Studying Nonverbal Communication

Nonverbal communication is not the special purview of the communication field. Quite a number of disciplines have studied it, each with its own unique assumptions about human behavior and their methods for studying it. The ethologist and biologist are interested in signals common to different species and their contribution to survival value. The physiologist and systems analyst are interested in the physical properties of the encoder, decoder, or channel in facilitating or impeding the transmission and reception of communication signals. The anthropologist is interested in the normative and routine nonverbal behaviors exhibited in a culture and how they reveal that culture. The linguist is interested in the structure of nonverbal codes and their relationship to verbal language. The psychiatrist and psychoanalyst are interested in deviant nonverbal behaviors and how they reveal personality or mental health problems. The sociologist is interested in how nonverbal patterns reveal something about group and organizational dynamics. And the psychologist is interested in the role of nonverbal cues as cause or effect in the larger study of human behavior.

If nonverbal behavior can be viewed as a crystal, each of these disciplines looks at a different facet of it, and it is through the totality of these perspectives that we can gain the fullest understanding of nonverbal phenomena. These various approaches are discussed in detail in *The Unspoken Dialogue* (Burgoon & Saine, 1978). The important point to recognize here is that the principles to be identified in this text draw at different times on all of these perspectives and their various methods for studying nonverbal behavior. We believe that an eclectic approach will bring the most rapid strides in our knowledge about the processes and products of nonverbal communication.

Although we do attempt to incorporate as much useful information as we can from these different fields, note that our approach to communication study has the most in common with social psychology, sociology, and linguistics. We subscribe to what Burgoon and Saine (1978) outlined as the functional perspective, which is to say that we are guided by the following assumptions:

1. **The nature of the specific communication function determines the nonverbal behaviors to be observed.** Some nonverbal codes may be irrelevant for some functions (e.g., clothing is an unlikely clue to deception).
2. **Every function has situational characteristics.** Certain contexts tend to be associated with certain functions and have associated verbal and nonverbal behaviors. Relational expressions of love, for instance, most often occur in face-to-face situations, and kinesic behaviors are more salient to such relational expressions than to a radio broadcast.
3. **Communication is an ongoing, dynamic process.** A given function rarely begins or ends in a single occasion. Although it is convenient to study episodes that cover a finite period of time, a particular purpose may be influenced by previous events and may have consequences beyond the specific interchange. Moreover, any episode may involve several functions that affect one another and evolve as the transaction unfolds.

4. **A single nonverbal cue may serve multiple functions.** Direct gaze, for example, may express relational involvement while facilitating learning and behavioral change.

5. **A single function may be accomplished through multiple nonverbal cues.** Fear may be expressed vocally, facially, posturally, proxemically, haptically, or through any combination of these channels.

6. **A single function typically requires the coordination of verbal and nonverbal behaviors.** Communication is usually a cooperative venture among several nonverbal channels and the verbal channel. To understand how communication goals are enacted, it is necessary to study how the various codes work together to attain their aim.

7. **Immediate causes of nonverbal behaviors are of greater interest than original causes.** Although causes and effects of a given function transcend a particular time period, the immediate situational features and the behaviors of other participants that might elicit one's own nonverbal behavior are considered more revealing about communication than are initial causes, such as a traumatic childhood.

The Roles of Context and Culture

For anyone who has traveled abroad, it becomes apparent immediately that many subtle and not-so-subtle differences exist in the ways people communicate in different cultures. Likewise, it is intuitively obvious that the kind of nonverbal communication mandated in the boardroom is inappropriate in the bedroom, and vice versa. Context and culture do make a difference.

The question is, just how large a difference do they make, and do they preclude stating any universal principles? The evidence to date suggests that there are indeed some signals that all members of the human species use and understand. Some of these are reviewed in more detail in Chapter 5. However, even some of these can be modified by culture (see Figure 1.3). Cultures formulate display rules that dictate when, how, and with what consequences these nonverbal expressions will be exhibited. This means that even though people the world over might use the same expression for grief in private, their public display may vary greatly. Thus even innate behaviors may appear with differing frequency, interpretations, and degree of social approval across cultures. This does not deny the universality of the behaviors, but it does reduce the ability to make pancultural generalizations about nonverbal communication.

Culture adds complexity to the picture in other ways. To the extent that cultures hold different world views (e.g., different social, religious, moral, and political values), their communication patterns may manifest these differences. Nonverbal repertoires in one culture may include behaviors not present in another. Mediterranean peoples have far more gestures, for instance, than North Americans. Traditional cultures may use colors and objects in more symbolic ways than technological societies.

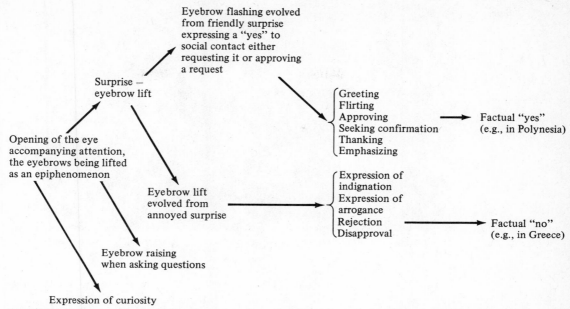

FIGURE 1.3 The eyebrow flash appears to be universal, but cultures differ in the meanings they apply to it.

Furthermore, cultures may use different behaviors to convey the same meaning (e.g., insult gestures) or use the same gestures to convey different meanings. A prime example is when then vice president Richard Nixon undertook a goodwill tour to Latin America. Photographers at his first airport stop flashed pictures of Nixon holding up both hands in the "A-OK" gesture. Unfortunately, that gesture in many Latin American countries means "screw you!" Those irretrievable pictures, splashed across the newspapers of several countries, did not do much for international relations.

Despite the apparent diversity, there are many commonalities across cultures in the basic messages, if not the specific forms, of nonverbal communication. What on the surface appear to be fundamental differences may in reality only be superficial variations on the same underlying theme. For example, all cultures have gestures symbolizing death, but each culture may use a different set that reflects the most common means of committing suicide in that culture. To determine commonalities, it is therefore necessary to look more closely at the behaviors in question to see if they are variants from the same class of behaviors.

More important, while the specific nonverbal "lexicon" may vary from place to place, larger patterns may be consistent across cultures. Acquaintanceship processes, for instance, should all progress through increasing degrees of intimacy, even though the specific intimacy cues used may differ somewhat.

Equally important, many of the differences that can be noted are what

This gesture has meanings ranging from "money" and "OK" to "worthless" and "screw you!"

Berger (1977) refers to as *irrelevant variety.* There are many interesting differences that actually don't make a difference as far as communication goes. It doesn't matter, for example, that Europeans hold their fork one way and North Americans hold theirs another. Before becoming carried away with all the evident variability across cultures, we need to discern what underlying principles operate in each situation and analyze whether these are the same or different for each cultural context.

All of this suggests that nonverbal behaviors cannot be neatly dichotomized as either universal or culture-bound. LaFrance and Mayo (1978a) contend that there are essentially three layers of behavior that range from complete commonality to great dissimilarity, depending on whether they bear content or relate more to form:

> The innermost core represents nonverbal behaviors considered to be universal and innate; facial expressions of some emotional states belong to this core. Next come the nonverbal behaviors that show both uniformity and diversity; members of all cultures display affect, express intimacy, and deal with status but the particular signs of doing so are variable. Finally, there are culture-bound nonverbal behaviors which manifest great dissimilarity across cultures—language-related acts such as emblems, illustrators, and regulators show this diversity most clearly. (p. 73)

Beyond the cultural facet of context are other specific features of the situation. These will almost certainly make a difference, but such differences should be systematic and predictable. A task or business setting evokes one set of routines or "scripts" and carries with it a set of assumptions about what is appropriate or inappropriate behavior. A social setting calls for a different set of appropriate and tolerated behaviors. As long as we can specify the salient features of the situation (e.g., formal or informal, social or task, acquainted or unacquainted, intimate or nonintimate), we should be able to specify regularities in nonverbal behaviors that occur or are expected to occur. Hence, even though the greeting ritual with an intimate friend differs from that used with a new business associate, we can predict that each interaction will open with a ritual and that the ritual will fall within certain bounds (e.g., a hug, kiss, or warm handclasp with the friend, a more reserved handshake and no prolonged touching with the business associate).

In sum, the importance of the context in which communication occurs cannot be overstated. Culture and other situational features can alter significantly the patterns of behavior that are observed. However, some of the observed differences are merely superficial and do not represent fundamental differences in function or meaning. And where real differences exist, these are often systematic and predictable. This makes it possible for us to derive quite a few generalizations about nonverbal communication, some of which are discussed in the next section.

The Role of Individual Differences

Just as some people believe that situational and cultural diversity makes the study of nonverbal communication impossibly complex, so do they believe that individual differences are too great to make any sense out of it all. It is true that no two individuals are alike in their nonverbal patterns and that the same individual may be changeable from one moment to the next. Moreover, when two or more people are paired together, their joint interaction pattern takes on additional uniqueness. Yet a moment's reflection will reassure us that there must be some consistency in behavior across and within people or we could never carry on a conversation; each encounter would be a new and foreign event.

Our expectations that people will commit certain behaviors and omit others are grounded in the normative or typical behavior patterns for a given class of people. While it may be difficult to say exactly how Person A will respond to Person B in Situation X, it is possible to develop some predictions about how people *like* Person A typically respond to people *like* Person B in contexts *like* Situation X. These predictions are based on the average response pattern of similar people under a given circumstance. If Person A is an extrovert and extroverts usually reciprocate direct eye contact, we can anticipate that Person A will do the same when Person B gazes at A. Our predictions will obviously not be error-free, but imperfect knowledge is better than none and allows us to gain greater control of our environment.

In the past, it has been common to rely on personality traits to explain and predict individual differences. But a shift seems to be taking place away from the imprecision and poor predictive power of personality variables to an emphasis on skills. As Friedman (1979a) notes, "The concept of nonverbal skill directs attention away from what people are to what they can do interpersonally" (p. 16). Not only can skills be measured more objectively (e.g., a person can be given a percentage correct score on a judgment test), but they also provide a more direct link to actual communication behavior.

Communication skill essentially can be broken down into two categories—sending ability and receiving ability. Among sending, or encoding, abilities are (a) sending nonverbal cues of affect, orientation, and intention to others, (b) integrating and coordinating verbal and nonverbal signals appropriately, and (c) choosing and implementing communicative acts in a socially appropriate manner. Decoding abilities include (a) accurately interpreting nonverbally expressed emotions, interpersonal orientations, and intentions, (b) integrating verbal and nonverbal meanings to detect sarcasm, joking, and discrepancies as well as amplifications of the verbal message, and (c) understanding social contexts and roles (Hall, 1979).

The amount of skill affects how a person behaves in a given situation and interprets the actions of others. Although it seems possible to come up with an infinite number of combinations and permutations of people and nonverbal behavior, in reality things are not that chaotic. Extensive research, summarized in Buck (1979a), DePaulo and Rosenthal (1979a), Hall (1979), Knapp (1978), Rosenthal, Hall, DiMatteo, Rogers and Archer (1979), and Rosenthal and DePaulo (1979b), reveals some systematic patterns. Based on over 100 studies, the following conclusions seem warranted:

1. **There is significant individual variability in encoding and decoding ability.** Some people are very expressive and easily read, while others are "opaque." By the same token, some people have excellent ability to interpret the expressions of others accurately, while some are very poor interpreters.
2. **Better encoders tend to be better decoders, and vice versa.** However, the relationship is a modest one. The good encoders are not necessarily the same people who are the good decoders. Although it is often reported that encoding and decoding skill go hand in hand, research findings have actually been all across the board, with the most likely conclusion being a relatively weak positive correlation (DePaulo & Rosenthal, 1979a).
3. **The various encoding skills are related to one another, as are the various decoding skills.** People who are better at encoding facially tend to be better at encoding vocally, for example. People who are good at decoding messages of liking and disliking also tend to be more accurate in judging ambivalent messages and deception.
4. **Women are more skilled at nonverbal communication than men.** They are better encoders of visual cues (especially facial cues) and may be better at sending vocal cues. This difference between males and females is not very pronounced in early childhood but becomes more so past preschool. They are also better decoders of nonverbal cues than men, regardless of age and the sex of the sender. This decoding superiority is greatest for facial expressions, followed by body movements, vocal cues, and brief visual cues. Women are less likely to have superiority in identifying discrepant messages.

    This pattern may be due to women being more "accommodating" than men, causing them to attend more closely to the intentional nonverbal messages of others and not to eavesdrop on unintentionally leaked cues. Other plausible explanations for why women might be better nonverbal communicators than men are that women gain more practice observing nonverbal communication because they are more often in passive or submissive roles; that they have an innate advantage; that they have different cognitive styles, possibly including greater ability to match affects with verbal labels; and that brain lateralization may differ for males and females. However, research by Hall (1979) has ruled out as possibilities that women are more skilled because they are more empathic, have more feminine attributes, or are more "oppressed" socially.

Although females do show a clear and consistent advantage over men in the sending and receiving of visual and auditory cues, the actual magnitude of the advantage is small (Hall, 1979). In other words, a lot of other things are as important as or more important than gender in predicting who will be a skilled communicator.

People's basic dispositions tend to parallel their encoding and decoding styles (see Applications, p. 32). Which comes first, the skill or the personality, is a question yet to be answered. But the answer of which is more useful to us in accounting for individual differences is clear. Focusing on skills replaces the need to look at a multiplicity of personality and demographic variables; it is much simpler and more direct to determine if Person A is a skilled encoder or not than to try to assess whether he or she is introverted, anxious, reticent, dogmatic, and so forth and from those attributes to infer how the person will communicate.

Of course, identification of skills isn't the whole picture. People also differ in their preferences, goals, and level of motivation, which results in considerable variability from one interaction to the next. As the study of nonverbal communication advances, we should gain greater understanding of how some of these other factors explain individual differences in behavior.

Competence Versus Performance

In considering the question of cultural, contextual, and individual differences, a helpful distinction is between the ideal or prescribed behavior, which becomes the standard for competent communication, and people's actual behaviors. If you were to ask people in the United States to describe the basic pattern for turn taking, for example, they would tell you that people speak one at a time; to speak simultaneously is a breach of the "taking your turn" rule. However, if you actually watch people talk, you see lots of interruptions, talk-overs, and simultaneous speech.

This is a good illustration of the competence-performance dichotomy. The rule of one turn at a time represents what this culture considers competent behavior. It is the appropriate or preferred way of behaving and is analogous to using grammatical speech. By comparison, people's actual behavior in normal day-to-day interaction may fall short of the ideal because

APPLICATIONS

The Successful Communicator

How can you tell if you have the makings of a skilled communicator? Beyond gender, encoding and decoding ability are related to personality, social predispositions, occupation, age, and training (but not race and intelligence) (DePaulo & Rosenthal, 1979a).

Compare yourself with the following research findings: encoding, or sending, skill increases with such personality and social traits as being more extroverted and nonreticent; being physically attractive; having more self-esteem; being less dogmatic; personalizing emotional experiences more; being more outgoing, socially participative, and adroit; engaging in more self-monitoring; being more socially anxious; being more likely to seek help; being more persuasive and influential; and holding a more complex view of human nature. People who avoid disconcerting or conflictful social situations do not do well at encoding discrepant or mixed messages. Those who see the world in more simple terms also have more difficulty encoding complex emotions; their messages are likely to lack subtlety.

Decoding skills also increase with gregariousness, sociability, experience, age, and training; they decrease as people become more Machiavellian and dogmatic. Interestingly, those who see themselves as persuasive may be good at sending nonverbal messages but are not particularly skilled at receiving them, suggesting that more careful listening and observation of others may be warranted.

If you see yourself among the categories of less skilled communicators, take heart. Training and instruction do improve ability. This book offers much practical information on how you can send the messages you mean to send and more accurately interpret the nonverbal messages of others. If you see yourself among the categories of more skilled communicators, we congratulate you and hope you too realize that you can improve your success with more education and experience.

they use colloquialisms and less formal speech. This is not to say that people are incompetent communicators. They may be fully aware of the proper forms of behavior and may be able to produce them on request. But their typical performance deviates from the standard.

This introduces two important considerations. One is that in describing cultural and situational differences, we need to distinguish between the preferred behavior pattern and the normative performance pattern. For example, even though people are expected to avoid certain kinds of personal behaviors such as twisting hair or rubbing the face during a job interview, they may actually perform these to the same degree that they do in a more private, informal setting. The standards for competent communication differ between the two types of settings, but the actual practice is the same. Conversely, two cultures may both require that subordinates maintain relatively erect posture while listening to a speech by a superior, but one culture may be more lax than the other in adhering to this standard, leading to observed differences in actual performance. Unless it is clear at what level a comparison is being made, this distinction can obscure real similarities and real differences.

The other consideration is that before an individual is classified as lacking communication skill because of a substandard performance, we need to ascertain whether the person knows the proper behavior. It is possible that situational factors are preventing the person from presenting a competent performance or are undermining the person's motivation to do so. Poor performance need not signal incompetence if competence is defined as cognitive knowledge rather than actual practice. If, however, competence is defined as executing the expected behavior at the appropriate time and in the ideal manner, the competence-performance issue is moot. We will try to reserve the term *competence* for cognitive knowledge of the appropriate behavior and to use the expression *competent performance* in circumstances when the actual performance matches the standard.

Summary

This chapter lays the groundwork for studying the codes, processes, and functions of nonverbal communication. Nonverbal behaviors are a central and essential part of the communication process. They contribute significantly to the meaning that is extracted from communicative episodes, and they influence communication outcomes. Possible reasons for this powerful impact include nonverbal cues being omnipresent; forming a sort of universal language system; adding to misunderstanding as well as understanding; expressing what verbal communication cannot or should not; having phylogenetic, ontogenetic, and interaction primacy; and being a trusted system of communication.

Before launching into detailed study of nonverbal communication, it is necessary first to clarify what it entails. A wide range of definitions is possible, some of which use the concepts of information, behavior, and communication interchangeably. In this text, we distinguish among these three. It is also possible to generate different definitions depending on whether one takes a source, receiver, or message orientation. In this text, emphasis is on the third approach, which regards as communication the behaviors that are used with regularity by a social community, are typically encoded with intent, and are typically decoded as intentional. In analyzing these perspectives, we have addressed a number of issues related to intentionally, awareness, propositionality, and meaning, including whether nonverbal behaviors are signs or symbols. The position advanced here is that the total nonverbal communication system includes a mix of signs and symbols with varying degrees of awareness, volition, and propositionality.

Contributing to that mix of signals are seven nonverbal codes that work together to serve a wide range of communication functions. To gain the fullest understanding of how these codes coordinate with one another and with the verbal code to achieve desired outcomes, nonverbal communication should be studied from a processual perspective and should take into account cultural, contextual, and individual differences. This is the approach that will be followed throughout this text.

Suggested Readings

Argyle, M. (1972b). *The psychology of interpersonal behavior.* Baltimore: Penguin.

Burgoon, J. K. (1980). Nonverbal communication in the 1970s: An overview. In D. Nimmo (Ed.), *Communication yearbook 4* (pp. 179–197). New Brunswick, NJ: Transaction Books.

Burgoon, J. K., & Saine, T. J. (1978). *The unspoken dialogue.* Boston: Houghton Mifflin.

Scheflen, A. E. (1967). On the structuring of human communication. *American Behavioral Scientist, 10,* 8–12.

Scheflen, A. E., & Scheflen, A. (1972). *Body language and social control.* Englewood Cliffs, NJ: Prentice-Hall.

Wiener, M., Devoe, S., Rubinow, S., & Geller, J. (1972). Nonverbal behavior and nonverbal communication. *Psychological Review, 79,* 185–214.

CHAPTER 2

Visual and Auditory Codes: Kinesics, Physical Appearance, and Vocalics

> The dominant organ of sensory and social orientation in pre-alphabet societies was the ear—"Hearing was believing." The phonetic alphabet forced the magic world of the eye. Man was given an eye for an ear. . . . The rational man in our Western culture is a visual man.
>
> Marshall McLuhan and Quentin Fiore (1967, p. 44)

Chapters 2 through 4 introduce the seven basic codes of nonverbal behavior. In this chapter, three codes will be examined: kinesics, physical appearance, and vocalics. Sometimes called performance codes, these three codes have the greatest impact on visual and auditory senses and are codes that often come to mind first when people think of nonverbal communication. In Chapter 3, approach-avoidance codes—proxemics and haptics—will be considered, and in Chapter 4 you will see how time, artifacts, and environments can be used to send messages and influence communication. The origin and acquisition of each code, its structural features or code elements, its potential for communication, and norms and standards for its use will be discussed.

Though nonverbal communication is broken into seven distinct codes, codes typically do not operate alone. Discussing them as separate entities is a matter of convenience and tradition, as well as a way of providing a foundation for understanding the processes and functions of nonverbal communication.

Kinesics

> The eyes of men converse as much as their tongues,
> with the advantage that the ocular dialect needs no
> dictionary, but is understood the world over.
>
> Ralph Waldo Emerson

The term *kinesics* derives from the Greek word for "movement" and refers to all forms of body movement, excluding physical contact with another's body. The popular expression "body language" is almost exclusively concerned with this code. Kinesics is one of the richest of the nonverbal codes, which probably accounts for the attention paid it by the popular press. Its preeminence is due in part to the large number of possible human body actions:

1. An estimated 700,000 different physical signs can be produced by humans (Pei, 1965).
2. Birdwhistell (1970) estimates that the face is capable of producing 250,000 expressions.
3. Physiologists estimate that the facial musculature is capable of displaying 20,000 different expressions (Birdwhistell, 1970) (not as large as the previous estimate but nonetheless impressive).
4. Krout (1935, 1954a, 1954b) observed 7,777 distinct gestures in classroom behavior and 5,000 hand gestures in clinical situations.
5. Hewes (1957) reports that 1,000 steady human postures are possible.

This list highlights the large encoding potential of kinesics. When one considers that a person displays more than a single behavior at any instance in an interaction, the many different messages that can be sent by this code are truly enormous. For example, how many ways can you think of to show someone you approve of something he or she has just done? You might engage in a very brief, almost imperceptible head nod or nod your head vigorously. You might smile or combine head nodding and smiling. You might even choose to be more enthusiastic by using arm movements such as shaking both arms with your hands clenched in fists. All these actions can signal approval to the other person, though each transmits a slight variation on that meaning.

The human capacity to receive kinesic messages is also large. We, as receivers, are able to make fine discriminations among the various kinesic actions. Observers can distinguish movements as short as 1/50 of a second. However, the multiplicity of meanings associated with kinesic behaviors often makes the reception of the messages confusing. The Zen parable provides an amusing example of this.

A Zen Parable

In a temple in the northern part of Japan two brother monks were dwelling together. The elder one was learned, but the younger one was stupid and had but one eye.

A wandering monk came and asked for lodging, properly challenging them to a debate about the sublime teaching. The elder brother, tired that day from much studying, told the younger one to take his place. "Go and request the dialogue in silence," he cautioned.

So the young monk and the stranger went to the shrine and sat down.

Shortly afterward the traveler rose and went in to the elder brother and said: "Your young brother is a wonderful fellow. He defeated me."

"Relate the dialogue to me," said the elder one.

"Well," explained the traveler, "first I held up one finger, representing Buddha, the enlightened one. So he held up two fingers, signifying Buddha and his teachings. I held up three fingers, representing Buddha, his teachings and his followers, living the harmonious life. Then he shook his clenched fist in my face, indicating that all three come from one realization. Thus he won. . . ." With this, the traveler left.

"Where is that fellow?" asked the younger one, running in to his elder brother.

"I understand you won the debate."

"Won nothing. I'm going to beat him up."

"Tell me the subject of the debate," asked the elder one.

"Why, the minute he saw me he held up one finger, insulting me by insinuating that I have only one eye. Since he was a stranger I thought I would be polite to him, so I held up two fingers, congratulating him that he has two eyes. Then the impolite wretch held up three fingers, suggesting that between us we only have three eyes. So I got mad and started to punch him, but he ran out and that ended it!"

Source: From *The Gospel According to Zen* (pp. 3–4) by R. Sohl and A. Carr, Eds., 1970, New York: New American Library. (Originally published in *Zen Flesh, Zen Bones* by P. Reps, 1957, Tokyo: Tuttle.)

Origins and Acquisition

When discussing the origin and acquisition of a nonverbal code, it is necessary to consider both the evolution of the act in humans and the development of the behavior in children. The famous biologist Charles Darwin was one of the first scholars to become interested in the evolutionary origin of kinesic behavior. In his classic book, *The Expression of the Emotions in Man and Animal,* Darwin (1965) noted similarities between emotional expressions of humans and those of primates and other lower animal forms. It was his belief that in the development of humans, facial expressions were programmed into the brain due to their importance to survival. For example, closing the eyes, flaring the nostrils, expelling breath, and extending the tongue in the disgust expression were useful in protecting early humans from harmful things in the environment such as rotten food. These facial expressions, though not as essential for survival in today's world, are still evoked when strong emotions are felt or used intentionally to communicate an emotional message.

Another kinesic behavior that has innate origins is tongue showing (Smith, Chase, & Lieblich, 1974). When people are intensely involved in activities requiring concentration, when the interaction contains negative characteristics such as a reprimand, or when communicators feel a loss of physical control or stress, they tend to display their tongue. Smith et al. report that other primates such as gorillas and orangutans show their tongues under similar conditions.

Studies of infants provide evidence for innate development of kinesic behavior. Newborns display many kinesic reflexes. Among the most important may be innate, genetic facial expressions (Andersen, Andersen, & Landgraf, 1985; Buck, 1981; Camras, 1980a, 1982; Ekman, 1978; Ekman & Friesen, 1969b; Izard, 1979; Johnson, Ekman, & Friesen, 1975; Saarni, 1982; Shennum & Bugental, 1982; Trevarthen, 1984). These expressions are similar to adult expressions and are linked directly to emotional states. Two important expressions in this newborn period relate to distress or anger and positive feelings (Emde, 1984). The infant very quickly learns to emit these expressions in response to other people and to use these expressions to control others' behaviors (Argyle & Cook, 1976; Cappella, 1981; Saarni, 1982; Stern, 1980; Trevarthen, 1984).

Like facial expressions, gestures originate at a very early age (Davidson, 1950; Wood, 1981). The pointing gesture usually emerges in the first year. Many gestures are likely learned, but they develop with such regularity that they seem to have some inborn basis.

Table 2.1 summarizes some of the key encoding and decoding abilities that emerge in the first year.

Eye contact, too, has innate properties. Within a few days of birth, infants engage in eye contact and appear to fixate on the caregiver's eyes (Argyle & Cook, 1976; Roedell & Slaby, 1977). Interestingly, the distance at which newborns focus best is the distance from the infant to the mother's eyes when breast feeding. At this very young age, it is likely that the child's gaze is more a signal of attention than any more complex social message (Stechler & Latz, 1966). Further, eye gaze from others innately arouses infants. Argyle and Cook report that in the weeks immediately after birth, simply seeing the eyes of a caregiver is sufficient to produce a smiling reaction. Finally, eye contact is necessary for proper maturation of infants.

TABLE 2.1 Development of Kinesic and Vocalic Encoding and Decoding Abilities

First Week	One to Three Months	Four to Six Months	Seven to Nine Months	Ten to Twelve Months
Kinesics				
Reflexive eye opening and closing. Grasp reflex. Moro reflex in response to sudden noise. Smiles spontaneously to soft sounds or other sensory stimuli.	Smiles, stares at faces and voices. Smiles and grunts differently to mother than others. Visually follows a moving person. Shows distress, delight, excitement. Makes eye to eye contact. Calmed by a face. Moves arms and legs.	Discriminates faces from other patterns. Differentiates among faces. Expresses emotions of fear, disgust, anger. Tries to imitate facial expressions. Smiles, tries to pat other children.	Begins imitating human behaviors. Beginning to point with index finger. Developing manual coordination, ability to stand.	Imitates facial expressions, gestures and movements of adults and other children. May stand and wave. Displays moods and preferences, emotions of anger, happiness, sadness, discomfort. Recognizes emotions in others.
Vocalics				
Cries often. Makes animal-like sounds. Distinguishes pitch and loudness. Prefers high-pitched voices. Tries to focus on voices, aware of their location.	Attentive to voices. Recognizes parent's voice. Can distinguish speech sounds. Develops cooing and vowel-like sounds. Vocalizes frequently. Calmed by voices. Expresses excitement. Crying begins to diminish.	Begins to babble (syllable-like sounds). Squeals and coos when talked to. Laughs, giggles. Expresses pleasure and displeasure. Imitates different tones. Vocalizes to initiate socializing. May use vocalizations to interrupt conversations.	Imitates sounds, sound sequences and intonations. Listens to own vocalizations. Alert to repetitive sounds. Shouts for attention.	Imitates vocal rhythms and inflections better than speech sounds. Controls intonations.

Source: Adapted from *The First Twelve Months of Life* by F. Caplan, 1973, New York: Grosset & Dunlap.

The lack of mutual gaze harms infant interaction and perceptual and social development (Andersen et al., 1985; Robson, 1967).

Not all kinesic behaviors displayed by adults and children are innate. Many are learned through environmental and social experiences. Ekman and Friesen (1969b; also Ekman, 1976; Ekman & Friesen, 1972; Johnson et al., 1975) suggest that some behaviors, though not innate, arise from experiences that all humans acquire through interacting with any environment. They provide two examples: All humans eat with their hands, and all humans have witnessed death. Thus almost all people possess kinesic behaviors representing eating and dying.

However, many of these behaviors show differences across cultures due to experiences that vary from culture to culture. An American emblem for suicide resembles placing a gun to one's temple; the Japanese equivalent involves extending the arms, grasping the hands, and pulling the arms and hands in toward the stomach to represent use of a sword.

Hewes (1957) has documented differences across cultures in common sitting and standing postures that he says are a product of the conditions and tools present in a culture (e.g., the chair-sitting posture in the United States differs from sitting in a deep squat in parts of Asia and Africa due to the lack of chairs in the latter regions). See Figure 2.1 for examples of different postures. Other behaviors that appear to be culture-specific include forms of greeting and parting rituals, occasions for and degree of facial expression usage, and kinesic turn-taking behaviors, to name only a few. Many behaviors are specifically taught by older members of the culture to infants and children. Others are learned through conscious or unconscious imitation. Either way, by school age, children appear to possess a rich repertoire of kinesic behaviors.

Acquisition of nonverbal behaviors continues into the elementary school years. Here, however, it is not the development of new behaviors but the ability to use the behaviors in socially acceptable ways that is learned. Improvements in the performance of facial expressions continue into late elementary school age, when ability stabilizes (Buck, 1977; Ekman, Roper, & Hager, 1980; Odom & Lemond, 1972). At the same time, children learn display rules for the use of these expressions and the ability to mask or inhibit facial expressions (Saarni, 1979, 1982; Shennum & Bugental, 1982), as well as how to use a facial expression symbolically to transmit an emotion that is not felt (Morency & Krauss, 1982; Moyer, 1975). Finally, many kinesic turn-taking behaviors improve during this period (Andersen et al., 1985).

Thus kinesic behavior is acquired in three ways:

1. From innate neurological processes passed on genetically and developed through evolution.
2. From experiences common to all humans as they interact with the environment.
3. Through culture-specific tasks and social interactions that produce varying experiences across cultures, subcultures, and individuals.

Before leaving this discussion of origins and acquisition, we must comment on the other side of the process: recognition of kinesic behavior. The ability to recognize kinesic behavior is partly innate and develops very rapidly during the first year of life. Orienting gaze toward others appears very early in a newborn's life (Argyle & Cook, 1976). Stern (1980) observed that between the ages of 6 weeks and 3 months, infants begin smiling in response to other faces, suggesting an ability to decode facial cues during this period. By 3 months infants recognize familiar faces. Recognition of affect displays also comes quickly (Andersen et al., 1985; Odom & Lemond, 1972). In general, the ability to decode kinesic cues increases with age, peaking during the teens (Buck, 1981; Camras, 1977, 1980b; Hamilton,

FIGURE 2.1 Posture types from the classification scheme of Hewes. The figures numbered 301 through 306 (top row) are common resting positions; the arm-on-shoulder postures of the next four figures are found mainly among western American Indians. In the next row are variations of the one-legged Nilotic stances, found in the Sudan, Venezuela, and elsewhere. Chair sitting (third row) spread from the ancient Middle East, but the Arabs there have replaced it with floor sitting.

1973; Honkavaara, 1961; Morency & Krauss, 1982; Odom & Lemond, 1972; Pendleton & Snyder, 1982; Rosenthal, Hall, DiMatteo, Rogers, & Archer, 1979; Zabel, 1979).

Structural Features

In response to the vast number of kinesic behaviors, classification methods have been developed to make the study of kinesics more manageable. Two ways of classifying behaviors have been used, focusing on structure or function.

The system developed by Birdwhistell (1970) is by far the most elaborate and famous example of a structural approach. In his system, Birdwhistell has sought to identify discrete, universal kinesic behaviors that are combined to produce nonverbal communication. He refers to it as the linguistic-kinesic analogy because it is modeled after the linguistic classification system that distinguishes discrete units of language behavior like phonemes and morphemes. Phonemes are units of sound in human speech, and morphemes are combinations of phonemes, like words and sentences, that carry meaning. Birdwhistell reasons that since kinesics appear to be tied to speech, they should exhibit similar structures as language.

In Birdwhistell's system, the smallest meaningful unit of behavior is a *kineme.* Birdwhistell has identified 50 to 60 kinemes that he considers culturally universal. That is, cultural differences in kinesic behavior come from variations within kinemes, not from the use of different kinemes. Birdwhistell has identified kinemes in eight regions: total head; face; trunk; shoulders, arms, and wrists; hand and finger activity; hips, legs, and ankles; foot activity (including walking); and neck. As Figure 2.2 shows, there are 32 or 33 kinemes in the head and face regions alone.

Kinemes are actually comprised of ranges of behaviors that are recognizable in a culture but do not possess unique meaning. These are known as *kines.* Variations in the intensity, duration, or extent of these behaviors are called *allokines* or *kine variants.* Although trained observers have noted as many as 23 different eyelid positions (Birdwhistell himself claims to observe 15), only four positions appear to change the meaning. Thus muscular adjustments of the eyelid around these four kineme positions are considered allokinic. Other groups of allokines are based on the side of the body used to display the kines. Winks by the left and right eye can be considered allokines, as can movements by left and right forefingers. The test is whether it makes a difference which side of the body displays the kine. If it does not, the kines are allokines.

When used, kinemes are combined into *kinemorphs,* which are similar to words in the linguistic system. Kinemorphs are grouped by classes and often occur in concert with other kinemorphs to produce complex kinemorphic constructions similar to sentences. It is at the level of kinemorphic constructions that the meaning of kinesic behavior becomes fully understandable. For instance, if you want to comfort a distraught friend, you might lower your head, lower your eyelids slightly, and lean your body in her direction. These behaviors singly and separately may not communicate

FIGURE 2.2 Birdwhistell's notation symbols for facial kinemes.

sympathy, but displayed together, they indicate your compassion and understanding.

Additional behaviors classified by Birdwhistell include kinesic *markers, stress,* and *juncture.* Kinesic markers are movements that occur with or stand for syntactic arrangements in speech. Markers can stand for pronouns, indicate pluralizations, mark verbs, designate area, and indicate the manner of events. Kinesic stress includes movements that occur regularly, marking special linguistic combinations such as clauses, phrases, adjectives with nouns, and the like. Four levels of stress are *primary stress* (strong movements), *secondary stress* (weak movements), *unstressed* (normal flow with speech), and *destress* (reduction of kinesic behavior below normal). Finally, kinesic junctures are behaviors that serve to connect or separate kinesic phenomena, such as a slight lengthening of movement at the end of a complex kinemorphic stream.

The approach used by Ekman and Friesen (1969b) focuses instead on functions of kinesic behaviors. Their system divides kinesics into five categories—emblems, illustrators, affect displays, regulators, and adaptors—each performing different functions or displaying different meanings.

Emblems are kinesic behaviors that meet the following criteria (Ekman, 1976; Ekman & Friesen, 1969b):

1. They have a direct verbal translation and can be substituted for the word or words they represent without affecting the meaning.
2. Their precise meaning is known by most or all members of a social group.
3. They are most often used with conscious intent to transmit a message.
4. They are recognized by the receiver as meaningful and intentionally sent.
5. The sender takes responsibility for them.
6. They have clear meaning even when displayed out of context.

Common American emblems include palms turned up and lifted shoulders meaning "I don't know," running an extended forefinger across the front of the neck meaning "stop what you are doing," and outstretched arm with waving hand meaning "hello."

Illustrators are kinesic acts accompanying speech that are used to aid in the description of what is being said, trace the direction of speech, set the rhythm of speech, and gain and hold a listener's attention. They may accent, complement, repeat, or contradict what is being said. Ekman and Friesen isolate eight types of illustrators: *Batons* emphasize a phrase or word, *ideographs* draw the direction or path of thought, *deictic movements* point to an object, *spatial movements* show a spatial relationship, *kinetographs* display a bodily action, *pictographs* sketch a picture of the referent, *rhythmic movements* show timing or rhythm of an event, and *emblematic movements* repeat or substitute for words in illustrating the spoken words.

Affect displays reveal emotions. In their extensive work in this area, Ekman and Friesen have identified a number of universal emotions that are tied to neurological processes. Thus they may be intentional or unintentional, accompany speech or stand alone, and transmit true emotions or be used symbolically, like emblems. These affect displays will be discussed more fully in Chapter 10.

Regulators are kinesic behaviors designed to maintain or regulate turn taking between two or more interactants. Rather than commenting on the verbal stream, regulators coordinate conversational flow and pacing and carry no message content. These behaviors are learned at a very young age, are displayed at very low levels of awareness, and are produced almost involuntarily. Regulatory cues will be discussed in Chapters 11 and 12.

Adaptors are behaviors that typically occur in private to satisfy physical or psychological needs. These behaviors satisfy personal needs, perform bodily functions, manage emotions, maintain interpersonal contact, and complete instrumental activities. Because they are designed to help the individual adapt to stresses or needs, adaptors are habits that usually are not intended to communicate a message. However, they can be quite informative about the source's internal state and occasionally are used with intent as an insult or message of disrespect.

There are three types of adaptors—*self-adaptors, alter-directed adaptors, and object adaptors*—distinguished by the target of the behavior. Scratching your arm, playing with your hair, or picking your nose are self-adaptors. Alter-directed adaptors are movements related to interpersonal contacts. When nervous about talking with someone, you might cross your arms on your chest to protect against the other communicator or release anger by swiping at someone. Finally, object adaptors involve the manipulation of objects in the environment, such as tapping a pencil or smoking a cigarette.

Structural and functional approaches are both useful in the study of kinesics; however, the functional approach with its emphasis on the purposes of behavior conforms more with our approach to nonverbal communication.

Eye Contact. One of the most important facets of kinesic behavior is eye behavior. Eye gaze or eye contact is often separated from discussions of

Adaptors are behaviors that satisfy physiological and psychological needs. Which kinds of adaptors are present on the left and the right? What needs do they satisfy?

kinesics, with many scholars preferring to treat it as a separate channel. Neither Birdwhistell nor Ekman and Friesen include eye behavior in their classification systems.

Eye behavior is included in our definition of kinesics because it is a body movement, is encoded along with other kinesic behaviors, and is integral to the total kinesic repertoire. Moreover, the eyes are used to perform many of the same functions as other kinesic behaviors, including expressing interpersonal attitudes or emotions, regulating interactions, signaling attention, and producing anxiety or arousal in another person (Argyle & Cook, 1976). Eye behavior does have a special function—gathering information from others (Argyle & Cook, 1976; Rutter, Pennington, Dewey, & Swain, 1984; Rutter & Stephenson, 1979; Rutter, Stephenson, Ayling, & White, 1978); however, this function is insufficient reason to separate eye contact from the other kinesic behaviors.

While eye behavior has garnered a good deal of research attention, very few systems identifying the units of eye behavior exist. Von Cranach and Ellgring (1973) have proposed a structural system based on the length, direction, duration, and reciprocation of gaze. For these authors, a *one-sided look* is a gaze in the direction of the partner's face that is not reciprocated by the partner. There are two types of one-sided looks: *face gaze* (unreciprocated gaze at the partner's face) and *eye gaze* (unreciprocated gaze at the partner's eyes). Gaze by both partners directed at each others' faces is considered a *mutual look,* whereas gaze by both partners directed at each others' eyes that both partners are aware of is *eye contact.* Finally, *gaze avoidance* occurs when one partner intentionally avoids the partner's eyes, and *gaze omission* happens when a partner fails to look at partner without intent to avoid eye contact.

More recently, Rutter and his colleagues (Rutter et al., 1984; Rutter & Stephenson, 1979; Rutter et al., 1978) have distinguished *looking* and *eye contact* on the basis of their functional nature. Looking is face gaze or mutual gaze intended to discover how the partner is reacting to the communication. Eye contact is mutual gaze with no need for information. As yet, Rutter's distinctions have not been adopted extensively by other scholars; however, his research suggests that this distinction is useful for classifying eye behavior (Rutter et al., 1984).

Norms and Standards

Although individual variability exists, kinesic behaviors are highly normative at the cultural and subcultural level. To identify norms of behavior, it is essential to understand the background against which the behavior is performed—characteristics of the individuals, their relationship, and the context. Allport and Vernon (1937) identified 11 personal characteristics that influenced the selection and frequency of behaviors: personality, sex, race and culture, age, body deformities, health, metabolic or structural peculiarities, body type, strain or fatigue, transitional emotional states or moods, and special habits from unique training (athletic or dramatic training). Individual goals should also be added to this list. You can no doubt come up with many examples of how these variables might influence the choice of kinesic behaviors and the perceptions of kinesic norms. Chapter 6 is devoted to discussion of cultural, racial, gender, and personality characteristics because of their large impact on how we communicate nonverbally.

The relationship between the communicators has a great effect on kinesic norms and usage. How well two people like each other and the degree to which they have equal or unequal status will affect what kinesic patterns are normative and preferred. Length of the relationship is particularly important to this relational definition. In newer relationships, interactants are more likely to misinterpret the meaning of a kinesic cue, especially if it is used in an unusual way by the relational partner. The longer people are in a relationship, the more likely they are to negotiate a definition specific to that relationship (Miller & Steinberg, 1975), thus the less likely outside persons or groups are to determine the norms.

Another consideration is the purpose of the interaction. Interactions can be distinguished loosely as task-oriented or social-oriented and as formal or informal. Each calls for a different set of kinesic behaviors. Many behaviors are determined by the norms of a culture or social group; these can be labeled conventions.

Finally, environmental features place constraints on what kinesic patterns emerge. For instance, emblems are more likely to be displayed when noise or distance blocks verbal communication (Ekman, 1976). A more extended discussion of this is presented in Chapter 11.

The people characteristics, relationship variables, and context factors combine to produce large variability in the use and interpretation of kinesic cues. This is not to say that predictable, consistent patterns are always evident, but the interrelationship of these factors produces a complex system where no behavior exists in isolation. With this qualification in mind, let us examine the norms and standards for each of Ekman and Friesen's kinesic categories, as well as eye contact.

APPLICATIONS

Learning Emblems

Be it for pleasure or business, someday you are likely to need to learn new emblems. If you travel to a foreign country, one of the most obvious communication differences you will encounter is the use of emblems. Paul Ekman and his colleagues (Ekman, 1976; Ekman & Friesen, 1969b, 1972; Friesen, Ekman, & Wallbott, 1979; Johnson et al., 1975) report that emblems are common in every culture. Some cultures, like middle-class U.S. culture, have less than 100 emblems, while others, like Israeli student culture, have over 250 emblems. Luckily for you, some emblems carry cross-cultural meaning. Ekman reports that emblems perform six functions in all cultures: (a) insulting others, (b) giving interpersonal directions

Learning Emblems (*Continued*)

("come here" or "be quiet"), (c) greeting others, (d) signaling departure, (e) replying to questions or requests ("yes" or "no"), and (f) commenting on physical or emotional states. Further, all cultures seem to use emblems in similar places in conversations—at the beginning or end of a turn, in filled pauses, and preceding or accompanying the words they repeat. Emblems such as those deriving from facial affect displays carry common meaning across cultures. Other emblems, such as eating and drinking emblems, bear some cross-cultural similarity because they arise from common experiences with the environment.

Unfortunately, the majority of emblems have meaning only for members of a particular culture. Generally, this simply means that the person to whom you are communicating will not understand your meaning when you use an emblem from your home culture. However, the use of some emblems may have more disastrous results, because they have entirely different meanings in another culture. If you like, turn ahead to Figure 6.1 and see if you know what each emblem means.

Intercultural interactions are not the only places where you will encounter unfamiliar emblems. Many businesses and professions develop emblems that improve communication among their members. Like cultures, many of these emblems carry meaning only among employees of a particular business or members of a particular profession. Beyond improving communication, knowing these emblems identifies you as a member of that business or profession. For example, Davidson (1950) documented emblems used by grain traders on the floor of the Chicago Board of Trade. The noise and chaos make verbal communication almost impossible, so traders must indicate their intentions through emblems: palm of hand held up and inward ("buy"), palm of hand held outward ("sell"), fingers held vertically to indicate quantities traded (5,000 bushels per finger), fingers held horizontally to indicate price (⅛ cent per finger). Emblems are also used to identify the brokerage house the trader works for.

Thus learning emblems and their norms for use is an important ongoing facet of nonverbal communication.

Illustrators. Norms of illustrator usage have not been well documented, although it is evident some cultures and subcultures are more "illustrative" than others. Exaggerated and stylized gestures used to be more common among actors and public speakers. At the turn of the century, the Del Sarte School of Oratory believed that particular forms and loci of gestures would dictate particular meanings. In more recent years, public speakers have gained more flexibility in the illustrators they use. (See Figure 2.3.)

The Hand Purse   The Thumb-and-Forefinger Touch   The Air Hold   The Hand Bend   The Air Grasp

The Hand-Chop   The Hand Scissor   The Hand Jab   The Air Punch   The Raised Forefinger Baton

The Palm Up   The Palm Down   The Palm Front   The Palm Back   The Palm Side

FIGURE 2.3 Selected illustrators.

Affect Displays. At a basic level, all cultures share a limited set of facial affect displays (Ekman, Sorenson, & Friesen, 1969); however, cultures have unique rules governing when affect displays are appropriate and inappropriate (Ekman & Friesen, 1969b). For example, U.S. culture encourages boys to mask negative emotions such as sadness or grief and not to display an overabundance of tenderness, affection, or emotionality in general. Conversely, women are allowed to show more emotions than males, but they have been trained to maintain a pleasant front. A more extended discussion of gender differences in affect displays appears in Chapters 6 and 10.

Regulators. Regulator behaviors are the most rule-governed of all kinesic behaviors and are displayed almost involuntarily in interactions. One regulator for which norms have been investigated is eye behavior. The following facts have been established (Ellsworth & Ludwig, 1972; Kendon, 1967, 1978):

1. The normal amount of gaze in an interaction ranges from 28% to 70% of the time.
2. Under stress conditions, the range broadens to from 8% to 73% of the time.

3. Eye contact increases when listening (30%–80% of the time) and decreases when speaking (25%–65% of the time).
4. Individuals are consistent in their looking patterns.
5. Interactants coordinate their looking patterns.
6. Gaze aversion is more frequent when discussing difficult topics, when uncertain, or when ashamed.
7. Sex, race, and personality affect the amount of eye contact.

Not all gaze serves a regulatory function; gaze also performs surveillance, information-gathering, attention-signaling, and relational functions. Rutter has suggested that looking increases when information is needed from another person and that the amount of looking is influenced by the interpersonal relationship. The need to monitor behavior and to be seen by the other person influences the frequency of gaze (Rutter et al., 1984; Rutter & Stephenson, 1979; Rutter et al., 1978).

Adaptors. The primary norm governing adaptor display is to avoid using adaptors in public. This is especially true of self-adaptors, which are permitted only in the privacy of one's own home and in the presence of very intimate relational partners. The comedian Bill Cosby has noted that at home, only fathers are allowed to have "gas." Alter-oriented and object adaptors are more permissible in public. Cigarette smoking is acceptable in many social situations, though recently, nonsmokers have started demanding rules limiting smoking in public places. Gum chewing is less acceptable in many social situations and is considered déclassé behavior in many countries, such as Germany. Often object adaptors are used to signal membership in a particular group. In some academic circles, pipe smoking by professors and their protégés is quite common. Beyond the public versus nonpublic and group-specific rules, few other norms for adaptor behavior exist.

Communication Potential

When considering a code's communication potential, it is important to examine how well it lends itself to use by a source—its encoding potential—and to perception by a receiver—its decoding potential. A number of characteristics make kinesics one of the most powerful codes in the nonverbal communication system, perhaps the most powerful.

Encoding Potential. The enormous number of kinesic behaviors at a source's disposal has already been mentioned. This code easily exceeds any other in the sheer number of possible cues. In addition, a single source can perform many of these cues at the same time. This produces a multichanneled message capable of many shades of meaning. A source can perform multiple functions simultaneously. At a given point in a conversation, kinesic cues can signal an emotion, coordinate the switch between speaker and listener, comment on the relationship of the source and receiver, and maintain a desired front. Only the vocalic code rivals kinesics in its ability to transmit multiple meanings and perform multiple functions simultaneously.

Finally, the innate basis of many of the kinesic cues makes it almost an unconscious choice to transmit many messages. Though some cues are unintentional, children learn very early in life to manipulate kinesic cues to affect the people around them.

Decoding Potential. Humans have a strong bias to attend to kinesic cues, due to the innate tendency to orient to others visually, the overtly noticeable and attention-getting characteristics of kinesics, and the many functions kinesic cues serve.

There is, though, a down side to the communication potential of kinesics. First, the large number of cues and their many combinations are often ambiguous or confusing, leading to misunderstandings and conflict. Also, the intrinsic relationship between many kinesic cues and communicators' feelings and emotions often leads to unintentional displays. Since receivers are likely to consider kinesic cues as intentional and truthful, communicators are sometimes faced with unexpected or undesirable reactions due to unwitting displays. Finally, people learn to mask or substitute kinesic cues, which makes accurate decoding more difficult. This is especially true for facial expressions and thus does not bode well for communicators biased toward attending to facial cues. All in all, though, the many advantages of kinesics outweigh these few disadvantages, leading to the conclusion that kinesics is a powerful nonverbal channel for communication.

Physical Appearance

> Being well groomed is an asset.
>
> Dry cleaner's slogan

Physical appearance has been an important issue for humans since prehistoric times. Natural features and body adornments are overt, attention-getting, and diverse. They are especially important in impression formation and management. What impressions do you form of a slender woman with jet-black hair and olive complexion wearing a luxurious white fur coat over a black dress? In encounters with others, we frequently make judgments of others based only on physical appearance cues. These are essential to the communication process because they allow us to communicate successfully with strangers, about whom we have little information. As communicators, each of us manipulates these physical appearance cues.

Origins and Acquisition

Most natural features are genetic and have developed through the evolution of the human species. Differences in facial structure, skin color, hair texture, eye color, and the like stem from independent evolutionary development. Natural features are passed from generation to generation because natural characteristics have survival value for the species (Darwin, 1965; Freedman, 1969).

Beyond natural features, cultures and subcultures determine a person's conception of what is attractive, how natural features should be styled, and how the body should be adorned. Excavations of human burial sites from Neanderthal times have found evidence of natural pigments used to paint the body. Drawings, carvings, and writings from the earliest civilizations reveal that ancient peoples painted the skin, constructed elaborate jewelry, created clothing and uniforms, and applied perfumes and oils, all in an effort to enhance the body's appearance. Here are some examples:

1. Face painting by Asians, Africans, and American Indians is thought to be a forerunner of today's cosmetics.
2. There are many biblical accounts of perfumes, oils, essences, and lotions used to anoint the body.
3. During Renaissance times, Italian women applied belladonna to their eyes to enlarge the pupils, making them more attractive.
4. In Roman and medieval societies, purple robes were symbols of authority.
5. Body disfigurations such as tattoos, foot binding, circumcision, and flesh piercing have occurred at various times in history.

For many of us, physical appearance needs rank alongside food and shelter needs. In today's society, beauty and fashion are multibillion-dollar industries. We purchase enormous quantities of cosmetics, perfumes, deodorants, soaps, clothing, jewelry, and shoes. Many people are employed in service industries related to physical appearance, including fashion consultants and retailers, hairdressers and barbers, manicurists, orthodontists and dentists, and plastic surgeons. Some of these industries are among the most financially stable even in the worst economic times. Many fads revolve around physical appearance. Each day many people rearrange work, leisure, and sleep habits to sweat, hurt, and moan in the name of beauty. Although there are many health benefits to jogging, aerobics, weight training, and other participatory sports, a major purpose of these physical fitness programs is improving the body's attractiveness. Moreover, people strive to look good while exercising. Grubby sweatsuits have been replaced by stylish designer outfits.

Notions of attractiveness develop early. Infants get a sense of their own body and those of others through touch, sight, and smell. Parents, other adults, and peers instill in the child the appearance norms of the culture and subculture. Babies learn accepted clothing norms through the clothes they wear and see on others. Children are taught to wear clothing appropriately; keeping pants and dresses on in public is an important norm that must be learned. By nursery school age, children's notions of beauty are surprisingly similar to adult perceptions, and like many adults, as they get older, children prefer attractive friends (Berscheid & Walster, 1972, 1974).

One way adults reinforce appearance norms for children is through

"Shape Up or Ship Out," Navy Personnel Ordered

NORFOLK, VA. (AP) — It's shape up or ship out for service-men under the command of an admiral who thinks "people are beginning to wonder what has happened to the clean-cut American sailor."

Rear Adm. Clinton W. Taylor, head of the Atlantic Fleet Training Command, has banned civilian clothes for sailors in Navy apprentice schools. . . .

Taylor . . . also has told officers and enlisted men to follow haircut regulations. . . .

Dress codes that have existed for years in the Navy have not been enforced lately by the senior enlisted men and officers respon-sible, Taylor said. . . .

A Navy captain who wore his insignia improperly and had hair considered too long was chastised. And an enlisted man dressed more for the disco than the military was kicked off base by officers.

"Personal appearance, pride, performance and professional-ism are the attributes of any first-class organization," [Rear Adm. Joseph F.] Frick told a base publication.

Source: Lansing State Journal, February 17, 1981, p. A3.

their reactions to children's appearances. Brody (1963) found that the ways in which black mothers dealt with blacks and whites affected their children's concept of being black. Berscheid and Walster (1972, 1974) and Dion (1972) conducted a series of studies on teacher perceptions of attractive and unattractive students. Their results showed that teachers hold more favor-able impressions of attractive students, which could lead to special treat-ment, cuing other children that beauty is preferred. Dion's experiment is particularly interesting because it focused on teacher reactions to physical aggression by children. Unattractive students were regarded as engaging in more chronic antisocial behavior and severe transgressions, as more likely to transgress in the future, and as more dishonest and unpleasant overall than attractive children, even though the transgressions were identical. The Ann Landers letter exemplifies the effect of parental reactions on children's notions of physical attractiveness.

Another important source of attractiveness and appearance norms is the media. Actors and actresses in most programs and advertisements are "beautiful people," conforming closely to cultural stereotypes of appear-ance. Even "hidden camera" commercials of "real" people show at least moderately attractive people. The effect of pop stars' taste in clothing on the dress styles of young people is testament to the media's ability to shape appearance norms and fads.

Parent Views Can Hurt Kids

Dear Ann Landers: Your advice to the mother who was worried about her baby's large nose was excellent. Concern about a child's looks comes through as "rejection" and can ruin a child's life. I speak from experience. It happened to me.

My mother focused on my homeliness as far back as I can remember. If it wasn't my hair, it was my teeth, my height or my posture. She made me self-conscious and miserable. I hated to look in the mirror. . . .

All this changed when a 19-year-old boy whose life I saved fell in love with me. I was convinced that he was just grateful. It took a lot of convincing before I would believe he really loved me. . . .

Tell the world my story, Ann. So many people need to know.

J. in D.C.

Dear J: . . . The lesson is clear. Unfortunately, in our culture, too much emphasis is placed on good looks, not only by mothers but [by] society.

This unkind sword can cut two ways. Sometimes the "beauty" feels she doesn't need to develop any talents or reach out to others. She expects the world to sit at her feet and admire her. The not-so-beautiful girl is obliged to put herself out to become involved, productive and friendly. Ask any man with a working brain cell which kind he prefers. He will also tell you that beauty alone can be empty, dull and boring.

Source: Ann Landers, May 12, 1981, *Lansing State Journal,* syndicated column, p. D2.

Structural Features

Natural Features. Unlike kinesics, little effort has been directed at classifying units or cues of physical appearance. However, a few researchers have been interested in *body shape* or *somatotype,* the most prominent natural feature. Somatotype relates to the general shape of the body. Because body shape is for the most part genetic, it is usually not considered part of the nonverbal communication system. However, somatotypes can be altered by diet, exercise, and surgery, to a limited extent, and may be communicative if a person intentionally alters it to manipulate impressions. Although intentional encoding of body shape is restricted, we sometimes treat it as an indication of personality traits (Cortes & Gatti, 1965).

Cortes and Gatti (1965) identify three somatotypes: endomorph, mesomorph, and ectomorph (see Figure 2.4). The *endomorph* is round, short, plump, and soft. Dom DeLuise and Oprah Winfrey are endomorphs. The *mesomorph* is athletic, trim, muscular, average in height, and V-shaped, with wide shoulders and a body that tapers to a thin waist. Tom Selleck and Chris Evert are mesomorphs. The *ectomorph* is tall, thin, and frail. Michael Jackson and Cher are ectomorphs.

A second prominent natural feature is *physiognomy,* which is one's hereditary facial structure, skin color, hair texture (and to some extent color), eye shape, and eye color. There are three general classes of physiognomies. *Negroid* characteristics include generally large round brown eyes, flat nose with flared nostrils, very full lips, brown skin pigmentation, and thick, tightly curled dark brown or black hair. *Caucasoid* characteristics generally include medium round brown or blue eyes, large thin nose, thin to medium-full lips, white skin, and straight or slightly curly blond to dark brown hair. *Mongoloid* features entail thin to medium slanted brown or black eyes, small and slightly flat nose, thin lips, light yellow or red skin, and straight dark brown

FIGURE 2.4 The three somatotypes.

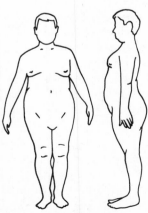
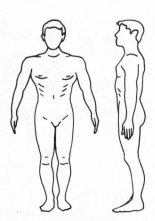
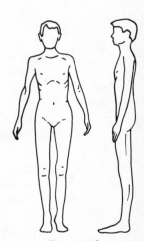

Endomorph   Mesomorph   Ectomorph

or black hair. An individual may closely fit the central characteristics of one of these groups or may show a blend of features. Consequently, physiognomy is not a very dependable predictor of racial or ethnic background. Moreover, because these features are involuntary and remain relatively stable throughout a person's life, they should not be considered part of a communication code.

Similarly, because *skin color* is inherited and largely a static cue, it has limited communication capacity, although it can be manipulated slightly through makeup and tanning. As a source of information, skin color may identify cultural and subcultural boundaries. In turn, some subcultures have preferences for, and reactions to, skin color that determine who will or can communicate with whom.

Hair, including *body, facial,* and *cranial hair,* is a highly variable natural feature. It can be stiffened, frizzed, curled, braided, perfumed, tinted, cropped short, grown out, shaved off completely, and covered with a wig. For body hair, amount and location are the main considerations. Facial hair shows more variation, with amount, location, color, and style being most important. Cranial hair is by far the most varied in amount, location, color, texture, and style. A whole industry has developed around the maintenance of cranial hair.

Adornment Features. Clothing, jewelry, accessories, and cosmetics are adornment features, so called because they are worn on the body. Adornment features are more communicative than natural features due to perceptions of intentional choice and placement on the body. *Clothing,* often thought to be an extension of the skin (Frank, 1971), has the most variability and the largest number of cues of any adornment feature. Color, style, location, amount, fabric texture, pattern and design, neatness, and fashionableness can all be varied. People also decode or interpret clothing on numerous dimensions. These include fashionability, color, pattern, decoration, comfort, interest, conformity, conventionality, and economy (Aiken, 1963; Bickman, 1974a; Birren, 1952; Compton, 1962; Gibbons & Gwynn, 1975; Pinaire-Reed, 1979). Many times, however, selection is based on personal preference or moods (Compton, 1962; Rosenfeld & Plax, 1977) and is less communicative. Nevertheless, the effect of dress on impressions of one's physical, socioeconomic, and personality characteristics makes clothing cues very important to the communication process.

Jewelry, accessories, and *cosmetics* also are highly variable in color, style, location, amount, construction, materials, pattern and design, and fashionableness. As with clothing, though, selection is not always communicative.

Norms and Standards

Generally in the North American culture, the preferred body types are mesomorphic males and ectomorphic females. This does not correspond to the average body type of the population, since most people are slightly overweight. However, obesity is definitely a stigma in this culture (Cahnman, 1968). Obese people are avoided by others and the subject of jokes and ridicule. In some other cultures, obesity is favorably regarded: "Where affluence is attainable only by a privileged few, obesity, especially in women, is likely to be regarded as prestigious and therefore attractive" (Cahnman, 1968, p. 287). Unfortunately, obesity is not always controllable; sometimes, it is genetically or physiologically determined.

Iliffe (1960) had 4,355 British subjects rank pictures of 12 women on degree of attractiveness. Males and females of all ages and occupational groups reported the same general ranking. Singer and Lamb (1966) reported a consistent norm of feminine beauty: 5 ft. 5 in. tall, 120 lbs., bust 35 in., waist 22.5 in., hips 35 in., 11.3-in. neck, 5.7-in. wrist, and 7.22-in. ankles. Preferences for height, weight, bust, waist, and hip measurements were more consistent across the respondents, suggesting that people do not have stereotypes for neck, wrist, and ankle sizes. Even more interesting is the finding that respondents distorted perceptions of their own characteristics in the direction of these ideals. This is a convenient strategy that allows us to live with imperfections in our appearance.

Stereotypes of male attractiveness are less well documented. One study reports that women prefer V-shaped men to pear-shaped men. That is, they like broad arms and upper trunk and thin lower trunk and legs (Lavrakas, 1975).

There appears to be a general preference for Caucasoid features in this culture. In 1964, Martin found that beauty standards among American black respondents placed black women with Caucasoid features higher than women with Negroid features. (This was not true for a Nigerian sample, who rated Negroid features as equally attractive.) Although campaigns such as the "black is beautiful" movement may have increased the attraction toward Negroid and Mongoloid features, the Caucasoid-like features of Vannessa Williams, the first black Miss America, suggest that the old standard still prevails.

Tanning is a related skin color norm, developed among Caucasians in this century. Prior to the 1900s, white skin was prized, because a tan indicated that you were poor and worked in the fields. Now tanned skin is a symbol of status and wealth in our culture.

Currently, among males, shorter cranial hair and little facial hair is normative. However, we still see mustaches and beards, though sideburns and goatees are not as popular as they were only 10 or 15 years ago. Facial hairstyles for men have changed greatly throughout history, as have cranial hairstyles. Abraham Lincoln is a good example. He was the first president to sport a beard and established a norm that was followed by a number of subsequent presidents. The Pentagon recently changed the hair norm for Marine embassy guards, as a result of terrorist attacks. The government felt that the short hairstyle of Marine guards is too well known, making them more vulnerable to identification and attack by terrorists.

For women, cranial hair styles are more varied and changeable. However, lack of body hair remains a fairly strict norm for women in American culture.

There are, of course, subcultural and individual differences in what is

Abraham Lincoln started something of a fad of beards on presidents.

considered attractive. The old cliché that beauty is in the eyes of the beholder is indeed valid. Physical appearance preferences fluctuate across age groups, socioeconomic levels, occupations, regions, and races, as well as across time (see Figure 2.5 for different eras in hemlines). Fashions seem to originate in metropolitan areas on the East and West coasts in the United States then move into suburban and rural areas. People in colder climates tend to wear darker colors, while people in warmer climates wear brighter and lighter colors. People in equatorial locations often wear less clothing than those in colder climates. The use of a veil to cover a woman's face is still seen in a few Middle Eastern countries. Covering of the genital region is nearly a universal norm, and in many cultures women cover their breasts. Athletic teams specify uniforms to be worn on the field, and sometimes they specify the attire to be worn off the field (Harris, Ramsey, Sims, & Stevenson, 1974). Other groups do not specify uniforms but have implicit or

Skirts Up—The Roaring Twenties   Skirts Down—The Great Depression

Skirts Up—Active Wartime Economy   Skirts Down—Post-War Austerity

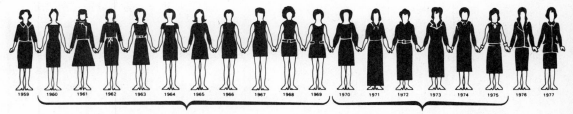

Skirts Up—The Swinging Sixties   Skirts Down—The New Recession

FIGURE 2.5 One interesting clothing norm is skirt length. In this century, skirt length norms have correlated with economic conditions. When economic conditions are poor, skirt lengths tend to go down; when the economy improves, skirt lengths go up.

explicit dress codes. You and your friends probably dress similarly. This similarity can be considered an implicit dress code. Businesses frequently have formal explicit dress codes.

In one of the few studies on dress norms, Ramsey (1976) was able to identify groups in a prison population by the clothes and other adornments they wore. For instance, Black Muslims were characterized by neat, pressed clothes; short, trimmed hair; and similar hats. "Tough" guards wore neat, pressed uniforms, while "easy" guards wore wrinkled uniforms.

Communication Potential

Encoding Potential. In number of cues and visual impact, physical appearance has great communication potential. Some natural and most adornment features lend themselves to variation in amount, location, color, texture, style, pattern and design, and fashionableness, allowing a communicator to construct a complex appearance. Because such cues stimulate the tactile and

Physical Attractiveness on a Date

Apart from academic progress, students are concerned about their social life, and in this social life, physical appearance plays a large role.

Using an ingenious method, Berscheid and Walster (1974) arranged dates for college dances through computer matching. Dance attendees completed a predance questionnaire concerning characteristics they desired in a date. They were also rated on their physical attractiveness. Unknown to the participants, dates were matched on the basis of physical attractiveness only. At intermission, attendees completed a questionnaire assessing liking for the dates, attendees' perceptions of how much their dates liked them, attitude similarity of dates, and desire to date the same people in the future.

The results showed that for first impressions, beauty is best. Both males and females expressed a desire for physically attractive dates; however, physical beauty was much more important for males. Females, meanwhile, had stronger preferences for intelligent, considerate, and outgoing dates and frequently placed more weight than males on these perceptions (Berscheid & Walster, 1969, 1972, 1974; Berscheid, Dion, Walster, & Walster, 1971; Brislin & Lewis, 1968; Coombs & Kenkel, 1966; Walster, Aronson, Abrahams, & Rottman, 1966).

Congruence in physical attractiveness between partners, however, may be more important than absolute attractiveness, which offers hope for the less attractive. Both predance desires and postdance reports showed a matching affect. That is, more attractive individuals desired more attractive dates and had a better time with more attractive dates, while less attractive participants desired less attractive dates and had a better time with them (Berscheid & Walster, 1969, 1972, 1974; Berscheid et al., 1971; Brislin & Lewis, 1968; Coombs & Kenkel, 1966; Walster et al., 1966). Congruence in physical attractiveness also seems to be expected by others. The match or mismatch of attractiveness affects perceptions of a couple. Bar-Tal and Saxe (1976) found that matched spouses were thought to be happier in their marriage. In unmatched couples, unattractive males married to attractive females were rated higher on income, occupational status, and professional success than attractive males married to attractive females. It seems judges felt that these positive characteristics of the unattractive males balanced the attractiveness of their female partners. However, unattractive women married to attractive men were not given the same benefit. This may be changing, as more women have entered the labor force in the past decade and assumed financial responsibilities in their marriages.

Physical Attractiveness on a Date (*Continued*)

The conclusions of this research are clear. Physical attractiveness is an advantage in social interactions with others. However, physical attractiveness is much more important to males. Females judge dates on other dimensions such as intelligence, social skill, and etiquette. Further, people seem to gravitate to partners at the same level of attractiveness. This supports two clichés: "Beauty is in the eyes of the beholder" and "There is someone for everyone." Physical attractiveness is also important to people who interact with the couple. That is, the attractiveness of one partner "rubs off" on the attractiveness of the other, though not always in a positive manner.

olfactory senses as well as the visual ones, these cues have high potential for arousal, attracting immediate attention from the decoder. Communicators may use this property to advantage. Further, many of these cues are available at a distance, before interaction takes place, giving physical appearance cues a significant primacy effect in establishing an impression. They also play a limited role in emotional expression (to the extent that selection is based on moods), social influence, and relational communication.

However, physical appearance cues are not always selected to encode a message. The ambiguity of whether a cue is communicative or not limits its communication value. People can consciously choose and manipulate many elements of physical appearance, but those choices are not always made with communication in mind. Purchase decisions on clothes, for example, commonly occur without considering communication. Preferences for a particular style or color and decisions to conform to appearance norms are influenced by personality, desire to be accepted by peers, desire to be liked, interest in fashion, exhibitionist tendencies, degree of practicality and comfort, femininity or masculinity, and interest in fashion design (Compton, 1962; Gibbons & Gwynn, 1975; Iliffe, 1960; Rosenfeld & Plax, 1977; Taylor & Compton, 1968). Further, daily decisions on what to wear, how to style one's hair, and the like are often based on such noncommunication factors as mood, amount of preparation time, tasks for the day, and what is still clean in the closet. Because intent is often not clear, appearance cues become ambiguous as to their message value. This is exacerbated by the fact that an appearance choice may be an intentional statement one day and not the next. You may purchase a particular blouse or shirt because you think it looks "sexy"; however, you do not always wear it with the intent of sending a message of sexual receptivity. For these reasons, appearance cues are not always communicative; however, decoders do make inferences about them and feel that at some level choice is intentional.

A second communication limitation of physical appearance is the lack of variability within a single interaction. This is especially true of natural features. They can only be changed by special methods (plastic surgery, hairstyling, tanning booths). Adornment features are relatively more changeable. Yet after initial selection and arrangement, we generally do not manipulate them for a large part of the day, except for occasional straightening or reapplication. Consequently, in a single interaction, physical appearance cues are static. We do not quickly modify their meaning or use them to transmit specific messages. A few exceptions do come to mind. A male supervisor can communicate relaxation by loosening his tie late on a Friday afternoon. Lovers can communicate sexual interest by removing their clothes. However, to carry on the equivalent of a conversation with only physical appearance cues would be nearly impossible.

Over time, there is more opportunity to communicate through appearance. An employer may communicate that task-oriented norms are being followed by wearing a suit to the office; however, the same boss communicates that social-oriented norms are in effect by wearing jeans and a knit shirt to the company picnic. A boyfriend or girlfriend who becomes increasingly slovenly in appearance for dates may signal less concern for the relationship.

Decoding Potential.   From a decoding perspective, physical appearance has moderate communication potential. On the plus side, many physical appearance cues are symbolic, so they are easily and readily understood. Second, humans have an excellent ability to make fine discriminations between cues. Third, though much of the information transmitted by physical appearance cues is stereotypic, it is often accurate. Fourth, the high potential for arousal by this channel is likely to increase attention to these cues.

There are a few decoding disadvantages that limit the communication potential of physical appearance cues. The interpretation of cues is often ambiguous, as is the degree to which cues are intentionally manipulated. Finally, there are fewer communication functions to which the cues can be applied, limiting both its decoding and encoding potential.

In sum, the communication potential of physical appearance is only moderate. There are many cues, and they have great attention-getting and arousal value. Decoders notice these cues and make consistent inferences about the source. At the same time, ambiguity of meaning, unintentional cue selection, and limited manipulability reduce the communication potential of physical appearance.

Vocalics

most people are perfectly afraid of silence.

e. e. cummings

The voice is a rich channel in the nonverbal communication system. It contains many behaviors besides the spoken word that are used to comple-

Many famous public figures are known by their voices. Can you recall the characteristic vocal patterns of each of these famous people?

ment, accent, emphasize, and contradict what is said, as well as to send additional messages. Pitch, loudness, silences, pauses, laughs, sighs, coughs, and sneezes are a few examples of cues in the code. Vocalic cues are among the most powerful in the nonverbal repertoire. They rival kinesics in number and variety, ability to use them, and tendency to attend to them. Cultures have dominant vocalic patterns, with numerous subcultural variations.

The vocal aspect of nonverbal communication has been alternately labeled paralanguage ("along-with language") and noncontent speech behaviors. We consider the former label too broad because it frequently encompasses kinesic behaviors. The latter, generally confined to pitch, loudness, tempo, pauses, utterance duration, and the like, is too narrow.

The label *vocalics* is preferable and encompasses any vocal-auditory behavior except the spoken word.

Origins and Acquisition

Vocalics are by no means exclusive to the human species. Many living beings depend on vocalics for communication with other members of their species. Vocal-auditory communication has been observed in crickets, grasshoppers, finches, thrushes, doves, mynahs, whales, and porpoises, as well as humans (Thorpe, 1972). Vocal behavior in primates is strikingly similar to that of humans. Van Hooff (1972) documents numerous examples of laughlike behavior in primates, comprised of a relaxed open-mouthed facial expression accompanied by screeches and squeals. In fact, during play involving children and chimpanzees, children engage in laughter, while chimps engage in the relaxed open-mouthed facial expression with squealing. Moreover, pitch levels and contours appear to be used for the same purposes in humans and other vertebrates. Vocalic threats and dominance displays invariably entail deep-pitched, harsh vocal patterns, while nonthreatening, nurturing contexts, such as mothers cooing at infants, show high-pitched, softer patterns.

An important process in language acquisition is auditory feedback. Children listen to their own voices as they pronounce words. This feedback helps them adjust vocal sounds to conform to adult standards. It also reinforces attention to the voices of others. The importance of auditory feedback is highlighted by the retarded speech development of deaf infants. At age 3 months, crying subsides in normal infants and is replaced by noncrying speech sounds. In deaf infants, crying subsides but is not replaced by speech sounds, because the infant cannot hear its own voice (Roberts, 1987).

Children continue to learn to use pitch after acquiring language to modify the meaning of their sentences (Menyuk, 1971, 1972). Yes/no questions appear about age 3, and children learn to encode vocalically such concepts as similarity/difference, expectedness/unexpectedness, finality/nonfinality, doubt/certainty, and subordination/superordination between ages 3 and 10.

Fundamental pitch changes from birth to puberty. The greatest changes occur between infancy and 2 years and at puberty. The number of pitches a child can encode also expands from five tones at birth to approximately 10 tones by age 7 (McGlone, 1966; Sheppard & Lane, 1968). Use of pausing and hesitations in speech is almost adultlike and highly stable by the time a child enters kindergarten (Levin, Silverman, & Ford, 1967; Wood, 1981). Children display a high degree of conversational congruence (matching pause behavior with conversational partners) by this time, and congruence continues to improve as they progress through elementary school. Tempo and loudness patterns are well established and adultlike by school age (Wood, 1981).

Perception of vocalic cues also undergoes developmental changes. Infants appear to attend to vocalic cues innately from birth (Harris & Ruben-

APPLICATIONS

Bringing Up Baby

You may think that it is nearly impossible for newborn babies to communicate with parents; however, there is growing evidence that they do just that. Infants are capable of vocalization at birth and can change their vocalizations (principally crying) to reflect physiological needs during this *prebabbling period* (Menyuk, 1971, 1972; Wood, 1981). For example, a hunger cry is moderately pitched and very loud, with a regular rhythm and short pauses to breathe, while a pain cry is extremely high-pitched, with long squeals (Wood, 1981). Parents are able to distinguish between different types of cries, an ability that is greater among mothers than fathers (Roberts, 1987). Further, parents respond to crying in some characteristic ways. Roberts (1987) believes that the attempt to comfort a crying baby may be an innate response. Another innate response she reports is that when a mother hears her baby crying, the milk in her breasts becomes warmer. Beyond communicating their needs, crying helps the baby develop the use of pitch, pausing, loudness, and tempo.

Some time between the third and sixth month, infants enter the *babbling period.* At the beginning of this period, crying subsides and is replaced by noncrying speech sounds (Roberts, 1987). Originally, it was thought that infants encoded only sounds specific to their own language. More recently, babbling has been shown to consist of sounds outside of the language as well. As the infant progresses through the babbling period, vocalic cues specific to the language are rewarded by parents, while other vocalizations become less frequent (Menyuk, 1971, 1972; Wood, 1981).

Babies learn a very important skill during this period, the use of intonation (Lieberman, 1967). Research using intonagrams, which measure the fundamental frequency, duration, and intensity of vocalic cues, has found that by 2 months of age infants produce intonation patterns similar to those of adults. Narration and assertion utterances appear at this time. These involve a gradual rise and fall in intensity and fundamental frequency. Between 6 and 8 months babies begin to imitate intonation patterns in their noncry utterances. At 7 months, requests appear. Calling and responses to calling by another person occur at 9 months, and infants encode commands by age 10 months. All these patterns involve only vocalic cues; no language has yet emerged.

As infants approach 12 months, their babbling becomes more characteristic of their own language sounds and word lengths. By the 11th or 12th month, most children begin to use single-syllable words, which are quickly followed by multisyllabic utterances.

In the first year, then, there is a rich communication exchange

Bringing Up Baby (Continued)

between the infant and its parents. (See Table 2.1 for a summary.) This exchange enables the infant to signal its needs and desires. The exchange also helps the parents care effectively for the infant. Finally, in this exchange the infant learns from the parents important basic communication skills that it will continue to use once it develops language.

stein, 1975), and the ability to discriminate between intonation patterns improves markedly during the babbling period (Menyuk, 1971, 1972). Discrimination at this stage is between large vocal units such as statements and questions. Attention to smaller, wordlike utterances comes later in the babbling period when the infant begins to acquire words. Improvements in decoding vocalic behaviors continue as the child matures (Pendleton & Snyder, 1982; Rosenthal et al., 1979); however, children have a difficult time perceiving messages where the vocal behavior conflicts with kinesic cues. A common example of such messages is sarcasm. Children generally do not understand sarcasm until they reach their teens, though with practice they can learn to interpret sarcasm accurately at a younger age (Bugental, 1974; Bugental, Kaswan, & Love, 1970). It is therefore unwise to tell your 5-year-old niece sarcastically that you are "happy" she dumped over your favorite houseplant if you want the others to remain untouched.

Structural Features

Next to kinesics, vocalics possess the largest number of nonverbal cues. The earliest systems for classifying vocal behavior, developed in the late 1950s, are similar to the structure-centered approaches to classifying kinesics. In fact, many of the researchers interested in vocalics worked or corresponded with those examining kinesics.

The best example of these early approaches is Trager's (1958, 1961) classification system. Actually, Trager's system encompasses the entire communication process, including both speech and body movement. He believed that vocalic behavior was only one facet of speech, intimately related to language, kinesics, and background characteristics of the speaker.

Voice set is the elementary level of Trager's system. It consists of the mental, physiological, and physical characteristics of a speaker, against which all vocalic and speech behaviors are judged. Sex, age, state of health, body build, rhythm state, position in a group, mood, bodily condition, and geographic location all influence the voice set. For instance, women generally encode higher fundamental pitch than men.

The next level of analysis is *speech*. Trager sees speech as a combination of language and paralanguage. *Paralanguage* includes voice qualities and vocalizations.

Voice qualities are vocalic behavior related to speech, including *pitch range, vocal lip control, glottis control, pitch control, articulation control, rhythm control, resonance,* and *tempo.* Each of these characteristics represents a vocalic continuum. That is, pitch control varies from spread to narrowed, vocal lip control from rasp to openness, glottis control from thick to thin tone, pitch control from sharp to smooth transitions in pitch, articulation control from forceful (precise) to relaxed (slurred), rhythm control from smooth to jerky, resonance from resonant to thin, and tempo from increased to decreased.

Vocalizations, by contrast, are specific vocal sounds or noises separate from language. These include vocal characterizers, vocal qualifiers, and vocal segregates. *Vocal characterizers* are laughing, crying, yelling, whispering, moaning, groaning, whining, breaking, belching, and yawning. These sounds can cover a large segment of language or occur between language segments. They are influenced by voice qualities and voice set. *Vocal qualifiers* are intensity, pitch height, and extent. Though these may seem similar to voice qualities, Trager (1958) considers them separate because they often " 'qualify' large or small stretches of language material as well as of the other vocalizations" (p. 6). Intensity ranges from overloud to oversoft, pitch height from overhigh to overlow, and extent from drawl to clipped. Finally, *vocal segregates* are sounds that do not fall easily into the other categories but are encountered often in speech. These include vocalic emblems like "uh-uh" for no, "uh-huh" for yes, "uh" for hesitation, and "sh" for quiet. Also included in this category are various clicks, pauses, and sounds produced by positioning of the tongue, lips, and diaphragm (nasalization, trill, vowel-like resonance, and inspiration or expiration of air as in coughs, snorts, and sniffs).

Birdwhistell (1970) tells a delightful story that illustrates the communicative power of this last category of noises:

> My mother's thin-lipped smile, which could be confined to her mouth, when accompanied by an audible input of air through her tightened nostrils required no words—Christian or otherwise—to reveal her attitude. My mother was a sniffer, a great sniffer. She could be heard for three rooms across the house. And, to paraphrase Mark Twain, her sniff had power; she could sniff a fly off the wall at 30 feet. I might even say she was an irresponsible sniffer, for she always denied her sniffing. When we'd say, "Well, you don't have to sniff about it," she'd respond firmly, "I have something in my passages—and a lady doesn't blow her nose." "Mark my words," she'd say and sniff again. (pp. 52–53)

Trager's remains one of the most comprehensive systems for categorizing the structural features of vocalics. More recent systems fail to offer unique distinctions. For instance, Crystal (1969) distinguishes between prosadic features (sounds linked directly to speech, similar to vocal qualities), paralinguistic features (sounds linked loosely to speech, like vocal characterizers), and nonlinguistic features (sounds not linked to speech, like vocal segregates). Harris and Rubenstein (1975) lump all vocalic behavior into nonsegmental features, as distinguished from segmental features (vowel and consonant sounds). By comparison to these, Trager's system is more thought out and useful in discussing and analyzing vocalic behavior.

One vocalic behavior that has been specified further is pausing. A common distinction is made between *unfilled* and *filled* pauses (Wood, 1981). The former are silences in a period of speech not filled by any vocal activity. Unfilled pauses frequently occur at the ends of sentences and at points of decision such as a difficult word choice. Filled pauses are periods between language containing excess vocalizations: elongated vowels ("ah," "eh," "uh"), repeated syllables, words, or word groups, and false starts. Filled pauses are often used to maintain a speaking turn.

Jaffe and Feldstein (1970) offer a more complex system for classifying pauses. They distinguish between *pauses* (intervals of joint silence bounded by vocalizations by the same speaker) and *switch pauses* (intervals of joint silence bounded at one end by vocalization by one speaker and at the other end by vocalization by another speaker). Three additional concepts are important in this system. *Vocalizations* are periods of uninterrupted vocal sound (usually speech) by a speaker, *speaking turns* are back-and-forth sharing of the speaker role, and *simultaneous speech* is overlapping speech, often indicating the absence of a switch pause.

Norms and Standards

All cultures have a preferred or standard vocalic pattern accompanying the "received" language for that culture. American English, British English, European French, Castillian Spanish, and Classical Arabic are preferred languages in the United States, Britain, Quebec, Spain, and Egypt, respectively (d'Angeljan & Tucker, 1973; Giles, 1973a; Giles & Powesland, 1975; Lambert, Hodgson, Gardner, & Fillenbaum, 1960; Ryan, 1979). Generally, these preferred vocalic and language patterns are evaluated as more prestigious by members of these cultures (Thakerar & Giles, 1981). Even speakers of nonpreferred dialects rate the preferred pattern more favorably.

An interesting example of the preference for a particular vocal style comes from Britain. Earlier in this century, accent training became an unofficial requisite of the British educational system. To promote the elitism of the educated class, students from London to Liverpool were subtly encouraged to adopt the accent of their Oxford masters. This "official" accent connoted intelligence and distinction. Many newscasters for the British Broadcasting Corporation adopted this vocal style, hence it acquired the nickname BBC English.

However, not every member of a culture follows the language and vocalic norms of the preferred pronunciation. Rather, subcultural variations persist in every culture. For instance, Southern, Appalachian, New England, Brooklyn, West Texan, Mexican-American, and Black English variations exist in our culture. These are generally rated lower on prestige but higher on benevolence and group solidarity dimensions (Giles, 1973a; Ryan, 1979; Thakerar & Giles, 1981). That is, if you encounter someone who speaks with an accent similar to your own, you will view them as friendlier, more similar to you, a member of your subculture, and more attractive. Positive relational perceptions and the maintenance of group identity promote the continuance of these nonpreferred patterns in a culture (Ryan, 1979).

Speech Accommodation Theory. While most people have stable accent patterns (regional or standard), they are capable of intentionally varying them within and across interactions to affect perceptions by others (Giles, 1973a, 1980; Giles, Bourhis, & Taylor, 1977; Giles & Powesland, 1975; Giles & Smith, 1979; Street & Giles, 1982; Thakerar, Giles, & Cheshire, 1982). Given the nature of the interaction (formal versus informal) and the perceived characteristics of the interactional partner (high versus low status), speakers either shift their accent toward the partner's accent, maintain their own regional accent, or shift toward a more regional accent. These shifts produce consistent changes in the evaluation of the speaker.

Giles proposed speech accommodation theory to explain these reactions to normative and nonnormative speech. The theory holds that people are motivated to change their language and accent patterns with respect to another's pattern to obtain a desired response from the other person. A receiver's response is dependent on that person's perceptions of the change (Street & Giles, 1982). Three types of changes in the vocalic pattern occur: convergence, maintenance, and divergence. *Convergence* is a shift toward the partner's language and vocalic patterns, motivated by a desire for social inclusion, identification with the partner, social approval by the partner, and effective communication. *Maintenance* is a no-change strategy, performed to maintain group identity and distance from the interactional partner. *Divergence* is a shift away from the partner's language and vocalic patterns, motivated by a desire to increase the distance between the speaker and interaction partner.

Beyond accent, the theory has explained reactions to shifts in speech rate (Putman & Street, 1984; Smith, Brown, Strong, & Rencher, 1975; Street & Brady, 1982), utterance duration (Street & Giles, 1982), response latency (Street, 1982), pause duration (Jaffe & Feldstein, 1970; Welkowitz & Feldstein, 1969), and interaction length (Stang, 1973). Converging shifts in these vocalic cues generally produce more positive perceptions on benevolence, liking, attractiveness, and the like, and diverging shifts produce more negative perceptions on these dimensions.

Other Vocalic Norms. In later chapters, vocalic norms related to regulation of conversations, communication of affect, and communication of relational meaning will be described. Before leaving this section, however, let us consider the types of vocalic patterns that occur in everyday speech. Heinberg (1964) identified a series of voice types based on common combinations of vocalic cues. Rather than classifying them by normative usage, he focused on their quality—pleasant or unpleasant. He considered one voice pattern as desirable and appropriate and another 14 as deviant.

The *good* voice involves maintaining sufficient muscle tone in the vocal folds to produce a highly complex vocal tone at a desired frequency and intensity; positioning the glottis at the correct vertical level; proper horizontal positioning of the tongue for articulation and audibility; proper use of the nasal cavity; and the right amount of sympathetic resonance. Confused?

An easier way of understanding what makes up a good voice is to consider the deviant voices:

1. **Breathy voice.** Produced by too much air escaping through the larynx because of insufficient muscle tone in the vocal folds and poor posture; more common in women then men; connotes immorality, stupidity, spinelessness, lethargy, seductiveness in women, and homosexuality in men; can express softness, awe, lightness, love, passion, and admiration.

2. **Tense voice.** Opposite of breathy voice; too little air is expelled through vocal folds; conveys uncooperativeness, emotional insecurity, bad temper, anger, rudeness, frustration, and cruelty.

3. **Breathy-tense voice.** Produced by both poor posture and a tense larynx; often perceived as weak and nervous.

4. **Husky voice.** Tense voice that sounds like a series of impulses; perceptions same as for tense voice.

5. **Harsh voice.** Tense voice that sounds like rubbing coarse sandpaper; perceptions same as for tense voice.

6. **Hard voice.** Tense voice that sounds like continuous grating; perceptions same as for tense voice.

7. **Strident voice.** Tense voice that sounds like metal hitting metal; uncommon but often found in neurotic or psychotic individuals; perceptions same as for tense voice.

8. **Nasal voice.** Produced by too much resonance in nasal passages (may be twangy); persons with voice perceived as dull, lazy, and whiny; can express repugnance, ugliness, boredom, complaint, and self-deprecation.

9. **Denasal voice.** Opposite of nasal voice, often due to colds or other blockages that prevent resonance in nasal cavities; generally does not carry meaning.

10. **Orotund voice.** Big, full voice produced by too much resonance in mouth cavity; commonly used by preachers and politicians; connotes idealism, authority, and pomposity.

11. **Flat voice.** Low monotone that occurs when glottis blocks out some tone qualities; unemotional and unenthusiastic perceptions; can communicate laziness, boredom, and displeasure.

12. **Thin voice.** High pitched voice that comes from the glottis blocking out a different set of tone qualities than in the flat voice; person may be considered immature, insecure, and indecisive; connotes doubt, apology, and weakness.

13. **Throaty voice.** Results from moving the tongue upward and toward the back of the mouth; often difficult to understand because of its muffled quality; frequently perceived as stupid or aristocratic; expresses surprise.

14. **Fronted voice.** Produced by moving the tongue forward and depressing it; very precise and clipped; often seen as supercilious, cold, disdaining, and aloof; communicates precision and irritability.

Communication Potential

Encoding Potential. Because of their primacy, frequency of manipulation, number of cues, and range of information and functions, vocalic behaviors possess great communication potential from the encoder's perspective. Research on the origins and acquisition of vocalics clearly shows that they are primary in human development. An infant begins to communicate with vocal cues long before words appear, and reliance on vocalics as a communication channel continues throughout life. Vocalic behaviors are encoded during every conversation. In addition, there are many vocal cues from which to choose in any given conversation. We actively manipulate them simultaneously to produce a variety of meanings. The range of information transmitted by vocal cues and the functions that they serve in human communication are as large as kinesics. Vocal cues communicate emotional reactions, comment on relationships, indicate social attitudes, and regulate the back-and-forth exchange in conversations.

As with other codes, intentionality is not always certain, but vocalics seems to be used intentionally more often than many other codes, probably due to the intimate connection to language, which is almost always encoded intentionally. However, the level of awareness of vocalic cues is probably lower than awareness of the words they accompany, and nonlinguistic expressions, such as emotional cues, may be far less intentional or conscious.

Decoding Potential. On the decoding side, the vocalic channel also possesses characteristics that make it an important nonverbal communication vehicle. Along with reliance on vocalic cues to communicate messages, an infant decodes meaning from the vocalic behavior of others. In fact, decoding ability develops before encoding ability. As adults, the focus on vocalic cues remains strong, due in part to attention to the spoken word. As people listen to words, they cannot help but process vocalic meaning, giving vocalic cues a perceptual advantage over other nonverbal channels. Finally, humans are capable of making very fine discriminations among vocal cues.

One qualification to this glowing appraisal of decoding ability must be made. Given their nature, some ambiguity exists in vocalic cues. Few vocal behaviors are tied to specific meanings. Further, multiple vocal dimensions, such as pitch, tempo, and rhythm, are generally encoded at the same time. Thus mistakes in decoding are common.

This qualification notwithstanding, vocalics is very important and powerful in the nonverbal communication system, ranking second only to kinesics in overall impact.

Summary

This chapter has examined the visual and auditory codes: Kinesics, physical appearance, and vocalics. Kinesics and vocalics are the two most powerful nonverbal codes, and exceed physical appearance in their encoding and decoding potential. All three codes, and the codes discussed in Chapters 3 and 4, are acquired by three means: They are inherited genetically; they arise from common experiences with the environment; and they emerge from culture-specific tasks and social interactions. All three codes share a high attention-getting and arousal value that increases their communication potential. In addition, all three codes contain many elements that can be varied to send messages. Kinesics and vocalics, though, possess more code elements than physical appearance because it is difficult to vary most natural appearance features (with the exception of hair and skin), and adornment features are relatively static. All three codes are governed strongly by cultural and subcultural norms that are learned at an early age, while kinesics and vocalics also include significant innate components. Together, these three visual and auditory codes play a major role in accomplishing the communication functions we will be discussing in Part II.

Suggested Readings

Berscheid, E., & Walster, E. (1972). Beauty and the best. *Psychology Today, 5,* 42–46.

Birdwhistell, R. L. (1970). *Kinesics and context.* Philadelphia: University of Pennsylvania Press.

Buck, R. (1981). The evolution and development of emotion expression and communication. In S. S. Brehm, S. M. Kassin, & F. X. Gibbons (Eds.), *Developmental social psychology* (pp. 127–151). New York: Oxford University Press.

Ekman, P., & Friesen, W. V. (1969). The repertoire of nonverbal behavior: Categories, origins, usage, and coding. *Semiotica, 1,* 49–98.

Gibbons, K., & Gwynn, T. K. (1975). A new theory of fashion change: A test of some predictions. *British Journal of Social and Clinical Psychology, 14,* 1–9.

Ramsey, S. J. (1976). Prison codes. *Journal of Communication, 26,* 39–45.

Rutter, D. R., & Stephenson, G. M. (1979). The functions of looking: Effects of friendship on gaze. *British Journal of Social and Clinical Psychology, 18,* 203–205.

Trager, G. L. (1961). The typology of paralanguage. *Anthropological Linguistics, 3,* 17–21.

Woods, B. S. (1981). *Children and communication: Verbal and nonverbal language development* (2nd ed.). Englewood Cliffs, NJ: Prentice-Hall.

CHAPTER 3

Contact Codes: Haptics and Proxemics

Touch is the basic mammalian mode of communication,
one warm-blooded creature's way of saying to another,
"You're not alone. I'm here."

Anne Gottlieb (1980, p. 80)

The flow and shift of distance between people as they
interact with each other is part and parcel of the
communication process.

Edward T. Hall (1973, p. 180)

One of the fundamental dimensions of human relationships is that of coming together and coming apart, of union and separation, of closeness and distance. We are constantly in a state of approaching or avoiding others, a basic tension well illustrated in a famous German fable:

> Once upon a wintry night, the porcupines gathered together for a little socializing. Because of the chill night air, they tried to move close together to gain a little warmth. But every time they did, they would prick each other with their quills. So they moved farther apart, but once again became cold. They continued to rearrange themselves until they found a distance at which they could be both warm and comfortable. Henceforth, that distance became known as good manners.

Like the porcupines (and many other members of the animal kingdom), we attempt in our day-to-day social relations to strike a proper balance or equilibrium between desires for closeness and affiliation and desires for separation and privacy. On the one hand, the drives for propagation and for protection from predators create pressures toward approach. On the other hand, the need for individual access to food, water, and shelter and the need for insulation from physical threats from other group members lead to pressures toward separation and the establishment of individual territories.

Whether the human species is governed by similar biological forces or is responding more to psychological needs for intimacy and privacy, humans display the same approach-avoidance patterns. When we choose to live in cities rather than the country, to plan social get-togethers with friends and family, and to congregate in crowds at political rallies, we are manifesting approach tendencies. When we seek solitude or attempt to limit the amount of sensory input we are receiving, we are manifesting avoidance tendencies. Have you ever noticed how quickly you attempt to escape the crowd after a football game or how annoyed you are by someone accidentally brushing against you on a subway or bus? Although we are more likely to display avoidance tendencies toward strangers and approach ones toward significant and familiar others (friends, family, coworkers), we sometimes need distance and time alone from even our closest friends. Thus our daily encounters entail continual choices about approaching and avoiding others.

These forces give rise to two different communication codes: haptics and proxemics. *Haptics* refers to the *perception and use of touch as communication*, and *proxemics* refers to the *perception, use, and structuring of space as communica-*

tion. Because these two codes are intimately linked, we will not treat them separately but rather examine them together in this chapter. We will first take a biosocial perspective on how these two codes originate out of powerful and pervasive biological needs for touch, distancing, and territory and how social learning further shapes their acquisition and use. We will then explore their structure and interrelationships with other nonverbal codes; what the norms, standards, and expectations are for their use; and what potential they have as communication vehicles.

Origins and Acquisition

We are a touch-starved society.

Desmond Morris

Frequent, loving physical contact with other human beings: cuddling, snuggling, stroking, hugging, holding hands, walking arm-in-arm, arms around each other's shoulders, arms around each other's waists. All of us need it. And most of us probably don't get enough of it.

Anne Gottlieb (1980, p. 80)

The Need for Touch

It is well documented that touch is essential to the physical, emotional, and psychological well-being of human infants and to their intellectual, social, and communication development (Fisher, Rytting, & Heslin, 1976; Frank, 1971, 1972; Montagu, 1978; Morris, 1967, 1971).

Physical Impact. The physical importance of tactile stimulation is grounded in the need for comfort and protection and begins before birth. The first sensory experience of the fetus is through the skin. At about 2 months, the skin develops sensitivity around the nose and mouth, and by 14 weeks, the entire body is responsive to its environment in the womb. From 17 weeks until birth, touch reactions to stimuli are largely the same as those shown after birth (Hooker, 1952).

In the womb, the developing fetus is well protected by the warm, fluid environment of the uterus that both cushions it from sharp or jarring movements and provides a controlled temperature. It is pleasantly stimulated by the heartbeat and rhythms of the mother and coordinates its own rhythms to hers (Meerloo, 1955). Birth, therefore, provides the newborn with a radical change in tactile experiences. Besides the trauma of labor contractions and passage through the birth canal, the infant is thrust into an alien environment that includes light, changes in temperature and atmospheric pressure, and contact with humans and foreign objects. Even the experiences of the infant's own respiratory system taking control are novel.

This is a time of great vulnerability and dependence for the newborn. Physical contact with others, particularly the mother, produces an essential element of security. Physical contact buffers the infant from impact, shelters it from hostile stimuli, alleviates fear, and provides needed warmth. Holding, rocking, and patting restore the familiar, soothing rhythms of the womb and can quickly calm a crying baby. Furthermore, the synchrony of rhythm developed between mother and child may regulate the infant's own cardiac, respiratory, and digestive systems.

The warm, protective touch that normally accompanies feeding forges a link between pleasurable human contact and satisfaction of basic human needs. Pediatricians stress that frequent holding and cuddling are as important as the form of feeding itself (breast or bottle). This belief in the value of touch is reinforced by the famous Harlow monkey studies (Harlow, 1958; Harlow & Zimmerman, 1958; Harlow, Harlow, & Hansen, 1963), which raised infant monkeys in isolation from their mothers. When given a choice between a wire mesh surrogate "mother" that supplied food and a terrycloth contraption equipped with a light bulb for warmth, the infant monkeys would spend up to 18 hours a day clinging to the cloth mother, only visiting the wire mother briefly for nourishment. Harlow concluded that this deep attachment toward cloth mothers was indication of the overriding importance of *contact comfort* and intimacy to the development of the organism.

Other evidence of tactile deprivation among humans further confirms the critical importance of touch to human physical well-being (Montagu, 1978). During the 19th century and the early part of the 20th, the mortality rate among infants in orphanages and children's hospitals was a staggering 90% to 100% from a disease called *marasmus*, which means "wasting away." Even in institutions providing the best care, babies progressively showed signs of becoming listless, unresponsive to stimuli, depressed, and hysterical. They would engage in autistic rocking, self-biting, and head banging. Eventually, many would develop serious illnesses and die. Those who survived were often seriously retarded or maladjusted for life. What caused this tragic pattern of death and debilitation? The absence of adequate stimulation, including touch. Because the addition of a modicum of caressing and holding significantly reduced the death rate, tactile experiences were regarded as essential:

> These are the reassuringly basic experiences the infant must enjoy if it is to survive in some semblance of health. Extreme sensory deprivation in other respects, such as light and sound, can be survived, as long as the sensory experiences at the skin are maintained. (Montagu, 1978, p. 79)

Less extreme forms of tactile deprivation, such as those experienced by premature babies placed in incubators, have also been associated with health problems later in life, including allergies, eczema, and vulnerability to illness (Montagu, 1978). It has even been argued that infants delivered by cesarean section, who fail to experience the normal birth process, may be prone to more ailments.

The health benefits of touch are not limited to the first years of life. Physical contact appears to have positive effects on adults as well. Petting an animal, for example, is reported to reduce blood pressure in nursing home patients.

Perceptual and Intellectual Impact. Touch not only affects physical development but also contributes to the proper development of mental abilities. Physical contact with the mother in just the first 2 days of life produces a more adaptive infant (Hill & Smith, 1984). The infant's initial rooting and grasping behaviors provide its first awareness of objects in the environment. These early tactile experiences help the infant begin to integrate a number of sensory stimuli into complex patterns. Tactile explorations with the tongue, lips, and hands promote the perceptual discrimination of size, shape, weight, and texture. They facilitate recognition of spatial and temporal relationships, abilities that are essential to mental growth. By contrast, inadequate tactile stimulation leads to limited abstract thinking and conceptualizing and has been associated with learning disabilities and speech difficulties in later years (Despert, 1941; Frank, 1957, 1971; Montagu, 1978).

Emotional and Psychological Impact. As the developing infant explores its environment and its own body through touch, it begins to acquire a sense of self as separate from the world. The child's body becomes a source of great fascination and preoccupation. The quality of these early self-explorations shapes the child's self-identity and body image. Frank (1971) writes,

> The baby begins to communicate with himself by feeling his own body, exploring its shapes and textures, discovering its orifices and thereby begins to establish his body image which, of course, is reinforced or negated by pleasurable or painful tactile experiences with other human beings. (p. 37)

Children who are discouraged from touching their own or others' bodies or punished for doing so may develop negative body images and guilt feelings about self-touch. Monkey studies also suggest that deprivation of physical contact with others may lead to limited self-awareness (Mitchell, 1975).

Other-touch and a certain amount of self-touch also appear necessary for healthy emotional development. Touch brings comfort and reassurance, pleasure and self-gratification. Its palliative effects are evident in the positive response of emotionally disturbed children to stroking and rhythmic slapping. Studies show that infant monkeys raised in isolation resort to self-clinging and rocking to satisfy their need for tactile comfort (Mitchell, 1975). Human infants display the same need for pleasurable contact in their attachment to blankets or stuffed animals and in thumb sucking.

The absence of adequate touch can have serious consequences on mental health. A study of children who were later diagnosed as psychotic found that home movies of their interaction patterns with their mothers differed from those of normal infants. Over a 6-month period, mothers of disturbed children reduced reciprocal touch with their infants and increased avoidance of them (Massie, 1978).

Why We Touch Ourselves the Way We Do

If we were to monitor self-touch, we would find that our need to relieve stress triggers by far the greatest number of our touches. We touch ourselves many times a day as we displace our anxiety and tension from internal to external expression. . . .

Stress gestures are actually healthy outlets. Nature wisely forces us to engage in motions that help work off the adrenaline coursing through our blood. Adrenaline prepares us for "fight or flight," a major motor activity. Most of the time, we cannot fight or take flight—we may be behind the wheel of a car, sitting in a business conference, standing in a slow checkout line at the market. Nature helps us to get rid of some of our pent-up tension with the small motor activity of touching ourselves.

. . . We touch ourselves for other purposes as well. . . . A classic World War II photo shows a small boy in a foreign country ecstatically hugging himself because he has been given a pair of new shoes. Like this child, you may throw your arms around yourself when you are feeling euphoric. Or you may spontaneously clasp both hands, one on top of the other, in the center of the chest, your gesture saying, "I can't believe this wonderful, marvelous thing is happening to me." . . . Interestingly, the gesture of hugging ourselves as an expression of joy is also used to heal ourselves when we are sad or depressed. When a friend was overwhelmed with despair, she would wrap herself in her own arms and rock back and forth. The rocking and self-hugging were her way of saying, "I'm all I've got." . . .

That's psychological healing. We are also constantly using self-touch for physical healing. We bang an elbow or stub a toe. Instinctively, we grab the injured part, rub it, and press on it to relieve pain. Napoleon, in his familiar gesture of keeping a hand inside of his jacket, was actually massaging himself to ease the pain of a stomach ulcer.

Source: Helen Colton, June 1983, *Cosmopolitan*, pp. 140–142.

Social and Communicative Impact. Most important to our interests in nonverbal communication, adequate touch experiences are essential to the social and communication development of humans. Instinctively, the newborn seeks physical contact and responds to human touch. Its sucking and grasping at the mother's breast express its primal needs for sustenance and protection. In turn, the mother fondles, kisses, pats, rocks, and gently cleans the infant, establishing the roots of intimacy and sealing the bond between child and parent (Morris, 1971). This pattern of infant actions and maternal reactions sets up a mutual feedback system that results in mutual modification of behavior. The more contact between infant and mother, the more synchronization of behavior cycles and the more coordination of communication (Hill & Smith, 1984). Thus the infant's rudimentary communication system originates through touch.

Early tactile experiences in turn set the stage for satisfactory relationships in later life. Children experiencing tactile deprivation show greater difficulty developing attachments to others; they are more prone to introversion and alienation. As Montagu (1978) writes:

> The body-feeling image we have of ourselves as sensitive or insensitive, sensuous or unfeeling, relaxed or tense, warm or cold, is largely based on our tactual experiences in childhood. The skin of those who have been tactually deprived is "turned off" to those experiences which the tactually satisfied enjoy. (p. 206)

Other aspects of social behavior also depend on adequate touch experience as a prerequisite to healthy development. Animal studies provide inferential evidence. Mice that are allowed physical contact with littermates show more positive behavior than those separated by wire mesh (Porter, Matochik, & Makin, 1983). Monkeys raised in isolation fail to learn appropriate play and courtship rituals, become increasingly aggressive, exhibit sexual dysfunction and inadequate mothering, fail to develop normal gaze avoidance behaviors exhibited by mature monkeys, cannot decipher the dominance hierarchy, and cannot combine unlearned behaviors such as postures, gestures, and vocalizations into meaningful communication patterns (Harlow, 1959; Harlow & Harlow, 1962; Mitchell, 1975). In short, they lack social and communicative competency.

Anthropological research on human behavior shows similar aberrant behavior associated with the absence of touch. Prescott (1975), summarizing a study of 49 primitive cultures, reports that limited physical contact in infancy and/or adolescence was strongly correlated with high levels of adult violence. In 36 of the societies, high degrees of affection and physical contact corresponded to low degrees of adult violence, while low amounts of infant affection corresponded to high incidences of violence, including killing, torturing, and mutilating enemies. Of the remaining 13 societies, those that were repressive regarding premarital sex also showed high violence, while those that were permissive sexually showed low violence, despite low levels of infant contact. In other words, opportunities for pleasurable body experiences during adolescence compensated for any detrimental effects from deficient physical affection in infancy.

Even though Prescott (1975) concluded, "The deprivation of physical pleasure is a major ingredient in the expression of physical violence" (p. 65), his anthropological studies along with the animal studies do not establish direct causation between the absence of pleasurable tactile stimulation and antisocial behavior. They do imply that touch is a necessary ingredient in the healthy development of individuals and societies, but what is not clear is how much touch is needed, when, and by whom. It has been argued that the need for touch diminishes as people mature into adulthood. Based on writings by Frank (1957) and Morris (1971), among others, Burgoon and Saine (1978) state:

> To some extent, physical contact is supplanted as a means of communication and self-gratification because we learn other ways of communicating messages that we could originally transmit only through touch. Mothers talk and sing to their children while they hold them, comfort them and reassure them. Slowly the child learns to associate the mother's voice with comfort and security, and eventually learns the words. At the same time, the child is learning his or her own verbal and gestural language systems with which to communicate needs and wants. Thus, touch is slowly replaced by other kinds of communicative signals. The pleasure gained from contact is also partially replaced by other kinds of stimuli that indirectly impinge upon the sense of touch—things like clothing and the rhythm of music. These socially acceptable forms are slowly substituted for self-touching and touching others. (p. 68)

Nevertheless, the desire for touching remains. Morris (1971) suggests that we go through cycles of seeking and avoiding touch throughout our life span. The frequent contact of infancy gives way to reduced contact with parents as the child begins to assert independence and to shed "babyish" ways. In adolescence, child-parent contact is at a minimum but is offset by the desire for intimate and sexual contact with others. Intimate touch again becomes extensive and, as young people establish pair bonds, is supplemented by intimate touch with new offspring. The cycle then repeats itself within the new family unit. Research by Mosby (1978) implicitly supports these patterns. She reports that people aged 18 to 25 and 30 to 40 engage in the most touching. She also reports that regardless of how much touching they actually engage in, people at all ages would like more. This discrepancy between actual and ideal touch testifies to the continued desire for touch beyond early childhood. What changes, then, is not the desire for pleasurable contact with others but the contexts in which it occurs. A child may hug a stranger without compunction; adults are far more selective. The important point to realize is that relatively infrequent touch in a given culture is not an accurate barometer of the need or desire for it.

The Need for Territory and Personal Space

> The history of man's past is largely an account of his efforts to wrest space from others and to defend space from outsiders. . . . To have a territory is one of the essential components of life; to lack one is one of the most precarious of all conditions.
>
> Edward T. Hall (1973, p. 45)

A counterpoint to affiliation and contact needs are needs for privacy and distance. These are satisfied by establishing territories and maintaining personal space, behaviors that can act as potent nonverbal messages.

Definitions. Before considering the extent to which such needs exist, we should distinguish between the two concepts of *territory* and *personal space.* A territory is a *fixed geographic area that is occupied, controlled, and defended by a person or group as their exclusive domain* (Altman, 1975; Altman & Haythorn, 1967; Goffman, 1963; Hall, 1959; Hediger, 1961; Lyman & Scott, 1967; Pastalan, 1970; Sommer, 1966, 1969; Stea, 1965). Typically, territories function to regulate access to scarce resources such as food, water, and shelter; to guard accumulated resources; to protect the family unit from disease and physical harm; to provide privacy for mating and child rearing; to permit protracted action or thought without disruption; and to create solidarity within a social unit. Thus they are strongly associated with species survival and physical needs. The existence of a territory is revealed through the territorial behavior of its owners/occupants. Key elements of territoriality include (a) marking boundaries and personalizing a space to declare ownership, (b) using warning signs or displays to alert intruders that they are trespassing, (c) patrolling perimeters or creating barriers to access, and (d) defending the territory from intrusion (Altman, 1975; Bakker & Bakker-Rabdau, 1985; Vine, 1975).

Personal space, by contrast, is an *invisible, portable, adjustable bubble of space surrounding an individual that is actively maintained to protect the person from physical and emotional threats* (Burgoon & Jones, 1976; Ciolek, 1983; Dosey & Meisels, 1969; Hall, 1966; Hayduk, 1978; Horowitz, Duff, & Stratton, 1964; Sommer, 1959). As originally conceived by Katz (1937), it is a person's perceived self-boundary and has been referred to as a "body-buffer zone" (Horowitz et al., 1964). Because it is grounded in individual needs and idiosyncrasies, it expands and contracts depending on who is approaching and under what circumstances. The main distinctions between personal space and territory are that the former moves with the person, whereas the latter is relatively stationary (one's automobile being an exception); personal space boundaries are invisible, whereas territorial boundaries are marked; and personal space has as its center the individual's body, whereas territory does not (Sommer, 1959). Intrusions on either personal space or territory typically arouse discomfort, but personal space invasion is more likely to prompt a withdrawal or flight response, while a territorial invasion may provoke threats or fights.

Although the extent to which territoriality and personal spacing patterns are inborn or learned is the subject of considerable controversy (e.g., Altman, 1975; Ardrey, 1966, 1970; Bakker & Bakker-Rabdau, 1985; Vine, 1975), that humans show strong spatial needs seems indisputable. The evidence supporting this conclusion comes from a variety of perspectives, including ethological, anthropological, biological, sociological, psychological, and communication observations and experiments.

Anthropological, Ethological, and Biological Evidence. The case for human territoriality begins with a biological perspective that humans are subject to the same evolutionary processes as other species and share some of the same underlying survival response patterns as other vertebrates (Hediger, 1961). Often observations of territorial behavior in other mammals are used to bolster the claim that territoriality is a necessity for many species including humans and that failure to secure adequate territory has serious consequences.

Two of the most famous studies are Christian's (Christian, Flyer, & Davis, 1961) of Sika deer and Calhoun's (1962, 1966) of rats, both of which demonstrate the detrimental effects of overcrowding. In the 1950s, Sika deer were thriving on James Island in Chesapeake Bay, an ideal habitat that was free of natural predators and had ample supplies of food and water. Suddenly, the deer population began to die in large numbers until the population had dropped from 300 to 80. The autopsies conducted on the deer were compared to earlier samples and revealed that the deer did not die from disease. Their only abnormality was greatly enlarged adrenal glands. Because the adrenal cortex responds to stress by producing larger quantities of adrenaline, which, over time, can be fatal, Christian concluded that the lack of adequate living space had created such stress for the deer that it literally caused their deaths. He further argued that mice, dogs, guinea pigs, monkeys, and even humans would be prone to respond to density-induced stress in the same way.

Calhoun studied the deleterious effects of excess population density and inadequate space by observing rats in a controlled laboratory setting. He built a pen that had ample water, food, air, nesting material, and opportunities for social contacts. All was well until the rats began to propagate. Soon there were too many rats for the small space, and bizarre behaviors began to appear, including a change in female nesting and nursing habits, premature births and aborted fetuses, sexual dysfunction, cannibalism, homosexuality, hyperactivity, vicious attacks by some males and cringing withdrawal by others, and increased illness. Calhoun labeled this deterioration of behavior in the face of excess population density a "behavioral sink."

These studies, among others, are used as illustrations of the harmful consequences of animals having inadequate territory. The inference drawn is that humans will respond in a similar fashion. A chief proponent of this position is Ardrey (1966, 1970), who argues that Homo sapiens are territorial creatures whose territoriality is partly a function of biological heredity and partly a function of culturally learned patterns of behavior. He cites examples of modern-day warfare as evidence that territorial and aggressive instincts have not been extinguished. His position is an intuitively appealing one because it relies on familiar incidents of individuals, groups, and countries creating and defending territories.

However, many scholars (e.g., Altman, 1975; Boulding, 1968; Edney, 1976; Gorer, 1968; Leach, 1968; Montagu, 1968; Schneirla, 1968; Vine, 1975) do not share Ardrey's conviction that territorial behavior is innate and criticize his position as overly simplistic and anecdotal. They caution that humans cannot be compared directly to other species. Such factors as complex social organization, the existence of cultural norms, nomadic patterns or high mobility among some cultures, unique human motives, and cognitions regarding territory and space challenge the comparability of circumstances between humans and other mammals. Vine (1975) notes that many

Human territoriality (top) has been compared to that of other species (bottom).

lower primates, who are humans' closest relatives, are themselves not strongly territorial. Edney (1976) also points out that humans invite people into their territories for visits and often take flight rather than engage in aggressive defense of a territory. Nevertheless, both men believe that human individuals and societies do display territorial proclivities.

A different form of biological evidence comes from work on brain processes (Esser, 1971, 1972), which indicates that the more primitive areas of the brain (i.e., the R-complex and the limbic system) govern territorial and fight-or-flight behavior. These parts of the brain, which are oldest in an evolutionary sense, are most closely tied to instinctive and innate response patterns. This suggests that territorial defense is an inborn reflex.

Equally important to territoriality is the need to maintain a certain amount of personal space, which may in fact be the more fundamental drive. Many experts on animal spacing (e.g., Leyhausen, 1971; McBride, 1971; Schneirla, 1965; Vine, 1975) contend that members of the same group characteristically adopt a distance between themselves and others that reconciles approach and withdrawal forces. Because personal space is mobile, it is possible simultaneously to preserve spatial insulation and to avoid aggressive encounters by simply moving out of range of another individual or group. This makes defense of a fixed territory less essential. Many species also permit overlapping territorial boundaries without conflict, and "time sharing" of the same location may even occur to regulate use of prime spaces. Because needs for territory and space intermingle, the distinction between territoriality and personal space motives is often blurred. When aggressive or withdrawal behaviors are observed, it is unclear whether they are reactions to a territorial intrusion, a violation of personal space, or both. It may well be that a main purpose for establishing territories is to ensure adequate personal space.

Sociological, Psychological, and Communication Evidence. Most of the research by social scientists falls into one of four categories: naturalistic observations of territorial definition and defense, observational studies of overcrowding, experimental (controlled laboratory) studies of overcrowding, and experimental studies of personal space invasion. The inference to be drawn from this large body of research is that if humans carve out territories and/or experience ill effects from inadequate territory or space, they must have a basic need for it.

Personal experience alone attests to people's strong habit of establishing territories. At school, you may choose a particular seat in class and return to that seat repeatedly. If someone else then sits in it, you may feel vaguely violated. At home, the person who does most of the cooking may treat the kitchen as his or her territory and may resent interference from well-meaning relatives or friends. Videotaped observations of home patterns (Scheflen, 1971) and questionnaire data (Altman, Nelson, & Lett, 1972) confirm that most U.S. households have clearly defined territories. Observations of other types of residences (such as mental institutions, delinquent residences, and dormitories) and of workplaces likewise reveal strong inclinations for people to claim territories and for others to respect those territories (Goffman, 1971; Lipman, 1970; Roos, 1968; Sommer, 1969; Vinsel, Brown, Altman, & Foss, 1980).

Where home territories are inadequate or nonexistent, individuals may band together to create a group-controlled space. Sociological observations of adolescent street gangs and urban criminal gangs reveal that such groups use a wide variety of means to block entry to their "turf" and often resort to violence to expel intruders (R. N. Johnson, 1972; Whyte, 1943). This proclivity to declare and defend a territory is especially pronounced in areas where poverty and overcrowding are the norm and is an adaptation to stressful circumstances. Census data and observations of congested areas, ranging from midtown Manhattan to inner-city Paris, show that as population density increases, so do such serious health and mental problems as crime, tuberculosis, respiratory ailments, mental illness, infant mortality, suicide, and juvenile delinquency (e.g., Davis, 1971; Dubos, 1965; Newman, 1972; Stokols, 1972). Illness complaints in prisons are likewise systematically related to crowding-induced psychological stress (McCain, Cox, & Paulus, 1976), and crowding has been cited as a major contributor to prison riots. Conversely, where residents of urban areas have "defensible spaces" and clearly recognizable territorial boundaries, conflict, crime, and social disruption are less frequent (Newman, 1972). Even in a college dormitory setting, those who use diverse means to regulate privacy in their dorm room are more likely to stay in school; those who fail to develop such territorial control mechanisms during their first year are more likely to drop out (Vinsel et al., 1980). Although the connection between congestion and these problems is only correlational and not casual, it does suggest that inadequate territory or territorial control leaves people more susceptible to physical, emotional, and health dangers.

Territorial violations occur when there is unauthorized use, unwanted surveillance, direct intrusions, or contamination from the leavings of others (Lyman & Scott, 1967). One way people take preventive or restorative action is to use *markers.* These may include boundary markers (such as hedges, fences, and "No Trespassing" signs), which identify the perimeter of the space, or central markers, which locate the middle of a locale. Vagrants can lay claim to part of a public park just by erecting a cardboard box with their meager belongings in it. A simple bottle of suntan oil can reserve your favorite spot on a public beach. Sociological and experimental evidence reveals that where space is at a premium or where occupancy is long-term, territorial marking increases and typically deters encroachments by others (Altman, 1975; Becker, 1973; Edney, 1972; Edney & Jordan-Edney, 1974; Sommer & Becker, 1969).

Another way that people prevent contamination and repel intrusions is through *barriers to entry* such as walls, door locks, guard dogs, and security guards. One of the main attractions to having one's own secretary or receptionist at work is the gatekeeping function the person serves, limiting others' access to one's office territory. Finally, *occupancy* itself will often prevent violations by others because it represents the potential for forcible resist-

These Cons Weren't Surprised: They Expected Riot

Residents at the Michigan Parole Camp stood at the edge of the camp property Tuesday and watched as flames shot up from temporary inmate housing units across the street. They watched as a thousand prisoners in the north complex at Jackson Prison swarmed around the yard, armed with sticks and clubs, flinging rocks and sticks through windows.

Later, as the prison tried to pull itself back together, there were no outward signs of emotion as the parole camp residents related what they had seen—just a resigned acceptance.

"You have to do time over there to know what it's like," said 43-year-old camp cook Joe Weems, convicted of armed robbery and a veteran of the Michigan prison system. "There's more tension inside those walls than you can find anywhere else in the world.

". . . They [prison officials] brag about the school and the recreation facilities, but it's not geared to the number of people they put in there. [The north complex] was designed for about 750 inmates. Then they bring in these [temporary housing] modules and cram 1000 people in there.

". . . It's just like packing sardines in a can. If you keep stuffing them in there, the pressure builds up inside and pretty soon the top's going to blow."

Source: Joyce Walker-Tyson, May 31, 1981, *Detroit Free Press*, pp. 1B, 4B.

ance. Rightfully or not, occupancy is usually taken as a sign of ownership of a space and is sufficient to keep others from intruding. That may explain why law enforcement people are so reluctant to evict squatters.

All these defensive maneuvers imply that people are distressed by violations, intrusions, or contamination of their territory. Experimental research by psychologists and communicologists confirms that deprivation or intrusion upon territory or space elicits all the characteristic features of stress. These fit under what is called the *general adaptation syndrome* (GAS), which consists of behavioral and physiological indicators of alarm, resistance, and exhaustion (Evans & Eichelman, 1976; Selye, 1956). Specifically, research on personal space invasion, excess density (too many people in a locale), and overcrowding (perceived deficient supply of space relative to demand) reveals all the following effects:

1. **Physiological responses.** Consistent with the GAS, laboratory experiments have found increased blood pressure and heart rate, increased skin conductance, and heightened EEG activity with personal space violations and crowding (Aiello, DeRisi, Epstein, &

Karlin, 1977; Aiello, Epstein, & Karlin, 1975; Epstein, Woolfolk, & Lehrer, 1981; Evans & Eichelman, 1976; Gales, Spratt, Chapman, & Smallbone, 1975; McBride, King, & James, 1965).

2. **Anxiety cues.** A number of ingenious experiments, such as having an accomplice join a stranger at a library table or invade the personal space of a salesperson, have demonstrated anxiety reactions to territorial or personal space invasion. The nonverbal responses to such intrusions include avoiding gaze (sometimes preceded by a threat stare), body blocking, building barriers with possessions, leaning away, adopting an indirect body orientation, and increasing postural tension, nervous gestures, self-touching, and random hand and foot movements (Argyle & Dean, 1965; Baxter & Deanovitch, 1970; Burgoon & Aho, 1982; Daley, 1973; Epstein et al., 1981; Felipe & Sommer, 1966; Garfinkel, 1964; Garner, 1972; Goldberg, Kiesler, & Collins, 1969; Patterson, Mullens, & Romano, 1971; Patterson & Sechrest, 1970; Sommer, 1959, 1969; Sundstrom, 1975).

Another coping strategy is to develop a nonperson orientation. This is exactly what people do when confronted with strangers in an elevator—they pretend others are not there by treating the strangers as objects rather than persons. Experiments have shown that people are far less anxious when approaching or being approached by an object such as a picture or a hat rack than by another person (Horowitz et al., 1964; McBride et al., 1965). Sommer (1969) notes, "A nonperson cannot invade someone's space any more than a tree or chair can. It is common under certain conditions for one person to react to another as an object or part of the background" (p. 24). He points out that we often treat maids, janitors, and hospital patients the same way. By ignoring them, their presence no longer constitutes a spatial intrusion.

3. **Interaction avoidance, withdrawal, and flight.** Although people may respond to invasions of their home territory with physical defenses, verbal aggression, arguments, or pleading, surprisingly, in other social situations people rarely use verbal means to get an intruder to depart. Rather, most people respond by reducing or avoiding interaction and ultimately, if the intrusion continues, taking flight (Ahmed, 1980; Baum & Greenberg, 1975; Baum, Harpin, & Valins, 1975; Baum, Riess, & O'Hara, 1974; Felipe & Sommer, 1966; Greenberg & Firestone, 1977; Griffitt & Veitch, 1971; Knowles, 1972; Konečni, Libuser, Morton, & Ebbesen, 1975; Milgram, 1970; Smith & Knowles, 1979; Stokols, 1976; Valins & Baum, 1973). This pattern was demonstrated in a series of experiments designed to study the effects of extended confinement in a small space such as a submarine or a bomb shelter (Altman, 1971; Altman & Haythorn, 1967; Altman, Taylor, & Wheeler, 1971; Smith & Haythorn, 1972). Pairs of sailors were placed in isolation together for 8 to 20 days. The most striking finding was that a majority of

the subjects in one study were unable to complete the experiment. They found the experience too stressful and literally bailed out. Moreover, both aborters and incompatible pairs who completed the experiments showed increased territoriality over time, while compatible pairs showed a high degree of territoriality early on. The designation of separate territories and withdrawal from interaction, labeled *cocooning* behavior, was interpreted as attempts to adapt to a perceived stressful situation.

4. **Decreased task performance.** People subjected to crowding in the form of personal space invasion perform less well on cognitive tasks than people who are not crowded (Aiello et al., 1977; Evans & Howard, 1973; Heller, Groff, & Solomon, 1977; Paulus, Annis, Seta, Schkade, & Matthews, 1976; Worchel & Teddlie, 1976; Worchel & Yohai, 1979). Even shoppers do less well completing shopping tasks when under crowded conditions (Langer & Saegert, 1977).

5. **Perceived discomfort and crowding.** When people are placed in a high density environment, are surrounded by a lot of people in a small space, or have their personal space invaded, they report more uneasiness, discomfort, and feelings of crowding (Baum et al., 1975; Epstein et al., 1981; Evans & Howard, 1973; Greenberg & Firestone, 1977; Rodin, Solomon, & Metcalf, 1978; Stokols, Rall, Pinner, & Schopler, 1973; Sundstrom, 1975; Valins & Baum, 1973; Walden, Nelson, & Smith, 1981; Webb, 1978; Worchel & Teddlie, 1976; Worchel & Yohai, 1979). The sensation of crowding is especially pronounced when the person has lack of control over the situation.

6. **More verbal aggressiveness and/or less affiliativeness.** The discomfort of crowding also results in victims expressing more verbal hostility, showing less friendliness nonverbally, or being less disclosive than those in uncrowded circumstances (Baum et al., 1975; Sundstrom, 1975). Just the expectation of crowding causes people to dislike others in the environment (Baum & Greenberg, 1975). Citing the stimulus overload that confronts people in large metropolitan areas like New York City, Milgram (1970) notes that "a city dweller blocks inputs by assuming an unfriendly countenance, which discourages others from initiating contact" (p. 1462). Evidence of this effort to minimize social contacts comes from a study in which interviewers asked to use a respondent's home telephone. Three-fourths of small-town residents permitted the interviewer to enter their home, while only a fourth of the city residents did so; the remainder yelled answers through their door or peered through peepholes.

Of course, as with other human behavior, territoriality and personal space defense are complex processes that do not operate in the same way

APPLICATIONS

Space in the Workplace

The research on personal space and territory has implications for how workspace should be designed to accommodate employees' needs. To give employees some sense of physical integrity and separation, their work area should allow for distance and insulation from others. The lack of such distance is one reason employees dislike open-pit or "bull pen" office arrangements, that is, arrangements where several people have desks in the same open space. One TV sitcom *(WKRP in Cincinnati)* played on this idea. Les Nesman, a radio announcer who rankled at sharing space with a receptionist and a salesman, drew an invisible line around his desk and would always pretend to open an invisible door before ushering people into his "office." Even small cubicles are preferable to open area arrangements because they provide a buffer against personal space invasions and permit employees to mark their own territory with personal possessions and the like.

Supervisors can also show greater sensitivity to spatial and territorial needs by not invading an employee's territory without permission. The manager who walks into an employee's office without knocking or, worse yet, rifles through an employee's desk and mail is intruding on a fundamental need. Such intrusions may trigger all the reactions described in the GAS. A sensitive supervisor or employer recognizes such signals from an employee as a possible plea for more distance or space.

for all people. Males tend to show more stress, aggressiveness, and poor task performance in crowded situations than women; in some circumstances, women are actually more affiliative and effective (Aiello et al., 1977; Epstein & Karlin, 1975; Evans & Howard, 1973; Freedman, 1975; Freedman, Levy, Buchanan, & Price, 1972; Griffitt & Veitch, 1971; Leibman, 1970; Stokols et al., 1973). Males and females react differently to side-by-side versus face-to-face approaches (Fisher & Byrne, 1975). Age also alters reactions. Younger people find close proximity stressful and debilitating, while older people, who have less opportunity for affiliative contact, find it pleasant and facilitative of performance (Smith, Reinheimer, & Gabbard-Alley, 1981). Furthermore, the nature of the task, the cognitive experience of crowding, personality factors, and interference with goal attainment make a difference (e.g., Ahmed, 1980; Aiello et al., 1977; Freedman, 1975; Langer & Saegert, 1977; McCallum, Rusbult, Hong, Walden, & Schopler, 1979; Rodin et al., 1978; Stokols, 1972; Thalhofer, 1980; Worchel & Yohai, 1979). Nonetheless, the evidence is substantial that humans' affiliative drives are matched by powerful drives toward territoriality and spatial insulation. These strong needs underlie the potency of haptics and proxemics as communication codes.

Development of Haptics and Proxemics

The ability to send and interpret haptic and proxemic messages begins with an infant's first human contacts after birth. As Table 3.1 illustrates, the first year of life is a crucial period in the infant's acquisition of tactile abilities and, particularly, the use of touch as a means of expressing needs and affection. At the same time, the newborn develops the spatial and depth perception necessary for understanding proxemic messages and in the latter half of the first year shows signs of having established a personal space zone. Research indicates that by the end of their first year, children who initiate approaches toward strangers typically get no closer than 4 or 5 feet, while approaches initiated by strangers typically evoke apprehension in the child (Horner, 1983).

Although the earliest touch and proxemic behaviors of infants are undoubtedly grounded in innate response patterns, very early in their development, infants and children begin to acquire the patterns of behavior that are appropriate for their culture, subculture, and gender (Hall, 1966). They also learn the norms for different social contexts (Andersen & Sull, 1985). These patterns develop because of the different experiences to which children are exposed and because of active modeling and reinforcement by adults.

In the case of touch, boy and girl infants have different touch experiences in their first year of life. Prior to 6 months of age, boys apparently receive more touching, rocking, holding, and kissing, while after 6 months, girls receive more (Lewis, 1972; Lewis & Goldberg, 1969). At preschool age and into adolescence, boys and girls engage in more same-sex touch than opposite-sex touch, but girls have more contacts than boys (Williams & Willis, 1978; Willis & Hoffman, 1975; Willis, Reeves, & Buchanan, 1976). Boys are also more likely to touch a male teacher, while girls touch male and female teachers equally. Teachers reinforce the pattern by engaging in more same-sex touch than opposite-sex touch with children and by using different types of touch by gender (Perdue & Connor, 1978). Other research shows that girls generally engage in more reciprocal touch than boys (Berman & Smith, 1984), a pattern paralleling adult behavior. Overall, use of touch decreases among all children as they age, with white children reducing their touch rates faster than black children (Willis & Hoffman, 1975; Willis & Reeves, 1976; Willis et al., 1976).

The use of touch for communication purposes is also linked to language development. A study of language-impaired and normal-speaking children found that children with language difficulties used far more touch than their nonimpaired peers and were equivalent in touch use to younger children at the same level of language development. Among normal-speaking children, touch use declined with age (Rom, 1979). Thus touch appears to be a compensation for lack of ability to communicate effectively through

TABLE 3.1 Development of Haptic and Proxemic Encoding and Decoding Abilities

One to Three Months	Four to Six Months	Seven to Nine Months	Ten to Twelve Months
Haptics			
Quiets when held. May start or stop crying, depending on who is holding baby. Adjusts posture to body of person holding baby. Grasps, clasps people. Roots and sucks at breast. Voluntary grasp develops. Most significant stimulation is haptic and oral.	Responds to and enjoys handling. Wants to touch, hold, turn, shake, mouth objects. Shows anticipation, waves and raises arms to be picked up. Tries to get close to person near crib. Clings when held.	Explores body with mouth and hands. Pushes away unwanted objects.	Gives affection to humans and to objects like toys.
Proxemics			
Clearly discriminates proximity and object size. Distinguishes near and far objects in space. Experiments with changes in proximity by extending and contracting arm. Orients and signals distinctively to each of several people.	Aware of differences in depth and distance.	Approaches and follows mother. Rejects confinement. Aware of vertical space. Recognizes dimensions of objects. Fears heights.	Ranges distant space into regions of differing depths. Senses self as distinct from other things. Perceives objects as detached and separate and related in time and space. Reacts to approach of strangers.

Source: Adapted from *The First Twelve Months of Life* by F. Caplan, 1973, New York: Grosset & Dunlap.

language. This conforms to the argument that touch is a more primitive form of communication that eventually gives way to more sophisticated, precise forms of expression (such as language).

In the case of interpersonal distance, children likewise soon learn adult patterns of behavior. The older they get, the farther away they generally position themselves from others (Aiello & Aiello, 1974; Andersen, Andersen, Wendt, & Murphy, 1981). Whereas a 3-year-old may sit close enough to touch a playmate while working on a task, 5- and 7-year-olds space themselves farther apart (Lomranz, Shapira, Choresh, & Gilat, 1975). Between the ages of 5 and 10, children begin to show the same distance patterns as adults. This means that they learn to vary their distance according to circumstances (Hutt & Vaizey, 1967). Guardo and Meisels (Guardo, 1969; Guardo & Meisels, 1971; Meisels & Guardo, 1969) conducted a series of studies on what kinds of spatial differentiations are made and when. They found that by third grade, children have well-established schemas that associate proximity with interpersonal closeness (that is, they decrease distance with people they like). By sixth or seventh grade, they also make discriminations on the basis of such contextual factors as familiarity and gender, with girls showing a more refined schema earlier than boys (a pattern consistent with their earlier acquisition of language skills).

Other observational research supports that children adapt their distancing behavior to sex, ethnicity, and social roles (Berman & Smith, 1984). By fifth grade, males adopt greater distances than females (Pedersen, 1973). Males also exhibit more indirect body orientation than females (Jones & Aiello, 1973). Although children may begin to restrict touch to members of the same sex, they display some evidence for opposite-sex attraction in that they generally adopt the least distance from opposite-sex peers, followed by opposite-sex adults (Pedersen, 1973). Racial or ethnic differences may also be a factor, but the research evidence to date is inconclusive. One study found that black and Puerto Rican children (6 to 8 years old) stood closer together than whites and that blacks adopted the least direct orientation (Aiello & Jones, 1971). However, another study found that while very young black children adopted closer distances and less direct orientation than whites, by fifth grade the differences had disappeared. Finally, the nature of the social relationship makes a difference: The distance between children at play correlates with the number of friendly or unfriendly acts committed by a playmate (King, 1966). Thus children acquire the norms of their culture, subculture, and gender by the time they complete elementary school. This development is clearly gender-linked, with girls developing more adultlike management of distance sooner than boys (Altman, 1975).

Two other aspects of proxemic development that have received far less attention are the use of territory and the acquisition of the concept of privacy. Although all children become more aggressive in response to increased density (Loo, 1972), which would suggest that they are predisposed to maintain some degree of territory or spatial integrity, this need appears to differ by sex. One study found that boys maintain more space, spend more time outdoors, and enter more areas than girls (Harper & Sanders, 1975). This tendency for boys to "claim more territories" for themselves is consistent with the findings that males require more personal space and respond to crowding with more aggression, hostility, and discomfort than females. This should in turn result in their communicating territorial needs under different levels of crowding and possibly responding to territorial encroachments in different ways.

Only two studies have considered the issue of privacy in child development. Wolfe and Laufer (1974) report that the concept of privacy becomes increasingly complex with age, although children have a good understanding of it by age 9. Whereas at age 7, controlling information is of primary concern, at age 17, aloneness is also an important part of privacy. This increasing need for independence, solitude, and secrecy is evident in the expressions of privacy that develop. Parke and Sawin (1979) had parents complete detailed questionnaires on their family rules and patterns of access in their homes. The results showed that as children develop, they use more privacy markers (e.g., closing doors) and follow more privacy rules (e.g., knocking on doors), with these expressions of privacy becoming especially prevalent in adolescence and in cross-sex relationships (such as father-daughter or brother-sister).

The combined haptics and proxemics literature reveals mature patterns of touch and spacing behavior long before children leave adolescence.

Structural Features of the Codes

The Haptic Code

Until recently, touch was not even recognized as a communication code. Many nonverbal texts subsumed tactile expressions under kinesics or proxemics. However, evidence of its significant impact on human relations has kindled a growing interest in its role as a communication vehicle.

The approaches taken to determining the code elements of haptics can be divided roughly into structural and functional categories.

Structural Approach. This approach, patterned after that used in linguistics, focuses on the basic forms and features that comprise the haptic code and its semantic content. Kauffman (1971) and Harrison (1974) have suggested that types of touch comparable to the kineme and kinemorph can be identified. These basic building blocks, called either *tacs* and *tacemorphs* or *haptons* and *haptemes,* presumably consist of the types of movements listed below (many of which come from Argyle, 1975):

hit	slap	pat	hug	pinch
kiss	tug	caress	brush	stroke
kick	punch	shake	poke	grasp
rock	hold	pull	tap	lick
embrace	tickle	guide	groom	tackle
jab	grab	tweak	push	restrain
bite	shove	nibble	rub	nuzzle

As yet, no systematic work has deciphered which of these (or similar types of touch designations) are regarded as separate units and which are merely variations on the same type of touch (i.e., are they tacs or allotacs?). For example, is a tap actually different from a pat?

A different structural approach considers the *dimensions* or physical properties that distinguish one type of touch from another. Immediately apparent dimensions are (a) the intensity or amount of pressure used (soft to hard), (b) the duration of touch (brief to prolonged), (c) the location of the touch on the body (e.g., shoulders, face, hands), (d) the body part delivering the touch (e.g., hand, foot, upper torso, lips), and (e) the frequency of contact (single to multiple contacts). To illustrate, a pat is a soft, relatively brief, often repetitive movement delivered by the hand to various body locations but usually occurring in the upper body region. Because a pat to the derriere may signify something quite different from a pat on the head, the dimensional approach, by including location as one distinguishing feature, adds some descriptive specificity missing from the simple labeling of types of touch.

Of course, the ultimate goal of a structural approach is to identify meaningful semantic units or dimensions. In pursuit of this goal, Nguyen, Heslin, and Nguyen (1975; 1976; Heslin, Nguyen, & Nguyen, 1983) conducted a series of studies to identify the meanings associated with various types of touches and locations of touches. They found that different types of touch do convey different meanings. Among a pat, a stroke, a squeeze, and a brush, a pat is seen as the most playful and friendly; a stroke is the most loving, pleasant, and sexual; a squeeze is also relatively playful, warm, and pleasant; and a brush is nonsexual. (Some of these meanings differ by gender.) Interestingly, different body locations also carry different meanings. A touch to the leg is playful. A touch on the hands is loving, friendly, and pleasant. And a touch to the genital area conveys sexual desire. Finally, they found that certain meanings, such as loving, pleasant, friendly, and playful, are highly related to one another.

Functional Approach Functional approaches are also after the meanings associated with touch but focus instead on the purposes of touch rather than their form and on the contextual or relationship factors that constrain meaning. Heslin (1974; Heslin & Alper, 1983) proposed five different types of situations or relationships under which various touches can be classified:

1. **Functional/professional.** This is the least intimate category and consists of one-sided, instrumental touches (those needed to complete some task such as a physician's examination or a golf pro's lesson). Edwards (1981) proposes some forms of touch that also fit this category: (a) information pickup touch (e.g., taking a pulse), (b) movement facilitation touch (giving someone a boost or carrying someone to safety), (c) prompting (providing manual guidance in learning), and (d) ludic touch (touch as part of games such as holding hands during ring-around-a-rosy).

2. **Social/polite.** These touches are relatively formal and governed by social norms. Included are touches that are social amenities such as handshakes and other kinds of contact during greeting and parting rituals.

3. **Friendship/warmth.** These are moderately intimate touches, usually exchanged between well-acquainted individuals. Congratulatory, comforting, or nurturing touches fit here. Because such forms

of touch may be easily confused with more intimate, sexual touches, they are more likely to occur in public than private.

4. **Love/intimacy.** This highly intimate contact is usually regarded as pleasant and welcome in close relationships and a source of discomfort if committed by a nonintimate.

5. **Sexual arousal.** The most intense and most intimate class of contacts.

To see how various touches relate to one another, Edwards (1984) asked counseling subjects to report their own touching and their receipt of touch during a co-counseling course. Nurturant, celebratory, ludic, and cathartic touches were found to be highly interrelated. Caring touch and sexually arousing touch were seen as separate, as were the perception of touch as threatening and one's own ability to threaten others with touch. The inclusion of aggressive and threatening touches adds an important antisocial dimension of touch that is missing in the Heslin-Alper classification.

An even more elaborate classification comes from Jones and Yarbrough (1985), who arrived at their categories on the basis of participant logs of nearly 1,500 actual contacts. They found that touches could be classified as one or more of the following types, depending on the context:

1. **Positive affect touches.** Communicate unambiguous positive emotions, including support (nurturing, reassuring, promising protection), appreciation (expressing gratitude), inclusion (enhancing togetherness and psychological closeness), sexual intent or interest (expressing physical attraction), and affection (expressing generalized positive regard).

2. **Playful touches.** Designed to lighten an interaction and possibly give double meaning to a verbal message, including playful affection and playful aggression.

3. **Control touches.** Direct the behavior, attitude, or feeling state of another, including compliance, attention giving, and announcing a response (emphasizing the feeling state of the initiator).

4. **Ritualistic touches.** Involved in greetings and departures.

5. **Hybrid touches.** Combine other types, including greeting/affection and departure/affection.

6. **Task-related touches.** Associated with the performance of a task (such as the functional/professional touches of the previous system).

Except for the omission of negative affect and aggressive touches, which are less likely to be reported by participants, this taxonomy appears very complete. Grounded as it is in actual observations of touch across a wide range of circumstances, it represents an excellent compendium of the meanings and purposes for which touch is employed. What is needed next is to cross the structural approach with the functional approach to determine more precisely which types of touch convey which meanings independently or in combination with other cues. For example, what types of touch qualify as playful aggression, and what specific accompanying nonverbal and verbal behaviors signal that a punch is playful aggression rather than serious hostility?

The Proxemic Code

Less progress has been made in establishing the basic code elements of proxemics. Although the animal literature makes distinctions among home range, living space, true territory, social distance, individual distance, personal spheres, and personal fields (e.g., Hediger, 1950, 1961; McBride, 1971), the three categories that have received the most attention for humans are territory, personal space, and conversational distance.

Territories. Altman (1975) distinguishes among *primary, secondary,* and *public territories.* Primary territories are those that are most central to the daily lives of the individuals or groups within them. They are occupied or owned on a consistent, exclusive, and usually permanent or semipermanent basis, enough so that others identify the space as belonging to the owner or occupant. Homes, offices, bedrooms—even a patient's bed in a hospital qualify as primary territories. These territories represent physical and psychological retreats and are so significant that people's identities are often connected to them. To violate such a territory is a serious affront.

Secondary territories, by contrast, are more peripheral to day-to-day functioning, may involve more temporary and nonexclusive use, and generally have more permeable boundaries. They are "semipublic" territories and as such have less definite rules about their use and what constitutes encroachment. A country club or a neighborhood bar would be examples of secondary territories. Formal or implicit membership in the group often determines who has access to the territory.

Public territories are those to which almost anyone has free access and no occupancy privileges. Use of such spaces is also more transitory by any one individual or group. Playgrounds, beaches, sidewalks, and the like are available for use by the public at large and are regulated only by the society's laws and customs.

Another similar system for classifying territories comes from Lyman and Scott (1967), who distinguish four types: *body, home, interactional,* and *public.* Body territory, as the label implies, is one's own person and the space immediately surrounding it (which corresponds to what we have called personal space). Usually the individual has complete autonomy over who has access to it, and touching is allowed only with permission. This is not the case, however, in cultures that permit slavery or in which the husband can give his wife to his guest for an evening's pleasure. In the U.S. culture, as with other Western cultures, the body territory is the most private and inviolate. We are outraged by rapes, assaults, and murders precisely because they are ultimate violations. Opponents of capital punishment view executions the same way.

Home territory, similar to primary territory, is any geographic territory, be it grass hut, tent, or private estate, that a person or group regards as their exclusive and private domain. Residents or occupants have ultimate control of such space and are justified in using force to expel intruders. Offices, desks, and automobiles also qualify as home territories.

Interactional territory, like secondary territory, is semipublic, with loosely defined rules and customs over who is entitled to access. Movie theaters and classrooms are interactional territories. You are supposed to enter only if you buy a ticket or pay tuition. In practice, encroachments are far more common in interactional territories because social sanctions are not always enforced against intruders.

Public territory in Lyman and Scott's system coincides with Altman's category of the same name.

It is probably the case that competent communicators in this culture can distinguish conceptually among these various types of territories. However, in actual performance there appears to be considerable confusion about use and misuse of these territories. For example, when school cafeterias are extremely busy, there are often disputes between studiers and diners about who has rights to the tables. Leaving your possessions at a table may not guarantee that the table will be vacant when you return with your food. By the same token, if you ask to join someone else's table in a crowded dining room, the person may feel reluctant to refuse you. The reason is that it is not clear whether such territories qualify as interactional ones or public ones. If they are interactional, then the diner, who is conforming to the legitimate activity for the territory—eating—has more claim to a table than does a studier. And the person who marks a space with possessions or occupies it first has the right to treat it as his or her own. But if they are public territories, then no one's rights prevail over anyone else's, so long as no one is violating any law.

This confusion over definitions of territories can take a humorous turn, as in the true story of an impoverished couple who, due to a broken-down auto, took up residence in the basement of a college office building. Because the building had at one time been the president's home, it was equipped with servants' quarters that had been converted into faculty offices. The squatter couple soon discovered that a faculty office with a couch, carpet, bathroom, and refrigerator was far more accommodating than their makeshift arrangement of a wicker basket for food and sleeping bags on the concrete floor. So they gradually began shifting their living activities into the faculty office. The professor to whom the office was assigned returned one evening to find laundry hanging from the ceiling pipes, a trail of clothes leading to the bathroom, and the sounds of giggles and splashes wafting through the bathroom door. What he presumed to be his home territory had now become theirs! Moreover, as others learned about the couple's activities, they, too, began taking liberties with the office, turning it into a lounge—an interactional territory. The confusion over what kind of territory it was eventually got resolved through a time-sharing arrangement: The professor reclaimed his office as his own territory during the day and early evening but relinquished it to the couple at bedtime.

Personal Space and Conversational Distance. These two concepts refer to dynamic, mobile (nonfixed) space. Although writers have traditionally referred to the spacing patterns between two or more individuals as personal space, as originally conceived, personal space is the minimum amount of spatial insulation a person requires. Yet people may space themselves at much greater distances than their protective needs dictate. The concept of interpersonal or conversational distance reflects the normal distances that people maintain between themselves and others. We will use the latter label because we are most interested in communication contexts.

The prevailing system for classifying dynamic spacing patterns remains the one originally proposed by anthropologist Edward Hall (1959, 1966). His four perceptual categories of distance represent simultaneously an actual range of physical distance, a degree of psychosensory involvement, and a designation of the level of intimacy and formality of an interaction (see Figure 3.1). Each category has a close and a far phase, for a total of eight distance ranges.

1. **Intimate distance (0 to 18 in.).** This range is reserved for the most private and intimate of interactions. At this distance, people's kinesthetic receptors are highly aware of the presence of another. You can feel another's breath, smell body odors, perhaps even sense body heat. The other person dominates your visual field, your detail vision is blurred, and the person's facial features look distorted and enlarged. You can easily touch his or her trunk region, and accidental touch is likely. The other person literally "fills up your senses." At such close range, you are also likely to speak in soft, barely audible whispers about secret or highly confidential topics.

2. **Personal-casual distance (1½ to 4 ft).** This category's close phase (1½ to 2½ ft) is noticeably different from its far phase (2½ to 4 ft). The close phase is commonly used with family, friends, and close acquaintances and is likely to be used for self-disclosive, private conversations. The far phase is more common for casual acquaintances and less personal topics. In the close phase, it is easy to hold hands but not easy to touch other body parts; in the far phase, the other person is "at arm's length." As you increase distance in this category, it becomes increasingly difficult to sense odors and body heat from the other person (unless they are excessive). Facial features begin to appear more normal in your vision. At the close end, you may still use a softer voice; as you move to the far phase, speaking tone and loudness become more conventional.

3. **Social-consultive distance (4 to 10 ft).** This distance is used for activities ranging from impersonal social conversations in the close phase to business transactions in the far phase. Sensory involvement is significantly reduced compared to the two previous categories, and the other person moves out of touching range. In the far, consultive phase, other people become visible in one's peripheral vision, communication styles become more formal, voices begin to

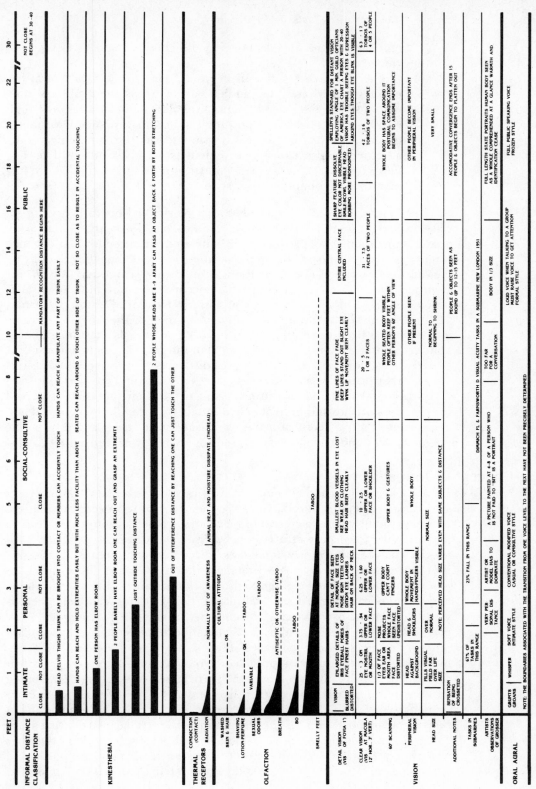

FIGURE 3.1 Chart showing the interrelationships among sensory channels in each distance zone.

get louder, and the distance is less conducive to carrying on a conversation.

4. **Public distance (10 ft and beyond).** This distance is typical between speakers and their audience, royalty and their subjects, holy men and their devotees, dignitaries and their admirers, or high ranking military leaders and their subordinates. At this distance, other people and objects easily compete with the communicator for attention, and sensory involvement is greatly reduced. This distance forces people to speak louder and usually elicits a more formal, frozen communication style.

Although Hall (1959) cautioned that he derived his categories from observations of predominantly white, middle-class North Americans, many students and scholars of proxemic behavior have embraced his four distance ranges as precise and widely generalizable. We feel that they should be viewed only as rough approximations. Our own research has shown, for example, that "intimate" distances may occur under nonintimate circumstances, such as in side-by-side seating in a classroom (Heston & Garner, 1972). This makes the "intimate" range inaccurate or the label inappropriate. Research by Altman and Vinsel (1977) also reveals that most people conduct standing interactions at personal or intimate distances and conduct seated interactions at personal or social distances. These combined results suggest that distance categories may be better captured by the following three zones: (a) a very narrow intimate zone of 0 to 12 inches that is reserved for the most private and intimate encounters, (b) a very large personal and social zone of 1 to 7 feet that is the "normal contact" zone, and (c) a public zone of 7 feet and beyond that is used for more formal encounters.

The Concept of Immediacy

Before leaving the code elements of haptics and proxemics, another category needs to be introduced. Nonverbal behaviors rarely occur in isolation; they are usually part of a system of behaviors. In the case of proxemics and haptics, they form part of a larger system called *immediacy behaviors.* Immediacy has been variously defined as "directness and intensity of interaction between two entities" (Mehrabian, 1967, p. 325); as abbreviated approach behaviors that heighten sensory stimulation, signal attentiveness, and communicate one's liking (Mehrabian, 1981); as multichanneled behaviors that promote psychological closeness (Andersen, 1979; Andersen, Andersen, & Jensen, 1979); and as a combination of affection, inclusion, and intensity of involvement messages (Burgoon & Hale, 1984). In short, immediacy behaviors express approach or avoidance and, in the process, affect the level of sensory involvement of the participants. Moreover, it is assumed that people approach things they like and avoid things they dislike, so immediacy behaviors also communicate positive or negative evaluations of the interaction partner. All the definitions of immediacy stress that it involves a combination of nonverbal and verbal behaviors working together as a system to increase or decrease the degree of physical, temporal, and psychological closeness between individuals. Mehrabian (1981) argues that this closeness-distance dimension is so important that immediacy is one of the three main metaphors governing interpersonal relations.

The nonverbal cues most often associated with immediacy and its opposite, nonimmediacy, are interpersonal distance, touch, gaze, body lean, head orientation (facing), body orientation, and smiling (Andersen, 1979; Andersen, Andersen, & Jensen, 1979; Argyle & Cook, 1976; Burgoon, Buller, Hale, & deTurck, 1984; Mehrabian, 1967, 1981; Patterson, 1973a, 1973b). Increases in one of these behaviors is often accompanied by decreases in one or more other behaviors so that the total level of sensory involvement remains relatively stable (Argyle & Cook, 1976; Argyle & Dean, 1965; Firestone, 1977; Hale & Burgoon, 1985; Knowles, 1980; Patterson, 1973a, 1976; Schaeffer & Patterson, 1980). For example, an increase in proximity may be offset by a decrease in gaze. This pattern of compensation occurs both within the individual, to maintain a comfortable level of approach or avoidance for oneself, and at the interpersonal level, to create the appropriate level of intimacy for the relationship at any given time.

The fact that nonverbal immediacy behaviors compensate for one another (and for the verbal level of immediacy) underscores their interrelatedness. It is not sensible to talk about what meanings are being expressed by touch or distance alone without simultaneously taking into account what is happening with the other immediacy components such as eye contact. It is possible, for example, to signal a close relationship, even if touch is inhibited, by adopting a close conversational distance and increasing gaze. By the same token, adding several cues together can intensify a particular meaning. In a study of five immediacy behaviors, Burgoon et al. (1984) found that even when a conflicting cue was present, two cues conveying the same level of involvement were sufficient to nullify the meaning of an opposite third cue. Thus touch and distance must be viewed as part of a larger system of immediacy behaviors, and any interpretations that are drawn must consider the co-occurring immediacy behaviors.

Haptic, Proxemic, and Immediacy Norms and Standards

Maturing communicators have a number of roles for which they must learn the appropriate behavior repertoires, roles related to culture, gender, family, social status, and social relationships (e.g., being a friend), among others. With each of these roles come norms and expectations for the use of touch and distance as communicative expressions. We will explore some of these norms and expectations in detail in Chapter 6 on identification, for it is through our conformity or nonconformity to expectations that we reveal our self-identity. At this juncture, we will limit ourselves to a brief overview of some of the important patterns that have been identified.

Cultural Similarities and Differences

At one level, cultures share a basic understanding of the meanings of touch and distance, in that they are grounded in innate signals of affection, hostility, association, and flight. For example, physical contact is an essential ingredient in the protection of newborns, in play behavior, and in mating. Members of societies also understand the underlying messages of approach and avoidance symbolized in distancing behavior. However, within these broad parameters, cultures still vary considerably in what touch and distance patterns prevail, as well as in what kinds of behavior are permissible or prohibited.

It has been popular to designate cultures as "contact" or "noncontact" (e.g., Hall, 1966; Montagu, 1978), with those falling in the former category being more prone to close interaction distances, direct body orientation, frequent physical contact, and direct gaze—in other words, more immediate and involving interaction styles—and those falling in the latter category engaging in more distant, nonimmediate types of exchanges. Arab, Indian, Mediterranean (e.g., Greek, Italian), and Latin American cultures are often classified as contact cultures, while North American and Northern European cultures are often classified as noncontact ones. However, this may be an overly simplistic distinction, as we shall see in Chapter 6.

Just as the frequency of contact varies across cultures, so do the purposes, meanings, and evaluations of touch. Social and religious values, status hierarchies, child-rearing practices, and long-standing traditions significantly influence the kinds of contacts that are sanctioned in each culture. In contrast to the restrictive and relatively punitive view toward touch that exists in the United States, many cultures are far more permissive and encouraging of physical contact. Nudity and open physical contact are common in more equatorial climes. Many cultures not only tolerate seeking physical pleasure through sexual contact and masturbation, but they may even incorporate sexual liaisons into their puberty rituals. In many primitive cultures, painful touch experiences may be central to the culture's traditions through scarification rituals, pain endurance tests, and other rites of passage. Meanings for behaviors also differ. Among the French, a handshake between an unacquainted man and an unmarried girl is frowned on because it conveys "a pact of friendship" that is presumptuous and improper; among Americans, it merely serves as a cordial greeting (Morris, 1971).

U.S. Cultural Norms and Expectations

Haptics. From what has been said already, it should be clear that the U.S. pattern is generally one of noncontact and nonimmediacy. This does not mean that touch is totally forbidden, for there are numerous types of relationships and occasions in which touch is appropriate and expected. But the total frequency of contact remains low relative to many other cultures.

This low frequency of contact, which is confined to the adult years, is apparently less than desired. A survey by Mosby (1978) found that no matter how much touching people receive, they want more, especially in satisfying relationships. Morris (1971) claims that the discrepancy between our desired and actual levels of touch leads to the use of "licensed touchers"— people such as hairdressers, barbers, manicurists, and masseurs whom we pay to supply the touch we are missing. Even though pleasurable contact is

Even though prolonged physical contact is occurring in both photographs, the location and amount of area involved in the touch, and the accompanying distance, distinguish between the contact culture (top) and the noncontact one (bottom).

not the primary reason for seeking these people's services, it is a desirable by-product that may reinforce repeat visits.

Burgoon and Saine (1978) discuss various speculations about why this pattern of noncontact has developed in the United States and other Western societies. One possibility is the shift from tribal to urban, mass societies. As long as people lived in small villages, they were all well acquainted and felt security within the group. With the rise of the industrial society and its concomitant mobility and growth of cities, people were no longer living in the midst of familiar and safe others. This may have led to avoidance of physical contact as a defensive reaction to too many strangers and uncertainty about whom to trust. Also, urban environments bring with them excessive levels of sensory stimulation—too much noise, too many sights, too little space, too much activity—that may lead to noncontact as a way to reduce stress.

Another explanation for the touch taboo is its strong association with sex. Because most religions in Western culture teach that premarital and extramarital sex are immoral and because intimate touch is the usual prelude to sexual relations, many forms of intimate contact become restricted except under ritualized circumstances. At the earliest ages, children are often discouraged from exploring their own or others' private parts. Little hands that attempt to examine a breast or genitals are nudged away. As they age, children are taught that self-manipulation and masturbation are naughty. Families that prohibit nudity reinforce the belief that the naked body, with its implicit invitation to touch, is somehow shameful. In adolescence, teens are warned by advice columnists and counselors to avoid petting because it leads to sex, and teenage girls are urged to protect their virginity. Adults may scrupulously avoid prolonged contact with members of the same sex for fear that it will be mistaken as a sexual overture. The net result is that intimate touch often produces guilt, embarrassment, and uncertainty that may even carry over to relationships in which it is normally acceptable. Marital counselors report that one of the main problems distressed couples face is deeply ingrained inhibitions about touch and sex. In short, the culture's religious and moral values influence the meanings and hence the use of touch.

A third explanation for the low frequency of touch is economic. Private property is a valued concept in this culture, and with it comes prohibitions against touching other people's possessions. Children are constantly cautioned not to touch Mother's computer, Father's pipe, Grandma's china, or a playmate's favorite toy. Although this "don't touch" dictum is applied to things rather than people, it is likely that it generalizes to all forms of tactile experiences, making people hesitant about initiating tactile exploration.

A final explanation concerns the communicative ability of touch itself. It has been argued that as societies become more technologically advanced and develop more sophisticated ways of communicating, they abandon such primitive forms of communication as the beating of drums or the use of touch. Thus the decline of touch is seen as a natural concomitant of the rise of printing and of mass media for visual and auditory communication. Moreover, as touch falls into disuse as a means of communication, people become less able to interpret its meanings or to send messages with it effectively, further contributing to its limited use.

Whichever of these explanations is correct, it is clear that touch as a communication medium is less common in the United States and similar Western cultures. Nevertheless, there are circumstances under which touch is not only permitted but expected. The norms are a function of (a) the type or purpose of the occasion, (b) the nature of the relationship between the communicators, (c) the body site being touched, (d) the type or meaning of the touch, and (e) the characteristics of the communicators, including gender, age, race, personality, and geography, among others.

Some occasions and relationships call for touch. Greetings and departures are instances. These are a few of the times when public displays of affection are permissible, although the routines are highly ritualized. Studies of airport behavior (Greenbaum & Rosenfeld, 1980; Heslin & Boss, 1980) have found that most people touch each other when greeting, and the forms of contact during greetings and good-byes are fairly intimate: a solid hug, a kiss on the mouth or cheek, a touch to the upper body (head, arm, or back), an arm around the waist, holding hands and/or a handshake. The more intimate the relationship, the more intimate the greeting. Dancing, sporting events, and other forms of play are also acceptable occasions for touch. Football and basketball games afford males rare opportunities for friendly physical contact with other males. The congratulatory full embrace, what Morris (1971) calls the "sportsman's triumph," is also commonplace on the playing field and during other recreational activities. Smith, Willis, and Gier (1980), for example, found a high rate of touch among bowlers (16.2 contacts per hour), with blacks exhibiting a higher rate of contact after successful performances than whites. It may be that roughhousing among males provides one of the few outlets for men to touch male friends and fathers to touch sons. Morris (1971) observes that when a man feels the urge to touch another man's head, he may resort to mock aggression, delivering such "pretend attack" gestures as grasping the neck in the crook of the arm or ruffling the hair.

Henley (1977) offers a list of the communication situations during which one is likely to touch or be touched (Table 3.2). Touch is likely to be initiated for more dominant functions, such as giving instructions or trying to persuade, while receipt of touch is more associated with submissive communication functions such as asking advice. This is congruent with the finding that in unequal-status relationships, the person of higher status is usually the one to initiate contact. Thus the relationship between communicators makes a difference. Similarly, the likelihood of touch increases as the familiarity of the relationship increases. People do not expect contact from strangers; they do expect it and desire it from intimates.

The frequency of contact also varies with the location of touch and its meaning. Morris (1971) claims that the partial shoulder embrace is six times more likely to occur than the full frontal embrace, the reason being, in part, that a fragmentary embrace has been deemed by convention to be nonsex-

TABLE 3.2 Types of Touch Situations and Likelihood of Touching or Being Touched

	Others More Likely to Touch When	Others Less Likely to Touch When
Information	Giving	Asking
Advice	Giving	Asking
Order	They're giving	You're giving
Favor	Asking	Agreeing to do
Persuade	They're trying	You're trying
Worried	You're	They're
Excited	They're	You're
Conversation	Deep	Casual
Place	Party	Work

Source: From *Body Politics: Power, Sex, and Nonverbal Communication* (p. 105) by N. Henley, 1977, Englewood Cliffs, NJ: Prentice-Hall.

ual. The hand-on-shoulder is even more common because it is less intimate. In one of the classic studies of touch norms, Jourard (1966a) asked 300 students to recall where they had touched and been touched on various body locations in a year's time. His results and those of a more recent study with 200 students (Rosenfeld, Kartus, & Ray, 1976) support the common observation that erogenous zones and immediately surrounding areas such as the face, buttocks, and thighs receive the least touch, while the head, shoulders, arms, and hands receive the most.

Of the major communicator characteristics mediating touch behavior, the one that has received the most attention is gender. One's gender influences not only how much touch a person receives and initiates but also whether one likes to be touched and what interpretations are given to various kinds of touch.

It was noted earlier that in childhood, most touch is with parents, peers, and teachers of the same sex. By college age, this pattern has reversed so that opposite-sex touch has become more prevalent (Jones, 1984, 1986; Major, 1981) and more body parts are reportedly accessible to opposite-sex friends (Jones, 1984; Jourard, 1966a; Lomranz & Shapira, 1974; Mosby, 1978). More women than men touch and are touched by others (Jones, 1984; Major, 1981), partly because women touch each other more than men touch each other (Andersen & Leibowitz, 1978; Stier & Hall, 1984). This is especially true among the elderly (Dean, Willis, & Rinck, 1978).

Other communicator characteristics that affect touch norms are age, race, personality, and geographic residence. For example, people between 30 and 40 and between 18 and 25 report more touching than those in other age groups, while older people report the least amount (Mosby, 1978). Older people are more likely to touch younger people than vice versa (Henley, 1973), which may be a status factor as well as an age factor. Blacks may report less touch and less desire for touch than whites (Norwood, 1979), but in one observational study—the one of bowlers—they touched

APPLICATIONS

Touch and Romantic Relationships

The question of when to touch and when not to touch the opposite sex is often a puzzling one. Part of the answer lies in how pleasurable people find such touch and what meanings they attribute to it.

Men and women differ on how pleasurable touch is for them. Consistent with the stereotype, women generally find it more pleasant. They evaluate touchers and the context in which touching occurs more favorably than men do (Fisher, Rytting, & Heslin, 1976; Heslin, 1978; Maier & Ernest, 1978; Major & Heslin, 1982; Stier & Hall, 1984). However, this conclusion must be tempered by two considerations: whether the toucher is of equal or different status and whether the toucher is a friend or a stranger. Research evidence indicates that both men and women respond favorably to touch from someone who has higher status than they. Women also respond favorably to touch from someone of equal or uncertain status, but men are neutral to negative about such touch (Major, 1981).

By contrast, women become less open to touch if it comes from a stranger. They find the prospect of a touch from an opposite-sex stranger more negative than men do (Heslin, Nguyen, & Nguyen, 1983). Heslin (1978) asked people to rate how pleasant it is to be patted or squeezed in various regions of the body by a close friend or stranger of the same or opposite sex. His results, which are displayed in Figure 3.2, show that both men and women find touch from a same-sex person generally unpleasant and touch from an opposite-sex friend largely pleasant, but they diverge in their reaction to touch from an opposite-sex stranger. Men like it; women don't.

Men and women also differ in how they interpret touch. Single women and married men are more negative toward touch with sexual connotations than married women and single men, and men generally read more sexual connotations into any kind of touch than women do (Heslin, 1978; Heslin & Alper, 1983).

These findings speak to the advisability of initiating touch in potentially romantic relationships. If the object of your romantic intentions is female, keep in mind that single women object to touch from strangers, especially if it has sexual overtones. However, if you are already a friend or someone of higher status, she will probably like being touched, especially if the touches are playful, nurturing, or affectionate. And if you marry her, she will likely find sexual touch more pleasant than before. If the object of your romantic intentions is male and single, he is likely to interpret any touch as sexual and may find it especially appealing if you are a stranger.

Touch and Romantic Relationships (*Continued*)

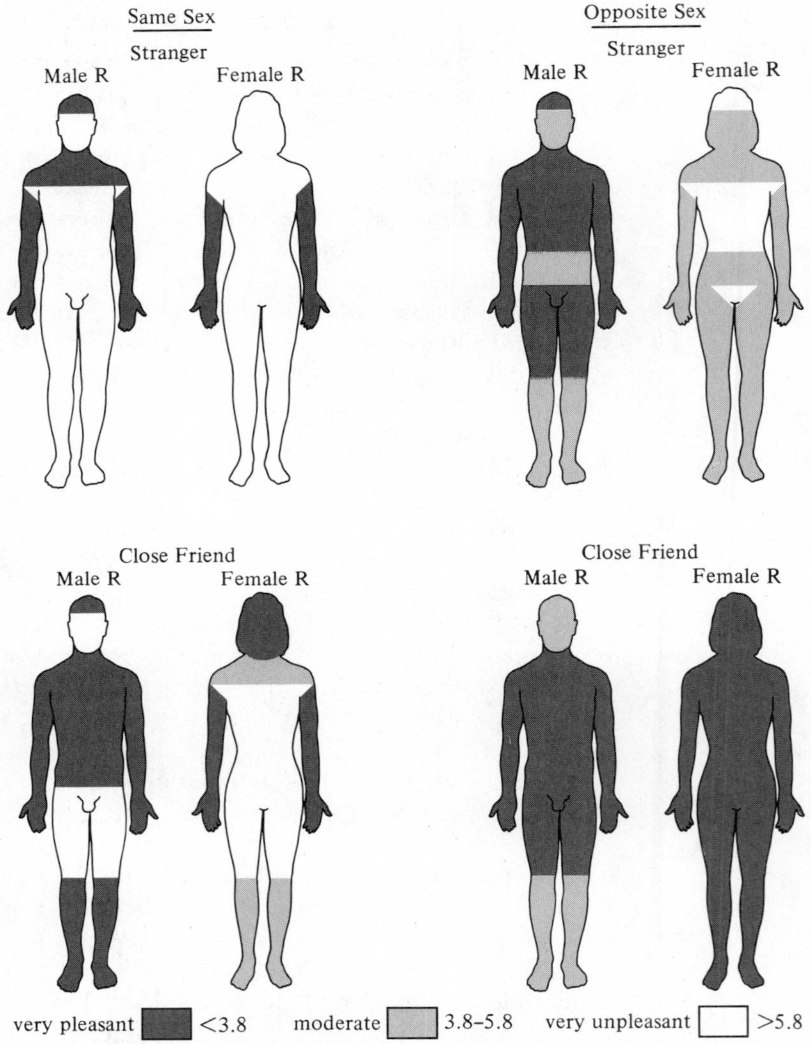

FIGURE 3.2 Perceived pleasantness of touch from same-sex and opposite-sex strangers and close friends for males and females.

each other more than whites did (Smith et al., 1980), and in another, they touched at the same rates as whites (Willis, Rinck, & Dean, 1978). By personality, such factors as one's conservatism, self-image, and body image may affect one's attitudes about touch (Norwood, 1979) and ultimately cause some people to be touch avoiders (Andersen & Leibowitz, 1978). Even where one lives can affect how much touch one experiences: Families in the South are more likely to touch each other than families in the North.

A capstone to this review of touch norms and preferences is the observational study by Jones and Yarbrough (1985), which takes into account all the kinds of influences on norms we have been discussing—the meaning of the touch, its location, the relationship between interactants, and character-

Embraceable USA—by Region

Southerners do it more than Northerners. Women are more willing to do it than men. And older people do it less but need it more.

"It" is touching.

Whether you're comfortable touching other people in social situations may depend on where you live, your age, and your sex.

A survey of 20,000 people in 25 states by Greg Risberg of Northwestern University Medical School found [that] families influence touching.

"No-touch doesn't mean no love," he said. "But low-touch families do not express affection physically. They save that for special occasions. High-touch families will hug or caress for all kinds of reasons, or no reason at all."

Among his findings:

In the South—80 percent come from medium- to high-touch backgrounds, 15 percent from low-touch and 5 percent from no-touch.

North—90 percent are from low- to medium-touch, 5 percent each from high-touch and no-touch.

Midwest—80 percent are from low- to medium-touch, 10 percent each from high-touch and no-touch.

Westerners—85 percent from medium- to high-touch, 10 percent low-touch, 5 percent no-touch.

Only 5 percent felt touched enough; 98% wanted more; 89% held back their inclinations to touch.

Women are much more comfortable touching, Risberg said; the elderly are more reluctant because they expect to be touched less.

Source: L. Howard, May 31–June 2, 1985, *USA Today*, p. A1.

istics of the individual communicators. Their summary of the frequency of various types of touches, the manner in which they are enacted, and the constraining circumstances on their uses provides an excellent depiction of touch practices in mainstream U.S. culture. Shown in Table 3.3, these 18 categories are the result of 1,069 observed cases of individual touches.

Proxemics. In comparison to haptics, far more research has been devoted to proxemic norms and expectations. Much of the early research is summarized in Altman (1975), Burgoon and Jones (1976), Burgoon and Saine (1978), Evans and Howard (1973), Hayduk (1978), Hickson and Stacks (1985), Knapp (1978), and LaFrance and Mayo (1978a; 1978b). Because this work is so voluminous, we will present an abbreviated summary here, along with more recent updates. A more detailed discussion of some of these factors also appears in Chapter 6.

The factors influencing conversational distance norms can be divided into three general categories: communicator characteristics, relationship characteristics, and context characteristics. *Communicator characteristics* are the demographic and individual features that are identifiable for each participant in an interaction. Among the features found to influence distancing are these four:

1. **Gender.** Although many studies fail to find gender differences, most research continues to confirm that female dyads sit and stand closer together than male dyads (e.g., Sussman & Rosenfeld, 1982). People also approach, sit, and stand closer to women than to men. In cross-sex dyads, research is mixed, with most finding that male-female pairs converse at closer distances than female-female pairs but some finding them at greater distances. However, mixed-sex pairs consistently adopt closer distances than male-male pairs.

2. **Age.** Interpersonal distance generally increases with age. For example, photographs of people walking with companions reveal that average distance increases from preschool and grade school children through teens and young adults to senior adults (Burgess, 1983). People also adopt closer distances with peers than with those who are younger or older.

3. **Race/ethnicity.** The research in this area is more sporadic and confusing. Some studies have found that blacks maintain greater distance among themselves than whites while conversing, others have found just the reverse, and yet others have found no racial differences. Mexican Americans are reported to adopt the closest distances among the three groups, but the research is very limited.

4. **Personality.** Different personality types have different distance requirements. Introverts and anxiety-prone individuals, for example, require greater interaction distances than extroverts and perceive distances between themselves and others as less than they really are.

Relationship characteristics are the features that capture the joint relationship between two or more people. They describe dyads and groups rather

TABLE 3.3 Characteristics of Meaning Categories for Individual Touches

Category (definition, number of cases)	Key Features	Range of Permissible Variation
A. Positive Affect Touches		
1. *Support*—serves to nurture, reassure or promise protection (39 cases)	(1) Situation calls for comfort or reassurance (100%) (2) Hand (100%), and sometimes an arm, directed to 1–2 body parts (89.7%) (3) Initiated by person who gives support (84.6%)	(1) Almost any relationship among the acquainted, but mainly close relationships (71.8%) (2) VBP and NVBP touched about equally (51.3% to 48.7%) (3) Verbalization common (82.1%), usually demands/commands or inquiries about welfare, but may be redundant or missing when situation is clear (4) Mainly holding (46.5%), although prolonged holding is rare; also spot touches, pats, and squeezes (41%), with a few caresses (10.3%) (5) Mainly cross-sex (71.8%), with some female-female (17.9%) and male-male (10.4%)
2. *Appreciation*—expresses gratitude (16 cases)	(1) Situation: receiver has performed service for toucher (100%) (2) Touch initiator verbalizes appreciation, usually some version of "thanks" (87.5%)	(1) Verbalization usually comes during or after, not before, touch (81.3%) (2) Divided between VBP (43.8%) and NVBP (56.3%); mainly hand-to-body touches, with a few kisses (18.8%) (3) Mainly holding (68.8%), but also brief touches (spot, pat, squeeze, or handshake) (4) Mainly cross-sex (68.8%), although male-male (12.5%) and female-female (18.8%) touches occur (5) When act of service occurs just before touch, verbalization may not be essential (12.5%) (6) Mainly close relationships (75%)
3. *Inclusion*—draws attention to act of being together; suggests psychological closeness (32 cases)	(1) Sustained touch (100%) (2) Close relationship (90.6%), mainly sexual intimates and close friends; only 2 cases involve immediate family members other than spouses	(1) Situation is usually involvement in a common task, rather than just conversation, but both occur (2) Half mutual, half initiated touches (3) Mainly holding (71.8%), especially holding/pressing against (46.9%), with some prolonged spot touches (12.5%) and repeated brushes (12.5%) (4) Mainly VBP (71.9%) touches (5) Verbalization usually occurs (71.9%) but is seldom related to the act of being together (9.4%)

TABLE 3.3 Characteristics of Meaning Categories for Individual Touches (*Continued*)

Category (definition, number of cases)	Key Features	Range of Permissible Variation
4. *Sexual*—expresses physical attraction or sexual interest (21 cases)	(1) Cross-sex relationships (100%) (2) Holding and/or caressing (100%) (3) VBP (95.2%), including or restricted to "sexual" body parts—chest (women), pelvis, and/or buttocks (85.7%)	(1) Most relationships are sexual intimates (76.2%); 4 of 5 exceptions are reported by a single participant (2) Mainly when people are alone, occasionally in crowds or focused small groups (3) Mainly initiated (61.9%), with some mutual hugs (38.1%)
5. *Affection*—expresses generalized positive regard beyond mere acknowledgement (56 cases)	(1) Close relationships (85.7%) (2) A residual category: absence of a more specific positive affect meaning suggests affection	(1) Mainly cross-sex relationships (75%), with some female-female touches (21.4%); male-male touches are rare (3.6%) (2) Holding and some caresses (64.3%), but some spot touches and pats (33.9%) (3) Divided between VBP (60.7%) and NVBP (39.3%) (4) Hugs and/or kisses more common than other positive affect categories (26.7%), except sexual meanings (5) Mainly initiated touches (82.1%)

B. Playful Touches

1. *Playful Affection*—serves to lighten interaction; seriousness of affection qualified (26 cases)	(1) Affectionate or sexual messages with play signal (100%)	(1) Mainly close relationships (76.9%), principally intimates (38.5%) and close friends (30.8%) (2) Mainly cross-sex (80.8%), with some male-male touches (19.2%) (3) VBP contacts common (80.8%) (4) Spot touches (38.5%), holding (23.1%), but also wrestle, tickle, punch, pinch, bump, pat (5) Touches are mostly initiated (76.9%) but may be mutual (23.1%)

TABLE 3.3 Characteristics of Meaning Categories for Individual Touches (*Continued*)

Category (definition, number of cases)	Key Features	Range of Permissible Variation
2. *Playful Aggression*— serves to lighten interaction; seriousness of aggression qualified (26 cases)	(1) Aggressive message with play signal (100%) (2) Initiated, not mutual (100%)	(1) Aggressive touches include mock strangling, mock wrestling, punching, pinching, slapping, grabbing, and standing on toes, while touches acting as play signals are mainly spot touches and pats (2) Mainly male-male (38.5%) and cross-sex (50%) touches (3) Not restricted by relationship: not-close (53.8%), close (46.2%) (4) VBP contacts somewhat more common (61.5%) than NVBP contacts (38.5%) (5) Verbalization usually occurs (80.8%); instances of silent playful aggression appear to be relationship-specific

C. Control Touches

Category (definition, number of cases)	Key Features	Range of Permissible Variation
1. *Compliance*—attempts to direct behavior and oftentimes also attitudes or feelings of another (75 cases)	(1) Initiated by person attempting influence (92%) (2) Verbalization occurs (states or implies requested action) (90.7%)	(1) Words are direct or implied demands/commands or requests for information and action (question form); situation may make touch clear in itself so words only reinforce (18.7%) or are absent (9.3%) (2) Close relationships most common (76%) but can occur in any relationship among the acquainted (3) Both sexes initiate to same and opposite sex, although female-to-male touches (33.3%) are somewhat more common than male-to-female (18.7%) (4) NVBP touches somewhat more common (62.7%) than VBP (37.3%) (5) Holding (46.7%), spot touches (45.3%) and pats (6.6%); mainly hand to body part (81.3%)
2. *Attention-getting*— serves to direct the recipient's perceptual focus (66 cases)	(1) Initiated by person requesting attention (100%) (2) Initiator verbalizes (clarifies purpose) (100%) (3) Brief touches (spot, pat, brush) directed to 1–2 body parts (84.8%)	(1) Attention is called to an object or event or to the verbalization itself (2) Most touches initiated by hand alone (80.3%) (3) NVBP more common (74.2%) than VBP (25.8%) (4) Both sexes initiate to same and opposite sex, although most touches are female-initiated (75.8%) (5) Any kind of relationship, including strangers (16.7%)

TABLE 3.3 Characteristics of Meaning Categories for Individual Touches (*Continued*)

Category (definition, number of cases)	Key Features	Range of Permissible Variation
3. *Announcing a Response*—calls attention to and emphasizes a feeling state of initiator; implicitly requests affect response from another (46 cases)	(1) Initiated by person announcing response (91.3%) (2) Verbalization by toucher(s) announces feeling directly or indirectly (97.8%)	(1) Mutual touches, while rare (8.7%), all express congratulations (2) Primarily hand to 1–3 body parts (80.4%); a few hugs (13%) (3) Primarily close relationships (80.4%) (4) Mainly female-initiated (67.4%), although both sexes initiate to both sexes (5) Mostly NVBP (63%)

D. Ritualistic Touches

Category (definition, number of cases)	Key Features	Range of Permissible Variation
1. *Greeting*—serves as part of the act of acknowledging another at the opening of an encounter (43 cases)	(1) Situation is beginning of interaction (100%) (2) Verbalization of standard greeting phrase (93%), before or during touch, not after (88.4%) (3) Hand to one body part (90.6%) (4) (Near to key feature) Minimal form of contact (handshake, spot touch, pat or squeeze) (83.7%)	(1) All sex composition types (2) All kinds of relationships (3) NVBP touches more common (74.4%) than VBP (25.6%)
2. *Departure*—serves as part of the act of closing an encounter (20 cases)	(1) Situation is end of an encounter (100%) (2) Verbalization of standard departure phrase (90%), before or during touch, not after (85%) (3) Hand to one body part (85%)	(1) Unlike greeting touches, handshakes are rare (10%) (2) Mainly pats and spot touches (55%); also holding, caresses (3) Mainly NVBP (75%) (4) Rarely occurs between family members or intimates (5%); mainly close friends (55%) and not-close friends (35%) (5) Mainly same-sex touches (80%)

TABLE 3.3 Characteristics of Meaning Categories for Individual Touches (*Continued*)

Category (definition, number of cases)	Key Features	Range of Permissible Variation
E. Hybrid Touches		
1. *Greeting/Affection*—expresses affection and acknowledgement at the initiation of an encounter (79 cases)	(1) Situation is beginning of interaction (100%) (2) Verbalization occurs (88.6%) (3) Close relationships (86.1%) (4) VBP touches (86.1%)	(1) Most words are standard greeting phrases (72.1%), while expressions of endearment accompanying greetings (24.1%) and direct expressions of affection (3.8%) are less common (2) Some "borderline" touches resemble pure greetings (few body parts) (22.7%), but most touches involve hugs and/or kisses (70.9%) (3) Mainly cross-sex touches (75.9%), with some female-female contacts (17.7%); male-male handshakes (6.3%) appear to be idiosyncratic interpretations
2. *Departure/Affection*—expresses affection and serves to close an encounter (72 cases)	(1) Situation is end of interaction (100%) (2) Verbalization occurs (94.4%) (3) Close relationships (94.4%) (4) VBP touches (91.6%), principally hugs and/or kisses (84.7%)	(1) Most words are departure phrases; some direct expressions of affection (18.1%) (2) A few "borderline" cases, resembling pure departure (hand-to-body contacts) (12.5%) (3) Mainly cross-sex touches (81.9%), with some female-female contacts (13.9%); male-male contacts rare (4.1%)
F. Task-Related Touches		
1. *Reference to Appearance*—a touch which points out or inspects a body part or artifact referred to in a verbal comment about appearance (11 cases)	(1) Words accompany and justify the touch, intrinsically coded so the definition is a key feature (100%) (2) Spot touch by a hand to a VBP (100%) (3) Female-initiated (100%) (4) Close relationships (90.1%)	(1) Verbalizations are compliments or expressions of interest (2) Mainly close friends; 2 mother-daughter touches; no touches among intimates (3) Female-to-female and female-to-male (4) Some translations suggest a secondary meaning of affection or flirtation

TABLE 3.3 Characteristics of Meaning Categories for Individual Touches (*Continued*)

Category (definition, number of cases)	Key Features	Range of Permissible Variation
2. *Instrumental Ancillary*—a touch which occurs as an unnecessary part of the accomplishment of a task (56 cases)	(1) Intrinsically coded, so the definition is a key feature (100%) (2) Hand-to-hand contacts (91.1%) (3) Instrumental act is clear in itself (100%)	(1) Although touches are self-explanatory, verbalization usually occurs (83.9%) (2) Mainly cross-sex (53.6%) and female-female (39.3%) contacts (3) Variety of relationships, including acquainted persons who are not close (25%) and strangers (17.8%), but few contacts between cross-sex close friends (8.9%) and none among intimates (4) Divided between mutual (53.6%) and initiated (46.4%) touches (5) Some touches carry apparent secondary meanings (flirtation, compliance, inclusion, affection)
3. *Instrumental Intrinsic*—touch which accomplishes a task in and of itself (54 cases)	(1) Intrinsically coded, so the definition is a key feature (100%) (2) Instrumental meaning is clear from the touch itself (100%)	(1) Principally initiated (87%), although this does not seem essential to the meaning (2) Verbalization usually occurs (77.8%), despite the fact that touch is self-explanatory (3) Either VBP (61.1%) or NVBP (38.9%), depending on task (4) Cross-sex (53.7%) and female-female (42.0%) contacts account for almost all incidents (5) Mostly close relationships (74.1%), but all kinds of relationships represented; seldom sexual intimates (5.6%) (6) Some translations suggest secondary message of flirtation, inclusion or affection

G. Accidental Touches

1. *Accidental*—touches which are perceived as unintentional and therefore meaningless (86 cases)	(1) Touches consist of single, momentary contacts, principally brushes (89.5%), with a few spot touches (9.3%) (2) Accepted, unrepaired touches occur principally among the acquainted (88.4%)	(1) VBP (45.3%) and NVBP (54.7%) (2) All kinds of relationships, but most touches between strangers are rejected and/or repaired (3) Words seldom occur (31.4%) and are unrelated to the touch (4) All sex-composition types, although cross-sex touches are most common (73.3%) (5) Some touches may be motivated since some persons who seldom initiate touches of other types have many accidental touches

Note. VBP stands for *vulnerable body parts* (e.g., legs, buttocks, neck) and **NVBP** stands for *nonvulnerable body parts* (hands, arms, shoulders, upper back).

Source: From "A Naturalistic Study of the Meanings of Touch," by S. E. Jones & A. E. Yarbrough, 1985, *Communication Monographs, 52,* pp. 28–35.

than individuals. Three of the most salient factors influencing proxemic patterns are:

1. **Familiarity.** The better acquainted two people are, the closer the distance they are likely to adopt for conversation. Greatest distances from strangers are consistently maintained.
2. **Attraction and liking.** As personal experience attests, people sit and stand closest to those whom they like.
3. **Status.** The greater the status inequality, the greater the distance. Leaders also tend to select interaction positions that maximize their eye contact and opportunity to control others. Thus they gravitate to the head of the table or sit opposite the most other people.

Context characteristics are the unique features of the occasion and environmental setting that distinguish one interaction situation from another. Chief among the important influences are the following:

1. **Formality.** All else being equal, a formal setting elicits larger conversational distances than an informal one. Recall that Hall's system for classifying distances makes degree of formality a major distinguishing characteristic among distance zones. One need only envision an important business meeting or a job interview to recognize the greater interaction distance that is likely, compared to a social chat over coffee.
2. **Purpose of the interaction.** Research on preferred seating arrangements shows that people differ in their patterns and preferences, depending on whether they are carrying on a social conversation, cooperating on a task, working independently on a task (coacting), or competing. For social conversations, seating arrangements that increase proximity while allowing good eye contact are preferred— such as side-by-side seating at a circular table or corner-to-corner and near-across seating at a rectangular table. For cooperative tasks, even greater proximity is preferred—such as side-by-side seating at a rectangular table. Competition yields preferences for greater distance but with opportunities for surveillance—such as is provided by across seating. Coaction produces a desire for the greatest distance, presumably to minimize distractions.

   In a classroom, the preferred seating pattern is a U shape, which focuses most attention on the instructor and facilitates discussion. Eating and drinking occasions add further considerations. In restaurants, the norm is for people to seat themselves opposite one another, no doubt to afford themselves ample elbow room and conversational ease. In a bar, side-by-side or corner-to-corner seating is more common, presumably because it promotes intimacy. Hall's four distance zones also incorporate purpose of the interaction as a distinguishing characteristic: Highly intimate conversations are reported to occur at the closest distances, more social and business-oriented conversations at intermediate distances, and public presentations at the greatest distances.

3. **Familiarity with the setting.** Just as people move closer together as they become better acquainted, people become more proximate as they gain familiarity with a particular setting. In fact, anticipating future interaction in a locale can bring people closer together.

4. **Space availability and density.** The volume of available space relative to the number of people in an environment can significantly affect how people distance themselves. The more space available, the closer together people sit or stand. This may be because they feel less trapped and freer to retreat in a large space, or it may be partly a function of the poorer acoustics in larger spaces. Whichever the reason, people in museums or hotel lobbies are more likely to cluster together than those in an office or living room. Similarly, people in outdoor environments tolerate greater closeness than people in indoor environments (Cochran, Hale, & Hissam, 1984).

5. **Furniture style and arrangement.** The perceived comfort of furniture is likely to be the first determinant of where people sit. Everyone has had experience trying politely to avoid the stiff, uncomfortable-looking sofa and chairs in someone's formal living room. Where the first entrants to a room choose to sit in turn affects the choices of later arrivals. Interior designers claim that the arc for comfortable conversation is about 6 to 8 feet. Some research by Sommer (1959, 1962) reveals that people prefer to sit across from one another—say, on facing couches—until the distance across is uncomfortable for conversation and exceeds that of the side-by-side option. Then people choose side-by-side seating. Usually, the shift to side-by-side choices occurs at about 5½ feet.

6. **Sensory stimulation.** Finally, the total level of noise, crowding, heat, odors, clutter, and other sensory stimulation in an environment can affect distancing. A tentative finding is that men, but not women, reduce the permeability of their personal space zone in the presence of stressful environmental conditions (Bell & Barnard, 1984).

Communication Potential of Proxemics and Haptics

As communication systems, haptics and proxemics have both strengths and weaknesses. A significant advantage is their innate importance to the developing human. The essential roles that physical contact, tactile stimulation, and spatial perception play in growth, development, and protection of the organism argue for a primacy of touch and proxemic messages that may be unequaled by other codes.

A second advantage of these codes is their arousal value. They have the capacity to arrest the attention of a receiver. A researcher at Princeton's Cutaneous Communication Laboratory notes that "cutaneous sensations, especially if aroused in unusual patterns, are highly attention-demanding. It is possible, therefore, that the simplest and most straightforward of all messages—warnings and alerts—should be delivered cutaneously" (Geldhard, 1960, pp. 1583–1584).

A third advantage, in the case of haptics, is that the skin is capable of making discriminations along several dimensions. Although the discriminations are somewhat crude, the skin can distinguish both spatial (locational) differences and temporal ones based on frequency of contact. It can also distinguish duration of contact, making about 25 distinctions, and intensity of pressure, making about 15 distinctions (Geldhard, 1960). These are cutaneous judgments. When kinesthetic features of haptic communication are also considered, there is good potential for accurate recognition through touch (Goldberg & Bajcsy, 1984). Moreover, these discriminations tend to be more accurate than visual ones, which are subject to perceptual distortions. Of course, the perceptual biases involved in visual judgments also plague distance judgments, which explains why personal space perceptions do not always match reality.

Compared to other codes, however, one weakness of haptics is the rather small range of decoding abilities among humans. The eye and ear have far greater physical capacity to handle a wide array of stimuli than the skin. Similarly, the range of code values appears somewhat smaller for haptics and proxemics than for other codes. The number of specific cues or dimensions that can be varied is somewhat limited. For example, if one accepts Hall's system, there are only four distinguishable categories of interpersonal distance. And the haptic code systems identify a finite, albeit sizable, set of touch types.

A third weakness of proxemics and haptics is the cultural variability in use, which not only limits experience with such codes in noncontact cultures but also restricts the generalizability of some of their meanings. North Americans and other Westerners, who are not permitted as many opportunities for tactile communication, become far less competent in its encoding and decoding, thereby reducing its utility as a communication vehicle. Cultural differences also mean that a close distance in one place may have a very different interpretation in another. This ultimately reduces reliance on touch and distance as sole carriers of messages.

Fourth, touch and distance messages are subject to high ambiguity even within the same culture. This further reduces their viability as primary message vehicles. Imagine, for example, trying to convey a need for assistance through touch or distance alone, and you can see how behaviors such as tapping another person or moving into close proximity could easily be misinterpreted without the benefit of other accompanying nonverbal and verbal cues.

Finally, proxemics and haptics are somewhat more restricted than other codes because they are not relevant to all communication functions. For example, these two codes are less important in deception, and proxemics is not particularly salient to emotional communication. Because these codes are often relegated to the supporting cast for certain communication

How can you tell that this apparently aggressive touch is merely play?

purposes (as is the case with touch in expressing emotions), they cannot be considered to be as powerful as kinesics or vocalics. Nevertheless, as part of the totality of the nonverbal complex, they play a significant role. In the case of some of the most fundamental messages of danger or affection, they are the central actors.

Summary

The interrelated codes of haptics and proxemics appear to arise out of competing drives for approaching and avoiding others and reflect strong personal preferences and social norms for their enactment. Humans share fundamental needs for human contact, for territoriality, and for personal space, needs that are central to their healthy development and functioning. The detrimental effects of inadequate tactile stimulation and space, and reactions to territorial or personal space invasion, such as the general adaptation syndrome, offer compelling evidence of how fundamental tactile and proxemic patterns are to human existence. Consequently, haptic and proxemic behaviors become potent means of expressing those needs and establishing satisfactory relationships with others. At the same time, cultural and group norms shape how these behaviors are transformed into acceptable or unacceptable communication patterns and what meanings are associated with the behaviors.

As a communication code, touch can be classified according to (a) the forms of touch, (b) the dimensions that produce a given touch, or (c) the functions and meanings associated with touch. Proxemic behaviors can be categorized according to type of territory or degree of conversational distance. Another concept, immediacy, incorporates proxemic and haptic behaviors with kinesic and vocal cues to signal approach or avoidance. Immediacy underscores the importance of examining nonverbal codes as systems rather than isolated behaviors.

Although all humans experience needs for touch and needs for distance at various times, such factors as gender, race, age, personality, and culture all shape what communication patterns become normative and expected. Patterns become fairly well-established in childhood and undergo little modification into adulthood.

Because cultures vary dramatically in whether they are contact or noncontact cultures, the potential for haptics and proxemics to serve as communication vehicles also differs dramatically. Beyond the possible primacy of these two codes stemming from their innate importance, haptics and proxemics also have significant potential to arouse the receiver, thereby gaining attention. Humans are also able to make relatively accurate but not widely ranging discriminations of tactile stimuli, which limits the haptic code. The proxemic code has an infinitely large range of possible distance and spatial behaviors that could be encoded, but it is likely that humans only recognize a few gross distinctions, and the proxemic code is plagued by the same biases in visual perception as kinesics. Cultural differences in frequency of use and meaning, ambiguities in meaning within the same culture, and the inapplicability of haptics and proxemics to some communication functions are further limitations on their communication potential. Nevertheless, they can act as very subtle and potent forms of communication.

Suggested Readings

Altman, I. (1975). *The environment and social behavior.* Monterey, CA: Brooks/Cole.

Ardrey, R. (1979). *African genesis.* New York: Dell.

Bakker, C. B., & Bakker-Rabdau, M. K. (1985). *No trespassing! Explorations in human territoriality.* San Francisco: Chandler & Sharp.

Esser, A. H. (1972). A biosocial perspective on crowding. In J. F. Wohlwill & D. H. Carson (Eds.), *Environment and the social sciences: Perspectives and applications.* Washington, DC: American Psychological Association.

Frank, L. K. (1971). Tactile communication. In H. A. Bosmajian (Ed.), *The rhetoric of nonverbal communication.* Glenview, IL: Scott, Foresman.

Hall, E. T. (1959). *The silent language.* Garden City, NY: Doubleday.

Hall, E. T. (1966). *The hidden dimension* (2nd ed.). Garden City, NY: Anchor Press/Doubleday.

Hayduk, L. A. (1978). Personal space: An evaluative and orienting overview. *Psychological Bulletin, 85,* 117–134.

Hediger, H. P. (1961). The evolution of territorial behavior. In S. L. Washburn (Ed.), *Social life of early man.* Chicago: Aldine.

LaFrance, M., & Mayo, C. (1978). *Moving bodies.* Monterey, CA: Brooks/Cole.

Major, B. (1981). Gender patterns in touching behavior. In C. Mayo & N. M. Henley (Eds.), *Gender and nonverbal behavior.* New York: Springer-Verlag.

Montagu, A. (1978). *Touching: The human significance of the skin* (2nd ed.). New York: Harper & Row.

Morris, D. (1971). *Intimate behavior.* New York: Random House.

Morris, D. (1977). *Manwatching: A field guide to human behavior.* New York: Abrams.

Sommer, R. (1969). *Personal space: The behavioral basis of design.* Englewood Cliffs, NJ: Prentice-Hall.

CHAPTER 4

Place and Time Codes: Environment, Artifacts, and Chronemics

No species can exist without an environment, no species can exist in an environment of its exclusive creation, no species can survive, save as a nondisruptive member of an ecological community. Every member must adjust to other members of the community and to the environment in order to survive. Man is not excluded from this test.

Ian McHarg (1963, pp. 57–58)

Environment and Artifacts

It is a human characteristic to affect and change the environment. Humans are affected by their physical surroundings as well. As a nonverbal code, environment and artifacts include a very diverse set of elements. We can define the environment and artifacts code as *the physical objects and environmental attributes that communicate directly, define the communication context, or guide social behavior in some way.* Environmental cues and other artifactual features serve as a communication code in three main ways. First, they often communicate some meaning directly to us. A building may be designed to convey some symbolic meaning. For example, churches often communicate very clear religious meanings. Similarly, people arrange their homes and offices to reflect their personalities, values, and preferences; thus their surroundings reveal something about who they are. Even our personal possessions, such as our choice of automobile or an attaché case, can carry meaning.

A second means of communication occurs when the environment and

These home exteriors suggest different things about the inhabitants.

its artifacts define the context in which social interaction takes place. Something as subtle as the colors used in a room can create a context for good social conversations (rather than task-oriented meetings). Or it may be something more obvious, such as the arrangement of chairs in rows so that people seated in the back row cannot speak to those in the front row.

Third, the environment and artifacts can tell us what is appropriate communication behavior and what is not. Picking up on these cues causes us to behave correspondingly. Or the environment may act more directly to affect our behavior, as when posted signs indicate how to communicate ("Quiet, Please" signs in libraries and hospitals, for example). This role will be discussed in detail in Chapter 11.

Our knowledge of the communicative role of environment and artifacts comes from a multidisciplinary group of people: architects, urban designers and planners, environmental psychologists, human factors psychologists, and cultural anthropologists, among others. The volume of research in this area has grown so large that environmental psychology is now considered a subfield of psychology itself (for an interesting overview of the development of environmental psychology, see Proshansky and Altman, 1979). Although not all of this work is directly applicable to communication, we shall focus on the studies that shed light on how the environment communicates meaning, sets a context for interpersonal interaction, or guides communication behavior.

Origins and Acquisition

Unlike other nonverbal communication codes, one does not really "acquire" the environmental code in any direct sense. Rather, we acquire *reactions* to the environment; that is, we learn (a) to interpret meaning from the environment, (b) that certain contexts prompt different kinds of interaction, and (c) that certain environmental cues imply sets of rules and guides for behavior. It is likely that most of our reactions to the environment are learned through socialization and involve a mix of classical, operant, and modeling learning strategies. The meanings interpreted from the environment are heavily influenced by one's cultural background. As a result, when we travel to another country, the meanings we gather from these new and novel environments are often different from those that the local population interprets from the same environment. For example, Westerners may not draw much meaning or significance from a formal Japanese rock garden, whereas the Japanese interpret quite important meanings from it. Similarly, most Westerners find the formal Japanese teahouse ceremony simply a quaint way to enjoy tea in a serene setting. However, for the Japanese, the teahouse and ceremony constitute a rich context full of cues and prompts for appropriate behavior.

Edward T. Hall has spent much of his career investigating the cultural aspects of the environmental code (see Hall, 1959, 1966, 1981). One distinction that can be made is between *high context* and *low context* cultures:

What does the arrangement of artifacts in this room suggest to you? A room for the tea ceremony, it holds a great deal of meaning for members of the Japanese culture. Notice how the arrangement of objects provides a focus for interaction.

> A high-context communication (HC) or message is one in which most of the information is either in the physical context or internalized in the person, while very little is in the coded, explicit, transmitted part of the message. A low-context (LC) communication is just the opposite; i.e., the mass of the information is vested in the explicit code. (1981, p. 91)

High context cultures use messages with implicit meanings that the communicators are presumed to know or meanings that are obvious in the context of the interaction. In such cultures, context and environment assume a very important communicative role. Low context cultures use explicit verbal messages that depend very little on the context as a carrier of meaning. Hall often uses the Japanese culture as a prime example of a high context culture. As you might guess, American culture is classified as low context (along with others such as the German and the Swiss). This distinction does not mean that environments and artifacts are meaningless for low context cultures, simply that they are less important than for high context cultures. The high/low context distinction indicates that one's culture determines how much attention is paid to the environmental context and how much communicative meaning is invested in it. Rules and expectations are also inculcated at an early age. Parents teach children how to behave in different environments (such as when to use "inside" voices versus "outside" voices). When a child unknowingly breaks a rule, a parent's usual immediate response is to get the child to conform.

Are there any innate features to this code? Yes, at least in one basic sense. Humans have always altered the environment for their purposes, interpreted meaning from it, and relied on environmental cues for guides to behavior. These are all adaptations to the environment that have survival value. For example, the way a culture works out the issues of crowding, privacy, and allocation of space allows the culture to mediate conflict about these issues and thus has survival value. Further, we can say that simply solving the problem of shelter for members of a culture has survival value. Clearly, different cultures have evolved different forms of adapting to the environment, but all cultures have had to adapt. In sum, most of what we consider to be pertinent to the environmental code is learned and culture-bound; however, the basic factor of making some kind of adaptation to the environment has had survival value and may be innately based.

Structural Features

Potentially, a large number of structural features of artifacts and the environment could play a role in communication. Research in architecture, urban design, and other areas focuses on the relevant features to consider. These may vary from culture to culture, and even across subcultures. Hall (1966) provides very useful distinctions for categorizing environmental features: *fixed-feature elements, semifixed-feature elements,* and *nonfixed-feature elements* (Hall calls this last category "informal elements").

Fixed-Feature Elements. This category consists of all elements of the environment that are relatively permanent and slow to change. Standard architectural elements, such as floors, ceilings, and walls, fall into this category.

As Rapoport (1982) indicates, the *spatial organization* of such basic elements may communicate something about the people who inhabit an environment or those who designed it. The ways in which urban and suburban areas are spatially organized vary greatly, even within one culture. The spatial organization of a New England town differs quite dramatically from that of an Indian pueblo or a large city like Los Angeles. These spatial organizations have a very basic effect on the communication networks people develop.

Another fixed-feature element is the *size and volume of space.* We have all been in a room or space that we considered too big or too small for the activity in which we were involved. Too many students in a small classroom can be distracting. The smoothness and success with which an event or activity proceeds also often depends on having an appropriate amount of space. Public events and political rallies can be erroneously perceived as failures because the volume of space available made a substantial turnout appear small.

The volume of space and size of architectural features in an environment can have other effects as well. Large, high ceilinged rooms, a huge pipe organ, or a large staircase may create feelings of expansiveness and grandeur and may make a person feel insignificant.

The *linear perspective* of an environment is another fixed-feature element. Linear perspective refers to the lines that are created by walls and objects in a given space and the relationship of the lines to each other. Work in landscape architecture (Simonds, 1961) suggests that various kinds of lines in an environment can create different impressions. In American culture, there is a heavy and almost exclusive use of right angles and straight lines, which may reflect a culture in a modern and technologically oriented stage of development. Since many more traditional cultures tend to use curved lines in their designs and architecture, this may reflect closer ties to the natural environment. Thus linear perspective may reflect a culture's position on a traditional-technological continuum. Another possibility, however, is that straight-line architecture simply reflects the standardization of building materials that we have at our disposal to construct environments, even though Buckminister Fuller's work with geodesic domes has shown that straight-line architecture is not always the most desirable or efficient. The impact of straight-line architecture on communication is, for the moment, an open question. However, curved lines in a space create more lines of convergence and perhaps more opportunity for eye contact and communication between individuals.

Materials used in the environment—permanent materials used in the walls and floors and changeable items such as wall hangings and carpet—have both fixed and semifixed aspects. Ruesch and Kees (1970) have described the effects of this element in the following way:

> Wood, metal, brick, and textiles produce a variety of anticipation of touch sensations. Wood against wood, metal against brick, a stiffened fabric against a soft and pliable one—all set up "chords" of tactile images that often produce sharp and immediate physical and emotional reactions. Metal may be highly polished or finished with a dull patina; containers may be opaque, translucent, or transparent. Surfaces—whether raised, carved, rough, or smooth—when exposed to light reflections, are likely not only to express the moods of those who shaped them, but also to suggest such subtle and abstract manners as interpenetration or merely the simple adjoining of boundaries. (p. 146)

As Ruesch and Kees suggest, materials have much to do with setting up how the context "feels." Soft, plush, and textured materials may create a relaxed atmosphere, while hard surfaces and bright, angular objects may create feelings of energy or anxiousness. The soft, textured environment may be more inviting for conversation than the hard-surfaced one.

Semifixed-Feature Elements. This category comprises relatively mobile and changeable features of the environment. One element is the *arrangement of objects and artifacts* in the environment. The placement of furniture, paintings, rugs, and so forth can affect the kind of interaction that takes place and whether any particular object in the environment will be perceived as significant or not. Several studies have shown that the placement of chairs in a room can encourage or discourage interaction. For example, people who wish to discourage conversation in their office place their desk so that their back is to others. The arrangement of seating has an effect on other nonverbal codes, particularly kinesics and proxemics, and may affect other communicative functions such as role definition (leader/follower emergence), mode of interaction (cooperative versus competitive), and status. These functions are discussed in detail in later chapters.

Finally, the arrangement of objects in an environment may provide a focal point for interactants in the environment. For example, judges in courtrooms often sit behind a large dais in the front of the room, elevated above everyone else. The environment clearly states who is most important in the room. The focal point in an environment may also be occupied by an object, such as an expensive piece of art that is placed in a prominent location to signal the owner's values or possibly status.

The second semifixed-feature element is the *selection of objects and artifacts* used in the environment. Beyond their arrangement, the objects and artifacts themselves can provide strong and distinct messages about an environment and the people who inhabit it. Objects and personal possessions may be used to "personalize" an environment. For example, one of our relatives has a large wall display of telephone memorabilia. This display not only provides a focus for conversation but also reveals that the owner is a telecommunications history buff.

The *lighting and shading in an environment* is the third semifixed feature to consider. A number of studies have investigated the effects of amount of light on work performance, but relatively few have explored the effects of lighting level on communication. Lighting and shading may influence whether a setting is seen as social or task-oriented. All other factors being equal, lower levels of light are conducive to social conversation, while higher levels of light set a task tone. Sometimes lighting is set inappropriately, as, for example, in a bar where the lights are too bright for social and intimate conversation. Similarly, many of us have found ourselves in a classroom with inadequate lighting. Academic performance often suffers under such situations.

The fourth semifixed feature, *color,* can significantly affect human behavior (see Birren, 1950). The available evidence suggests that color is associated with people's mood states (Mehrabian & Russell, 1974; Wexner, 1954) and level of arousal (Acking & Kuller, 1972; Wilson, 1966). Specifically, blue and green tones have been found to be relaxing, yellows and oranges to be arousing and energizing, reds and blacks to be sensuous, and grays and browns to be depressing. One reason that these colors set such moods is that colors also have symbolic meanings. Some of the more common moods and symbolic meanings associated with colors in our culture are presented in Table 4.1.

Color also affects our perceptions of other dimensions of the environment, such as temperature. One study (Lewinski, 1938) that examined reac-

TABLE 4.1 Color in the Environment: Moods Created and Symbolic Meanings

Color	Moods	Symbolic Meanings
Red	Hot, affectionate, angry, defiant, contrary, hostile, full of vitality, excitement, love	Happiness, lust, intimacy, love, restlessness, agitation, royalty, rage, sin, blood
Blue	Cool, pleasant, leisurely, distant, infinite, secure, transcendent, calm, tender	Dignity, sadness, tenderness, truth
Yellow	Unpleasant, exciting, hostile, cheerful, joyful, jovial	Superficial glamor, sun, light, wisdom, masculinity, royalty (in China), age (in Greece), prostitution (in Italy), famine (in Egypt)
Orange	Unpleasant, exciting, disturbed, distressed, upset, defiant, contrary, hostile, stimulating	Sun, fruitfulness, harvest, thoughtfulness
Purple	Depressed, sad, dignified, stately	Wisdom, victory, pomp, wealth, humility, tragedy
Green	Cool, pleasant, leisurely, in control	Security, peace, jealousy, hate, aggressiveness, calm
Black	Sad, intense, anxiety, fear, despondent, dejected, melancholy, unhappy	Darkness, power, mastery, protection, decay, mystery, wisdom, death, atonement
Brown	Sad, not tender, despondent, dejected, melancholy, unhappy, neutral	Melancholy, protection, autumn, decay, humility, atonement
White	Joy, lightness, neutral, cold	Solemnity, purity, chastity, femininity, humility, joy, light, innocence, fidelity, cowardice

Source: From *The Unspoken Dialogue: An Introduction to Nonverbal Communication* (p. 110) by J. K. Burgoon and T. Saine, 1978, Boston: Houghton Mifflin.

tions to different colors of light found that blue and green were associated with feelings of coolness, while red created a feeling of being hot. In fact, in one case, cafeteria customers complained that a particular room was always too cold. The problem was eliminated by changing the color of the walls. Note that symbolic reactions to color are culture-bound. So our reactions to color in the environment, in terms of mood state, mode of interaction, and other variables, will differ from those of members of other cultures.

The actual *temperature in the environment* is a fifth semifixed feature. People report feeling most comfortable at 79°F and feeling only "slightly cool" to "slightly warm" across a range of temperatures from a low of 68°F to a high of 80°F (Rohles, 1971). Other factors, such as humidity level, physical activity level, air movement, and amount of clothing worn also affect how comfortable a temperature feels (McCormick, 1976). Interestingly, Holahan (1982) indicates that other factors that we would expect to

Pink Jails and Inmate Violence

One controversial example of the use of color to affect behavior has occurred in the corrections institutions in this country. A number of jails and penal institutions around the country have begun to paint some of their inmate cells pink (actually, a very specific shade of pink—hot pink; Johnston, 1981; Pellegrini, Schauss, & Miller, 1978). On the advice of Alex Schauss, a corrections consultant, jails in New Orleans; Mecklenburg County, NC; San Bernardino, CA; San Jose, CA; and elsewhere now sport pink holding cells for inmates. According to Schauss, the specific shade of pink he advocates drastically reduces inmates' violent behavior by weakening human muscles, thus calming the inmates. This reasoning is based on the possibility that visual processing of light may affect neurological and endocrine functions and that shades of pink and orange can result in loss of strength. Anecdotal reports by some jail directors support Schauss's claims. However, one empirical study (Pellegrini et al., 1978) of the pink jail failed to show any long-term effects due to the color, and a number of environmental design researchers have expressed skepticism. How will the "pink clink" controversy be resolved? When empirical evidence clearly indicates whether there are any effects or not. In the meantime, it does appear that changing environmental colors from the usual industrial green to another color (even pink) does have some effect on inmates, even if it is only to make them think that corrections officials are more responsive to their environmental needs.

be related to temperature comfort, such as age and gender, have not been confirmed in empirical research.

Temperature in the environment probably affects communication much in the way that color does—by affecting interactants' moods and prompting certain modes of interaction. Although no research has directly addressed the effect of temperature on communication, extended exposure to uncomfortable temperatures may induce fatigue, boredom, and irritability (Holahan, 1982). We would expect communication to become more difficult and less effective under those circumstances. We might also expect temperature to be related to context perception within the thermal comfort range, warm temperatures being associated with social interaction and cooler temperatures with task interaction. Cold and hot temperatures outside the comfort range have been shown to have detrimental effects on task performance, although the evidence suggests these relationships are complex (see Holahan, 1982, pp. 137–138, for a review).

The sixth semifixed element is *noise* present in the environment. As Holahan (1982) points out, this factor has been heavily investigated in recent years, probably because of government regulations on noise levels. But what precisely is noise? Holahan has suggested that noise is any sound that a listener doesn't want to hear. It is also important to note that noise is not dependent on simple physical characteristics. Instead, noise is *psychologically defined.* Loud sounds are not necessarily noise to some people, while soft sounds may be. Someone whispering next to you can be as noisy and distracting as a fire engine passing outside.

Primarily, we expect noise to have negative and detrimental effects on communicative processes. We have all tried to carry on a conversation in a noisy room, felt too distracted to do so, and given up. Most research on noise has examined its effects on performance of simple mental and psychomotor tasks or more complex experimental tasks that require attention and vigilance. A review of this research (Cohen & Weinstein, 1981) indicates that noise produced in laboratory settings does not adversely affect performance on simple tasks. However, it does adversely affect performance on complex tasks (Boggs & Simon, 1968), tasks that require a high level of concentration (Jerison, 1959; Woodhead, 1964), and tasks that require handling a large amount of information (Glass & Singer, 1972; Woodhead, 1966). It is likely that communication fits a complex task description in that it requires the handling of large amounts of information and a high level of concentration. Even though this research has not investigated noise effects on communication per se, it does suggest that communication processes will be negatively affected by noise.

Research has also shown that noise characteristics and timing can affect performance. Intermittent noise is more annoying than continuous or aperiodic (irregular) noise (Eschenbrenner, 1971; Theologus, Wheaton, & Fleishman, 1974). Interestingly, Acton (1970) has shown that intelligible speech is the most disruptive of several types of noise. Moreover, longer exposure produces more negative performance effects (Hartley & Adams, 1974), and performance continues to suffer even after one leaves a noisy situation (Glass, Singer, & Friedman, 1969).

Given that intelligible speech may be one of the more distracting forms of noise, one might wonder about the implications of this for open office plans. Since these arrangements provide little or no control over nearby noise, workers may be highly distracted by the conversations of coworkers. The stress and fatigue felt at the end of the day when working in an open office may be due in part to noise exposure.

Other forms of sound in the environment that are often considered noise may not be, depending on one's reaction to the sound. Background or elevator music, for instance, may be very pleasant to some and thus not noise, while very irritating to others.

The seventh and last semifixed element is the *overall level of sensory stimulation* in the environment. It is a composite of fixed and semifixed elements, such as lighting, windows, color, materials, and noise, all of which may contribute to the level of stimulation present. A certain amount of stimulation in an environment is necessary for humans to feel comfortable and be productive. Too much or too little is undesirable. In fact, studies indicate that total lack of sensory stimulation over a period of time can be uncomfortable and frightening.

Moderate rather than extreme stimulation appears to be the ideal. Sensory stimulation affects the inhabitants' level of arousal, which in turn affects performance. The Yerkes-Dodson Law (Yerkes & Dodson, 1908), developed in early experimental psychology, posits an inverted U-shaped function between level of arousal and performance: Moderate levels of arousal are optimum for good performance, while low or high levels of arousal are detrimental. Thus environments that provide a moderate level of stimulation, and hence a moderate level of arousal, should be optimal for communication.

However, two factors qualify the stimulation-performance relationship. Research on task complexity suggests that more complicated tasks (which probably includes communication processes) achieve an optimum level of performance at somewhat lower levels of arousal, although the function still has an inverted U shape. Further, people seem to adapt to different levels of stimulation, some liking less and others liking more. For example, you may be the kind of person who needs quiet and sedate environments for study, contemplation, or communication. But you probably also know someone who needs stereo music, a TV, or even both in order to study, think, or communicate.

How can we explain these idiosyncratic differences? Helson's (1964) adaptation-level theory suggests that people adapt to and become habituated to different levels of stimulation over time. As a result, idiosyncratic preference levels for stimulation may develop. This would help explain why some find a given level of stimulation in an environment suitable while others find it unpleasant. It may be, for example, that family experience sets an initial norm for environmental stimulation. After that, stimulation preferences may change gradually over time. The best or optimum level of sensory stimulation for communication in an environment appears to depend on idiosyncratic preference as well as the complexity of the task at hand.

Norms and Standards

The norms and standards of the environmental code are reflected in the ways that the elements are used for communicative purposes in any given culture. According to Rapoport (1982), in our culture, the semifixed elements are more likely to be used in a communicative way:

> Thus in our own culture, both in domestic and non-domestic situations, semi-fixed feature elements tend to be used much—and are much more under the control of *users;* hence they tend to be used to communicate meanings. Yet they have been ignored by both designers and analysts who have stressed fixed-feature elements. (p. 92)

As a result of the different points of view of creators and users, environments often do not fulfill the functions and purposes for which they were designed. Sommer (1974b) has described architecture that does not respond to the needs of the user as "hard architecture," while "soft architecture" is design that takes user needs into account.

In some cases, users are denied the ability to modify semifixed elements to meet their needs. When CBS designed its headquarters in New York City, an aesthetician was placed in charge of choosing art, colors, plants, furniture, and all other environmental elements so that the semifixed elements would be consistent with the overall building design (Rapoport, 1982). The designers prohibited the use of any personal objects (calendars, pictures, plants, etc.) by the workers in order to preserve the aesthetic ideal of the building.

As you might guess, the users of the building disagreed with the designers and attempted to bring in personal effects anyway. Some of the workers even brought suit against the company. To the users of the environment, the prohibition against modifying the semifixed elements of their workspace was going too far. Similarly, in the past on many college campuses, students have been prohibited from decorating the walls of their dorm rooms because the maintenance costs of painting every year are too great (Sommer, 1974b). These prohibitions violate inhabitants' needs to personalize the environment and to give it meaning with which they can identify. Such prohibitions have negative effects on motivation and productivity. Incidentally, CBS eventually relented and allowed the workers to personalize their offices, but not before a very open and public quarrel.

We might wonder whether this state of affairs is found in other cultures. The answer seems to be: not always. As Rapoport (1982) has indicated, in cultures that are less technologically standardized and specialized, decisions about both fixed and semifixed features of the environment are still often left to the user. The culture may prescribe a range of choices, but it is the user who makes those choices. One broad overall norm, then, has to do with the environment and artifacts elements that are considered pertinent to environmental meaning in a culture. Developed and specialized cultures appear to place most emphasis on semifixed elements, whereas more traditional cultures emphasize both fixed and semifixed elements. For example, in Navajo culture, both the dwelling's structure (the hogan) and the settlement pattern (very dispersed) are meaning-laden and reflect historical values of the culture.

But within a culture there are more specific norms and standards to consider. Perhaps the best way to examine those norms is to analyze a few specific kinds of environments and the effect these norms have on the communication processes that occur in these environments. We have chosen two environments to analyze: homes and schools.

Homes.   Residences are among the most important environments for members of a culture. As noted in Chapter 3, they are primary territories that provide the most environmentally direct expressions of crowding and privacy functions in a culture, and in our culture, they allow the highest degree of personalization and communication of identity. Such elements as the styles of furniture, colors, levels of lighting, objects in the environment, and materials and textures do not always communicate (unless used symbolically), but they clearly provide a great deal of personal information about the inhabitants of a residential space.

APPLICATIONS

Communication Characteristics of American Homes

Several design features of American homes indicate how the environment is structured for communication purposes. One striking aspect of American homes when compared with homes of other cultures is that the space is divided up by permanent walls. In other cultures (in Polynesia, for example), the residence floor plan is almost completely open. The compartmentalization of space in the American home reflects the specialization of functions and tasks in space and the notions of privacy that operate in our culture. These space arrangements are very likely to affect the communication patterns of the inhabitants, particularly in terms of content (intimate versus nonintimate) and level of disclosure. We might say certain things to our spouse only in the privacy of our bedroom; other cultures might handle that content differently. The amount of space allocated to a given room often indicates the importance of that space for family and communication activities. Larger rooms often imply more use, and therefore more interaction in that space by families. The kitchen was once one of the largest rooms in the home. This probably reflected a rural lifestyle that centered around food preparation and other activities (many farmhouses today still retain this design). However, today's kitchens appear no longer to be the family gathering place. Instead, the family room or den has taken over. It is likely that a completely different set of activities is associated with this space (watching TV being the predominant one) and that family communication patterns are different as a result. For a cultural contrast to the use of space in American homes, consider the fact that in many other countries, the total living space is equal to that of an average American living room.

Finally, the external features of a residence often communicate something about the inhabitants. Clearly, the size and style of a house, as well as its location in a neighborhood, provide information about the inhabitants' status, social standing, and wealth. Landscaping and gardens are important features as they provide the "front stage," the most visible and most easily evaluated aspect of the residence (see Rapoport, 1982, ch. 5, for a review). Must houses

---

Communication Characteristics of American Homes (*Continued*)

always have similar external features, as they do in many places in America? Rapoport has noted that there are often locally imposed bounds on what a house in a given neighborhood can look like. This typically has something to do with the way in which a residential area was developed, but the residents also come to prefer it that way. Rapoport gives a number of examples where a house of an unusual and innovative design was built in an established neighborhood. Often in such cases, the residents complain that the new house "doesn't fit in" and turns the neighborhood into an "eyesore." Consistency in the residential environment is apparently important for our culture—something to consider should you ever contemplate an "innovative and different" remodeling job on a home.

Schools. Another significant environment in which we all spend a great deal of time is the classroom. Education in our culture is a very important basis for improved opportunity in life. Despite this, it is likely that you can recall educational experiences that were impeded by the classroom environment. The standard classroom that most of us encounter is the teacher at the front and students arranged in a rectangle of columns and rows. Little use of color (other than industrial green) is evident, and often there is little variation on other semifixed features. The overall effect is to produce a very somber, almost boring environment that hampers communication among students and limits the possibilities for communication between students and teachers.

Recently, a new kind of classroom design called the open-space classroom has been employed in some schools. This design is literally a school without walls where large open spaces are partitioned into smaller usable spaces for as many as five classes. The aims of this classroom design are to create more flexibility in the use of space for educational processes and to encourage more interaction among teachers and between teachers and students (Educational Facilities Laboratories, 1965).

Few studies have evaluated the effectiveness of open-classroom design, and their limited results are not clear-cut. One study found that open-space design leads to the use of more spaces in the classroom for educational activities (Gump & Good, 1976). Others (Brunetti, 1972; Burns, 1972) find that the open-space design results in a greater level of visual and auditory distraction for students. Another investigation (Rivlin & Rothenberg, 1976) discovered that the use of space in an open classroom was very unevenly distributed, with students and teachers spending most of their time in one area of the room. Further, students spent most of their time engaged in individual activities instead of the group-focused activities open classrooms are designed to encourage. However, when open-space classroom design was modified with sound-absorbing partitions to correct for some of the noise, distraction, and privacy problems, students asked more work-related questions, and the rate of verbal and nonverbal interruptions in the classroom dropped off sharply (Evans & Lovell, 1979).

User Participation in a Navajo School Design

One interesting attempt to integrate user needs and views into environmental design can be found in the work of members of the Institute for Environmental Education (1978) at the University of New Mexico. A Navajo school in northwestern New Mexico decided to design a new educational facility that would (a) be a departure from standard Anglo building design, (b) better reflect Navajo values and culture, and (c) focus in particular on the role that design has in prompting traditional forms of communication in the Navajo culture. Surveys and small group discussion methods were used to assess Navajo users' views of the best and most appropriate design features for their new facility. Results indicated a wish for design features that would indeed depart from standard design and included use of openings instead of doorways throughout the building, incorporation of natural materials from the environment and landscaping, use of earth colors to blend the building internally and externally with the environment, abundant use of natural lighting via skylights, sloping floors and different floor levels in rooms to be consistent with cultural activities, and inclusion of sizable common areas that would accommodate the communication activities of the Navajo. In general, many of these features resemble hogans and other traditional buildings in the Navajo culture. Interestingly, the Navajo view these building features as ones that will enhance communication and be consistent with their cultural values.

Communication Potential

Now let us consider the degree to which the structural elements we have discussed actually meet the criteria for a nonverbal code in the strict sense of the word. This is particularly important for the environment and artifacts code, as the elements we have considered often play a contextual and situational role and are not part of the communicative act itself. At other times, though, they clearly do play a communicative role, as when they communicate symbolically or via sign or prompt the use of certain rules for interaction.

As we have said earlier, one key criterion for deciding if something is communication is whether it has consensually recognized meaning. It is clear that we all have perceptions of the environment and its elements, some of which are very detailed and elaborate (for a review of work on environmental perception and cognition, see Holahan, 1982, ch. 2–3; or Ittelson, 1973). Those that have symbolic value, such as architectural forms for churches, colors, and certain artifacts, will be interpreted consensually. The environment and its artifacts may also communicate on a sign level. A very common example is international signs. These signs often employ icons (visual images), such as the shape of males and females on rest room doors, to communicate content.

Additionally, environment and artifacts have great communication potential by virtue of the behavioral routines that they cue. Rapoport (1982) described the "mnemonic function" of the environment: The environmental cues elicit appropriate emotions, behaviors, interpretations, and transactions. These environmental cues remind people of what is expected of them. Goffman (1963) has referred to "occasioned places" as environments that contain regulative indications of how to behave. Such environmentally based prescriptions to behave confirm that we all share perceptions of indicators in the environment.

The communication potential of the environment and artifacts elements can be demonstrated on other grounds as well. First, there are a relatively large number of structural elements. As we have already discovered, the potential combinations of those elements to produce different communication messages and effects are numerous. Second, humans have the visual and tactile capacity to decode subtle variations in artifactual patterns. Third, most of the senses—sight, sound, touch, and smell—can be stimulated by the structural elements we have been discussing. Since most of the senses are stimulated by the structural elements, the coding potential is bolstered. Fourth, our reactions to environment and artifacts cues are not only cognitive and perceptual but also emotional and attitudinal, which indicates a strong coding potential. Reactions to the environment are often not simply a matter of taste but a function of the attitudes we have about environmental elements. Seeing a home decorated with lime green carpet, art deco clocks and lamps, and floral-print furniture, we know immediately whether we like it or not, an opinion that reflects our attitudes about living spaces. Finally, environmental and artifactual elements, because of their static nature, serve as a constant statement in any communicative setting and may serve as a framework for interpreting the interactions that take place.

However, many environmental and artifactual elements are mistaken for communication when they are merely information. Moreover, their static nature means that they can make only one statement at a time and are incapable of adapting to the ongoing interaction. Finally, although environmental and artifactual elements are relevant to several functions, there are some for which they are irrelevant (e.g., expressive communication, relational communication). Compared to codes such as kinesics and vocalics, then, they may be somewhat more limited in their communication potential.

Chronemics

> You may delay, but time will not.
>
> Benjamin Franklin

> Time talks. It speaks more plainly than words. The
> message it conveys comes through loud and clear. . . . It
> can shout the truth where words lie.
>
> Edward T. Hall (1959, p. 15)

Philosophers, biologists, and physicists alike have been intrigued by the concept of time. Our interest is in its biological, psychological, and cultural implications for communicators. As Fisher (1978) notes, "Time is, without a doubt, one of the most crucial, yet most neglected, variables of communication" (pp. 79–80). The very concept of communication as process implies that it is a time-bound activity. At the same time, the way time is structured may send messages to others. Chronemics, then, is *how humans perceive, structure, and use time as communication.*

Consider a few examples of how time affects our daily communication. Our work and school activities revolve around schedules and deadlines. Waiting too long for an appointment may make us impatient or angry. Some consultants now advocate a "one-minute manager" approach, whereby employee problems are dispensed with in this time frame (thus saving valuable time). We regard the amount of time a friend spends with us when we are in need as a statement about the importance of our relationship. Many parents now say it is the "quality" of the time they spend with their children that is important, not the quantity.

Acquisition

Infants have no sense of time other than their awareness of their own biological cycles. Young children likewise have limited understanding of the passage of time and future events. They may be disturbed, for example, when a parent goes away on a brief business trip. Yet by age 6, children have learned such formal time categories as the days of the week, and by age 12, they have mastered the key elements of a given culture's time system.

Piaget (1981) has suggested that a child's sense of time depends on the child's operational stage of development. A child cannot develop an adult-like sense of time until reaching the higher stages of cognitive development, which begin around age 12. Cognitive maturation is partly a biological process. Nevertheless, ideas, expectations, and rules about the chronemic code are likely to be learned via socialization in one's culture. The great cultural diversity that exists in chronemic behavior is best explained through social learning.

Structural Features

The perception of time is partly due to the perception of patterns of events—their starting, stopping, cycling, frequency, and duration (Bruneau, 1980; Doob, 1971). Those patterns, which can be linked to our biological, psychological, and cultural levels of experience, form the structure of the chronemic code. We will first review the biological and psychological levels and then consider cultural patterns under "Norms and Standards."

Biological Cycles. Although the exact relationship of biology to the use of time as a communication vehicle remains unknown, there is little doubt that our sense of time is affected by biological cycles. Most biologists believe that most species, including humans, have some kind of internal *biological clock* (Cloudsley-Thompson, 1981; Hamner, 1981) that governs such diverse phenomena as plant flowering, migration, navigation, and sleep rhythms. When you experience jet lag after a long plane trip, you are actually experiencing a lag between your biological clock time and the clock time in the local environment. Recent research on work schedules at manufacturing plants shows that rotating shift schedules adversely affect worker health, alertness, and productivity. Giving workers more time to adjust their biological clocks to a new work schedule can overcome these negative effects.

One of the most well-known biological cycles that affects behavior is the *circadian rhythm* (circadian meaning "about day"), an approximate 24-hour cycle exhibited by almost all organisms (Hamner, 1981). This rhythm tends to persist despite environmental changes. For example, one study took participants to a northern latitude where the sun shines continuously and subjected them to daily cycles of varying lengths (21 hours, 27 hours, etc.) by speeding or slowing the clocks. Although participants changed their activities to match the new clock times, basic physiological cycles such as secretion of urine and salts remained in circadian rhythm (Hamner, 1981). Further evidence of the persistence of such biological rhythms comes from the discovery of Seasonal Affect Disorder (SAD), which occurs in people who are particularly sensitive to light and darkness cycles. As days shorten in the fall and winter, individuals with SAD become increasingly depressed. It is thought that the shortening light cycles throw the hormone melatonin out of balance. Exposure to artificial light in the morning hours helps SAD sufferers reduce their depression.

It is possible that other biological cycles such as biorhythms affect our

communication behavior. Biorhythms have physical, sensitivity, and intellectual cycles. The physical cycle involves endurance and energy levels, the sensitivity cycle involves fluctuations in emotional states, and the intellectual cycle reflects changes in mental alertness and accomplishments. When "critical days" occur—days when the cycles change from positive to negative or vice versa—behavior is supposedly most vulnerable to impairment. Although empirical evidence of the impact of biorhythms is lacking, many industries take cognizance of biorhythms in planning work schedules for employees in risk-related occupations. Even if we view biorhythms with some healthy skepticism, it should be evident that biological rhythms provide the most fundamental time framework we have.

Psychological Orientations. Our ideas and expectations about time form four basic psychological time orientations (Reinert, 1971). Individuals with a *past* orientation dwell on events in the past, relive old times, and take a sentimental view toward time. Such people often see events as recurrent and time as circular. ("Those who fail to learn from the past are condemned to repeat it.") Individuals with a *time-line* orientation literally see time as a continuum integrating past, present, and future, a linear and systematic progression of events. These people often view time analytically and scientifically. Individuals with a *present* orientation are focused on the here and now. They pay little attention to the past or future and tend to deal with events, activities, and problems spontaneously. Finally, individuals with a *future* orientation are focused on anticipating and planning for future events and relating them to the present.

These time orientations can affect communication in many ways. The content of conversation may be affected: those with a past orientation may spend time retelling old stories, while those with a future orientation may talk about predictions for the future. The urgency of communication may be affected: those who are present-oriented may be far less concerned about achieving closure on decisions or plans, while those who are time-line and future-oriented may be insistent upon it. The structure of communication likewise may be affected: people with past or present orientations may see little need for punctuality or adherence to others' time pressures, while those with a time-line or future orientation may see schedules, calendars, and deadlines as necessities.

APPLICATIONS

Time Orientation and Your Career

Has it ever occurred to you that the way you deal with time could affect the occupational choices you make? A *Psychology Today* survey report (Gonzales & Zimbardo, 1985) suggests that time orientation may be quite complex and related to income, gender, and occupational choice. Since the survey was limited to *Psychology Today* readers, we cannot say that it is representative of the population at large.

Time Orientation and Your Career (*Continued*)

However, as the authors indicate, the results are suggestive and useful at what is still an early stage of research.

Past orientation was found to be rare among respondents (1% of the sample; this is consistent with previous research), and present orientation was also infrequent (9%). Fully 57% of the respondents indicated a time-line orientation and 33% a future orientation. Responses to the Stanford Time Perspective Inventory were subjected to factor analysis, a statistical technique that identifies underlying traits or abilities accounting for people's replies. The analysis identified seven different time perspectives (see Table 4.2). Four are future-oriented, two are present-oriented, and one reflects an emotional reaction to time pressure. These results suggest that time orientation is more complex than earlier work indicated and that it is a function of several things, including work motivation, perseverance, goal seeking, and planning. These factors relate to age, income, and occupation. Both men and women become more future-oriented as they age. Sensitivity to time pressures also increases with age in this sample. Those with higher incomes tend to be more future-oriented, whereas lower incomes are more associated with a present orientation. Finally, job choice is related to time orientation. For example, the most characteristic occupation for Factor 1 was white-collar manager; for Factor 4, professional or teacher; and for Factor 5, retired manager.

How well do your career plans match with your time orientation according to the seven factors identified in Table 4.2? If your time orientation is associated with an occupation that you currently hold or plan to hold in the future, the news is good. Gonzales and Zimbardo suggest that people gravitate to jobs with matching time orientations, and job success and satisfaction depend on intensifying that time orientation. Moreover, one's time orientation may depend on one's socioeconomic background and upbringing; children with skilled and professional parents may acquire the kind of time orientation that allows them to succeed in skilled and professional occupations; children raised by unskilled parents may develop a present orientation that predisposes them to unskilled and semiskilled occupations. If so, the researchers recommend remedial time training for those from unskilled backgrounds who aspire to professional-level jobs. Finally, they suggest that we would all be better off if we could be flexible enough to shift time orientations when the situation called for it. At work, a future orientation is best for productivity and success. But when it is time to socialize, relax, and enjoy friends, a present, hedonistic orientation is more appropriate. Given the number of workaholics that many of us encounter on a daily basis, this sounds like good advice. More research in this area may support the maxim: Work hard, play hard.

TABLE 4.2 Time Orientation Factors

Factor 1: Future, work motivation, perseverance

    A. Meeting tomorrow's deadlines and doing other necessary work comes before tonight's partying.

    B. I meet my obligations to friends and authorities on time.

    C. I complete projects on time by making steady progress.

    D. I am able to resist temptations when I know there is work to be done.

    E. I keep working at a difficult, uninteresting task if it will help me get ahead.

This factor embodies a positive work motivation and a stereotypical Protestant work ethic of finishing a task despite difficulties and temptations.

Factor 2: Present, fatalistic, worry-free, avoid planning

    A. If things don't get done on time, I don't worry about it.

    B. I think that it's useless to plan too far ahead because things hardly ever come out the way you planned anyway.

    C. I try to live one day at a time.

    D. I live to make better what is rather than to be concerned about what will be.

    E. It seems to me that it doesn't make sense to worry about the future, since fate determines that whatever will be, will be.

People with this orientation live one day at a time, not to enjoy it fully but to avoid planning for the next day and to minimize anxiety about a future they perceive as being determined by fate rather than by their efforts.

Factor 3: Present, hedonistic

    A. I believe that getting together with friends to party is one of life's important pleasures.

    B. I do things impulsively, making decisions on the spur of the moment.

    C. I take risks to put excitement in my life.

    D. I get drunk at parties.

    E. It's fun to gamble.

In contrast with the present-oriented people described by Factor 2, hedonists fill their days with pleasure seeking, partying, taking risks, drinking, and impulsive action of all kinds. Many teenagers fall into this category. Among older hedonists, gambling is often an important element.

Factor 4: Future, goal seeking, planning

    A. Thinking about the future is pleasant to me.

    B. When I want to achieve something, I set subgoals and consider specific means for reaching those goals.

    C. It seems to me that my career path is pretty well laid out.

Compared to future Factor 1, the items here center less on work per se and more on the pleasure that comes from planning and achieving goals.

Factor 5: Time press

    A. It upsets me to be late for appointments.

    B. I meet my obligations to friends and authorities on time.

    C. I get irritated at people who keep me waiting when we've agreed to meet at a given time.

TABLE 4.2 Time Orientation Factors (*Continued*)

This factor doesn't fall neatly into a present or future orientation (although it does correlate positively with the future factors). It centers on a person's sensitivity to the role time plays in social obligations and how it can be used as a weapon in struggles for status.

Factor 6: Future, pragmatic action for later gain

    A. It makes sense to invest a substantial part of my income in insurance premiums.

    B. I believe that "a stitch in time saves nine."

    C. I believe that "a bird in the hand is worth two in the bush."

    D. I believe it is important to save for a rainy day.

These people act now to achieve desirable future consequences. The researchers thought that item C would be characteristic of present orientation. Instead, the respondents saw it as advice to do or have something concrete now rather than gambling on an uncertain outcome. Thus it is a conservative strategy to safeguard future options.

Factor 7: Future, specific, daily planning

    A. I believe a person's day should be planned each morning.

    B. I make lists of things I must do.

    C. When I want to achieve something, I set subgoals and consider specific means for reaching those goals.

    D. I believe that "a stitch in time saves nine."

This factor describes individuals obsessed with the nitty-gritty of getting ahead. They adopt a somewhat compulsive attitude toward daily planning, make lists of things to do, set subgoals, and pay attention to details.

Source: From "Time in Perspective" by Alexander Gonzales and Philip G. Zimbardo, March 1985, *Psychology Today,* pp. 20–26.

Even though much of what we have said about time orientation suggests that it is a somewhat permanent and traitlike concept, we should not lose sight of how changeable our perception of time is. Some authors have ventured that our perception of time passing slowly or quickly may depend on communication factors. For example, Bruneau (1980) has suggested that the novelty of events results in time being perceived as passing quickly. Brodey (1969) has advanced similar arguments. This "time-binding" aspect of the chronemic code is an important feature to consider. We turn next to the cultural level of the chronemic code.

Norms and Standards

Perhaps the best way to understand the parts of the chronemic code that are most relevant to daily life is to examine time at the cultural level. The elements at this level are the ones we are most often aware of on a day-to-day basis. These elements reflect a culture's view of time and include its norms and standards for time.

Cultural Time Orientations. It is often difficult for us to realize that there is any time orientation other than our own. Yet in many cases, the chronemic code in other cultures has little in common with our own. Hall's work in *The Silent Language* (1959) still stands as one of the best accounts of how cultures vary in terms of chronemic behavior. For a better grasp of how other cultures deal with chronemics, we need first to examine our own culture's view of time.

That our culture is obsessed with time is an understatement. Time in the United States is infused with a strong sense of urgency. We play an endless game of beat the clock. Time is seen as a precious resource, a valuable and tangible commodity. We spend time, save it, make it, fill it, and waste it. It is seen almost as a container with defined boundaries. This tangible view of time is also reflected in how we mark its passage. It is highly divisible: We break it into years, months, weeks, days, hours, minutes, seconds, tenths of seconds, and even nanoseconds. The average American thinks of time in 5-minute blocks, which are very small chunks of time. The way we schedule events also reflects the urgent and precise way we deal with time. We expect classes to start on time (within a minute or so), and when they don't, we wait only so long (20 minutes at the most) before leaving. Imagine how restless students would become if professors lectured to the end of their train of thought before dismissing class.

Our mass media also reflect a highly structured approach to scheduling. We expect newspapers to be delivered at a certain time, and television programs begin and end precisely to the second at the same time each day. Compare this to Italian television, where programs continue until they are finished. This may seem chaotic or irresponsible, but it is no less peculiar than forcing television plots into uniform 30-minute blocks. News programs are also highly compressed: most half-hour broadcasts devote only 18 minutes to news, a brief time to cover the day's events in a complex world.

Few aspects of our culture do not reflect the fast pace of our lives, from fast food to fast banking to instantaneous Dow Jones quotations. For many of us, the workday is strongly governed by the clock. We must arrive at work at an appointed time (certainly within a minute or two), typically take only an hour for lunch, and leave at an appointed time (though working "late" is sometimes acceptable). The more we consider the way our culture deals with time, the clearer our obsession with it becomes. Hall (1959) claims that Americans are surpassed only by the Germans and the Swiss in having an urgent, precise, and fast-paced orientation to time.

Keep in mind that various groups within our culture deviate significantly from this general time orientation. Subcultures, ethnic groups, and even the population of entire regions can have a different orientation to time than that of the mainstream culture. For example, the Sioux have no words for *late* or *waiting* in their language. Pueblo Indians start many of their ceremonies "when the time is right," not at some scheduled time. For the traditional Navajo, time and space are very much the same; only the here and now is real, and the future is a foreign concept (see Hall, 1959, for a

Americans always seem to be on the go. Our fast pace of life is reflected in the variety of services we can access from a car.

more thorough discussion of these subcultural differences). It is well known that the pace of life is slower in rural regions than in urban areas. Native Hawaiians operate under two time systems. *Haole time* reflects the influence of the early missionaries in the islands and is very much like the mainstream culture's time system. *Hawaiian time,* on the other hand, is very lax. When you meet someone in Hawaii and plan to meet again at a given time, it is important to know under which time system. If the islander says to you, "See you at three," you can expect to meet at that time. However, if the islander says, "See you at three Hawaiian time," that really means that you will see each other whenever you both happen to arrive.

Hall (1959) has suggested that three distinct time systems operate in any culture: technical time, formal time, and informal time. *Technical* time is probably the least relevant to the chronemic code. It is concerned with the scientific and precise measurement of time. The setting of a standard time (such as Greenwich Mean Time) via an atomic clock and the difference between a solar, sidereal, and anomalistic year are other examples.

Formal time is the traditional way a culture views time. It is the conscious, formally taught system for measuring time. In our culture, we are regulated by a calendar comprised of many cyclical and hierarchical units. Other cultures do not always use this system. Some cultures use phases of the moon, summer and winter solstices, or the fall and spring equinoxes as formal time systems. For example, the ancient Southwest Indian culture, the Anasazi, probably used the spring and fall equinoxes to mark important cultural events and rites. It was recently discovered at Chaco Canyon National Historical Park that features of the pueblo buildings line up with the angle of the sun so that the sun strikes these architectural features (often portals in a kiva wall) on the equinox. By closely examining the architectural arrangements and sun position, researchers now think that the Anasazi could know on what day an important ceremony (and the equinox) would fall and could anticipate the arrival of that day (see Zeilek, 1985a, 1985b).

Other elements of this system that we learn formally are how our culture orders events, the kinds of cycles it recognizes, the values it places on time, what duration means for the culture, and the degree of depth and tangibility the culture assigns to time. Thus North Americans see the days of the week following a fixed order; we are highly aware of weekly, monthly, and seasonal cycles; we place a monetary value on time; we judge duration by the clock rather than by natural events; we attribute some depth to time as we often profess to be interested in our own history; and there is no doubt that we see time as something concrete.

Other cultures treat these elements quite differently. Many cultures mark the order of time on the basis of natural events and not by clock or calendar time as we do. A striking example of this contrast is that some North African cultures view the clock as the "devil's mill" (Levine & Wolff, 1985). We view the clock as indispensable and a source of order, whereas they associate it with something evil. Further, cycles in time are often marked differently. Hall (1959) has noted that the Tiv of Nigeria name days according to what is to be sold at market each day.

The different values that cultures place on time is also evident in the treatment of waiting time. In our culture, waiting is considered a waste of time and often provokes anger. In other cultures, such as Japan, India, and many of the Arabic cultures, waiting is not seen as unproductive. The duration of an event is for us a matter of clock time, but it may be "as long as it takes" for people in other cultures.

The level of depth we attribute to time does not approach that of many Arabic cultures. According to Hall (1959), Arabs view time as an endless process and the individual as an insignificant speck in its huge expanse. Many other cultures do not attribute tangibility to time as we do. For those cultures, time just is, and it is not something to be spent, controlled, or wasted.

Our formal time system, because it is deeply rooted in traditions, has the power to evoke strong emotions. Old ways are valued and new ones are viewed with suspicion. This was no more clear than when Daylight Savings Time was first instituted. A Kansas farmer wrote to his legislature to protest, saying that the extra hour of sunlight would burn up his tomatoes.

Informal time is probably the most interesting and yet difficult to understand time system of the three. Informal time elements are loosely defined, are not explicitly taught, and typically operate outside consciousness. They most often take the form of rules and expectations we learn from our culture, but it is not clear when or if we all learn these rules.

Punctuality is one of the most prominent concepts in the informal time system. Arriving for an appointment or an event at the appropriate time is often a very important part of having a successful interaction with others. What constitutes being "on time," however, varies across different types of situations. Being on time for a business appointment most often means literally arriving at the appointed time. Arriving more than 5 minutes late is a violation of this rule and often requires an apology or an explanation. We can classify these kind of situations as formal and task-oriented. Social situations that can be characterized as informal imply a different rule. If you are invited to a party by friends that starts at 8:00 P.M., arriving "on time" may mean showing up at 8:30 or 9:00, possibly later. No explanation for lateness is given because you are not perceived to be "late." But some situations can be described as both formal and social. For example, if you are invited to dinner at a friend's house at 7:00 P.M., most often the expectation is that you will arrive either at 7:00 or shortly thereafter. The formality of this situation is introduced by the effort your friend goes through to prepare dinner. It is expected that you will respect that effort by arriving promptly so that the food does not spoil.

To complicate matters, different regions of the country often have different versions of these informal rules. In New York City, going to a party that starts at 9:00 P.M. often means arriving at 10:30 and staying until the event is over. Being invited to dinner in a Mormon community often means that you are expected to arrive early, as Mormons tend to be quite punctual. Imagine, however, that you followed this rule in another part of the country. You might arrive to find your hosts madly rushing about in robes and curlers, attempting to clean house and prepare food at the same time. Needless to say, this would not be a good way to start the evening. Since these kind of rules are rarely communicated explicitly, people who move from one region of the country to another are likely to follow the wrong rules and be perceived negatively.

There are also individual differences in the way that people follow these informal time rules. Some adopt a *displaced-point* time pattern. These individuals view an appointment time as an end point, arriving either at or before the appointed time, but rarely after. For example, the wife who is to pick up her husband at 6:00 P.M. at a given place will arrive shortly before or at 6:00 P.M. Others adopt a *diffused-point* pattern, viewing appointed times as approximate. Such people arrive somewhere around the appointed time, either early or late, within an acceptable deviation. Interesting things happen when people of different patterns have an appointment. If the displaced-point wife arrives at 6:00 P.M. and the diffused-point husband shows up at 6:20, it is likely that conflict will ensue. Knowing that each operates on a different time pattern may help in such situations. However, given that

waiting is such an onerous experience for everyone in our culture, knowing about someone else's time pattern may not help much.

Rules for punctuality in other cultures are quite different, as Levine and Wolff (1985) report. Levine, who is a professor of psychology, discovered when teaching at a university in Brazil that Brazilian students arriving as late as 11:00 for a class held from 10:00 to 12:00 showed few signs of concern for their "lateness." Equally disconcerting was that unlike American students, when the end of class arrived, only a few students left. Even 15 minutes after the end of class, many of the Brazilian students were still there, asking questions. At 12:30, Levine himself ended class, as it appeared that some of the remaining students were settling in for an even longer stay! Such behavior in an American university class is unheard of. In an informal survey, Levine found that Brazilian students feel less personally responsible for lateness, they express less regret for their lateness, and blame others less when they are late. This work is consistent with earlier observations made by Hall (1959). Clearly, the informal time sense for punctuality is very different in Brazil from our own culture.

Despite cultural differences in what is meant by being punctual, the timing of one's arrival can have strong message value in each culture. A related chronemic message is *waiting time.* Here again is an area ripe for misunderstanding because the informal rules are not known. A common problem for North American business people traveling to Latin America is adapting to the local time system. Corporate executives may find themselves waiting up to an hour and a half to meet their Latin American counterpart, and they may find that several appointments have been scheduled at once, so that there is no clear sequence for seeing visitors. North Americans, who have no tolerance for waiting or going out of turn, find this system incomprehensible and often take such treatment as a personal insult when no insult is intended.

However, it is also possible to use such behaviors as punctuality and waiting time to send an intentional message. The story is told about Harry Truman, who, shortly after becoming president, was visited by a newspaper editor. After waiting 45 minutes in the outer office, the editor asked an aide to tell the president he was becoming annoyed by the long wait. Truman replied, "When I was a junior senator from Missouri, that same editor kept me cooling my heels for an hour and a half. As far as I'm concerned, the son of a bitch has 45 minutes to go!"

Other informal time system elements that have message potential are duration, urgency, monochronism, activity, and variety. Hall (1959) has suggested eight informal levels of *duration* in our culture: immediate, very short, short, neutral, long, very long, terribly long, and forever. When someone says, "I'll do that immediately," does it mean 1 minute, 5 minutes, or 3 weeks? It probably depends on whether the person is promising to turn on the television or process your loan application. *Urgency* similarly concerns the immediacy and importance of events. The amount of lead time between the assignment of a task and its due date can be used to communicate urgency. The less lead time, the greater the urgency. The timing of an event can have the same effect. A knock at the front door at 3:00 A.M. connotes far more urgency than one at 3:00 P.M.

Contrast these patterns with the Truk Islanders, who treat the past as if it were the present and who have no past tense in their language (Hall, 1959). Events are indefinite in duration and old conflicts never lose their immediacy because they are treated as if "they happened just yesterday."

Monochronism, or doing one thing at a time, can be contrasted with *polychronism,* or doing several things at once. In a culture where monochronism is the norm, doing several things at once can carry a potent message. Imagine, for example, you are meeting with a professor about a serious grade problem and the professor proceeds to rifle through files on his desk while listening to you. Or imagine that you are trying to clinch an important sale and the client accepts several telephone calls during your meeting. When someone gives us their divided rather than their undivided attention, we may take offense. Elsewhere it may be quite common for people to conduct several activities simultaneously, and consequently, polychronism doesn't take on communicative import.

Finally, *activity* and *variety* refer to the degree to which time is filled with activity or not and whether such activities are varied or repetitive. For Westerners, to be inactive is to be lazy, unambitious, and wasteful. Novelty and variety are stimulating and prevent boredom. In oriental cultures, too much paripatetic activity and variety may be a sign of inadequate thought, reflection, and maturity.

In sum, the informal time system consists of at least six elements, punctuality, duration, urgency, monochronism, activity, and variety. Further, within these elements are some specific chronemic patterns that may reflect intentional use, as in the waiting time pattern and the punctuality element. Informal time systems, provide us with some of the most striking differences in chronemic behavior across cultures. They also cause many difficulties when members of different cultures communicate.

Communication Potential

Current evidence indicates that the communication potential of the time code is somewhat limited. Its chief advantages are its subtlety and its ability to evoke strong emotional reactions. Its chief disadvantage is its ambiguity, in terms of both the meaning that can be ascribed to a particular behavior and its intentionality. People's chronemic behavior may reflect a response to their own internal cycles or to cultural norms, rather than an intentional message. Moreover, this code is often part of the situational framework in which interaction takes place and thus may serve as either information or communication. Such diverse chronemic actions as following a schedule, being early or late to an appointment, and filling our time with activity are certainly informative behavior. We may infer several things about a person on the basis of this behavior. But the behavior does not qualify as communication if it is unintentional, is not interpreted as intentional, and is not used regularly by members of a social community to mean something in particular.

Another limitation is that the accuracy of the perception of code elements varies. The formal and technical elements of the code tend to be perceived quite accurately, but the informal time system, which contains the elements most likely to affect behavior, tend not to be. Subcultural and ethnic background, region of the country, and some individual difference factors complicate our perceptions of the informal elements so that our culture there is often less than consensual agreement on what a given informal element (such as duration) may be taken to mean. Further, since these elements are often not explicitly taught, there may be additional room for misperception. In general, this lowers the communication potential of chronemics.

Third, the number of identified elements in the chronemic code is relatively low. It is not clear just which forms of time manipulation qualify as messages in each culture. Finally, chronemics is not relevant to some primary communication functions, such as emotional expression and message processing. All these factors limit communication potential for the chronemic code.

Keep in mind that we know very little about this code. Most of what we know stems from Hall's (1959, 1974) work. Further, most of that work presents only anecdotal evidence at best. Although personal observation and anecdotes are useful as basic descriptions, they do not provide evidence that helps us understand or explain. Recent work on the importance of time for relational development and other relationship processes (Werner & Haggard, 1985) indicates that there is a great deal more to understand about this code. Thus our assessment of the communication potential of chronemics may change as our understanding of the code develops.

Summary

Both the environment and the chronemic codes play very important roles in communication. Elements from these codes are often used in a communicative fashion and may also provide a great deal of situational and contextual information. Environmental code elements act as communication cues by communicating meaning directly in symbolic form, providing a context for interaction, or by guiding behavior by prompting rules for interaction. The elements of the environment and artifacts code can be classified into one of two basic categories: fixed-feature elements, which are relatively permanent and slow-to-change features, and semi-fixed elements, those features that are mobile and easily changed. In general, people in our culture have a much greater degree of control over semi-fixed than fixed features. Other cultures have a greater degree of control over features in both categories. Finally, some recent analysis indicates that some cultures are more oriented towards the use of elements of this code for communicative purposes (high context cultures), while other cultures are less likely to do so (low context cultures). Although the American culture qualifies as a low context culture, this chapter has shown that we still make extensive use of these code elements as part of communication.

Although we are still discovering the importance of the chronemic code elements, it is already apparent that they are very relevant to all cultures. The elements of this code exist on three levels: the biological, psychological, and cultural. The biological elements appear to provide a fundamental framework for the experience of time. The psychological elements indicate the kinds of expectations we hold for time and the activity and behavior that people wish to engage in. The cultural elements indicate how each culture perceives time and uses it as a means of sending messages. Given that the elements of this code are often learned on an implicit basis and that there is great cultural and subcultural variation in their use and meaning, many communication difficulties can be explained by an analysis of chronemic elements. Much is yet to be learned about this interesting and subtle code, especially in interpersonal and relational contexts.

Suggested Readings

Doob, L. W. (1971). *Patterning of time.* New Haven, CT: Yale University Press.

Hall, E. T. (1959). *The silent language.* Garden City, NY: Doubleday.

Hall, E. T. (1966). *The hidden dimension* (2nd ed.). Garden City, NY: Anchor Press/Doubleday.

Holahan, C. J. (1982). *Environmental psychology.* New York: Random House.

Ittelson, W. H., Proshansky, H. M., Rivlin, L. G., & Winkel, G. H. (1974). *An introduction to environmental psychology.* New York: Holt, Rinehart and Winston.

Lauer, R. H. (1981). *Temporal man.* New York: Praeger.

Meerloo, J. A. M. (1970). *Along the fourth dimension.* New York: Harper & Row.

Mehrabian, A. (1976). *Public places and private spaces.* New York: Basic Books.

Rapoport, A. (1982). *The meaning of the built environment: A nonverbal communication approach.* Beverly Hills, CA: Sage.

CHAPTER 5

Relationships Between Verbal and Nonverbal Communication

> While verbal and nonverbal communication may be different, they are not separate. There is a dynamic tension, an inseparable bond between them.
>
> A. M. Katz and V. T. Katz (1983, p. xvi)

> "I can never bring you to realize the importance of sleeves, the suggestiveness of thumbnails, or the great issues that may hang from a bootlace."
>
> Sherlock Holmes to Watson

In Chapters 2, 3, and 4, we examined the various nonverbal codes and detailed the differences and similarities among them. Now we shall examine how they compare and contrast with the verbal code and the ways in which the two communication systems—verbal and nonverbal—interrelate.

It should be evident that we believe the verbal and nonverbal codes to be inextricably linked. We share with many other scholars (e.g., Argyle, 1972a; Knapp, 1978; Patterson, 1983; Poyatos, 1983, 1984) the view that "it is impossible to study either verbal or nonverbal communication as isolated structures. Rather, these systems should be regarded as a unified communication construct" (Higginbotham & Yoder, 1982, p. 4). In this chapter, the interconnectedness of these systems should become more apparent as we compare verbal and nonverbal communication in terms of origins, structure, brain processing, functions, and impact. We begin with the last first.

Channel Reliance

> What I hide by language, my body utters.
>
> John Barthes

The social impact of nonverbal communication relative to verbal communication is addressed in research on channel reliance, that is, the channels or codes that most influence people when assigning meaning to communicative interchanges. This issue has been addressed in a variety of contexts, including judgments about speaker dominance or credibility; personality assessments; impressions of a job interviewee; assessments of a therapist's empathy; emotional and attitudinal interpretations; and determinations of the "objective meaning" of verbal statements.

Approaches

People have studied the question of channel reliance in two main ways. One is to manipulate experimentally some combination of verbal and nonverbal cues and measure what interpretation receivers assign to the cue combination. For example, three versions of a verbal message—positive, neutral, and negative—might be paired with three levels each of facial expression (positive, neutral, and negative) and vocal tone (positive, neutral, and negative), for a total of 27 different verbal-facial-vocal combinations. Receivers are asked to judge the meaning of a given combination on a positive-to-negative continuum. In cases where the cues are not consistent with each other—say, the facial cue is negative and the other two are positive—it is possible to determine if the facial cue carries more weight than the verbal and vocal cues by seeing if the meaning is negatively skewed or is judged as positive.

The other approach is to look at naturally occurring conversation or monologues, to measure the nonverbal and verbal behaviors that appear, and to determine statistically which ones most influenced the outcomes. For example, observers might watch videotaped segments from a job interview and rate the applicant on intelligence, personality, and hirability. The nonverbal and verbal behaviors appearing on the tapes could then be coded and correlated with the observer evaluations of the applicants.

The first approach allows examination of all possible combinations of a particular subset of cues so that congruent and incongruent combinations can be studied. It also ensures that each cue can be presented with equal frequency and strength. It usually means looking at a very limited number of cues, however. The second approach permits studying the full range of verbal and nonverbal behaviors that normally occur, but those cues may not arise with equal frequency, extremity, or consistency. Also, cues typically do not appear in all possible combinations; incongruent patterns are especially rare. The second approach is therefore much more informative about consistent cue patterns than about contradictory ones.

Propositions

Fortunately, enough research has used both approaches to permit making some generalizations. On the basis of close to 100 studies, a number of conclusions can be drawn. These kinds of generalizations are often called propositions.

1. **On average, adults place more reliance on nonverbal cues than on verbal ones in determining social meaning.** The figure most often cited to support this claim is the estimate that 93% of all meaning in a social situation comes from nonverbal information, while only 7% comes from verbal information. This estimate has found its way into almost every popular article about nonverbal communication.

   Unfortunately, it is erroneous. It is based on extrapolation from two studies, one comparing vocal cues to facial cues (Mehrabian & Ferris, 1967) and one comparing vocal tone to single words (Mehrabian & Wiener, 1967), rather than a study comparing all three. In the vocal-verbal study, only single words were used, which provides a very limited test of the impact of verbal information. In the vocal-facial study, the verbal component was held constant—the word "maybe" was used in all cue combinations—so it never had a chance to make a difference to receivers' interpretations. The two studies also dealt only with attitude inference, not the full range of meanings available in a social encounter. Hence the verbal component was not given a fair test. These and other faults have led many scholars to treat Mehrabian and Ferris's (1967) proposed weighting as highly suspect and exaggerated (see, for example, Hegstrom, 1979).

   Nevertheless, other, more temperate estimates still give priority to nonverbal cues (e.g., Danziger, 1976). Birdwhistell (1955), for example, asserted that 60% to 65% of the meaning in a social context is conveyed nonverbally. A recent summary of much of the channel reliance literature has provided statistical support for Birdwhistell's claim (Philpott, 1983). It showed that approximately 35% of social meaning is derived from verbal behaviors, leaving the remaining 65% to be accounted for by nonverbal behaviors or their interplay with verbal information. Typical of the kinds of investigations that have confirmed the general superiority of nonverbal over verbal cues is a series of experiments by Argyle and associates (Argyle, Alkema, & Gilmour, 1971; Argyle, Salter, Nicholson, Williams, & Burgess, 1970). In one version, subjects saw videotaped segments of speakers reading friendly, neutral, or hostile passages accompanied by friendly, neutral, or hostile kinesic-vocalic nonverbal presentations. In another version, the segments displayed verbal and nonverbal combinations of superior, neutral, and inferior attitudes. Subjects were asked to determine what meanings were being expressed. Results showed that if the verbal and nonverbal cues were relatively equal in strength when judged separately, the nonverbal cue dominated the verbal one when they were paired together. The nonverbal elements were actually 12.5 times as powerful as the verbal message in one experiment.

Even when the verbal message was subsequently strengthened to give it a better chance to influence meaning, it still lost out to the nonverbal channel when the two channels were presented together.

Nonverbal cues prevail over verbal ones when people are making judgments of a communicator's leadership ability and credibility (Gitter, Black, & Fishman, 1975), and people are more accurate judging interpersonal styles from nonverbal than verbal behaviors (Perlmutter, Paddock, & Duke, 1985).

People place greater reliance on facial and gestural expressions than on words when completing certain comprehension and behavioral tasks (Wahlers, 1976). Vocal cues carry more weight than verbal ones for both consistent and inconsistent expressions of attitudes, feelings, and ideas, even when the vocal cue is neutral and the verbal cue is extreme (Fujimoto, 1971; Mehrabian & Wiener, 1967). People are also more accurate in answering interpretive questions when they have nonverbal as opposed to verbal information available to them (Archer & Akert, 1977). (Also see Applications, p. 157.)

All of this research points to the superiority of nonverbal over verbal behaviors in contributing to meaning. Though this is indeed the general trend, a number of circumstances alter the pattern. Thus this generalization needs to be qualified by the specific conclusions that follow.

2. **Children place greater reliance on verbal cues than adults do.** In fact, most of the research suggests that children believe the words more than they do facial expressions or intonations (Bugental, Kaswan, Love, & Fox, 1970; Reilly & Muzekari, 1979; Solomon & Yeager, 1969a; Wass, 1973; Woolfolk & Woolfolk, 1974). For example, if you tell your 3-year-old nephew in an affectionate, teasing voice that he is a "weirdo," he will think you really don't like him. A teacher who tempers criticism with a smile will still be regarded as critical, not helpful. Philpott (1983) estimated that children are five times as likely to believe the words as the nonverbal behaviors. However, one study (James, 1969) found that children were much like adults in relying more heavily on nonverbal than verbal cues; they just didn't discount the verbal content as much as adults did when the verbal and nonverbal channels were in conflict.

Whether children are truly more literal is hard to say. It is also not clear at what age they make the transition to greater reliance on the nonverbal channel. But it would be safest not to use sarcasm with a small child if you want the true intent of your message to be understood.

3. **Reliance on nonverbal cues is greater when the verbal and nonverbal channels conflict than when they are congruent.** Research showing that the verbal content equals or exceeds the nonverbal content in importance usually comes from studies in which the two channels are not completely contradictory. For example, two studies on impressions and hiring of job interviewees (Hollandsworth, Kazelskis, Stevens, & Dressel, 1979; Sigelman & Davis, 1978) showed that verbal and nonverbal cues were nearly equal in their impact on impressions, and verbal content

APPLICATIONS

Importance of Nonverbal Cues in Therapy and Medicine

A wide range of studies have found that patients place more weight on a therapist's or doctor's nonverbal behavior than on what is said. In the counseling realm, nonverbal cues are far more important than verbal ones in judging a therapist's empathy, genuineness, and respect for the client (Haase & Tepper, 1972; Seay & Altekruse, 1979; Tepper, 1972; Tepper & Haase, 1978). For example, forward trunk lean, direct eye contact, a concerned voice, and a concerned facial expression are better at conveying empathy than words are. When positive verbal statements are accompanied by contradictory negative kinesic and vocal behaviors rather than positive nonverbals, counselors are rated as less effective and as having less regard for their clients (Reade & Smouse, 1980). Nonverbal cues may also be more sensitive in distinguishing distressed from nondistressed couples (Rubin, 1977).

Likewise, the nonverbal stream, especially vocal intonation, is more significant than the verbal stream in physician-patient interactions and becomes increasingly important with more visits (Friedman, 1979c; Hall, Roter, & Rand, 1981; Waitzkin, 1984).

The photograph of the hospital patient Ron is illustrative. Although the poster greeting is nice, the nonverbal expressions of caring, affection, and concern from the nurses doubtless meant a lot more to this young cancer patient.

Which conveys more affection and caring for this cancer patient—the nurses' facial expressions, postures, and proximity or the verbal posted birthday card?

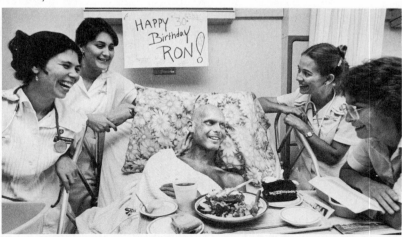

157

appropriateness was the biggest predictor of hiring likelihood. Because ratings were made on naturally occurring interview behaviors, it can be assumed that the interviewees attempted to coordinate their verbal and nonverbal behavior and did not engage in blatant contradictions. Similarly, people making evaluative judgments based on excerpts from the Dole-Mondale vice presidential debates or on interviewees' replies to positive, negative, and neutral questions based more of their judgments on the verbal information than the nonverbal cues (Krauss, Apple, Morency, Wenzel, & Winton, 1981).

Two final experiments using both congruent and incongruent conditions found different patterns under each condition. McMahan (1976) had people respond to four different combinations of dominant and submissive verbal and nonverbal presentations. When respondents rated interpretations of the statements and the speaker's intent, the presence of incongruent nonverbal cues significantly altered their ratings compared to the congruent conditions, indicating that conflicting nonverbal cues influenced their judgments. Zahn (1973) combined verbal and vocal elements on a friendly-to-hostile continuum. Although he found that nonverbal cues generally affected interpretations more than verbal cues, when the verbal and vocal cues were consistent with each other, the verbal component carried more weight; when they were in conflict (e.g., one positive and one negative), the nonverbal component carried more weight.

Overall, these results suggest that people are especially inclined to turn to nonverbal cues when they are receiving mixed messages. They rely on the nonverbal cues to resolve the conflict in meaning. When the verbal and nonverbal channels are relatively consistent, the verbal information is more readily accepted.

4. **Channel reliance depends on the communication function at stake.** Verbal content is more important for factual, cognitive, abstract, and persuasive interpretations, while nonverbal content is more important for judging emotional and attitudinal expressions, relational communication, and impression formation. In McMahan's (1976) study involving judgments of communicator dominance, respondents were asked to determine the factual content of the speaker's statements and to form evaluations of the speaker. When they were asked to reconstruct the overt statements, they relied most on the verbal information. When they had to volunteer impressions of the speaker, they relied more on nonverbal cues. Friedman (1978) likewise found that judgments of what grade a teacher might give a student were influenced more by verbal information, while judgments of a teacher's friendliness toward a student were influenced most by facial cues. Similarly, Solomon and Yeager (1969b) found that verbal content prevails when one is assessing "objective meaning" and intonation prevails when one is inferring a speaker's liking for a listener. In a deception context, verbal content is also better at helping one detect factual lying, while nonverbal cues are more helpful in detecting emotional deception (Hocking, Bauchner, Kaminski, & Miller, 1979; Kraut, 1978; Maier & Thurber, 1968).

In fact, most of the research cited to support the general superiority of nonverbal cues (Proposition 1) comes from studies involving relational, affective, or impression-leaving outcomes, while those showing increasing impact for verbal content (Proposition 3) come from studies involving interpretations or reconstructions of verbal meanings. In his synthesis of research, Philpott (1983) attempted to divide research along functional lines. He concluded that for symbolic or persuasive communication, verbal information accounts for far more of the meaning than nonverbal information does. For emotive, relational, or attributional (impression formation) outcomes, nonverbal cues account for varying but greater amounts of the meaning than verbal ones. This is consistent with Noller's (1985) conclusion that "the importance of the verbal channel increases with the amount of information contained in the words and is greater for more cognitive (rather than affective) tasks" (p. 44).

5. **When the content in different channels is congruent, the meanings of the cues tend to be averaged together equally; when content is incongruent, there is greater variability in how information is integrated.** Scholars who are interested in information processing are intrigued by the issue of how people combine information from different channels. Does each channel get counted equally? Do some channels consistently carry more weight than others? Are some cues ignored when they are inconsistent with other cues? Although these questions have yet to be answered definitively, it appears that when the information in the various channels is not totally at odds, people tend to add up their individual

Talking to You

They are earnestly
telling you something

they are telling you about themselves

they are telling you
with all their might
something they want you to know
and the story is not them

the words are not them

it is the movement the twisting mouth the
eyes trying to pinion you the
face crying for attention the
shoulders squared the
breath fast and even
to push forth the words that
don't matter only the gesture does

Source: From *The Blue Scar and Other Poems* (p. 54) by A. Grilikhes, 1988, New York: Folder Editions.

meanings and arrive at an average meaning based on all the contributing channels (Apple, 1979; Philpott, 1983; Zahn, 1973). For example, in judging a speaker's nervousness, audiences will tend to add together the separate bits of information presented by the kinesic and vocal cues of anxiety.

However, when mixed messages are being sent, different people may handle such conflicting information differently (Zahn, 1973). In some cases, people may use a discounting strategy, that is, ignoring one noncongruent cue when two others are consistent with each other (Anderson & Jacobson, 1965). In a study of immediacy cues, Burgoon, Buller, Hale, and deTurck (1984) found that is what people did when judging the relational meaning of a set of five cues: If two were consistent, a third inconsistent one was usually unable to reverse or neutralize the interpretation drawn from the other two. Other research has shown that people believe whichever cue is the most extreme or most negative (e.g., Bugental, 1974; Bugental, Kaswan, & Love, 1970; Friedman, 1979b; Hegstrom, 1979).

But this is not always the case. The bulk of evidence reviewed so far would suggest that visual cues tend to be counted more strongly than vocal cues, which in turn are counted more heavily than verbal ones. Fujimoto's (1971) finding that vocal cues carried more weight even when the verbal cue was extreme and the vocal cue was neutral tends to support this interpretation. But firm conclusions await further research.

How people combine information channels has a number of interesting implications. If people are most biased toward visual information, this may help explain the immense popularity of television. It may also suggest some instructional strategies for improving classroom learning (e.g., more films, videotapes, and slides). If, however, people place great faith in the voice, it may explain why so often people have their most intimate conversations over the telephone rather than in person. The relative weight each channel carries may also account for why people are easily deceived in some situations and not in others. (We consider this channel issue in more detail in Chapter 8.) Finally, it may help us decide as communicators the best vehicle for sending important messages to others—letters, telephone, or face-to-face conversation.

However, before you decide that there is one best way to send information, you should be aware of the next conclusion, which places further limitations on our generalizations about channel reliance.

6. **Individuals have biases in their channel dependence.** Some people consistently rely on certain nonverbal channels, some usually rely on verbal content, and some are situationally adaptable. One study shows that each person is consistent in relying on either facial cues or language when judging incongruent emotional expressions (Shapiro, 1968). Another shows that people making judgments of a speaker's level of stress can be classified into one of three groups: those who are verbal-reliant, those who are nonverbal-reliant, and those who shift back and forth in their channel preference, depending on the context or type of judgment being made (Vande Creek & Watkins, 1972).

No doubt people's channel preferences are related to which channel they have the greatest ability to encode and judge accurately. Since individuals differ in their skill at sending and interpreting linguistic, facial, or auditory information (Berman, Shulman, & Marwit, 1976; Krauss et al., 1981; Levy, 1964; Rosenthal, Hall, DiMatteo, Rogers, & Archer, 1979; Thompson & Meltzer, 1964), it makes sense that they might come to rely on those channels that they are best able to use and "read." This is just speculation at this point, however, and would be an interesting hypothesis to test.

Explanations and Speculations

As important as who relies most on nonverbal versus verbal channels and when, is why the nonverbal stream so often dominates people's determinations of meaning. A number of intriguing conjectures have been advanced.

Argyle et al. (1971) offer three possibilities. One is that we are innately programmed to signal affective states through nonverbal displays and are likewise programmed to recognize such signals. As support for this position, they note that many nonverbal behaviors are universal and unlearned. To the extent that all humans come equipped to send and recognize nonverbal cues, this would give nonverbal behaviors an edge over verbal expressions, which must be learned.

A second possibility is that there is an efficient division of labor such that verbal communication handles more abstract, nonsocial tasks such as problem solving while nonverbal communication handles more social, interpersonal matters. Because verbal and nonverbal communication occur simultaneously, the nonverbal channels can silently handle monitoring, feedback, and relational definition functions that are crucial to interpreting what is happening in the verbal stream. The nonverbal cues thus become the frame of reference against which verbal interpretations are checked. Scherer (1982b) makes the same point when he notes:

> Through speech, humans can at the same time communicate symbolic meaning via language, with all the advantages that the design features of language command, and reveal information about their biological and social identity, transitory states, and relationship to the listener via a nonverbal vocal signalling system. (p. 138)

This distinction between the content and relational facets of communication recurs in Chapter 9.

A third, related possibility is that because of their ambiguity, subtlety, and deniability, the nonverbal channels may be especially well suited to expressing sensitive and risky interpersonal information. As we noted in Chapter 1, nonverbal codes can express what the verbal code cannot or should not. If you offer verbal criticism of a friend's behavior and it is rebuffed, you may find yourself very embarrassed, with little ability to retract your statement. But if you express the same concern through looks, touches, and vocal tones rather than words, this gentle approach may be more effective. If not, you can always disclaim any unkind intentions.

Some other possible reasons for the power of nonverbal cues were cited in Chapter 1. The primacy of nonverbal communication as a means of expression for the species and for infants may predispose us to rely more on nonverbal behaviors as dependable and familiar sources of information. The temporary shift in early childhood to greater reliance on words may be due to the novelty and challenge of learning the verbal communication system. We may also rely more on nonverbal cues because we believe they are more spontaneous, uncontrolled expressions of "true" feelings.

One other possible explanation concerns the structure of verbal and nonverbal coding systems and how the brain is able to handle such information. It may be that the more continuous, nonsegmented nature of many nonverbal signals makes them especially well designed for right-hemispheric processing, where more holistic, impressionistic, and affective judgments are made. That is, the structural properties of the code system may determine how and where such information is processed and, consequently, what types of interpretations are made. We consider this possibility in more detail later.

Origins

> Is there a signalling code—a language without
> words—common to all men?
>
> I. Eibl-Eibesfeldt (1972, p. 297)

Nature or Nurture?

A major controversy regarding human behavior in general and communication in particular is the nature-nurture debate. Are behavioral patterns biologically and genetically determined, or are they shaped by environmental and cultural influences? As noted in previous chapters, to the extent that nonverbal signals are innate or part of a pattern of experience common to all humans, they will form a universal communication system. This would make nonverbal codes unlike verbal languages, which are largely learned, culture-bound systems.

The evidence on the innateness or universality of nonverbal behaviors is highly mixed, with staunch proponents at both ends of the nature-nurture spectrum. Those who take the inborn position rely on three types of evidence: (a) comparative studies between humans and other mammals, particularly primates, which imply a genetic heritage; (b) cross-cultural similarities, which may produce evidence of inborn or at least universal behavior patterns; and (c) studies of child development, particularly of handicapped children, which reveal patterns common to all developing humans.

Ethologists have observed a number of similarities between human behavior and that of lower primates. For example, the broad smile and wide-mouth laugh in humans resemble closely the silent bared-teeth and relaxed open-mouth displays in primates (Figure 5.1; van Hooff, 1972). Analogues between humans and other mammals include alarm vocalizations, alert responses such as eye widening, and play behaviors such as mock aggressive touch (e.g., see Andrew, 1972; Smith, 1974; Thorpe, 1972).

Underlying these comparisons is a belief that commonalities across species demonstrate the evolutionary character of behavior. Consistent with Darwin's theory of natural selection, it is assumed that behaviors retained in the human repertoire over the millennia have *survival value;* that is, they have served the species well in surviving dangers and adapting to environmental changes. According to the theory, behaviors that are useful become part of the permanent signal system of the species, while those that are nonfunctional eventually disappear, leaving a largely universal communication system.

As noted in Chapter 2, Darwin's (1965) observations in 1872, which predated "scientific" study of human behavior by many decades, documented some hereditary and apparently universal communication patterns. Especially interesting were his cross-generational comparisons. He found children using the same finger-rubbing gesture, for instance, as a grandparent whom they had never met. He noticed that British adults don't display the shoulder shrug, but British children do. This led him to conclude that many behaviors are mistakenly assumed to be culture-specific because adults have learned *not* to exhibit them when in reality they originate as universal behaviors. Darwin's speculations about the commonality of many emotional expressions across cultures have since been confirmed by con-

FIGURE 5.1 Note the similarity between the wide-mouth laugh of the boy and the relaxed, open-mouth display of the chimpanzee.

temporary research (for summaries, see Chapter 10; Ekman, 1973; and Knapp, 1978).

Anthropologists have produced further examples. One is the eyebrow flash—a quick, almost imperceptible raising of the eyebrows, common in friendly greetings in a number of widely different cultures.

Another form of evidence for the innate position comes from developmental studies revealing that all infants display the same reflexes and emotional expressions, regardless of culture. It might be argued that children

Examples of the eyebrow flash from the Waika Indian, French, and Papuan cultures.

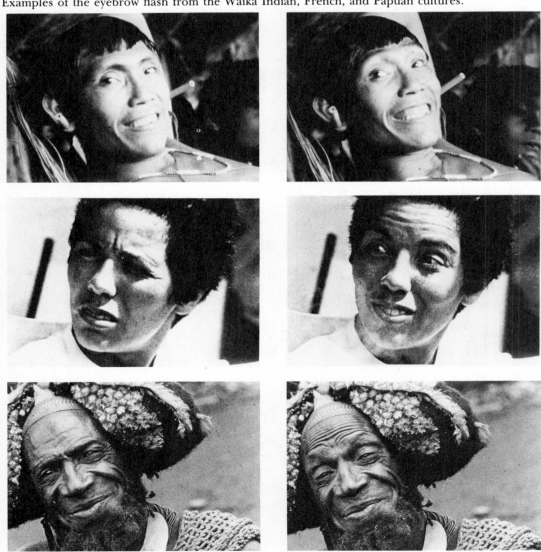

learn these expressions from their caretakers. But this possibility is disputed by observations of blind, deaf, and limbless children, who display the same smiling and grief expressions as sighted and hearing children (e.g., see Eibl-Eibesfeldt, 1973). Deaf and blind children could not have learned these behaviors through auditory or visual imitation, and institutionalized limbless babies (born to mothers who took thalidomide during pregnancy) are especially limited in their ability to learn nonverbal signals from adult models because they lack opportunities for tactile exploration or frequent reinforcement from contact with caretakers. That they present many of the same vocal and kinesic expressions as normal babies is taken as evidence that there are some basic behavior patterns endemic to all members of the human species.

At the opposite end of the nature-nurture continuum are theorists who believe that all behavior is learned and culture-specific (e.g., Birdwhistell, 1970; La Barre, 1947). They contend that surface similarities in the structure of behavior across cultures or species mask real differences in function and meaning. Further, the rules for usage and interpretations of behaviors are culture- and context-specific and therefore must be learned.

For example, even though various cultures display the eyebrow flash, its usage and meanings vary considerably. In North American cultures, it is a very common gesture that may express everything from pleasure at greeting to attentiveness to approval. By contrast, in some Oriental cultures it is an inappropriately demonstrative behavior that may be regarded as rude and "very forward." (A professor learned this, much to her embarrassment, after nearly a week of "flashing" a group of Chinese nationals whom she was teaching, ironically, about nonverbal communication.)

Other examples of cultural differences abound. Belching after dinner is polite in some countries, rude in others such as ours. Americans and Europeans point with the forefinger; many Africans and Asians point with their lips or head. As noted previously, emblem gestures may look the same but have entirely different meanings across cultures, or different-appearing behaviors may have the same meaning. And patterns of behavior may appear in one country that are totally absent in another. This tremendous variety in form and function of nonverbal signals across cultures is taken as evidence that there is no universality to nonverbal communication and therefore no innateness.

A third position is a blend of these two extremes. It holds that a common core of expressions shared by all humans is grounded in our genetic and neurological heritage but that these expressions are also embedded in a matrix of learned cultural rules and environmental influences (e.g., see Buck, 1984; Eibl-Eibesfeldt, 1972; Ekman, Friesen, & Ellsworth, 1972). Such things as facial expressions, glances, spacing behavior, and touch may have biological roots, but their use and interpretation have been modified and adapted by each culture to meet its own needs and values. Further, a number of behaviors, such as emblems or vocal inflections, are strictly learned and unique to a given culture. Even Darwin acknowledged that many behaviors require instruction and practice before they are performed in a useful or socially acceptable manner. The end result is great diversity in the kinds of nonverbal displays and meanings that appear but a universal ability to understand some basic displays such as the smile or territorial defense postures.

We subscribe to this third position. It seems likely that some behaviors do have an evolutionary base but may have to conform to cultural or contextual rules, while others originate within a particular culture and are idiosyncratic to it. Given this middle-of-the-road nature-nurture position, how do nonverbal codes compare to verbal ones?

Comparison to Verbal Communication

Intuitively, it seems as if the verbal languages that have been developed are totally acquired affairs. After all, one cannot travel to Moscow or Nairobi and automatically speak the local dialect. Children do not inherit language; they must be taught vocabulary and the rules of grammar. And the words themselves are largely arbitrary human creations that may or may not survive to the next generation.

This is not to say, however, that nature plays no role in language. It has been argued that humans may be inherently predisposed to develop language. Eisenberg and Smith (1971) write:

> We know that the capacity for language is innate, for all human beings display a predisposition to use a language composed of discrete sounds linked together by syntactical rules. Regardless of the culture in which he is raised, a child learns to use language in the same chronological sequence as all other children. For instance, he will utter sentences at the same age in all cultures. (p. 42)

Beyond this developmental evidence of the inherency of language, prominent linguists believe that language may be patterned after the way the brain organizes information, lending a further innate dimension to language. Add to this some nonarbitrary elements of the lexicon such as onomatopoeia (words that sound like the thing they represent) and the consistent use across different languages of sounds that evoke the colors associated with the words in which they appear (Marks, 1975), and it becomes apparent that language is also not strictly a learned system.

Clearly, one cannot put nonverbal communication at the nature end of the continuum and verbal communication at the nurture end. The situation is far more complex than that. Moreover, many vocal and kinesic behaviors are part and parcel of speech, so that wherever they are placed on the continuum, they must be placed together with language. Probably the most accurate conclusion to be drawn is that both verbal and nonverbal communication share some biologically governed properties, including an inherent inclination of humans to develop a *communication* system, and both share many learned features. But of the two, nonverbal has a more innate base than verbal communication. This foreshadows some differences in the structure of each system.

Structure

Analogic Versus Digital Coding

Nonverbal codes have been commonly characterized as *analogic,* to distinguish them from verbal communication, which is said to be *digital.* The distinguishing features of an analogic code are that it is comprised of an infinite, continuous range of naturally occurring values. The color spectrum and the natural number system are good examples of analogic systems. By contrast, a digital code consists of a finite set of discrete and arbitrarily defined units. An A-to-E grading system is a good example: It has only five finite categories, each is mutually exclusive and distinguishable from the next (i.e., discrete), and the number of grade levels is an arbitrary, human decision. There could as easily be 10 grade levels or 100.

Although there is no quarrel with labeling language a digital system, to call all nonverbal codes analogic is overly simplistic and inaccurate. True, many nonverbal signals have intrinsic, or naturally arising, meaning (for example, crying to signal pain or unhappiness) and may take on an infinite range of values. But many others must be regarded as digital, either because they are arbitrarily concocted (such as the A-OK sign) or because they are discrete (such as the greeting kiss). Dittmann (1978) presents a compelling case that many other apparently continuous behaviors become essentially discrete units for communication purposes. Examples of behaviors that we regard as single or stand-alone units: the smile, the nod, eye contact (present or absent), postural shifts, hairstyles, vocal characterizers such as a shriek, emblems, and various other types of gestures such as the ear tug or the pointing gesture. Moreover, most of the classification schemes for nonverbal codes (such as kinemes or tacemes) reduce behaviors to discrete categories on the assumption that they represent what is meaningful.

Hence the nonverbal codes (and it should be emphasized that we are talking in the plural) include a mix of analogic and digital elements. It may be that the more we treat a given nonverbal behavior or pattern as communicative, the more we treat it as digital. That is, we may mentally transform a continuous, naturally arising behavior into a more manageable, digital form to make sense out of it.

Properties of Language

To the extent that nonverbal signals take on digital form, they may begin to resemble verbal languages. To consider the question of whether nonverbal codes do in fact form a language system requires first considering the special properties of language.

Numerous treatises have been written about the features of language. We will examine only some of them here as an introduction to this issue. The most complete analysis of formal design features of verbal human language can be found in Hockett (1960). Other structural and organizing features of language in use are discussed in Ellis (1982). Applications to nonverbal and animal communication can be found in Burgoon (1985b), Lyons (1972), and Thorpe (1972), among others.

Here is a baker's dozen of the most obvious and most important properties:

1. **Discreteness.** As already noted, language is comprised of recognizable, separable units. In spoken language, there is actually a dual system of sound units (phonemes, phones, allophones, etc.) and symbol units (letters) that are combined to form semantically meaningful components called morphemes (words, prefixes, etc.). Units are combined in increasingly complex hierarchies, but at each level, the separate units are distinguishable.

2. **Syntax rules.** Language has rules for combining and sequencing elements, for example, rules for what letters or sounds can follow each other, rules for noun-verb order in sentences, and rules for the positioning of prepositions.

3. **Semantic rules.** Language follows rules for associating words with their referents and assigning literal meanings to utterances. Dictionaries tell us what a given word denotes at a particular point in time. Other rules exist for extracting meaning from the ordering of elements in sentences (e.g., a noun-verb-noun sequence is to be interpreted as agent-action-object).

4. **Polysemy.** Words may have multiple denotations. The word "run" may denote rapid locomotion, a score in a baseball game, a batch of goods in a factory, or a snag in hosiery.

5. **Arbitrariness.** A major feature of symbolic communication is that meanings are assigned by convention. There is no necessary connection between a referent and the symbol selected to stand for it.

6. **Culture- and context-bound meaning.** A corollary of the arbitrariness principle is that words in one language do not carry over to another language. Meanings are therefore tied to a specific language community, and even cultures that use the same language may assign different meanings to the shared lexicon. A corollary of the polysemy principle is that contextual information is often necessary to determine which meaning to select. The net result of these two properties is that no verbal language qualifies as universal.

7. **Displacement.** Language can refer to things removed in space and time, to the "not here" and "not now." For example, changes in tense allow us to talk about the past or the future, rather than just the present. The use of the negative allows us to talk about things that are absent or nonexistent.

8. **Reflexivity.** Language has the special property that it can be used to talk about itself. In other words, it need not refer to something out in the world. It can reflect on itself—theoretically, an infinite

number of times. The sentence "My last statement was nonsensical" is an example of self-reflexivity.

9. **Prevarication.** Language need not be truthful. It can be used to lie and intentionally mislead.

10. **Transformation.** A given meaning can be transformed into a number of alternative expressions. This refers to the linguistic distinction between deep structure and surface structure. The same underlying meaning can give rise to several actual sentence forms. For example, "The man gave the girl a balloon" is equivalent in meaning to "The girl was given a balloon by the man." The surface differences are superficial.

11. **Productivity.** The language system is open in that words and sentences can be put together in novel ways to create an infinite variety of new messages that are readily understood. Although the initial pool of elements is relatively small, the number of new utterances that can be created is limitless. Language is therefore "productive."

12. **Coherence mechanisms.** Language includes devices such as prepositions and question-answer sequences that allow speakers and listeners to draw connections between series of utterances in a larger discourse.

13. **Pragmatic rules.** Just as there are rules for how to construct language and assign meaning to it, there are rules for its use in actual practice. These are socially dictated prescriptions for when and how to use various language forms.

Linguistic Properties of Nonverbal Codes

Let us now consider the extent to which these properties apply to the nonverbal code systems.

Discreteness and Arbitrariness. We have already said that many nonverbal cues are discrete or are treated as such in communication. All of the nonverbal codes have some discrete elements: gestures in kinesics, vocalized pauses in vocalics, symbolic colors for clothing in physical appearance, formal seating arrangements in proxemics, categories of touch such as a slap in haptics, appointment time in chronemics, and status symbols in artifacts. Some of these, such as emblems or status symbols, are created by convention and are therefore arbitrary. Others, such as the laugh or the slap, are natural behaviors rather than linguistic inventions. Thus nonverbal codes meet these criteria partly but not completely.

Syntactic and Semantic Rules. It has been popular to claim that nonverbal communication is not rule-governed. Yet closer inspection shows that we follow rules both in the construction of nonverbal expressions and in their interpretation. At the syntactic level, there are rules of combination and rules of ordering. For example, a smile and scowl do not appear together because they would create a bizarre expression. Certain parakinesic and paralinguistic behaviors are consistently used to punctuate spoken language. Illustrator gestures accompany speaking, not listening. Greeting rituals follow the order of eye contact before handshake, not vice versa. At the semantic level, individual cues and sets of cues have consistently recognized meanings. Laughter may express happiness, anxiety, or contempt; it never means "I want a turn at talk." Close proximity may have several meanings, but when combined with smiles, caresses, and constant gaze, it becomes restricted to meanings of intimacy or physical attraction. Meanings are also derivable from larger cue patterns and sequences, as in the departure ritual (see Exline and Fehr [1978] and Kendon [1983] for additional examples). Thus nonverbal codes used in a communicative sense are indeed rule-governed. The best evidence of this is our ability to recognize "ungrammatical" expressions—unorthodox combinations of signals and uninterpretable sequences.

Polysemy and Culture- and Context-bound Meaning. The fact that a nonverbal cue such as gaze has no single meaning is often cited as evidence against nonverbal behavior forming a language. Yet this is no different from the property of polysemy in verbal language. It merely means that one must rely on context and culture to decide which interpretation to select. Many nonverbal behaviors depend on simultaneously occurring verbal and nonverbal information for their interpretation. Similarly, one may need to know the culture before choosing an interpretation. Downcast eyes may mean sadness in the United States but respect for elders in an African village. Much nonverbal communication, then, is like verbal language in being context- and culture-bound.

Displacement. Some parakinesic and paralinguistic behaviors act as tense and place markers (e.g., Birdwhistell, 1970). Otherwise, nonverbal codes tend to be tied to the here and now. Although one might display anxiety cues in anticipation of an uncomfortable situation or long after an unpleasant occasion has passed, the time referent of the anxiety, in the absence of further information, would be unclear to an observer. Pantomime narratives occasionally attempt flashes backward or forward in time, but they are usually accompanied by some verbal explanation. By contrast, verbal languages explicitly index tense through morphemic, phonological, or paralinguistic changes.

Reflexivity. It is difficult to envision an example of nonverbal behavior that can reflect on itself indefinitely. A smile might comment on a preceding smile or a laugh on a previous laugh, but it is hard to imagine this going beyond one iteration. Nonverbal codes are therefore probably best regarded as not self-reflexive.

Prevarication. Can one dissemble nonverbally? Can one misrepresent or misdirect nonverbally? The obvious answer is yes. People are continually masking true emotions and constructing self-presentations that are more favorable than reality. And it is easy to deceive others through the omission of some nonverbal information or the addition of false information. The defendant in a child molestation case, for instance, shaved his beard, cut his hair, dressed in conservative clothing, and wore a cross so as to seem a moral and upstanding person on the witness stand.

Transformation. Nonverbal codes display transformation just as verbal codes do. There are alternate ways to signal that you want to relinquish a turn, numerous ways to initiate a courtship ritual, and different cue combinations that express surprise.

Productivity. The feature of transformation in itself ensures that a code has productivity. This means that nonverbal codes are capable of endless varieties of utterances and that they are open and evolving systems.

Coherence Mechanisms. Birdwhistell (1970) has identified a number of kinesic behaviors analogous to paralinguistic cues that serve many of the same coherence functions as markers in verbal language. They cross-reference what is going on verbally, work at a syntactic level to connect larger sequences of utterances, may distinguish different personal pronouns, and may identify tense. All of these features help a listener make sense of discourse. Similarly, familiar nonverbal sequences allow a person to interpret a proffered hand in a greeting context not as a request for money but as a desire to shake hands. The extent of coherence mechanisms in nonverbal communication is only beginning to be understood.

Pragmatic Rules. The concept of display rules provides evidence that there are rules for the management of nonverbal behaviors in public. Each culture can easily articulate what behaviors are considered appropriate or inappropriate for use in various contexts.

Based on the features compared so far, it is clear that nonverbal codes include many of the same properties as verbal languages. However, some additional code properties are unique to nonverbal systems.

Unique Properties of Nonverbal Codes

1. **Analogic coding.** We have said that nonverbal codes include some digital and some analogic elements. Some behaviors are truly analogic in that they form a natural continuum. These include conversational distance (although we may reduce it to a few simple categories), sociopetal-sociofugal furniture arrangement, length of eye gaze, touch intensity and frequency, colors used in clothing and artifacts, and most vocal features. Because of the infinite range and intensity of values that are possible, analogic codes permit subtle shadings of meaning.

2. **Iconicity.** Behaviors are iconic to the degree that they resemble directly what they refer to and preserve a one-to-one correspondence in size. A hologram or life-size statue of a person would be the most iconic form of representation; a photograph is less iconic, although it preserves the proportionality of the physical features that are visible; a stick figure would be less iconic; and a verbal description would have no iconicity.

   Many emblems are iconic because they attempt to mimic what they represent. For example, the death emblem of the finger drawn across the throat imitates slashing the throat with a knife. Facial emotion expressions, some illustrators, and some artifacts are iconic. Iconicity gives nonverbal behaviors a vividness that is missing from verbal versions of the same referent.

3. **Universality.** Only the nonverbal codes can claim some universally used and understood behaviors, such as smiling or crying.

4. **Simultaneity.** The nonverbal codes have the potential for simultaneous multiple message transmission. Within each nonverbal code, several features can be manipulated at the same time. In kinesics, for instance, gaze and facial expression may together send one message while posture sends another and gestures send a third. With touch, one can tickle another in a playful manner with one hand while holding the victim in a not so playful, viselike grip with the other. If one considers all the nonverbal codes as an interdependent system, the opportunity for cross-modality multiple messages increases dramatically. Because of this capacity for simultaneous message encoding, nonverbal codes may be used in combination, all sending the same message—thereby greatly increasing message redundancy and the likelihood of accurate reception—or they may modify and complement each other to produce a complex and possibly incongruent message. A variety of thoughts and feelings can be conveyed much faster this way than through the sequential transmission required with verbal expression.

5. **Directness of sensory stimulation.** Because nonverbal behaviors can impinge directly on the senses, they may produce more rapid, automatic, and emotional responding in receivers. By contrast, verbal descriptions require an intermediate cognitive translation step before the individual can respond. The maxim "A picture is worth a thousand words" takes some of its truth from this principle that direct stimulation of the visual senses has far more impact than the most elaborate verbal description of the same phenomenon. (See Applications, p. 173.)

6. **Spontaneity.** Just as the reaction to nonverbal cues may be more rapid because of the direct link to the senses, much nonverbal encoding may be rapid and relatively uncontrolled, especially behaviors that are intrinsic biological signals and those that are overlearned, habitual expressions. A by-product of the ease of such encoding is that receivers come to believe nonverbal communication is more spontaneous and therefore more "truthful." As noted in Chapter 1, this may partly account for the power of nonverbal behavior in communication. Although in reality many nonverbal behaviors are controlled and manipulated deliberately, the faith placed in their verisimilitude gives nonverbal codes yet one more unique property.

It should be clear from these unique features that verbal communication and nonverbal communication do not have identical linguistic and message properties. But they do share enough similarities to regard nonverbal acts as integral to the functioning of language. Leach (1972) in fact

APPLICATIONS

Impact of Television and Photography

A vivid example of the directness of sensory stimulation comes from the Vietnam War era. While many people watched their TV during the dinner hour one night, much to their horror, they watched a South Vietnamese officer parade a prisoner before the camera, put a pistol to his head without warning, and summarily execute him. Viewers not only saw the man's body crumple to the ground, his blood spattering on the street, but they also heard the gun firing and the shocked vocal responses of the onlookers. Seeing this event produced powerful visceral responses in the viewers that could not be captured by the next day's newspaper account of it. You can partially re-create the experience by viewing the accompanying photos here and on the following page. Compare the photograph of the moment prior to the shooting to the written account. Similarly, look at the other photograph. Which is more compelling, this photograph of the innocent victims of war or a written description of the accidental napalming of South Vietnamese children?

Saigon police chief Nguyen Ngoc Loan summarily executes a Viet Cong suspect at the height of the Tet offensive, 1968.

Impact of Television and Photography (*Continued*)

After a South Vietnamese plane napalmed Trang Bang, Vietnam, in error, Phan Thi Kim Phuc flees, having torn off her flaming clothes.

concludes that nonspeech behaviors (nonverbal communication) do form a sort of language and notes some of the same comparisons we have been making:

> It does not consist of isolated sets of trigger signals . . . but of gestures and symbols which are related to one another as a total system after the fashion of a language. Such non-speech "languages" are both simpler and more complex than "normal" spoken or written language. They are simpler because the syntactic rules are fewer in number and more explicit—the difference between right and wrong nonverbal behaviour is more clear-cut than the difference between right and wrong speech forms—but they are more complex because non-speech is a multi-channel phenomenon. . . . The receiver of a message is likely to be subjected to communicative signals through several different sense channels simultaneously. Sound, sight, smell, taste, touch and rhythm may all be "relevant," not only singly but in combination. (p. 318)

The verbal and nonverbal codes are also so inseparable in producing a total communication system that the more relevant question for future analysis may be what *code* properties are significant in achieving human goals and social organization rather than what *linguistic* ones are important (see Table 5.1).

TABLE 5.1 Comparison of Verbal and Nonverbal Codes on Linguistic Coding Properties

Linguistic Properties	Present in Verbal Code?	Present in Nonverbal Codes?
Discreteness	yes	yes (but not all are)
Syntax rules	yes	yes
Semantic rules	yes	yes
Polysemy	yes	yes
Arbitrariness	yes	yes for many behaviors and codes
Culture- and context-bound meaning	yes	yes for many behaviors and codes
Displacement	yes	to a limited extent
Reflexivity	yes	to a limited extent if at all
Prevarication	yes	yes
Transformation	yes	yes
Productivity	yes	yes
Coherence mechanisms	yes	yes
Pragmatic rules	yes	yes
Analogic coding	no	yes for many behaviors and codes
Iconicity	no	yes for some
Universality	no	yes for some
Simultaneity	no	yes
Direct sensory stimulation	no	yes
Spontaneity	no	yes

Neurophysiological Processing

We alluded earlier to the possibility that nonverbal codes have different structural features from verbal codes because they are processed differently by the brain. The crux of this argument lies in the designation of the left hemisphere of the brain as the "verbal" side and the right hemisphere as the "nonverbal" side. There is some basis for this distinction. There is ample evidence that many verbally related activities such as word and symbol recognition occur in the left hemisphere, and the left side of the brain is typically dominant for rational, logical, and analytic tasks (which themselves involve verbal abilities). Conversely, the right hemisphere is said to be dominant for spatial, pictorial, musical, geometric, and emotional stimuli, including such nonverbally related activities as voice recognition and depth perception (see Campbell, 1982; Restak, 1979; Springer & Deutsch, 1981). This lateralization of many functions led Andersen, Garrison, and Andersen (1979) to propose that nonverbal and verbal communication can be distinguished from one another by where they are processed in the brain.

This view is too simplistic, however. Most of the literature only applies to where stimuli are initially *perceived.* It does not address where the stimuli are interpreted as communication signals. It is possible, for example, that the right hemisphere initially apprehends that a person is 6 feet away but the left hemisphere takes over in determining what message is implied by that choice of conversational distance. The lateralization literature also applies largely to the decoding of stimuli but not the encoding. If you choose to stand 6 feet from someone as a message of detachment, where does that communicative decision take place?

Contemporary work on information processing suggests a far more complex, synchronized relationship between the two hemispheres in the perception, comprehension, retrieval, and encoding of social information. For example, both hemispheres are involved in speech production. The left hemisphere governs vocabulary, rhythmic patterns, and free movements that accompany speech, while the right hemisphere processes social gestural speech and automatic speech. Interpretation responsibilities are also shared. Right hemispheric involvement is necessary to understand jokes, metaphors, stories with a moral, and emotions; people who have had the right hemisphere damaged give inaccurate, disjointed, or overly literal versions of these. Where interpretation takes place may also shift, depending on how familiar the person is with the code. Most people initially process music in the right hemisphere; they respond to it as an analogic code. However, once musicians become familiar with a particular piece of music, they process it in the left hemisphere, treating it like a digital code. It is a reasonable hypothesis that communicative stimuli that are treated in a holistic, gestalt fashion are processed as analogic information and therefore handled by the right hemisphere, while those are segmented into finer, discrete categories are processed as digital information by the left hemisphere. This conclusion is consistent with Campbell's (1982) contention that the left brain is better for deductive, convergent, discrete, intellectual, objective, literal, and denotative tasks, while the right brain is better for imaginative, divergent, continuous, sensuous, subjective, metaphorical, and connotative tasks. As Campbell puts it:

> The right brain is not a linguistic idiot. It has its own codes, its own rules, and these are worth examining. It does have some comprehension of spoken language, and it is good at detecting pitch, intonation, stress, cadence, loudness, and softness. It knows whether a sentence is asking a question, giving an order, expressing a condition, or making a statement. . . . It can recognize the ridiculous and inappropriate, and be aware that words are embedded in a wide matrix of relationships. (pp. 244–245)

One other interesting line of discovery casts further doubt on the simple nonverbal right–verbal left distinction. The brain can also be viewed as tripartite, consisting of the *R-complex,* the most primitive brain, located at the end of the brain stem; the *paleomammalian brain,* composed of the limbic system surrounding the R-complex; and the *neomammalian brain,* which is the cortex itself. Each brain controls different aspects of communication and nonverbal behavior. The R-complex controls instinctive behavioral and aggressive displays (e.g., territorial defense). The paleomammalian brain controls emotional expression and experience, as well as bodily functions. The neomammalian brain controls higher order thought processes and symbolic activity, presumably including such nonverbal symbols as emblems. Stacks (1982) argues that one can better understand the interrelationships between verbal and nonverbal communication by analyzing

The President's Speech

What was going on? A roar of laughter from the aphasia ward, just as the President's speech was coming on, and they had all been so eager to hear the President speaking . . .

There he was, the old Charmer, the Actor, with his practised rhetoric, his histrionisms, his emotional appeal—and all the patients were convulsed with laughter. . . . The President was, as always, moving—but he was moving them, apparently, mainly to laughter. What could they be thinking? Were they failing to understand him? Or did they, perhaps understand him all too well?

It was said of these patients, who though intelligent had the severest receptive or global aphasia, rendering them incapable of understanding words as such, that they none the less understood most of what was said to them. . . . [Why?] Because speech—natural speech—does *not* consist of words alone. . . . It consists of *utterance*— an uttering-forth of one's whole meaning with one's whole being— the understanding of which involves infinitely more than mere word-recognition. And this was the clue to aphasiacs' understanding, even when they might be wholly uncomprehending of words as such. For though the words, the verbal constructions, *per se,* might convey nothing, spoken language is normally suffused with 'tone,' embedded in an expressiveness which transcends the verbal—and it is precisely this expressiveness, so deep, so various, so complex, so subtle, which is perfectly preserved in aphasia, though understanding of words be destroyed. . . .

In this, then, lies their power of understanding—understanding, without words, what is authentic or inauthentic. Thus it was the grimaces, the histrionisms, the false gestures and, above all, the false tones and cadences of the voice, which rang false for these wordless but immensely sensitive patients. It was to these (for them) most glaring, even grotesque, incongruities and improprieties that my aphasic patients responded, undeceived and undeceivable by words.

This is why they laughed at the President's speech.

Source: From *The Man Who Mistook His Wife for a Hat and Other Clinical Tales* (pp. 76–79), by Oliver W. Sacks, 1985, New York: Summit Books.

the interplay among these three levels of the brain and which is in control during a particular nonverbal or verbal expression. Thus some communicative activities, such as threatening others, may be primarily controlled by the R-complex. Other activities, such as emotional expressions, may require the careful coordination of both verbal and nonverbal channels but rely more heavily on the spontaneously generated nonverbal signals of the limbic system. Finally, symbolic expressions may relegate nonverbal channels to a lesser though necessary role by providing complementary relational and connotative information.

Functions

> The functions of any given communication behavior are
> not realized in isolation from the other communication
> components but are dependent on the organization of
> the entire system for the expression of meaning.
>
> D. J. Higginbotham and D. E. Yoder (1982, p. 5)

The interrelatedness of verbal and nonverbal codes in producing a total communication system becomes most evident when we analyze communication according to the functions it serves. It has been popular to use Ekman and Friesen's (1969b) five basic functions of nonverbal behavior as the basis for such analysis. However, their analysis essentially treats nonverbal behaviors as subordinate or supplementary to verbal communication, which is at odds with our position that nonverbal communication serves a multiplicity of functions beyond enhancing the verbal message. As such, their categories elaborate the role of nonverbal behaviors in producing comprehensible messages, which is only one, albeit important, function of nonverbal communication. Here we briefly preview all the major functions of nonverbal communication that we will cover in this text, emphasizing how verbal communication relates to each.

Message Production, Processing, and Comprehension

Ekman and Friesen (1969b) claim that nonverbal behaviors may perform five functions:

1. **Repeat what is said verbally.** Nodding one's head while saying yes is one example of repetition. Typically, much of what people do nonverbally is somewhat redundant with the verbal message. In that way, accuracy of communication is improved.
2. **Substitute for portions of the verbal message.** Visual symbols may replace words. A simple smile may replace the need to say "yes." A loud laugh may signal that a joke is understood.
3. **Complement or clarify the verbal message.** The nonverbal cues may add surplus meaning to that expressed by the words alone.

Verbal hesitancy in the midst of a heated conflict may be accompanied by nonverbal avoidance cues that amplify the person's desire to escape the battle.

4. **Contradict the verbal statement.** This produces a mixed or ambiguous message in some cases, sarcasm in others. The statement "How nice of you to come," expressed in a flat voice, becomes condescending and insincere.

5. **Emphasize the words.** Pointing gestures, table pounding, and yelling are all ways to underscore what is being said.

These functions imply that we rely heavily on nonverbal behaviors to facilitate understanding of verbal communication in face-to-face contexts. This same position is articulated by Poyatos (1983), who refers to language, paralanguage, and kinesics as the "basic triple structure." He contends that these three channels are the primary vehicles for creating messages and are closely coordinated into a total communication system from early childhood on.

The integration of these channels is especially apparent when people attempt to construct messages. Some nonverbal behaviors may "prime the pump," so to speak. Kinesic expressiveness is such a natural part of the encoding process that even when it serves no benefit to the listener, it helps us get our thoughts out in a smooth fashion. Moreover, gestural forms tend to mirror the semantic meaning of an utterance. This suggests that our thoughts give rise to words and actions simultaneously. Just as nonverbal behaviors play a central role in encoding messages, they also affect decoding significantly. They may facilitate attention, comprehension, and recall or serve as distractors.

Other Social Functions

Identification, Impression Formation, and Impression Management. In expressing one's identity and creating first impressions, nonverbal and verbal behaviors must be coordinated to produce a consistent and sincere presentation. However, as noted previously, first impressions tend to be far more influenced by nonverbal information. This may be partly because verbal self-disclosure is constrained by social norms. Except for the research on channel reliance, little research has looked at the interrelationship of verbal and nonverbal channels to communicate identification and to manage impressions.

Mixed Messages and Deception. Here the research on verbal and nonverbal codes has been far more integrated. The mixed messages work addresses (a) how individuals differ in their skill in interpreting incongruent messages and (b) the impact of message congruity on such other functions as comprehension and persuasion. Most deception research has looked at (a) how accurately receivers can detect deception from verbal, nonverbal, and combination channels, (b) what kinds of verbal and nonverbal behaviors people exhibit while lying, and (c) what verbal and nonverbal strategies people might attempt when perpetrating deception.

Relational Communication. Most relational work has centered on nonverbal behavior. An exception is Sillars, Coletti, Parry, and Rogers' (1982) study of how nonverbal behaviors complement verbal conflict tactics. Other integrative work along this line should be forthcoming. During times of relational stress, when couples and families are more likely to verbalize their conflicts, it seems likely that coordination of verbal and nonverbal behaviors should be an especially sensitive issue and one worth studying more fully.

Emotional Expression. Most work in this area again focuses on nonverbal behaviors. Verbal behavior mostly becomes relevant when identifying the labels that are applied to emotional expressions rather than examining verbal emotional expressions themselves. However, some recent work (e.g., Knudsen & Muzekari, 1983; Plazewski & Allen, 1985) has examined how congruent verbal contextual information affects receiver agreement and consistency in judging emotions and how incongruent context may alter interpretations. Given that context plays a major role in people's interpretations, this type of work is likely to generate further interest.

Structuring Interaction and Conversational Management. In the areas of turn taking, greetings, and termination rituals, researchers have tended to look at the total picture of verbal and nonverbal behaviors used. Verbal behaviors are more prominent markers of the beginnings and endings of conversations.

Social Influence and Facilitation. Most research on persuasion processes has looked either at verbal behavior or at nonverbal behavior but rarely at the two in combination. This breach needs to be closed, especially as more attention turns to persuasive strategies, which inevitably involve multiple nonverbal and verbal codes.

Summary

We have reiterated throughout this chapter that nonverbal and verbal codes are part of an indivisible communication system. Although nonverbal information prevails over verbal information for much of our interpretation of the meaning of social situations, the verbal stream carries important and sometimes overriding information for many functions and receivers. We have discussed possible reasons for the nonverbal dominance effect. One explanation resides in the relative differences in origin between the verbal and nonverbal codes. Nonverbal behavior appears to have more innate features than the verbal code. Another area of difference is the structural properties of the respective verbal and nonverbal codes. Although nonverbal codes share many linguistic features with the verbal system, there are a few differences, and nonverbal codes include many coding features not present in verbal language. The differences in code structure may be well adapted for different forms of neurophysiological processing. Nonverbal behaviors that are treated analogically may be handled by the right hemisphere, while those that are treated digitally may be handled by the left hemisphere. It is also likely that instinctive and emotional nonverbal behaviors are governed by subcortical regions of the brain, whereas more symbolic nonverbal content and verbal content is governed by the cortex. Despite differences in cerebral processing of verbal and nonverbal material, the verbal and nonverbal codes are closely coordinated to produce messages, and they are well integrated for achieving most other communicative functions. To treat them as independent systems is therefore an artificial and counterproductive distinction.

Suggested Readings

Burgoon, J. K. (1985). Nonverbal signals. In M. L. Knapp & G. R. Miller (Eds.), *Handbook of interpersonal communication* (pp. 344–390). Beverly Hills, CA: Sage.

Burgoon, J. K. (1985). The relationship of verbal and nonverbal codes. In B. Dervin & M. L. Voight (Eds.), *Progress in communication sciences* (Vol. 6, pp. 263–298). Norwood, NJ: Ablex.

Dittmann, A. T. (1978). The role of body movement in communication. In A. W. Siegman & S. Feldstein (Eds.), *Nonverbal behavior and communication* (pp. 69–95). Hillsdale, NJ: Erlbaum.

Key, M. R. (Ed.). (1980). *The relationship of verbal and nonverbal communication.* The Hague: Mouton.

Leach, E. (1972). The influence of cultural context on nonverbal communication in man. In R. A. Hinde (Ed.), *Non-verbal communication* (pp. 315–344). Cambridge: Cambridge University Press.

Lyons, J. (1972). Human language. In R. A. Hinde (Ed.), *Non-verbal communication* (pp. 49–85). Cambridge: Cambridge University Press.

Noller, P. (1985). Video primacy—A further look. *Journal of Nonverbal Behavior, 9,* 28–47.

Thorpe, W. H. (1972). The comparison of vocal communication in animals and man. In R. A. Hinde (Ed.), *Non-verbal communication* (pp. 27–47). Cambridge: Cambridge University Press.

PART II

Nonverbal Communication Functions

CHAPTER 6

Identification of Culture, Race, Gender, and Personality

The language of behavior is extraordinarily subtle. Most people are lucky to have one subcultural system under control—the one that reflects their own sex, class, generation, and geographic region within the country. . . . [Nonverbal communication] systems are interwoven with the fabric of the personality and into society itself, even rooted in how one experiences oneself as a man or a woman.

Edward T. Hall (1981, p. 82)

Japanese, Polynesian, Pakistani, Arab, Nigerian, Russian, French, Brazilian, Canadian, black, white, Hispanic, male, female, introvert, extrovert . . . What nonverbal pictures do these labels bring to mind? How would you know a member of one of these groups if you encountered one? Would you expect similar communication behaviors from each of them?

You have probably encountered these questions in communicating with others. Successful communication across cultural, racial, gender, or personality groups hinges on the ability to predict where similarities and differences in communication behavior exist. One way we are able to make such predictions is by noting nonverbal "badges," behaviors that identify members of cultural, racial, gender, or personality groups. Communicators use their nonverbal demeanor to declare who they are or think they are. Receivers rely on the same cues to categorize communicators. While the most apparent of these nonverbal badges are physical appearance differences, many other nonverbal cues also signal such identities.

Communication behaviors are encoded and interpretations of messages are made on the basis of stereotypic classifications of culture, race, gender, and personality. Moreover, these broad sociological characteristics are central to an individual's own sense of self-identity and are key elements in that individual's self-presentation. People think of themselves as introverted or extroverted; as male or female; as black, white, or Oriental; as Indian, German, Chinese, and so on, and they act according to the norms of these groups. It is no wonder, then, that we rely on these behaviors in first attempts to label someone and make predictions about his or her behavior.

Because cues identifying culture, race, gender, and personality are critical to impression formation and can affect many nonverbal functions in intercultural, interracial, and intergender communication, it is essential that we be aware of them. In so doing, we may avoid communication problems and increase communication successes. As Hall (1959), one of the most prolific writers on cross-cultural communication, states:

> I am convinced that much of our difficulty with people in other countries stems from the fact that so little is known about cross-cultural communication. (p. 10)

Throughout the following discussion, several barriers and limitations that have the potential to distort one's understanding of the cues identifying culture, race, gender, and personality (Jensen, 1985) must be kept in mind.

1. **Overgeneralization.** Variations within large groups such as cultures, races, and genders are enormous, and highlighted differences are frequently simplified.

2. **Mythical "average person."** The average person, often referred to in this discussion, is not likely to exist in the exact form described. Rather, this "average person" is an amalgamation of characteristics possessed by individual group members.

3. **Equality of cues.** Not all cues identified occur with equal frequency or effect.

4. **Exaggeration of differences.** Since discussion of similarities is generally omitted, differences identified will seem more frequent than they actually are.

5. **Exaggeration of effects.** In highlighting these differences we risk overstating the likelihood that they will cause communication problems; however, even minor irritants can become major problems.

6. **Distortion of primary causes.** Some of the problems attributed to misunderstanding of these nonverbal cues actually can be attributed to problems in the personalities of the interactants. The "Ugly American" who refuses to learn and use the language and nonverbal behavior of another culture is a good example of such personality problems.

7. **Prejudice.** In viewing these differences, one must keep an open mind, remembering that notions of appropriate and inappropriate behavior are determined by culture, race, and gender.

8. **Viewing culture as static.** Cultural, racial, and gender groups are

constantly changing, albeit slowly; therefore, communication norms and nonverbal badges also change.

Thus what we present in this chapter is, at best, an incomplete atlas of identifiers; however, this sampling should heighten your sensitivity to cultural, racial, gender, and personality group differences in nonverbal communication.

Identifiers of Culture

In his novel about South Africa, *The Covenant,* James Michener (1980) writes about the interaction between Europeans and Africans, often highlighting each culture's misunderstanding and accompanying mistrust of the other by relating mistakes in cross-cultural communication. Describing the first meeting between a European (Adriaan) and a native African (Sotopo), Michener writes:

> Sotopo thrust out his hand to grasp Adriaan by the arm, but the Dutch boy was frightened by the unexpected movement and drew away. By the time he recovered his senses and wanted to accept the farewell touching, Sotopo had stepped back, mortified that his gesture had been rejected. (pp. 334–335)

This exchange exemplifies how misinterpretation of culture-specific nonverbal behaviors can lead to unfavorable outcomes in cross-cultural communication. Cross-cultural communication is more frequent than one might imagine, and this frequency is increasing as distances shrink through advances in aerospace and telecommunications technology. Such cross-cultural interactions can have long-term effects on the relationships between cultures. Thus it becomes important to recognize what behaviors in each nonverbal channel act as cultural identifiers and set cultures apart.

Kinesics

Emblems. As noted in Chapter 2, emblems exist in every culture; however, the form of these emblems varies greatly between cultures (Ekman, 1976). Figure 6.1 shows emblems identified in various cultures for greeting, parting, replying to questions, beckoning to others, and commenting on others.

There are several considerations when using emblems for cultural identification. First, the unique emblems in a given culture make it possible to recognize people from, say, a Mediterranean culture or a Northern European one. At the same time, there is some commonality across cultures: All cultures use gestures for the same functions, but the same meanings may be expressed through different gestural forms. Rubbing noses; pressing lips to hand, cheek, arm, or lips of another; juxtaposing noses and inhaling; and smelling heads all signal affection. Many emblems, though, possess contradictory meaning when displayed cross-culturally. For example, the head throw for "no" displayed by Greeks, Southern Italians, Bulgarians, and

FIGURE 6.1 These 20 common emblems have different meanings in different cultures. How many meanings can you identify for each?

Turks could be mistaken for "yes" in cultures where nodding signifies affirmation. The Bulgarian turn of the head for "yes" is likely to appear to be shaking the head, a sign of negation in many cultures. Beckoning gestures are also a source of misunderstandings. The palm-down fluttering-fingers beckoning gesture observed in Asian and Latin American cultures may be interpreted as "go away" by North Americans. In sum, although emblematic differences allow us to identify cultural group membership, they can also create cross-cultural misunderstandings and unfavorable attributions.

Lest you think these emblematic contradictions are trivial, consider where contradictory meanings led to geopolitical embarrassment (Harrison, 1974). We noted previously the example of Richard Nixon displaying the "A-OK" emblem, which is considered obscene in Latin America, denoting the female genitalia. Nearly 15 years later, when Soviet premier Leonid Brezhnev visited the United States to meet with President Nixon, he exited his plane with his hands clenched over his head. This Russian emblem signifies gracious receipt of a tribute, and Brezhnev was acknowledging the welcoming ceremony he was receiving. But this emblem was inappropriate in the host culture, because in North America this emblem denotes superiority and victory. Needless to say, neither man's emblematic mistake did much to promote international goodwill.

Emblems can vary between groups within a culture. Social and occupational groups develop special emblems to identify group membership (such as a fraternity handshake) and to facilitate accurate task communication (drawing an extended finger across the neck to indicate "stop the program"

Nonverbal behaviors can identify social group membership. Here the chanting, marching style, artifacts, and costumes identify members of the Hare Krishna.

in radio broadcasting). Sometimes emblems originating in social or occupational groups enter into general usage and become identifiers of culture. The "peace" emblem (fist with index and second fingers raised in a V) came into general usage in the United States in the early and mid-1970s. A similar emblem was adopted by the British during World War II, but it had an altogether different meaning: Victory!

Illustrators. Differences in illustrator usage have not been identified as frequently as differences in emblems. There is a stereotype that Italians and Jews use illustrators more frequently and more expansively than Northern Europeans and North Americans. Efron (1972), examining first-generation Italians in the United States, found that they tended to use broad, full-arm gestures. By comparison, he found that first-generation Jews gestured close to the body, and their gestures appeared to trace the flow of their speech. Shuter (1979) found few differences in the frequency of illustrators between Jews and Protestants in the United States beyond the Jews' use of more frontal than peripheral gestures. The lack of differences in this latter study is likely due to adoption of North American norms by American Jews and Protestants. Efron in fact found that cultural differences in illustrator use faded in second-generation Italians and Jews. Thus the stereotype may be valid only in Italy, Israel, and insular Italian and Jewish communities in the United States.

Another illustrator that shows some culture specificity is the facial cutoff gesture used by Japanese women (Ramsey, 1981), particularly those adhering to traditional sex roles (see Figure 6.2), to communicate shy femininity. Less frequent and less varied cutoff gestures have been observed in European, African, South American Indian, and Indonesian flirting behavior (Eibl-Eibesfeldt, 1972). Desmond Morris (1977) has observed Americans and Europeans using cutoff gestures when under stress, to reduce or block reception of environmental stimuli rather than to block transmission of a facial cue.

Finally, Michael and Willis (1969) have identified a German variation of deictic or pointing behavior. Where North Americans generally point with the index finger, Germans were observed to point with the little finger.

Eye Contact. The major distinguishing feature in the cross-cultural use of eye contact is the focus of the listener's eyes. In North America and England, listeners are socialized to gaze in the direction of the speaker's face, particularly the eye region. English listeners gaze more continuously at a speaker, while North American listeners look away more than English listeners (Hall, 1959). By contrast, African listeners are taught to avoid eye contact when listening, especially with a person of higher status (Byers & Byers, 1972).

As for frequency of looking, Watson and Graves (1966) found that Arabs engaged in more eye contact than Americans. Noesjirwan (1978) reported that Indonesians engaged in less direct gaze than Australians in a waiting room.

FIGURE 6.2 Facial cutoff gestures used by Japanese women.

Posture. Cultures may vary in the directness of body orientation that interactants assume. Indonesians have been observed to use less direct body orientations than Australians (Noesjirwan, 1978), and Arabs use more direct body orientations than Americans (Watson & Graves, 1966).

Differences in sitting or resting postures display large cultural variability. Hewes (1957) documented over 1,000 such postures (see Figure 2.1 in Chapter 2). As he points out, many of these postures result from the types of furniture and other environmental features present in a culture. However, Smutkupt and Barna (1976) show that sometimes cultural beliefs dictate posture. Apparently, Thais consider feet to be the lowest, most objectionable part of the body and deem it insulting to have a foot pointed at them. Thus Thai communicators may be embarrassed by an American with crossed legs who points a foot in their direction.

Facial Expressions. Facial expressions possess many universal characteristics (see Chapter 10). Cross-cultural differences do occur, however, because each culture has unique display rules dictating what facial expressions can and cannot be displayed and what object or event triggers an expression (Cuceloglu, 1970; Ekman & Friesen, 1975). For instance, smiling in response to a smile from a stranger is expected in the United States, and failing to respond is interpreted as a lack of social competence. However, in Israel, smiling in response to a smile is not socially prescribed, and omission of the smiling response carries no social sanctions (Alexander & Babad, 1981).

Beyond display rules, some cultures possess facial expressions whose meanings are recognizable only by other members of those cultures. New Guineans encode a blend of a sad brow and angry mouth not recognizable by North Americans. The North American "smug" expression is not universally recognized (LaFrance & Mayo, 1978b). Also, non-British communicators have difficulty recognizing the British wry smile—one corner up (partial smile) and the other corner down (doubt) (Brannigan & Humphries, 1972).

Proxemics and Haptics

A cross-cultural difference that has received extensive attention is the amount of contact (proxemic and haptic) between interactants in various cultures. Hall (1966) argued more than two decades ago that cultures can be distinguished by the distances at which members interact and how frequently members touch. He proposed that some cultures are characterized by tactile and olfactory (smell) modes of communication while others are based on visual communication. The former are labeled *contact* cultures and the latter *noncontact* cultures. In his preliminary analysis, Hall suggested that Latin Americans, French, and Arabs, among others, live in contact cultures while Germans and North Americans live in noncontact cultures (Hall, 1966).

Early studies of proxemic patterns and preferences (e.g., Little, 1968; Watson, 1970; Watson & Graves, 1966) tended to confirm this distinction. So have reports of touch norms. Desmond Morris (1971, 1977), one of the most prodigious observers of nonverbal behavior, states that people of Anglo-Saxon cultures engage in far less frequent contact in daily encounters than do, say, people from Mediterranean and Latin countries and are far less intimate in what public contact does occur. To illustrate, the friendly full embrace between males is far more acceptable among Latin men than among British or American men. Likewise, the arm link between two men is much more common in Latin countries than in non-Latin Western ones. Jourard (1966a) observed the amount of touch people displayed in cafés in four different cultures. Couples in San Juan averaged 180 contacts per hour, those in Paris averaged 110, those in Florida averaged only 2, and those in London made zero contacts. Henley (1973) found similarly low levels of public touch in Maryland.

However, it has become increasingly apparent that the contact/noncontact distinction is too simplistic. Cultures that are geographically contig-

APPLICATIONS

East Meets West

Increasingly, people from the United States and Western Europe are coming into contact with countries along the Pacific Rim, most prominently Japan. If you are faced with this prospect, you need to be prepared for important differences in communication style. One is the use of emblems. Bowing is prevalent in Japanese society and carries different meaning depending on its initiation, depth, and duration. The significance of this emblem is often lost on Westerners. The emblem for beckoning others also differs from Western usage. In Japan and other Asian countries, the palm up, backward hand scoop gesture, common in the West, is restricted to children and is considered insulting to adults. Instead, one should beckon an adult by holding the palm down and fluttering the fingers. Also, in Japan, extending the little finger upward indicates a female, and extending the thumb upward indicates a male. Finally, if you want to invite your Japanese friends for a drink, mime drinking from a small sake cup with the index finger and thumb extended. In general, however, Japanese communicators use fewer gestures overall and consider extremely frequent gesturing childish (Ramsey, 1983).

The cutoff gesture, beyond communicating self-consciousness, shyness, coyness, and cautiousness, can be used as an impression management device to hide negative facial expressions (Morsbach, 1973; Ramsey, 1981). Japanese are taught to mask negative facial expressions with smiles and laughter and to display less facial affect overall, leading some Westerners to consider the Japanese inscrutable (Friesen, 1972; Morsbach, 1973; Ramsey, 1983). The masking of facial expressions in Japanese culture appears contrary to the high premium that culture seems to place on nonverbal communication over verbal communication. Morsbach (1973) traces this restraint back to the Tokugawa Period (1603–1867) when the Samurai ruling class was very influential. During this period, inappropriate behavior that offended an authority figure could result in immediate execution. Further, Zen Buddhist teaching supposedly placed a high value on the unspoken portion of interpersonal communication, favoring a high sensitivity to nonverbal communication (Ishii, 1973; Kunihiro, 1976; Ramsey & Birk, 1983). However, this historical view has recently come under fire. Miller (1982) asserts that this "antimyth of silence" was propagated by the ruling class in pre–World War II Japan to inhibit the common Japanese from questioning ruling-class decisions. Regardless of how and when these norms developed, the Japanese appear to be one of the least expressive cultural groups.

A potential communication problem in East-West interactions

East Meets West (*Continued*)

is the normal eye contact of Japanese communicators. They are taught to avoid eye contact when listening by focusing on the speaker's neck (Bond & Komai, 1976; Byers & Byers, 1972; Morsbach, 1973). This is contrary to Western cultures, where listeners are trained to look directly at the speaker's eyes. Thus Westerners may consider Japanese listeners less attentive, and the Japanese may consider Westerners rude. The Japanese commonly indicate attention by the word *hai,* which literally means "yes." *Hai* in this context, though, does not mean the Japanese listener is agreeing with you but simply that he or she is attending to your statements (much like the American *uh-huh*). One American mistook this behavior for agreement to deliver services, only to find out later that the Japanese listener actually disagreed with the American's requests (Morsbach, 1973).

Japanese communicators use the same distances as Americans when interacting with authority figures like parents and teachers (Engebretson & Fullman, 1972). In general, their public pattern is one of noncontact. They maximize distance by adopting larger conversational distances, touching less, and scrupulously avoid public displays of affection (Cathcart & Cathcart, 1976; Elzinga, 1975; Engebretson & Fullman, 1972; Morsbach, 1973; Ramsey, 1983; Sussman & Rosenfeld, 1982). However, in private, with family members and close friends, Japanese communicators adopt much closer distances. Japanese families often sleep in the same room under a large quilt with their feet touching for warmth. Japanese are also more tactile with their children, holding them more frequently than North American infants when they cry, and children frequently sleep with parents until puberty. These sleeping arrangements are not simply due to lack of space; rather it seems that contact norms for babies, infants, and children, even in public, are much less restrictive than those for adults in Japanese society. Further, in their homes and gardens, the Japanese exploit space by filling it to capacity or creating the illusion of spaciousness in small areas (Condon & Kurata, 1974; Engebretson & Fullman, 1972; Morsbach, 1973; Ramsey, 1983). Hall notes:

> The Japanese are pulled in two directions. . . . There is a deep need to be close, and it is only when they are close that they are comfortable. The other pole is as far away as one can get. In public and during ceremonial occasions. . . . there is great emphasis on self-control, distance, and hiding inner feelings. (Blonston, 1985, p. 80)

Status affects posture. Whereas high status communicators are generally relaxed in North America, in Japan they assume stiff, erect postures with feet firmly planted on the floor (Taylor,

East Meets West (*Continued*)

1974). The bowing ritual in Japan is also marked by status differences. Higher status communicators decide when the bowing ritual is terminated, and lower status communicators bow deeper (Morsbach, 1973).

One of the trademarks of Japanese culture is the great importance it places on dress and adornments, especially as cues of social rank (Morsbach, 1973; Ramsey, 1983). Japanese frequently wear badges, costumes, and uniforms characteristic of their place of employment, sports group, city, or other group. In the West, Japanese tourists are frequently stereotyped as wearing the same clothes, carrying expensive cameras, and traveling in large groups. These nonverbal group membership cues, which many Westerners find odd and humorous, are very common in Japan. In fact, sunglass manufacturers encountered problems marketing their products in Japan in the early 1970s. Most Japanese would not buy sunglasses because they were considered a physical appearance badge worn only by hoodlums and gangsters (Morsbach, 1973).

Finally, the home environment in Japan is structured differently from Western homes. Unlike homes in the West, Japanese place furniture in the middle of rooms that have semifixed walls, and many different activities are performed in a single room.

This brief discussion is intended to sensitize you to communication differences you may encounter when you interact with a Japanese communicator. In turn, you should be able to identify quickly which nonverbal communication patterns would present difficulties for a Japanese visiting the West.

---

uous and similar in values may develop different norms. A study of Central and South American cultures (Shuter, 1976), which have often been grouped together as "Latino," reveal that they differ in the amount of touch that occurs and the distances typically adopted for conversation. Costa Ricans adopt closer distances and engage in more touch than Panamanians and Colombians. In Western Europe, too, differences appear: French men kiss each other on the cheek in greeting; British men rarely do (Morris, 1971).

Cultures may be high contact for certain behaviors or certain contexts and noncontact for others. A number of cultures also display gender differences in the spacing and touching. In a comparison of Italian, German, and American adult speakers, Shuter (1977) reported that the Italian culture is characterized by tactile males and nontactile females, while German and American cultures contain tactile females and nontactile males.

Observed similarities may also mask real differences due to context, status, and degree of acquaintance. For example, a laboratory setting may minimize actual differences between people of different cultures. Although all cultures generally adopt closer distances as familiarity increases, absolute preferred distances for interactions with friends, acquaintances, and family members may differ markedly across cultures (see LaFrance & Mayo, 1978a, for a summary of such mitigating factors).

The relationship among the various behaviors comprising the immediacy complex also may differ between cultures. A study of proxemic patterns of Indonesians and Australians (two supposedly noncontact cultures) showed that Indonesians adopted closer distances, touched more, and smiled more than Australians but were less direct in orientation and gaze (Noesjirwan, 1978). Cultures may need to be classified in terms of both degree of affiliativeness in interaction (as seen through closeness, touching, and smiling) and degree of dominance (as seen through gaze and body orientation). This would make the Indonesians more affiliative and deferent than the Australians. Alternatively, cultures may simply differ on which of the immediacy cues they prefer to express in high degrees and may compensate with other, less immediate cues to achieve a comfortable level of conversational involvement.

Finally, the language interactants speak may be associated with space and touch norms. Researchers have noted similarities in proxemic and haptic behavior among groups speaking the same language. Prosser (1978) has suggested that cultures that employ Anglo-Saxon-derived languages are noncontact, and Montagu (1971) considers cultures employing Latin-derived languages or Russian as contact cultures. Also, Montagu suggests that nonliterate cultures are more contact-prone, consistent with Hall's (1966) suggestion that contact cultures rely less on visual and more on tactile and olfactory communication.

In a direct examination of this association, Sussman and Rosenfeld (1982) compared Japanese, American, and Venezuelan communicators. Japanese adopted the largest interaction distances, Americans adopted intermediate distances, and Venezuelans adopted the closest distances when each group was speaking their native language. However, when Japanese and Venezuelan communicators spoke English, they adopted distances similar to those of Americans! Japanese decreased their interaction distances and Venezuelans increased their distances. These findings, though, do not indicate that language use causes contact norms. It may be that the association between language and contact norms is a result of common cultural backgrounds of people in a given language community. People learning a language also may learn some of the cultural norms; when they switch languages, the new language may cue the new norms.

The adaptation of conversational distance to the language suggests that language and nonverbal behaviors are inextricably interwoven into a conversational style associated with each culture. This reinforces the argument that the relationship among immediacy behaviors is more complex than previously thought and that the contact/noncontact designation may no longer be appropriate. It may also explain some otherwise contrary findings (e.g., Forston & Larson, 1968, failed to find differences between North American and Latin American students).

Nevertheless, some broad trends can be detected. North Americans generally use large interaction distances. Watson and Graves (1966) compared American and Arab students on sitting distance. They found that Americans preferred farther distances than Arabs. In addition, North Americans adopt greater distances than Venezuelans (Sussman & Rosenfeld, 1982), Latin Americans (Hall & Whyte, 1966; LaFrance & Mayo, 1978a), Italians (Shuter, 1977), members of Mediterranean cultures (Little, 1968), and Pakistanis (Sommer, 1968).

Many Northern European cultures are characterized by interaction distances similar to those in North America. Research by Sommer (1968) found that American, English, and Swedish communicators use essentially the same interaction distances. Little (1968) also reported similar distances for North Americans and Northern Europeans. Some cultures, such as Germans and Danes, prefer even larger interaction distances than Americans (Hall, 1966; Sommer, 1968).

Consistent with proxemic norms, Americans, Britons, and Australians are less tactile than people in many other cultures. Arabs, Middle Easterners (Watson & Graves, 1966), Latin Americans, Russians (Montagu, 1971), Italians (Shuter, 1977), and Indonesians (Noesjirwan, 1978) live in highly tactile cultures. Japanese (Barnlund, 1975; Elzinga, 1975; Morsbach, 1973; Ramsey, 1983) and other Asians (Sechrest, 1969) tend to be less prone to contact in public.

Space and touch norms appear to be learned at very young ages. Culture-specific patterns of proxemic and haptic behavior appear between parents and children. For example, upper-class Britons engage in almost no contact with their children, employing governesses and sending children to boarding schools as soon as they are old enough (Montagu, 1971). Contact between parents and children in North America is also restricted compared to other cultures, though there is a very strong sex difference. Male children are touched less by parents than female children (Jourard, 1966a). Interestingly, Arab parents touch male children more than female children (Lomranz & Shapira, 1974).

Vocalics

Although researchers have paid less attention to documenting cross-cultural differences in the vocalic channel, a few interesting differences have been reported. Loudness shows the most cultural dissimilarity. Arab cultures are characterized by loud speech. For Arabs, loudness connotes strength and sincerity while softness communicates weakness and deviousness (Hall & Whyte, 1966; Watson & Graves, 1966). By contrast, Britons and other Europeans use softer volumes relative to Americans (Hall, 1966). It is not unreasonable to speculate that Americans are likely to be seen as brash by Britons and Europeans, and Arabs are considered pushy and rude by non-Arabs.

Vocalic backchanneling also displays cultural differences. British listeners may use less vocal backchanneling than Americans, substituting eye blinks (Hall, 1959).

Culture can also be readily identified by dress and adornment features.

Chronemics

Cultures possess characteristic tempos that reflect the dominant time orientation (Bruneau, 1979). One of the most prominent differences is the extent to which a culture is clock-bound in its perception of time. North American culture and Northern and Western European cultures are clock-bound cultures. Time is based on an arbitrary, objective system (a mechanical clock). Members of these cultures have a linear perspective on time, one event following another in an orderly progression. Not surprisingly, these cultures are distinguished by a monochronic use of time (see Chapter 4).

Asian, African, and Latin American cultures are non-clock-bound cultures. Time is based on subjective, personal, and often natural time systems (daylight cycle, seasons, etc.). Members of these cultures view time holistically, employing a point perspective on time. Events occur in a less orderly fashion than in the clock-bound cultures. The present may or may not have a relationship with the past or the future. Polychronic time usage is the norm. It is quite common to schedule many events at the same time, a practice that clock-bound people find exasperating. In non-clock-bound cultures, emphasis is placed on activities, not time units (Hall, 1981; Morsbach, 1973).

Sensitivity to Cultural Identifiers

It should be apparent by now that cultures have distinct ways of using nonverbal communication and that failure to be sensitive to these differences can cause communication problems. However, simple exposure to another culture does not seem to guarantee more accurate nonverbal communication (Michael & Willis, 1969); rather, training in culture-specific cues is necessary. Collett (1971) trained British communicators to behave nonverbally like Arab communicators. Arab communicators evaluated the trained British communicators more favorably than untrained British communicators. Thus display of and sensitivity to culture-specific nonverbal communication can go a long way in achieving high quality cross-cultural relationships.

Identifiers of Race and Ethnicity

Cultures are far from homogeneous. Groups within cultures, known as subcultures, often display nonverbal cues in unique ways. As with culture, differences in nonverbal behavior can and often are used to distinguish members of one subculture from another. Although most cultures possess more than one subculture, the number varies considerably. Due in large part to colonization and mass immigrations, cultures in the Western Hemisphere contain many subcultures. A few cultures (Japan is a good example) remain very homogeneous, having had few immigrants over the centuries (Morsbach, 1973).

Much of the research on subcultural differences in nonverbal communication, especially in the United States, focuses on normative differences among blacks (usually urban black groups), whites, and Hispanics, because these are the predominant racial and ethnic groups. Most research centers on black-white comparisons. The limitations listed at the beginning of this chapter are especially applicable to this research.

Kinesics

Eye Contact. Children in the various racial subcultures learn different norms for appropriate eye behavior with adults in authority. Black and

Puerto Rican children are taught to look down out of respect when interacting with an adult superior, while white children are taught to engage in eye contact with a superior. Byers and Byers (1972) relate many problems encountered by white teachers who expect black and Puerto Rican students to look at them during conversations. This pattern of eye behavior among blacks may be a carryover from eye contact norms in Africa, where it is not permissible for a child to look an adult in the eye. This caused problems for at least one Peace Corp teacher in an African town. The teacher required her students to look her in the eyes when she reprimanded them. This was such a violation of social norms that the elders of the tribe had the teacher sent elsewhere. (Also see Applications, p. 201.)

Posture. A small amount of research indicates that racial subcultures use different postures. Jones (1971) found that black and Chinese males adopted more indirect body orientations when interacting with other males of their racial subgroups. However, in a second study, Jones found no difference in body orientations.

K. R. Johnson (1972) described two postures characteristic of black males: the *pimp strut* and the *rapping stance.* The pimp strut is a walking posture used to gain attention. It is generally a slow, casual, rhythmic stroll. The head is often slightly elevated and tilted slightly to the side. One arm is stationary, while the other arm swings at the side with the hand slightly cupped. An example of this can be found in the movie *Stir Crazy* when Richard Pryor attempts to disguise Gene Wilder as a black man. After having Wilder apply dark brown facial makeup, Pryor teaches him an exaggerated version of this pimp strut. The rapping stance is used by black males as a masculinity display when interacting with a black female. The male adopts an indirect body orientation, with his head tilted toward the female, eyes partially closed, one hand limp at the side, and the other hand in the front pocket.

Johnson also identified a posture used by black females when communicating hostility. This posture is performed by placing the hands on the hips with the weight on the heels and the buttocks extended.

Proxemics

Proxemic norms of ethnic subcultures have been examined, with mixed results. Some studies suggest that blacks prefer closer interaction distances than whites (Aiello & Jones, 1971; Bauer, 1973; Hall, 1966; Jones & Aiello, 1973). Others have found that blacks use greater distances than whites (Baxter, 1970; Willis, 1966). One researcher found no ethnic differences when comparing blacks, Puerto Ricans, and Italians (Jones, 1971). Research on Hispanic communicators is also mixed. Baxter (1970) reported that Hispanic communicators used less distance than blacks but the same distance as whites. Aiello and Jones (1971) found that blacks and Hispanics adopted the same distances, both closer than whites.

For distancing norms, the socioeconomic status of the interactants is probably more important than race. Two studies (Aiello & Jones, 1971;

APPLICATIONS

Eyeing Race Relations

Eye behavior during conversations shows distinct differences between white and black communicators. When speaking, whites look away from listeners continuously and look at listeners only intermittently, particularly at "listener response-relevant moments" (LRRMs—points in a conversation where the speaker expects a response from the listener and nonverbally signals this expectation to the listener). White listeners are expected to look at the speaker continuously, and looking away is interpreted as a sign of inattention (Erickson, 1979; Fugita, Wexley, & Hillery, 1974; Hall, 1974; Kendon, 1967; LaFrance & Mayo, 1976). Among blacks, conversely, speakers maintain constant gaze, while listeners are expected to look at the speaker only intermittently. Black listeners frequently use speaker-directed gaze as a "listener response" (LR) to LRRM cues from speakers.

You may think these differences are trivial, but they can create profound problems when whites and blacks interact (Erickson, 1979). Whites often consider black listeners to be inattentive and uninterested in the conversation, since whites expect constant eye contact from black listeners but receive intermittent eye contact instead. White speakers also fail to see LRs by blacks listeners. Blacks use nods *or* vocal backchanneling *or* eye contact as LRs; white listeners give a combination of head nods *and* vocal backchannels *and* eye contact. Thus black LRs are often insufficient for white speakers, causing white speakers to repeat their previous statements. Black listeners may believe that these repetitions signal that white speakers consider them incompetent or stupid. Blacks also often perceive white interactants to be hostile or overbearing, since whites engage in continuous eye contact when listening, less eye contact when speaking, and multicue LRs.

Thus a subtle difference in eye contact norms can have dramatic and undesirable effects on interracial interactions. Smoother race relations may ensue when whites and blacks become more cognizant of this and other nonverbal differences and strive to modify their behaviors when interacting with one another.

Scherer, 1974) found that middle-class interactants preferred farther distances than lower-class interactants. Also, gender mediates distancing norms within ethnic groups. For example, when black and white males and females are compared, black males require the greatest distance during an interview, while black females require the least, with white males and females adopting intermediate distances. Black females also exhibit more synchronous leaning than black males or white females (Smith, 1983). Finally, it is possible that blacks use distance more fluidly than other subgroups, moving in and out of proximity as the conversation unfolds. If so, results that attempt to state a stable interaction distance for blacks can be highly misleading.

Haptics

Research comparing haptic behavior of black and white interactants is more consistent. Blacks engage in more touching than whites (Smith, Willis, & Gier, 1980; Willis, Reeves, & Buchanan, 1976). Also, touching among white children appears to decline significantly from kindergarten to sixth grade, but touching among black children does not decrease during this same time span (Willis & Hoffman, 1975).

A tentative conclusion is that the black subculture may be more contact-oriented than the white subculture, particularly when one considers haptic behavior. However, the mixed results of research on proxemic behavior and the possible influence of socioeconomic status (yet to be applied to haptic research) may temper this conclusion. The research is presently insufficient to form any strong conclusions about space and tactile norms in other racial subcultures.

Vocalics

Vocalic differences between racial subcultures, though not as pronounced as gaze and other kinesic differences, do exist and can cause difficulties in interracial interactions. In Chapter 2, it was noted that subcultural dialects, such as Mexican-American and Black English, are less preferred and less prestigious than the "received" General American dialect. Ethnic group membership is often identified by the vocalic pattern associated with each dialect. Further, people have learned to manipulate vocalic differences either to accentuate or minimize ethnic group membership.

Specifically, French and von Raffler–Engel (1973) showed that white and black children are taught to pause at different points in verbal conversation. White children pause at the beginning of clauses or before conjunctions, while black children pause whenever a significant change in pitch occurs. Sometimes these pauses by black children are within clauses, causing white children to perceive black children's speech as less grammatical than the speech of other white children.

Erickson (1979) has identified racial differences in nonverbal cues that white and black speakers use to mark LRRMs. White speakers typically mark LRRMs by simple junctures or pauses. Black speakers mark such LRRMs by sharply falling intonation. These differences are likely to be confusing in interracial interactions, producing inappropriate or nonexistent LRs.

Finally, Gallois and Markel (1975) found that Hispanic interactants use longer switch pauses (silences between one person's turn and another's turn) than white interactants.

On the surface, these differences appear likely to cause communication problems, but members of nondominant racial subcultures (blacks and Hispanics in the United States) display a learned ability to code switch. That is, black and Hispanic communicators frequently adopt white communication behaviors when interacting with whites, thereby avoiding many potential problems (Erickson, 1979; Gallois & Markel, 1975; Wylie & Stafford, 1977). Such code switching does not occur as frequently among white interactants.

Physical Appearance

The most prominent physical appearance identifier of race is physiognomy (see Chapter 2) and its accompanying skin color differences. Beyond this, there are differences in dress and adornment styles, though these are likely to be influenced by other factors such as urban versus rural locale, socioeconomic status, and gender.

Sensitivity to Identifiers of Race

Garratt, Baxter, and Rozelle (1981) have shown that as with culture cues, it is possible to train members of one subculture to encode cues indicative of another racial subculture with positive results. They trained white policemen to use nonverbal behavior typical of black interactants (larger distances, less direct body orientation, and less eye contact when speaking) during interviews with black subjects. The black interviewees rated the trained white policemen more favorably on personal, social, and professional competence than untrained white policemen.

Identifiers of Gender

You may think that differences between men and women are so obvious that discussion of these differences is unnecessary. After all, there are genetic, as well as physical, differences in the human body. Birdwhistell (1970) has labeled the former primary gender differences and the latter secondary gender differences. However, as he points out, there are also many tertiary, or behavioral, gender differences in the way nonverbal communication is performed by men and women that are not the result of chromosomal or anatomical differences and that help us identify gender group membership.

One origin of communication differences between men and women is the sex-role expectations taught by our society (LaFrance & Mayo, 1979). Some scholars argue that women are trained to be affiliative and reactive (being sensitive to and adjusting to behaviors of others), while men are taught to be dominant and proactive (controlling and creating their own and others' behavior). These socialized feminine and masculine sex roles are manifested in the communicative behaviors of men and women. Women are passive, submissive, expressive, and accommodating communicators. Men are active, controlling, and less expressive communicators (LaFrance & Mayo, 1978b, 1979; Mulac, Studley, Wiemann, & Bradac, 1987; Weitz, 1976).

While this proactive/reactive classification is convenient, it oversimpli-

How many physical appearance cues can you identify that distinguish the man from the woman?

fies gender differences. One must keep in mind that (a) gender differences are most apparent in children and young adults (older adults display fewer differences); (b) context frequently overrides gender differences; (c) gender differences vary by culture and subculture; and (d) people differ in their degree of sex-role acceptance (Epstein, 1986; LaFrance & Mayo, 1979).

These last two qualifications deserve additional comment. Variance of gender-related communication norms between cultures and subcultures is very common. In some groups, adherence to very traditional feminine and masculine roles is dictated. Other groups are less strict in their expectations, allowing women to display masculine traits and men to display feminine traits. Further, sex-role expectations are constantly in flux. The North American culture, where much of the research reported in this section was conducted, has experienced significant changes in sex-role expectations in the past 20 years. It has become more acceptable for women to assume roles previously reserved for men (especially in the business environment) and for men to assume roles previously reserved for women (especially in the home environment). This adaptation has led to increased androgyny (Bem, 1974), the display of both feminine and masculine traits. Thus one must be careful not to pigeonhole another person solely on overt biological sex differences. A competent communicator, instead, bases notions of sex-role acceptance on the behaviors and opinions expressed by the interactant.

Kinesics

Emblems. Limited evidence suggests that social norms may permit more frequent emblem usage by women, and women have been observed to use more emblems than men. Baglan and Nelson (1982) found that both men and women thought it was more appropriate for women to use beckoning gestures than men. Poling (1978) observed that women use more emblems of all kinds than men. This is especially true for physically attractive women, suggesting a norm for usage by this group. Contrary to the proactive/reactive explanation, emblem usage is greater for dominant rather than submissive women communicators, especially in cross-sex interactions.

Illustrators. Research on gender differences in illustrator usage is mixed. Ickes and Barnes (1977) and Rosenfeld (1966a) found women use more illustrators overall than men, but Duncan and Fiske (1977) and Kennedy and Camden (1983) observed no differences in illustrator usage by women and men. It may be that differences exist in the types of gestures used rather than overall frequency. One study found that women use more palms-up gestures and men use more pointing gestures. Palms-up gestures frequently accompany the shrug emblem (Friesen, Ekman, & Wallbott, 1979), signifying uncertainty or hesitancy. Pointing gestures, conversely, can be interpreted as more dominant gestures. Thus these findings may support the proactive/reactive explanation of gender differences.

Adaptors. One study found that women use more adaptor behavior than men (Peterson, 1976); however, this difference may be a matter of type, not frequency. Kennedy and Camden (1983) found no differences in overall frequency of adaptor usage. Women, though, used more self-adaptors and men used more object-adaptors.

Eye Contact. Female dyads engage in more eye contact than male dyads (Dabbs, Evans, Hopper, & Purvis, 1980; Exline, 1963; Exline, Gray, & Schuette, 1965; Libby, 1970; Mulac et al., 1987). The greater amount of gaze occurs while speaking, while listening, and during silence (see Table 6.1). This is consistent with the finding that women are more sensitive

TABLE 6.1 Time Engaged in Eye Contact (%)

	Mutual	Listening	Speaking	Total
Males	3.0	29.8	25.6	23.2
Females	7.5	42.4	36.9	37.3

Source: From "Explorations in the Process of Person Perception: Visual Interaction in Relation to Competition, Sex, and Need for Affiliation," by R. Exline, 1963, *Journal of Personality and Social Psychology, 31,* p. 11.

communicators (Rosenthal, Hall, DiMatteo, Rogers, & Archer, 1979). Increased visual surveillance is likely to improve sensitivity to nonverbal cues. Mulac et al. (1987) speculate that there may be less mutual awareness in dyads that include a male because of more one-sided gazing in these dyads. Further, there may be a norm or expectation in the North American culture that women engage in more eye contact during conversations than men. Kennedy and Camden (1983) found that women who did not engage in eye contact were more likely to be interrupted by men in small group interactions. They surmised that the lack of eye contact by a woman is considered a cue of inattention or disinterest, making her more vulnerable to an interruptive attempt. This same interpretation did not occur when men failed to engage in eye contact.

Posture. Mehrabian (1981), in his early analysis of posture, observed that men assumed more potent, more dominant, less affiliative, and less intimate postures than women. In other studies, men have been observed to use less direct body orientations and more backward lean than females in interpersonal conversations (Jones, 1971; Mehrabian & Friar, 1969; Shuter, 1976, 1977). Further, it may be more appropriate for men to lean backward and to display more postural relaxation than women (Baglan & Nelson, 1982). By contrast, in small group interactions, men were observed to lean forward while women leaned backward. Backward lean by women may indicate less involvement and lead to more interruptions of women by men (Kennedy & Camden, 1983). Another study found that men tilt their heads forward, while women cock their heads to the side (Kendon & Ferber, 1973).

Facial Expressions. A prevalent sex-role stereotype is that women are more expressive communicators than men. This stereotype is, in general, upheld by research on facial expressions. Women are more expressive facially than men (Eakins & Eakins, 1978; LaFrance & Mayo, 1979) and display warmer cues than men (Weitz, 1976). Women appear to be better encoders than men (Buck, Miller, & Caul, 1974); however, this varies on the type of emotion expressed. In a study by Zaidel and Mehrabian (1969), women were more accurate senders of negative emotions and men were more accurate senders of positive emotions. Androgynous males (those possessing a mix of masculine and feminine traits) may also be better senders than traditionally masculine males (Weitz, 1976).

One explanation for why encoding ability varies by the type of emotion is that the baseline or at-rest facial expressions are different for women and men. That is, women generally display a positive baseline facial expression; therefore, negative emotions are more distinctly displayed by women. Conversely, men generally display a neutral or negative facial expression. Thus positive facial expressions become more noticeable.

Consistent with this speculation is the general finding that women smile more than men, regardless of the emotion they feel at the moment (Eakins & Eakins, 1978; Henley, 1977; Kennedy & Camden, 1983; LaFrance & Mayo, 1979; Mackey, 1976; Rosenfeld, 1966a). In some of these same studies, women encoded more positive head nodding than men. Moreover, communicators seem to expect women to smile more frequently than men.

Haviland (1977) showed a group of people pictures of infants and asked them to identify the sex of the infant. Infants with positive facial expressions were more likely to be judged females, and those with negative facial expressions were more likely to be judged males.

For a woman, smiling is an interactional phenomenon, whereas for a man, it is an emotional expression (LaFrance & Mayo, 1979). Communicators seem to recognize this distinction. Bugental et al. (1971) found that children attributed greater friendliness to their fathers who smiled than to their mothers who smiled. Another study found that women, who smiled more than men even when alone, increased their rate of smiling when paired with another woman more than did men who were paired with men. Women were also more likely than men to respond to a smile of greeting with a smile of their own. Beekman (1975) found that a woman's smile was associated with her feelings of social anxiety, discomfort, deference, and abasement whereas a man's smile was correlated with his desire to be affiliative and sociable. It appears, then, that women are socialized to use the smile as an interactional tool in this society. Men, by contrast, are taught to reserve it for times when they feel genuinely happy or friendly.

Proxemics

In interpersonal and small group interactions, women use less space than men (Evans & Howard, 1973). Females use closer distances than males (Aiello & Jones, 1971). Female dyads sit closer than male dyads (Aiello & Aiello, 1974; Baxter, 1970; Evans & Howard, 1973; Giesen & McClaren, 1976; Mehrabian & Diamond, 1971; Patterson & Schaeffer, 1977; Pellegrini & Empey, 1970; Shuter, 1976, 1977; Sussman & Rosenfeld, 1982), and women are approached by other communicators more closely than men. Women also adopt postures that take up less space than men (Mehrabian, 1981); they are even less likely than men to use the armrests in airplane seating (Hai, Khairullah, & Coulmas, 1982). Women allow others to approach them more closely than men (Hartnett, Bailey, & Gibson, 1970; Willis, 1966), though women tolerate side approaches better, whereas men tolerate frontal approaches better. Women are more cooperative and less aggressive than men under conditions of high density (Freedman, Levy, Buchanan, & Price, 1972). In addition, women seem to have less control over space. They are more likely to yield space to men when passing on a sidewalk (Silveira, 1972), and female territorial markers are more likely to be violated than male markers (Shafer & Sadowski, 1975).

Space usage in cross-sex interactions is more mixed. In general, male-female interactions are characterized by closer distances than male-male interactions. Frequently this distance is even smaller than that assumed by female-female dyads (Baxter, 1970; Evans & Howard, 1973; Patterson & Schaeffer, 1977; Shuter, 1976, 1977).

Haptics

Women give and receive more touch than men (Elzinga, 1975; Fisher, Rytting, & Heslin, 1976; Henley, 1973; Jones, 1984; Jourard, 1966a; Major, 1981; Rosenfeld, Kartus, & Ray, 1976). Moreover, female dyads are characterized by more touching than male dyads or cross-sex dyads (Andersen & Leibowitz, 1978; Shuter, 1976; Stier & Hall, 1984; Willis & Hoffman, 1975). In cross-sex dyads, women are touched more by men than men are touched by women (Jourard, 1966a; Rosenfeld et al., 1976).

Unfortunately, the procedure used by Jourard and many people who have since tried to replicate his work was faulty, which makes his findings somewhat suspect. Jourard asked his respondents simply to record in which of 14 body regions they had been touched by their mother, father, best same-sex friend, and best opposite-sex friend in the preceding 12 months. His division of the body into regions, much like a butcher's chart, appears in Figure 6.3. He did not ask people how often they touched or were touched in each region. Nor did he distinguish between intentional and accidental touches. In an attempt to test the validity of Jourard's procedure, Jones (1985) replicated Jourard's study, with three important modifications. Some of his subjects completed the original Jourard Body Accessibility Questionnaire. Others completed an altered version in which they reported what body parts ordinarily would be touched on 1 or 2 typical days with the target person (rather than over an entire year). Two weeks after completing the questionnaire, the student subjects were trained to observe and log actual touch behaviors with the same four target people. They kept logs of actual initiated and received touches over 3 full days. Finally, 2 weeks after completing the logs, the "typical day" subjects were asked to recall what body parts had been touched during the log period. Results from the initial questionnaire

FIGURE 6.3 Front and rear body segments as identified in Jourard's body accessibility research.

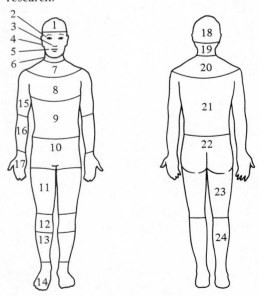

showed that those reporting on a 12-month period claimed far more body parts being touched than those reporting on a 2-day period, and the 12-month figures had less correspondence to the actual logs than the 2-day figures did. Thus reports over a long time span may inflate the estimates of amount of contact. More important, the original 2-day questionnaire and the postlog recall questionnaire were highly correlated with one another but not with the actual log data. What this means is that the questionnaires tend to reflect people's expectations and stereotypical views of touch rather than their actual touch behavior. This makes any recall data, especially that covering long time periods, suspect. It may explain why so many studies have produced conflicting results on whether males or females touch more and who initiates and reciprocates touch.

Henley (1977) hypothesized that men initiate more touch than women as part of a general pattern of dominant behavior by males and submissive behavior by females, but more recent research (e.g., Jones, 1984; Stier & Hall, 1984) finds women equaling or exceeding men in their initiation of touch. Women also more often reciprocate others' touch and have their own touch reciprocated than men do (Major & Williams, 1980). The results of one observational study of 799 instances of intentional touch (Major & Williams, 1980), shown in Table 6.2, are illustrative.

Jones (1984) proposes that the greater total amount of touch and reciprocation of touch for women occurs because touch is a feminine-appropriate role behavior and a masculine-inappropriate one. Thus girls and women are encouraged to touch and be touched as part of their feminine, nurturing role, and males are discouraged from touching because touch becomes synonymous with feminine rather than masculine behavior. As further evidence of this, he reports that males who are verbally aggressive are least likely to initiate touch. Major (1981) similarly contends that women are expected to be more passive, affiliative, and emotional than men and that the patterns of touch between men and women reflect these stereotypes.

These gender-specific space and touch differences are believed to originate in mother-child interactions (Frank, 1957). Mothers have been observed to touch female infants more than male infants (Goldberg & Lewis, 1969), and female children seek and offer more nonaggressive touch than male children (Whiting & Edwards, 1973). It seems that women are taught

TABLE 6.2 Responses to Intentional Touch (%)

	Reciprocated	Unreciprocated	Total
Male to female	21	15	36
Male to male	6	9	15
Female to male	14	13	27
Female to female	11	11	22

Source: Adapted from *Frequency of Touch by Sex and Race* by B. Major and L. Williams, 1980 (unpublished manuscript). In *Gender and Nonverbal Behavior* (p. 20) by C. Mayo and N. M. Henley, Eds., 1981, New York: Springer-Verlag.

to have a different attitude toward touch than men (Heslin, 1978; Major & Heslin, 1982; Stier & Hall, 1984). In a study by Fisher et al. (1976), women reacted positively to touch, while men reacted ambivalently. Similarly, Whitcher and Fisher (1979) found that touch by nurses in a therapeutic setting resulted in positive evaluations and increased reciprocal touching by female patients. Male patients, however, gave more negative evaluations of touching nurses and were less likely to reciprocate the nurses' touch.

Vocalics

The most obvious gender difference in vocalic behavior is in fundamental frequency or pitch. Adult males have a lower pitch than adult females. This is due in part to men having larger larynxes and longer, thicker vocal cords as a result of physiological changes at puberty (LaFrance & Mayo, 1978b, 1979; Sachs, Lieberman, & Erickson, 1973; Schwartz & Rine, 1968). Men also have lower resonances due to larger supralaryngeal vocal tracts.

There is some evidence, though, that gender-linked pitch differences are not entirely due to physiological differences. Boys and girls are socialized into different speaking styles at a very early age (Siegman, 1978). Sachs et al. (1974) found that boys and girls who had not yet reached puberty could be distinguished by voice alone. They offered as a further explanation that girls, and subsequently women, smile more than boys and men. Smiling changes the vocal cords by shortening them, thereby increasing overall pitch (Mattingly, 1966; McConnell-Ginet, 1974; Meditch, 1975).

Women also seem to encode vocalic patterns containing a more varied range of tone changes than men (Brend, 1975; McConnell-Ginet, 1974). One pattern is the "high-low down-glide" frequently used to indicate surprise ("Oh, how awful!"). Another is a "request confirmation pattern" ("You do?"). Still others are a "hesitation pattern" ("Well, I studied . . .") and a "polite cheerful pattern" ("Are you coming?"). Finally, women often answer questions with declarative statements that end in rising pitch, an intonation pattern characteristic of a question. This can make women appear uncertain or hesitant when making statements (Lakoff, 1973).

From these differences, it is apparent that women's vocalic patterns are not due just to physical differences in their vocal tract. Rather, social norms prescribe different vocalic patterns for men and women, and children learn to encode these patterns at a very early age (LaFrance & Mayo, 1979).

When it comes to overall time talking, it is quite clear that men talk and women listen (LaFrance & Mayo, 1979), contrary to the stereotype of the "chatty" female. Studies on mixed-sex dyads consistently find that men dominate the talking time (Argyle, Lalljee, & Cook, 1968; Hilpert, Kramer, & Clark, 1975; Soskin & John, 1963; Strodtbeck, 1951; Strodtbeck & Mann, 1956). Further, men seem to talk with greater intensity than women (Markel, Prebor, & Brandt, 1972). Interruptions also have been offered as evidence of men's domination of talk. Men tend to interrupt women more than women interrupt men (Argyle et al., 1968; Zimmerman & West, 1975). However, Kennedy and Camden (1981, 1983) have shown that interruptions by men are more likely if women display low involvement cues (backward lean, lack of eye contact) or a pleasant facial expression (smiling). Thus interruptions by men may be a product of misinterpreting female nonverbal cues rather than just a desire to dominate the conversation. The findings for total speaking time, though, do support the notion of a dominant male speaker.

APPLICATIONS

Nonverbal Battle of the Sexes

Gender differences are interesting and often humorous, but in actual practice, they can cause tension in male-female conversations.

The first place where tension may exist is in the eye behavior of men and women. As noted, women are expected to engage in more eye contact. Moreover, when females fail to make eye contact, they are more likely to be interrupted by males, especially in group situations. Lack of eye contact by women may be interpreted as inattention or disinterest, making them more vulnerable to interruptive attempts. Men, however, do not seem to fall victim to a similar interpretation.

Eye contact and interruption differences may also contribute to perceptions of women as submissive and men as dominant (see Chapter 9 for additional discussion). Women may also accede control to men by occupying less space, assuming less relaxed postures, and occupying less conversational time. Mulac et al. (1987) recently found that women are more accommodating than men in eye contact patterns. That is, women are more likely to adopt the eye contact pattern of the men they communicate with (i.e., more averted gaze), but men are less likely to adopt women's eye contact patterns. This might also indicate that women code switch more than men.

As previously noted, the sex role adopted by parties in an interaction may be more important to communication between males and females than biological sex differences. Ickes, Schermer, and Steeno (1979) showed that interaction patterns changed when the interactants were either sex-typed (i.e., masculine or feminine) or androgynous. An interaction between two traditional males or two traditional females is characterized by less nonverbal involvement than an interaction between two androgynous individuals. They suggested that androgynous communicators have more skills, being both instrumental (masculine) and expressive (feminine), that they can use to communicate effectively. The lack of one or the other of these skills in traditional sex-typed interactions leads to less involving conversations. Ickes et al. also suggested that androgynous individuals may be more likely to compensate for the interac-

Nonverbal Battle of the Sexes (*Continued*)

tion skills of sex-typed opposite sex partners. That is, androgynous males may bring both their instrumental and expressive skills to bear in conversations with traditional females who lack instrumental skills. Similarly, androgynous females may bring their instrumental and expressive skills to bear in conversations with traditional males who lack expressive skills, resulting in more involved conversations. However, this same compensation does not seem to occur when an androgynous communicator interacts with a sex-typed same-sex partner (Ickes & Barnes, 1977).

The differences in nonverbal behavior can create relational stress between males and females and reduce relational satisfaction. The avoidance of close interactions and touch by men and the desire for more contact by women may produce dissatisfaction. Women may also be uncomfortable with men's common association of touch with sexual intentions, while men may be confused by women's need for touch that does not culminate in sexual intercourse.

As important to satisfaction as gender may be gender role. Ickes et al. found higher satisfaction when two androgynous communicators interacted. It is interesting to note that sex-typed males were also more satisfied with their interactions, perhaps because they desired and experienced less conversational involvement. Finally, opposite-sex interactions may also be satisfying if they contain an androgynous partner, because of this partner's ability to compensate for the skill deficiencies of the sex-typed partner.

Thus, gender differences are far from trivial, humorous anecdotes. They have the potential to create tension, conflict, and dissatisfaction between men and women. This may be increasingly true as more women move into male-dominated areas in business and politics. In these areas, power and influence are important considerations, and to the extent that women's behaviors handicap their abilities to exercise control, their success may be limited. On the social front as well, these differences may bode ill for male-female relationships as men's and women's communication styles come into conflict.

Identifiers of Personality

Within cultural, racial, and gender groups, communicators display many individual differences in nonverbal communication that often identify particular personality types and provide self-perceptions of personality. Much of what is known about the nonverbal identifiers of personality falls into one of two categories of investigation—research on personality characteristics, such as introversion and communication reticence, and studies of psychological disorders, such as schizophrenia and paranoia. The following brief discussion is admittedly very selective in the information presented.

Personality Types

Eye Contact. Much of the research on personality types is not usually thought of in terms of nonverbal identifiers, although occasionally research has found some connection. There is evidence that need for affiliation is related to amount of eye contact. People who have a great need for being affiliated with others give more eye contact than those with less need for affiliation (Exline, 1963). The relationship seems almost intuitive, since eye contact is one means of achieving affiliation and recognition. Conversely, introverts often resist visual interaction as if fearing involvement (Mobbs, 1969).

Proxemics. What is known about eye contact parallels closely proxemic identifiers of introversion and extroversion. Highly introverted people tend to require greater distance between themselves and others than extroverted people do (Mobbs, 1969).

On the deviant side of personality, aggressive and violence-prone individuals have larger personal space zones. Work with violent prisoners, for example, shows that they begin to feel discomfort at double the distance at which others express discomfort. Work on touch avoidance indicates that those who are predisposed to avoid touch adopt greater interaction distances (Andersen & Sull, 1985). Although there has been less research on spacing patterns among the psychologically and emotionally disturbed, it appears that various neuroses and psychoses produce deviant proxemic behavior patterns.

Somatotypes. Somatotypes may be related to personality insofar as they may indirectly affect one's view of self and others. Stereotypes exist of the jolly, easygoing fat person and the sensitive, high-strung thin person, and many traits stereotypically associated with each of the somatotypes show up when people rate their own temperament (Cortes & Gatti, 1965, 1970). They also show up in parents' and teachers' evaluations of children (Walker, 1963). The commonly found associations are listed in Table 6.3.

These findings have caused speculation as to why clusters of behaviors and personality traits are associated with somatotype. One line of thought suggests that temperament has physiological determinants and that the genetic, organic, and metabolic processes that produce a certain somatotype also influence temperament. An alternative line of thought that makes some sense is that communicators respond to children according to their appearance—plump endomorphs and skinny ectomorphs get negative reactions and teasing; mesomorphs receive a lot of positive reinforcement because they are considered more attractive. Research on somatotypes and body attractiveness as they relate to self-esteem seems to support this view (Berscheid, Walster, & Bohrnstedt, 1973; Jourard & Secord, 1955). One should

TABLE 6.3 Personality Traits Commonly Associated with Somatotypes

Endomorph	Mesomorph	Ectomorph
Affable	Active	Aloof
Affected	Adventurous	Anxious
Affectionate	Argumentative	Awkward
Calm	Assertive	Cautious
Cheerful	Cheerful	Considerate
Complacent	Competitive	Cool
Cooperative	Confident	Detached
Dependent	Determined	Gentle-tempered
Extroverted	Dominant	Introspective
Forgiving	Efficient	Meticulous
Generous	Energetic	Reflective
Kind	Enterprising	Reticent
Leisurely	Hot-tempered	Sensitive
Placid	Impetuous	Serious
Relaxed	Optimistic	Shy
Soft-hearted	Outgoing	Tactful
Soft-tempered	Reckless	Uncooperative
Warm	Social	Withdrawn
	High need for achievement	Low need for achievement
	Nonconforming	Conforming

Source: Compiled from "Physique and Propensity," by J. B. Cortes and F. M. Gatti, April 1970, *Psychology Today*.

be careful, though, not to overinterpret these associations. There is no direct evidence that possessing a particular somatotype causes one to adopt certain behavioral patterns and personality traits.

Dress and Adornment. Choice of clothing and other features of adornment is related to personality. In Chapter 2, it was reported that Aiken (1963) found that clothing and adornment choices could be classified along five dimensions: (a) interest in dress, (b) economy in dress, (c) decoration in dress, (d) conformity in dress, and (e) comfort in dress. Choices on these dimensions were related to personality. For example, those who showed great interest in dress were conventional, conscientious, compliant before authority, stereotyped in thinking, persistent, suspicious, insecure, and tense. Although the results may now be outdated, they support the relationship of personality to clothing and adornment choices.

Rosenfeld and Plax (1977) conducted a study that was designed to follow up and extend Aiken's work. Male and female subjects were given a clothing questionnaire and an extensive set of personality measures. Again, the dimensions of attitudes identified in the study were related to the personality characteristics of both males and females. Here are some of the results:

1. **Clothing consciousness.** "The people I know always notice what I wear." Females strong on this dimension were inhibited, anxious, compliant before authority, kind, sympathetic, and loyal to friends.

2. **Exhibitionism.** "I approve of skimpy bathing suits and wouldn't mind wearing one myself." Males strong on this dimension were aggressive, confident, outgoing, unsympathetic, unaffectionate, moody, and impulsive.
3. **Practicality.** "When buying clothes, I am more interested in practicality than beauty." Females strong on this dimension were clever, enthusiastic, confident, outgoing, and guarded about personal self-revelations.
4. **Designer image.** "I would love to be a clothes designer." Males strong on this dimension were cooperative, sympathetic, warm, helpful, impulsive, irritable, demanding, and conforming.

Another study, conducted by Gurel, Wilbur, and Gurel (1972), found that conformity was related to clothing choices. "Greasers," who scored highest on conformity, wore black leather jackets, knit pullovers, and teased or greased hair. "Hippies," who scored lowest on conformity, wore old grubby clothes, peace symbols, and beards.

Color preferences also appear to be related to personality (see, for example, Lüscher, 1971). The predominant colors in a person's wardrobe can produce stereotypic impressions of personality. The personality traits most associated with preferences for various colors are listed in Table 6.4.

The combination of color and design preferences in clothing is also related to personality. Compton (1962) found that people who preferred small designs were concerned about making a good impression. Those who chose less bold prints were modest and conveyed an image of naturalness. Assertive, sociable women preferred deep shades and saturated colors, while submissive, passive women preferred lighter tints.

Vocalics. Intuitively, we are all aware of the personality associations conjured up by various voices. Who, for instance, does not get a clear image of false bravado from Don Knotts' voice? Beneath the sensuality, Marilyn Monroe's voice seemed to reveal her vulnerability. Clint Eastwood's masculinity is quite evident when he asserts, "Go ahead, make my day."

Research on many aspects of the voice has yielded evidence of a significant number of relationships to personality. Early research found that inflection correlated with intelligence and breathiness related to neuroticism, introversion, and submissiveness (Crawford & Michael, 1927; Moore, 1939). In 1934, Allport and Cantril concluded that (a) the voice conveys correct information about inner as well as outer characteristics of personality; (b) although there is no uniformity in expression of personality from the voice (that is, certain personality traits are not consistently evidenced by certain vocal features), many features of personality can be determined from the voice; and (c) the more highly organized and deep-seated traits and dispositions are judged more consistently and more accurately than physique and appearance features.

Contemporary research has added more information on the relationship between vocalics and personality. Markel, Phillis, Vargas, and Howard (1972) examined loudness and tempo. They found that *loud, fast* voices correlate with being self-sufficient and resourceful, expecting the worst of

TABLE 6.4 Color and Personality

Color	Personality Characteristics
Red	Extroverted, impulsive, stimulating, action-oriented, physical, youthful, athletic, competitive, sensual, dramatic, other-directed, strong sex drive, productive
Blue	Highly educated, cultured, high income, introverted, sensitive to others, respected, steady character, cautious, secure, relaxed, empathetic, loyal, dedicated, normal sex drive, need for contentment
Yellow	Moderately stimulating, intellectual, idealistic, high-minded, attracted to cults, safe friend, theoretical, philosophical, confident, industrious, fitful, future-oriented, difficult to understand, compulsive
Orange	Sympathetic, friendly, extroverted, athletic, active
Purple	Affectionate, pompous, solemn, artistic, good mind, keen wit, observant, verbose, creative, needs discipline, easy to live with, insecure, not cheerful, possible homosexuality and emotional insecurity
Green	Fair, respectable, a joiner, good citizen, sensitive to etiquette and social custom, frank, normal sex drive but not prudish, stable, wants to impress and be recognized, wants to be independent
Black	Vain, sophisticated, worldly, mysterious, wise, revolting against fate, acts hastily
Brown	Earthy, conscientious, shrewd, obstinate, parsimonious, dependable, steady, sensuous, conservative, responsible in love, wants security, may be ruthless
White	Simple, young, decent, venial, flirtatious, likes to be alone

Source: From *The Unspoken Dialogue: An Introduction to Nonverbal Communication* (p. 163) by J. K. Burgoon and T. Saine, 1978, Boston: Houghton Mifflin.

people, and being intrapunitive (blaming oneself for problems). The *loud, slow* voice is associated with being aggressive, competitive, confident, self-secure, radical, self-sufficient, and resourceful; tending toward rebelliousness for its own sake; being low on introspection; and responding to stressful situations with hypochondria. The *soft, fast* voice correlates with being enthusiastic, happy-go-lucky, adventuresome, thick-skinned, confident, self-secure, radical, phlegmatic, composed, optimistic, nonconforming, independent, and composed under stress. Finally, the *soft, slow* voice is associated with being competitive, aggressive, enthusiastic, happy-go-lucky, adventurous, thick-skinned, reckless, and carefree, but withdrawn and introspective under stress. Other investigations that have looked at such vocal features as resonance, loudness, pitch, and tempo have found that vocal profiles correlate with personality profiles (Mallory & Miller, 1958; Markel, 1969). In sum, voices are often good indicators of actual personality traits. You might want to compare your own voice qualities to personality features listed in this section to see if they apply to you.

Communication Reticence

Researchers in the field of communication have long been interested in a relatively stable communication predisposition called communication reticence. Originally, the phenomenon was labeled stage fright, but it has come to mean something much more than freezing in the presence of large audiences. Communication reticence can be prompted by almost any situation calling for interpersonal or public communication. The reticent communicator may be unable to respond coherently to others in even the most informal situation.

Reticent communicators are, in general, more anxious, tense, depressed, and unanimated; detached, apathetic, and uninvolved; and nonaffiliative, nonintimate, and possibly submissive in their nonverbal communication (Burgoon & Koper, 1984). Specifically, reticents, as opposed to nonreticents, encode more negative forms of arousal by increased bodily tension, more self-adaptors, and more protective behaviors such as body blocking, face covering, and leaning away from their communication partner. Their behavior is often more restrained and rigid, and they display more uncoordinated, random movements. Positive indicators of arousal such as facial animation and head nodding are less evident in reticent communicators. Finally, reticents engage in less eye contact, less facial pleasantness, indirect head and body orientation, and more cues of apathy than nonreticents. Anxious communicators also display a high rate of nonfluencies and other speech errors (Harper, Wiens, & Matarazzo, 1978). Frequent nonfluencies and other speech errors have also been linked to trait anxiety (Siegman, 1978). People high in trait anxiety exhibit shorter response latencies as well (Murray, 1971).

Not surprisingly, the nonverbal behavior of communication reticents can lead to unfavorable perceptions on relational communication, credibility, and attraction. This often makes it more difficult for reticents to establish friendships. However, Burgoon and Koper (1984) found that once friendships are established, friends may be more tolerant and sympathetic than strangers to the reticent's condition and resulting nonverbal communication.

Summary

In studying nonverbal communication, one must be cognizant of nonverbal "badges" of culture, race, gender, and personality that help place a person in psychological space and create self-identity. Cultures can be identified by their expressiveness, amount of contact, and degree to which they are clockbound. Each culture is also made up of subcultures that make cultural classification less accurate. Particularly important are racial and gender subcultures. The most important racial identifiers involve the use of eye gaze and vocalic cues. These differences appear to cause difficulties in interracial interactions. Gender identifiers are also prevalent, especially in kinesic expressivity, degree of contact, and use of vocalic cues. Somatotypes, dress and adornment, and vocalic cues are the most reliable identifiers of personality. Being sensitive to these nonverbal identifiers and encoding appropriate cues can improve the quality of intercultural, interracial, intergender, and interpersonal relationships and the communication that occurs within them.

Suggested Readings

Burgoon, J. K., & Koper, R. J. (1984). Nonverbal and relational communication associated with reticence. *Human Communication Research, 10,* 601–627.

Collett, P. (1971). On training Englishmen in the non-verbal behavior of Arabs: An experiment in inter-cultural communication. *International Journal of Psychology, 6,* 209–215.

Condon, J. C., & Yousef, F. (1975). *An introduction to intercultural communication.* Indianapolis: Bobbs-Merrill.

Eibl-Eibesfeldt, I. (1979). Similarities and differences between cultures in expressive movements. In S. Weitz (Ed.), *Nonverbal communication* (2nd ed.) (pp. 37–48). New York: Oxford University Press.

Erickson, F. (1979). Talking down: Some cultural sources of miscommunication in interracial interviews. In A. Wolfgang (Ed.), *Nonverbal communication: Applications and cultural implications* (pp. 99–126). Orlando, FL: Academic Press.

Hall, E. T. (1959). *The silent language.* Garden City, NY: Doubleday.

Hall, E. T. (1981). *Beyond culture.* Garden City, NY: Anchor·Press/Doubleday.

Henley, N. M. (1977). *Body politics: Power, sex, and nonverbal communication.* Englewood Cliffs, NJ: Prentice-Hall.

Jourard, S. M. (1966). An exploratory study of body-accessibility. *British Journal of Social and Clinical Psychology, 5,* 221–231.

LaFrance, M., & Mayo, C. (1979). A review of nonverbal behaviors of women and men. *Western Journal of Speech Communication, 43,* 96–107.

Morris, D. (1977). *Manwatching: A field guide to human behavior.* New York: Abrams.

Samovar, L. A., & Porter, R. E. (1985). *Intercultural communication: A reader* (2nd ed.). Belmont, CA: Wadsworth.

Shuter, R. (1977). A field study of nonverbal communication in Germany, Italy, and the United States. *Communication Monographs, 44,* 298–305.

Stier, D. S., & Hall, J. A. (1984). Gender differences in touch: An empirical and theoretical review. *Journal of Personality and Social Psychology, 47,* 440–459.

CHAPTER 7

Impression Formation and Management

Men trust their ears less than their eyes.

Herodotus

Beware, as long as you live, of judging people by
appearances.

Jean de La Fontaine

"As to your practice, if a gentleman walks into my
rooms smelling of iodoform, with a black mark of nitrate
of silver upon his right forefinger, and a bulge on the
side of his top hat to show where he has secreted his
stethoscope, I must be dull indeed if I do not
pronounce him to be an active member of the medical
profession."

Sherlock Holmes in "A Scandal in Bohemia," by Sir Arthur Conan
Doyle

Put yourself in the situation of meeting someone for the first time. Would
you employ as much skill as Sherlock Holmes in forming an impression of
that person? Assume that this person you meet at a public plaza is wearing
a jacket with the name of a well-known Japanese corporation emblazoned
across the back, and his name, John, monogrammed on the front left side.
Otherwise, he is dressed in dress slacks, white shirt and tie, and comfortable-
looking shoes. Ah, you think, a worker from the new Japanese microchip
factory. After he asks you what you do for a living, you say, "Well, you must
work in the new silicon chip factory just down the way here. Are you a

foreman on one of the production units?" He gives you a horrified look and says, "Oh no, I'm vice president for manufacturing at the plant." The conversation becomes awkward and stilted because both of you are embarrassed. Not quite a Holmes-like series of judgments, would you say?

What does this little scenario illustrate? (a) We tend to form impressions of others quickly and automatically and to draw inferences about them; (b) we often base our impressions of others on external and nonverbal characteristics, in this case dress and adornment features; and (c) impres-

What impressions do you think her classmates have of this girl's "punk" hairstyle?

sions and inferences can be incorrect, especially when we are unfamiliar with the person and the situation, such as the Japanese corporation in this example. Employees of Japanese companies, managers and workers alike, often wear the "company uniform" (*Newsweek,* Feb. 2, 1987). Indeed, David Halberstam, in his book *The Reckoning* (1986), reports that the president of the Nissan plant in Smyrna, Tennessee, wore the Nissan worker outfit at the workplace, a kind of blue fatigue outfit with his name, "Marvin," on the shirt pocket. Since executives in American companies rarely, if ever, wear such uniforms, one might incorrectly presume that someone wearing such a uniform would not be very high up in the company hierarchy. To be fair, it's not quite clear what Holmes would do in this situation.

In this chapter, we will consider the principles and nonverbal cues that allow one to form impressions of others. From this, you should gain a better understanding of how impressions affect the way you interact with others. We will also consider the kinds of strategies communicators can use to manage the impressions others form of them. *Impression management,* or *self-presentation,* is a growing area of research in communication and other social science disciplines. We will examine the nonverbal code elements that can be used to create desired impressions and the kinds of communicative and psychological factors that determine the effectiveness of impression management attempts.

Keep in mind that impression formation and impression management are really two sides of the same coin. Impression formation is studied from a decoder perspective and is concerned with how we form impressions of a communicator. It focuses primarily on the more static or uncontrollable features of nonverbal behaviors from which observers make attributions about communicators. Impression management takes an encoder perspective and is concerned with what we, as communicators, can alter and control intentionally to present ourselves positively. It focuses on the nonverbal strategies and tactics we can use to foster credibility, attraction, and other images.

Impression Formation

Principles of Impression Formation

A number of folk sayings reveal our culture's interest in impression formation. Phrases like "You can't judge a book by its cover" and "Beauty is only skin deep" suggest a cautious and hesitant approach to impression formation. By contrast, "What you see is what you get" suggests that impressions are straightforward and reliable. Like many commonsense views of social behavior, these phrases do not quite hit the mark. The principles that researchers have found to govern the formation of impressions provide a more thorough and systematic view.

People develop evaluations of others from limited external information. By necessity, what we know about someone when we first meet, and even after several encounters, is quite limited. Despite this, we form impressions comprised of an extensive series of judgments. What drives people to make judgments with so little information? Some research (Berger, 1979; Berger & Bradac, 1982; Berger & Calabrese, 1975) indicates that impressions are a product of the uncertainty about the other person (usually a stranger) and the situation. Impressions provide some level of predictability about how the interaction with the person will proceed. Alternatively, people make rapid judgments to estimate whether the relationship is likely to be a rewarding one or not (Sunnafrank, 1986). In either case, making judgments on the basis of limited information is presumed to be psychologically satisfying.

What kind of information does one rely on to make inferences and judgments? As Berger and Calabrese (1975) point out, in first impression situations, since most initial conversation is limited to social amenities and standard social topics such as the weather and movies, we are not likely to know a lot about the other person by verbal means. Therefore, nonverbal cues predominate in the impression formation process.

Impressions are partly based on stereotypes the perceiver holds. When forming impressions, humans rely on what they already know about others in general. Alternately called person schemas, personality stereotypes and attributes, person themes, and person memory, we rely on our "person knowledge" when forming an impression because the amount of external information that is gleaned about an individual is limited. Impressions, then, are a combination of the limited information one knows about an individual and what one knows about people in general. This process, reflects a general principle of comprehension and information processing called the *given-new* (Haviland & Clark, 1974) or *fact-inference* (Kintsch, 1974) distinction. This explains how individuals can go beyond given information to extract an understanding from a variety of new verbal materials and tasks. Interestingly, the way we form impressions of others parallels the way we comprehend things in other information domains.

Can nonverbal cues be linked to the general person knowledge most people have in our culture? The answer is clearly yes. As you will see shortly, there are a variety of nonverbal cues that elicit stereotypes about people. For example, many personality stereotypes are based on physical appearance features: The color of one's hair suggests personality traits (blondes are fun-loving, sexy, and not too bright, redheads are temperamental), as does one's height (tall men are aggressive and domineering). Vocal cues have also been linked to stereotypic judgments, with loud, deep, and resonant voices suggesting ambition and soft and hesitant voices implying shyness.

First impressions are often initially based on outward appearance cues. As we saw in the scenario that began this chapter, people rely heavily on physical appearance cues in first impression situations. There may be a variety of reasons for this, but one reason is that physical appearance information is readily available during first encounters. Before you know anything else about strangers, you know what they look like (presuming a face-to-face encounter). Other nonverbal cues come into play over time and subsequent encounters, but physical appearance cues are quite potent initially.

A number of studies have affirmed this principle. As discussed in Chapter 2, physically attractive individuals are seen as more responsive, sensitive, kind, sexy, modest, poised, sociable, extroverted, intelligent, well-adjusted, and interesting than unattractive individuals (Berscheid & Walster, 1974; Dion, Berscheid, & Walster, 1972). Taller and thinner men earn higher salaries. Finally, some jury simulation studies (Efran, 1974; Jacobson, 1981) have shown that guilty defendants who are physically attractive receive lighter sentences than unattractive ones.

The implications of these studies, and the principle in general, paint a somewhat unflattering picture of general social conduct in our culture. At least in initial encounters, people tend to judge books by their nonverbal covers. Subtle forms of prejudice and discrimination based on physical

Being Tall Pays

A recent survey of graduates of the University of Pittsburgh's MBA program has found that, in the world of business, the thinner and taller the male executive, the fatter the salary. Professors Irene Frieze and Josephine Olson surveyed 1,200 graduates and found that tall men earn more than their shorter colleagues, and that men who are at least 20 percent overweight make $4,000 less than their thinner coworkers. These researchers found that the average salary of those surveyed was $43,000, but that a typical 6-foot male professional earned $4,200 more than his 5-foot-5 counterpart. When weight and height were combined, the taller and trimmer man earned about $8,200 more than the shorter and heavier man. Olson explained the survey findings by pointing out that "people imagine a male manager as tall, strong and powerful. And the man who meets that image gets rewarded." The results for women were not conclusive because of the small number of female respondents who were significantly tall or overweight. However, Frieze indicated that being tall and slim are attractive attributes for men, and that "it's more complex for women than men. If a woman is seen as fairly attractive and she is doing these male-dominated jobs . . . there's a suspicion of how she's gotten there, how much she's used her attractiveness to get there." For tall and thin men, social stereotypes about physical appearance attributes and personal characteristics work advantageously. As for the rest of us, the implications are not so positive.

Source: Tucson Citizen, March 2, 1987, p. 9A.

appearance may affect a number of initial encounter situations, such as hiring interviews, court appearances, and even a teacher's initial assessment of a student's academic potential. Lip service is paid to basing judgments in these situations on relevant and meritorious attributes, but this unfortunately may not always be the case.

Initial impressions form a baseline of comparison for subsequent impressions and judgments. Initial impressions can have lasting impact, but their importance diminishes in proportion to the amount of new information gained over time. Some impressions formed at an initial encounter do not change very much because of limited contact with the individual. These impressions can sensibly be called first impressions and are most likely to be affected by the principles already discussed. Other impressions do change because we have subsequent contact and literally get to know the person. These impressions are more detailed, complex, and stable. The longevity of an initial impression thus hinges on the amount of subsequent communication and new information that becomes available between the parties involved. Even so, research indicates that first impressions often serve as a template, guiding the interpretation of subsequent information, so a bias in person perception may persist due to first impression information. If you commit a horrible social blunder during an initial encounter, it may leave a lasting impression that colors interpretations of your subsequent social competence. Repairing such impressions may require many counter examples of behavior.

Impressions consist of judgments on at least three different levels: physical, sociocultural, and psychological. Judgments on the physical level have to do with a person's age, gender, race, body shape, height, and weight. Sociocultural judgments are concerned with socioeconomic status, education level, occupation, place of residence, ethnic or cultural background, religious identity, political and social group membership, and attitudes that correspond to one's socioeconomic and cultural background. Psychological judgments have to do with psychological makeup, temperament, and moods, including inferences about personality and attributions of causality concerning behavior.

Accuracy Versus Consistency of Judgments

Many people wonder whether the impressions they form are accurate. After all, if you think of a friend in certain terms, it would be nice to know that your perceptions are accurate. Unfortunately, impression formation isn't that simple.

First, the level of a particular impression judgment affects the likelihood of its being accurate. Impression judgments are generally more accurate when made at the physical level, somewhat less accurate at the sociocultural level, and least accurate at the psychological level. In other words, as one moves from making judgments about external and fairly easily verifiable characteristics about a person to more internal and difficult-to-verify characteristics, the less accurate one becomes. Cook (1979) indicates that overall, "the most striking finding to emerge from the extensive, jumbled literature on 'accuracy of person perception' is how very inaccurate most people are most of the time" (p. 119).

A second complication has to do with the term *accuracy* itself. To determine the accuracy of any particular judgment, some reliable information about the judgment must exist. Reliable information usually exists for the physical and sociocultural judgments one makes about people. That is, if we think we know Sally as a white female weighing about 115 pounds, standing 5'4", from Little Rock, Arkansas, who has a bachelor's degree in education and is a member of the Tri-Delta sorority, information is available to verify all these judgments. However, when we make inferences about this individual's personality and psychological makeup, the reliability and availability of relevant information decreases. If you judge Sally as outgoing, vivacious, somewhat flippant, judgmental of others, rigid, and somewhat bigoted, what information could verify these judgments? You could cite several examples of Sally's behavior that back up these judgments, but you would still be relying on your *perception* of her behavior. Personality tests would not help much, either. The correlation between measured personality traits and behavior has been found to be low (Mischel, 1968), so the results from these tests would probably not be consistent with your impressions. Thus it may be more useful at a psychological level of impression formation to focus on whether inferences are *consensual,* that is, similar and consistent across a variety of individuals who are making the judgments. Not surprisingly, many judgments at this level *are* consensual and consistent: People often agree on the personality traits of a given individual. However, research on what nonverbal cues produce consensual judgments about personality says little about what nonverbal cues provide accurate impressions.

One further qualifying comment is in order about the research evidence we will review. Much of this research has only investigated one or two nonverbal cues at a time, so often what is known is the impact on impression formation of a fragmentary set of cues. The challenge of cementing these nonverbal pieces together into something that corresponds to everyday interaction remains before us, although there have been some recent attempts, which we will discuss later. Finally, realize that most of the research has not included situational and contextual factors, which are also likely to affect impression formation in unknown ways.

Physical and Demographic Judgments

Judgments about the physical characteristics of an individual—a person's age, gender, race, body shape, height, and weight—should be the easiest and most accurate to make, although they are not infallible. These judgments are typically made on the basis of physical appearance and vocal cues, with other codes such as kinesics, proxemics, haptics, and artifacts playing a secondary role.

Age. At first glance (no pun intended), judging the age of someone unknown to you wouldn't seem very difficult. However, the difficulty of determining someone's age depends in part on how exact the judgment needs to be. We are most successful at making estimates within broad age categories, particularly the infant, preteen, and elderly categories. Physical appearance cues are very likely to influence age discriminations. However, physical appearance cues can be misleading. Since our culture values youth so highly, a wide variety of cosmetics, drugs, preparations, and surgery are used to take years off one's physical appearance. As several nonverbal researchers have pointed out (Burgoon & Saine, 1978; Leathers, 1976), these factors complicate and increase the error in age judgment.

Clothing can also make specific and accurate age judgments difficult. Some clothing styles can identify the wearer as someone older. One of the safest clothing cues for age judgments is whether the clothing reflects current styles. If so, the person is more likely to be younger. Table 7.1 lists a sampling of clothing and accessories that reflect age, according to women's magazines of the mid-1970s. Interestingly, some of the items in the table will return in popularity among younger people as styles change. But the person who wears a preponderance of these styles will probably be judged older. On the whole, age judgments based on clothing may be accurate only within broad categories.

Vocal cues can lead to fairly accurate judgments of an individual's age. A number of studies (Addington, 1968; Nerbonne, 1967; Pear, 1931) have shown that judges can make fairly accurate estimates of age from vocal cues. The accuracy of these judgments is probably due to changes in a variety of vocal parameters that occur with aging. As one grows older, the pitch level of the voice drops, although in the elderly, gender may make a difference in this pattern (McGlone & Hollien, 1963). One study (Mysak, 1959) found that speaking rate drops with age: Middle aged and older age groups speak slower than college age groups. However, children increase their speaking rate as they get older due to less pausing and being more articulate (Kowal, O'Connel, & Sabin, 1975). These results indicate that vocal cues change with age in ways that one can implicitly recognize. Although these changes may allow some broad judgments to be made about age, Siegman (1978) suggests that more research is needed on vocal changes across the entire developmental time span before the relationships between age and vocalics are fully understood.

The relationship of other nonverbal codes to age judgments is speculative. Burgoon and Saine (1978) have suggested that kinesic cues such as a person's general posture, frequency of gestures, speed of movement, and apparent energy level could be related to age judgments. Similarly, proxemic cues could indirectly indicate differences in age among a group of individuals, with those at larger conversational distances being of different age than those at closer distances.

To sum up, of the cues we have covered, vocal cues appear to provide the most reliable information about individual's age. Convergence of a variety of nonverbal cues may also help the observer to make more accurate and specific age judgments than the research evidence has suggested so far.

TABLE 7.1 Apparel and Accessories That Reveal Age

Clothes

Women	*Men*
Stretch pants	Straight-legged knit pants that hit
Sack dresses	above the ankle
The basic black dress	White socks with dark shoes
Cotton housedresses	Thin nylon socks
Hose with seams	Polyester suits
Blouses with roll-up sleeves	Leisure suits
Coat dresses	Flowered cotton shirts
Straight-legged pants with elasticized	Suits with wide lapels
waist	Baggy pants
	Sleeveless undershirts

Prints and Fabrics

Women and men	
Seersucker	Fake denim
Madras	Loud or "cutesy" prints
Heavy wools	Small-flowered prints
Metallic brocades (for women)	Glen plaids
	Polka dots

Colors

Women and men	
Pale pastels	Navy blue
Dark, somber colors	Purples and magentas
White shirts and blouses	
Muddy colors	

Accessories

Women	*Men*
Jeweled-frame eyeglasses	Tie tacks
Eyeglass holders	Neck scarves
Poodle and owl pins	Penny loafers
Lace handkerchiefs	Pointed-toe shoes
Hats	Hats
White gloves	Loose-fitting plaid raincoats
Practical shoes	Galoshes
Rain boots	White belts with white shoes
Mink-collared coats	
Vinyl purses	

Source: Adapted from *The Unspoken Dialogue: An Introduction to Nonverbal Communication* (p. 150) by J. K. Burgoon and T. J. Saine, 1978, Boston: Houghton Mifflin.

Gender. Although judgments of gender are relatively accurate, many people have embarrassing stories to relate about being mistaken in this judgment, particularly people who grew up during the 1960s and early 1970s. Some young men who sported shoulder-length hair had to get used to being addressed as "ma'am" when approached from behind.

Physical appearance cues are often assumed to be very clear indicators of gender. However, these cues do not present as clear a picture as it would seem. Clothes can often mask gender-related characteristics, and since it is common for males and females to wear similar styles of casual clothes, judging gender from certain angles can be difficult. Body type can also be an unreliable indicator of gender. People come in all shapes and sizes, regardless of gender. As popular films such as *Tootsie* and *Victor/Victoria* have shown us, a he can certainly look like a she, and vice versa. Some styles of physical appearance conform to our stereotypical view of masculinity and femininity more than others, and the cues that are part of these styles are likely to lead to gender judgments about individuals that are at least consensual, if not accurate.

As with age, vocal cues seem to be reliable indicators of gender (Epstein & Ulrich, 1966; Hollien, Dew, & Philips, 1971; Pear, 1931). In Chapter 6 we noted many vocal cues that differ between males and females, and this wide variety of physiological and learned differences is probably what allows observers to distinguish between male and female voices. Other cues from the kinesic, proxemic, and haptic codes further confirm one's impression of an individual as being masculine, feminine, or androgynous.

Race and Ethnic Ancestry. Another fundamental part of an impression has to do with judgments of an individual's racial and ethnic heritage. It is important to realize that the inferences people make are based on racial stereotypes, not on the judgment of racial or ethnic ancestry per se. Better understanding of how such judgments are made may lead to less dependence on racial stereotypes in forming impressions.

Physical appearance features may allow categorization of an individual into one of three broad racial groupings, Mongoloid, Negroid, and Caucasoid. However, it is often difficult to place people in one of the three broad groupings, much less to make any finer distinctions, based on these features. North Americans, for example, are not very adept at distinguishing individuals of Korean, Japanese, Chinese, Vietnamese, and Thai background on the basis of facial structure, skin color, and hair features. Also note that even in the three broad racial categories, there is a great deal of individual variation in physiognomy, so any given individual may be difficult to categorize.

Another physical appearance feature that may be relevant here is clothing and dress. However, variations in dress are also due to other factors, such as geographic region, socioeconomic status, gender, and rural or urban location. For example, in India, distinct differences in the way that Sikhs and Hindus dress are immediately recognizable. In North American culture, however, because of the mass production of clothing, dress is not a reliable indicator of racial or ethnic group.

Vocal cues likewise do not provide a good basis for making race judgments. Although one study (Nerbonne, 1967) suggested that vocal cues allow the discrimination of an individual's race, other studies contradict this finding (Knapp, 1978). This is somewhat surprising because, as we discovered in Chapter 6, research has identified some vocal differences among racial groups. Several factors help to explain this seeming contradiction. First, it may be that some vocal differences are too subtle for the untrained ear to hear and cannot be used by most people to discriminate another person's race. For example, the finding that black children pause primarily at pitch changes in utterances, while white children pause at the beginning of clauses or conjunctions (French & von Raffler–Engel, 1973), is probably not noticeable to most people; it would take the trained ear of a sociolinguist and systematic research to pick up on the difference. Second, even though researchers have identified dialects such as Black English that are tied to race and ethnicity, the use of these dialects is a sociological rather than a racial or ethnic phenomenon. Not all blacks speak Black English; middle-class blacks may either code-switch or not speak Black English at all. Further, Dillard (1973) has shown that southern whites often use Black English forms. When a person hears the vocal cues associated with Black English, there is only a moderate probability that the speaker is actually black. To sum up, the most reliable information for racial background judgments appears to come from physical appearance elements. Other codes appear to play supplementary roles at best, and none are highly accurate.

Body Shape, Height, and Weight. Although these characteristics are fairly accurately estimated from physical appearance cues, some evidence suggests that they can be derived from other nonverbal cues as well. Studies have shown that extremes in height and weight can be inferred from vocal cues. However, height and weight in the middle ranges are apparently difficult to estimate from vocal cues (Fay & Middleton, 1940; Lass & Davis, 1976). Knapp (1978) makes two important points about these judgments: First, the precision required for the judgment to be considered accurate can affect whether vocal cues are found to be useful guides for these judgments. Interestingly, in the Lass and Davis study, the average difference between actual height and estimated height was only .8 inches, and the average discrepancy in weight was only 3.48 pounds. Second, it is still unclear what particular vocal cues are informative for extremes in weight and height judgments. It could be loudness, resonance, intonation, breathiness, or some other vocal cue. This area provides an opportunity for some interesting research.

In summary, judgments in the physical features category are often accurate, but not as accurate as one might guess. Physical appearance cues are usually good indicators of age, gender, and body shape but only moderately accurate indicators of race and ethnicity. Vocal cues provide good indicators of age and gender and somewhat accurate indicators of body characteristics but not very accurate indicators of race. Other codes appear to play a supporting and contextual role for these judgments.

Sociocultural Judgments

Included in this broad category are such judgments as socioeconomic status, region of residence, and religious and political group membership. As with

What do the clothing and artifact cues in this picture
suggest about the wearers' socioeconomic status?

the physical judgments, physical appearance and vocal cues are most relevant to these judgments, though cues from other codes play a supporting
role.

Socioeconomic Status, Occupation, and Education.
Judgments of socio-
economic status, occupation, and education level are highly correlated. The
judgment of one of these characteristics can lead to inferences about the
others. Therefore, we shall discuss all three together.

Imagine for a moment the following fellow travelers on a bus or subway: a woman dressed in a sweater and jeans, a woman in a blue pastel
business suit, a man in a three-piece pinstripe suit with overcoat in hand,
a man in corduroy pants and tweed sports jacket, and a man in jeans and
knit sportshirt. Do these clothing cues prompt you to make assumptions
about what these individuals do for a living and their socioeconomic status

(SES) and education? The answer is undoubtedly yes. You might conclude that the jeans-clad persons are students, the man in the pinstripe suit is a banker, the woman in the business suit is a middle-level manager in a corporation, and the man in the cords and tweed jacket is a college professor. These judgments may not be accurate, but they are likely to be consensual.

Studies by Douty (1963), Rosencranz (1962, 1965), and Fortenberry, Maclean, Morris, and O'Connell (1978) have shown that observers make consistent status distinctions on the basis of clothing cues. Other anecdotal evidence indicates that some groups and corporations stress clothing as a means of indicating status and prestige via dress codes for employees. Organizations such as IBM, Sears, Allied Stores, and May Company have established formal dress codes (Malandro & Barker, 1983).

Sybers and Roach (1962) note that clothing is a symbol of status, that people are acutely aware of the status cues that clothing provides, and that people rely on apparel as a means of signaling professional aspirations and personal values. Further, people expect others to recognize their status and socioeconomic aspirations from their clothing. As a result, many individuals believe that if they don't conform to the dress norms for their social level and occupation, advancement up the ladder of success will be retarded, if not blocked. In some sectors of our culture, this is likely to be so; many people, rightly or wrongly, take dress seriously. In fact, Sybers and Roach indicate that clothing often communicates not only the SES, occupation, and education that people currently have but also what they aspire to.

Before leaving clothing cues, it's worthwhile to note that one of the most straightforward clothing indicators of SES, education, and occupation is the uniform. Cultures formalize through the symbol of clothing the status of such occupations as police officer, judge, doctor, and clergy. This is further testimony to the need for readily accessible visual information about a communicator's social role.

Vocal cues are informative for some judgments, less so for others. Listeners can accurately identify a speaker's SES from vocal cues (Ellis, 1967; Harms, 1961; Moe, 1972). Although it is unclear from these studies exactly what vocal cues are responsible, pronunciation and pausing patterns are likely possibilities (Siegman, 1978). Siegman and Pope (1965), for example, found a correlation between silent pausing and SES in an interview study with female nursing students. In this study, lower-class and lower-middle-class subjects showed more pausing than upper-middle-class and upper-class subjects.

The judgment of occupation from vocal cues, however, is less precise. Some investigations (Allport & Cantril, 1934; Pear, 1931) have found limited support for accurate judgments of occupation from vocal cues. Another study that provided subjects with a wider range of occupational categories (Fay & Middleton, 1940) found a great degree of consistency among subjects' occupational judgments but little accuracy. Put in context, these results make a great deal of sense. A person's socioeconomic status is a constant feature of one's everyday life—people are born into a family at a

APPLICATIONS

Hair Length and Career Success

Hair length and beardedness (for males) may affect judgments of occupation and even whether one gets a job in the first place. Burgoon and Saine (1978) report the findings of a survey of 114 college recruiting officers and managers. The respondents in the survey were asked to rate a number of hairstyles and beards in terms of their effect on hiring decisions. The most favorable ratings were given to the moderately short-haired and clean-shaven male model. Although the survey was conducted in 1976 and the popularity of hairstyles and beards have changed somewhat since then, it is likely that these physical appearance preferences are still in place. It is commonplace for males to get a shorter than normal haircut and to shave any facial hair before job interviews. Thus there is still a perception in our culture that short hair and the absence of facial hair makes one *appear* more businesslike and serious and therefore more appropriate for employment.

In many workplaces, long hair and beards are in fact unacceptable for employees, even for those who have been on the job for some time. This may be particularly true in jobs where an individual has to deal with the public, and the organization is concerned with its image. (A notable exception is that if you plan a career in the music industry, longer hair and beards may be perfectly acceptable, even required.) So while some occupations have lessened their restrictions on hair length and beards, many jobs in our culture regulate them, either implicitly or explicitly. Further, it is still the case that some hairstyles (e.g., punk or Rastafarian) rule the wearer out of most careers.

Are women's career concerns affected by hairstyles as well? Little systematic evidence is available on this question, but some authors (e.g., Richmond, McCroskey, & Payne, 1987) suggest that longer hairstyles on women are perceived as sexy and may contribute to perceptions of incompetence from female coworkers and low intelligence from male coworkers.

given social stratum and are socialized by that family. As language researchers have shown, verbal and vocal behavior are affected by socialization at different levels of SES. Occupational choices, by contrast, are typically only made as an adult and thus do not have the powerful socializing effects that a person's socioeconomic background does. Short of very specialized occupations that require some kind of vocal training (such as radio announcer), it is unlikely that occupation has much recognizable effect on vocal cues; therefore, it is not used by listeners to make occupational judgments.

In sum, both physical appearance and vocal cues can be consistent, if not accurate, indicators of education, occupation, and SES. Being able to judge one of these three characteristics accurately greatly increases the odds of accurately judging the other two.

Geographic Residence. Both physical appearance and vocalic cues can be indicators of the region in which a person resides. Of course, the communicators must dress and use vocal cues that are typical of their own region. Cowboy hats and western boots are at home in Albuquerque and Tucson but would be quite out of place in Baltimore and Cincinnati. Similarly, eastern seaboard "preppie" styles of clothing might look appropriate in Boston but less so in Boise. There are two important qualifications to the accuracy of inferences about geographic residence on the basis of clothing. First, because of the increased mass marketing of clothing in this country, a variety of styles are now available in most areas of the country. As a result, distinctive regional clothing styles may be disappearing. Second, often a particular regional clothing style becomes popular and is mass-marketed. That clothing style, then, is no longer a reliable indicator of region of residence.

Most of us are aware of the role that regional accent plays as an indicator of geographic residence. Trained and knowledgeable linguists can often accurately determine not only the state a person comes from by features of accent but the county or community as well. Most communicators do not have that precise an ear for accent, and the empirical evidence indicates that listeners can determine only the general region from which a person hails (Nerbonne, 1967; Pear, 1931). These broad regional discriminations may be easiest when a speaker uses a dialect that is not of one's own region. Brooklyn listeners can immediately recognize a speaker's southern accent (doesn't sound like he comes from around here), and residents of Mobile, Alabama, will know that a person with a Chicago accent is from the North.

Two factors complicate the judgment of regional residence from vocal cues. First, some parts of the country, like Florida and California, have experienced great influxes of people from other regions. As as result, it is difficult to determine what the local and regional dialects and accents are, and very mixed patterns of regional accent may result. Second, researchers have discovered that communicators often accommodate to the surrounding linguistic community's accent patterns. A person from Pennsylvania who moves to Oklahoma will after a while begin to sound like an Oklahoman.

Culture. Cultural judgments can be more difficult than one might think, and to some extent they overlap with judgments of racial background. While features of physiognomy and skin pigmentation can often help define a person's ethnic and cultural ancestry, other physical appearance cues, such as clothing and grooming, are more useful in defining one's current cultural membership. Unfortunately, most observers may not know enough about other cultures to recognize clothing and grooming cues that would indicate ethnicity. For example, most westerners do not know enough about different traditional Asian folk costumes to distinguish between a kimono (traditional Japanese attire for females) and a hanbuk (traditional Korean attire). In our own culture, there are many subcultures whose members could potentially be identified by clothing cues if traditional forms of clothing are worn. If individuals from Navajo, German, and Italian communities wear traditional costumes, an observer should be able to identify the ethnic backgrounds of these individuals. However, since traditional forms of dress are infrequent these days, such cues are of little use.

The ability of a typical observer to make ethnic or cultural judgments on the basis of vocal cues also appears to be limited. Different languages do have different vocal patterns and parameters in terms of rhythm, inflection, rate, and other vocal qualities. One study has indicated that listeners may be best at identifying vocal patterns of their own language (Cohen & Starkweather, 1961). American subjects who heard filtered samples of Chinese, English, German, and Italian identified the English voice more accurately than any of the others. However, the extent to which a speaker exhibits these vocal cues and the degree to which a listener is familiar with them may be limited.

Group Membership and Related Attitudes. An individual's membership in social, political, religious, civic, and other groups is often communicated nonverbally, primarily through physical appearance cues. Whether the group is the Kiwanis, Campus Crusade for Christ, a local softball team, or a group of punkers and skinheads, a variety of physical appearance cues will identify an individual as a member. Beyond inferences about group membership, observers will also make inferences about an individual's social, political, moral, and religious views, which are linked to these groups. In one study (Kelley, 1969), subjects were shown drawings of different clothing styles and then asked to indicate whether the wearer was liberal or conservative, supported or opposed the Vietnam War, was religious or not, and was politically active or apathetic. Results of the study showed that unconventional dress was associated with the political left, greater activity in politics, and use of various drugs. Although this study is somewhat dated, some similar results would probably be obtained if it were replicated today. On the whole, though, physical appearance cues allow observers a rather straightforward way of making inferences about another person's group membership and related attitudes.

Psychological Judgments and Attributions

Here we are concerned with a whole range of judgments that people make about others' psychological states, personalities, traits, and moods. Many judgments in this category are evaluative in that they represent a person's attitudinal response to another individual. Also, these judgments tend to rely heavily on stereotypes, scripts, implicit personality theories, and other person-relevant information. As a result, these judgments are often more consensual than accurate. Further, unlike physical and sociocultural judgments, these inferences rely on a broader range of nonverbal cues. In a sense, these inferences are among the most interesting to investigate because they show how willing we are to attribute internal characteristics to an individual on the basis of external cues.

Personality Perceptions and Attributions. Perception of a personality trait in another person involves not only relying on one or more nonverbal cues but also linking those cues to a stereotype about others. Personality traits themselves are stable and enduring internal characteristics that persist across situations. As noted earlier, the accuracy of these judgments is at best difficult to assess and in many cases quite low. More important is the fact that such inferences and judgments are commonly made by observers about others.

A variety of physical appearance cues lead to personality perceptions. One of the most basic is body type. Recall that people describe themselves according to a set of stereotypes that are associated with one's body type or somatotype—endomorph, mesomorph, ectomorph (see Table 6.3 in Chapter 6). These stereotypes are used to perceive not only oneself but other people as well. Walker (1963) has shown that these stereotypes are used by parents and teachers to evaluate children. Though the accuracy of these stereotypes can certainly be questioned, the more important point is that as part of the impression formation process, people often invoke such stereotypes based on the somatotype of the person being perceived. Further, if such stereotypes are applied early in life (as Walker suggests), children are consistently responded to and interacted with as if they actually possessed the personality traits associated with their particular body type. As a result, a child's self-concept and personality can be shaped by the expectations that others have on the basis of the child's somatotype. This line of reasoning could help to explain why there is some correspondence between somatotype and self-description in terms of these traits.

Another physical feature that may affect personality attributions is facial hair. Freedman (1969) asked male and female subjects to describe clean-shaven and bearded men. Male subjects (all beardless) described bearded males as more independent and extroverted, while the female subjects described bearded men as more sophisticated, mature, and masculine. Pellegrini (1973) went so far as to devise a study for which he took photos of men with beards and mustaches, had the confederates shave to goatees, photographed them, had them shave completely, and then photographed them again. These photos were then shown to subjects who were asked to rate them in terms of a series of personality traits. The results consistently showed that the more hair on the face, the higher the ratings on masculinity, maturity, self-confidence, dominance, courage, liberality, nonconformism, industriousness, and good looks. This finding seems a bit curious in light of our earlier discussion of beardedness and careers. It may be that while some of the traits cited are desirable for males in careers, others, such as nonconformism, liberality, and dominance, are not. So from a personnel manager's point of view, beardedness presents a mixed picture at best. Personality stereotypes about hair for females also exist, regarding length and color in particular. However, these stereotypes have so far received little empirical attention.

Finally, there may be a link between clothing and personality stereotypes. Given that people's preferences and attitudes about clothing are linked to their personality traits, it is possible that observers rely on the same dress cues to make personality attributions.

Vocal cues have also been associated with personality. Studies in this area fall into one of three categories: (a) studies that focus on the actual relationship between voice characteristics and personality traits, (b) studies that focus on the accuracy of judges in identifying personality traits, and (c) research that focuses on the perceptions attached to various vocal features. We are concerned with the last category of studies here.

One of the most extensive studies in this area was conducted by Addington (1968). Addington understood that certain vocal cues, in this case voice qualities, are closely linked to personality perception. He devised a study where male and female speakers simulated breathy, thin, tense, flat, throaty, nasal, and orotund voice qualities. Subjects then rated the perceived personality traits. Table 7.2 presents the results of the study. They

TABLE 7.2 Personality Traits Associated with Voice Qualities

Voice Quality	Personality Stereotypes in Males	Personality Stereotypes in Females
Breathy	Young, artistic	Feminine, pretty, petite, effervescent, high strung, and shallow
Thin	No relationships	Social, physical, emotional, and mental immaturity; high sensitivity; sense of humor
Flat	Masculine, sluggish, cold, and withdrawn	Same as for males
Nasal	Unintelligent, short, lazy, immature, fat, boorish, unattractive, sickly, uninteresting—all socially undesirable traits	Same as for males
Tense	Old; unyielding	Young; emotional, feminine, and high-strung; unintelligent
Throaty	Old; realistic, mature, sophisticated, and well-adjusted	Unintelligent, masculine, lazy, boorish, unemotional, ugly, sickly, neurotic, quiet, careless, unartistic, naive, humble, uninteresting, apathetic
Orotund	Energetic, healthy, artistic, sophisticated, proud, interesting, enthusiastic	Lively, gregarious, increased aesthetic sensitivity, proud, humorless

Source: Compiled from D. W. Addington, "The Relationship of Selected Vocal Characteristics to Personality Perceptions," *Speech Monographs*, 1968(35), 492–503.

indicate that some rather specific personality stereotypes are associated with voice qualities.

In summary, a variety of physical appearance and vocal cues prompt observers to attribute personality characteristics to others. Further, some of these cues are actually linked to rather specific personality stereotypes. Since personality judgments represent the attribution of stable and enduring traits, they constitute a powerful form of judgment. It is important, then, to keep in mind that nonverbal cues may lead observers to make these inferences and that such judgments can have effects on other interpersonal outcomes as well.

Impression Management

One provocative way to view social behavior is from the perspective of impression management theory. Underlying several impression management theories is the assumption that people behave in particular ways in social situations to engender positive images of themselves in other people. Among the reasons for managing behavior so that others will have positive impressions, Tedeschi and Reiss (1981) contend that communicators do so to make others (a) trust them more, (b) accept and believe their accounts, claims, and messages more readily, (c) harm them less, and (d) reward them more.

Three main theories of impression management have been advanced. The earliest and most comprehensive is Goffman's (1959, 1961b, 1963, 1967, 1969, 1971, 1974) dramaturgic analysis of self-presentation. Using terms derived from the theater, Goffman has provided an informally stated theory that features nonverbal illustrations and principles of successful and unsuccessful performances. Tedeschi (1981) and his colleagues have also provided a series of impression management principles that focus more centrally on interaction, and in a more specialized vein, Jones (1964) has developed ingratiation theory.

Goffman's work has provided a very broad and general view of self-presentation. So we will review the concepts and principles of Goffman's dramaturgical analysis first, along with their implications for nonverbal behavior. Then we will examine impression management principles and finally move on to research on nonverbal behavior linked to the impression management dimensions of social attractiveness and credibility.

Self-presentation: Dramaturgical Concepts and Principles

Though many authors in literature have noted the similarities between theater and everyday life, the implications of this analogy were not clear for social science until Goffman provided his dramaturgical analysis. Starting with *The Presentation of Self in Everyday Life* (1959), Goffman adopted a theatrical model to explain everyday human interaction. *Self-presentation,* according to Goffman, is the process whereby we constantly attempt to communicate impressions of ourselves to others. Much as in the theater, we present ourselves to others within the framework of playing various roles. Although most of us play a variety of roles on any given day, the overall goal of promoting positive views of ourselves in others transcends any particular role.

Goffman uses the term *performance* to refer to the total range of a particular interactant's behaviors that might influence any other interactant. Performances occur in the presence of observers, who constitute the audience, and at particular locations, which the dramaturgical model terms the *stage*. The *front region* of the stage encompasses the areas that the communicator actually uses for performance purposes. Thus people are seen as actors playing a role in the front stage area.

Goffman (1959) defines *front* as follows:

> that part of the individual's performance which regularly functions in a general and fixed fashion to define the situation for those who observe the performance. Front, then, is the expressive equipment of a standard kind intentionally or unwittingly employed by the individual during his performance. (p. 22).

Three elements define the front:

1. *Appearance* includes cues that indicate the performer's social status. As discussed in Chapter 2 and earlier in this chapter, physical appearance cues such as clothing may indicate a great deal about a person's status.
2. *Manner* includes cues that indicate the interaction role about to be taken or the actor's attitude toward the role. A variety of kinesic cues, such as facial expression, posture, and rate of movement, are relevant to this front component.
3. *Setting* includes physical environment cues that assist in defining the dramatic situation for observers. A variety of the environment and artifacts code elements discussed in Chapter 4, particularly the changeable semifixed elements, are relevant here.

According to Goffman, all these components should act in concert and be consistent with one another; if not, observers may begin to doubt the performance. Indeed, if you were referred to a well-known and expensive accountant and showed up at his office only to find it in a run-down building and the office in a dirty, disorganized, and chaotic state, you might doubt the accountant's performance.

In contrast to the front region where performances occur, Goffman has also defined a backstage area. In the *backstage region,* an actor is beyond the sight and sound of the audience and therefore feels free to act and speak in a more informal, less consistent, and more spontaneous way. Actors are allowed to relax, rehearse lines, and prepare for future interactions. A professor's office can be considered a backstage region, for example, from the performance of lecturer. According to Goffman, the backstage region is often used by performers as a place for engaging in behavior that would contradict a performance, such as smoking, swearing, or belching. Further,

 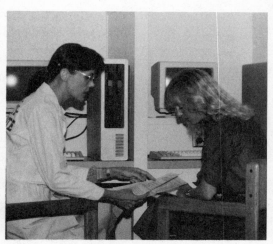

Compare the women in both photos. How are setting and personal front altered to suit two different performances?

actors may express dissatisfaction with their roles and derogate the audience in this area, actions that would be unacceptable in the front region.

The wings in a theater are regions to either side of the stage that hold equipment, props, the prompter, and aids to the performance. Goffman defines *wings* in his dramaturgical analysis as areas that contain people and equipment that can assist a performer in a role. A kitchen during a party, for example, may be a wings area for the hosts, containing equipment and props that are vital to the performance of the role of host.

Finally, Goffman has defined supporting roles that can facilitate an individual's performance. Much as a theatrical actor might consult a dialect specialist about certain dialect sounds for a part, everyday actors consult *specialists* to help in preparation for a given performance. There are two types of specialists. A *technical* specialist provides a skill or performs a function required by the performance. A caterer that you hire for a party may play this supporting role. A *training* specialist instructs the performer in the various actions that make up a performance. An etiquette specialist that you might consult for a formal party would fit here. Anyone who acts as an adviser, teacher, or counselor can be considered a training specialist. In defining this concept in dramaturgical analysis, Goffman points out that performances are rarely successful without the support and help of other people.

As a next step in dramaturgical analysis, Goffman has identified several principles that lead to a successful performance.

1. **A performer must segregate audiences.** Because of the variety and complexity of roles, it is likely that some of those roles are somewhat inconsistent (or appear to be inconsistent). As a result, the members of one audience should not see the actor performing an

inconsistent role for another audience. If an actor fails to segregate audience members, the performances may be compromised or invalidated.

2. **A performer should be aware of and adhere to requirements of decorum that accompany dramatic action.** One must follow a variety of social and interactional rules to be successful at self-presentation. Playing by the rules allows one to be seen in a positive light by others. Violating social rules may invalidate a performance, allowing the actor to be seen as possessing negative traits. For example, if one inappropriately gains the floor by repeatedly interrupting and not following turn-taking rules, such behavior is likely to lead to an unsuccessful performance. However, as we shall see shortly, in certain circumstances, rule violations may be advantageous.

3. **A performer must coordinate verbal and nonverbal codes to create an impression.** We have already discussed how contradictory messages can lead to confusion in interactions. Successful performances must have consistency between verbal and nonverbal cues. Goffman (1959) has argued that many nonverbal cues are difficult to control (he terms them ungovernable aspects of behavior), but more recent research has shown that there are individual differences in the ability to control and manipulate a variety of nonverbal behaviors (we will return to this point later). Thus some communicators will be better than others at achieving verbal-nonverbal consistency in self-presentation.

4. **For a performance to be accepted by an audience, the actor must be judged to be sincere.** Messages of sincerity are often conveyed via nonverbal cues. If an actor does not appear to be sincere in a performance, observers will not view the performance as successful. Rather, they may become suspicious and make negative attributions about the performer. It is important, then, that sincerity be effectively portrayed both verbally and nonverbally.

5. **An actor must appear satisfied with the role.** According to Goffman, it is important that an actor convey an attitude of liking the role that is being played and being compatible with it. If an actor gives nonverbal indications of disliking the role or being uncomfortable with it, the performance will suffer. For example, some teaching assistants at universities appear ill at ease because they are put in the classroom with students who are only slightly younger (and in some cases older) than they are. Their youthfulness alone may prevent them from feeling comfortable with a role. Consequently, their presentations as knowledgeable instructors may suffer.

Goffman has identified three typical factors that lead to unsuccessful performances. First, an actor may momentarily lose muscular control and accidentally convey incapacity, impropriety, or disrespect. Continuous coughing, stuttering, sneezing, and other similar behaviors may cause an audience to doubt the validity of an actor's performance and question the actor's self-control. Second, an actor can invalidate a performance by conveying either excessive involvement and interest or not enough of it. Audience members may be put off by an actor who appears overeager or apathetic in a role. Third, a presentation may suffer from "inadequate dramaturgic direction." This reflects an actor's lack of familiarity with the props and available equipment, architectural features of the staging area, and other requirements of the performance. Inadequate dramaturgic direction can also stem from not consulting specialists for a performance. For example, showing up for a day of deep-sea fishing in a neatly pressed white pantsuit demonstrates inadequate dramaturgic direction. Not consulting specialists about appropriate attire for the occasion could cost both the performance and an outfit!

APPLICATIONS

The Doctor As Dramatist

How often do people engage in self-presentation performances? In a "My Turn" column in the February 1, 1988, issue of *Newsweek,* Dr. Stephen A. Hoffmann suggests that self-presentation concerns enter into situations and role performances that we might not consider self-presentational. Hoffmann details a variety of self-presentation tactics he uses on a patient to convince her that he has provided a good diagnosis of her medical problem:

> Hoping to put her at ease, I adopt a calming manner. After I'm far enough into my examination to see that her strength and sensation are normal, I tell her I understand why she came in; that many women who start the Pill are concerned about developing a stroke, a heart attack or a blood clot. Then, pausing for effect, I smile and give her the good news, thinking it will allay her fears: "Fortunately, it takes much longer for the risk of a stroke to increase."

Unfortunately, this does not convince Hoffmann's patient, who is still very much aware of her symptoms. Hoffmann then decides to pursue the examination further.

> And so, I resort to theater. I stage a dazzlingly detailed neurologic exam. There are props: a reflex hammer and an ophthalmoscope, each of which I move about in carefully choreographed patterns. There are dramatic asides—thoughtful "hmmm's"—and flourishes, too, like the motions I put my patient through to test for rare, abnormal reflexes. I even bring in special effects, such as black and white striped tape which I move back and forth hypnotically before the woman's eyes, testing for subtle changes in her vision. Throughout it all, I'm careful to concentrate on my delivery,

The Doctor As Dramatist (*Continued*)

> timing my words, smiles, and gestures for best effect. . . . It's often said that doctors "play God," but the comment misses the point. Whether or not we're trying to be God's understudies, we always play to our audience. The truth is that people expect it of us.

Whether patients expect such behavior, and whether, as Hoffmann asserts, "Good bedside manner, in fact, is good theater," is debatable. What is interesting to note is Hoffmann's extensive use of nonverbal cues to manage his impressions with the patient. Hoffmann claims that these cues helped in a successful performance:

> Returning to her side, I sit down, maintain eye contact and explain as gently as I can that a thorough workup has shown that nothing is awry. Yet I carefully try to deal with her concern and to leave the door open to further care. "These symptoms are clearly bothering you a lot and they will hopefully resolve on their own," I say, "but we should consider doing more studies if they persist." I encourage her to call, shake her hand and wish her well. She's clearly pleased and thanks me profusely.

Many professionals engage in what amounts to self-presentation performances, using a variety of nonverbal cues. Some would claim that this is part of professional behavior and is expected by clients. Others would say that such behavior represents a less than honest approach to professionalism. What is your reaction?

The value of Goffman's work is that it has provided general principles that help to explain both successful and unsuccessful self-presentation performances. Further, some of the principles directly involved the use of nonverbal cues, while others imply their use. However, a number of facets of impression management can be linked more specifically to nonverbal cue displays. We turn next to impression management concepts and principles to explore these issues.

Principles and Tactics of Impression Management

As noted earlier, impression management theory is concerned with how social actors engender positive views of themselves in others while avoiding negative views. Impression management theorists have attempted to identify tactics and strategies that would allow interactants to achieve these goals. Recently, Tedeschi and Norman (1985) have synthesized a variety of impression management tactics into an overall taxonomy of impression management behaviors. Though not all the tactics they cover are relevant for our purposes, some clearly are and others have the potential to be.

Tedeschi and Norman's taxonomy rests on two basic distinctions concerning impression management tactics. First, impression management tactics can be described as either defensive or assertive. *Defensive* impression management occurs whenever an actor experiences or anticipates a predicament. In such situations, actors may believe that others will attribute negative qualities to them and will consequently employ a variety of impression management tactics to avoid negative judgments by others. *Assertive* impression management occurs when actors attempt to establish particular attributes in the eyes of others. Thus an actor who wishes to be perceived as a skilled computer hacker will presumably engage in a variety of assertive impression management tactics to establish that identity with others.

The second distinction is that impression management can be characterized as either tactical or strategic (note that the terms *tactics* and *strategy* are used in different senses later in this text). Similar to military uses of these terms, *tactical* impression management behaviors have short-term goals and objectives, while *strategic* impression management behaviors have long-term consequences over time and situations. A 2×2 matrix that employs these distinctions provides a taxonomy of impression management tactics (see Table 7.3).

Impression management behaviors can be classified as *defensive-tactical, defensive-strategic, assertive-tactical,* and *assertive-strategic.* Interestingly, nonverbal cues have mostly been linked to assertive-strategic impression management (attraction, esteem, prestige, status, credibility, trustworthiness)—behaviors that promote impressions in others over the long term.

Social Attractiveness, Friendliness, and Likability. One of the most basic aims of impression management is to prompt perceptions of friendliness

---

TABLE 7.3 A Taxonomy of Impression Management Behaviors

	Tactical	**Strategic**

Defensive	Accounts
	   Excuses
	   Justifications
	Disclaimers
	Self-handicapping
	Apologies
	Restitution
	Prosocial behavior
		Alcoholism
		Drug abuse
		Phobias
		Hypochondria
		Mental illness
		Learned helplessness

Assertive	Entitlements Enhancements Ingratiation Intimidation Exemplification Self-promotion Supplication	Attraction Esteem Prestige Status Credibility Trustworthiness

and liking in others. In Tedeschi and Norman's scheme, this would involve the assertive-strategic goal of attraction, alternately called affiliativeness, affect, warmth, and immediacy (Mehrabian, 1981). A number of dimensions have been used by researchers to measure these types of impressions, including sociable-unsociable, friendly-unfriendly, warm-cold, likable-unlikable, socially attractive-unattractive, kind-unkind, and pleasant-unpleasant. Despite the variety of concepts and measurement dimensions, we can assume that the general conceptual domain is the same across terms, methods, and studies.

Many of the behaviors that promote an attractive image are the same ones we use to communicate to others that we are attracted to them. This literature is discussed in detail in Chapter 9. Here we focus on behaviors that are used to create generalized impressions of the communicator as attractive. Further, we consider a closely related set of credibility judgments, perceptions of sociability and benevolence, later in this chapter. A variety of kinesic cues make major contributions to perceptions of social positiveness. One of the most basic is, of course, the smile. A substantial number of studies (Andersen, Andersen, & Jensen, 1979; Argyle, 1972; Bayes, 1970; Burgoon, Buller, Hale, & deTurck, 1984; Gutsell & Andersen, 1980; Mehrabian, 1971a, 1981; Mehrabian & Ferris, 1967; Reece & Whitman, 1962; Rosenfeld, 1966a, 1966b) have found smiling to be a potent and important cue for engendering perceptions of social attractiveness and warmth. Another cue that often occurs simultaneously with smiling is head nodding. One investigation (Woodall, Burgoon, & Markel, 1980) examined the impact of smiling, head nodding, and eyebrow raising, both singularly and in combination, on perceptions of social attractiveness. Participants in the study were shown videotaped segments of an actor verbalizing a standard phrase while performing one of the cues, two of the cues in combination, or all three. Participants then rated the stimulus they had just seen along social attractiveness dimensions. The results showed that the single most powerful cue in promoting social attractiveness perceptions was the smile, followed by the head nod and then the eyebrow raise. Smiling and head nodding turned out to have the most impact on social attractiveness of any cue combination.

Another kinesic cue that results in perceptions of social positiveness is eye contact and gaze. Wiener and Mehrabian (1968) devised a study in which an interviewer looked more at one interviewee than the other. Interviewees receiving more gaze perceived the interviewer to be more positive toward them than interviewees receiving less gaze. LaCrosse (1975) had confederates role-play either "affiliative" or "nonaffiliative" counselors, which included 80% or 40% levels of eye contact, respectively. Participants who viewed videotapes of the role plays rated the affiliative role plays as more attractive. Similarly, Wiemann (1974) had subjects interview confederates who gazed at them 100%, 75%, 25%, or 0% of the time. As predicted, as confederate gaze decreased, subjects rated the confederates as less friendly. Other studies, using different methodology and communication situations, have found similar results (Beebe, 1980; Goldberg, Kiesler,

& Collins, 1969; Kendon, 1967; Kleinke, Meeker, & LaFong, 1974). For reviews of this literature, see Exline and Fehr (1978), Harper, Wiens, and Matarazzo (1978), and Andersen (1985).

Other kinesic cues that have been linked to perceptions of social positiveness include increased use of gestural activity, relaxed body positions, open body positions, direct body orientation, and forward leaning (Andersen, Andersen, & Jensen, 1979; McGinley, McGinley, & Nicholas, 1978; Mehrabian, 1968c, 1969, 1971a, 1981).

Some studies have taken a broader, more integrative approach by assessing the effects of a combination of nonverbal cues on social attractiveness perceptions, often along with verbal behavior. Fretz, Corn, Tuemmler, and Bellet (1979) investigated the effects of high and low levels of eye contact, direct body orientation, and forward lean on perceptions of attraction and facilitativeness in simulated counseling interactions. Results showed that counselors who displayed high levels of the nonverbal behaviors were rated as more attractive and facilitative than those with low levels of the behaviors. However, in a follow-up study, subjects actually interacted with counselors who displayed either high or low amounts of the nonverbal behaviors. The results showed no difference in the perceptions of facilitativeness and attractiveness between the high and low nonverbal behavior conditions. Two factors may help explain these contradictory results. First, as other researchers have pointed out, rating a tape and rating a live interaction in which one is a participant are two quite different evaluative tasks. Second, in addition to the high or low levels of nonverbal behaviors in the live interactions, counselors were very supportive verbally and vocally, which may have washed out differences in perceptions that might have otherwise been obtained. Overall, the study underscores the importance of studying nonverbal behaviors in naturalistic contexts.

Another counseling study (Barak, Patkin, & Dell, 1982) investigated the relative contributions of responsive or unresponsive nonverbal behavior, counselor jargon, and formal or casual attire on perceptions of attractiveness of the counselor. In this study, participants viewed a simulated counseling session on videotape that had the counselor engage in either responsive or unresponsive nonverbal behavior, use two levels of jargon (professional or lay), and dress in either formal or casual attire. Responsive nonverbal behavior included positive facial expressions, gestures, head nodding, and forward trunk lean; unresponsive nonverbal behavior lacked these. Results of the study showed that responsive nonverbal behavior yielded significantly higher ratings of attractiveness than nonresponsive nonverbal behavior. Further, of the three variables, counselor nonverbal behavior accounted for 61% of the variance, while jargon and attire accounted for 17% and 4%, respectively. Similar findings have been reported in other counseling research studies (Claiborn, 1979; Roll, Crowley, & Rappl, 1985; Seay & Altekruse, 1979; Tepper & Haase, 1978), as well as other research (e.g., Imada & Hakel, 1977).

Culture is also likely to play a role in the use of nonverbal cues in impression management attempts. One study that examined the effects of cultural background on perceptions of attraction (McGinley, Blau, & Takai, 1984) showed Japanese and American subjects a series of slides of a Japanese confederate who either smiled frequently or infrequently while displaying an open or closed body position. American participants rated the confederate most attractive when she smiled frequently and displayed open body positions and least attractive when she smiled infrequently and displayed closed body positions. By contrast, Japanese participants found the confederate most attractive when she smiled frequently and exhibited closed body positions. In this case, perceptions of attractiveness are strongly affected by cultural perspective.

Vocal cues are certainly important contributors to perceptions of friendliness, likability, and attractiveness. In telephone conversations, we often make judgments about the friendliness of an individual on the basis of vocal cues. In one interesting study that employed a Moog synthesizer, Scherer (1979c) found that variations in pitch and tempo produced positiveness ratings. In a similar study (Scherer & Oshinsky, 1977), a number of acoustic parameters resulted in pleasantness ratings, including small amplitude variation, large pitch variation, downward pitch contour, and fast tempo. Because of its reinforcing properties, the use of positive backchannel vocalizations like "mm-hmm" probably produce positive social perceptions (Matarazzo, Wiens, & Saslow, 1965). Note that to some extent research on vocal cues and perceptions of credibility overlap with this area since some credibility factors include a sociability dimension. That work will be reviewed shortly.

Finally, use of touch and close proximity may promote perceptions of a communicator as more attractive, especially when used according to cultural guidelines (Andersen et al., 1979; Argyle, 1972; Fisher, Rytting, & Heslin, 1976; Heslin, 1974; Heslin & Boss, 1980; Mehrabian, 1981; Mehrabian & Friar, 1969; Mehrabian & Ksionzky, 1970; Patterson, 1977). However, as we shall see, a communicator may also sometimes promote greater attraction by violating the cultural norms.

To sum up, a wide variety of kinesic, vocalic, haptic, and proxemic code elements result in fostering perceptions of social attraction, liking, and immediacy with others. Smiling, head nodding, eye contact, gestural activity, relaxed and open body positions, variations in vocal pitch and tempo, close proximity and increased amounts of touch are among the cues that engender these impressions in others and provide communicators with a means to manage attractiveness impressions for both short-term and long-term aims.

Credibility and Related Evaluative Judgments. Concerns about communicator credibility can be traced back to the earliest writings of the classical rhetoricians, the historical roots of the field of communication. Contemporary treatments of credibility conceive it to be a set of perceptions that are held by one communicator about another communicator. In impression management terms, the fostering of perceptions of credibility in others may give a communicator a greater ability to influence others across interpersonal, public, and mass media contexts (see Chapter 13).

Three points need to be made about credibility. First, research has led to numerous dimensions of credibility, with little agreement on the main or central elements of this set of judgments; however, the ones most widely recognized in communication research are competence (expertise), character (trustworthiness), composure, dynamism (extroversion), and sociability. Second, as noted earlier, to some degree, some credibility judgment dimensions (primarily sociability) overlap with the foregoing discussion of liking and immediacy. As much as possible, we have tried to keep the research concerned with credibility separate and will discuss it in the following sections. Third, other evaluative dimensions of impression management (e.g., prestige and benevolence) fall into the same conceptual domain and will be discussed here as well.

Numerous vocal cues significantly affect credibility perceptions. One of the most extensively studied is speech tempo or rate. The preponderance of research shows that faster speaking enhances competence-related perceptions such as intelligence, objectivity, and knowledgeability (Buller & Aune, 1988; Giles & Street, 1985; Gunderson & Hopper, 1976; Mehrabian

APPLICATIONS

Effective Nonverbal Cues in Job Interviews

A recent study explored which nonverbal cues might lead to being hired by an organization (Gifford, Ng, & Wilkinson, 1985). Though not focused on credibility judgments per se, the study examined the nonverbal cues a job applicant could use to bolster an interviewer's perceptions of social skill and motivation, as well as the relationship between these cues and the applicants' views of their own social skill and motivation. The judgments being drawn about the applicants are similar to judgments of credibility since perceptions of social skill are similar to credibility judgments.

Results indicated that three applicant nonverbal cues led to high perceptions of social skill by interviewers: gesturing during the interview for a brief amount of the interview time, talking an average of 6.3 minutes when answering questions during the interview, and being moderately formally dressed. The cues were also strongly correlated with the applicants' own perceptions of their social skill, suggesting self-confidence plays a role in these kinds of situations.

For the motivation judgments, interviewers and applicants differed on what nonverbal cues they relied on: interviewers relied on the amount of time talked, rate of gesturing, and smiling, while applicants relied on body posture, dress, and gender. It is worthwhile for an applicant to know that interviewers infer motivation from talkativeness and friendliness. Effective use of these cues may be the most useful in creating a favorable impression and possibly obtaining an offer.

& Williams, 1969; Pearce & Brommel, 1972; Ray, 1986; Siegman & Reynolds, 1982; Smith, Brown, Strong, & Rencher, 1975; Stewart & Ryan, 1982; Street & Brady, 1982), perceptions of dominance (Buller & Aune, 1988), and perceptions of dynamism (Addington, 1971; Brown, Strong, & Rencher, 1973, 1974; Burgoon, 1978b). Greater variety in tempo also contributes to higher perceived sociability (Birk, Pfau, & Burgoon, 1988). Marketing research on the effects of compressed speech, which essentially speeds up the audio portion of a radio or television broadcast, finds similar beneficial effects for faster tempo (LaBarbera & MacLachlan, 1979; MacLachlan, 1979). However, research on the effects on sociability, composure, and character-related judgments has produced mixed findings. Some experiments have found that a faster rate is more credible (Miller, Maruyama, Beaber, & Valone, 1976; Street & Brady, 1982; Street, Brady, and Putman, 1983), while others have found that a moderate or slower rate is perceived as more composed, honest, people-oriented, and benevolent (Brown, 1980; Brown, Strong, & Rencher, 1973, 1974, 1975; Burgoon, 1978a; Pearce & Conklin, 1971; Ray, 1986; Schweitzer, 1970; Smith et al., 1975; Woodall & Burgoon, 1983). The relationship may actually be curvilinear such that both slow and fast rates are less desirable than a moderate one.

Street and Brady (1982) offer one explanation for this complex set of relationships between tempo and various credibility judgments. They suggest that a linear relationship indeed exists between tempo and competence, such that faster is better, but that similarity between the receiver's own speaking rate and that of the speaker mediates judgments related to social attractiveness. Since moderate rates are most likely to be similar to listeners' own tempo, moderate rates of speech would be judged most socially attractive. Thus, although preferences for fast speech may determine competence ratings, tempo similarity between speakers and listeners may determine attractiveness and sociability judgments. Two studies by Street (Street & Brady, 1982; Street et al., 1983) and a recent one by Buller and Aune (1986) support these claims. Street et al. (1983) concluded that interactants prefer speech rates that are similar to or somewhat faster than their own speech rates.

Other factors that influence speech judgments are communication context, gender, and mode of presentation. The negative perceptions of slow speech rate can be canceled out if the listeners can favorably account for the slow rate of the speaker, for example, helping listeners understand an unfamiliar or difficult topic (Giles, Brown, & Thakerar, 1981). Research on gender has produced conflicting findings. Most research in this area has employed male voices for stimuli and generalized results to both males and females. When both genders are taken into account, different results are obtained. Although for both male and female speakers, faster rates are associated with high ratings of competence and status, speaking rate appears to be *unrelated* to perceived social attractiveness of female speakers (Aronovitch, 1976; Crown, 1980; Siegman & Reynolds, 1982). Finally, Woodall and Burgoon (1983) found that subjects hearing audio-only messages were more influenced by speaking rate than those who received the message in the audiovisual mode. The results suggest that when listeners have only the audio channel present, vocal behaviors such as speech tempo have a greater impact on credibility perceptions than situations where both audio and visual channels and cues are present.

A second vocal feature that affects credibility is pausing. Two types of pausing have been studied: within-turn pausing, sometimes termed *hesitation pauses,* and between-speaker pauses, called *response latency.* Several studies have shown that short pauses of both types result in positive credibility evaluations (Lay & Burron, 1968; Newman, 1982; Scherer, 1979c; Scherer, London, & Wolf, 1973; Siegman & Reynolds, 1982; Street, 1982). Another study (Baskett & Freedle, 1974) found differential effects for response latency pausing, with short latencies (1 sec or less) being perceived as most competent and moderate latencies (1–3 sec) as most trustworthy. Finally, Street (1982, 1984) found that *similarities* in response latency between interactants produce positive social and credibility perceptions.

Loudness and pitch affect credibility. Research indicates that up to a moderately high level of intensity, increases in loudness or vocal intensity enhance a range of credibility judgments, including impressions of dominance, competence, emotional stability, boldness, sociability, and extroversion (Aronovitch, 1976; Birk et al., 1988; Burgoon, 1978a; Ray, 1986; Scherer, 1979c). However, a softer voice combined with a varied pitch may be best for fostering benevolence judgments (Ray, 1986). Research results on pitch level itself and impressions appear to be inconsistent (Giles & Street, 1985). Some work indicates that higher levels of vocal pitch result in favorable impressions of competence, dominance, and assertiveness (Scherer, 1978; Scherer et al., 1973). Other research reports negative impressions being drawn with increasing levels of pitch (Apple, Streeter, & Krauss, 1979) and instead finds that deeper pitch is more credible (Brown, Strong, & Rencher, 1973, 1974). The conflicting findings may be due in part to different acceptable pitch ranges for male and female voices. Increases in male pitch may result in positive credibility impressions up to a point, that point being pitch ranges associated with female voices. Once a male voice enters this range of pitch, negative attributions result. Research on pitch variation, however, consistently shows that greater pitch variation enhances credibility perceptions across the board (Addington, 1971; Brown, Strong, & Rencher, 1973, 1974; Burgoon, 1978a; Scherer, 1979c). It is especially effective in creating competence impressions when coupled with a fast tempo (Ray, 1986). Closely related to pitch variety is vocal pleasantness. Voices perceived as more pleasant foster impressions of sociability (Addington, 1971; Birk et al., 1988).

The amount of vocalization affects credibility perceptions as well. Some research has indicated that interactants who engage in long conversational turns are perceived positively in terms of competence and conscientiousness (Hayes & Meltzer, 1972; Scherer, 1979c). Stang (1973) has reported that medium-length turns by interactants are perceived as more attractive. Street (1982) has shown that either a consistent turn duration or modifying turn duration toward the other interactant's length results in positive social attractiveness perceptions. Thus it appears that competency ratings are best served by lengthy turns, while sociability ratings are most positively affected by medium-length turns or consistent or matching turn lengths, a pattern somewhat similar to the speech rate findings.

Many of us assume that speech errors and disfluencies affect others' perceptions of us negatively. To a large extent, this is true. Two studies show that disfluency negatively affects perceived competency but does not diminish trustworthiness (Miller & Hewgill, 1964; Sereno & Hawkins, 1967). It also affects composure and sociability. Birk et al. (1988) found that a speaker's fluency was the best predictor of the speaker's being judged as composed, while fluency and pleasantness were the best predictors of sociability judgments.

Two broader vocal styles that reflect a combination of vocal cues have been studied for their impact on credibility perceptions (Pearce & Brommel, 1971; Pearce & Conklin, 1971). One style, the conversational delivery style, contains a smaller range of inflection, greater consistency in rate and pitch, less volume, and lower pitch, while the dynamic style involves more pausing, higher pitch range, and more variations in volume. The conversational delivery style results in perceptions of honesty and people-orientedness, while the dynamic delivery results in perceptions of tough-mindedness, task orientation, assertiveness, and confidence.

Finally, regional and ethnic dialects have been studied for their effects on communicator perceptions. Although a dialect or accent is comprised of variations in verbal behavior, variations in vocal behavior make up an accent as well (vocal qualities, pronunciations of various words, rate, etc.). The amount of research on dialect and accent is extensive and will not be covered in detail here (for reviews, see Giles, 1979; Ryan, 1979; Street & Hopper, 1982). After reviewing this literature, Giles and Street (1985) drew the following conclusions concerning accent and credibility: (a) Receivers generally perceive dominant or prestigious group accents and dialects as more competent, higher in status, more intelligent, and more successful; (b) Regional or inferior group accents are perceived as trustworthy and likable and are preferred by in-group members, especially in informal contexts such as neighborhood bars and homes. Finally, Burgoon and Saine (1978, p. 182) assembled the following conclusions:

1. Regional dialects are not always rated highest by regional occupants. (Delia, 1972)
2. The General American dialect (what is spoken in the Midwest) is viewed as more credible and especially more competent than southern or New England dialects. (Delia, 1972; Toomb, Quiggins, Moore, MacNeil, & Liddell, 1972)
3. People with a New York accent are rated more dynamic and competent but less sociable than those with a southern drawl. (Toomb et al., 1972)
4. Speech with native accents is rated as more dynamic, more aestheti-

cally pleasing and reflective of higher socio-intellectual status than that of foreign-accented speech. (Mulac, Hanley, & Prigge, 1974)
5. Both blacks and whites rate speakers of standard English higher than speakers using nonstandard dialect. (Buck, 1968)

To sum up, the evidence overall indicates that perceptions in the competence domain are enhanced by fast speaking rate, greater fluency, short pauses, moderately high intensity (loudness), deeper and more varied pitch, longer conversational turns, dynamic style, and the preferred (General American) dialect. Perceptions in the sociability and attractiveness domain are enhanced by a vocal tempo that is similar to or slightly faster than the perceiver's, moderate latency or a latency that is similar to the perceiver's, greater fluency, deeper and more varied pitch, vocal pleasantness, medium-length turns or turn length similar to the perceiver's, conversational vocal style, and a regional or in-group accent. A number of studies have shown that these vocal cues can affect communication outcomes in educational, job interview, therapeutic, and legal settings. Quite clearly, vocal cues have a strong effect on how others see us and how we see others.

One of the most potent kinesic cues is eye contact or gaze. Increased eye contact results in perceptions of dynamism, likability, believability, and persuasiveness (which can be viewed as a component of credibility) (Beebe, 1980; LaCrosse, 1975). Hemsley and Doob (1978), in a courtroom simulation study, found that witnesses who averted their gaze were perceived as less credible. Further, the defendant for whom the witness was testifying was also judged as more likely to be guilty. Similar results have been obtained in other studies (Kleck & Nuessle, 1968; LeCompte & Rosenfeld, 1971).

When gaze is combined with other immediacy cues, it further enhances credibility. Public speakers who use more immediacy and who are more expressive facially and gesturally are perceived as more sociable, more extroverted, and of better character.

Burgoon and Saine (1978) have suggested that good posture and a walk that effuses confidence are likely to affect perceptions of credibility positively. Recent research has tended to support this conjecture. Birk et al. (1988) determined that postural rigidity led to lower ratings of sociability and quite low ratings of composure. Curiously, higher rates of self-manipulation in this study led to higher perceptions of relaxation.

Finally, the synchronization of kinesic cues (rhythmic hand gesturing and head nods) affects perceptions of credibility. Woodall and Burgoon (1981) created videotapes wherein actors either closely synchronized rhythmic hand gesturing and head nods to primary stress points in phonemic clauses or displayed them either immediately before or after the stress points. Synchronous displays were perceived as more competent, composed, trustworthy, extroverted, and sociable than the dissynchronous displays.

A growing number of studies are demonstrating that proxemic variations have an impact on credibility perceptions. In one early study (Patter-

The speaker's hand gestures are likely to enhance perceptions of credibility in audience members.

son & Sechrest, 1970), a curvilinear relationship between distance and social activity ratings (friendly, extroverted, dominant, aggressive) was found. Ratings were highest when confederates were 4 feet from the subjects and were lowest at distances of 2 feet and 6 feet. A series of studies designed to test a nonverbal expectations and violations model (to be discussed shortly) has also demonstrated that conversational distance affects credibility.

In an age of media presidents, most of us need not be reminded of the impact of physical appearance on perceptions of credibility. Political candidates pay a great deal of attention to physical appearance in an attempt to bolster their image and credibility. Even the news broadcasters who report on the candidates often take care that their physical appearance cues enhance their audience image as well as their audience share.

Several physical appearance factors are at work here. One study that investigated the effects of body types on credibility perceptions (Toomb & Divers, 1972) found that female ectomorphs were rated most sociable, followed by male mesomorphs. These results may be due to our culture's preference for thin females and muscular males. Some studies on hair length (Andersen, Jensen, & King, 1972; Peterson & Curran, 1976) have found that short-haired males are rated as more competent, dynamic, intelligent, masculine, mature, wise, and attractive than long-haired men.

Although there is little systematic and empirical evidence concerning the effects of clothing on credibility, it is reasonable to believe that mode of dress has an impact. For example, in legal settings, astute trial lawyers have their clients dress so as to convey sincerity, believability, and innocence. Many people believe that dressing well and appropriately can make a difference in their status and credibility in an organization. Nowhere has this view been more popularized than in John Molloy's *Dress for Success* books. Molloy (1975, 1977) offers very specific advice about the kind of clothing choices that will work best in business settings. Unfortunately, there are two important drawbacks to Molloy's work. First, Molloy states that the advice he gives is based on research he and his associates conducted. However, his research methods, statistical analysis, and results are not well-documented, so it is not possible to verify the soundness of his advice. Second, his advice may be overly restrictive. It is unlikely that the limited range of clothing choices he suggests are the *only* options that will produce "successful" results. In fairness, Molloy himself has begun to recognize the value of developing a wider range of clothing styles so that one can better adapt to a particular audience. His latest advice suggests that matching one's audience in dress style may be preferable to emphasizing power and competence.

The New Dress Code for Success

. . . Whereas [Molloy] championed the all-purpose power uniform in 1975, now he's advocating different suits for different folks.

"In the first book, I said '*this* is the right tie' and '*this* is the right suit'," Molloy says. "Now the world is a little more sophisticated."

In the new version, Molloy gets very specific indeed. For instance, he advises the businessman traveling to Jacksonville, Florida, to wear a "midrange blue or gray suit with a blue shirt and striped tie"; a professional destined for St. Paul would do better in a dark-brown pinstripe.

For the salesman whose appointment is with a hip architect, Molloy's advice is to dress cleverly—in three shades of blue, for instance. If the client is a military man, the seller should avoid an off-putting gray suit and Ivy League tie.

This approach worked for Phil Dusenberry, chairman and chief creative officer of the New York advertising agency BBDO. When pitching the Apple computer account . . . , Dusenberry says his team "left our six-piece suits at home and dressed down—in sports jackets—for the presentation."

The folks at Apple wear jeans and open-collar shirts, "and we didn't want to come off as slick New Yorkers," Dusenberry says. It worked. BBDO landed the account.

Source: Elizabeth Sporkin, *USA Today*, January 12, 1988, p. D2.

Finally, chronemic code elements can potentially affect perceptions of credibility. One study (Baxter & Ward, 1975) asked 84 secretaries what their impressions would be if someone arrived 15 minutes early, 15 minutes late, or on time for an appointment. Late arrivers were regarded as highly dynamic but low on competence, composure, and sociability. Prompt arrivers were considered the most competent, composed, and sociable but not very dynamic. Early arrivers were rated low on dynamism and only moderate on other dimensions. While secretaries' views may not be representative of the whole population, the results do suggest that promptness overall has the best credibility outcome.

As this review shows, a large number of cues from the vocalic, kinesic, proxemic, physical appearance, and chronemic codes can be used to enhance perceptions of credibility. As the research on vocal cues and credibility shows in particular, a given nonverbal cue typically affects only certain dimensions of credibility (dynamism or sociability, for example) and not others. Other nonverbal cues from codes not mentioned above may also have the potential to be used for credibility-related impression management purposes (a variety of environmental cues may lend themselves to such use). Now let us consider the possibility of violating expectations as an impression management strategy.

Expectancy Violations

A common theme running through popular advice on communication and explicitly stated in Goffman's self-presentation theory is that to be a successful communicator requires conforming to social norms. Violators are supposedly regarded as deviants and evaluated negatively. Though this principle may seem intuitively appealing, evidence is coming to light that there may be occasions when nonverbal violations of expectations are a better strategy than norm conformity for enhancing one's credibility and influencing others. Burgoon and colleagues (Burgoon, 1978b, 1983; Burgoon & Jones, 1976; Burgoon, Stacks, & Woodall, 1979) first explored this possibility in the realm of proxemic behavior. After reviewing the literature on reactions to spatial invasions and other adjustments in proxemic behavior, they advanced the first model of nonverbal expectancy violations. They began with the assumption that people hold expectations about how others will behave in communication situations. This includes expectations about how close or far away another person will sit or stand. These expectations are grounded largely in social norms. For example, it is normative for two males to interact at a farther distance than two females.

Burgoon and Jones (1976) were interested in predicting what happens when a communicator violates these expectancies. They proposed that a major determinant of whether a violation yields positive or negative communication consequences is how the communicator is regarded by other interactants. If the communicator is initially regarded favorably, perhaps because of attractiveness, credibility, high status, similarity of attitudes, or positiveness of feedback, the communicator is classified as having *high reward value*. A number of considerations may come into play in sizing up a person's reward value. The key is that the receiver sees the source as someone with whom it is rewarding to interact. Conversely, a person with *low reward value* is seen as repulsive, untrustworthy, hypercritical, boring, of low status, or the like.

The expectancy violations model then requires taking into account the *direction* of a nonverbal violation (is the violator moving closer or farther away than expected?) and the *magnitude* of the violation. In the case of a high reward communicator, it is proposed (in the most recent revisions of the model) that a violation closer or farther than expected will produce better outcomes than conforming to the norm. The greater the deviation from expectation, the greater the benefit. However, if the violation is so close as to be perceived as a physical threat, it is hypothesized to produce negative consequences.

In the case of a low reward communicator, it is predicted that the greater the deviation from the expected nonverbal pattern, the greater the negative consequences. Thus a high reward person may gain a more favorable image by engaging in a violation, whereas a low reward person will end up with an even more negative image.

On what are these predictions based? Several elements are involved in the process (Burgoon, 1978b, 1983, 1985b, 1986; Burgoon & Aho, 1982; Burgoon, Coker, & Coker, 1986; Burgoon & Hale, 1987a, 1988; Burgoon, Manusov, Mineo, & Hale, 1985; Burgoon, Stacks, & Burch, 1982; Hale & Burgoon, 1984). One is the concept of *arousal.* It is argued that violations create physiological and psychological arousal in the violatee. This arousal in turn creates *distraction.* The violatee's attention is subdivided, shifting from primary focus on the verbal content of the interaction to the cause of arousal—in this case, the violator. This makes the communicator's reward characteristics and the nature of the relationship between the two more salient. If the violator is well regarded, his or her rewarding features should become more noticed. The same should be true of the negative qualities of the low reward violator.

Furthermore, the violation behavior itself may be *interpreted and evaluated.* A move closer may be interpreted as a desire for affiliation, attentiveness, liking, or dominance, among other things. When a high reward person engages in such a violation, we may interpret it favorably and evaluate it favorably. We like having a high reward person show interest in us, for example. When a low reward person engages in the same behavior, however, we may interpret it negatively ("This person is being very pushy and aggressive") or evaluate it negatively ("This person is trying to be friendly but I don't want to be friends with her").

To summarize, the process of predicting whether violations have positive or negative consequences depends on (a) the reward level of the communicator, (b) the direction and magnitude of the violation, (c) the presence of arousal change and distraction, and (d) the interpretations and evaluations given to the behavior itself.

Several studies have attempted to test this expectancy violations model. We focus here on those that have tested the effects on impressions of attraction and credibility. In the first test, Burgoon (1978b) had one group of subjects establish what were expected (normative) and threatening distances and then had other subjects engage in a sentence creation task while an interviewer interacted at a far, normative, close, or threatening distance. High reward interviewers gave positive feedback; low reward interviewers gave negative feedback. High reward interviewers were seen as higher in character when they engaged in a distance violation (i.e., adopted a far, close, or very close distance). Conversely, low reward interviewers earned their *lowest* ratings on character, composure, and physical attraction when they engaged in a violation, especially at the very close distance. The next set of experiments (Burgoon, Stacks, & Woodall, 1979) examined sex, race, and physical attractiveness as possible bases of reward. Only physical attractiveness worked to mediate the impact of distance violations. Physically attractive interviewers were again rated more positively on credibility and attraction if they engaged in a violation, whereas unattractive interviewers were rated most favorably if they conformed to the norms and earned lower ratings when they committed a violation. A subsequent experiment by Stacks and Burgoon (1981) likewise found that physically attractive student confederates, who in this case gave persuasive speeches to other students waiting for the "experiment" to begin, earned highest ratings on competence, sociability, composure, extroversion, social attraction, and physical attraction when they adopted extremely close or extremely distant positions.

In the next experiment (Burgoon, Stacks, & Burch, 1982), rewarding and nonrewarding violators were compared to rewarding and nonrewarding confederates who conformed to the norms. Using a mock trial context, subjects interacted with two confederates, one who presented the prosecution case and one who presented the defense case in a murder trial. The subject was to decide at the end of the session whether the defendant was innocent or guilty of the charges. During the discussion, violating confederates either moved in closer or moved farther away than the original distance, while the other confederate remained stationary. High reward confederates were made to appear as physically attractive as possible, were introduced as having previous jury experience and a prestigious major, and expressed interest in the task. In the low reward conditions, the same confederates were made to appear unattractive, claimed to have no prior jury experience, had an undeclared major, and were enthused about the task. Consistent with the model's predictions, high reward confederates were seen as more credible and attractive when they violated norms, especially when they moved farther away, than when they maintained the initial distance. For low reward confederates, the biggest effect of their violations was to confer greater credibility on the other confederate, who did not engage in a violation. Nonrewarding communicators were better off conforming to the original distance.

These studies all demonstrate that proxemic violations can have positive consequences in terms of image management when they are performed by a highly rewarding communicator. They can also have negative consequences for a low reward communicator. Hence it becomes important for a person to estimate his or her regard by others before deciding whether to violate or conform to proxemic norms.

The next set of experiments attempted to extend the expectancy violations model beyond conversational distance to other nonverbal cues and to predict more clearly which kinds of violations are likely to be interpreted or evaluated as positive and which as negative. It was argued that some forms of nonverbal violations, such as avoiding eye contact or greatly decreasing involvement, should be unequivocally negative violations, while others, such as greatly increasing gaze or immediacy, might be positive violations, depending on who commits them.

Three experiments (Burgoon, Coker, & Coker, 1986; Burgoon, Manusov, Mineo, & Hale, 1985; Manusov, 1984) tested eye gaze violations, and two experiments (Burgoon & Coker, 1987; Burgoon & Hale, 1988) tested immediacy or involvement violations. Although these investigations failed to produce truly low reward interactions, the results did consistently show that decreased gaze, immediacy, and involvement lowered credibility and attraction ratings and that increases in gaze, immediacy, and involvement frequently improved them. These findings suggest that other forms of violations may also enhance one's image but that one must know in advance whether the violating behavior itself has unambiguous meanings and evaluations or not. If the behavior or set of behaviors clearly qualify as a negative violation of expectations in a given culture, they will undoubtedly yield unfavorable image assessments. If instead they typically would be read as a positive violation, they should enhance image more than conforming to the norms. Finally, if the behavior is subject to multiple interpretations and evaluations, the reward value of the communicator should determine whether the violation is ultimately defined as positive or negative.

Factors Affecting Attempts at Impression Management

At least two factors limit and affect the scope of nonverbal cues and impression management. First, there are individual skill differences in managing nonverbal cues for impression management purposes. Among the concepts that could reflect such individual differences, self-monitoring (Snyder, 1974, 1979) is likely to be one. Snyder describes high self-monitors as sensitive to their self-presentation and expression to relevant others out of concern for the appropriateness of their social behavior. High self-monitors, then, carefully monitor their verbal and nonverbal behavior (Giles & Street, 1985). Low self-monitors are less concerned about appropriate self-presentation and typically do not have well-developed self-presentational skills. Some initial research has shown that high self-monitors are better able to express emotional states through facial and vocal channels than low self-monitors. In turn, Riggio and Friedman (1986) have confirmed that high self-monitors and those who are more skilled at encoding emotional expressions create more favorable first impressions. Males seem to do so through greater speaking and gestural fluency and body movement, while women do so primarily through the use of more facial expressiveness. On an anecdotal level, we have all met individuals who make a great number of social mistakes and faux pas and others who are very slick and smooth in social situations. The latter may be more successful at managing their impressions because they are high self-monitors or more expressive, extroverted communicators.

Given that self-monitoring may affect an individual's skill in using nonverbal cues, one might wonder whether communicators know what kinds of impressions they are making. A recent study that addressed this question (DePaulo, Kenny, Hoover, Webb, & Oliver, 1987) found that subjects involved in an interaction knew what impressions they were conveying to partners over time, how their impression management attempts changed over time with different partners, and how their competence was perceived. Clearly, then, not only are communicators able to control and use nonverbal cues for impression management purposes, but they are also aware of the nature of the impression that they are managing.

A second factor that limits the scope of nonverbal cues and impression management is the situation. Analyses of situations (examined in Chapter 11) suggest that some situations are marked for impression management tactics, strategies, and behaviors while other situations are not. Impression management efforts are appropriate in formal or goal-related situations, for example. Familiar and commonplace situations may not be appropriate for such efforts. To put it another way, going to a bank to talk to an officer about a loan is certainly a situation that calls for impression management; going to the local 7-Eleven for a Slurpee is not. Further work needs to be done to develop links between situational analyses and impression management theory. Such links would allow nonverbal communication researchers to specify in what situations nonverbal cues would be used for impression management and the extent of success of such efforts.

Finally, as Giles and Street (1985) suggest, a great deal of work is yet to be done in closely connecting impression management theory with communication research and theory. That is particularly true for nonverbal communication research, for at the moment, impression management theory mostly allows a reinterpretation of preexisting research. In addition to nonverbal cues being used for impression management purposes, Giles and Street suggest that nonverbal cue patterns, such as speech accommodation, compensation patterns, and divergence patterns (described in Chapter 12) could be linked to impression management tactics.

Summary

Impressions formed on the basis of nonverbal cues are guided by several principles, including these: (a) Impressions are based on limited information, (b) they incorporate stereotypes, (c) first impressions often make use of physical appearance cues, and (d) first impressions often form a baseline for subsequent impressions. Nonverbal cues from a number of codes have been shown to affect impressions on the physical, sociocultural, and psychological levels. In general, the evidence indicates that impressions are more consensual and less accurate when they are concerned with internal and psychological characteristics than with external and objective characteristics. Further, a wide variety of nonverbal cues affect impressions on all three levels of judgment.

Self-presentation concepts and principles dictate that a performer should (a) attempt to segregate audiences for different performances, (b) adhere to the rules that accompany a social act, (c) coordinate verbal and nonverbal cues, (d) be judged sincere, and (e) be satisfied with the role being played. The importance of these principles for nonverbal communication was discussed. A review of impression management tactics pointed out that most nonverbal cues have been linked to assertive-strategic impression management goals, which include the enhancement of perceptions of social attractiveness, credibility, esteem, status, and prestige. Nonverbal violations of expectations research was examined for impression management findings, and that research indicates that in some cases, violations of nonverbal expectations can result in positive impression management outcomes. Finally, self-monitoring and situational factors were suggested as constraints on the effectiveness and scope of impression management tactics.

Suggested Readings

Burgoon, J. K., & Saine, T. J. (1978). *The unspoken dialogue: An introduction to nonverbal communication.* Boston: Houghton Mifflin.

Cook, M. (1979). *Perceiving others: The psychology of interpersonal perception.* London: Methuen.

Goffman, E. (1959). *The presentation of self in everyday life.* Garden City, NY: Doubleday.

Goffman, E. (1967). *Interaction ritual.* Garden City, NY: Doubleday.

Kleinke, C. L. (1975). *First impressions: The psychology of encountering others.* Englewood Cliffs, NJ: Prentice-Hall.

Schlenker, B. R. (1980). *Impression management: The self-concept, social identity, and interpersonal relations.* Monterey, CA: Brooks/Cole.

Tedeschi, J. T., & Norman, N. (1985). Social power, self-presentation, and the self. In B. R. Schlenker (Ed.), *The self and social life* (pp. 293–322). New York: McGraw-Hill.

CHAPTER 8

Mixed Messages and Deception

The face is the mirror of the mind, and the eyes, without speaking, confess the secrets of the heart.

St. Jerome

When enacting multichannel nonverbal presentations, common sense says that one should coordinate the channels to produce a consistent message. For instance, if you want to communicate love to your romantic partner, you might simultaneously sit very close, look deeply into your partner's eyes, caress your partner's body, periodically kiss, and whisper "sweet nothings." Unless your partner is terribly insensitive or distracted, your "pure" multichannel message will successfully communicate your love.

Now let's suppose that your partner's response to your pure message of love is to sit very close, stare off into the distance, caress your body, kiss you only when you initiate the kiss, and whisper affectionate things. How would you interpret this message? The words, the closeness, and the touching are right. But the lack of eye contact and passionate kissing are inconsistent with the affection communicated by the other cues. Does your partner love you or not?

Mixed Messages

Communicators frequently encounter "mixed" messages in which the nonverbal cues do not provide a clear, unambiguous message. Sometimes these mixed messages are deliberate. Jokes and sarcasm rely on mixed messages for their effect. Other times, mixed messages are indicative of internal confusion. Uncertainty, indifference, and ambivalence (e.g., simultaneously liking and disliking another person) produce mixed messages. Finally, deceptive communicators inadvertently display mixed messages that can clue others in on their duplicity.

Mixed messages are difficult to decode. One must sort out the conflicting cues and make an interpretation based on less certain information than in pure messages. Receivers, though, can and do decode mixed messages (DePaulo & Rosenthal, 1979a; Johnson, McCarty, & Allen, 1976). The process involves three phases: (a) confusion and uncertainty when first encountering mixed messages, (b) increased concentration and interest in mixed messages as one deliberately decodes the mixed cues, and (c) negative reactions and withdrawal as a result of the uncertainty of interpreting the mixed message (Leathers, 1979).

A receiver's ability to decode mixed messages is quite separate from the ability to decode pure messages, and decoding visual mixed messages requires a different ability from decoding mixed vocalic messages. People rely on these skills to varying extents, depending on the type of cues displayed, nature of the emotion communicated, degree of cue discrepancy, sex, and age.

Visual Cue Primacy

In attempts to resolve the inconsistency in mixed messages, receivers rely heavily on information communicated by visual cues (i.e., kinesic cues) (Hegstrom, 1979; Philpott, 1983; Tepper & Haase, 1978). In one of the earliest studies on mixed messages, Mehrabian and Ferris (1967) found that people rely most on visual cues, less on vocal cues, and least on verbal cues when decoding inconsistent messages. Bugental, Kaswan, and Love (1970) also found a visual primacy among their adult and child subjects, as did subsequent studies by DePaulo and her colleagues (DePaulo, Rosenthal, Eisenstat, Rogers, & Finkelstein, 1978; DePaulo & Rosenthal, 1979a). In research on nonsocial visual (e.g., lights) and auditory (e.g., tones) cues, subjects engage in perceptual tasks that require them to indicate whether a light flashes or a tone sounds on their right or left. Though neither channel contains more information, subjects display a strong visual bias in these studies (Posner, Nissen, & Klein, 1976).

At least four explanations have been offered for this visual bias (Keeley-Dyreson, Bailey, & Burgoon, 1988). First, when it comes to decoding emotional information, visual cues provide more information and possess more meaning than vocal cues (Berman, Shulman, & Morwit, 1976; Buck, 1980). Visual cues are more semantically distinctive and more efficient transmitters, providing more units of meaning per time unit (DePaulo & Rosenthal, 1979a). Second, Posner et al. (1976) argue that humans attend deliberately to the visual channel because unlike auditory cues, it is not automatically alerting. This deliberate attention reduces the input from auditory cues, giving visual cues more impact. Third, encoders have greater control over the face, thereby giving decoders more intentional information. Fourth, Berman et al. (1976) speculate that people rely more on visual cues because they can quickly scan the face and then concentrate on the most informative facial cues, whereas with the voice, decoders can only process the cues sequentially and fleetingly. Thus the amount of emotional information in the visual channel, its lower alerting capacity, its greater intentionality potential, and the longer duration of facial cues cause people to rely more on visual cues when decoding mixed messages (DePaulo & Rosenthal, 1979a).

Visual cue primacy is greater when mixed messages involve the face rather than the body (DePaulo et al., 1978; DePaulo & Rosenthal, 1979a). The face has long been recognized as a rich source of emotional content (Ekman & Friesen, 1967), so it is not surprising that receivers place more weight on facial cues when resolving inconsistencies.

Visual cue primacy also is stronger when decoding emotions related to positivity (agreeableness, conscientiousness, positive or negative attitude), especially when visual cues include the face. Conversely, body and vocalic cues become more important when decoding dominance, assertiveness, and anxiety (Burns & Beier, 1973; DePaulo et al., 1978; DePaulo & Rosenthal, 1979a; Scherer, Scherer, Hall, & Rosenthal, 1977; Zuckerman, Amidon, Bishop, & Pomerantz, 1982). The face is particularly important in judging positivity because receivers associate the smile with positivity, a link that has no analogue in the body and voice. Dominance, by contrast, is communicated very well by intense, emphatic body movements and vocal loudness, leading to greater reliance on these two channels when judging mixed messages of dominance, assertiveness, and anxiety (DePaulo et al., 1978; DePaulo & Rosenthal, 1979a).

In the nonsocial research on visual primacy, as the discrepancy between visual and auditory cues increased, the ability to distinguish between the differences in the two channels increased and auditory cues had more impact (Posner et al., 1976). This effect seems to apply to mixed nonverbal messages as well. DePaulo (DePaulo et al., 1978; DePaulo & Rosenthal, 1979a) reports that as the discrepancy between visual and vocalic cues increases, visual cue primacy decreases and receivers increase their reliance on vocalic cues.

Women are more likely to display visual cue primacy, especially when the visual cues involve the face and judgments of positivity (DePaulo et al., 1978; DePaulo & Rosenthal, 1979a). This may be due to greater visual interaction by females. Women engage in more eye contact than men in interpersonal interactions and are uncomfortable when they cannot see their conversational partner. Further, women have been observed to increase their visual interaction in positively valenced interactions (Argyle, Lalljee, & Cook, 1968; Exline, Gray, & Schuette, 1965; Exline & Winters, 1965). The attention to visual cues may also be the result of a learned tendency for women to be "polite" communicators by paying less attention to vocalic channels likely to "leak" information the source did not intend to send (Rosenthal & DePaulo, 1979b).

Finally, children encountering mixed messages use decoding processes somewhat different from those of adults. DePaulo and Rosenthal (1979a) found that younger children can detect mixed messages communicating positivity but have difficulty decoding those communicating dominance. Further, when decoding positivity, children seem to discount positive visual cues when they are paired with negative vocalic cues, especially when the positive cue is a smile by a woman. Younger children appear to assume the worst, placing more weight on the negative meaning in these mixed messages, whereas adults counterbalance negative vocalic cues with positive visual cues. In sum, the ability to decode mixed messages increases with age, and the ability to decode mixed messages containing positive emotions develops earlier than the ability to read mixed messages containing dominance cues (Bugental, Kaswan, & Love, 1970; Bugental, Love, Kaswan, & April, 1971).

Affective Reactions

As noted earlier, receivers find inconsistent messages less preferable (Mehrabian, 1970b) and react unfavorably when encountering them (Argyle, Salter, Nicholson, Williams, & Burgess, 1970). Also, receivers frequently question the veracity of mixed messages. That is, mixed messages beget suspicion and are decoded as deceptive (DePaulo & Rosenthal, 1979a; Zuckerman & Driver, 1985; Zuckerman, Driver, & Koestner, 1982). In fact, one study (DePaulo, Rosenthal, Green, & Rosenkrantz, 1982) found that receivers could not distinguish between deceptive mixed messages and ambivalent mixed messages, seeing both messages as equally deceptive.

Deception

Despite most people's assumption of truthfulness in interpersonal interactions and their belief that deceit is reprehensible and immoral, lying is a common communication strategy (Bok, 1978; Zuckerman, DePaulo, & Rosenthal, 1981). Deception can be indispensable for controlling information, maximizing rewards, and minimizing costs (Bok, 1978; Knapp & Comadena, 1979; Lippard, 1988; Turner, Edgley, & Olmstead, 1975; Wolk & Henley, 1970; Zuckerman, DePaulo, & Rosenthal, 1981). It is a highly adaptive and competent communication strategy essential for survival (Camden, Motley, & Wilson, 1984; Zuckerman, DePaulo, & Rosenthal, 1981). Some researchers have even argued that skillful liars and lie detectors have arisen through natural selection (Kraut, 1980; Leakey & Lewin, 1978). Thus many of us find in our everyday interactions that honesty is not always the best policy (Turner et al., 1975).

Deception, as a method of controlling information, is a communication strategy, the morality of which is determined by the motives of the deceiver. Sometimes these motives are selfish and harmful to partners, while at other times they are unselfish and beneficial to partners. Turner et al. (1975) asked a group of individuals to keep a log of their conversations and their motives for these conversations. Surprisingly, only about one-third of the exchanges were entirely honest. When asked why they encoded their deceptions, participants identified five primary motivations: (a) to save face (either their own, the partner's, or some third party's), (b) to maintain, maximize,

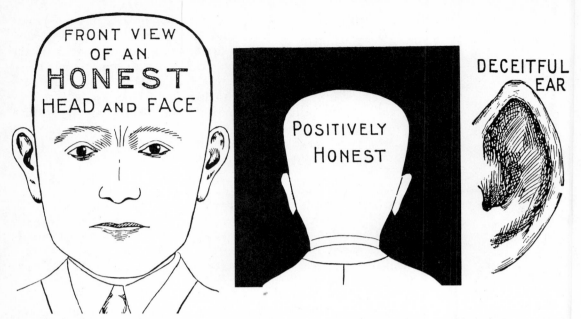

Deception and the ability to detect it have fascinated people for a long time. Unfortunately, knowledge of the cues that reveal deception has often been imperfect. For example, early in this century, L. A. Vaught was convinced that the shape of the head, face, and ears reveal the liar.

or terminate a relationship, (c) to establish, maximize, or maintain power or influence over the partner, (d) to avoid tension or conflict, and (e) to maintain, redirect, or terminate social interactions. In a later study, Lindskold and Walters (1983) identified six motivations ranging from altruistic through individualistic to exploitative: (a) to save partner from minor hurt, shame, or embarrassment, (b) to protect self or partner from punishment or disapproval for a minor failing or mistake, (c) to influence people in official positions to achieve a reward for self or partner, (d) to make self appear better or protect some gain received in the past to which self was not really entitled, (e) to persuade partner to do something for self-gain that will harm partner or cause partner to lose some resource, and (f) to hurt partner for self-gain. Camden et al. (1984) provided a taxonomy of deception motivations, all of which can be performed for the benefit of self, conversational partner, or a third party. In their taxonomy, there are four primary groups of motivations: basic needs, affiliation, self-esteem, and other motivations. Most recently, Metts and Chronis (1986) found that deceivers cite partner-focused, self-focused, and relationship-focused motivations for their deceptions (see Table 8.1).

It is apparent that many lies are told for selfish reasons; however, many are not "viciously selfish" and may be designed to assist another person (Camden et al., 1984). Metts and Chronis reported that 40% of all motivations cited for deception are partner-focused, 34% were relationship-

TABLE 8.1 Motivations for Deception

Camden, Motley, and Wilson	Metts and Chronis

I. Basic Needs
  A. Acquisition of resources
  B. Protection of resources
II. Affiliation
  A. Positive
    1. Initiate interaction
    2. Continue interaction
    3. Avoid relational conflict
    4. Obligatory acceptance
  B. Negative
    1. Avoid social interaction
    2. Leave taking
  C. Conversational control
    1. Redirect conversation
    2. Avoid self-disclosure
III. Self-esteem
  A. Competence
  B. Taste
  C. Social desirability
IV. Other
  A. Dissonance reduction
  B. Practical joke
  C. Exaggeration for effect
	I. Partner-focused Motivations
	  A. Avoid hurting partner
	  B. Regulate or constrain partner's self-image
	  C. Permissible deception due to partner's previous deception
	  D. Maintain partner's face or self-esteem
	  E. Uncertain about partner's attitudes, feelings, preferences, etc.
	  F. Concern for partner's mental or physical state
	  G. Protect partner's relationship with a third party
	  H. Avoid worrying partner
	II. Self-focused Motivations
	  A. Self would suffer "stress" and abuse from partner
	  B. Protect partner's presumed image of self
	  C. Enhance self-image
	  D. Fear of being resented for telling truth
	  E. Protect or retain own resources
	  F. Ensure continued reward or service from partner
	  G. Issue too trivial
	  H. Issue too private/forbidden to tell
	  I. Own feelings too confused to express
	III. Relationship-focused Motivations
	  A. Avoid conflict
	  B. Avoid relational trauma
	  C. Avoid unpleasant, repetitive episodes
	  D. Avoid violation of role expectation

Source: Adapted from "White Lies in Interpersonal Communication: A Taxonomy and Preliminary Investigation of Social Motivations," by C. Camden, M. T. Motley, and A. Wilson, 1984, *Western Journal of Speech Communication, 48,* 309–325; *An Exploratory Investigation of Relational Deception,* by S. Metts, and H. Chronis, paper presented to the annual meeting of the International Communication Association, Chicago, 1986.

focused, and only 27% were self-focused. More specifically, deceivers are most likely to lie to avoid hurting the partner, avoid relational trauma, and protect the deceiver's image in the eyes of the relational partner. Beyond these reasons, many deceptions are encoded in the interest of tact or politeness, to convince oneself as much as the partner (particularly lies for self-esteem), and to gain a margin of success when in a low power position.

A number of interesting gender differences in these motivations have been observed. Lindskold and Walters (1983) reported that men feel deceit is more permissible than women do. Camden et al. (1984) found that women's lies are motivated more by affiliation concerns, especially when trying to avoid relationships. Further, with self-esteem motivations, women are more likely to deceive to protect the partner's self-esteem, while men are more likely to lie to protect their own self-esteem. Finally, in male-female interactions, males are likely to deceive to protect their images in the eyes of the women, and women lie for affiliation reasons (particularly relational avoidance). Metts and Chronis (1986), however, found that women are just as likely as men to lie to protect their own image, though women are more likely than men to lie to protect the partner's image. Women are also more likely to lie for partner-focused reasons and less likely to cite self-focused motivations, whereas men select equally from among partner-focused, self-focused, and relationship-focused motivations. Although these gender differences may apply only to young adults, they suggest that the sexes differ in their approach to deception.

Defining Deception

Much of the research has defined deception as an intentional, conscious act that "fosters in another person a belief or understanding which the deceiver considers false" (Zuckerman, DePaulo, & Rosenthal, 1981, p. 3). This definition rules out self-deceptions, intentionally transparent lies (such as sarcasm, joking, and social amenities), and mistaken lies (communicating information that the source believes is true but is actually false). However, this definition is somewhat restrictive when one considers the nature of deception in everyday life. Granted, people frequently do offer information that they know is false, but they also often conceal, omit, or exaggerate information, acts that also are deceptive. Thus be aware that the information presented in this chapter applies primarily to situations in which a source intentionally communicates false information. The extent to which these findings can be applied to concealments, omissions, and exaggerations is only now being investigated.

Other limitations in the research also restrict our understanding of the deception process (Knapp & Comadena, 1979). First, most of the research has focused on a single participant, the liar, and is characterized by brief, one-way communication. Rarely does the lie detector interact with the liar. Also, most of the experiments employ strangers, ignoring the relationship between deceiver and deceived. Many of the deceptive situations are characterized by low motivation, high awareness, and trivial consequences for the deceiver, which are not characteristics of all lies in everyday life (DePaulo,

Zuckerman, & Rosenthal, 1980a; Kraut, 1980). Finally, a receiver's expectation of deceit is artificially increased in many of the studies. The receiver is told to discriminate between truth telling and lying; however, in real life, a receiver usually has no special prior knowledge that the source will deceive (Miller & Burgoon, 1982).

Even in the face of these limitations, research on deception has provided a number of interesting findings, as well as puzzling contradictions. Most of it has been concerned with two processes: the behaviors encoded during deception and the ability of receivers to detect deception (and truth) when it occurs.

Behaviors Encoded During Deception

Among the first to suggest that deception was characterized by a specific pattern of nonverbal behaviors were Ekman and Friesen (1969a), who offered a "leakage hypothesis" to account for a deceiver's behavior. They proposed that deceivers attempt to control their nonverbal presentations so that their behaviors do not clue the receiver to the fact that deception is occurring (deception cues) and to the nature of their true feelings (leakage cues).

Deceivers' success is determined by internal reactions to the deceptive act and the controllability, sending capacities, and external feedback of the nonverbal channels.

Ekman and Friesen speculated that when people deceive, they experience some internal emotional reaction to the deceptive act. Such reactions are generally negative, in the form of guilt and anxiety about the possibility of detection. Deceivers also at times experience overeagerness and "duping delight" (delight about their deceptive success). Generalized arousal, which is the basis for polygraph measures of deception, often accompanies these internal reactions (Waid & Orne, 1981) and may be automatically exhibited in the deceiver's overt nonverbal display.

The controllability and sending capacities of the nonverbal channels determine whether a particular channel will display cues to the internal reactions. Controllability relates to the encoder's conscious awareness of the cues in a channel and ability to recall, repeat, or specifically display a planned sequence of cues. Sending capacity concerns the number of different messages that can be sent, the speed with which messages can be sent, and the visibility and salience of messages in a channel. The extent to which a receiver attends to, comments on, reacts to, and holds a person responsible for the messages in a channel determines the external feedback an encoder receives to a channel. Deceivers are less likely to display nonverbal cues that reflect their internal reactions in channels that are highly controllable, have a large sending capacity, and receive extensive external feedback. Conversely, a channel is most likely to reflect a deceiver's internal reactions if it is less controllable, has a low sending capacity, and receives little external feedback.

The leakage hypothesis suggests that a leakage hierarchy exists among the various nonverbal channels (DePaulo, Stone, & Lassiter, 1985a;

DePaulo, Zuckerman, & Rosenthal, 1980b; Ekman & Friesen, 1969a, 1974; Zuckerman & Driver, 1985). Facial cues are least likely to leak information about deception, because (a) encoders are highly aware of them, (b) the cues are highly visible, can send many different messages, and can send messages rapidly, and (c) receivers are likely to attend and react to facial cues (recall the facial primacy identified in the research on mixed messages). Body cues are more likely to display clues to deception because they are less controllable, have a lower sending capacity, and receive less external feedback. Many of the characteristics of vocalic cues suggest that they would be less likely to leak information about deception. The encoder should obtain excellent internal feedback and have the ability to control the larynx. Vocalic cues are able to transmit rapidly a wide range of messages, and receivers attend and react to vocalic cues. However, for reasons not fully understood, vocalic cues leak as much as body cues (DePaulo et al., 1980a; Zuckerman & Driver, 1985). It seems that the automatic link between internal affective reactions and vocalic cues is particularly strong, and encoders may pay less attention to the vocalic portion of speech than is commonly assumed.

Zuckerman, DePaulo, and Rosenthal (1981) have provided the most significant extension of the leakage hypothesis. They propose that four factors influence cue display: attempted control, arousal, affective reactions, and cognitive processing. Deceivers attempt to control their nonverbal display, but due to differences in internal feedback, sending capacities, and external feedback, attempted control produces more deliberate and discrepant presentations. Deceivers will experience autonomic arousal while lying. Just why arousal occurs is not completely clear. It may be that the question that evokes the lie or the lie itself is linked with unpleasant, traumatic experiences during previous deceptions. Arousal can also result from conflicting desires to tell the truth and to lie or may result from the anticipation of punishment if detected (Davis, 1961). It may also be due to feelings of guilt or the motivation to succeed. Regardless of how it occurs, Zuckerman and colleagues believe that arousal produces behavioral changes such as increased pupil dilation and blinking rate, higher vocal pitch, and more speech disturbances. Like Ekman and Friesen, Zuckerman et al. suggest that deceivers experience affective reactions to their duplicity, most commonly

FRANK AND ERNEST   **by Bob Thaves**

Reprinted by permission of NEA, Inc.

guilt and anxiety, which are reflected in their nonverbal display. Deceivers are likely to exhibit less pleasant facial expressions and vocalic cues, more adaptors, and less immediacy (less eye contact, less direct body orientation, less proximity, and fewer illustrators). Finally, deception is seen as a more difficult and complex process than telling the truth. Increased cognitive processing is likely to result in more pauses during speech, increased response latencies (time from end of question to beginning of response), more pupil dilation, and fewer illustrators.

As we shall see, the evidence supports the role of these four factors, especially attempted control and arousal. The leakage hierarchy has also received strong support. At the same time, the assumption that there are consistent nonverbal cues to deception has been questioned (Hocking & Leathers, 1980; Kraut, 1978, 1980). More recent compilations of the evidence, though, show some consistent cues as well as a number of factors that influence cue display, including personality, planning, motivation, and age.

Cues to Actual Deception

One of the most striking results of the research on nonverbal behavior during deception is the lack of consistent associations between specific cues and deceptive intent. For instance, among vocalic cues, three studies found that pitch increased during deception (Ekman, Friesen, O'Sullivan, & Scherer, 1980; Ekman, Friesen, & Scherer, 1976; Streeter, Krauss, Geller, Olson, & Apple, 1977), but Zuckerman, DeFrank, Hall, Larrance, and Rosenthal (1979) found that pitch did not discriminate honesty from deception. Liars have been found to talk for shorter periods than truth tellers (Knapp, Hart, & Dennis, 1974; Kraut, 1978; Mehrabian, 1971a; Motley, 1974), although Matarazzo, Wiens, Jackson, and Manaugh (1970) found that response length did not differ significantly for liars and truth tellers. Mehrabian (1971a) and deTurck and Miller (1985) reported that deception was associated with more speech errors, but this same association was not found by Knapp et al. (1974). In the kinesic channel, two experiments showed that liars smiled more or exhibited more positive facial cues (Ekman et al., 1976; Mehrabian, 1971a, 1972), while four studies showed that liars smiled less or displayed less facial pleasantness (Feldman, Devin-Sheehan, & Allen, 1978; Kraut, 1978; McClintock & Hunt, 1975; Zuckerman, Larrance, Hall, DeFrank, & Rosenthal, 1979). Liars engaged in shorter periods of eye contact and fewer glances in the study by Knapp et al. (1974), showed no difference in experiments by Matarazzo et al. (1970) and McClintock and Hunt (1975), and displayed more eye contact than truth tellers in Riggio and Friedman's (1983) investigation. Ekman and Friesen (1972), Ekman et al. (1976), and Hocking and Leathers (1980) reported that gesturing decreased during deception, but deTurck and Miller (1985) found that gesturing increased among their liars.

This lack of consistency has led some theorists to question whether nonverbal cues are reliable indicators of deception. Kraut (1978, 1980) asserts that few nonverbal behaviors are strongly and consistently associated with deception. He believes that nonverbal cues are important only to the extent that they reinforce judgments of truth derived from verbal statements. That is, more important cues to deception exist in verbal communication, and changes in the deceiver's nonverbal behaviors are so idiosyncratic that receivers use them simply to confirm their suspicions (of either deception or truth). There is some evidence that receivers are more accurate in detecting deception when verbal cues are present (DePaulo et al., 1985a). DePaulo et al. (1980a), however, take issue with this position, believing that some consistency in cue display has been shown. They also argue that the lack of consistency could be interpreted as added flexibility, from the receiver's point of view. The cues associated with deception are available when needed to detect deception, and at the same time they are subtle enough to be overlooked when the receiver finds it easier, safer, or more adaptive to ignore deception.

Knapp et al. (1974) and Miller and Burgoon (1982) also believe that nonverbal behavior during deception is somewhat idiosyncratic to liars and contexts, but they propose that changes in nonverbal behavior during deception consistently occur in six behavioral categories: (a) cues indicating underlying anxiety or nervousness, (b) cues indicating underlying reticence or withdrawal (including nonimmediacy), (c) excessive behaviors that deviate from the liar's truthful response patterns, (d) cues showing underlying negative affect, (e) cues showing underlying vagueness or uncertainty, and (f) incongruous responses or mixed messages. These categories are consistent with the contention of Ekman and Friesen and of Zuckerman et al. that behaviors associated with lying are determined by the liar's attempt to control the nonverbal display (reticence, excessive behaviors, and incongruous responses), by autonomic arousal (anxiety, nervousness, and excessive behaviors), by negative affective reactions (withdrawal, negative affect, and vagueness), and by complex cognitive processing (reticence and vagueness).

Recently, Buller and Burgoon (in press) suggested that the categories of deception behavior can be distinguished on whether they contain strategic cues or leakage cues. Strategic cues are encoded to establish the veracity of the deceptive message, to distance or disassociate the deceiver from the deceptive message, to reduce the deceiver's responsibility for the deceptive statement, or to reduce the negative consequences if the deception is detected. Buller and Burgoon identified four categories of strategic deception cues: (a) uncertainty and vagueness cues, (b) nonimmediacy, reticence, and withdrawal cues, (c) disassociation cues, and (d) image-protecting cues (originally suggested by DePaulo et al., 1985a). By contrast, leakage cues inadvertently signal deceptive intent and are not designed to substantiate the truth of the deceptive message. They include (a) arousal and nervousness cues, (b) negative affect cues, and (c) incompetent communication performances (e.g., nonnormative, awkward, discrepant, or substandard performances).

In three extensive reviews of the data on cues to actual deception, Zuckerman, DePaulo, and Rosenthal (1981), Zuckerman and Driver (1985), and DePaulo et al. (1985a) showed that several nonverbal cues are, in fact, consistently related to deception. They found that 58% of the behaviors that had been examined in two or more studies consistently discriminated deceivers from their truthful counterparts (see Table 8.2). Deceivers display increased pupil dilation, blinking rates, and adaptors, more segments of body behavior, and fewer segments of facial behavior. These latter two variables relate to the amount of deliberate control exercised over cues in a channel. Naturally occurring segments of behavior generally decrease as the amount of deliberate control over behavior increases. Thus liars' facial cues are more deliberate and controlled than their body cues. Deceivers' voices are characterized by shorter answers, more errors, more hesitations, and higher pitch. Finally, there is more discrepancy between the nonverbal channels during deception than during truthful communication.

Pupil dilation, blinking, and adaptors appear to be indicators of underlying arousal in the deceiver, confirming the contention of Ekman and Friesen and of Zuckerman et al. that heightened arousal contributes to changes in the deceiver's nonverbal display. However, arousal is not the sole

TABLE 8.2 Nonverbal Behaviors Associated with Deception

Nonverbal Behavior	Associated with Actual Deception	Stereotypically Associated with Deception	Decoded As Deception
Kinesic			
Pupil dilation	+	+	×
Gaze	0	−	−
Blinking	+	+	×
Smiling	0	+	−
Facial segmentation	−	×	×
Head movements	0	+	×
Gestures	0	0	×
Shrugs	0	+	×
Adaptors	+	+	0
Foot and leg movements	0	+	×
Postural shifts	0	+	+
Body segmentation	+	×	×
Vocalic			
Response latency	0	+	+
Response length	−	+	0
Speech rate	0	+	−
Speech errors	+	+	+
Speech hesitations	+	+	+
Pitch	+	+	+
Channel discrepancy	+	×	×

+ indicates that the behavior increased during actual deception, was believed to increase during deception, or increased in association with attributions of deception; − indicates that the behavior decreased during actual deception, was believed to decrease during deception, or decreased in association with attributions of deception; 0 indicates that a change in the behavior was not related to actual deception, beliefs about deception, or attributions of deception; × indicates that the role of the behavior was not investigated.

cause of these changes. Recently, deTurck and Miller (1985) compared the behavior of deceivers and aroused truth tellers. They found that both deceivers and aroused truth tellers increase their rate of adapting and decrease their message duration, but these changes are much greater among deceivers. Deceivers displayed a 300% increase in adaptors, compared to a 30% increase among aroused truth tellers, and deceivers decreased their message duration twice as much as aroused truth tellers. Moreover, compared to aroused truth tellers, deceivers gestured more, made more speech errors, and had longer response latencies. DeTurck and Miller conclude that changes in deceivers' behavior are not due to general arousal but rather to a special deception-induced arousal. This special deception-induced arousal probably results from deceivers' attempts to control their behavior, their affective reactions to their deceit, and/or their increased level of cognitive processing during deception. This is similar to the Buller and Burgoon (in press) argument that some deception behaviors result from strategic activity rather than all being the result of inadvertently leaked anxiety. Thus to attribute all cues of deception to changes in general arousal is far too simplistic.

Factors Affecting Cue Display

We have provided a general picture of deceivers' nonverbal behavior; however, several factors affect which cues a particular deceiver encodes.

Machiavellianism. Machiavellianism has received the most attention of any personality factor in deception research. A Machiavellian individual is highly manipulative of others and often finds deception a necessary strategy to achieve desired ends (Christie & Geis, 1970). Since highly Machiavellian sources see lying as a justified means to an end, they should not experience the negative internal reaction that less Machiavellian liars experience. Further, Machiavellian sources are more skilled at controlling their spontaneous presentation; thus highly Machiavellian sources *should* be more successful liars (Christie & Geis, 1970; DePaulo & Rosenthal, 1979b; Geis & Moon, 1981; Knapp & Comadena, 1979; O'Hair, Cody, & McLaughlin, 1981).

The evidence for the superiority of highly Machiavellian liars is mixed. In some studies highly Machiavellian liars engaged in more eye contact, exaggerated their dishonest display ("hammed"), were less likely to confess when accused, and were believed more by receivers than less Machiavellian liars (DePaulo & Rosenthal, 1979b; Exline, Thibaut, Hickey, & Gumpert, 1970; Geis & Moon, 1981). However, some studies have found no difference between high and low Machiavellian liars (Knapp et al., 1974; O'Hair et al., 1981). It appears that Machiavellianism does not consistently affect deception, but when it does, it usually results in more successful nonverbal presentations.

Self-monitoring. This is another personality trait that may influence a deceiver's behavior. Self-monitoring concerns the ability to control expressive behavior (Snyder, 1974). Individuals with this ability should be more effective deceivers. Again, the results are mixed. Hemsley (1977), Lippa (1976),

Krauss, Geller, and Olson (1976), and Elliot (1979) reported that high self-monitors were less detectable deceivers than low self-monitors. Zuckerman, DeFrank, Hall, Larrance, and Rosenthal (1979), however, found that high self-monitors were more detectable than low self-monitors, and Zuckerman, DePaulo, and Rosenthal (1981) concluded that self-monitoring does not consistently affect the ability to deceive.

Character Traits. Other personality characteristics that may be associated with the ability to deceive include *dominance, extroversion,* and *exhibitionism.* Riggio and Friedman (1983) reported that dominant, extroverted, and exhibitionist deceivers control their nervous movements and increase their facial animation relative to deceivers low in these traits. The reduction in nervous movements and increased facial animation misleads receivers who believe that these behaviors are encoded by truthful communicators.

Planning. The ability to plan a deception also seems to increase the deceiver's success by allowing more control over the nonverbal display, though its effect is not as great as that of motivation (Littlepage & Pineault, 1979; O'Hair et al., 1981; Zuckerman, DePaulo, & Rosenthal, 1981; Zuckerman & Driver, 1985). Compared to lies with little or no planning, planned lies are characterized by increased pupil dilation, more smiling, less gesturing, increased postural shifts, shorter response latencies, shorter response lengths, and faster speech. The reduction in response latencies may be particularly important, since unplanned lies typically have longer response latencies. However, some of the other cues encoded during planned lies correspond to actual cues of lying: increased pupil dilation and shorter response lengths. So planning does not result in complete control of the nonverbal display.

Age. In general, the ability to deceive successfully increases with age (DePaulo et al., 1985a; Feldman & White, 1980; Zuckerman, DePaulo, & Rosenthal, 1981). A child's ability to deceive during early elementary school is very poor. There seems to be an increase in deception ability during fourth and fifth grade and a progressive increase through high school. Further, there appears to be a developmental progression in nonverbal deception strategies. Very young children have no strategies: They leak cues and are easy to detect. The first real strategy that emerges is the naturalistic reproduction of emotions. This is followed by the ability to exaggerate affect. This latter skill, called "hamming," is very effective and seems to be a general skill among adults as well. This developmental change applies mainly to facial and body cues; the voice remains a very leaky channel at all ages (DePaulo & Rosenthal, 1979b; DePaulo et al., 1985a). Children, though, are successful liars mainly with peers and adult strangers. They have difficulty deceiving their parents (Allen & Atkinson, 1978; DePaulo et al., 1985b; Morency & Krauss, 1982). Also, among female children, the ability to control facial cues increases with age, but the ability to control body cues appears to decrease. Male children show just the opposite trends (Feldman & White, 1980).

APPLICATIONS

Deceiving Friends and Lovers

As we mentioned, deception is a relatively common interpersonal tactic. This is no less true in conversations with intimates such as best friends, lovers, and spouses. But the amount and nature of motivation to deceive may differ in such relationships. Whereas strangers may be motivated primarily by the desire to date an attractive partner (DePaulo, Stone, & Lassiter, 1985b), intimates have far more at stake. In her research on relational deception, Metts (Metts & Chronis, 1986; Metts & Hippensteele, 1988) found that friends, dating partners, and spouses deceive to avoid harming the partner, to protect the partner's image, and to avoid relational conflict. Dating partners and spouses often also lie to protect the partner's self-esteem, but friends rarely cited this motivation. Dating partners are more likely than spouses and friends to deceive to avoid relational trauma. In a follow-up study, Metts found that friends deceive to protect their resources and that dating partners deceive to protect their relationships. Spouses, though, are unlikely to deceive for these two reasons and are more likely to deceive in order to protect the partner's self-esteem.

What does all this mean for nonverbal communication during deception? For one thing, the degree of motivation to succeed at deception directly affects cue display. Zuckerman, DePaulo, and Rosenthal (1981) and Zuckerman and Driver (1985) have shown that highly motivated liars decrease blinking, have more neutral facial expressions, display fewer head movements, adaptors, and postural shifts, provide shorter responses to questions, and talk slower. When compared to the behavior of less motivated deceivers, highly motivated deceivers monitor and control their nonverbal display better and more closely resemble truthful communicators. However, DePaulo (DePaulo et al., 1980b; DePaulo et al., 1985b) suggests that highly motivated deceivers will only be able to control cues in channels such as the face, which are amenable to control. Also, control decreases as emotional reactions to deception increase, suggesting that friends may control cues better than intimates.

Second, the type of motivation may affect the degree of arousal and type of emotion a deceiver experiences during deception. Metts notes that partner- and relationship-centered motivations may be more common in established relationships because they are more acceptable and excusable. Thus people who deceive to protect the partner or the relationship may experience less anxiety about lying and fewer negative emotions, allowing them to monitor and control deception cues more effectively. Compared to

> ## Deceiving Friends and Lovers (*Continued*)
>
> strangers, relational partners seem to monitor and control their nonverbal behavior during deception, particularly arousal, negative affect, and immediacy cues (Buller & Aune, 1988b). That is, relational partners encode cues that make them appear more relaxed, more positive, and more involved in the conversation. Such patterns may make it more difficult to detect when someone we care for is lying to us.

Demeanor Bias. Finally, you probably know people who are good liars and people who are always caught at their lies. You may be very adept at lying, or you may avoid lying because you are usually found out. The research on deception shows that some people are consistently successful, while others are consistently detected (Kraut, 1978; Miller & Burgoon, 1982; Zuckerman, Larrance, Spiegel, & Klorman, 1981). Also, some people have a truthful look about them; other people look and sound suspicious. Zuckerman, DePaulo, and Rosenthal (1981) term this a "demeanor bias." They found that demeanor bias is particularly prevalent in the vocalic channel for lies that exaggerate emotions, display spontaneous emotions, and suppress emotions. Demeanor bias occurs in the facial channel only when the liar is suppressing emotions.

In sum, while there is a general pattern of nonverbal cues associated with deception, the set of nonverbal cues each liar will enact is a function of the deceiver's personality, motivation, relationship with the target, opportunity to plan, and age. Some deceivers are generally successful, whereas others are consistently unsuccessful in their duplicity.

Detecting Deception

Given that deception is a frequent event in everyday communication, receivers must be sensitive to deception (and truth) when it occurs. Research has focused extensively on a receiver's skill at detecting deception. It appears that receivers can at times distinguish truth from deception enacted by a stranger. Across most of the studies, though, accuracy is only slightly above chance when receivers have access to only the deceiver's nonverbal behavior. That is, receivers would be almost as accurate if they relied entirely on guessing (DePaulo et al., 1985a; Hocking, Bauchner, Kaminski, & Miller, 1979; Hocking & Leathers, 1980; Knapp & Comadena, 1979; Kraut, 1980; Miller & Burgoon, 1982; Stiff & Miller, 1986; Zuckerman, DePaulo, & Rosenthal, 1981). Kraut (1980) found that in 10 studies, accuracy ranged from 36% to 72% and averaged only 57% (50% is chance accuracy). Likewise, Miller and Burgoon (1982) reported that in six experiments, accuracy ranged from 46% to 64%. Receivers are even less accurate when it comes to detecting the true underlying affect hidden by the deceiver. Usually they decode the emotion intended by the deceiver

I JUST CAN'T GET THAT CANDOR EXPRESSION!!

TRICKY!

rather than the true emotion the deceiver is hiding. Thus accuracy at detecting deception cues exceeds accuracy at detecting leakage cues (DePaulo & Rosenthal, 1979b).

Some theorists have suggested that in everyday interactions a certain level of inaccuracy is functional (Knapp & Comadena, 1979). Being unaware of deception at times may be safer, easier, quicker, and beneficial (DePaulo et al., 1980a; DePaulo, Rosenthal, Green, & Rosenkrantz, 1982). DePaulo speculates that people who are too sensitive to deception will be less popular and have less satisfying relationships than less sensitive people. Further, people learn certain norms of polite interaction that lead them to place more weight on the meanings intended by sources than on covert information leaked during deception (DePaulo, 1981; DePaulo & Rosenthal, 1979a; Rosenthal & DePaulo, 1979b). In many interactions, therefore, people usually believe that a source is being truthful (DePaulo et al., 1985a; Goffman, 1959; Kraut, 1978; Stiff & Miller, 1986). Still, some receivers are more suspicious than others, attributing deception frequently. Zuckerman, DePaulo, and Rosenthal (1981) labeled this tendency a perceiver bias, analogous to a deceiver's demeanor bias.

The poor detection skills may also be a function of the inferential process by which receivers attribute deception. In everyday interactions, deception detection involves a two-step process. First, a receiver must perceive and attend to relevant cues and then interpret the cues (of which deception is only one possible interpretation) (Zuckerman, DePaulo, & Rosenthal, 1981). Since nonverbal cues are not directly indicative of deceptive intent but rather signal attempted control, arousal, negative affect, and heightened cognitive processing, a receiver must make an inferential leap from these perceptions to deceptive intent. Receivers may be reluctant to attribute deception simply on the basis of a source's behavior without contextual cues that strongly suggest deceptive intent because deception is a socially unfavorable attribution (DePaulo, Rosenthal, Green, & Rosenkrantz, 1982). Instead, receivers may make "safer" interpretations, such as ambivalence, discrepancy, tension, or indifference. In DePaulo, Rosenthal, Green, and Rosenkrantz's (1982) experiment, receivers interpreted deceptive messages as more discrepant, ambivalent, indifferent, and tense as well as more deceptive than truthful messages. Most notably, ambivalence judgments distinguished deceptive from truthful messages better than did direct judgments of deception. Receivers, however, do not always make the link between ambivalence and deception, even though they do observe differences in the behavior of deceptive and truthful communicators.

Researchers have also examined the nonverbal cues that a receiver relies on in making attributions of deception and truth in order to explain their poor detection skills. It appears that receivers hold beliefs about how a deceiver will behave. Some of these beliefs are accurate and some are not. Further, a receiver's beliefs or stereotypes about deception cues differ somewhat from the cues that are actually associated with a receiver's attribution of deception.

Stereotypical Cues to Deception. Several investigations surveyed individuals about the nonverbal cues they believe are encoded by liars. Hemsley (1977) reported that people believe that liars display less gazing, more smiling, nervous hand gestures, and postural shifts, longer response latencies, and disfluent speech. Respondents to a survey by Hocking, Miller, and Fontes (1978) believed that liars also display less eye contact, unnatural smiles, and tight faces, more tension and nervousness, longer response latencies, and disfluent speech. In addition, liars were thought to gesture more, engage in more adaptors, squint, and be stiffer in their nonverbal display than truthful communicators. Hocking and Leathers (1980) found that people thought liars show less eye contact, more shaking, trembling, and fidgeting, and more defensive gestures and extraneous movements.

In the most extensive survey of receivers' stereotypes, Zuckerman, Koestner, and Driver (1981) asked respondents to indicate the changes they would expect in 16 nonverbal behaviors during deception. Respondents thought deceivers would display less gazing and increased pupil dilation, blinking rates, smiling, head movements, shrugs, adaptors, foot and leg movements, and postural shifts. Deceivers' voices were believed to contain longer response latencies, longer responses, faster speech rates, more errors and hesitations, and higher pitches (see the middle column of Table 8.2). These stereotypes do not correspond completely to the actual behavior changes accompanying deception. The predictions of increased pupil dilation, blinking rates, adaptors, speech errors, speech hesitations, and pitch are correct. However, the beliefs about gazing, smiling, head movements, shrugs, foot and leg movements, postural shifts, response latencies, response lengths, and speech rate are erroneous.

Cues Decoded As Deception. Although stereotypes exist concerning the way deceivers behave, people do not rely on them entirely when judging veracity. Further, the cues that receivers do rely on do not correspond exactly with a deceiver's behavior, though they are somewhat more dependable than general stereotypes. Zuckerman and Driver (1985) report a less than perfect correlation ($r = .64$) between cues associated with actual deception and cues associated with attributions of deception. The rightmost column in Table 8.2 identifies the cues Zuckerman and Driver found to be associated most with attributions of deception. It is apparent that receivers rely on a small number of nonverbal behaviors when attributing deception. They are more likely to think the source is lying when observing less eye contact and smiling, more postural shifts, longer response latencies, slower speech, frequent speech errors and hesitations, and higher pitched voices. Of these, only increased speech errors and hesitations and higher pitch are accurate indicators of deception. The remaining behavioral changes are not dependable indicators of deception because liars and truth tellers do not differ systematically in their gazing, smiling, postural movement, response latencies, or speech rate. Further, receivers seem to ignore two consistent indicators of deception: changes in adaptors and response lengths.

Miller and Burgoon (1982) also concluded that detectors frequently ignore or are misled by gestures, facial cues, speech rate, and response length. Riggio and Friedman (1983) found similar faulty attribution processes. Their receivers attributed deception to sources who engaged in less eye contact, more nervous behaviors, and greater facial animation. These attributions, however, were incorrect, because liars in that study actually displayed more eye contact, less nervous behaviors, and less facial animation. The only dependable cue that receivers used was body adaptors: Deceivers engaged in more body adaptors, and receivers attributed deceit to sources who displayed more body adaptors. Stiff and Miller (1986) also reported that attributions of deceit were more likely when sources blinked and smiled more, gestured less, and took longer to respond to a question. Again, most of these cues—smiling, gesturing, and response latencies—are inaccurate. Riggio, Tucker, and Widaman (1987) reported that observers felt sources were less believable when encoding less verbal fluency, more positive affect, less head movement, and less eye contact. Socially skilled sources, though, effectively controlled their fluency and head movements to appear more believable. Finally, although Buller and Aune (1988b) found that deception caused changes in forward lean, one-sided gazing, gaze avoidance, adaptors, gestural animation, vocal activity, and vocal pleasantness, Buller (1988) reported that trust and honesty attributions by the targets of the deceptions were affected only by one-sided gazing, gaze avoidance, one type of adaptor (brief body adaptors), and vocal activity. Further, gaze avoidance and body adaptors had more influence on attributions about deceiving relational partners, whereas vocal activity was more influential on attributions about deceiving strangers.

Why do receivers hold incorrect theories about deceptive behavior? Hocking and Leathers (1980) speculate that sources also know these stereotypes and try to inhibit the behaviors that cause a receiver to attribute deception. Consistent with this, one study found that deceivers controlled their nonverbal behavior more when they believed they were being observed than when deceivers did not think they were being observed (Krauss et al., 1976). In another study, deceivers exerted more effort to control their nonverbal presentations when an interviewer questioned the veracity of the deceivers' answers (Stiff & Miller, 1986). A third study showed that deceivers monitored and controlled arousal, negative emotional displays, and immediacy cues (Buller & Aune, 1988b). Apparently, receivers expect a particular pattern of nonverbal behavior from liars, but deceivers are aware of this expectation and control their nonverbal display so as to show little change in their behaviors. It is not surprising, then, that many of the behavioral changes that produce attributions of deception do not occur during actual deception.

Receivers also do not seem to learn through experience. Two studies have shown that people who must detect deception as part of their professional responsibilities (customs inspectors and police detectives) are no more accurate than laypeople (Hendershot & Hess, 1982; Kraut & Poe, 1980; see the box on page 280). DePaulo et al. (1985a) believe that receivers do not always obtain the necessary feedback to change their faulty theories; therefore, they continue to rely on inaccurate cues to deception:

> Consider, for example, customs inspectors. . . . What kind of feedback do they get? From the many travelers whom they decide not to search, they get virtually no feedback at all. Some of those persons may in fact be smugglers, but once the inspectors let them pass unsearched, they will almost never find out that they made a mistake. Even when inspectors do decide to search travelers who are in fact smuggling illegal goods, they may not always find those goods. In those instances, the inspectors would classify the travelers as nonsmugglers, when in fact they are smugglers. (p. 345)

People are likely to receive incorrect feedback in interpersonal interactions as well. With some conversational partners, you neither suspect nor attribute deception (recall that people have a strong bias toward attributing truthfulness) and are unlikely ever to find out if your attributions are wrong. At other times, you may be suspicious but conclude that the person is telling the truth even though the person is lying. Again you receive improper feedback. Only when you successfully detect deception or attribute deception and subsequently find out you were misled do you have the possibility of modifying your theories. However, you may not be completely aware of the cues you relied on to attribute deception. Table 8.2 shows that people's stereotypes about deception do not correspond entirely to the cues that

Fallible Customs Inspectors

Do customs inspectors have a secret formula for detecting deception? Not likely. Despite their experience, in a recent simulation they and a group of untrained adults used identical commonsense signs of nervousness in deciding whom to search for contraband— and were equally unsuccessful in fingering smugglers.

Through newspaper advertisements, social psychologists Robert Kraut and Donald Poe recruited 39 United States customs inspectors from three ports of entry along the border of New York State and Canada [and] 49 adults with occupations ranging from housepainter to cook.

Because federal officials forbade making tapes of real customs inspections, the inspectors and amateurs had to judge a simulated inspection arranged by Kraut and Poe and complete with smugglers. The researchers paid passengers waiting in the Syracuse, New York, airport $2.50 for participating and hid "contraband," such as bags of white powder and cameras, on half the group. The researchers urged the participants to try passing inspection without being selected for a search . . . and offered a $100 prize to "the most convincing traveler."

The amateur and professional inspectors agreed on half the travelers. To identify the behavior they might have used in making their decisions, Kraut and Poe had coders categorize smugglers and nonsmugglers on the basis of 15 verbal and nonverbal cues that had helped people in previous studies detect deception. The inspectors turned out to have tapped people whom the coders had noted shifting their weight from foot to foot, swaying back and forth, hesitating before responding to questions, giving very brief answers, and avoiding eye contact. These nervous nellies tended to be young, lower-class travelers.

Source: From *Psychology Today,* March 1981, p. 27.

actually trigger their attributions of deception. To the extent that your basis for this attribution is faulty, you will reinforce an incorrect attribution process.

Do not conclude from this that to be more accurate you simply need to be more suspicious of others. Heightened suspiciousness does not necessarily increase accuracy. Suspicious receivers often rely more heavily on their imperfect theories and are less accurate than trusting receivers (Toris & DePaulo, 1985). Rather, you should rely on the information in this chapter to change your theories about the nonverbal behaviors that signal deception. Recent research shows that learning to pay more attention to the nonverbal channels likely to leak deception cues can increase accuracy (DePaulo, Lassiter, & Stone, 1982). Pursuant to this, we shall examine detection accuracy in the kinesic and vocalic channels.

Factors Affecting Detection Accuracy

Channel Accuracy. Recall that body and vocalic cues should display more deception cues than facial cues. It follows, then, that receivers who attend to body and vocalic cues will make more accurate deception attributions than receivers attending to the face. This is exactly what happens. Receivers who are able to view only the deceiver's body are more accurate detectors than receivers who view only the deceiver's face (DePaulo et al., 1985a; Ekman & Friesen, 1974; Riggio & Friedman, 1983; Zuckerman, DePaulo, & Rosenthal, 1981). Similarly, receivers exposed to vocalic cues are more accurate than receivers exposed to facial cues and are sometimes more accurate than receivers exposed only to body cues (DePaulo et al., 1985a; DePaulo et al., 1980b; Hocking et al., 1979; Maier & Thurber, 1968; Zuckerman, Amidon, Bishop, & Pomerantz, 1982; Zuckerman, Larrance, Spiegel, & Klorman, 1981). Detection accuracy is lower when receivers have access to only facial cues, as would be expected given greater control over these cues (DePaulo et al., 1985a; DePaulo et al., 1980b; Feldman, 1976; Hocking et al., 1979; Littlepage & Pineault, 1979; Zuckerman, Larrance, Spiegel, & Klorman, 1981).

Thus when suspecting deception, receivers should pay more attention to leakier channels such as the body and voice. DePaulo, Lassiter, and Stone (1982) experimentally directed receivers to attend to the voice, the visual presentation, or the words of a deceiver. Receivers who attended to the voice made the most accurate attributions of deceit. Those who attended to the visual presentation were least accurate and no more accurate than a control group who received no special instructions.

Charles Van Doren correctly answered question after question on the quiz show *Twenty-one* in 1956. Van Doren's performance was later exposed as a hoax, a masterpiece of deception.

Some of you may already realize the need to increase your reliance on vocalic and body cues when attributing deception. In a study by Zuckerman, Spiegel, DePaulo, and Rosenthal (1982), receivers who believed that the source was more likely to lie relied less on facial cues (showed less visual primacy) and more on vocalic cues. When the receivers believed that the source would be truthful, they relied more on facial cues and less on vocalic cues. Some receivers seem to realize that facial cues are less informative than vocal cues when they suspect deception. Receivers who expected deception were also more sensitive to channel discrepancies. This is an effective strategy, since liars often encode inconsistent nonverbal displays (see Table 8.2) (DePaulo et al., 1978; Hocking et al., 1979; Zuckerman & Driver, 1985). However, receivers were not able to discount facial cues entirely in these experiments. In multichannel nonverbal presentations (visual and vocal cues), receivers find it difficult to attend only to the cues in a single channel; therefore, detection may be more difficult when the liar interacts with the receiver face to face than, for example, over an intercom or telephone where only vocalic cues are present (Feldman, 1976; Feldman, Jenkins, & Popoola, 1979; Krauss et al., 1976). From a practical viewpoint, if you suspect deception, you might be more accurate if you talked with the source over the telephone rather than confronting that source in person.

Attention to the verbal portion of a deceiver's presentation may be more advantageous than relying entirely on nonverbal cues. Accuracy is highest when receivers have access to the deceiver's verbal channel alone or along with nonverbal channels (DePaulo et al., 1985a; DePaulo et al., 1980a; Hocking et al., 1979; Zuckerman, DePaulo, & Rosenthal, 1981). These results are counterintuitive. One would think that the verbal channel is less likely to leak information about deception than the nonverbal channels because of its sending capacity, a source's ability to control it, and the attention sources and receivers pay to it. However, deceivers display many changes indicative of deceit in their verbal messages: more negative statements, irrelevant information, leveling (overgeneralized statements containing terms like all, none, everybody), and less verbal immediacy (DePaulo et al., 1985a; Zuckerman, DePaulo, & Rosenthal, 1981; Zuckerman & Driver, 1985). Moreover, implausible, self-serving, and ingratiating responses can clue receivers to deception (DePaulo et al., 1985b; Kraut, 1978; Riggio & Friedman, 1983). Finally, the relationship between nonverbal cues and verbal statements may be critical to attributional accuracy. Kraut (1978) suggested that receivers first judge the veracity of the verbal statement, then search the nonverbal channels for confirming evidence. In his study, receivers who observed a long pause prior to a statement they believed was false were more convinced of the source's duplicity. For receivers who thought the same statement was true, the long pause prior to the statement reinforced their conclusions that the statement was true. Thus another potentially revealing cue is the discrepancy between verbal and nonverbal channels.

Familiarity with Deceiver. Beyond attending to a particular nonverbal channel, prior experience with the deceiver's truthful communication improves accuracy (Knapp & Comadena, 1979; Zuckerman, DePaulo, & Rosenthal, 1981). Many of the behavioral indicators of deception represent changes from honest behavior. Prior knowledge of a source's truthful nonverbal pattern provides a benchmark against which to evaluate current communication behavior. The first evidence for this came from Ekman and Friesen's (1974) initial test of their leakage hypothesis. They found that receivers were better at detecting deception in the body than in the face only when they were initially presented with a short segment of the source's truthful communication. Brandt, Miller, and Hocking (1980b) experimentally varied the receivers' exposure to the deceiver's truthful communication. Respondents were exposed to a segment in which the deceiver was communicating truthfully once, three times, or six times prior to judging a segment in which the deceiver was lying. A fourth group did not see the truthful segment. Detection accuracy was highest with moderate familiarity (three exposures to the truthful segment). Receivers were also most confident about their judgments in this condition. The same authors replicated this effect in two subsequent experiments (Brandt, Miller, & Hocking, 1980a, 1982).

A logical extension of these results would be that receivers become more accurate detectors as the relationship between the deceiver and receiver develops. Limited research, however, suggests that this may not be the case. In the first studies on this issue, Bauchner (1978) and Miller, Bauchner, Hocking, Fontes, Kaminski, and Brandt (1981) found that detection was more accurate by friends than by strangers, but spouses were less accurate than friends. In contrast, Comadena (1982) reported a trend toward spouses' being more accurate detectors than friends, and McCornack and Parks (1985) found no correspondence between accuracy and relationship development.

These authors advanced two different explanations for the effects. Bauchner (1978) and Miller et al. (1981) speculated that in intimate relationships, partners scrutinize each other's behavior less closely and look for only a certain pattern of cues while ignoring many revealing cues. Friends, in contrast, are more accurate because they are in the "discovery phase," actively seeking information about the partner by closely monitoring the partner's behavior. Strangers are inaccurate because they are unfamiliar with the partner's normal behavior. McCornack and Parks reject this argument because they believe the familiarity concept is too narrow to "generalize to the far richer historical and social cognitive environment of actual interpersonal relationships" (1985, p. 18). They assert that as a relationship develops, partners become biased toward honesty attributions. They showed that in the highly intimate context of well-developed relationships, detectors become rigid and confident in their judgments of honesty. This "truth bias," not insensitivity to behavior changes, reduces accuracy by intimates.

Taking a slightly different approach, Buller (1988) suggests that a truth bias due to relational context is consistent with a general bias in judgments about others called the overattribution effect (Jones, 1979; Jones & Harris, 1967; Quattrone, 1982). Initial impressions of a source can anchor subsequent attributions about a message that is inconsistent with or contradicts the initial impressions. That is, interpretations of the message change less than they should from an objective analysis of the contradictory message.

Zuckerman, Koestner, Colella, and Alton (1984) and Zuckerman, Fischer, Osmum, Winkler, and Wolfson (1987) demonstrated that this effect can occur in attributions of honesty. When subjects judged the content of a message before assessing its honesty, they were inclined to think that the message was truthful. Thus message content anchored honesty judgments.

Building on the overattribution notion, Buller (1988) proposed that positive impressions of relational partners based on trust, intimacy, self-disclosure, and sharing would bias interpretations about the honesty and trustworthiness of messages communicated by friends and intimates. He had subjects interact with an intimate, friend, and stranger who were either lying or telling the truth. As expected, messages from friends and intimates were judged more trustworthy than messages from strangers. Interestingly, though, once targets were informed that deception may have occurred, they attributed more dishonesty to friends and intimates. Buller speculated that once warned about the deception, targets relied on their greater familiarity with the friend and intimate and were more accurate in judging honesty. Consistent with this speculation, honesty attributions about friends were based on three actual deception cues, increased chair twisting, fewer adaptors, and less frequent one-sided gazing (Buller & Aune, 1988b), whereas the honesty attributions about strangers were not affected by any of the deception cues present in the conversations.

In sum, your intimate partners and close friends may be successful when deceiving you because you are likely to believe in the trustworthiness of their messages. If, however, contextual cues are present that warn you about possible deception, you may be able to detect their deceptions because you are familiar with their truthful behavior. Recall, though, that suspiciousness may cause you to rely too heavily on imperfect stereotypes about deceivers' behavior (Toris & DePaulo, 1985). Thus, you must make an effort to focus on those channels that are likely to display reliable deception cues, such as the voice and body, to detect their deception accurately.

Age and Sex of Receiver. A receiver's age and sex are other important factors in the detection process. Young children do not have the same understanding of moral values; cultural, social, and interpersonal norms; or experience with deception as adults. Therefore, they cannot be expected to make the same attributions about deception (DePaulo, Jordan, Irvine, & Laser, 1982; DePaulo et al., 1985a; Piaget, 1965). DePaulo, Jordan, Irvine, and Laser (1982) found that as age increases, a child's ability to detect ambivalence, discrepancies, and deception increases. Further, the researchers identified a developmental progression in these ratings. Younger children (sixth to eighth graders) distinguished deceptive messages from truthful messages solely on the basis of the affect expressed in them. That is, younger children rated the emotion expressed in truthful messages as more

APPLICATIONS

Detecting Deceit

Last month, you ordered a new bicycle for commuting to and from your nonverbal class. Unfortunately, after 6 weeks the bike has still not arrived. What's more, you're beginning to suspect that the salesperson is not being honest with you. She first told you that the bike would arrive in a week but now, when you called to see if the bike was in, she told you that it will arrive next week. What would you do in order to tell, most accurately, whether or not the salesperson is deceiving you?

1. Tell her you are coming down to the bike shop later that same afternoon to talk with her about the delay.
2. Continue quizzing her about the reasons for the delay over the phone.
3. Accuse her of deceiving you and see what she says.
4. Go unannounced to the bike shop 2 days later and ask her when the bike will arrive.

If you chose Option 1, you probably harmed your chances of detecting deceit. By forewarning the salesperson of your later visit, she will probably spend some time planning her defense. This should make her more relaxed when talking to you that afternoon, and you will be less likely to detect arousal cues.

If you chose Option 2, you will tend to increase your chances of detecting her deceit. Remember, the voice is among the most leaky nonverbal channels. Particular attention should be paid to the salesperson's pitch, response latency, speech errors, and response length. This fact also works against Option 1. People tend to focus on facial cues, so confronting the salesperson face to face may distract you from important deception cues.

Option 3 is also not a particularly good strategy. Granted, it is conducted over the phone, and vocal cues are often very telling deception cues. However, a direct accusation of deceit may arouse a negative reaction in the salesperson that will be difficult to distinguish from the arousal and negative emotions produced by deception.

Option 4 is a potentially successful strategy. The salesperson is not likely to expect to see you 2 days later, particularly if you sound satisfied with her explanations today. Thus you may catch her off guard, forcing her to create spontaneous deceptions that are more likely to be accompanied by nonverbal clues. However, you must be careful not to be overly influenced by facial cues. Instead, you should pay closer attention to cues in her body and voice.

extreme than the emotion expressed in deceptive messages. Slightly older children (tenth graders) were able to discriminate deceptive and truthful messages on the presence or absence of mixed feelings. The oldest children (twelfth graders) separated deceptive messages and truthful messages in their judgments of deception. These children, though, were less accurate when detecting leakage cues (interpreting the true emotion felt by the liar) than younger children. It may be that children learn a politeness norm that causes them to interpret the emotional meaning intended by the source even though they suspect that the message is false. Younger children, who are unaware of this politeness norm and who do not possess the ability to decode mixed messages and deception cues, decode the emotional content of the nonverbal cues more accurately (DePaulo, Jordan, Irvine, & Laser, 1982; Rosenthal & DePaulo, 1979b).

Rosenthal and DePaulo (1979b) report that this politeness norm seems to be stronger among women than men. Women are more likely than men to decode the meaning intended by the source. Also, women's greater visual primacy implies that they are less likely to attend to leaky body and voice cues. Women, therefore, may be less accurate detectors of deception and less likely to decode leakage cues.

Summary

In everyday interactions, sources sometimes encode messages in which the nonverbal channels provide inconsistent information. These mixed messages can be deliberate or inadvertent. Receivers find mixed messages difficult to decode and generally rely more on visual cues, particularly facial cues, when doing so. This visual primacy is more pronounced among women and with messages of positivity. Receivers often question the veracity of mixed messages, since deceivers, in attempting to control their communication, inadvertently encode mixed messages.

Deception is a frequent, essential, and adaptive strategy in human communication. In many conversations, communicators are not completely truthful. Deception as a strategy to control information is amoral. It is motivated by a need for resources, affiliation desires, relational considerations, and self-esteem requirements, and the evaluation of these motives determines the morality of a particular deception. While many deceptions are selfishly motivated and could be construed as immoral, liars often deceive for the benefit of others and their relationships. These latter motives may be considered altruistic and ethical.

Research on deception has been concerned with two issues: the behaviors a deceiver encodes during deception and a receiver's ability to detect deception. Nonverbal behavior during deception often leaks information concerning the deceptive intent of the source, due to the source's attempted control, internal arousal, affective reactions, and cognitive activity. Only a few behaviors—pupil dilation, blinking, adaptor gestures, shorter response length, speech errors, speech hesitations, higher pitch, and channel discrepancies—appear to be consistently linked with deceptive intent. The nonverbal cues displayed by a particular deceiver are a function of the deceiver's personality, motivation, planning, and age.

Receivers are not particularly skilled detectors of deception. It may be that a certain level of inaccuracy is safer, easier, quicker, and beneficial. Also, the process of attributing deception requires an inferential leap from perceptions of control, arousal, negative emotions, and heightened cognitive activity to deceptive intent. Due to the socially unfavorable nature of deception, receivers may be reluctant to make such an inference without contextual cues.

Even if receivers do suspect deception, their stereotypes about liars and the nonverbal behaviors that trigger their attributions of deception are unreliable. Sources appear to inhibit the behaviors that receivers expect liars to display. Also, receivers often ignore highly revealing deception cues. Receivers can improve their accuracy by learning to attend to body and vocalic channels, which are more likely to leak deception cues than the face, but heightened suspiciousness is not uniformly effective. Familiarity with a deceiver's honest behavior can increase detection skills, though familiarity does not guarantee accuracy. The positive context of intimate relationships may introduce a truth bias in honesty judgments. Finally, young children are less accurate at detecting deception, and women may be less accurate detectors than men.

Suggested Readings

Camden, C., Motley, M. T., & Wilson, A. (1984). White lies in interpersonal communication. A taxonomy and preliminary investigation of social motivations. *Western Journal of Speech Communication, 48,* 309–325.

DePaulo, B. M., & Rosenthal, R. (1979). Ambivalence, discrepancy, and deception in nonverbal communication. In R. Rosenthal (Ed.), *Skill in nonverbal communication: Individual differences* (pp. 204–248). Cambridge, MA: Oelgeschlager, Gunn & Hain.

DePaulo, B. M., Stone, J. I., & Lassiter, G. D. (1985). Deceiving and detecting deceit. In B. R. Schlenker (Ed.), *The self and social life* (pp. 323–370). New York: McGraw-Hill.

Ekman, P., & Friesen, W. V. (1969). Nonverbal leakage and clues to deception. *Psychiatry, 32,* 88–105.

Knapp, M. L., & Comadena, M. E. (1979). Telling it like it isn't: A review of theory and research on deceptive communications. *Human Communication Research, 5,* 270–285.

Miller, G. R., & Burgoon, J. K. (1982). Factors affecting witness credibility. In N. L. Kerr & R. M. Bray (Eds.), *The psychology of the courtroom* (pp. 169–194). Orlando, FL: Academic Press.

Zuckerman, M., DePaulo, B. M., & Rosenthal, R. (1981). Verbal and nonverbal communication of deception. In L. Berkowitz (Ed.), *Advances in experimental social psychology* (Vol. 14, pp. 1–59). Orlando, FL: Academic Press.

Zuckerman, M., & Driver, R. E. (1985). Telling lies: Verbal and nonverbal correlates of deception. In A. W. Siegman & S. Feldstein (Eds.), *Multichannel integrations of nonverbal behavior* (pp. 129–148). Hillsdale, NJ: Erlbaum.

CHAPTER 9

Relational Communication

The unspoken dialogue between two people can never
be put right by anything they say.

Dag Hammarskjold

There's a language in her eye, her cheek, her lip;
Nay, her foot speaks. Her wanton spirit looks out
At every joint and motive of her body.

William Shakespeare, *Troilus and Cressida* (4:5.55)

> The pained look in his eyes told her that he was deeply hurt. She
> tried to speak, to apologize, but he just shook his head as he turned
> away. She gently touched his face, turning it toward her, and kissed
> him tenderly on the cheeks, the eyes, the mouth. The tears in her
> eyes weakened his resolve as his lips responded to hers. He took her
> in his arms and held her tightly in silence. . . .

Such is the stuff of which pulp novels are made. But it is also the stuff out
of which interpersonal relationships are crafted. Through such nonverbal
dialogues, we come to define and redefine the nature of our relationships
with other people. That is what relational communication is all about.

Nature of Relational Communication

More specifically, relational communication addresses the processes and
messages whereby people negotiate, express, and interpret their relationships with one another. Through relational messages, people may signal
how they regard each other, the relationship itself, or their own identity in
the context of the relationship. Expressions of love, noncommitment, or
anxiety in another's presence are examples of relational messages. The
evolution of relational definitions is part of the relational communication
process.

289

Definitions

It has been said that every communication includes both a *content* and a *relational* component. That is, it includes not only the subject matter under discussion but also a frame of reference for interpreting the content. Because the nature of the relationship may dictate how an exchange is to be understood, relational communication is often referred to as metacommunication. (*Meta-* means "about"; thus these are messages about messages.) A request made by one's boss, for instance, takes on greater force than a request made by a stranger. Much, but not all, of relational work is handled by the nonverbal channels, leading many people to equate nonverbal behavior exclusively with an auxiliary metacommunicative role. However, the content is sometimes the relationship itself. In such cases, nonverbal expressions become a central part of the content and therefore should not be viewed as only augmenting the verbal stream but as making meaningful statements in their own right.

The function of relational communication resembles impression formation and management in that people may attempt to foster images of themselves as likable, trustworthy, or powerful. However, there are at least four notable differences between the two functions. One is that impression formation and management are more concerned with cause-and-effect relationships (e.g., what behaviors produce credibility or attributions of intelligence), whereas relational communication is more concerned with structural properties (e.g., what behaviors carry what relational meaning). Second, impression formation tends to take an observer perspective, examining the judgments observers make about a communicator's behavior, whereas relational communication tends to take a participant perspective, examining the behaviors the communicators encode and how they interpret them. How communicators engender attraction toward themselves is an impression management question; how they express their attraction toward another is a relational communication question. Third, impression management techniques are directed toward a generalized audience; relational communication behaviors are targeted to the specific parties in a relationship. This makes impression management more pertinent to public and mass media contexts, and relational communication to interpersonal contexts. Finally, impression formation and management focus on the single individual—the communicator about whom an impression is being formed—whereas relational communication ultimately requires examining the dyad or group as the unit of analysis. For example, a person is not regarded as communicating relational dominance unless the dominating act elicits a subordinate response from the partner. Although it is possible to study individual intentions and perceptions in the production and interpretation of relational communication, relational communication, by definition, must finally concern itself with the dynamic interaction between people.

Relational Escalation, Maintenance, and Dissolution

Interpersonal relationships do not materialize instantly; they develop gradually. Some remain stunted, some grow to maturity, some stagnate, and

The man's relational message of hostility is clearly targeted to one person. His gaze direction, the wincing of the displeased recipient, and the amused expression of the bystander are all metasignals that the relational message is intended for the woman on the right.

some dissolve. Recognition that relationships evolve over time requires that relational communication be studied from a developmental and processual perspective. Issues that are important in the early stages of a relationship— such as emphasizing similarity—may be far less so in later stages, and behaviors may take on new or different meanings as relationships change. Reliable interpretation of relational communication therefore requires knowing the current stage of a relationship.

A number of typologies are available to classify stages of relational development. Knapp's (1984) is particularly useful because in specifying several gradations during the escalating and deescalating phases, it calls attention to the changing communication concerns that occur at different stages of development. Table 9.1 presents the 10 proposed stages and a brief description of each.

One important feature of treating relational definitions as evolving and dynamic rather than static is the identification of *critical events* that change the nature of the relationship. Rare but significant acts of commission and omission are often more critical markers of a relationship than frequently occurring behaviors. The first kiss may propel a friendship into courtship; an act of physical aggression may be the most telling barometer of a marriage in trouble; the absence of an expected handshake may signal that a business relationship has gone sour. In studying relational communication, it is difficult to catch glimpses of these critical behaviors, both be-

TABLE 9.1 Stages of Relational Escalation and Dissolution

Coming Together

Initiating	Behaviors involved in first encounters, including determining if person is cleared for interaction, sizing up attractiveness, presenting self as attractive and likable. Typical communication behavior: conventional greetings.
Experimenting	Trying to discover the unknown. Typical communication behavior: demographic questions, small talk, casual and uncritical interaction.
Intensifying	Becoming "close friends," greater awareness of relationship, more active participation. Typical communication behavior: more self-disclosure, informal and personalized language, direct expressions of commitment.
Integrating	Becoming a couple, fusing two identities into a single relational identity. Typical communication behavior: synchronized routines, exchanges of intimate gifts, increased similarity in dress and manner, increased nonverbal and verbal expressions of intimacy.
Bonding	Formalized public commitment of the relationship, including engagement and marriage. Typical communication behavior: same as in integrating, plus public evidence of bond, such as wedding rings.

Coming Apart

Differentiating	Process of disengaging, making differences more important than similarities, more emphasis on *I* than *we*. Typical communication behavior: less disclosure, conflict over differences.
Circumscribing	Constriction of communication and information. Typical communication behavior: reduced depth and breadth and quantity of communication.
Stagnating	Marking time. Communication is at a standstill. Typical communication behavior: very cautious language choice, avoidance of many topics, especially the relationship itself.
Avoiding	Eliminating any form of face-to-face or voice-to-voice interaction. Typical communication behavior: antagonism, brevity of encounters, nonperson orientation.
Terminating	Complete dissolution of the relationship. Typical communication behavior: varies with the length and level of commitment of the relationship and degree of acrimony over its termination.

Source: Adapted from *Interpersonal Communication and Human Relationships* (pp. 32–44) by M. L. Knapp, 1984, Boston: Allyn & Bacon.

cause of their rarity and because many are behaviors that only appear in private circumstances. Yet personal experience confirms that these definition-altering behaviors are often the most vivid in memory and have the most impact on how a relationship progresses. Knapp (1983a) underscores this point when he writes:

While observers and researchers are often preoccupied with behaviors that are shown, participants in a relationship may be primarily concerned with behaviors *not* shown. Feelings of intimacy may depend as much on the absence of nonintimate or unpleasant behaviors (such as nose picking or staying in the bathroom too long) as on the revelation of intimate ones. Similarly, some intimate behaviors, once performed, need not become common fare, so intimate feelings often rest on a behavioral potential that may only be infrequently or intermittently realized. (p. 182)

Communication Constraints

A number of things may constrain the what, when, and how of relational communication. One is *culture.* Cultural norms may limit the relational message repertoire by prohibiting some behaviors and requiring others. This removes any relational content from such behaviors, making them useful only for social or cultural identification. For example, dress in both nonegalitarian (hierarchical) and communistic (e.g., Chinese) cultures may be so controlled by cultural dictates that no personal statements are possible through changes in costume. In other cases, it may be difficult to differentiate relational statements from conformity to normative or expected behavior. When gentlemen routinely held doors for women, the gesture could not be taken as a sign of special respect for a particular recipient. Today, the act may take on relational meaning among younger people because for them it is not an ingrained habit.

Context may similarly prescribe some behaviors and proscribe others. A hushed whisper might connote intimacy if it occurred in the midst of a social gathering but not if it occurred during a church service. The key to whether a behavior has the potential to carry relational meaning is whether it is obligatory or voluntary in the given situation. Only in the latter case is it likely to be a relational message. The exception is when one violates the normative or expected behavior. Such violations may have especially strong relational import because of their novelty. The midnight serenade is such a case.

Code structure may limit which behaviors are salient for which types of messages. A distinction introduced earlier is among *static, slow, and dynamic signals.* Static behaviors do not vary during the course of an interaction; physical appearance is an example. Slow signals show only infrequent changes; postural shifts or changes in proximity are slow signals. Dynamic signals involve moment-to-moment changes; most vocalic behaviors and facial expressions are dynamic. Static signals may be responsible for cuing basic role relations such as high or low status, while slow and dynamic signals express subtle nuances in the tone of the relationship.

Channel primacy may likewise influence which codes and behaviors have the most relational significance. The consistent finding that visual information has primacy over auditory information (see Chapters 5 and 8) gives preference to kinesics, physical appearance, proxemics, haptics, and artifacts as primary vehicles for conveying relational messages. However, there is some evidence that for dominance messages, auditory cues have primacy (Rosenthal & DePaulo, 1979a; Zuckerman, Amidon, Bishop, & Pomerantz, 1982).

A fifth constraint is the *communication skill* of the participants. As noted previously, some people are far better than others at encoding and decoding nonverbal communication. This applies to relational communication as well. People with learning disabilities, among others, have difficulty decoding relational messages (Wood, 1985). The accuracy of relational message exchange can only be as good as the least skilled participant.

Finally, the *multifunctional nature* of nonverbal behaviors makes it difficult at times to determine whether a given behavior has relational meaning, is serving some other communication function, or both. A case in point is eye contact. Gazing at another may convey such relational meanings as involvement, affiliation, and dominance; it may be used to request a turn at talk; or it may be part of an effort to persuade someone. Deciphering which of these interpretations to assign to gaze can be a challenge. This illustrates that not all nonverbal behaviors are intended or interpretable as relational signals.

All these factors place limitations on what constitutes relational communication, when and how it will take place, and its likelihood of success.

Relational Themes and Messages

So far we have discussed relational communication without specifying the content of such exchanges. Now we shall consider the traditional and more recent views of the basic themes that are possible and the nonverbal behaviors that express them.

Traditional Perspective on Relational Themes

The concept of relational communication can be traced to anthropological observations by Bateson (1935, 1958) of symmetrical and complementary relationships among New Guinea tribesmen. In symmetrical relationships, parties emphasized equality between themselves. In complementary relationships, they maximized differences, usually in the form of dominant behavior by one person being followed by submissive behavior from the other. This sparked interest in symmetrical and complementary interaction patterns, later applied to psychiatric contexts by Watzlawick, Beavin, and Jackson (1967). Issues of dominance versus submission and relational control became a focus of investigators of healthy and distressed interpersonal relationships.

Other work in the psychiatric realm on interpersonal needs and interpersonal behavior (Leary, 1957; Schutz, 1958) added two additional interpersonal relationship dimensions to the dominance dimension: inclusion (the need to establish associations with a satisfactory number of other people) and love or affection (the need to achieve intimacy with others and have it returned). These early directions gave impetus to the study of relational communication, and with it, the assumption that its primary dimensions for message exchange were dominance-submission, inclusion-exclusion, and affection-hostility (love-hate).

A Contemporary Multidimensional View

Recently, Burgoon and Hale (1984, 1987b) have challenged this traditional view as too narrow. They argue that relational definitions entail far more facets of meaning than just three and that the communication process involved in such definitions consists of a much broader range of messages than these. Based on a synthesis of ethological, anthropological, sociological, psychological, and communication literature, they concluded that there are as many as 12 different *topoi* (basic generic themes possible in relational communication). These interdependent but distinctive themes represent the underlying continua along which people send and interpret relational messages and ultimately define their interpersonal relationships.

1. **Dominance-submission.** The extent to which a relational partner is dominant, persuasive, aggressive, controlling, and ingratiating, or the opposites of these. Closely related to this is the degree of equality or inequality that is perceived in the relationship.
2. **Emotional arousal (activation).** The degree to which a person indicates being aroused and stimulated by the partner's presence.
3. **Composure.** How poised, relaxed and calm, or tense and nervous a person is in the context of the particular relationship.
4. **Similarity.** The extent to which relational partners signal being alike or different from each other.
5. **Formality-informality.** The extent to which interactants make their exchanges casual and informal or proper and formal.
6. **Task-social orientation.** Whether in a task situation a person remains work-oriented or is more interested in the social side of the situation.
7. **Intimacy.** A composite of all the following subthemes:
   a. **Affection-hostility.** Degree of positive or negative feelings related to attraction and liking.
   b. **Inclusion-exclusion.** Messages related to openness, receptivity, rapport, and affiliation or closedness and desire for privacy and distance.
   c. **Intensity of involvement.** Degree of engagement in the conversation or relationship. Together with affection and inclusion, this dimension signals approach or avoidance, which is what we have labeled elsewhere as immediacy.
   d. **Depth-superficiality.** Degree of acquaintance and familiarity that is stressed.
   e. **Trust.** Messages related to sincerity, honesty, and mutual trust.

The literature on relational communication generally falls into related clusters of these themes. Before looking at the nonverbal patterns as-

APPLICATIONS

Relational Themes in the Classroom

You can verify that you use Burgoon and Hale's 12 relational themes to interpret the communication of others by thinking of two professors you have who differ significantly in the way they relate to their classes. Try rating each of them on the following set of relational communication scales (from Burgoon & Hale, 1987b) to see if they appear to be sending their students different relational messages. (Note that some items measure composite themes.) For each statement, 5 = strongly agree, 4 = agree somewhat, 3 = neither agree nor disagree, 2 = disagree somewhat, 1 = strongly disagree.

1. Attempts to persuade the students.
    (dominance)   5 4 3 2 1
2. Dominates class discussions. (dominance)   5 4 3 2 1
3. Is calm and poised around students.
    (composure/arousal)   5 4 3 2 1
4. Seems irritated with students.
    (composure/arousal)   5 4 3 2 1
5. Tries to establish common ground with
    students. (similarity/depth)   5 4 3 2 1
6. Wants to keep the relationship at an
    impersonal level. (similarity/depth)   5 4 3 2 1
7. Makes class interactions formal. (formality)   5 4 3 2 1
8. Is more interested in a social conversation
    than the task at hand. (task-social orientation)   5 4 3 2 1
9. Communicates coldness rather than warmth.
    (affection-hostility)   5 4 3 2 1
10. Is interested in what students have to say.
    (involvement)   5 4 3 2 1
11. Is sincere in communicating with students.
    (receptivity/trust)   5 4 3 2 1
12. Wants students' trust. (receptivity/trust)   5 4 3 2 1

sociated with each, a note about research methods is needed. Some of the research to be reviewed uses an *encoder approach.* Communicators are induced to behave in a certain way (e.g., to be friendly), and the nonverbal behaviors they enact are then studied. Sometimes these actors are told explicitly what meanings to project; in other cases, the possible meanings must be inferred. Other research uses a *decoder approach.* Subjects are exposed as participants or observers to manipulated or spontaneous nonverbal behaviors and rate the meanings of the behaviors (e.g., rapport). Finally, some of the research looks at the effects of nonverbal cues on such relational outcomes as attraction and liking. In these cases, the researchers or analysts draw inferences about whether people might use these same behaviors to communicate reciprocal meanings. Seldom is the situation so simple that a given behavior can be taken to have one and only one meaning. More often than not, a combination or sequence of cues is needed before a fairly

Testing Your Myth Quotient

To test how many popular myths you believe about nonverbal communication, first try taking the following true-false test:

———— 1. People express their liking by being completely relaxed.

———— 2. The person with the most power in a group is the one who looks most often at others.

———— 3. The longer a couple is together, the more they touch.

———— 4. To be seen as more dominant, women should increase the amount of time they spend making eye contact with others.

———— 5. Leaning forward is interpreted as being overly eager and submissive.

———— 6. Close proximity and direct gaze always signal attraction.

———— 7. Slow, deliberate speaking conveys power.

———— 8. Extended silence is a sign of communication breakdown and stress.

Now see how others do on these same questions. Give the quiz to 10 other people and see what the average score is. You may want to add some new questions to the quiz, based on your reading. What do the quiz results tell you about people's stereotypical views of nonverbal relational communication?

ANSWERS TO "Testing Your Myth Quotient" 1. *False.* Moderate relaxation is most likely. 2. *False.* High power people receive, not give, the most frequent eye contact. 3. *False.* Married couples engage in less touch than newly formed couples. 4. *False.* Such behavior by women is seen as submissive. 5. *False.* Forward lean is associated with dominance. 6. *False.* Not always—they may also accompany a hostile confrontation. 7. *False.* Faster tempo is more dominant. 8. *False.* Complete agreement and harmony may also be accompanied by extended silences.

unambiguous interpretation is possible. We therefore caution you not to assume that you know unequivocally what signals what. People who hold such simplistic and certain views often find themselves bogged down in relational quagmires.

Nonverbal Patterns Associated with Relational Themes

> The history of man's past is largely an account of his efforts to wrest space from others and to defend space from outsiders.
>
> Edward T. Hall

> By and by a proud-looking man about fifty-five—and he was a heap the best-dressed man in that town, too—steps out of the store, and the crowd drops back on each side to let him come.
>
> Mark Twain

Messages of Power, Dominance, and Equality

Of all the dimensions that characterize interpersonal relationships, the two primary ones are dominance-submission and intimacy. The need to define patterns of inequality and control is no doubt an outgrowth of more primitive survival needs based on identifying friend or foe and establishing a social order. Our instinctive fight-or-flight responses mark the extremes of a continuum of dominance and submission behaviors that are present (in varying forms) in all species.

Definitionally, the concept of dominance is murky and is often treated as synonymous with power and status. Though interrelated, these concepts can be distinguished from one another. *Status* denotes a position within a hierarchy: socioeconomic status, political status, organizational status, and so on. High status often fosters power and dominance (Patterson, 1985), since one is higher up in the "pecking order," but it is not a guarantee of powerful or dominant behavior. *Power* refers to control of resources, which usually enables control of others. *Dominance* refers specifically to the ability to influence others. Although some scholars have been inclined to treat dominance as an individual trait (e.g., Weisfeld & Linkey, 1985), it is more commonly regarded as a relational phenomenon. That is, dominance is determined by the subservient or submissive responses of others. It is not dominance unless it works. Even in lower primates, there is growing evidence that dominance is more a social skill that emerges through interaction than an individual trait based on aggressiveness (Mitchell & Maple, 1985; Shively, 1985).

Writing in this area often does not distinguish among these concepts.

Hence our review includes messages of status, power, dominance, and individual dominance-proneness (what some have called domineeringness). The literature is organized by code because most of the research has looked at one or two isolated behaviors as they correlate with status, dominance, or dominant personality traits. However, the clear communication of dominance usually relies on the presentation of several cues simultaneously. The greater the number of cues present, the less ambiguous and more intense the message (Henley & Harmon, 1985).

Proxemics and Haptics. The most elemental signals of fight and flight, of power and powerlessness, are embedded in these two codes. Territory is a key resource: People display status, dominance, and power by owning, controlling, and accessing more, and qualitatively better, territory (Hall, 1966; Henley, 1977; Lott & Sommer, 1967; Sommer, 1969, 1970, 1971; Sundstrom & Altman, 1976). Territorial privilege may be used to reinforce relational dominance. The chief executive officer of a major publishing company reserved full time a string of presidential suites around the country for his occasional visit to each city. He insisted that the staff of one hotel completely rearrange his room to suit his tastes. His prerogative to make such demands clearly signaled to subordinates and service personnel who was in control. In diplomatic negotiations, the person to enter a room first is presumed to be the ranking representative of state. In one set of U.S.-Soviet discussions, a second doorway had to be cut into the conference room so that diplomats from both countries could enter the room simultaneously.

Illegitimate bids for territory may also indicate one's relative power position, as the following anecdote from Gay Talese's book *The Kingdom and the Power* (1969) reveals:

> Where one sits in *The Times'* newsroom is never a casual matter. It is a formal affair on the highest and lowest level. Young reporters of no special status are generally assigned to sit near the back of the room, close to the Sports department; and as the years go by and people die and the young reporter becomes more seasoned and not so young, he is moved up closer to the front. But he must never move on his own initiative. There was one bright reporter who, after being told that he would cover the labor beat, cleaned out his desk near the back of the room and moved up five rows into an empty desk vacated by one of the labor reporters who had quit. The recognition of the new occupant a few days later by an assistant city editor resulted in a reappraisal of the younger reporter's assets, and within a day he was back to his old desk, and within a year or so he was out of the newspaper business altogether. (p. 131)

Power may be reinforced by insisting that interactions occur within one's own territory. People entering someone else's domain automatically become more deferent and submissive (Edney, 1976), while those on their "home court" gain confidence from the familiarity of their surroundings. Voluntarily to allow yourself to be summoned to someone else's home turf is a show of weakness. Inexperienced diplomats and politicians unfortunately often learn this only after having made too many concessions to adversaries or having lost the respect of allies. The recognized territorial advantage is the reason for insisting on a neutral locale for summit meetings and other serious talks.

To intrude on someone else's territory is the boldest of power ploys. One popular book on nonverbal communication advises power seekers to spread their briefcase and possessions on another person's desk so as to gain the upper hand or at least tip the balance of power back toward their favor. A woman executive reports that a salesperson carried this idea to the extreme by sweeping into her office and taking over her desk. She was so unsettled by this violation of her territory that she lost control of the business deal.

Part of the greater territorial control that accompanies power is the right to demand and gain privacy through the use of gatekeepers, barriers, locks, and other protections against visual, auditory, and spatial intrusions. Older children often have their own room, while younger siblings share a bedroom. Employees whose desks are placed in the middle of an open area without benefit of walls or doors are symbolically told that they have very low status relative to others in the organization. In turn, having to deal with low status functionaries is a relational statement in itself. A student who had several meetings with her insurance company thought nothing of being turned over to one of the clerks in the "pit" until she noticed older clients being ushered into enclosed offices.

With greater territory comes the use of more territorial markers (Gillespie, 1978). People of prominence may mark property boundaries more explicitly (e.g., fences, hedgerows, No Trespassing signs) and may personalize claimed territories with more possessions, as in the case of a celebrity "taking over" a hotel lobby with luggage and a personal retinue. Verbal or gestural references to markers in one's territory may also be used to reinforce awareness of a position of dominance. A study in which subjects alternated playing student and teacher roles found that when they were in the high status (teacher) role, they pointed more often toward their possessions (Leffler, Gillespie, & Conaty, 1982).

The use of personal space parallels the use of territory. Dominant and high status people claim and are accorded more personal space and conversational distance, take up more space with expansive postures, and may initiate more intimate or invasive distances (Altman & Vinsel, 1977; Burgoon, 1978b; Dean, Willis & Hewitt, 1975; Gillespie, 1978; Leffler et al., 1982; Lott & Sommer, 1967). Both close (Burgoon, Buller, Hale, & de-Turck, 1984; Patterson & Sechrest, 1970) and far (Goffman, 1971; Henley, 1977; King, 1966; Sommer, 1969) interaction distances have been associated with being perceived as high status and dominant. This is because dominant individuals are freer to deviate from normative distances than submissive individuals and may initiate a more formal or intimate interaction pattern, whereas low status individuals must maintain deferential intermediate distances in conversation. Control over distance is well practiced

Territorial markers strongly reinforce a position of dominance and status.

in the military. One must have approval to approach an officer or anyone of higher rank, and even at social events, no one enters a banquet hall until the highest in command has made an entrance.

Dominance and status are also signaled by centrality of position. Leaders sit or stand in more central positions in a group, such as at the head of a table or wherever visual access to the most other people is maximized (Hare & Bales, 1963; Sommer, 1971; Strodtbeck & Hook, 1961; see also Bass & Klubeck, 1952). High status mental health professionals choose more central seating in dining rooms (Heckel, 1973), and child leaders position themselves in the middle of peer groups (Barner-Barry, 1980). Similarly, proximity to people in authority confers status by association. The closer one's home is to "prestigious" neighborhoods or one's office is to the company president's, the more status one is presumed to have.

Body orientation may connote power. An indirect body orientation conveys dominance, whereas a direct orientation conveys deference (Mehrabian, 1968b, 1981). Indirect orientation, which is often accompanied by gaze aversion, increases psychological distance.

Finally, dominance may be displayed by approaching others' territory in a more rapid and deliberate fashion (Mehrabian, 1981) and by being less likely to yield space when approached by another. By contrast, submission is communicated by hesitantly approaching others (implying a reluctance to risk a confrontation), giving way to others, or taking flight.

Touch behaviors show similar patterns. Dominant individuals initiate touch. They determine the frequency, intensity, and intimacy of touch. Among status unequals, there is a nonreciprocal pattern of touch analogous to forms of address: High status people have the prerogative and are expected to be more familiar than low status people (Goffman, 1967; Henley, 1977; Stier & Hall, 1984). Just as employers and physicians can call you by your first name, so are they free to touch you and to use such intimate touches as a shoulder squeeze or a congratulatory hug. You, however, must refer to them by title, must refrain from touching them if they have not touched you first, and must limit your contact to more formal varieties. Under no circumstances can you pat them on the head or pinch their derriere.

By contrast, status equals engage in more reciprocal touching, especially if they are intimately acquainted. Henley (1977) contends that the one-way pattern of familiarity from high to low status mirrors the pattern of nonverbal intimacy among equals, not only for touch but for other nonverbal behaviors as well (see Table 9.2). Thus initiating touch may be interpreted as an assertion of dominance. Conversely, reciprocating touch may be taken as an assertion of equality. In cases of uninvited nonreciprocal touch, the use of touch increases the perceived dominance of the toucher and reduces the dominance of the recipient, compared to people who do not touch (Frieze & Ramsey, 1976; Harper, 1985; Henley & Harmon, 1985; Heslin & Alper, 1983; Major & Heslin, 1982; Stier & Hall, 1984; Summerhayes & Suchner, 1978). Consistent with this pattern, nondominant personalities expect to be touched more and to touch others less (Henley, 1973).

Touch, like spatial invasions, may underscore dominance by being a violation of expectations, something only people in positions of power are entitled to do. Powerful people use touch and pointing as well as proxemic encroachments to intrude on others (Leffler et al., 1982). Again, it is a question of who has access to whom.

As further evidence of the dominance connotations of touch, Henley (1973) reports that touch more frequently accompanies communication functions that are dominance-related, such as trying to persuade someone, giving advice, or giving an order. It is also more common in superior-subordinate relationships. Finally, it should be remembered that the ultimate expression of dominance—physical aggression—is a haptic behavior.

Artifacts. Closely related to territorial control is the use of physical objects and surroundings to symbolize power and status. As already noted, people in power reveal their influence through possession or access to valued resources, which can include not only larger, more spacious, and prized locations but also luxurious furnishings in homes and offices, expensive automobiles, membership in exclusive clubs, ownership of rare art collections, and the like.

Hitler was a master of such symbols and carefully designed his surroundings to reinforce his power. For example, his Berchtesgaden window,

TABLE 9.2 Gestures of Power and Privilege: Examples of Some Nonverbal Behaviors with Usage Differing for Status Equals and Nonequals and for Women and Men

	Between Status Equals		*Between Status Nonequals*		*Between Men and Women*	
	Intimate	Nonintimate	Used by Superior	Used by Subordinate	Used by Men	Used by Women
1 Address	Familiar	Polite	Familiar	Polite	Familiar?[a]	Polite?[a]
2 Demeanor	Informal	Circumspect	Informal	Circumspect	Informal	Circumspect
3 Posture	Relaxed	Tense (less relaxed)	Relaxed	Tense	Relaxed	Tense
4 Personal space	Closeness	Distance	Closeness (option)	Distance	Closeness	Distance
5 Time	Long	Short	Long (option)	Short	Long?[a]	Short?[a]
6 Touching	Touch	Don't touch	Touch (option)	Don't touch	Touch	Don't touch
7 Eye contact	Establish	Avoid	Stare, ignore	Avert eyes, watch	Stare, ignore	Avert eyes, watch
8 Facial expression	Smile?[a]	Don't smile?[a]	Don't smile	Smile	Don't smile	Smile
9 Emotional expression	Show	Hide	Hide	Show	Hide	Show
10 Self-disclosure	Disclose	Don't disclose	Don't disclose	Disclose	Don't disclose	Disclose

Source: From *Body Politics* (p. 181) by Nancy M. Henley, 1977, Englewood Cliffs, NJ: Prentice-Hall.

[a] Behavior not known.

before which he received statesmen, provided a massive backdrop of sky and mountains that dwarfed his visitors.

In many organizations, entitlement to such symbols of position is closely regulated. In the military, for instance, rank determines the size of office, the size of desk, the number of filing cabinets, the type of wastebasket (metal or wood), and even the number of plants a person can have. The same is true at many universities. Corporate America routinely uses such office accouterments as well as access to company cars, limousines, and jets as indicators of status. If you can command a company jet at will, you are obviously in a position of power. If you get to ride occasionally in the jet, you are still part of an inner circle. If you fly commercial airlines but go first class, you have some rank but haven't yet made the big time. And if you fly coach or don't fly at all, you are down somewhere in the lower echelons.

Even when no formal or informal rules of allocation exist, more dominant individuals will lay claim to scarce and desirable resources. This pattern develops early. Dominant children were found to play longer with desired objects (a pair of gerbils) at the expense of their more submissive peers (Camras, 1984).

Status symbols are a fact of life in every culture, no matter how much it strives for a classless society. In communist China, the latest status symbols are possession of American tennis shoes and portable stereos. In other communist countries, the current status symbols are ownership of major appliances or an automobile. What is valued in one country, however, may not be in another. Shuter (1984) reported that a business delegation from the American Midwest,

> wishing to give Chinese government officials a quintessentially
> American product as a gift, gave them wheels of cheddar cheese.
> What they did not realize is that the Chinese consider cheese to be
> barely edible. Moreover, the Chinese officials display gifts from
> foreigners as a mark of pride, and a perishable product defeats the
> whole purpose. (p. F1)

What constitutes a status symbol in a given culture is also constantly in flux. The fact that 9 out of 10 people could probably report current status symbols accurately, however, is testimony to their significance.

The key features that seem to distinguish power and status symbols are that they have scarce availability, entail exclusivity, or are associated with some special accomplishment or position of prestige. Displays of wealth usually reflect possession or access to things outside the economic means of the average person. But expense isn't the only indicator of status. Plaques and trophies have small monetary value but are important symbols of achievement. Flaunting such symbols becomes a way of relationally emphasizing one's status. It is told that Richard Nixon was so taken with the trappings of the presidency that he dressed his White House guards in uniforms befitting royalty and insisted that he eat only out of the president's dishes, which were flown with him whenever he traveled abroad.

Kinesics. The similarity between many human kinesic displays of dominance and submission and those of our primate cousins has led to specula-

Hard Times for the Status-minded

He may never have been a Galileo of the social firmament, but as a journalist Vance Packard is clear-eyed enough to have seen, before anybody else, that the post–World War II U.S. has got caught up in a compulsive competition for status. The proof came in *The Status Seekers* (1959), a dissection of those Americans who, as the author put it, were "continually straining to surround themselves with visible evidence of the superior rank they are claiming." Since that happened to include just about the entire U.S. population, the great status game, once focused, provoked a great many fears that it would damage the egalitarian ideal and hasten the evolution of sharp class lines. What none of the fearful saw was that, given the services of mass production and sustained prosperity, universal chasing after prestige would engender such a gorgeous and gaudy muddle of status symbols as to reduce the game to a farce—which it has now plainly become.

Status in its diverse forms still exists, no doubt, and many an American is still out there grabbing after some of it. What makes the spectacle ridiculous now is that, except in some rare cases, people who have latched onto some status cannot be sure how to flash the news to the world, and people who are watching cannot be sure who is dramatizing what sort of status with what symbol. Order Gucci loafers and you only risk winding up shod the same way as the boy who delivers them. A Cadillac today signifies nothing about the owner except that he might well pull in at the next Burger King. . . . A privately owned yacht still symbolizes high financial status, but Sperry Top Siders—now worn by landlubbers of all varieties—no longer symbolize the status of yachtsman as they once did. Initialed handbags of the Louis Vuitton sort signaled uppering status in the days when people spoke of "going abroad"; now such bags have been so replicated that they represent little but the exhaustion of pop imagery. . . . Those beepers that summon people to unseen telephones? Years ago, when they were rare, beepers emanated some prestige, but today, in profusion, they signal little but duty. . . .

Status, as notion or fact, is inseparable from the human condition. Given the nature of the U.S. as an open society cherishing the premise that anybody is free to rise, a good deal of status chasing was inescapable from the outset. If the chase had indeed rigidified the lines of class in society, the symbols of status could only have become ever more clear. Reflecting upon that fact, one contemplates the present symbolic (and hierarchical) muddle with a light heart.

Source: Trippett, December 21, 1981, *Time,* p. 90.

tion that such behaviors share a common evolutionary origin. Though the variability and complexity of dominance patterns among monkeys and apes argues against direct comparisons to humans (Keating, 1985; Mitchell & Maple, 1985), there are enough analogues to support a sociobiological interpretation of such behaviors. This is another way of saying that many of the behaviors have universal meaning for humans.

The behavior that shows the most commonality across primate species is gaze. The threat stare is a primary dominance display, and visual access is such that dominant animals freely scrutinize the group, without too much attention to any one member, while subordinates constantly watch the dominant one (Chance, 1967; Dovidio & Ellyson, 1985).

This parallels human behavior. People in positions of power or status are more likely to engage in unwavering, direct looks or stares and to break eye contact last; submissive individuals are more likely to avert gaze or break eye contact first (Exline, Ellyson, & Long, 1975; Fromme & Beam, 1974; Levine, 1972; McDowell, 1973; Modigliani, 1971; Moore & Gilliland, 1921; Rosa & Mazur, 1979; Snyder & Sutker, 1977; Strongman & Champness, 1968; Weisfeld & Linkey, 1985). We are taught to show deference to our elders and authority figures by lowering our eyes (Argyle, 1972b), while they are free to look at us. Moreover, we perceive their extended gazes at us as dominant and their stares as threatening (Burgoon et al., 1984; Ellsworth, Carlsmith, & Henson, 1972; Thayer, 1969). The power of the stare is captured in Secretary of State Dean Rusk's metaphor for the Russian response to President Kennedy's blockade during the Cuban missile crisis: "Eyeball to eyeball, they blinked first."

Although powerful or high status people may engage in looks of long duration, they tend to look less *frequently* at specific others, while themselves being the recipients of more frequent gaze and facing (Collins & Guetzkow, 1964; Efran, 1968; Exline, 1963, 1972; LaFrance & Mayo, 1978b; Mehrabian, 1969). In groups, the least amount of eye contact is directed to low status group members. Interestingly, though, the highest status person receives less than a person of moderate status (Hearn, 1957). The notion of deference may explain this tapering-off effect. At the most extreme, powerful people may avoid looking at the speaker altogether. Speakers attribute more authority and control to listeners who either subject them to extended unbroken looks or do not look at them at all (Argyle & Kendon, 1967; Mehrabian & Williams, 1969; Thayer, 1969).

The differences in gaze pattern between dominant and nondominant individuals becomes more evident if the speaking role is separated from the listening role. A higher ratio of looking while speaking to looking while listening is both encoded and decoded as dominant. Exline, Ellyson, and Long (1975) have labeled this *visual dominance behavior*. Whereas submissive people spend far more time looking at others while listening than while speaking, dominant people look about equal amounts of time while listening and while speaking. Also, increasing the amount of gaze during speaking is perceived as dominant, while increasing it during the listening phase is perceived as submissive. The normal pattern among people equal in status is to look more while listening than while speaking, but the amount of gaze while listening is far more pronounced by submissives. The visual dominance pattern holds true of both men and women and across such definitions of dominance as high status, control orientation, and expert power (Dovidio & Ellyson, 1982, 1985; Ellyson, Dovidio, & Corson, 1981; Ellyson, Dovidio, Corson, & Vinicur, 1980; Exline et al., 1975; Fugita, 1974; Whitehurst & Derlega, 1985). Figure 9.1 shows some typical results from encoding and decoding studies demonstrating these relationships.

The explanation for the difference in looking while speaking and looking while listening makes sense. During speaking, the amount of cognitive load influences how much we look at others: The more difficult the task, the less we look (so as to minimize distractions). This limits the amount of time speakers will look at listeners, regardless of dominance. But during the listening role, the norm of paying attention is a prevailing consideration, and such factors as situational constraints, personality, and relational definition influence the extent to which someone adheres to the norm or violates it. This makes the listening phase more sensitive to differences in dominance level. (It also makes the listening phase more sensitive to gender differences: Women spend far more time looking while listening than men.)

Like gaze, smile and brow position may have universal significance for dominance. Smiling, which is comparable to the primate grimace, and raised eyebrows connote deference, submission, and possibly appeasement; the absence of a smile and lowered brows convey dominance (Henley, 1977; Keating, 1985; Mehrabian & Williams, 1969; Romano & Bellack, 1980). Nonsmiling is recognized as a dominance cue across a variety of cultures and equally among boys and girls. The consistent interpretation of brow lowering is less certain. Keating (1985) says that "most of the evidence targets brow position as a potential universal dominance cue in humans" (p. 91), but her own cross-cultural research reveals that only some cultures clearly differentiate raised and lowered brows. Whether this is the result of cultural display rules overriding a biologically based signal remains to be seen.

Dominant postures and gestures rely on principles of elevation, precedence, expansiveness, and dynamism (Mehrabian, 1968b, 1969, 1972; Morris, 1977; Poling, 1978; Schwartz, Tesser, & Powell, 1982; Spiegel & Machotka, 1974; Weisfeld & Linkey, 1985). Standing rather than sitting, looming over someone's shoulder, or positioning oneself higher or in front of someone else connotes dominance. Followers keep their heads lower and walk behind leaders. Erect, full-height, open, or asymmetrical postures, raising the head, leg-apart stances, standing with arms akimbo (elbows extended), hands clasped behind the head, hands on hips, and "looser" seated postures that take up a lot of space convey power by expanding apparent body size. Large, sweeping gestures also extend the individual's spatial sphere of control and add an air of dynamic energy. Frequent gesturing, use of emblems and pointing gestures, and a confident, rapid gait likewise contribute to the sense of potency. Together these behaviors also imply a defensiveness, a readiness to hold one's ground, that corresponds to a fight response.

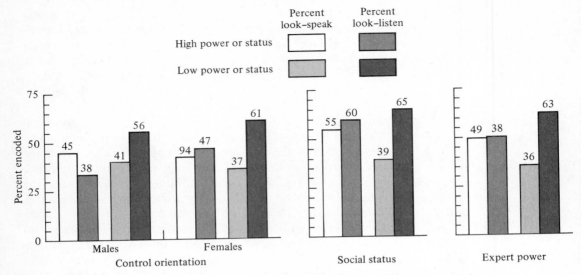

Higher proportions of look–speak time to look–listen time are more commonly encoded by more powerful or dominant communicators.

(a)

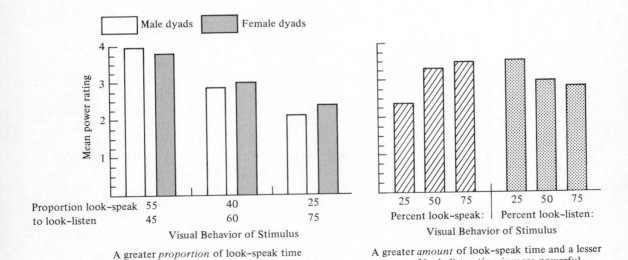

A greater *proportion* of look–speak time is more powerful.

A greater *amount* of look–speak time and a lesser amount of look–listen time is more powerful.

(b)

FIGURE 9.1 Sample results from encoding and decoding studies of visual dominance. (a) Encoding studies: percent looking while listening and looking while speaking for different types of encoders. (b) Decoding studies: attributions of power based on relative and absolute percentages of looking while speaking and looking while listening.

Conversely, submissive individuals tend to be more circumspect and "tighter" in their behavior. They appear to "shrink in," using closed, symmetrical postures and small gestures or gestures that convey vulnerability such as palm showing, uncrossed arms, and uncrossed legs. A particularly symbolic one is the head tilt, which is reminiscent of the ultimate show of submission in the animal kingdom—exposing the jugular vein to the victor. The head tilt may in fact be a vestige of more primitive forms of human communication.

Another sign of status and power is postural relaxation (Goffman, 1961b; Henley, 1977; Mach, 1972; Mehrabian, 1969, 1970a; Weisfeld & Linkey, 1985). In a mixed status group, people with higher rank exhibit more relaxation, feeling free to slump in chairs or put feet up on a desk. Those of lower rank tend to mirror the postures and level of relaxation of high status members, but they don't match it fully, maintaining some degree of postural restraint. As similarity of status increases, so do postural congruency and relaxation. This pattern of high status people using more relaxed postures and more informal demeanor while subordinates are more tense and circumspect again parallels the pattern between intimates and nonintimates of equal status (Table 9.2). This implies that dominance displays involve some of the same relational messages as intimacy displays. In the absence of other contextual information clarifying the status relationship, there is sometimes confusion about the relational meaning of such displays. Is the person presenting such behavior being aggressive or merely affiliative? When such behaviors are directed by lower status individuals toward higher status ones, they may often be regarded as illegitimate challenges to power when they are only intended to be shows of affection (or worse yet, reflect lack of social competence on the part of their exhibitor).

One of the more extreme forms of relaxed behavior is the public display of self-adaptors. Picking one's nose or passing gas in the presence of someone other than a close intimate is taken as a blatant show of disrespect. In fact, prisoners often engage in such displays as spitting to show their disdain for their captors. A female employee reports the experience of being in a mailroom when her supervisor, who was not speaking to her at the time, entered, checked his mail, then paused in the doorway and scratched his derriere before exiting. He had so internalized treating her as a nonperson that he forgot her presence. He would have been sorely embarrassed if caught in the act in a more public situation.

The importance of relaxation and tension cues is documented in an interesting analysis by Exline (1985) of the 1976 presidential debates between Gerald Ford and Jimmy Carter. He objectively coded such tension-release adaptors as lip licking, postural sway, shifting gaze, eyeblinks, and speech nonfluencies and then had observers rate various segments of the speeches. Observers rated more favorably segments that showed less tension leakage, and Ford—the winner of the first debate—showed less leakage at the outset of his speech. The implication is that power correlates with greater relaxation and poise. To communicate dominance therefore requires minimization of adaptor behaviors unless they are deliberate and recognizable as such.

Of these three people—the governor of Oregon, the state assembly speaker, and the state senate president—which is the most powerful? What proxemic, artifactual, and kinesic cues convey his relational communication of dominance?

Finally, it appears that people in lower ranks become most expressive facially when interacting with someone of higher rank, whereas those in higher status positions have greater flexibility in how expressive they are (Patterson, 1985). This is consistent with the prerogatives of high status people to adopt highly immediate or nonimmediate interaction patterns.

Vocalics. As noted earlier, the voice is more influential than visual cues in determinations of dominance. This may be because it is an innately used and recognized signal. One striking finding from comparative studies is that the same deep-pitched, loud vocal patterns are used across a number of species to signal dominance and threat (Public Broadcasting System, 1984). Common experience tells us that we try to make our voice more imposing when attempting to influence someone or give orders. The louder, deeper voice connotes greater size and implicitly greater physical strength. Conversely, people use soft, high pitched tones when trying to be nonthreatening. This is the universal vocal pattern mothers use when soothing infants.

Perceptual research also confirms that voices perceived as higher status, dominant, and confident display (a) lower pitch, (b) greater loudness, (c) moderately fast tempo, (d) clearer articulation and enunciation, (e) more intonation, and (f) no accent (Apple, Streeter, & Krauss, 1979; Argyle, 1975; Brooks, 1975; Delia, 1972; Giles, 1973a; Mehrabian & Williams, 1969; Mulac, Hanley, & Prigge, 1974; Packwood, 1974).

Another way in which people may demonstrate dominance is by controlling the conversational floor (Wiemann, 1985). Dominant people talk more and interrupt others more (Brandt, 1980; Lamb, 1981; Leffler et al., 1982; Markel, Long, & Saine, 1976; Scherer, 1982a; Starkweather, 1964; Stephan, 1952; West, 1979; West & Zimmerman, 1977; Zimmerman & West, 1975). In turn, they are more often perceived as the leader in a group (Kleinke, Lenga, Tully, Meeker, & Staneski, 1976; Sorrentino & Boutillier, 1975; Stang, 1973).

Finally, if silence is regarded as a vocalic cue, one of the more emphatic indicators of dominance is the use of extended silences. Silence shows respect for authority. Protocol dictates that subordinates must wait for superiors to break the silence first, and their refusal to do so can be a very potent reminder of the status difference (Bruneau, 1973). The ultimate form of silence—failing to acknowledge another's presence with a greeting—is a powerful symbolic message of status inequality, even if unintentional. A person who receives no greeting from a preoccupied equal or superior can easily stew for a week about the perceived snub. Because the "silent treatment" causes frustration, it can provoke behavior that reinforces power:

> Silence can also protect power by aggravating those seeking to destroy or discredit persons in power. This can be done by forcing subordinates into awkward positions whereby they exhibit behaviors detrimental to their own cause—because their frustration is aggravated by silent response to their efforts. Silence as absence of response to or lack of recognition of subordinates may very well be the main source of protection of power in socio-political orders where physical restraint has lost repute. (Bruneau, 1973, p. 39)

Physical Appearance. We have said that proxemic, kinesic, and vocalic behaviors convey dominance in part through implications of physical size and strength. Physical appearance elements that themselves convey these qualities likewise connote dominance. For example, even such uncontrolled features as a square jaw, broad face, smaller eyes, and receding hairline convey dominance, while rounded jaws, large head and eyes, and thicker lips convey weakness and helplessness (Keating, 1985). The reason is that the former features are associated with age and maturity (and hence strength) and the latter with infancy and immaturity. Taller people are also assumed to be more powerful. The taller of the two candidates typically wins the U.S. presidency. Carter was an exception and was reportedly so concerned by his stature that for a time he stretched his neck in an odd manner to look taller. The importance of height is reflected in a study that found that we actually see higher status people as taller (Wilson, 1968).

Individuals cannot use such genetically controlled features to encode relational messages, but they can use other appearance elements that emphasize or minimize size and strength. Women may wear young hairstyles, youthful apparel, clothing that makes them look thinner or more petite, and makeup that enlarges the eyes. These efforts create an impression of helplessness and elicit caretaking behavior on the part of males. (Women who have such nondominant appearances are also judged more attractive.) Males, by contrast, adopt hairstyles and clothing that make them appear taller, more muscular, and more mature. The initial popularity of "masculine" clothing and hairstyles among professional women reflected a desire to appear more powerful to colleagues and supervisors.

Other obvious appearance indicators include uniforms, more formal attire, and other status symbol accessories. High status shoppers dress up more, even for shopping trips (Sybers & Roach, 1962). That such dress cues express dominance is evident in the way others respond to them. Passersby are less likely to intrude on a group of people with high status dress (Knowles, 1973), and anyone who has attempted to purchase a new car has realized that the deference and attention paid to customers is in direct proportion to the formality and expensiveness of their clothing. Because of their high visibility and constancy in an interaction, appearance cues are readily available markers of the dominance hierarchy in any set of interpersonal relationships.

Chronemics. How people use their own time and that of others can be a very subtle but effective signal of dominance. People in power set schedules. They determine the frequency and duration of contact. A senior faculty member may insist on Saturday meetings with research assistants. The corporate executive who routinely schedules mandatory-attendance company retreats from 7:30 A.M. until 11:00 P.M. is letting subordinates know who is in control.

Powerful people are free to violate time norms. They may arrive later, stay longer, appear at odd hours, or keep others waiting but are themselves less likely to be violated. One newspaper publisher kept his editor waiting 4 hours while his wife and family packed before driving to an out-of-town meeting. They arrived an hour late to the meeting but made no apologies to the assembled group. Such behavior no doubt enhanced their perceived power. In this culture and others, those who arrive late are seen as higher in status (Levine & Wolff, 1985).

Dominant people also have more access to and demand more of other people's time. They may buy it, request it, or intrude on it. High status shoppers demand more attention from salesclerks and are more patronizing toward them (Sybers & Roach, 1962). An employer may require an employee to give up a weekend or a planned holiday to work on a report. We know of an executive who missed his 25-year retirement celebration because he was called away for one last service to his employer. Even the matter of "hogging the conversational floor" is a matter of taking a disproportionate share of the talk time.

Status is also revealed through greater leisure time and varied activity. The freedom to take a 1½-hour lunch or to plan a spur-of-the-moment ski trip implies a relative position of importance.

Finally, dominance and power may be expressed through polychronistic use of time. People in authority are free to give others divided attention. The job interviewer who sifts through a pile of applications while interviewing you is signaling a relative inequality in status, as is the manager who interrupts staff meetings to take telephone calls.

Some popular books advise using these and other chronemic maneuvers as ploys in the power game. But as you will see, some of these behaviors carry negative relational meanings in terms of intimacy and immediacy. The cost of successfully communicating dominance may therefore be some other unintended relational statements.

Gender and Power. One of the most provocative questions surrounding dominance is whether the fundamental distinction between men's and women's nonverbal displays is one of dominance, with men's displays paralleling those of power and women's those of powerlessness. This issue has

Richard Nixon shows mastery of polychronistic use of time. What relational messages does his behavior express?

generated considerable research and speculation (see, for example, Aries, 1982; Axelrod, 1980; Ellyson & Dovidio, 1985; Gillespie, 1978; Greenberg, 1979; Hall & Halberstadt, 1986; Henley, 1977; Henley & Harmon, 1985; Jones, 1986; LaFrance, 1985b; Leffler et al., 1982; Stier & Hall, 1984). Table 9.2 lists some of the key behaviors cited to support the claim. Although it is true that many behaviors exhibited most frequently by women connote submissiveness and weakness, female displays, as noted in earlier chapters, can also be characterized as affiliative, positive, sensitive, and engaged. Moreover, in same-sex interactions, women are capable of displaying the same dominance behaviors as men. It is not clear, therefore, that female displays are uniformly nondominant. It may be, as two studies have shown, that women are more likely to monitor their partner's behavior and to accommodate their behavior to their partner's when the partner is male, whereas men maintain a more fixed pattern of behavior (Greenberg, 1979; Mulac, Studley, Wiemann, & Bradac, 1987). Some women's displays may also be more the result of social nervousness and unease than dominance (Hall & Halberstadt, 1986). Time will tell whether societal change in male and female roles brings a corresponding change in nonverbal dominance displays.

Messages of Intimacy

Intimacy is a composite of several interrelated themes, each of which contributes to the total degree of intimacy that characterizes a relationship. Generally, the more involvement, affection, inclusion, depth, and trust that is expressed, the more intimacy.

Unlike dominance, most of the research relevant to intimacy has looked at combinations and sequences of cues as they relate to a particular outcome, such as liking. Despite differences in labels, most of the research tends to follow the thematic dimensions that Burgoon and Hale (1984, 1987b) found. Conversational involvement fits with immediacy and includes cues specifically concerned with approach or avoidance and engagement or detachment. Research on the depth (familiarity) dimension invariably includes similarity elements as relationships proceed through the stages of acquaintanceship. Work on attraction and liking corresponds to the affection dimension. Research on such related topics as warmth, responsivity, trust, empathy, rapport, and genuineness fits the combined themes of inclusion, receptivity, and trust, as does work on the opposite end of the inclusion continuum, privacy. A culminating line of work is that on the courtship process.

Involvement and Immediacy. Involvement behaviors are voluntarily expressed behaviors that signal participation, interest, and occupation with the other person in an interaction. Sometimes involvement is considered synonymous with immediacy, which encompasses behaviors specifically reflecting the degree of psychological distance between participants. However, involvement may also be communicated through expressiveness, good interaction management, altercentrism (focus on the other), and lack of social anxiety (Coker & Burgoon, 1986).

We rely on immediacy behaviors primarily to judge the level of involvement in a specific encounter rather than the status of the entire relationship (Forgas, 1978). The behaviors most often cited as indicative of immediacy are (a) close conversational distance, (b) direct body and facial orientation, (c) forward lean, (d) increased and direct gaze, (e) positive reinforcers such as smiling, head nods, and pleasant facial expressions, (f) postural openness, (g) frequent gesturing, and (h) touch (Andersen, 1979; Argyle & Cook, 1976; Argyle & Dean, 1965; Beier & Sternberg, 1977; Burgoon et al., 1984; Cappella, 1983; Cappella & Greene, 1984; Coker & Burgoon, 1986; Edinger & Patterson, 1983; Exline, Gray & Schuette, 1965; Henley, 1977; Keiser & Altman, 1976; LaFrance & Ickes, 1981; Mehrabian, 1968c, 1971b, 1972, 1981; Mehrabian & Ksionzky, 1972; Mehrabian & Williams, 1969; Patterson, 1973b, 1976; Sobelman, 1973). Other kinesic behaviors that people encode to demonstrate expressiveness, good interaction management, and lack of anxiety are more facial animation, more gestural animation and use of illustrators, coordinated movement, use of fewer adaptors, less random movement, and greater postural attentiveness (Coker & Burgoon, 1986). The opposites of these signal detachment and noninvolvement. Although the addition of more cues tends to make a message more pronounced, some cues such as proximity carry more weight than others (Burgoon et al., 1984; Fisher, Rytting, & Heslin, 1976; Henley, 1977). For instance, moving to a far distance may be sufficient to communicate nonimmediacy.

Vocal cues have received far less study. Those mentioned as indicative of involvement are speech rate, speech latency, loudness or intensity, speech duration, and interruptions (Cappella, 1983; Patterson, 1983). In a study designed to see what behaviors people actually enact to signal high or low involvement, Coker and Burgoon (1986) found that people expressing higher involvement spoke louder and faster, lowered their pitch, used more pitch variety, had fewer silences or latencies and more coordinated speech, and generally had warmer, more relaxed, resonant, and rhythmic voices with frequent relaxed laughter.

One chronemic element that expresses involvement is monochronistic versus polychronistic use of time. To do more than one thing at once is to show lack of involvement in the interaction. Miss Manners provides some lighthearted guidelines on when it is not acceptable to do two things at once.

Although many of these cues are also interpreted as signals of affiliation, taken individually they may only indicate intensity of involvement and should not be taken as reliable indicators of intimacy (Cappella, 1983). Gaze is a case in point. Two people engaged in a heated and hostile argument may make as much eye contact as two people who are attracted to one another. One study found that decreased gaze indicated disapproval, reduced intimacy, or reduced power, depending on the circumstances (Lochman & Allen, 1981). Thus gaze is primarily an intensifier of affect. Other cues may

Advice from Miss Manners

Is it proper to do two things at the same time? . . . It all depends on what two things and where and with whom.

It is proper to drink champagne and make eyes over the top of the glass at the same time. It may not always be wise, but the combination itself is considered socially proper.

However, it was not gallant of dear Gustave Flaubert to smoke a cigar and make love at the same time. Miss Manners dares say he meant it to be improper. . . .

It is never proper to have a television set on when visitors arrive except on election night, but visitors who drop in aren't proper themselves, so they may be told that one is busy just then. Miss Manners thinks it improper to have even so-called background music on when people are talking, but then she thinks such music improper all by itself.

It is proper and even decorative (meaning nicely old-fashioned) for ladies to do needlework in their own homes when company is present on all but the most formal occasions, and on very informal visits to others.

If they are challenged, they may use an old argument left over from Miss Manners' college days about how it is actually easier to pay attention to what someone is saying when one is knitting. The reasoning is that no one can pay constant attention to a lecture anyway, and it is better to have one's hands active than one's thoughts wandering.

This comes with the warning that the professors didn't care for it. It should be kept in mind that the two things anybody who is talking believe that the other person ought to be doing are (1) listening and (2) committing it all to memory.

Source: "Miss Manners" by J. Martin, *The Knoxville News-Sentinal,* March 16, 1986.

be similarly ambiguous unless coupled with a sufficient number of other intimacy cues to make the meaning clear.

Depth and Similarity. As members in a relationship progress from strangers to acquaintances to friends to intimates, many of the involvement behaviors become more prevalent. For example, friends gaze more, smile more, show more facial pleasantness, and adopt closer conversational distances than strangers, and such cues are taken as indicative of more familiar relationships (Coutts & Schneider, 1976; Hale & Burgoon, 1984; Keiser & Altman, 1976; Little, 1968; Russo, 1975; Sundstrom & Altman, 1976;

Thayer & Schiff, 1974). Subtle nonverbal differences may even distinguish harmonious couples and conflicted couples (those who may be presumed to be in one of the deescalation stages). Happy couples sit closer together and touch each other more, while discordant couples touch themselves more and adopt such closed postures as crossed arms (Beier, 1974; Beier & Sternberg, 1977).

An integral part of moving a relationship to a deeper, more familiar level is shows of commonality and similarity. These include adopting similar dress and appearance, vocal patterns, and kinesic mannerisms in addition to modeling each other's language use. Romantic couples universally use appearance to publicly proclaim identification as a duo. They may dress alike, exchange matching rings, or even wear identical hairstyles. The lifelong habit of married couples' mimicking each other's facial expressions often results in their faces looking alike over time.

The use of attire and adornments as a form of shared identity is not confined to romantic relationships. Youth gangs rely on various badges, clothing styles, and colors to proclaim their separateness. Religious cults often enforce a common dress code to promote group identity over individ-

Gaze, facial pleasantness, smiling, relatively direct body and facial orientation, postural relaxation, and proximity combine to signal affiliation and friendliness.

ual identity. Law enforcement agencies, parochial schools, corporations, and renegade groups such as survivalists likewise know the value of a recognizable uniform in fostering group solidarity.

Vocally, affiliated pairs and groups may converge their speech patterns. By matching a partner's speech style, a person may emphasize similarities and enhance attraction. Conversely, one may signal dissimilarity by diverging from the other's speech pattern. Specific behaviors on which people match or contrast speech include accent, pronunciation, speech rate, loudness, pause length, vocalization length, utterance length, interruptions, and language choice (Feldstein & Welkowitz, 1978; Giles, 1977; Giles & Powesland, 1975; Matarazzo & Weins, 1972; Siegman, 1978; Street, 1982; Street & Giles, 1982). Observers and dyadic partners rate more favorably those who converge their speech patterns with their partners on latency, tempo, duration of vocalization, and accent, as well as on content (Giles & Powesland, 1975; Giles & Smith, 1979; Street, 1982; Street & Brady, 1982; Street, Brady, & Putman, 1983; Welkowitz & Kuc, 1973).

Kinesically and proxemically, people may show similarities through proximity and postural sharing. People who have similar personalities and attitudes adopt closer interaction distances (Byrne, Ervin, & Lamberth, 1970) and echo each other's body positions or adopt mirror-image postures (Morris, 1977; Scheflen, 1964). In turn, people who are induced to share posture perceive themselves to be more similar (Navarre, 1982). Attitudinally and demographically similar dyads also display more affiliative behaviors such as gesturing, self-grooming, and more gaze, while dissimilar pairs show more nonaffiliative behaviors such as self-touching and nervous laughter (Gonzales, 1982; Murray & McGinley, 1972). Better adjusted marital couples, too, show more reciprocal gaze (Noller, 1980a, 1980b).

Other indicators of the depth of a relationship are what Morris (1977) calls *tie-signs*. These are signals that a couple is to be treated as a bonded pair. Many are haptic gestures, such as linked arms, handholding, arms around waists, hand-to-face touches, and the arm-to-elbow assist. Many other cues exchanged among courting and bonded couples qualify as tie-signs. Interestingly, tie-signs are more prevalent among dating and courting couples than among marrieds. Once a relationship is well established, the need for public displays of affection and oneness are no longer necessary. Thus the stage of the relationship dictates which of these behaviors will be present.

At a more general level, Knapp (1984) hypothesizes that as relationships escalate, styles of communication move from (a) narrow to broad ranges of expressions (such as more facial and vocal blends, fewer dichotomies, and more time together); (b) stylized, conventional forms of communication to more unique, idiosyncratic, and relationally negotiated forms; (c) difficult to more efficient, accurate communication; (d) rigid to flexible patterns of interaction; (e) awkward to smooth, synchronized, convergent communication; (f) public to personal and private revelations (such as previously unknown information and use of adaptors); (g) hesitant to spontaneous, rapid, and relaxed communication; and (h) suspending overt judgment

Two types of body contact tie-signs.

to making such judgments, including negative feedback, explicit. Conversely, as relationships deescalate, they move back toward the narrow, stylized, difficult, rigid, awkward, hesitant, nonjudgmental ends of the stylistic continua. Table 9.3 shows the dimensions that Knapp believes underlie relational communication styles.

Affection, Attraction, Liking, and Love. The signals of love and attraction hold a fascination for most of us. They are essential not only to the mating game but also to the development of satisfying friendships, family relations, and work relations. The courtship process is detailed later, so here we consider behaviors that singly or in combination communicate positive or negative affect toward the partner.

The ubiquitous immediacy behaviors are especially significant. People display more immediacy toward someone they like (Coutts, Schneider, &

TABLE 9.3 Knapp's Dimensions of Relational Communication Styles

Narrow ———————————	Broad
Stylized ———————————	Unique
Difficult ———————————	Efficient
Rigid ———————————	Flexible
Awkward ———————————	Smooth
Public ———————————	Personal
Hesitant ———————————	Spontaneous
Overt judgment suspended ———————————	Overt judgment given

Montgomery, 1980; Mehrabian, 1970a), and people who are induced to show more immediacy come to like the target more (Slane & Leak, 1978). Immediacy cues can even leak unintended evaluations. Tutors who thought they were working with bright children gazed, nodded, smiled, and leaned forward more than those who thought they were working with dull children (Chaikin, Sigler, & Derlega, 1974).

Of special significance are the eyes. Literary passages abound with references to the power of the eyes to attract and arouse. Consider this one from *The Sleepwalkers:*

> So they smiled frankly at each other and their souls nodded to each
> other through the windows of their eyes, just for an instant, like two
> neighbors who have never greeted each other and now happen to
> lean out of their window at the same moment, pleased and embar-
> rassed by this unforeseen and simultaneous greeting. (Broch, 1964)

People in love spend more time gazing into each other's eyes, especially at close range (Givens, 1978; Rubin, 1970). People also gaze longer at someone they like or are attracted to and gaze less at a disliked other (Exline, 1972; Exline & Winters, 1965; Goldberg, Kiesler, & Collins, 1969; Harper, Wiens, & Matarazzo, 1978; Lochman & Allen, 1981; Mehrabian, 1968c, 1969; Murray & McGinley, 1972). There is an interesting sex difference, however: Men adjust their gaze behavior to express liking during the listening role, while women adjust it during the speaking role (Exline & Winters, 1965; Murray & McGinley, 1972). More gaze is also rated as indicative of liking, friendliness, and similar positive evaluations (Argyle, 1972a; Beebe, 1980; Goldberg et al., 1969; Kleinke, Meeker & La Fong, 1974; McDowell, 1973; Patterson, Jordan, Hogan, & Frerker, 1981; Reece & Whitman, 1961).

Another uncontrolled signal of attraction is pupil dilation. When people see someone or something they like, their pupils dilate (Hess, 1975; Hess & Polt, 1960; Janisse & Peavler, 1974). At the same time, widened pupils make people more attractive, a discovery that led women centuries ago to use belladonna to artificially enlarge their pupils. Suppose two people's eyes meet across a crowded room. If the man is attracted to a woman, his pupils will automatically dilate, which makes him appear warmer and more attractive. If her pupils dilate in turn, the pair will have the beginnings of mutual physical attraction. This is one way people know that someone is interested in them.

Facial and bodily expressiveness are also important barometers of attraction. Smiling and facial pleasantness are equated with liking, friendliness, and intimacy (Burgoon et al., 1984; Harper et al., 1978; Patterson et al., 1981; Waldron, 1975). Postural mirroring, in addition to signaling perceived similarity, occurs more often between people who like each other (Mach, 1972).

Proximity and touch are major carriers of attraction and liking messages. People adopt closer distances to those they like or evaluate positively and greater distances from those they dislike (Byrne et al., 1970; Gilbert, Kirkland, & Rappoport, 1977; Kleck, 1969; Lott & Sommer, 1967; Patterson & Sechrest, 1970; Rosenfeld, 1965; Sommer, 1971). Proximity is the most important immediacy behavior in decoding liking and intimacy (Burgoon et al., 1984). Touch is likewise perceived as warm, loving, intimate, and friendly (Breed & Ricci, 1973; Burgoon et al., 1984; Fisher et al., 1976; Kleinke et al., 1974). Interestingly, when touch is nonreciprocal, it increases ratings of warmth of the toucher and decreases them for the person touched (Heslin & Alper, 1983; Major & Heslin, 1982). Touch also engenders more liking from recipients (Boderman, Freed, & Kinnucan, 1972) and is expected in intimate relationships (Henley, 1977). Even with nonreciprocal touch, romantic pairs perceive it as expressing warmth or love rather than dominance (Pisano, Wall, & Foster, 1986). Its potency is best expressed by Thayer (1986):

> Touch is a signal in the communication process that, above all other communication channels, most directly and immediately escalates the balance of intimacy. . . . To let another touch us is to drop that final and most formidable barrier to intimacy. (p. 8)

The absence of touch may also be a powerful message of repugnance. A study on the frequency of touch in a nursing home found that the staff engaged in much less touching with extremely handicapped patients, even though touch is frequently a necessary part of medical care (Watson, 1975).

Beyond immediacy behaviors, vocal tone may communicate affection. In particular, a louder voice is associated with negative affect (Kimble, Forte, & Yoshikawa, 1981). Conversely, people in love may express their feelings by using oversoft, slurred, drawling, resonant, high pitched voices (Costanzo, Markel, & Costanzo, 1969; Givens, 1978).

One final indicator of level of affection is the use of silences. Silences may be associated with complete harmony or complete conflict. When people are completely comfortable in a relationship, there is no need to talk. When relationships are just developing, silences become less common. People who are attracted to each other may use fewer silent pauses (Siegman, 1979). At the other extreme, silences may indicate aversion and disdain (Bruneau, 1973):

> Fat persons, dwarfs, very tall persons, crippled persons with mobility problems, blind persons, persons with pronounced speech or hearing disorders, etc., have known nervous silences toward them. Differences in appearance, such as perceived ugliness, dress and color of skin, when different than the situational norm, seem to be greeted by initial silences. (p. 32)

Equally important to the specific cues of intimacy is their sequencing. If people are subjected to cold behavior and then warm behavior by a partner, they are likely to be more attracted to that person than someone who exhibits consistently warm behavior. Conversely, a sequence of warm behavior followed by cold is more detrimental to attraction than all cold behavior. The finding that people place greater importance on the contrast between cold and warm behavior follows gain-loss theory (Aronson & Linder, 1965; Clore, Wiggins, & Itkin, 1975a, 1975b). Gains or losses in apparent affection are more telling than consistent behavior. This probably explains why we feel we have made more strides with a person who initially seems aloof to us and then warms up to us. We take it as a significant relational statement.

Trust, Receptivity, Warmth, and Rapport. Not surprisingly, many of the same kinesic, proxemic, and haptic behaviors that communicate relational depth, similarity, and affection also express empathy, rapport, and other receptive themes. The amount and directness of eye contact increases in response to warm nonverbal cues from a tutor, which suggests greater receptivity; it increases with preferences for intimate relationships (McAdams, Jackson, & Kirshnit, 1984) and is seen as expressing more empathy and warmth (Haase & Tepper, 1972; Ho & Mitchell, 1982; McAdams et al., 1984). However, too much gaze may be counterproductive. One study found that moderate eye contact earned the highest ratings on genuineness and empathy (Reed, 1981).

More smiling, facial pleasantness, head nods, frequent and open gestures, and eyebrow raises have the same effects as more gaze: They accompany a desire for intimacy, are a likely response to an immediate partner, and are interpreted as expressing more empathy, warmth, affiliativeness, and friendliness (Bayes, 1972; Clore et al., 1975b; D'Augelli, 1974; Gutsell & Andersen, 1980; Harrigan & Rosenthal, 1986; Hillison, 1983; Ho & Mitchell, 1982; Janzen, 1984; McAdams et al., 1984; McMullan, 1974; Mehrabian, 1981; Patterson et al., 1981; Sobelman, 1973). Coldness is expressed by such acts as blank stares, gazing away or at the ceiling, and engaging in such adaptor behaviors as knuckle cracking, hair twisting, or smoking (Clore et al., 1975b).

Postural mirroring or congruence is also a key indicator. Occurring more frequently among cooperative pairs, it is associated with rapport, empathy, and trustworthiness in the short term and over time, and can lead to more liking of the partner when a person is induced to display it (Charney, 1966; Fraenkel, 1983; LaFrance, 1979, 1985a; LaFrance & Broadbent, 1976; Mansfield, 1973; Navarre, 1982; Sandhu, 1984; Trout & Rosenfeld, 1980). However, it is possible that postural sharing is only actually associated with long-term relationships; in brief encounters, it may signal a desire for rapport but be accompanied by discomfort (LaFrance & Ickes, 1981). Facial, postural, and vocal motor mimicry—mimicking someone else's expression of emotion such as pain or leaning in the same direction during a recounting of a near accident—is another form of mirroring that occurs most when it is visible to the sufferer (suggesting that it is an intentional show of sympathy) and is interpreted as knowing and caring how another feels (Bavelas, Black, Chovil, Lemery, & Mullett, 1988; Bavelas, Black, Lemery, & Mullett, 1986).

Close proximity, direct body orientation, forward lean, and the use of touch also communicate greater empathy, warmth, affiliation, and rapport, which in turn produce perceptions of greater trustworthiness (Breed & Ricci, 1973; Claiborn, 1979; Fisher et al., 1976; Haase & Tepper, 1972; Hillison, 1983; Kleinke et al., 1974; Major & Heslin, 1982; McMullan, 1974; Patterson, Powell, & Lenihan, 1986; Sobelman, 1973; Trout & Rosenfeld, 1980). However, touch may be a vital relational message of sincerity and intimacy only among friends and family. It may not express the same meanings among strangers, or at least not to the same degree. This was the conclusion of two experiments (Breed & Ricci, 1973; Burley, 1972). In one, actual touch increased more positive feelings among stranger recipients, but empathy was perceived to be even greater when accompanied by no touch or imagined touch. In the other, touch or no touch was coupled with warm or cold behavior. It turned out that the warmth cues made more of a difference than touch. Thus it may be that the affiliative behaviors typically accompanying touch are more responsible for the effects of touch than touch itself. One other interesting observation is that interviewers who are more favorable toward an interviewee touch their foot more (while seated in a foot-on-knee position) (Goldberg & Rosenthal, 1986). This may be a very subtle cue that someone is open to you. (Also see Applications, p. 324.)

Vocally, more laughter is associated with greater intimacy motivation (McAdams et al., 1984) and more vocal pleasantness with affiliation (Mehrabian, 1970a).

Privacy. At the opposite end of the inclusion and receptivity continuum are relational messages expressing the desire for exclusion, nonreceptivity, and privacy. As we noted earlier, people appear to have competing needs for approach and avoidance, even in their most intimate relationships. The nature of privacy and the means through which people express their need for it or a desire to restore lost privacy are not solely relational messages and are discussed in more detail in Chapter 11. However, it is important to recognize that the relational communication of privacy can be designed both to move a relationship to a more intimate level and to move it, even if temporarily, to a less intimate one. The kinds of behaviors that are most likely to signal a desire for greater privacy include a combination of nonimmediacy, nonaffiliation, and dominance behaviors. These are often coupled with manipulations of the environment, space, and time that afford greater control of accessibility, sensory stimulation, and surveillance (Altman, 1975; Burgoon, 1982).

So far we have considered the component nonverbal cues that together express messages about the relative intimacy of a relationship, regardless of whether it is a friendship, family relationship, work association, or romantic partnership. Now we turn specifically to the mating game.

APPLICATIONS

Empathy and Rapport in Doctor–Patient Relationships

Good rapport is essential to a successful relationship between physicians and their patients. Without it, patients may not comply with a doctor's recommendations or may even change doctors. We noted in Chapter 5 that empathy and rapport are better expressed through nonverbal channels than verbal ones. Just what are the nonverbal cues that physicians use to communicate this to patients?

Immediacy behaviors are very important. Doctors who sit or stand closer to their patients, face them directly, lean forward, nod frequently, and use touch are seen as warmer and more empathic. However, eye contact doesn't work in quite the same fashion. Doctors who gaze more *toward* their patients but engage in less *mutual* gaze are seen as having the most rapport (Harrigan, Oxman, & Rosenthal, 1985; Harrigan & Rosenthal, 1983, 1986). Whether posture is open or closed is also telling. Symmetrical, open arm positions and hands resting in the lap are associated with greater physician rapport, while crossed arms are seen as the coldest and least empathic expression (Harrigan et al., 1985; Harrigan & Rosenthal, 1986; Smith-Hanen, 1977).

Interestingly, more self-touching by doctors, rather than the absence of it, is associated with greater warmth and expressiveness. This may be because self-touching often accompanies efforts to encode or decode speech and may be taken as an indication that the doctor is intently interested in what the patient has to say (Harrigan, 1985; Harrigan, Kues, & Weber, 1986; Harrigan, Weber, & Kues, 1986). Gesturing is even more positively evaluated than self-touching, probably because it too expresses high involvement.

Doctors' vocal cues are also strong predictors of whether patients are satisfied with their relationship with the doctor. In particular, a nondominant, anxious, but warm voice leads to physicians' being perceived as warm (Blanck, Rosenthal, & Vannicelli, 1986). A friendly or neutral voice is also perceived as more receptive and trustworthy than an authoritarian voice (Parrott & LePoire, 1988).

Finally, doctors who are more accurate encoders of their emotional states, whether through audio, visual, or combined channels, have patients who are more affectively satisfied with them (Di-Matteo, Prince, & Hays, 1986). In other words, doctors who are more skilled at expressing nonverbal communication are seen as having greater understanding of and rapport with their patients.

Courtship and Quasi-courtship

Courtship consists in a number of quiet attentions, not
so pointed as to alarm, nor so vague as not to be
understood.

Lawrence Stern

Courtship runs on messages—on physical signals and
displays. Love may be intangible, but love
communication is concrete, real.

David Givens

Two of the most detailed analyses of the courtship process come from
Givens (1978) and Scheflen (1965, 1974). Givens's conclusions come from
an examination of commonalities between humans and other species in the
basic courtship sequence and signals. He finds a strong biological base for
these behaviors and concludes that they are universal. Scheflen's conclusions come from psychotherapeutic observations of therapists interacting
with families. He discovered that courting behaviors occur between female
patients and doctors. He labeled these flirtatious exchanges *quasi-courtship*
and attempted to distinguish between them and those that are intended to
culminate in an intimate, usually sexual, commitment.

The major distinguishing characteristics of courtship are (a) use of
attention-gaining signals, (b) use of submissive behaviors to minimize the
possibility of approach being interpreted as a threat, and (c) reliance on
patterns of interaction that parallel parent-child interactions. These various
signals unfold through five stages.

The first stage is *attention.* Before anything can happen, the two parties
involved must first gain each other's attention. This may be accidental—as
in two people catching each other's eye at a bus stop—or intentional—as in
an arranged introduction. In fact, Givens (1983) claims that "all the smiling,
firm handshakes, excited greetings, nervous laughter, clown-colorful costumes, and scurrying about you see at parties can be viewed in a detached
way as *attention* signals" (p. 11). A key feature of this stage is ambivalence—a
mix of tendencies to draw near and to avoid that reflect the tentativeness
of this initial period. The two may vacillate between glancing at each other
and glancing away or downward, smiling and compressing lips, yawning,
stretching, accelerating the tempo of behavior, and engaging in a lot of
self-touch as a sign of anxiety (Eibl-Eibesfeldt, 1975; Givens, 1978). They
may also display infantile or childlike expressions designed to elicit affectionate responses (Eibl-Eibesfeldt, 1971).

The next stage is *recognition,* or what Scheflen (1965) calls *courtship
readiness.* If the response of one party to these hesitant approach signals is
a stare, blank face, negative facial expression, or orienting away, that ends
it. However, if there is some interest, the recipient will display availability

signals. These include eyebrow raises and the typical immediacy behaviors of gaze, more direct body orientation, and smiling, but they are tempered by ambivalence signals such as demurely averting gaze downward and engaging in the same adaptor behaviors of yawning, stretching, self-touching, and the like.

A common indicator of readiness is increased muscle tone. Posture improves, sagging tummies and derrieres are pulled in, bags around the eyes tend to disappear. People appear more alert, eyes seem brighter, and skin may take on a rosier hue due to more blood flooding the capillaries of the face. Accompanying these physiological changes are preening behaviors—such self-grooming acts as smoothing the hair, straightening clothing, tugging at socks (by men), and checking makeup (by women) (see Figure 9.2a). You can see a good demonstration of these behaviors the next time you are in a public rest room or trying on clothes in a department store. People go through a range of preening behaviors in front of the mirror before presenting themselves in public again.

Anxiety is still evident in this stage and may even result in a "freezing" of behavior. Postural immobility is especially common after an embarrassing period of mutual gaze. It may serve to reassure the partner that no aggressive intentions exist.

A central characteristic of the displays in this stage, in fact, is their submissive quality. Docile behaviors, by disclaiming dominance, cue the approacher that he or she need not fear hostile responses to the overture. A complex of behaviors that Givens (1978) calls the *shoulder shrug composite* often occurs. This set of submissive behaviors, seen in both children and adults, includes the shoulder shrug itself, brow raising, the head tilt, and an open mouth or pout. In women, physical features reduce apparent aggressiveness even further: "Relative hairlessness, smooth complexion and voice tone [all of] which have a childlike character may contribute to this. They may also dispose the male toward caretaking and protective behaviors" (Kendon, 1975, p. 328).

The third stage is *positioning* for courtship and interaction. People place themselves in close face-to-face positions for direct and personal conversation. These positions also serve the function of closing others out. By leaning forward, crossing legs toward each other, orienting the body toward each other, and placing chairs in a way that prevents others from joining them, a couple may become an enclosed unit. If others are present, the upper body may be turned slightly to include them politely while the trunk and lower limbs clearly signal exclusion (Scheflen, 1965) (see Figure 9.2b). The topic of conversation is irrelevant to the formation of a bond; it is the manner in which it occurs that is significant. It is highly animated, responsive, immediate, and submissive. Heightened arousal may be evident in an accelerating tempo of activity and in exaggerated behaviors such as emphatic gestures and loud laughter. Responsivity may become evident (to both participants and onlookers) through extended gazes, increased head nodding, postural mirroring, and synchronized movements. Submissiveness is apparent through softer, quieter, higher pitched voices, demure gaze

Some preening behavior of male psychotherapists

A) Tie preen
B) Sock preen
C) Hair preen

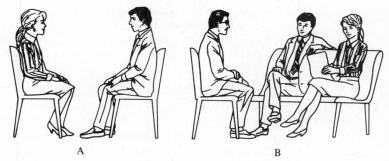

Positioning for courtship

A) With two people
B) With third party present

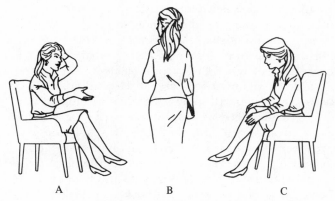

Appealing or invitational behavior of women

A) Presenting the palm with hair press
B) Rolling the hip
C) Presenting and caressing the leg

FIGURE 9.2 Behaviors typical of the second, third, and fourth stages of courtship.

downward (as opposed to away), and continuation of the shoulder shrug composite (Givens, 1978).

The fourth stage is *invitations and sexual arousal.* In this stage come the implicit appeals for a sexual liaison expressed through body language, verbal innuendo, and vocal orchestration. The expressions of affection that appear match those between caregiver and child:

> Barriers to physical closeness have begun to relax in this phase, and tentatively at first, touching, stroking, caressing, massaging, playing with the other's hands, all behaviors that may be observed in the earliest parental responses to the neonate, begin to be exchanged. Paralinguistically, speech continues in a soft and high-pitched manner; semantically, it may be well stocked with childcare metaphors (e.g., "baby," "sugar daddy," "little lady," "babe") and pet names (e.g., "cutie," "dollie," "sweetie"). Even varieties of baby talk may be used. The partners can be expected to give and receive certain activities related to breast-feeding. Nuzzling, licking, sucking, playful biting, kissing, and so on, which appear to have a broad geographical distribution as sexually meaningful signs, can be used to communicate the emotional intimacy that is prerequisite to sexual intercourse. (Givens, 1978, p. 352)

Other behaviors in this stage include grooming the partner (e.g., fixing the hair, adjusting or buttoning clothing), carrying and clutching activities (e.g., handholding, clinging, carrying across a threshold), and sexually provocative behaviors (e.g., rolling or protruding the pelvis, protruding the chest, cocking the head, turning wrists or palms outward to expose more skin, exposing the thigh when crossing legs, stroking the wrist or thigh, unbuttoning clothing) (see Figure 9.2c). The tempo might slow somewhat, and the couple might show increased relaxation but extreme attentiveness.

The final stage is *resolution.* In true courtship, the culminating act is copulation. Here is where courtship differs from quasi-courtship and flirtation. Many of the preceding stages and behaviors may be present when there is no intention of the relationship's moving to the level of sexual contact. Flirting behavior is common not only in bars but also in the boardroom. The expression of mutual attraction seems to be a rewarding activity in itself because it enhances self-esteem. How, then, does one tell the difference between true courtship and harmless flirtation?

Usually there are clues in the early stages to prevent the relationship from advancing to the brink of the resolution stage. One way to let a prospective partner know that this is not an intimate relationship in the making is to abbreviate or omit part of the ritual. Postural involvement may be incomplete, the leg and arm positions open enough to include others. Eye contact may be broken to make contact with others, or voices may be loud enough to be audible to others. Glances and nods in the direction of others serve as reminders that others are present, thereby invoking norms for appropriate conduct. Other cues such as intimate touch or the head tilt may be omitted. Another way is to add cues that conflict with the courtship ritual. Expressing dominance behaviors is at odds with true courtship, even among males (the movie-perpetuated stereotype of the strong male to the contrary). Finally, the context itself, by its inappropriateness, may make evident that true courtship is not taking place. Unfortunately, this last indicator may no longer work well. The rise in romantic relationships in the workplace suggests that locale may not be much of an inhibitor.

Before leaving the courtship process, it is worth noting that once a pair has bonded, many of the affectionate cues associated with courtship become infrequent. For example, established couples display far less self-grooming than developing couples (Daly, Hogg, Sacks, Smith, & Zimring, 1983). Flirting behaviors may become redundant and unnecessary to the negotiation of sexual accessibility and consequently eventually disappear. Public displays of affection likewise become minimal. This reduced level of nonverbal activity is often dismaying to married couples and victims of seduction, who find that "courtship seems to be only a *temporary* relationship that occurs between the first meetings and intercourse. After resolution, courting signals become scarce" (Givens, 1978, p. 353).

Theories of Intimacy Exchange and Development. How people respond to changes in intimacy and immediacy by a partner and how relationships escalate or deescalate intimacy is the focus of much theorizing. The first theory to address these questions was *affiliative conflict theory* (Argyle & Cook, 1976; Argyle & Dean, 1965). It proposes that people have competing approach and avoidance needs and will seek a level of conversational immediacy that balances the two. When this equilibrium level is disturbed, as by an interaction partner moving too close or reducing gaze, people compensate by changing their own nonverbal or verbal behaviors to restore a comfortable level of immediacy. Compensation may occur on the same behavior—reduced gaze being met by increased gaze—or on related immediacy behaviors. People may also engage in intrapersonal compensation, adjusting elements in their own interaction style to keep their net degree of involvement in balance. This theory has generated a profusion of research, much of it confirming that compensation occurs on some behaviors and under some circumstances (for reviews, see Firestone, 1977; Hale & Burgoon, 1984; Patterson, 1973a).

However, some research has shown that an opposite pattern occurs— just as people tend to match a partner's increased verbal self-disclosure with more intimate disclosures of their own, so do they often reciprocate increased verbal and nonverbal immediacy with more intimate nonverbal behaviors (see, for example, Chapman, 1975; Coutts et al., 1980; Goldberg, 1980; Schulz & Barefoot, 1974). The frequent occurrence of *reciprocity* rather than compensation led to several new theories that tried to predict under what circumstances compensation or reciprocity would emerge.

Patterson's (1976) *arousal labeling model* suggested that deviations from equilibrium create arousal and that how one labels the arousal dictates the response: Positive labeling of the experience leads to reciprocity, negative labeling to compensation. More recently, Patterson (1983) has suggested in his *sequential functional model* that the functions the behaviors are interpreted as serving (e.g., social versus task-related) influence the outcome, as does the degree to which an interaction is stable and conforms to expectations. When the level of actual involvement deviates significantly from what is preferred and expected, it leads to instability and compensatory adjustments.

Other models have followed Patterson's lead in recognizing the role of arousal in predicting outcomes. Burgoon and Hale (Burgoon, 1978a; Hale & Burgoon, 1984) propose that *expectancy violations* (any change from the expected behavior pattern) are arousing and that the combined reward level of the violator and direction of violation determine whether it will be met by reciprocity or compensation. Increased immediacy by a highly rewarding partner should be positively interpreted and responded to with reciprocity. Decreased immediacy by a nonrewarding partner should be negatively interpreted and likewise lead to reciprocity (a matched deescalation of intimacy and involvement). Conversely, decreased immediacy by a high reward partner should be troubling and lead to an effort to "warm up" the interaction, a compensatory response, whereas increased immediacy by a poorly regarded partner should lead to an effort to "cool down" the involvement level, also a compensatory response.

Two other approaches, Andersen's (1985; Andersen & Andersen, 1984) *arousal valence model* and Cappella and Greene's (1982) *discrepancy arousal model,* make the assumption that adjustments that are moderately discrepant from norms or expectations are moderately arousing and prompt reciprocity, while extremely discrepant behaviors are highly arousing, producing discomfort and prompting compensation. These models require knowing the level of arousal that is being experienced, since they predict a change from reciprocity to compensation once the threshold of high arousal is attained.

Research in these areas will continue to refine these theories and determine under which circumstances any of them apply. What is important is that they attempt to explain not just the impact of a single relational message but the ongoing, dynamic process of relational communication and the manner in which relationships may progress to increasingly intimate levels or degenerate into noninvolvement. They are of practical importance, because they can help us predict whether our efforts to move a relationship to a deeper, more intimate level are likely to be met with like behavior from our partner or by counteracting moves. They may also identify what strategies people in the helping professions should use to elicit more openness and commitment from their patients and clients.

Equally important is determining the outcomes that reciprocity or compensation yield. For example, which pattern promotes more satisfaction, liking, rapport, involvement, commitment, and the like? We have already noted that convergent or reciprocal patterns often lead to more positive evaluations and occur among more satisfied pairs. Developmental research has shown that reciprocal patterns lead to attachment between mother and infant (see Gewirtz & Boyd, 1976). Interestingly, this research indicates that the infant conditions the mother for reciprocal activity, not vice versa (which should dispel any notion that parents are in the driver's seat). Cappella (1985) came to the conclusion, based on the limited evidence available, that reciprocity contributes to positive outcomes but noted some limitations of the research:

> Although the evidence is certainly not overwhelming or broad enough in behaviors to warrant a strong claim, it is suggestive. Convergence, reciprocity, and similarity in behavioral expression tend to produce positive evaluation. The research has generally avoided studying the perceptions of participants in favor of studying the reactions of judges and has tended to study staged convergence rather than actual convergence. As we become more assured that mutual influence patterns are associated with outcomes, unstaged convergence and participant responses will need study. (p. 426)

Other research points to compensatory patterns as preferable for attaining influence and control. For example, one study (Burris, 1982) found that when two interactants in a decision-making context match the posture and gestures of a third, the third person is perceived as the leader. Thus one may lose control by matching another's behavior. Much more research is needed to determine under what conditions reciprocity or compensation is the optimal communication strategy.

Messages of Arousal and Composure

Little has been written about the deliberate encoding of messages about degree of responsiveness to a relational partner. How do people signal that they are stimulated or aroused, either pleasantly or unpleasantly, in the other's presence? That they feel composed, calm, and relaxed? That they feel depressed and lethargic? It appears that two dimensions are involved. One is the intensity or general degree of activation. The other is the degree of positivity or negativity. Simplified, this produces four combinations: aroused and pleasant, unaroused and pleasant, aroused and unpleasant, unaroused and unpleasant.

Research on the unintentional leakage of anxiety and tension cues and on such affective states as attraction, anger, and embarrassment offers implications for the relational communication of aroused states. Relevant proxemic indicators of anxiety, avoidance, and withdrawal behaviors were reviewed in Chapter 3. Research on other sources of situational arousal and anxiety confirms that as negative arousal increases, so does distance (Brady & Walker, 1978; Nesbitt & Steven, 1974). Kinesic cues encoded during such negative arousal states as embarrassment, anger, and anxiety include both gaze aversion and longer glances, more nervous or forced smiles and facial tics, fewer positive feedback cues such as nodding and facial pleasantness, more indirect head orientation, greater postural rigidity and bodily tension, more postural shifts, more gesturing, and more self-manipulations and extremity movements (although the chronically anxious may display less random movement) (Boice & Monti, 1982; Burgoon & Koper, 1984; Cappella, 1983; Cappella & Greene, 1984; Edelmann & Hampson, 1981a, 1981b;

Exline et al., 1965; Jurich & Jurich, 1974; Kimble et al., 1981; Modigliani, 1971; Sainesbury, 1955). Amount of direct gaze increases with both intensely positive and intensely negative emotions (Kimble et al., 1981) and is therefore a good signal of the intensity of arousal.

Vocally, negative arousal states produce louder speech, nervous laughter (which may be used to reduce the level of anxiety), more speech disturbances, more silent pauses, faster tempo (although tempo may slow with extreme or chronic anxiety), and higher pitch (Brady & Walker, 1978; Cappella & Greene, 1984; Edelmann & Hampson, 1981a; Kimble et al., 1981; Scherer, 1982b; Siegman, 1985). Anxious communicators engage in fewer interruptions of others (Natale, Entin, & Jaffe, 1979).

If physical attraction can be viewed as a positive form of arousal, increases in positive arousal carry such indicators as closer proximity (Byrne et al., 1970), shorter pauses, shorter response latencies, faster tempo (Siegman, 1978, 1979), and the other attraction cues cited earlier. High levels of social arousal may also be accompanied by natural laughter, which may serve as an arousal release mechanism (Chapman, 1975).

At the opposite end of the arousal continuum are indicators of relaxation and composure or depression and lethargy. Mehrabian (1969; Mehrabian & Ksionzky, 1972) has identified a set of interrelated behaviors that he considers relaxation cues. These include asymmetrical leg and arm positions, sideways lean, arm openness, high rates of gesturing, and less swiveling and leg and foot movement. Burgoon et al. (1984) and Patterson et al. (1981) also have found through decoding studies that greater facial pleasantness, smiling, eye contact, and proximity convey messages of calmness, relaxation, and composure. Finally, Mehrabian (1970a) proposes that depressive tendencies and less responsiveness to others are revealed through lower nonverbal activity.

These combined findings suggest that the best way to signal arousal is through heightened physical activity and louder, higher pitched, rapid speech. When coupled with anxiety cues and the absence of positive feedback or affiliative behaviors, such behavior may signal noncomposure and discomfort in a relationship. Because the presence of facial pleasantness, smiling, increased gaze, and proximity may accompany either positive arousal or relaxation, immediacy behaviors by themselves do not reveal level of arousal. If arousal or nonarousal behaviors are evident only in the presence of one relational partner and not others, they can probably be taken as relational messages. Otherwise, they are best treated as indicators of the individual's personality traits or characteristic communication style.

Messages of Formality and Task or Social Orientation

These final two themes of relational communication are related in that what tends to communicate formality also communicates a task orientation and what expresses informality tends to express a social orientation.

As with arousal and composure, very little work has directly considered what nonverbal behaviors express these themes. Common sense would suggest that a more relaxed and asymmetrical posture, pleasant facial expression, smiling, and close conversational distance—in other words, cues of immediacy and relaxation—convey greater casualness and social orientation and that "proper" posture, less expressiveness, and a greater distance communicate a businesslike and formal demeanor. Altman and Vinsel (1977) did find that people stand or sit farther apart in more formal settings.

What has received a little attention is the difference the presence or absence of certain channels makes. The presence of visual information tends to make an interaction more intimate and informal. Thus speaking by telephone is more formal than meeting face to face (Stephenson, Ayling, & Rutter, 1976). This may explain why people don't like to fire someone or deliver bad news in person. The kinesic and proxemic immediacy cues present in face-to-face encounters reduce the sense of distance at a time when the sender wants to increase it. The absence of visual information also aids negotiation and competition (Argyle & Cook, 1976; Morley & Stephenson, 1969), probably because it eliminates the possibility of visual confrontation and the distraction of surveillance. This suggests that you can signal a task orientation by reducing the amount of sensory stimulation you give another and by closing the communication channel through gaze avoidance.

One final indicator of task orientation is undoubtedly monochronistic use of time. Giving only partial attention to the task at hand conveys less serious commitment to it. The receptionist who writes personal letters and paints her nails during work is sending a relational message to her employer of low task involvement.

Summary

In this chapter, we have seen that one of the major functions of nonverbal communication is to define the nature of the relationship between two or more people. Although not all nonverbal behavior has relational import and not all relational meaning is conveyed nonverbally, a wide range of nonverbal signals can and do carry relational messages. The themes they can convey include not only the central ones of (a) dominance-submission or equality and (b) intimacy, with its multiple facets of depth, similarity, immediacy, inclusion or exclusion, trust, liking, and attraction; but also (c) arousal, (d) composure, (e) formality, and (f) task or social orientation. The behaviors that convey these themes entail all the nonverbal codes. While many behaviors appear to be biologically based, universal signals with consistent meanings across contexts and relationships, other behaviors carry different meanings depending on whether the relationship is one of equality or inequality and of intimacy or unfamiliarity. The relational definition in turn colors the interpretation of the verbal text. Unlocking the meaning of the relational subtext is therefore crucial to making sense out of any communicative encounter.

Suggested Readings

Burgoon, J. K., Buller, D. B., Hale, J. L., & deTurck, M. A. (1984). Relational messages associated with nonverbal behaviors. *Human Communication Research, 10,* 351–378.

Burgoon, J. K., & Hale, J. L. (1984). The fundamental topoi of relational communication. *Communication Monographs, 51,* 193–214.

Cappella, J. N. (1983). Conversational involvement: Approaching and avoiding others. In J. M. Wiemann & R. P. Harrison (Eds.), *Nonverbal interaction* (pp. 113–148). Beverly Hills, CA: Sage.

Ellyson, S. L., & Dovidio, J. F. (Eds.). (1985). *Power, dominance, and nonverbal behavior.* New York: Springer-Verlag.

Givens, D. B. (1978). The nonverbal basis of attraction: Flirtation, courtship, and seduction. *Psychiatry, 41,* 346–359.

Givens, D. B. (1983). *Love Signals.* New York: Crown.

Goffman, E. (1961). *Encounters: Two studies in the sociology of interaction.* Indianapolis: Bobbs-Merrill.

Hale, J. L., & Burgoon, J. K. (1984). Models of reactions to changes in nonverbal intimacy. *Journal of Nonverbal Behavior, 8,* 287–314.

Harper, R. G., Wiens, A. N., & Matarazzo, J. D. (1978). *Nonverbal communication: The state of the art.* New York: Wiley.

Henley, N. M. (1977). *Body politics: Power, sex, and nonverbal communication.* Englewood Cliffs, NJ: Prentice-Hall.

Mehrabian, A. (1971). *Silent messages: Implicit communication of emotions and attitudes* (2nd ed.). Belmont, CA: Wadsworth.

Morris, D. (1977). *Manwatching: A field guide to human behavior.* New York: Abrams.

Scheflen, A. (1974). *How behavior means.* Garden City, NY: Anchor Books/ Doubleday.

CHAPTER 10

Expressive Communication

"He is the Napoleon of crime, Watson!" As my friend
spun round from his position before the fireplace, the
flames behind him and the shrill, unnatural quality of
his voice lent his attitude a terrible aspect. I could see
his nerves stretched to their highest limits. "He is the
organizer of half that is evil and of nearly all that is
undetected in this great city and in the annals of
contemporary crime. . . ." And so he rambled on,
sometimes incoherently, sometimes declaiming as if
from the stage of the Old Vic. . . . I listened to this
erratic recital with mounting alarm, though I did my
best to conceal it. I have never known Holmes to be
untruthful and I could see at a glance that this was not
one of his occasional practical jokes. He spoke in deadly
earnest, almost babbling with fear. . . . The tirade did
not so much conclude as run down. From shrill
statements Holmes gradually subsided into inarticulate
mutterings and from thence to whimpers. Accompanying
this modulation in speech, his body, which had been
striding energetically to and fro, now leaned up against
a wall, then flung itself absent-mindedly into a chair
and, before I realized what had happened, Holmes was
asleep.

Dr. J. H. Watson in N. Meyer, *The Seven-Per-Cent Solution* (1976,
p. 16)

Emotions and their nonverbal expression are an inescapable part of everyday life. We smile, laugh, frown, cry. We often appear and sound surprised,
angry, disgusted, contemptuous, interested, ashamed, happy, fearful. Emo-

The faces of these Beatles fans display a wide range of emotions and affect blends.

tions are a primary motivational force in human life, and the expression of emotion is a necessary reaction to this force. As a basis for understanding emotional expression, we shall first consider the origin and existence of emotions. Then we shall examine the link between emotional experiences and emotional expressions and shall conclude with a discussion of the encoding and decoding of emotional displays.

The Nature of Emotion

Scholars of the human psyche have attempted for years to explain the phenomenon of emotion. Currently, emotion is viewed as a complex of three processes: adaptation and maintenance of balance in the human system, direct subjective experience of the emotion, and external emotional expression (Buck, 1984).

Adaptation

At the neurological level, *emotion is an innate reaction to a stimulus that motivates the organism to behave in an adaptive way* with respect to the stimulus eliciting the emotion. Darwin (1965) was the first to suggest that emotional expressions are adaptive responses that communicate information about a person's internal state. Theorists such as Izard (1971, 1972, 1977) and Tomkins (1962, 1963) believe that emotion is the primary motivator that stimulates human cognition and organizes human consciousness throughout most of life. "Presence of emotion in consciousness insures a readiness to respond to events of significance to the organism's survival and adaptation" (Izard, 1978, p. 163).

In this view, basic emotions are universal; that is, all humans, regardless of culture, possess similar neural mechanisms that produce emotions. This prewired emotion system arose through the natural progression of human evolution (Buck, 1984). Today, emotions emerge innately during human maturation. For instance, distress at birth is adaptive because it motivates help from the caregiver. Later, the social smile emerges to motivate continued social stimulation and strengthening of interpersonal bonds. Still later, shame prompts the development of self-awareness and self-identity, and guilt prompts self-regulation (Izard, 1978). Table 10.1 details other emotions and the adaptations they motivate, which are necessary for physical and cognitive development. As each emotion emerges, consciousness becomes more complex, and the ability to process information increases.

Subjective Emotional Experience

The second component of emotion is direct subjective experience or the feeling one gets when a stimulus elicits an emotion. Imagine the feeling of joy you experience when meeting a close friend or receiving a much sought award, or the feeling of depression and sense of loss when a close friend dies or a goal is not achieved.

There is considerable debate concerning the source of these feelings. In 1890, James proposed that subjective emotional experience was a product of somatic and visceral changes caused by the eliciting stimulus. That is, a stimulus causes changes in facial expressions (somatic) and physiological arousal (visceral), and perceptions of these changes are the emotional experience. Without facial expressions and physiological arousal, you would not subjectively experience fear.

James's formulation has been criticized because research suggests that autonomic arousal is more general than he suggested. That is, changes in arousal do not distinguish among individual emotions (Buck, 1984). Recently, however, Ekman, Levinson, and Friesen (1983) demonstrated that the facial expressions of happiness, disgust, and surprise were associated with lower autonomic arousal, whereas anger, fear, and sadness were associated with higher autonomic arousal. Further, anger was distinguished from fear and sadness by higher finger temperature (another measure of arousal). Still, researchers have been unable to find a unique pattern of arousal associated with each distinct emotion. Beyond a lack of distinctiveness, changes in arousal are often too slow and appear to lag behind the actual subjective experience of the emotion (Buck, 1984).

Recently, two alternative explanations, related to James's formulation, have been proposed. Tomkins (1962, 1963, 1981) and later Izard (1971,

TABLE 10.1 The Development of Emotions and Their Adaptations

Emotion	Age at Emergence	Adaptation
Distress	Birth	Signals need for help from caregiver.
Startlelike movements[a]	Birth	Withdrawal from stimulus; signals caregiver about a potentially dangerous stimulus.
Disgust	Birth	Removal or rejection of distasteful substance from mouth; signals intolerance of substance and/or need for help in removing substance.
Interest	Birth	Attention; exploration; engages caregiver's interest; later regains and maintains perceptual contact, which stimulates learning.
Social smile	8–10 weeks	Continued social stimulation and strengthening of interpersonal bonds; invites attention from others.
Anger	3–4 months	Dealing with frustrations, restraints, and barriers.
Surprise	3–4 months	Increased surveillance and resetting of cognitive activities.
Fear	5–7 months	Self-regulation by defining limits; escape from harm; self-defense.
Joy	5–7 months	Development and maintenance of emotional attachments.
Shame	4–6 months	Development of self-identity and self-esteem; learn skills to increase self-worth and decrease likelihood of experiencing shame.
Contempt	6–12 months	Actions to overcome frustrations, restraints, and barriers.
Guilt[b]	12–18 months	Self-regulation by defining limits; cognitions about self-initiated actions that cause harm to others; understanding of self-responsibility.

Source: Adapted from "Emotions as Motivations: An Evolutionary-Developmental Perspective," by C. E. Izard, in R. A. Dienstbier (Ed.), 1978, *Nebraska Symposium on Motivation,* Vol. 25 (pp. 163–201), Lincoln: University of Nebraska Press.

[a] Not considered a basic emotion.
[b] Considered the principal emotional motivation in adult conscience.

1972, 1977, 1978, 1981), in their *differential emotions theory*, suggest that emotional feelings result from the adaptive actions triggered by the emotional reaction to the eliciting stimulus. So, like James, differential emotions theory views subjective experience as a process of self-perception. However, rather than autonomic arousal, overt behaviors determine subjective experience. The most important are reflexive facial displays that are more distinctive and occur more quickly than arousal (Buck, 1984). The theory also expands beyond James to include self-perceptions of the entire composite of adaptive nonverbal and verbal behaviors.

Alternately, Schachter and Singer (1962) maintain the belief that subjective emotional experience requires physical arousal. However, they assert that simply perceiving a change in arousal is not sufficient for subjective experience. Rather, arousal motivates the person to search the environment for clues to the meaning of the arousal. The cognitive label provided by the environment determines subjective emotional experience. This approach has come to be known as *cognitive appraisal theory* (Smith & Ellsworth, 1985). People label emotional arousal by appraising (a) whether to *attend* to the stimulus, (b) how *certain* one feels in the situation, (c) how much *control* can be exerted to cope with the stimulus, (d) how *pleasant* or desirable the stimulus is, (e) whether the stimulus is perceived as an *obstacle* in life, (f) who or what is *responsible* for the stimulus, (g) whether the outcome is *legitimately deserved,* and (h) the degree of *anticipated effort* in dealing with the stimulus (Roseman, 1984; Scherer, 1982a; Smith & Ellsworth, 1985).

These two explanations, though intriguing, have not yet been fully tested, and the tests that have been conducted provide confusing results. The major component of the differentiated emotions theory receiving critical research attention is the "facial feedback hypothesis": Perceptions of one's facial expression determine emotional experience. Laird (1974) and Lanzetta, Cartwright-Smith, and Kleck (1976) found that adopting facial expressions of aggression and pain increased the subjective experience of these emotions. By contrast, Tourangeau and Ellsworth (1979) found no effect on subjective experience by creating facial expressions of fear, sadness, and neutrality. (Also see Ekman's view in the box on p. 340.) The best conclusion that can be drawn at present is that facial expressions may affect the intensity of the felt emotion or create general emotional feelings such as pleasantness or unpleasantness, but facial expressions may not produce specific emotional experiences such as disgust, anger, and contempt (Buck, 1984; Ekman & Oster, 1979; Winton, 1986).

Two problems arise in the research on cognitive appraisal theory. First, as noted earlier, changes in physiological arousal often lag behind subjective emotional experience (Buck, 1984). Also, the structure of the appraisal mechanism is unclear. Smith and Ellsworth's (1985) research supported a strong pleasantness appraisal with weaker appraisals of responsibility, control, certainty, attention, and anticipated effort. Subjects unexpectedly evaluated the degree of situational control, along with self-control, but they did not appraise the extent to which the stimulus was an obstacle.

Paul Ekman Speaking on Facial Feedback

LOS ANGELES—The mere act of putting on an angry face or a disgusted look can trigger the corresponding emotion deep within the brain, researchers have found.

Part of the brain that controls the facial muscles is connected to the lower parts of the brain where the emotions are thought to reside, said Paul Ekman of the University of California at San Francisco.

"By making a face, you can create [or] generate emotions," Ekman said at a press conference Tuesday during the annual meeting of the American Association for the Advancement of Science. "These changes seem to be very strong."

Ekman has found that the effect occurs with fear, anger, disgust, and sadness. Strangely enough, it does not seem to occur with smiles and happiness, at least according to research done so far, Ekman said.

"Maybe because we smile so much, it's disconnected from the physiology," he said.

Furthermore, he said, the researchers do not yet know whether facial expressions can be used to turn off one emotion by triggering another—whether putting on an angry face can counteract sadness, for example.

Source: Associated Press, June 3, 1985.

Buck (1984) has rejected these two explanations in favor of direct neurochemical causes. He has compiled evidence that emotional feelings result when certain regions of the brain are activated, regardless of the person's state of arousal, facial expressions, and adaptive nonverbal and verbal behavior. For example, emotional feelings such as interest and surprise result from brain stem activation and are very primitive responses common to many animals. Feelings of pleasure and displeasure are produced by activation of certain regions in the hypothalamus. The hypothalamus also plays a key role in integrating information from other systems in the emotional process and is responsible for changes in physiological arousal during emotion. Pleasurable emotions associated with sexuality are triggered by the septal area. Interestingly, lesions or damage in this area increase feelings of viciousness and fear. Another brain structure, the amygdala, also produces fear experiences. This structure is responsible for feelings of anger and rage as well. Thus Buck believes subjective emotional experience is a by-product of biological processes in the human brain that exist because awareness of one's own emotional state is essential for human survival.

APPLICATIONS

The Runaway Truck

Given the indispensability of automobile travel, many of us have had the unfortunate experience of an actual or near accident. This situation presents a useful, albeit unpleasant, illustration of the ways in which people may subjectively experience emotion.

Suppose that you are cruising along a four-lane highway late one evening when suddenly you see a large truck swerve over the median and head directly toward you. You immediately become aroused, display a facial expression comprised of widened eyes and parted, tightened lips, scream "Oh,———!" slam your foot on the brake, violently yank the steering wheel to the right, and pray to your favorite deity. At the same time, you subjectively experience fear. What caused this feeling of fear?

James would say that your feeling of fear resulted from labeling your heightened autonomic arousal and facial expression. Moreover, if you did not display these reactions—say, if you simply remained calm and adopted a neutral facial expression—James would argue that you would not have subjectively experienced fear.

Differential emotions theory, as developed by Tomkins and Izard, also claims that your subjective experience of fear resulted from your overt reactions. However, this theory departs from James because it claims that (a) the total combination of overt adaptive responses, not merely the facial expression, contributed to your feeling of fear, (b) autonomic arousal was not a factor in your feeling of fear, and (c) it was the observation of the responses, not the labeling of responses, that produced the fearful feeling. The adaptive responses carried meaning, and you interpreted this meaning in much the same way you would have interpreted the same actions performed by another person.

In contrast, cognitive appraisal theory maintains that your fear resulted from applying a label to the sudden change in autonomic arousal you experienced upon observing the truck moving toward you. That label stemmed from the attention you devoted to the truck, the certainty, or perhaps uncertainty, that the truck would harm you, your inability to control the truck's movement, the unpleasant anticipated outcome of a collision, the obstacle the truck presented, your lack of responsibility for the event, your belief that the anticipated harm was not deserved, and the amount of effort required to avoid the collision.

Finally, Buck believes that your feeling of fear resulted from the chemical changes that occurred when certain regions of your brain were activated by the vision of the truck approaching you. That is, you did not observe your own action, nor did you label your

The Runaway Truck (*Continued*)

arousal, in order to experience fear. Rather, your feeling of fear was a chemical by-product or residue of brain activity, the brain activity that sensed the truck and activated coping behaviors, facial expression, and autonomic arousal.

Categories Versus Dimensions of Emotion

Within the analysis of subjective aspects of emotion is a concern over whether emotions are experienced as separate and distinct categorical phenomena or as a composite of feelings along several emotional dimensions. On one side of the issue, Tomkins (1962, 1963), Ekman (1971), and Izard (1977) believe that emotions are categorical. People experience happiness distinct from sadness, distinct from surprise, distinct from contempt. Each author offers a set of basic emotion categories that he believes are universal to all humans (see Table 10.2). The categorical perspective applies very well to overt facial display of emotion, which these three authors are most concerned with. There is ample evidence that at least the basic emotions are accompanied by unique facial displays.

The categorical approach, however, stands in the face of growing evidence for the dimensions of emotion. Studies of the way people judge emotional facial expressions, their own subjective experiences of emotion, and emotion words and terms consistently reveal two bipolar emotion dimensions: pleasantness and activity (Abelson & Sermat, 1962; Apple & Hecht, 1982; Bush, 1973; Cliff & Young, 1968; Daly, Lancee, & Polivy, 1983; DePaulo, Rosenthal, Finkelstein, & Eisenstat, 1979; Dittmann, 1972b; Neu-

TABLE 10.2 Universal Categories of Emotion

Tomkins	Ekman	Izard
Interest	Happiness	Interest
Joy	Sadness	Joy
Surprise	Fear	Surprise
Distress	Surprise	Sadness
Fear	Anger	Anger
Shame	Disgust/contempt	Disgust
Contempt		Contempt
Anger		Fear
		Shame
		Shyness
		Guilt

Source: From *Affect, Imagery, Consciousness,* Vol. 1: *The Positive Affects* and Vol. 2: *The Negative Affects* by S. S. Tomkins, 1962–1963, New York: Springer-Verlag; "Universal and Cultural Differences in Facial Expressions of Emotions," by P. Ekman in J. K. Cole (Ed.), 1971, *Nebraska Symposium on Motivation,* Vol. 19, (pp. 207–283), Lincoln: University of Nebraska Press; *Human Emotions* by C. E. Izard, 1977, New York: Plenum.

feld, 1975, 1976; Plutchik, 1962, 1980; Royal & Hays, 1959; Russell, 1978, 1980, 1983; Russell & Bullock, 1985; Russell & Steiger, 1982; Schaefer & Plutchik, 1966; Schlosberg, 1952, 1954; Shepard, 1962). People appear to have an implicit mental map in which the emotions are arrayed in a circle defined by the pleasantness and activity dimensions (Russell, 1978, 1980). Figure 10.1 shows that arousal is opposite sleepiness and defines the vertical activity dimension, while pleasure and misery are opposite emotions defining the horizontal pleasantness dimension. Distress is a highly active, unpleasant emotion. Excitement incorporates high activity and pleasantness. Contentment combines low activity and pleasantness. Depression is an inactive, unpleasant emotion. A more recent three-dimensional variation of this model is shown in Figure 10.2. Maintaining the pleasantness and activity dimensions, Daly, Lancee, and Polivy (1983) added an intensity dimension, which relates to the strength of the emotional reaction. Emotional intensity distinguishes emotions such as annoyance and rage, amusement and euphoria, disdain and disgust. Additional dimensions such as attention-rejection, dominance-submission, and spontaneity have been identified, but these tend to be weaker and related more to the antecedents and consequences of emotions than the emotions themselves (Russell, 1978, 1980).

The evidence, taken together, seems to support the dimensional nature of emotion, with pleasantness, activity, and intensity being the most important dimensions. Categorical proponents have taken issue with the dimensional approach, claiming that it is too simplistic and sterile and does not correspond to intuitive experiences (Ekman, 1971; Smith & Ellsworth, 1985). Russell and his colleagues (Russell, 1983; Russell & Bullock, 1985; Russell & Steiger, 1982), however, believe that the two approaches are complementary. They suggest that the dimensional representation of emotion is innate and universal in humans. Through the maturation process, children differentiate their feelings on these dimensions and learn to label

FIGURE 10.1 Universal dimensions of emotions: Two-dimensional model.

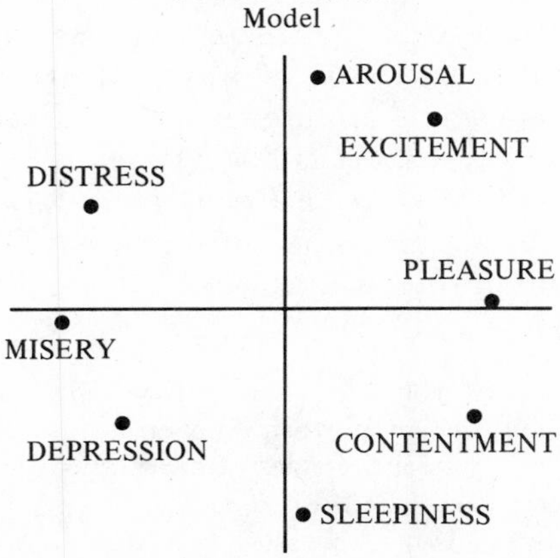

Two–Dimensional Model

AROUSAL

EXCITEMENT

DISTRESS

PLEASURE

MISERY

DEPRESSION   CONTENTMENT

SLEEPINESS

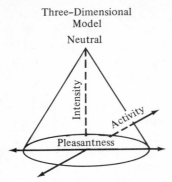

Three–Dimensional
Model

Neutral

Intensity

Activity

Pleasantness

FIGURE 10.2 Universal dimensions of emotions: Three-dimensional model.

combinations of pleasantness and activity as happiness, fear, disgust, and so on, by observing environmental cues, adaptive behaviors, and facial expressions. Buck (1984) also believes that the two approaches are complementary. Neurochemical processes in the brain produce dimensionlike emotions of pleasantness in the hypothalamus and activity in the brain stem, categorical emotions of happiness and sadness in the hypothalamus, sexual pleasure in the septal area, and fear and anger in the amygdala.

Emotional Expressions

The third component of emotion is external emotional expression. Several questions are important when considering the expression of emotion. First, why do these expressions exist? Next, what factors influence their production? Third, what is the specific nature of these expressions? Finally, how accurate are people at expressing emotion and decoding emotional expressions?

Emotion-Expression Link

The link between emotion and its overt expression has been a source of controversy for over 100 years. Most of this controversy has centered around whether emotional expressions are innate or learned. The *universalists,* including Darwin (1965), Allport (1924), Tomkins (1962, 1963), and Izard (1971, 1977), argue that emotional expressions are innate. Darwin proposed that emotional facial expressions are inherited. These expressions developed through evolution because they were biologically adaptive in early times:

> Actions, which were at first voluntary, soon become habitual, and at last hereditary, and may then be performed even in opposition to the will. Although they often reveal the state of mind, this result was not at first either intended or expected. Even such words as that "certain movements serve as a means of expression" are apt to mislead, as

they imply that this was their primary purpose or object. This, however, seems rarely or never to have been the case: the movements having been at first either of some direct use, or the indirect effect of the excited state of the sensorium. An infant may scream either intentionally or instinctively to show that it wants food; but it has no wish to draw its features into the peculiar form which so plainly indicates misery; yet some of the most characteristic expressions exhibited by man are derived from the act of screaming. . . . (Darwin, 1965, p. 356)

Darwin believed that the primary adaptive purpose of present-day emotional expressions is to signal or communicate internal emotional reactions to others.

The universalists have compiled compelling evidence of the cross-cultural, cross-generational, and cross-species consistency of expressions of the basic emotions. (The basic emotions are listed in Table 10.2.) Another source of evidence for the universalist position is studies of children born blind and deaf. These children, who have very little opportunity to learn emotional expressions, encode emotional expressions like laughter, anger, and resentment similarly to normal children (Charlesworth & Kreutzer, 1973; Eibl-Eibesfeldt, 1975; Fraiberg, 1971; Fulcher, 1942; Goodenough, 1932). Also, the consistent pattern with which emotional expressions emerge suggests that they are at least partly innate (Izard, 1978; Oster & Ekman, 1978). The development of emotional expressions will be discussed later.

In opposition to the universalists stand the *cultural relativists* (Birdwhistell, 1970; LaBarre, 1947; Leach, 1972; Mead, 1975). They see emotional expression as specific to a given culture. People learn which expression goes with which emotion in much the same way as they learn language. Cultural relativists argue that even when emotional expressions transcend culture, the rules for emotional expression and the social functions associated with expressions are determined by the cultural context. Cultural relativists have recorded a large number of cross-cultural differences in support of their position.

Paul Ekman and his colleagues (Ekman, 1971, 1975; Ekman, Sorenson, & Friesen, 1969; Oster & Ekman, 1978) have developed a third explanation, the *neurocultural theory,* which appears superior to either the universalist or cultural relativist positions. Essentially, the neurocultural theory assumes that emotional expressions are innately prewired in the human brain, but through experience people learn culture-specific rules for their display. The entire expressive process, illustrated in Figure 10.3, involves eliciting events that activate the neurological affect program. This affect program directs overt emotional expressions and other behaviors that cope with the emotion and elicitor. The link between the affect program and overt behavior is moderated by learned display rules. Let us examine each of these components more closely.

According to the theory, the first component of the emotional expression process is *elicitors:* events that stimulate emotion in the human brain.

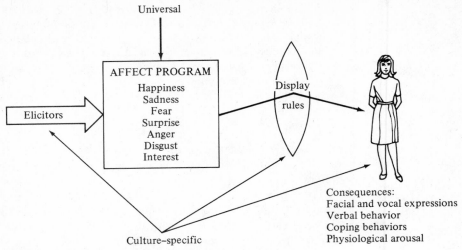

FIGURE 10.3 Process of emotional expression.

Ekman believes that basic noninterpersonal elicitors, such as hunger, are universal but that many interpersonal elicitors, such as messages from other people, are socially learned and vary from culture to culture. Early in life, noninterpersonal elicitors predominate in the emotional expression process, but by late childhood, learned interpersonal elicitors are more plentiful. Ekman also believes that humans have the capacity to analyze and evaluate elicitors, as suggested earlier by cognitive appraisal theory.

In most instances, an elicitor triggers the neurological emotion system, which Ekman labels the *affect program.* This innate neurological system controls facial and vocal responses, verbal responses, skeletal motor responses, more fully elaborated coping behaviors, autonomic and central nervous system changes, and the subjective experience of emotion. Within this affect system is a set of basic emotions: happiness, sadness, fear, surprise, anger, disgust, and interest. The affect program links each primary emotion to a distinctive pattern of adaptive behaviors, including a distinctive facial expression.

These innate emotion-expression links exist because (a) certain facial movements are required to sustain life and (b) it is adaptive to signal emotions and intentions to other humans. Ekman also recognizes the role of social learning in the emotion-expression linkage. He believes that as humans mature, they recognize that certain events signal the presence of elicitors. These anticipatory events are learned and linked with facial muscle performance. Through social learning, various objects, ideas, people, and behaviors are associated with the original innate elicitor or anticipatory elicitors and activate the emotion-expression linkage.

Humans do not display simply pure emotional expressions, such as happiness, sadness, or disgust. Rather, the affect program frequently blends pure expressions to create new expressions. People can simultaneously appear surprised and happy, angry and contemptuous, fearful and surprised. These blends are likely to be culture-specific because an elicitor that activates a blended expression is unlikely to be present in another culture. Also, blends often result from culture-specific rules governing emotional expression. Finally, a common cause of blends is intrapersonal reactions to one's own feelings, which are generally a product of culture (e.g., feeling ashamed of being angry).

The third component of the expressive process according to the neurocultural theory is *display rules.* Display rules are learned procedures for managing emotional displays. These include intensifying, deintensifying, neutralizing, and masking emotional expressions. Display rules are learned early in life and quickly become habitual. Because they are learned, they vary across individuals, situations, and culture. Ekman asserts that much of the evidence for culture-specific origins of emotional expressions is actually evidence for display rules.

An important assumption of display rules is that people have the ability to control the expressive process. People can alter the activation of the affect program by elicitors, inhibit activation of emotional expressions by the affect program, encode emotional expressions without activation of the affect program, and modify emotional expressions once they begin. This assumption underlies many of the theories of emotion, which propose that much of the emotion process occurs within the somatic neurological system, which is open to active control.

The final step in the expressive process involves the *consequences* of emotional arousal. These are the actual adaptive behaviors directed by the affect program and modified by display rules. These include facial expressions, vocalic responses, verbal behavior, other behaviors that cope with the aroused emotion or elicitor, and physiological arousal.

To review, consider the following example. You are out with a group of friends at a local nightclub. Midway through the evening, one of your friends comes back to the table with a man (the elicitor) she met dancing. It turns out that you know him from one of your classes, but you consider him a loud, obnoxious type and are annoyed (affect program activated) that she brought him to the table. However, because you are in a social situation and she is a close friend, you do not display an overt expression of dislike or anger, adopting instead a polite but weak smile while talking with the couple (display rules causing a deintensified polite smile to mask anger expression).

Universal Facial Expressions

Cultural Comparisons. In developing his neurocultural theory, Ekman and his colleagues explored the universal nature of facial expression (Ekman, 1971, 1975; Ekman & Oster, 1979; Ekman et al., 1969; Oster & Ekman, 1978). Research comparing American, Japanese, Argentinean, Chilean, and Brazilian communicators showed a high degree of cross-cultural similarity in the facial expressions of emotions and the meanings assigned to facial

APPLICATIONS

The Inscrutable Japanese and (Il?)Literate South Fore

Ekman and his colleagues have traveled extensively to other cultures to demonstrate the universal nature of facial expressions. In one series of studies, they found that Japanese and Americans were accurate judges of pleasant and unpleasant emotional expressions portrayed by communicators from the other's culture. Further, judgments by Japanese observers corresponded closely to judgments by American observers. When American observers thought the communicator expressed happiness, Japanese observers also thought the communicator expressed happiness. This correspondence occurred with both Japanese and American senders. A third study in this series compared actual facial expressions encoded by Japanese and American senders. Once again, broad cross-cultural agreement prevailed. The similarity in facial expressions was most pronounced for the primary emotions such as happiness, sadness, and fear. Displays of emotional blends were less similar, as predicted by Ekman's neurocultural theory.

In addition to cross-cultural similarities in expression, the research on Japanese communicators revealed the use of display rules. Japanese and Americans enacted similar disgust and anger expressions, but only when the Japanese were alone and unaware of being observed. When Japanese and American communicators were later interviewed about these reactions, the Japanese masked these expressions with a polite smile, whereas the Americans openly displayed their disgust and anger. Ekman attributed this difference to culture-specific display rules prohibiting public facial expressions of disgust and anger in Japan but permitting them in America. Thus the stereotype of the inscrutable Japanese has a kernel of truth and is partly the result of cultural display rules.

The evidence for universality is open to one criticism. Namely, members of literate cultures might learn to display and judge facial expressions similarly through direct contact with other literate cultures, especially via the mass media. To answer this criticism, Ekman's group traveled to the South Pacific to study the emotional expressions of members of a preliterate culture, the South Fore of New Guinea. This tribe had its own language and very limited contact with literate cultures and advanced technology. Ekman showed facial expressions of happiness, sadness, fear, surprise, anger, and disgust, portrayed by American communicators, to members of the tribe. Many of their emotional judgments were exactly what Ekman had expected. The South Fore were accurate when decoding expressions of happiness, sadness, disgust, and sur-

The Inscrutable Japanese and (Il?)Literate South Fore (*Continued*)

prise. They did have some problems with expressions of fear and anger, which they mistook for surprise and disgust, respectively.

Next, Ekman videotaped members of the South Fore expressing emotions facially. When his group returned to the United States, they asked American observers to decode the expressions of the South Fore. The American judges were accurate when decoding expressions of happiness, sadness, anger, and disgust. Interestingly, the Americans had difficulty distinguishing fear from surprise, as did the South Fore.

The results of these two experiments rule out the argument that cross-cultural similarities come about by exposure to other cultures and further reinforce the contention of the neurocultural theory that basic emotional displays are universal.

expressions. Further, this research produced evidence of culture-specific display rules, particularly those that govern the public and private display of emotions. Independent research by Izard (1971) with Japanese, American, English, Spanish, French, German, Swiss, and Greek communicators also confirmed this cross-cultural consistency in decoding facial expressions.

Ekman also was able to demonstrate that the cross-cultural similarity is not due to contacts between cultures, that is, one culture learning a similar expression or interpretation by interacting with another culture. In research on members of a preliterate culture, who had little contact with more civilized cultures, Ekman found remarkable cross-cultural similarity in facial expressions and their interpretations.

Child Development. Another area providing evidence for the universality of emotional expressions is child development. Both Ekman and Izard have examined the emergence of emotional expression in children and noted a universal pattern (Ekman & Oster, 1979; Izard, 1978; Oster & Ekman, 1978). It is assumed that the neurological emotion system, or affect program, and the facial musculature necessary for expression are fixed at birth. Thus expressions of the basic emotions are not learned. Oster and Ekman (1978) report observing all facial movements characteristic of adults in full-term and premature infants, except raising corners of lips in a smirk. Izard (1978) provides more specific details about the maturation process (Table 10.1). The neonate typically displays expressions of distress, disgust, and interest. Smiling begins at this time but does not become social until about 8 or 10 weeks of age. Expressions of anger and surprise emerge at 3 to 4 months, fear and joy at 5 to 7 months, and shame at 4 to 6 months. Expressions of contempt and guilt appear later, at 6 to 12 months and 12 to 18 months, respectively. The most important implication of these findings is that all children regardless of cultural background show the same maturation process when it comes to the basic emotional expressions. Once the emotional expressions emerge, though, children begin to learn that they can be controlled voluntarily, displayed without the presence of the emotion, used to achieve certain outcomes, and modified to conform with social rules. Thus as children mature beyond infancy, they develop a more complex, adultlike understanding of the emotion-expression linkage, display more expressive differences, and begin to use emotional expressions as part of their nonverbal code system.

Encoding Emotional Expressions

Research on emotional expression has tried to identify the nonverbal behavior or clusters of behaviors that transmit each emotional meaning. Facial and vocalic behaviors consistently outperform other nonverbal channels. The body and touch play a lesser but important role as well.

Facial Expressions. Behaviors in the face that influence the transmission of emotional meaning can be separated into three groups: static, slow, and

As children mature, they develop an understanding of the link between emotions and emotional expressions.

"MR. WILSON WAS HAPPY TO SEE US, BUT THE HAPPY NEVER MADE IT TO HIS FACE."

rapid (Ekman & Friesen, 1975). *Static signals* are permanent features of the face such as skin color and bone structure. *Slow signals* tend to alter gradually over time, as is the case with skin texture and wrinkles. Static and slow signals generally act as sources of information about sex, age, and race, but they can alter or complement the transmission of emotional cues. For instance, you may know people with crow's-feet, small wrinkles emanating from the outside corners of the eyes, who always appear to be expressing pleasant emotions, regardless of their other facial cues. Their negative expressions appear to be blended with at least weak pleasant emotion. Conversely, you may know others whose wrinkles form a permanent scowl. Static cues altered the appearance of President Jimmy Carter. His mouth was proportionately large; when encoding a smile, he appeared at times comical or insincere, even when attempting to convey a serious message.

The *rapid* signals are our main concern. They provide the primary cues about emotion, including all kinesic movements usually associated with facial expressions of emotion. In analyzing rapid facial movement during emotional expression, Ekman and Friesen found it useful to separate the face into three regions: (a) the brows and forehead, (b) the eyes, eyelids, and bridge of the nose, and (c) the cheeks, nose, mouth, chin, and jaw (Ekman, Friesen, & Tomkins, 1971). Each of these areas provide cues that contribute to the emotional meaning of an expression. That doesn't mean that cues from all regions are important to all emotional expressions. Observers may pay close attention to one region, using cues in the other regions only to check their interpretations.

Table 10.3 integrates the findings of two studies that Ekman and his colleagues conducted to determine the role of each of the three facial regions in expressing various emotions. In one study, trained observers identified fear, disgust, anger, surprise, happiness, and sadness in various facial regions, and these were compared with judgments of the entire face (Ekman et al., 1971). In a second experiment, Boucher and Ekman (1975) cut up photos depicting each emotion into the three regions. Both the slices of the face, and composites made up of a slice combined with a neutral expression in the remaining regions, were judged. From Table 10.3 it is apparent that disgust is best conveyed by the mouth and cheeks region, fear by the eyes and eyelids, sadness by both the brows and forehead and the eyes and eyelids, happiness by both the mouth and cheeks and the eyes and eyelids, anger by both the mouth and cheeks and the brows and forehead, and surprise equally well by all three regions.

In a separate experiment, Cuceloglu (1972) found that pleasant emotions were best revealed by the mouth, followed by a combination of the mouth with the eyes or the brows. Unpleasant emotions were much more difficult to decipher from a single feature. The single best indicator was the eyebrow position, but certainty was best when cues from all three regions were present. Receptive and nonreceptive emotions were displayed best by the eyes, but communication of receptive emotions was improved by combining the mouth with the eyes, nonreceptive emotions by combining the brows with the eyes.

TABLE 10.3 Emotional Expression in the Three Facial Regions

Emotion	Facial Region Involvement		
	Eyes and Eyelids	Brows and Forehead	Mouth and Cheeks
Pleasant (happiness, joy)	yes (skin gathered around eye sockets)	no	yes (mouth curved upward, cheeks raised)
Unpleasant (general)	no	yes	yes
Fear	yes	no	no
Sadness	yes	yes	no
Disgust	no	no	yes
Calm	yes	yes	yes
Irritation (general)	yes	yes	no
Anger	no	yes	yes (mouth shortened and opened)
Receptivity (attentive, open)	yes	yes (raised and constricted)	yes (mouth curved, cheeks raised)
Nonreceptivity (indifferent)	yes	yes	no
Certainty	no	no	yes (mouth stretched, cheeks raised)
Uncertainty (puzzled, bewildered)	no	yes (lowered and constricted)	yes (mouth curved down, dropped jaw)

Source: Adapted from "Facial Affect Scoring Technique: A First Validity Study," by P. Ekman, W. V. Friesen, and S. S. Tomkins, 1971, *Journal of Communication, 21,* 37–58; "Facial Areas and Emotional Information," by J. D. Boucher and P. Ekman, 1975, *Journal of Communication, 25* (2), 21–29.

More recently, Forsyth, Kushner, and Forsyth (1981) identified specific facial movements displayed when communicating pleasure, annoyance, interest, certainty, and puzzlement. Pleasure produced an upward mouth curvature accompanied by raised cheeks. This is the classic smile. (Ekman and Friesen, 1982, also report that the smile is accompanied by gathering the skin inward around the eye sockets.) Annoyance produced an expression combining a short mouth length and a slightly open mouth. Interest was expressed by curving the mouth slightly upward, raising the cheeks and eyebrows, tilting the head to the side, and constricting the forehead muscles. A combination of higher cheek rise and greater mouth stretch was displayed to communicate certainty. Puzzlement was displayed by curving the mouth downward, lowering the eyebrows and eyelids, dropping the jaw, and constricting the forehead muscles.

Out of their work, Ekman and Friesen (1976, 1978) developed the Facial Affect Code (FAC). This system of action units is based on anatomical analysis of facial movement or action. In this system, a user must learn the

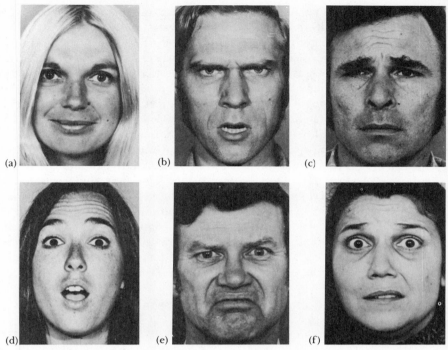

Facial expressions of primary emotions: (a) happiness, (b) anger, (c) sadness, (d) surprise, (e) disgust, and (f) fear.

muscular basis of facial action and the distinctive actions associated with muscular movement, such as "the movement of skin, the temporary changes in shape and location of the features, and the gathering, pouching, bulging, and wrinkling of the skin" (Ekman & Friesen, 1976, p. 62). Ekman and Friesen identified 46 action units in the face. For example, there are three action units involving the eyebrow: inner brow raiser, outer brow raiser, and brow lowerer. In actual facial expressions, action units are combined. Ekman and Friesen were able to identify combinations of up to eight action units that resulted in distinctive facial movements. The larger combinations of units occur in the lower region of the face.

Vocal Expressions. Along with facial expressions, the voice is a powerful channel for expressing emotion. In fact, the ability to express emotion in the face is linked to the ability to express emotion in the voice. People who are accurate expressors in the face tend to be good at expressing emotion in the voice as well (Zuckerman, Larrance, Hall, DeFrank, & Rosenthal, 1979). The primary questions stimulating research on vocal expressions of emotion concern the identification of vocalic qualities associated with each emotion. What this research shows is that the voice is every bit as complex a channel as the face.

In early research on vocal expressions of emotion, Costanzo, Markel, and Costanzo (1969) showed that soft, empathic emotions, such as grief and love, were expressed through variations in pitch. Harsh, hostile emotions, like anger and contempt, were expressed by changes in loudness. Neutral emotions (indifference) were expressed through tempo changes.

Klaus Scherer (1979a) has performed the best research into vocalic qualities of emotional expressions. He first identified five vocalic qualities fundamental to the display of affect: *pitch variation* (moderate, extreme, up contour, down contour), *amplitude variation* (moderate, extreme), *pitch level* (high, low), *amplitude level,* (high, low), and *tempo* (fast, slow). Next he used a Moog synthesizer to produce artificial voices characterized by every possible combination of the five vocal qualities. Judges then assigned emotional meaning to each combination. This first study was followed by a more comprehensive experiment (Scherer & Oshinsky, 1977), the results of which are shown in Table 10.4. As you might have guessed, an emotion such as happiness involves large pitch variation, moderate amplitude variation, and fast tempo. Fear voices have high pitch level, up pitch contours, small pitch variation, and fast tempo. Boredom is reflected by a voice that has little pitch variation, a generally low pitch level, and a slow tempo.

Differences in Encoding Emotional Expressions

Emotion.   The results of several studies suggest that pleasant emotions are expressed better than unpleasant or socially undesirable emotions. The study by Cuceloglu (1972) reviewed earlier found that pleasant emotions were easiest for judges to put together. In a study of children, Odom and Lemond (1972) found that children are least accurate at producing expressions of socially undesirable emotions. Mayo and LaFrance (1978) replicated this finding and showed that fear is difficult to encode even for the oldest age groups. This may be a result of display rules inhibiting unpleasant and socially undesirable emotional expressions. In a survey of college students, Sommers (1984) found that people who typically express negative emotions are rated most unfavorably and liked least. This is particularly true for women. Conversely, people who are always positive or typically positive are rated as most sociable and popular. People seem to accept and prefer others whose emotional expressions are predominantly positive; thus communicators may learn to repress expressions of negative emotions.

Intensity of the felt emotion may also influence encoding. Zuckerman, Hall, DeFrank, and Rosenthal (1976) found that accuracy of encoding emotional displays increases as the emotion experienced by the encoder becomes more intense. It is likely that intensity increases encoding accuracy because more intense emotional experiences trigger spontaneous emotional displays, which are less likely to be modified by display rules.

The foregoing explanation identifies another factor that affects emotional expression: whether the expression is *spontaneous* or *posed*. Spontaneous expressions appear very similar to posed expressions (Zuckerman et al., 1976; Zuckerman, Larrance, Hall, DeFrank, & Rosenthal, 1979); however, given the intensity of the emotion, spontaneous and posed expressions

TABLE 10.4 Vocal Characteristics of Emotional Expressions

Emotional State	Cues[a]
Pleasantness	Fast tempo, few harmonics, large pitch variation, sharp envelope, low pitch level, pitch contour down, small amplitude variation (salient configuration: large pitch variation plus pitch contour up)
Activity	Fast tempo, high pitch level, many harmonics, large pitch variation, sharp envelope, small amplitude variation
Potency	Many harmonics, fast tempo, high pitch level, round envelope, pitch contour up (salient configurations: large amplitude variation plus high pitch level, high pitch level plus many harmonics)
Anger	Many harmonics, fast tempo, high pitch level, small pitch variation, pitch contours up (salient configuration: small pitch variation plus pitch contour up)
Boredom	Slow tempo, low pitch level, few harmonics, pitch contour down, round envelope, small pitch variation
Disgust	Many harmonics, small pitch variation, round envelope, slow tempo (salient configuration: small pitch variation plus pitch contour up)
Fear	Pitch contour up, fast tempo, many harmonics, high pitch level, round envelope, small pitch variation (salient configurations: small pitch variation plus pitch contour up, fast tempo plus many harmonics)
Happiness	Fast tempo, large pitch variation, sharp envelope, few harmonics, moderate amplitude variation (salient configurations: large pitch variation plus pitch contour up, fast tempo plus few harmonics)
Sadness	Slow tempo, low pitch level, few harmonics, round envelope, pitch contour down (salient configuration: low pitch level plus slow tempo)
Surprise	Fast tempo, high pitch level, pitch contour up, sharp envelope, many harmonics, large pitch variation (salient configuration: high pitch level plus fast tempo)

Source: Adapted from "Cue Utilization in Emotion Attribution from Auditory Stimuli," by K. R. Scherer and J. S. Oshinsky, 1977, *Motivation and Emotion, 1*(4), p. 340.

[a] Single acoustic parameters (main effects) and configurations (interaction effects) are listed in order of predictive strength.

differ in their ability to communicate emotional meaning. Zuckerman et al. (1976) found that spontaneous expressions are superior emotional cues to posed expressions when extremely pleasant and extremely unpleasant emotions are communicated. In contrast, posed expressions are superior to spontaneous expressions when moderately pleasant or unpleasant emotions were communicated. It appears that for extreme emotions, the spontaneous expressions contain sufficient cues to communicate the emotional state of the sender, but for moderate emotions, the spontaneous expressions contain insufficient cues. Posing allows the sender to compensate by displaying either more cues or more stylized cues of emotion. In another study, posed expressions were superior to spontaneous expressions for pleasant emotions in general (Zuckerman, Larrance, Hall, DeFrank, & Rosenthal, 1979). As mentioned earlier, display rules may prescribe positive emotional displays. Hence the superiority of posed expressions of pleasant emotions may be due to a socially learned skill to appear positive when not experiencing pleasant emotions.

Physiology of Sender. The most interesting physiological difference in emotion expression is the *bilateral differences* in facial expressions. In 1978, Sackeim, Gur, and Saucy reported an experiment in which they sliced a series of photographs of facial expressions into left and right halves. They then recombined the halves to create faces that were composites of either the left side or the right side of the face. Observers judged left-side composites as displaying more intense emotions than right-side composites for all emotions except happiness. The authors suggested that the advantage of the left side of the face is a result of its connection to the right brain hemisphere, which appears to play a larger role in processing emotional stimuli. The emotion-dominant right hemisphere exerts more control in facial encoding, which is manifested in a more intense emotional expression in the left side of the face. They also suggested that the superiority of the left side of the face is advantageous from a decoding point of view. An observer's visual field is split bilaterally such that stimuli left of center in the visual field are projected to the right hemisphere and stimuli right of center are projected to the left hemisphere. When observing facial expressions, the superior left side of the face is in the right visual field and is projected to the emotionally inferior left brain hemisphere. Sackeim et al. proposed that the bilateral facial differences may have evolved to compensate for the emotional inferiority of the left hemisphere.

The bilateral differences and Sackeim et al.'s (1978) neurophysiological explanations are intriguing. They fit well with growing evidence for specialization of emotional processes in the brain (Buck, 1984; Andersen, Garrison, & Andersen, 1979). However, this explanation is not immune to criticism. Ekman (1980) points out that the bilateral differences observed by Sackeim et al. occurred only in posed emotional expressions. The happiness expression was the only spontaneous expression in the experiment—and the only one that did not show bilateral differences. Further, Ekman is not sure there is as yet sufficient evidence of right hemisphere superiority in emotional processes to warrant Sackeim et al.'s conclusions.

Sender Characteristics. Encoding ability is related to *age*. Odom and Lemond (1972) found that young children are less accurate encoders of socially undesirable emotions. Buck (1975) reported that children are better able to encode happiness than fear and anger. Mayo and LaFrance (1978) showed that encoding ability increases with age. Expressions of happiness and sadness are present at all ages, but expressions of anger and surprise improve up to age 10 or 11 years. Expression of fear is difficult at all ages.

Several studies have shown a strong effect for *gender* on emotional expression. Women in most of the studies are more expressive than men

(Buck, 1979a, 1979b; Buck, Miller, & Caul, 1974; Sabatelli, Buck, & Dreyer, 1980; Wagner, MacDonald, & Manstead, 1986). In the most recent experiment, Wagner et al. found that women were superior to men in overall encoding. This superiority was particularly pronounced for expressions of surprise and neutrality. Men outperformed women in expressions of sadness.

Female superiority in emotional expression is likely a function of culture-specific display rules. In the American culture, expression of emotion by women is more acceptable than by men. Research has shown that very young children appear to express emotions similarly regardless of gender; however, with age, girls become more accurate and more expressive and boys less accurate and less expressive encoders (Buck, 1975).

Apart from gender, there are two general types of encoders, *externalizers* and *internalizers.* Externalizers are particularly adept at portraying emotion, while internalizers are less skilled in sending cues (Buck, 1979a). Women tend to be externalizers, whereas men tend to be internalizers. These differences in overt expression also appear to be linked to certain personality traits. Externalizers are more extroverted, socially oriented, and higher in self-esteem than internalizers. Externalizing males may also be more self-confident, less self-deprecating, more dominant, and more heterosexually oriented (Buck, 1979a; Buck et al., 1974; Buck, Savin, Miller, & Caul, 1972; Harper, Weins, & Matarazzo, 1979).

Ekman and Friesen (1975) have identified eight idiosyncratic *styles* for displaying emotion in the face. The *withholder* is someone who tends not to

Although emotions are often communicated by voice and facial expressions, they can also be communicated by manipulating artifacts in the environment.

be very expressive. Withholders simply do not send the kinds of rapid signals that reveal emotion, and they know it. It is not that they are not emotional; it is just that their faces do not show emotion. The *revealer* is the opposite. No matter how hard they try to control the face to hide emotions, revealers seem automatically to reveal what they feel. *Unwitting expressors* are much like the revealers, only they do not know just how expressive they are. They are continually amazed that others are able to read their emotions. *Blanked expressors* think they are expressing emotions but they are not. For some reason their faces do not display the appropriate cues, appearing expressionless or ambiguous. The *substitute expressor* has a single expression that preempts other expressions. For example, a substitute expressor may encode happiness regardless of the actual emotional reaction. Unfortunately, such people are convinced that they are communicating what they feel. *Frozen-affect expressors* also tend to have one predominant facial expression, but it usually results from facial construction. Even when they display other emotions, traces of the primary expression remain. An *ever-ready expressor* is someone who has an initial expression for almost any situation. No matter what the emotion, the initial expression is always the same. As time passes, other expressions may take its place. Last, the *flooded-affect expressor* is rare indeed. This individual has one or two expressions that continually flood the face. Ekman and Friesen have only observed this style in people undergoing major trauma.

Finally, *training* in emotional expression can improve encoding abilities. Izard (1971) reports that people can improve their accuracy level by at least 6% and by as much as 51%.

Decoding Emotional Expressions

When considering the issue of decoding emotional expressions, two questions must be addressed. First, what behaviors, when observed, result in attributions of a particular emotion? Next, how accurately do people decode the overt expression of each emotion? The evidence for decoding ability has come from three major research groups: Ekman's work with facial expressions, Buck's work with his Communication of Affect Receiving Ability Test (CARAT), and Rosenthal's work with the Profile of Nonverbal Sensitivity (PONS). As with encoding ability, facial and vocal behaviors have received the most attention.

Facial Expressions. We have already identified the facial behaviors that people display when experiencing or attempting to communicate each emotion. It does not necessarily follow from these experiments, however, that receivers recognize each of these cues and attribute the emotional meaning intended by the sender. Table 10.5 presents the results of one experiment by Wiggers (1982), which directly examined the cues that affect receivers of emotional displays. As this table shows, a combination of two or more facial behaviors contributed to judgments of each emotion. Happiness was inferred when the source displayed a smile accompanied by raised cheeks. Fear judgments resulted when the brows and upper eyelids were raised, lips

TABLE 10.5 Cues That Affect Decoding of Emotional Displays

Emotion	Behaviors[a]	Accuracy (%)
Happiness	*cheeks raised; smiling*	64–100
Fear	brows raised; *upper eyelids raised; lips stretched;* mouth open	64–95
Disgust	*upper lip raised; nose wrinkled;* mouth open, tongue thrust out; chin raised	64–100
Sadness	*inner brow raised;* brows drawn together; lower eyelids raised; *lip corners depressed; lips parted*	67–95
Surprise	*brows raised;* jaw dropped; *upper eyelids slightly to moderately raised;* head moved up; eyes moved down	77–100
Shame	*lip biting;* lips parted; *upper eyelids dropped;* head lowered	87–100
Anger	*brows lowered;* upper eyelids raised; lips slightly tightened; upper lip raised; lower lip depressed; mouth opened	69–100
Contempt	single outer brow corner raised; one or both brows raised; *head moved up; eyes moved down;* one side of upper lip raised; lips parted; one mouth corner pulled inward producing a dimple; chin raised	72–100

Source: Adapted from "Judgments of Facial Expressions of Emotion Predicted from Facial Behavior," by M. Wiggers, 1982, *Journal of Nonverbal Behavior, 7,* 101–116.

[a] Behaviors in italics influence judgments of intensity of emotion.

stretched, and mouth opened. Lowering the brows, raising the upper eyelids, tightening the lips while raising the upper lip and depressing the lower lip, and opening the mouth produced anger interpretations.

While several behaviors had to be combined to produce emotion judgments, Wiggers found that each expression contains one to three cues that are particularly important to the emotion judgment (cues in italics in Table 10.5). These cues are unique to or distinctive of a particular emotion, and their presence is sufficient to cause the emotion interpretation. For example, smiling and raised cheeks are sufficient to cue happiness judgments; raised upper eyelids and stretched lips cue fear; and head moved up with eyes moved down cue contempt. The remaining behaviors may be redundant and relied on only to reinforce interpretations based on the primary cues.

Table 10.5 also reports the accuracy of observer judgments in Wiggers's experiment. Shame and surprise were decoded most accurately. Judgments of contempt, anger, disgust, and happiness were slightly less accurate; however, some observers demonstrated high accuracy on these emotions. Fear and sadness were decoded least accurately, with no observer attaining 100% accuracy. Still, over two-thirds of these expressions were decoded accurately.

In general, pleasant emotions, particularly happiness, are the easiest expressions to decode (Cuceloglu, 1972; Feinman & Feldman, 1982; Zuckerman, Lipets, Koivumaki, & Rosenthal, 1975). Unpleasant emotions, such as anger, disgust, sadness, and fear are more difficult to recognize (Wagner et al., 1986; Zuckerman et al., 1975). Part of this difficulty can be traced to similarity in facial expressions of different emotions. Although there are particular behaviors that are distinctive to each emotion, there seems to be enough similarity between emotional expressions that observers make consistent mistakes (Schlosberg, 1952, 1954; Wagner et al., 1986; Wiggers, 1982). For example, observers mistake anger for fear because of the brow movement. Fear and surprise are confused because of the brow and eye positions. Surprise is also sometimes confused with happiness. Schlosberg (1952, 1954) asserts that facial expressions can be arrayed along two or three dimensions much like the emotions they represent (see Figures 10.1 and 10.2). Emotions that are similar along pleasantness, activity, and intensity dimensions will be similar in expression and more likely to be confused by observers. Thus one is unlikely to confuse happiness with anger or disgust with surprise, but disgust may be confused with anger and happiness with surprise. This confusion increases when one encounters blended facial expressions. Many blends contain similar or related emotions; thus observers often are uncertain about their interpretations and make mistakes decoding blended expressions.

Another factor that influences accuracy is *gender.* Not surprisingly, women have a general superiority over men when it comes to decoding facial expressions (Wagner et al., 1986; Zuckerman et al., 1976; Zuckerman et al., 1975). This relationship may not hold for all females, however. Zuckerman, Larrance, Hall, DeFrank, & Rosenthal (1979) found that extroverted, socially competent females are better decoders of negative facial expressions, but extroverted, socially competent males are better decoders of positive facial expressions. Further, males improve their sensitivity to facial expressions as the relationship with the sender increases (Zuckerman et al., 1975). Thus males who are socially competent and males in developed relationships may be accurate decoders and no more disadvantaged than women. Increased sensitivity by males in developed relationships, though, may not produce more relational satisfaction. Sabatelli et al. (1980) reported that women in relationships with more sensitive males expressed less love for their partner. This may be a result of cultural rules prohibiting male sensitivity, or it may be that women are uncomfortable when males pay too much attention to their emotional expressions.

Another factor that influences accuracy is whether the facial expressions are *spontaneous* or *posed.* Like encoding, skillful decoders of spontaneous facial expressions are likely to be skillful decoders of posed expressions. People, though, are generally more accurate when judging posed facial expressions (Fujita, Harper, & Weins, 1980; Zuckerman et al., 1976; Zuckerman, Larrance, Hall, DeFrank, & Rosenthal, 1979). The advantage of posed expressions is not surprising in light of the fact that encoders often improve their facial expressions when they are allowed to pose them. Posed facial expressions may be richer in cues and more stylized than spontaneous expressions, especially expressions of less extreme emotions.

Since the beginning of research on facial expressions, there has been a debate over the role of *context* in judgments of emotion. Several researchers have argued that receivers incorporate information from the context into their judgments of facial expressions. These same researchers have expressed concern that much of the research on decoding facial expressions has taken place in contextually sterile environments (e.g., a photograph or videotape of facial display against a neutral background). As a result of these concerns, experiments have been designed that embed facial expressions in contexts. An immediately apparent conclusion from these experiments is that context is indeed important. Receivers do incorporate contextual information in their judgments of facial expressions, and this information can affect decoding accuracy (Cupchik & Poulos, 1984; Knudsen & Muzekari, 1983; Spignesi & Shor, 1981).

What is unclear from this research is exactly *how* contextual information is incorporated. In Spignesi and Shor's (1981) experiment, receivers sometimes placed more importance on context than facial expression, at other times they placed equal importance on context and expression, and at still other times they placed more importance on expression than context. Knudsen and Muzekari (1983) paired facial expressions with congruent and incongruent contexts. Congruent contexts produced greater agreement between judges on sadness, anger, and fear but did not affect judgments of happiness expressions. Incongruent contexts, as would be expected, reduced agreement between judges. Particularly interesting in these contexts was the fact that judges often rationalized the incongruencies by (a) devising an explanation for the expression-context pairing, (b) denying the existence of the emotion, or (c) seeing the context as implausible. At this point, the evidence is too mixed to make any conclusion beyond stating that context can provide information about emotions and is often incorporated in attributions about emotional expressions.

Vocal Expressions. The ability to decode vocalic expressions of emotion also varies according to the emotion displayed. Davitz and Davitz (1959) found that decoding accuracy ranged from 65% (for anger) to 21% (for pride) (see Table 10.6). Of those tested, nervousness, sadness, and happiness were identified more accurately, with over 40% of listeners making the correct judgment. Sympathy, satisfaction, fear, jealousy, and love were less accurately judged.

Subsequent studies have replicated these findings. Apple and Hecht (1982) found that sadness was most easily identified in the voice. Happiness and surprise also could be identified, but with less accuracy than sadness. Other studies have found that fear (Zuckerman et al., 1975) and love (Costanzo et al., 1969) are among the most difficult emotions to judge. Examinations of anger expressions have proved less consistent. Apple and Hecht's observers had more difficulty decoding anger than sadness but were just as accurate decoding anger as decoding happiness and surprise. Costanzo et al., meanwhile, concluded that anger was one of the hardest emotions to recognize in the voice.

**TABLE 10.6 Accuracy in Decoding Vocal
Expressions of Emotion**

Emotion	Accuracy (%)
Anger	65
Nervousness	54
Sadness	49
Happiness	43
Sympathy	39
Satisfaction	31
Fear	25
Jealousy	25
Love	25
Pride	21

Source: Adapted from "The Communication of Feelings by Content-free Speech," by J. R. Davitz and L. J. Davitz, 1959, *Journal of Communication, 9,* 6–13.

Mistakes in decoding vocal expressions of emotion show the same consistency as mistakes in decoding facial expressions. Davitz and Davitz (1959) reported that observers confused fear with nervousness and sadness, love with sadness and sympathy, and pride with satisfaction and happiness. Apple and Hecht (1982) found that observers confused surprise and happiness with sadness when the vocalic cues accompanied an emotionally loaded verbal statement. Like facial expressions, vocal expressions of various emotions share similar vocalic cues. A close examination of Table 10.4 makes this quite apparent.

Other factors affect the decoding process. Sensitivity to vocal expressions seems to increase as a relationship develops. Hornstein (1967) and Zuckerman et al. (1975) both found that observers who had a prior relationship with the sender were more accurate than observers who were unfamiliar with the sender. In Zuckerman et al.'s study, however, this improvement was limited to male observers. Decoding accuracy may also improve when the emotions expressed are more intensely felt by the encoder (Davitz & Davitz, 1959).

Relationship Between Encoding and Decoding Emotional Expressions

Before leaving the discussion of emotional expression, it is necessary to consider the relationship of the abilities to encode and decode emotional expressions. Are skilled encoders also skilled decoders? Yes, maybe.

It seems that in a general sense, encoding and decoding skills are positively correlated. Good encoders tend to be good decoders, and poor encoders are poor decoders. This conclusion seems to hold when one considers skill at encoding and decoding all emotions (Cupchik, 1973; Knower, 1945; Levy, 1964; Zuckerman et al., 1976; Zuckerman, Larrance, Hall, DeFrank, & Rosenthal, 1979; Zuckerman et al., 1975). However, when one examines the skill to encode and decode the same emotion, people perform poorly. Zuckerman and his colleagues have consistently found that the correlation between encoding and decoding of the same emotion is lower than between encoding a particular emotion and decoding all other emotions. In many instances, the correlation for the same emotion is negative. That is, people who are skillful encoders of, say, fear are not very accurate decoders of fear, but they are generally accurate decoders of happiness, sadness, anger, and disgust. Zuckerman has suggested two plausible explanations for this relationship. First, when the display rules do not allow expression of a specific emotion, people do not develop the skills to encode that emotion, but they learn to be particularly sensitive to the prohibited emotion in others. Alternately, people who find it difficult to decode an emotion may assume that others will have trouble decoding that emotion, so they take special care to encode that emotion accurately.

Summary

Emotion is a primary motivator in the adult, controlling adaptive responses to emotion-eliciting stimuli. The structure of the emotion mechanism in our brain is innate and contains a set of basic emotions. The subjective experience of emotion may be a product of three processes: (a) intrapersonal feedback from overt emotional reactions, (b) autonomic arousal causing us to appraise the environment, or (c) neurochemical changes associated with the activation of emotion-producing brain regions. There is debate on whether we experience emotions as dimensions or categories. The weight of the evidence supports the existence of pleasantness, activity, and intensity dimensions. However, we may learn to associate combinations of these three dimensions with categorical labels. Also, some brain regions produce dimensional experiences while others produce categorical experiences. Therefore, dimensional and categorical experience of emotion may be complementary processes.

The link between emotion and overt emotional expression is also innate. Ekman's neurocultural theory proposes that noninterpersonal (innate) and interpersonal (learned) elicitors activate the affect program, which controls adaptive responses to the elicitors, including facial and vocal emotional expressions. As we mature, we learn culture-specific display rules for managing emotional expressions. The interaction of these display rules with the affect program determines the emotional expression we encode.

Ekman has provided extensive evidence for universal facial expressions of happiness, sadness, fear, surprise, anger, and disgust. He has also observed display rules operating to create cultural differences in these primary emotional expressions. Child development research has revealed that infants can encode most of the facial behaviors of adults, and each emotional expression emerges in an innate progression.

An emotional expression is a combination of several cues, some of which are unique to a particular expression. People are more accurate encoders of pleasant and intensely felt emotions. Posing increases the ability to encode moderately felt emotions accurately. For various reasons, facial expressions appear to be more intensely encoded on the left side of the face. Encoding ability also increases with age, among females and externalizing communicators, and with training.

Decoding ability is generally high but varies by emotion. Pleasant facial expressions are easier to decode than unpleasant ones. Nervousness, sadness, and happiness are most accurately decoded from vocalic cues. Mistakes in decoding result from the similarity between expressions of similar emotions. For example, happiness is more likely to be confused with surprise than with sadness. Females are better decoders of facial expressions than males, and posed expressions are easier to decode than spontaneous expressions. When available, decoders integrate contextual information into their judgments of emotional expressions; however, just how they integrate this information is not clear. Finally, good encoders seem to be good decoders of emotional expressions, in general, but good encoders of a particular emotion may not be good decoders of that same emotion. This may be a product of display rules or compensation for an emotion that a person does not decode well.

Suggested Readings

Boucher, J. D., & Ekman, P. (1975). Facial areas and emotional information. *Journal of Communication, 25 (2)*, 21–29.

Buck, R. (1984). *The communication of emotions.* New York: Guilford Press.

Davitz, J. R. (1964). *The communication of emotional meaning.* New York: McGraw-Hill.

Ekman, P., & Friesen, W. V. (1975). *Unmasking the face.* Englewood Cliffs, NJ: Prentice-Hall.

Ekman, P., & Oster, H. (1979). Facial expression of emotion. *Annual Review of Psychology, 30*, 527–554.

Izard, C. E. (1977). *Human emotions.* New York: Plenum.

Russell, J. A. (1983). Pancultural aspects of the human conceptual organization of emotions. *Journal of Personality and Social Psychology, 45*, 1281–1288.

Smith, C. A., & Ellsworth, P. C. (1985). Patterns of cognitive appraisal in emotion. *Journal of Personality and Social Psychology, 48*, 813–838.

Spignesi, A., & Shor, R. E. (1981). The judgment of emotion from facial expressions, contexts, and their combination. *Journal of General Psychology, 104*, 41–58.

Wiggers, M. (1982). Judgments of facial expressions of emotion predicted from facial behavior. *Journal of Nonverbal Behavior, 7*, 101–116.

Winton, W. M. (1986). The role of facial response in self-reports of emotion: A critique of Laird. *Journal of Personality and Social Psychology, 50*, 808–812.

CHAPTER 11

Structuring Interaction

Often, it is not so much the kind of person a man is as the kind of situation in which he finds himself [that] determines how he will act.

Stanley Milgram (1974)

It is by the reading of these less perceptible signs that one person is able to respond to the sentiment of another. In a face-to-face group changes in facial expression, slight gestures, and the like, although largely in the field of unverbalized reactions, enable an individual to sense a situation instantly. Thus, they define the situation and promote rapport.

F. M. Thrasher (1927, p. 297)

A significant self-revelation for many people is that we behave differently in different situations. Depending on the situation in which we find ourselves, we may adjust how, with whom, and about what we communicate. Many of these adjustments are due to the influences of nonverbal cues that structure our behavior. This chapter is devoted to exploring some of the ways in which nonverbal cues frame and control our interactions with others.

Nature of the Interaction–structuring Process

In many situations, we merely respond to contingencies that are presented to us. We enter a doctor's office and passively accept the solitary wait, the uncomfortable seating on an examining table, the impersonal probing of our body by the physician. In other situations, we create and manage various aspects of the social situation to achieve our own goals. When we invite guests for dinner, we may make decisions about such nonverbal features as what time guests should arrive, where people should congregate before the meal, whether the meal is to be formal or informal, what seating arrangement at the dinner table will enhance conversation, and what attire guests should be told is appropriate. These decisions are not trivial, for they can affect how enjoyable the evening turns out to be. Failure to provide sufficient structure may result in immense discomfort for the friend who arrives promptly, dressed in suit and tie for a formal dinner party, only to find the other guests arriving an hour later, dressed in jeans for a casual outdoor barbecue.

The nonverbal features we shall discuss in this chapter are largely ones that elicit behavior without people being consciously aware of their influence. That is, people respond to them in relatively passive, unconscious ways. Although most of these nonverbal features can also be used deliberately to structure a situation to accomplish some instrumental goal, we will focus more extensively on their strategic use in Chapter 13. For the moment, our interest lies primarily in the elusive yet obvious background elements of which we are at once consciously unaware and yet unconsciously, profoundly aware. Such features, like a puppet's strings, appear to control our actions invisibly but are readily detectable if we choose to look closely.

Nonverbal code elements function to structure our behavior in at least three ways. First, some nonverbal elements control the occurrence of interaction. They affect with whom we interact, when, and how often. They can control whether interaction even takes place.

Second, nonverbal cues set expectations for situations yet to be encountered. They often "telegraph" upcoming interactions by suggesting what a given situation will be like. Environmental designs, for example, evolve out of a culture's customs and expectations and therefore evoke anticipations of what behaviors will be exhibited in a previously unencountered setting. Our ability to prepare for new interactions and situations is strongly based on nonverbal codes.

Third, nonverbal elements set the stage for current interactions. As an episode unfolds, nonverbal elements embedded in the situation provide elaboration of its definition. They may prompt certain kinds of behavior, identify or clarify role relationships among interactants, and imply rules for behavior (Goffman, 1967, 1974; Scheflen, 1974). In so doing, the totality of situational features, including the nonverbal cues that are present, create a *frame of reference* or lens through which to see and understand a situation and provide structure for the interaction that occurs. Moreover, once people arrive at an understanding of a situation, they typically conform in a habitual and relatively mindless fashion to the behavioral routines associated with it. This further reinforces the prevailing definition of the situation.

Erickson and Shultz (1982) refer to this process of cuing the appropriate behavioral programs as *telling the context:*

> People of varying ages and cultural backgrounds all seem to be actively engaged while they interact, in telling one another what is hap-

pening as it is happening. . . . The particular ways this telling is done—what signals are used and how the signals are employed and interpreted by the interactional partners—may vary developmentally across the life cycle and may also vary from one culture to another. But some ways of telling the context seem to be present in all instances of face-to-face interaction among humans. People seem to use these ways to keep one another on the track, to maintain in the conduct of interaction what musicians call "ensemble" in the playing of music. (p. 71)

Precursors to Interaction

One of the chief ways that nonverbal behaviors structure interaction is to determine if interaction will occur at all. Three nonverbal signals are posited to be especially influential in determining if and how much people will interact: propinquity, gaze, and physical attractiveness.

Propinquity

One of the intriguing discoveries of social scientists is just how much pressure propinquity, or geographic proximity, exerts on people to interact. Propinquity controls the opportunities for interaction. Mehrabian and Diamond (1971) note that environments can facilitate communication by providing an excuse for people in relatively close proximity to engage in similar activities. Moreover, proximity encourages interaction. You may have noticed your own urge to exchange pleasantries with someone who shares a bus seat or sauna with you. Goffman (1963) reports that when workers in businesses and medical offices are seated within 12 feet of each other, they seek interaction. The happenstance of propinquity often leads to communication.

One reason that proximity promotes interaction is that it connotes belonging: "Our expectancies about proximity—called *spatial schemata*—are closely related to our belonging schemas" (Wegner & Vallacher, 1977, p. 191). We use spatial relationships to infer with whom we are affiliated and to signal to others our expectancies of belonging. The result is that we tend to feel we belong with those close to us and use communication to express that bond.

Of course, the probability of interacting with others need not be a chance occurrence. By intentionally increasing or decreasing physical distance, people can control their own or others' interaction availability. The use of such privacy-gaining mechanisms as fences, walls, and hedges can override the power of propinquity. Conversely, the absence of territorial markers or an open-door policy in an office may promote the kinds of accidental contacts that open communication channels. Men and women who are successful at picking someone up in a singles bar rely in part on their quarry feeling the obligation to speak to them when at close ranges. In these ways, it is possible to structure the communication situation actively rather than passively react to it.

APPLICATIONS

Building Rapport Through Housing Propinquity

Several studies in the 1950s and 1960s (e.g., Blake, Rhead, Wedge, & Mouton, 1956; Byrne, 1961; Deutsch & Collins, 1951; Festinger, Schachter, & Back, 1950; Maisonneuve, Palmade, & Fourment, 1952; Mann, 1959; Priest & Sawyer, 1967) revealed that people in residences or classrooms are much more likely to interact and develop friendships with those who are physically closest to them. In a housing project, for example, those whose houses are closest together or who see each other frequently while checking mailboxes or sitting in the yard are more likely to develop friendships. In an apartment building, those who live adjacent to one another, reside on the same hall, or share the same elevator or stairwell are far more likely to become acquainted than those who live on different floors. The likelihood of interacting is directly proportional to the physical and psychological distance between dwellings. Early on, it was even observed that a disproportionate number of marriages occurred among people who lived within 20 blocks of each other (Kennedy, 1943).

A study of Maryland police trainees (cited in Wegner & Vallacher, 1977) confirmed that propinquity fosters interaction and friendship. The trainees were assigned classroom seats and living quarters alphabetically, so that those whose names were closest together in the alphabet sat and lived together. After 6 weeks of training, "the Andersons and Bakers preferred each other to the Youngs and Zimmermans" (p. 201). A similar study of naval apprentice trainees showed that those whose bunks were closest talked to each other the most (Sykes, 1983), leading to the conjecture that proximity leads to talk which leads to attraction.

Mann (1959) attempted to determine if increased contact between people could decrease racial prejudice. Black and white students were placed in leaderless groups (which gave everyone equal status) and interacted with one another for a 3-week period. Afterward, students were asked to rank who they would like to have as continuing friends. Their sociometric choices indicated that interracial exposure reduced their tendency to use race as a criterion for choosing friends. In other words, the sheer force of physical proximity and the interaction it fostered broke down some racial prejudices. This has obvious implications for avoiding segregated schools and neighborhoods. Such findings have caused scientists (e.g., Deutsch & Collins, 1951; Festinger, 1951) to encourage architects and planners to take greater account of propinquity when planning and anticipating the social consequences of various housing developments and residential designs.

Gaze

In most unfocused social situations, where there is no intention of carrying on a conversation, the rule is to engage in *civil inattention.* It is impolite to stare at strangers in a restaurant or a department store. Though it is often unavoidable to look briefly at a passerby on the street, this usually occurs while at a distance and is followed by "casting the eyes down as the other passes—a kind of dimming of lights" (Goffman, 1963, p. 84). The mere act of making eye contact, then, serves as an invitation to interact.

Its potency in establishing a social bond is evident in the words of the famous sociologist Georg Simmel, who wrote in his *Soziologie* about the union that is brought about by mutual gaze (cited in Parks & Burgess, 1924):

> Of the special sense-organs, the eye has a uniquely sociological function. The union and interaction of individuals is based on mutual glances. This is perhaps the most direct and purest reciprocity that exists anywhere. . . . The totality of social relations of human beings, their self-assertion and self-abnegation, their intimacies and estrangements, would be changed in unpredictable ways if there occurred no glance of eye to eye. This mutual glance between persons, in distinction from the simple sight or observation of the other, signified a wholly new and unique union between them. (p. 358)

Physical Attractiveness

We have noted elsewhere that beauty may be only skin deep, but the attractiveness of the veneer often determines whom we choose to approach or avoid. The fact that attractive people are often viewed as more curious, complex, outspoken, assertive, flexible, candid, amiable, happy, active, confident, and perceptive than unattractive people (Miller, 1970) suggests we may be more willing to interact with attractive strangers because we attribute appealing characteristics to them.

More direct evidence comes from the computer dating studies cited in Chapter 2 and a similar "Coke date" study (Byrne, Ervin, & Lamberth, 1970). Experimenters paired subjects with members of the opposite sex and asked them to spend 30 minutes getting acquainted over a Coke at the student union. Afterward, students evaluated their dates. Results showed that students were much more attracted to their date if the date was physically attractive (both as rated by the partner and by the experimenters). A follow-up study at the end of the semester also revealed that students were more inclined to see their Coke date partner again if the date was handsome or pretty. Thus physical attractiveness may affect not only with whom we interact but also the likelihood and amount of subsequent contact.

In Chapter 9, we noted the biological basis for many courtship practices. The importance of physical attractiveness in approach or avoidance decisions is strongly linked to sexual attraction and the mating process. It is natural for men and women to size up potential partners on physical appeal. It may be, however, that the sizing-up process works overtime, extending to social interactions that do not have sexual undercurrents. It would be interesting to study whether physical attractiveness governs same-sex interactions to the same extent that it does opposite-sex relations.

Nature of Situations

Because the situation is such an important feature of social behavior, situational concepts have been given prominence in a wide variety of communication and social behavior theories. Kurt Lewin, the founder of what we now know as social psychology, laid the basis for much research in social science by proposing the well-known equation $B = f(P, S)$. This asserts that behavior *(B)* is a function *(f)* of two main factors, the person *(P)* and the situation *(S)* (Lewin, 1935). Subsequent theories as diverse as attribution theory (see Jones & Nisbett, 1972), various personality theories (see Mischel, 1968, 1979), and cognitive schema theories (see Schank & Abelson, 1977) have given situational factors a significant role. Communication researchers have likewise turned their attention toward an analysis of situations as an important part of understanding interpersonal communication (see Cody & McLaughlin, 1985). The impact of the situational definition on how people communicate and behave thus cannot be overstated.

Situations, Settings, and Episodes

The term *situation* probably has intuitive meaning for you, but what does it really mean? Not surprisingly, it has a number of interpretations. Magnusson (1978) found in reviewing the literature on situations that definitions could range from the microscopic (including specific stimuli or small sequences of events known as episodes) to the macroscopic (including both physical settings not tied to any particular occasion and environments, which include social as well as physical factors).

Most scholars, however, see situations as some intermediate combination of physical, temporal, and psychological frames of reference tied to particular occasions. Furnham and Argyle (1981) offer a relatively concrete definition that captures most of what we consider relevant. A situation is made up of the following components:

1. **The elements of behavior used.** These are the specific verbal utterances and nonverbal behaviors accompanying the situation.
2. **The goals or motivations of the participants.** For example, is this a learning, selling, or socializing situation?
3. **The rules of behavior.** The rules for carrying on a dinner party differ from those for a classroom lecture.
4. **The roles different people must play.** A committee chair plays a different role and follows different rules from those of the secretary.
5. **The physical setting and equipment.** A classroom, with its chalkboard or overhead projector and straight row seating, creates a different situation from a living room with overstuffed chairs and a coffee table.

6. **Cognitive concepts associated with it.** Dominance may be a salient consideration in some situations, supportiveness in others.
7. **Relevant social skills.** A decision-making context implies that certain skills will be exhibited for the successful achievement of the goal.

Situation, then, refers to an overall gestalt that is the sum of all these factors.

From this perspective, the *setting* is one defining feature of a situation. As we shall see, many nonverbal environmental features are useful in symbolizing this aspect of a situation. An *episode*, by contrast, is any sequence of events that "has some principle of unity" (Harre & Secord, 1972, p. 154). An interview can be divided into four episodes: an opening, a period during which the interviewer asks questions, a time when the candidate asks questions, and a closing. A situation can often be defined by the nonverbal episodes within it or elicited by it. The style of an episode—an effusive, intimate greeting versus a polite handshake—may distinguish one type of situation from another.

The various features that differentiate settings and episodes, distinguish skillful performances, and are associated with rule and role following and rule and role violations are often nonverbal. Hence nonverbal cues play a prominent role in defining situations and in structuring interpersonal interactions. Typically, these nonverbal elements work together to create an overall gestalt. That is, we respond to the totality of the cue pattern rather than to individual cues. Because so much redundancy is built in across codes, we are able, instantly and effortlessly, to determine the kind of situation that is presenting itself and our corresponding behavioral obligations. An example of a gestalt perspective on situations is Simonds's (1961) sample environmental designs (Figure 11.1), which, through a combination of volume of space, linear perspective, materials, artifacts, lighting, color, and sound, create radically different moods and types of interaction.

It is possible that our recognition ability is also aided by reducing judgments of situations to a few categories or continua that underlie our cognitive perceptions of them.

Situational Dimensions

Interactants tend to perceive social situations along some stable *dimensions*. Such dimensions help distinguish, for instance, a business negotiation from a matrimonial proposal.

Researchers have proposed various sets of dimensions that can be used to represent and understand a situation. Forgas (1976) found that housewives judge social episodes according to the dimensions of *perceived intimacy* (is the situation intimate or nonintimate?) and *self-confidence* (would they feel self-assured or not in that situation?).

Mehrabian (1972, 1976) advocates three very general dimensions that represent the basic emotional responses to environmental stimuli. (They also parallel Mehrabian's three metaphors of human interaction discussed in Chapter 9.) These are *pleasure-displeasure, dominance-submissiveness,* and

Fright

Sensed confinement. A quality of compression and bearing. An apparent trap. No points of orientation. No means by which to judge position or scale. Hidden areas and spaces. Possibilities for surprise. Sloping, twisted, or broken planes. Illogical, unstable forms. Slippery, hazardous base plane. Danger. Unprotected voids. Sharp, intruding elements. Contorted spaces. The unfamiliar. The shocking. The startling. The wierd. The uncanny. Symbols connoting horror, pain, torture, or applied force. The dim, the dark, the eerie. Pale and quavering or, conversely, blinding garish light. Cold blues, cold greens. Abnormal monochromatic color.

Gaiety

Free spaces. Smooth, flowing forms and patterns. Looping, tumbling, swirling motion accommodated. Movement and rhythm expressed in structure. Lack of restrictions. Forms, colors, and symbols that appeal to the emotions rather than the intellect. Temporal. Casual. Lack of restraint. Pretense is acceptable. The fanciful is applauded. Often the light, bright, and spontaneous in contrast to the ponderous, dark, and timeless. Warm, bright colors. Wafting, sparkling, shimmering, shooting, or glowing light. Exuberant or lilting sound.

Sublime spiritual awe

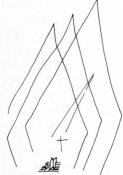

Overwhelming scale that transcends normal human experience and submerges one in a vast well of space. Soaring forms in contrast with low horizontal forms. A volume so contrived as to hold man transfixed on a broad base plane and lift his eye and mind high along the vertical. Orientation upward to or beyond some symbol of the infinite. Complete compositional order—often symmetry. Highly developed sequences. Use of costly and permanent materials. Connotation of the eternal. Use of chaste white. If color is used, the cool detached colors, such as blue-greens, greens, and violet. Diffused glow with shafts of light. Deep, full, swelling music with lofting passages.

Pleasure*

Spaces, forms, textures, colors, symbols, sounds, light quality, and odors all manifestly suitable to the use of the space—whatever it may be. Satisfaction of anticipations, requirements, or desires. Sequences developed and fulfilled. Harmonious relationships. Unity with variety. A resultant quality of beauty.

Displeasure*

Frustrating sequences of possible movement or revelation. Areas and spaces unsuitable to anticipated use. Obstacles. Excesses. Undue friction. Discomfort. Annoying textures. Improper use of materials. The illogical. The false. The insecure. The tedious. The blatant. The dull. The disorderly. Clashing colors. Discordant sounds. Disagreeable temperature or humidity. Unpleasant light quality. That which is ugly.

* It is to be noted that "displeasure" and "pleasure" are general categories, whereas "tension," "relaxation," "fright," and the others mentioned are more specific. With these more specific responses, we can list in more specific detail the characteristics of the volumes designed to induce them. The degree of "pleasure" or its opposite, "displeasure," would seem to depend on the degree of sensed fitness of the volume for its use, and a unified and harmonious development of the plan elements to serve this function. It can be seen that one could therefore experience pleasure and fright simultaneously (as in a fun house) or pleasure and sublime spiritual awe simultaneously (as in a cathedral), and so forth.

FIGURE 11.1 Sampling of environmental features that can create various moods.

Tension

Unstable forms. Split composition. Illogical complexities. Wide range of values. Clash of colors. Intense colors without relief. Visual imbalance about a line or point. No point at which the eye can rest. Hard, rough or jagged surfaces. Unfamiliar elements. Harsh, blinding, or quavering light. Uncomfortable temperatures in any range. Piercing, jangling, jittery sound.

Dynamic action

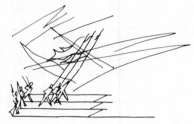

Bold forms. Heavy structural cadence. Angular planes. Diagonals. Solid materials as stone, concrete, wood, or steel. Rough natural textures. The pitched vertical. Directional compositional focus. Concentration of interest on focal point of action—as to rostrum, rallying point, or exit gate through which the entire volume impels one. Motion induced by sweeping lines, shooting lights, and by climactic sequences of form, pattern, and sound. Strong primitive colors— crimson, scarlet, and yellow-orange. Waving flags. Burnished standards. Martial music. Rush of sound. Ringing crescendos. Crash of brass. Roll and boom of drums.

Relaxation

Simplicity. Volume may vary in size from the intimate to the infinite. Fitness. Familiar objects and materials. Flowing lines. Curvilinear forms and spaces. Evident structural stability. Horizontality. Agreeable textures. Pleasant and comfortable shapes. Soft light. Soothing sound. Volume infused with quiet colors—whites, greys, blues, greens. *"Think round thoughts."*

Contemplation

Scale is not important since the subject will withdraw into his own sensed well of consciousness. The total space may be mild and unpretentious or immense and richly ornate— so long as the structural forms are not insistent. No insinuating elements. No distractions of sharp contrast. Symbols, if used, must relate to subject of contemplation. Space must provide a sense of isolation, privacy, detachment, security, and peace. Soft, diffused light. Tranquil and recessive colors. If sound, a low muted stream of sound to be perceived subconsciously.

Sensuous love

Complete privacy. Inward orientation of room. Subject the focal point. Intimate scale. Low ceiling. Horizontal planes. Fluid lines. Soft, rounded forms. Juxtaposition of angles and curves. Delicate fabrics. Voluptuous and yielding surfaces. Exotic elements and scent. Soft rosy pink to golden light. Pulsating, titillating music.

arousal-nonarousal. Relationships, situations, and environments can all be judged according to how much they make us feel happy, satisfied, and contented or annoyed, melancholic, and distressed (the pleasure dimension); the extent to which they make us feel dominant, important, and in control or restricted, weak, and impotent (the dominance dimension); and the degree to which they make us feel active, stimulated, alert, and responsive to external stimuli or unaroused, relaxed, sluggish, or inattentive (the arousal dimension).

Environments and situations can also be scaled along a general *sociofugal-sociopetal* continuum (Osmond, 1957). Sociofugal environments thrust people apart, whereas sociopetal ones bring them together and encourage interaction. We prefer to cast this dimension in terms of *publicness-privacy,* which is much broader and entails more than whether or not the environment encourages people to interact.

Studies of dyadic and group interaction (Wish, 1978; Wish, Deutsch, & Kaplan, 1976) have discovered four or five dimensions underlying people's perceptions of interpersonal relations that can also describe situations: *friendly/cooperative versus competitive/hostile, dominant versus equal, intense versus superficial, socioemotional versus task-oriented,* and *impersonal/formal versus personal/informal.* A birthday party is an example of a friendly, equal, socioemotional, informal, and somewhat intense occasion. Interestingly, Wish (1978) also found that these dimensional perceptions differed by communication channel. Verbal and nonverbal audio information contributed most to perceptions of cooperativeness, task orientation, and formality. The visual channel, by contrast, contributed most to perceptions of intensity and dominance. These results reveal that certain nonverbal channels and cues may be more important to some situational dimensions than to others.

Though not an exhaustive list, these dimensions provide a starting point for analyzing how nonverbal features structure interaction. Moreover, it appears that situational dimensions remain stable and consistent over time (Magnusson, 1971), which permits us to draw some valid cross-situational generalizations. We turn now to specific nonverbal cues and patterns that are associated with some of the most important dimensions.

Nonverbal Indicators of Situational Dimensions

The Private–Public Dimension

> The alternative to privacy is the ant heap.
>
> P. Kelvin (1973, p. 260)

One of the first features of a situation we are likely to apprehend is the degree to which it is public or private. Public situations invoke entirely different roles, rules, and behavioral repertoires than private ones.

The concept of privacy is complex. Consider just a few possible definitions of it:

1. Ability to exert control over self, objects, spaces, information, and behavior and to deny access to others (Warren & Laslett, 1977; Wolfe & Laufer, 1974).
2. Being protected from unwanted access from others, including physical access, personal information, or attention (Bok, 1982).
3. An interpersonal boundary process whereby a person or group regulates interaction with others (Altman, 1975; Derlega & Chaikin, 1977).
4. Freedom of choice in a particular situation to control what, how, and to whom the person communicates information about the self (Proshansky, Ittelson, & Rivlin, 1970).
5. Individual independence and reduced vulnerability to the power and influence of others (Kelvin, 1973).

These definitions reveal that privacy may pertain to an individual, dyad, or group; that it can be defined according to what is desired or what is actually achieved; and that it implies some degree of freedom and control.

Embedded in the various conceptualizations of privacy are four major types or *dimensions of privacy:* physical, social, psychological, and informational (Burgoon, 1982). *Physical privacy* refers to the degree to which an individual, dyad, or group is physically inaccessible to others. It involves freedom from intrusion on one's "body buffer zone," from the discomfort of overcrowding, from surveillance, and from excessive sensory stimulation. The number of nonverbal sensory channels through which people are accessible or inaccessible to others (sight, sound, touch, smell) provide one barometer of the degree of physical privacy that a situation affords (Kira, 1966). The more channels through which one is accessible to others, presumably the less privacy.

Social privacy refers to the ability to control the degree of social contacts at the individual, dyadic, or group level. It includes the capacity to control the who, when, and where of communication. A fundamental facet of privacy is the ability to withdraw from social intercourse and to limit approaches from others to a manageable number. This is necessary so that gratifications from such relationships can be maximized and annoyances and conflicts minimized (Calhoun, 1970; Desor, 1972; Milgram, 1970). When the number of social contacts becomes excessive, the amount of stimulation "overloads" the system, creating stress and a desire to withdraw. At the dyadic or small group level, social privacy becomes a means for facilitating intimacy within the relationship while inhibiting social overtures from others. A dating couple, for example, may engage in courtship behaviors that are designed to foster togetherness while simultaneously alerting others that their company is unwelcome. Such behaviors accomplish social privacy.

Psychological privacy refers to an individual's ability to control affective and cognitive inputs and outputs. On the input side, psychological privacy means a person is free to think, formulate attitudes, hold beliefs and values, develop an individual identity, engage in emotional catharsis, assimilate new experiences, and make plans without interference, undue influence, criticism, or distraction from others. On the output side, it means determining with whom and under what circumstances one will share thoughts and feelings, disclose intimate or secret information about oneself, offer emotional support, and seek advice (Burgoon, 1982; Goffman, 1959; Kira, 1970; Westin, 1970). The concept and its importance are well put by Simmel (1950):

> Just as material property is, so to speak, an extension of the ego, and any interference with our property is, for this reason, felt to be a violation of the person, there is also an intellectual private property whose violation effects a lesion of the ego in its very center. (p. 322)

Finally, *informational privacy* refers to the right to determine how, when, and to what extent personal data are released to others (Carroll, 1975). It is grounded in legalistic concerns such as protections over the gathering, computerization, and dissemination of information about private citizens. Because demographic, financial, legal, military, consumer, lifestyle, and even personality data about individuals or groups can be compiled and shared without their knowledge or permission, informational privacy differs from psychological privacy in that it is less under personal control.

These four dimensions of privacy represent four continua, from private to public, along which any situation can be evaluated. The nonverbal features responsible for signaling the degree of privacy desired or present in a situation can be divided into five categories: (a) environmental and artifactual, (b) spatial and haptic, (c) temporal, (d) kinesic and vocalic, and (e) physical appearance. It should be recognized that verbal behaviors may also play a significant role in establishing or restoring privacy. (For a discussion of these, see Burgoon, 1982.)

Environment and Artifacts. Included here are the features of fixed- and semifixed-feature space, plus specific artifacts, that define a setting as public or private. *Architectural design* fosters physical privacy by creating barriers (walls, fences, partitions, gated parking lots) and insulation that protect the individual from visual, auditory, olfactory, and bodily intrusions (Altman, 1975; Derlega & Chaikin, 1977; Marshall, 1972; Sommer, 1974b). Through the imposition of distance and gatekeepers, architectural design can also make access to the occupants of a locale difficult. Corporate executives often have offices in largely impenetrable spaces. They may be buffered by several stories, winding corridors, private elevators, multiple secretarial offices or desks, and personal receptionists that separate them from the public and subordinates.

Doors are a particularly significant barrier in our everyday experience. Schwartz (1968) refers to doors as "a human event of significance equal to the discovery of fire" because they can be used deliberately and selectively to regulate physical and social intrusion and because they contribute to psychological self-definition:

> Doors provide boundaries between ourselves (i.e., property, behavior, and appearance) and others. Violations of such boundaries imply

a violation of selfhood. Trespassing or housebreaking, for example, is unbearable for some not only because of the property damage that might result but also because they represent proof that the self has lost control of its audience. (p. 747)

The importance of doors to the achievement of privacy is evident in a study of first-year college students, 92% of whom reported they shut their door as a way of reducing contact with others (Vinsel, Brown, Altman, & Foss, 1980). It is further evidenced by a remark from one of Hall's (1966) informants: "If there hadn't been doors, I would always have been in reach of my mother" (p. 127).

Architectural design also signals implicitly whether spaces are private or semipublic by the number of enclosures and the degree of functional differentiation associated with them. The design of most American homes, for example, creates separate spaces for sleeping, bathing, elimination and personal hygiene, cooking, and so forth. The more spatial divisions in a setting and the smaller the volume of space in each, the greater the sense of physical and psychological privacy and social intimacy (Kira, 1966, 1970; Marshall, 1972; Simonds, 1961). Large, open spaces create a feeling of vulnerability and tend to define a situation as more public. Greater differentiation of the functions of each space also results in some spaces such as bedrooms and bathrooms being defined as highly private, intimate locales (Edney, 1976; Goffman, 1963).

Furnishings and artifacts supplement fixed architectural features by providing additional barriers and insulation in such forms as drapes, blinds, lamps, room dividers, bookshelves, and white noise from air conditioners or radios. These can carve settings into smaller spaces, block visual and auditory access, and cushion noise. Filing cabinets in small offices and book stacks in libraries serve such purposes (Sommer, 1970; Stea, 1970).

Compare these two environments. What kind of privacy messages do you get from each?

Architectural features and personal artifacts together may demarcate a particular place as someone's territory. Numerous scholars (Altman & Chemers, 1980; Edney, 1976; Edney and Buda, 1976; Goffman, 1961a; Stea, 1970) have noted the value of territories in ensuring physical protection, regulating social interaction, creating a sense of personal identity, and promoting group identity and bonding:

> Among many animal species there is broad recognition of a territory holder's "rights"—his claim to privacy and relative immunity to arbitrary challenge and interruption when he is on home ground. The complementary restrictions on a visitor on another organism's territory—his circumspection, inhibition, and restraint—seem to be tacit recognition of those rights. . . . The geographic separation of individuals into personal territories gives those individuals physical distinctiveness, but the effects of this spatial distinctiveness also appear on a psychological level . . . [Territory] is also likely to facilitate social bonding through a cognitive sense of similarity, and it may also help to preserve bonds because a person has to lose his territorial identity if he leaves the group. (Edney, 1976, pp. 37–40)

APPLICATIONS

Achieving Security Through Artifacts and Environmental Design

Defining a territory with markers elicits behaviors from others that are more respectful and deferential toward the owner or occupant. In turn, identifiable territories provide a sense of personal security, comfort, and permanence. Patterson (1978) found that when elderly people use such territorial markers as No Trespassing signs, welcome mats, and electronic surveillance devices, they have less fear of assault and property loss. Conversely, students who use fewer decorations such as posters, pictures, and mementos to personalize a dorm room are less likely to remain in school (Vinsel et al., 1980). This suggests that territorial markers are indicative of one's sense of belonging and security in an environment.

On a broader scale, Newman (1972) has identified general environmental design features that increase the security of high density living spaces such as low income apartment buildings in urban areas. In an extensive study of low income public housing in New York City and other major urban areas, Newman identified four environmental design features that reduce vandalism and crime and increase the occupants' sense of security, well-being, and control over their environment:

1. Providing a territorial definition of space that reflects the areas of influence of the inhabitants. This is done by dividing the areas surrounding the building into small

Achieving Security Through Artifacts and Environmental Design (*Continued*)

zones that encourage residents to adopt proprietary attitudes.

2. Position apartment windows so that residents can survey the exterior and interior of public areas of their living environment.

3. Using building forms that do not prompt perceptions of vulnerability and isolation of the inhabitants, achieved primarily through use of low rise and medium density buildings.

4. Enhancing safety by locating residential developments in areas that are not adjacent to activities that provide continued sources of threat.

In comparing developments that have employed these design considerations to those that have not, Newman (1972) found that "poorly designed buildings and projects have crime rates as much as three times higher than those of adjacent projects housing socially identical residents at similar densities" (p. 7).

Architecture and artifacts may symbolically designate a setting as private by creating a "forbidding" appearance. People are more inclined to behave formally and with restraint when surrounded by expensive interior decor. By invoking status and power connotations, massive exteriors, expansive properties, and exclusive locations tend to deter approach from all but vandals, thereby de facto defining a locale as socially and physically private. Or, as Newman suggests, architectural features that prompt surveillance and proprietary attitudes may catalyze residents to be more self-reliant and responsible for their own space, thus cutting down on crime and vandalism. It is not by accident, then, that most property crimes and muggings occur in squalid, run-down neighborhoods where inhabitants are socially isolated by building design and there are no physical symbols to inhibit approach and intrusion. These problems are much less likely to occur in exclusive, well-protected areas or neighborhoods where a sense of community and social contact is encouraged by residential design. Ironically, the massiveness of many public buildings such as libraries and government offices may also discourage people from entering them because people view the structures as either semiprivate settings reserved for an elite group of users or as so large and impersonal as to be overwhelming.

Arrangements of furniture and artifacts may also create sociofugal or sociopetal environments (Osmond, 1957). Institutional arrangements of benches along a wall, church pews, and rows of rigid, connected seats in airports inhibit interaction, while small conversational groupings of chairs facing each other in a home or hotel lobby encourage it. The arrangement therefore signals whether social encounters are permissible and expected. (See Figure 11.2.)

Proxemics and Haptics. How people space themselves in an environment and the degree to which touch occurs can likewise be interpreted as defining a situation as private or public. Recall that Hall's (1973) distance categories range from intimate (0 to 18 in.) to public (12 ft and beyond). Intimate distances tend to correspond to situations that are regarded as private. As conversational distance increases, so does the perception of the situation as more public. By the same token, frequent touch and touch to more intimate body regions are more likely to occur in private contexts and therefore define those situations as private (Evans & Howard, 1973; Jourard & Friedman, 1970; Rosenfeld, Kartus, & Ray, 1976). We are often surprised and offended by a couple's prolonged fondling and kissing in public precisely because such behavior seems out of place in nonprivate settings.

A number of other proxemic behaviors may color a situation as one of physical, social, or psychological privacy. In libraries and other public settings, people desiring privacy select seating positions at tables that are farther from others, permit greater surveillance of the entrances, and reduce their own vulnerability to surveillance (Sommer, 1970). When we enter a library or museum, we recognize the relatively private quality of what is otherwise a public setting and respond with appropriately quiet, unobtrusive, and nonintrusive behavior. Indirect body orientation and extreme sideways or backward lean connote the desire for individual privacy, whereas direct body orientation, moderate degrees of leaning and reclining, and side-by-side or adjacent seating may connote a situation of dyadic intimacy and privacy (Bond & Shiraishi, 1974; Cooper & Bowles, 1973; Morris, 1971).

Proxemic and haptic codes may also signal privacy loss. When people feel threatened physically or psychologically or when the amount of social involvement is excessive, they may attempt to compensate by increasing the behaviors just cited—greater distance, indirect orientation, leaning away, and gaze aversion (which increases psychological distance)—and they may erect body and artifact barriers (Argyle & Dean, 1965; Baum & Greenberg, 1975; Felipe & Sommer, 1966; Hayduk, 1978; Knowles, 1972; Patterson, 1973a; Patterson, Mullens, & Romano, 1971; Patterson & Sechrest, 1970; Stokols, 1976; Sundstrom & Sundstrom, 1977). In short, they respond with displays of nonimmediacy. If these fail, they may resort to flight or, rarely, fight (Baum, Riess, & O'Hara, 1974; Elman, Schulte, & Bukoff, 1977; Felipe & Sommer, 1966; Ginsburg, Pollman, Wauson, & Hope, 1977; Hayduk, 1978; Konecni, Libuser, Morton, & Ebbesen, 1975; Loo & Smetana, 1978; Matthews, Paulus, & Baron, 1979; Smith & Knowles, 1979; Stokols, 1976; Sundstrom & Sundstrom, 1977).

Finally, people may use a proxemic shift (Erickson, 1975) to signal their desire to end an episode within an encounter. If, for example, people

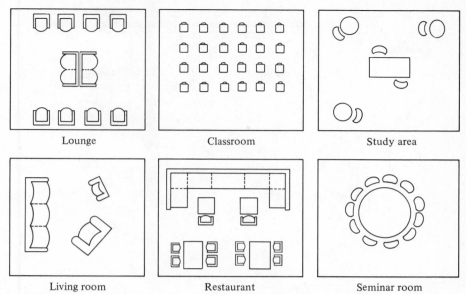

Lounge   Classroom   Study area

Living room   Restaurant   Seminar room

FIGURE 11.2 Which arrangements are sociofugal? Which are sociopetal?

find a discussion becoming embarrassing or too invasive of their psychological and informational privacy, they may use the proxemic adjustment as a cue that they are ready to change the subject.

In sum, the dynamic proxemic and touch behaviors participants use cue each other and onlookers as to whether they view the situation as private or public and whether they wish to alter that definition. The use of these and artifactual elements as privacy statements is nowhere more evident than in prison, as the excerpt from Ramsey (1976) on p. 382 reveals.

Chronemics. Use of time is another way of defining the degree of privacy of a situation. Time can be manipulated to regulate privacy in at least three ways. One is to segregate use of a particular setting by time. In the animal kingdom, different species may have territories that overlap but use the commonly held space at different times (Leyhausen, 1971). With humans, this may take the form of maximizing privacy in an otherwise heavily trafficked area by using it at times when one expects other people to be absent. A prime example is coordinating the use of a solitary bathroom in a large household or when guests come to visit.

A second way that people may declare a situation as private is by using interactional or public territories during nonpeak hours. A person who truly wants solitude may seek out a church sanctuary during the week, when it is not in use. A dating couple may seek out a secluded corner of a public park late at night when there is little traffic. Early risers or late-night workers may consciously alter their work schedule to avoid rush-hour traffic. And stu-

Prison Codes

Within the prison setting, where verbal communication is tightly controlled, an awareness and sensitivity to all types of nonverbal messages is vital to successful functioning. . . .

One may communicate invasion of privacy and rudeness by looking into another's cell without invitation. This is especially true if it occurs on a range other than one's own.

When in the yard or other open space, someone crossing the eight-to-ten-foot barrier is perceived as trespassing. In closed quarters, depending on the need for privacy, the distance is reduced to two or three feet. The outer limits become important when approached from the rear or when an approach is combined with direct constant eye contact. Conversational distance between two inmates is approximately two feet; between an inmate and a guard it increases to three feet. Invasion of boundaries communicates disrespect and violation of one's person. . . .

While one's cell is the only claim to privacy available, some inmates or groups of inmates stake out rights to seats in the auditorium and cafeteria. New inmates learn very quickly that violation of such space is strongly dealt with. When the auditorium is filled, there is usually a seat between every two men. An inmate would rather stand in the back than sit down right beside a stranger. . . .

Although most of the time spent in the cell is behind locked doors, the individual cell is perceived as an extension of one's self. It is the only place where an inmate may even begin to relax. Locked doors keep one inside, but they also keep others out. Any uninvited intrusion into the cell is considered a direct assault. Only guards have continual access and as long as their visits fall into expected patterns, the feeling of relaxation is not disturbed.

Source: "Prison Codes," by S. J. Ramsey, 1976, *Journal of Communication*, pp. 39, 43–44.

dents in dormitories report avoiding use of the bathrooms when they are most crowded (Vinsel et al., 1980).

Finally, a setting may be assigned different functions by time. In many parts of the world and in lower socioeconomic households, what is the living room during the daytime may become a bedroom at night. In dormitories, fraternities, and sororities, a common room may be designated as a study room during certain hours and a place for entertaining guests during other hours. Thus the kinds of social interactions that are permissible vary by time. When the time-space pattern for a setting affords inadequate privacy, people may cope by changing schedules or making more explicit rules about what functions are acceptable at what time. We know of a graduate student who became so annoyed by his officemate's public displays of affection with a girlfriend that he began coming to his office late in the day and working until the middle of the night. Both students saw the office as a private place, but the use of it for intimate behavior by one intruded on the felt privacy of the other. The radical change in schedule should have been a tip-off to the officemate that something was awry.

Kinesics and Vocalics. A wide variety of facial, body, and vocal behaviors can be used to judge how private or public the participants consider the situation. Most of these behaviors have already been discussed as relational messages, but they may also serve the function of establishing a situation as one of physical, social, or psychological privacy.

Especially important are turf defense and exclusion cues. These include (a) threat displays such as staring or tongue showing, (b) dominance displays such as expensive postures and loud voices, (c) body blocks and face covering, (d) emblems such as "go away" that express unapproachability, (e) dyadic postures and orientations that create a closed unit, (f) silences, (g) gaze aversion or reduced facial regard, and (h) other forms of reduced immediacy (Burgoon, 1982; Burgoon, Parrott, LePoire, Kelley, Walther, & Perry, 1988).

As a signal that a situation is affording inadequate privacy, people may also display anxiety and negative affect cues. Many of these were reviewed in Chapter 3 in the context of personal space invasions. Reduced smiling and increases in such behaviors as self- and object-adaptors, postural shifting, restless trunk and limb movements, negative facial affects, and vocal tension all frequently accompany situations that provide inadequate physical, social, or psychological privacy (Baum & Greenberg, 1975; Greenberg & Firestone, 1977; Hayduk, 1978; Maines, 1977; McCauley, Coleman, & DeFusco, 1978; Patterson, 1973a; Patterson et al., 1971; Sundstrom, 1975, 1978; Westin, 1970).

At a more general level, a key indicator of the privacy of a situation is the extent to which participants treat it as a backstage and engage in rule- and role-conforming or rule- and role-violating behaviors. You will recall that Goffman (1959), in his self-presentational approach to human interaction (see Chapter 7), distinguishes between frontstage behavior, which is the set of behaviors appropriate to a given role that one is performing, and backstage behavior, which includes behaviors that occur when one "lets down the mask." To engage in backstage behavior is to view a situation as private. Backstage, one is free to commit behaviors that violate general social norms, to engage in emotional release (Westin, 1970), "to escape from the compulsion of one's social role" (Chapin, 1951, p. 164), and even to denigrate that role. The ameliorative value of defining a situation as backstage is expressed by Burgoon (1982):

> The privacy associated with the backstage region enables one to recuperate from the traffic of day-to-day living and to regenerate energy and initiative. The metaphor of the backstage thus gives social privacy a spatial and temporal dimension. It is seen as a place—a

"behind-the-scenes" hideaway where people go to escape from the demands of daily social transactions, to heal after stressful encounters, to rehearse and prepare for future contacts—and also a duration of time—a "grace" period during which the normal rules of conduct can be suspended. (p. 219)

Beyond violating or digressing from general social norms and the behavioral repertoire of a given role, some specific behaviors that may be associated with the backstage include use of more adaptor behaviors, more emotional expression (especially of negative emotions), more postural and vocal relaxation, and more profane language (a verbal behavior).

Finally, because people may attempt to achieve psychological privacy through being "enigmatic" (Jourard, 1966b, 1971), they may suppress their felt emotional expressions and adopt impassive, "polite" ones. The "inscrutability" attributed to Orientals may be just because of this use of inexpressiveness to achieve psychological privacy in their culture.

Physical Appearance and Attire.

Finally, physical appearance may signal individual or group definitions of privacy. At the individual level, one may use clothing as a form of physical insulation that carries psychological connotations: In psychiatric settings, it has been recognized that more layers of clothing symbolize a closing-off of self from others and a greater desire for psychological privacy. Clothing may also establish *anonymity,* which minimizes self-identity but contributes to individual psychological privacy. Goffman (1961a) has observed that institutions strip people of individual identities by issuing regulation hospital garb, giving standard haircuts and forbidding facial hair, and enforcing restrictions on other aspects of personal grooming. The military and prisons rely on the same kinds of uniformity in appearance to create mass rather than individual identities. Organizations like the Ku Klux Klan also achieve individual anonymity and hence privacy through the use of identical costumes.

Conversely, clothing may establish one's identity and specifically one's level of status, which affects how much social and physical privacy one is accorded (Altman, 1975). Occupational uniforms and other role-related dress denote levels of social status. As status increases, approachability decreases. Military uniforms, police uniforms, business suits, or surgical scrubs are far less likely to invite approach than are jeans or a factory apron. Other clothing may directly signal approachability. Veils worn by women in the Middle East cue strangers that they are not to be spoken to, while the near nudity of beach attire in the West invites conversation and possibly even physical contact.

Finally, the clothing worn by an assemblage of people can directly define roles and the interactional context. If everyone is dressed in skiwear, the context can safely be assumed to be recreational and hence more public than private. If, however, people at the head of a congregation are wearing ceremonial robes, one may conclude that a religious or other special ritual is in progress and may only be accessible to a select group. Thus appearance

Which of these situations is a private business meeting, an invitation-only cocktail party, and a public fair? Identify all the nonverbal elements that permit you to make these judgments.

is one of the primary signals of the collective definition of a situation and, by implication, the amount of privacy associated with it.

The Informal–Formal Dimension

Closely related to the dimension of privacy is formality. The more informal a situation is, the more it tends to be viewed as private, and vice versa. But it is also easy to think of situations that are both private and informal (e.g., a parent consoling a child over losing a school election), so formality must be regarded as separate from privacy. Another set of terms often used in association with *informal-formal* is *personal-impersonal.* We will use *formal* to refer to situations that are also relatively impersonal and proper in nature and *informal* to refer to those that are relatively personal, casual, and relaxed.

Environment and Artifacts. The physical setting is an obvious influence on how comfortable and relaxed or restrained and formal we feel in a situation. Some environments put us at ease immediately; others make us feel that we must be on our best behavior. Volume of space is one influence. Simonds (1961) notes that the size of a room affects the kinds of activities and communication that occur in it. Large spaces produce formal activities like conversing, holding a banquet, or discussing serious topics. Small spaces correspond to far more informal activity such as chatting, arguing, or singing (see Figure 11.3).

Artifacts can set a formal tone for interaction. Objects that are meant to impress others primarily by their costliness can create a formal setting. Knowing that the office you have just entered has a real Monet or Van Gogh hanging on the wall may elicit formal behavior. Furniture and decorations that are traditional in style and design can have a similar effect. Other

FIGURE 11.3 The amount of space that is available is likely to affect the kind of communication that goes on. Activities appropriate for a small space are far more informal than those appropriate for a large space, as the sample activities listed under each space suggest.

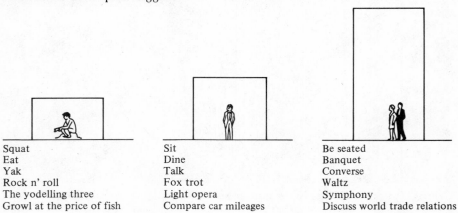

Squat	Sit	Be seated
Eat	Dine	Banquet
Yak	Talk	Converse
Rock n' roll	Fox trot	Waltz
The yodelling three	Light opera	Symphony
Growl at the price of fish	Compare car mileages	Discuss world trade relations

artifacts, such as family pictures on a desk, can set an informal and friendly tone. Interior designs that emphasize comfort are also likely to set an informal and personal pattern of interaction. It is difficult to imagine, for example, carrying on a formal discussion in a room where people are seated in recliners.

Lighting may contribute to formality or informality. Lighting that is moderately bright to bright lends a formal and impersonal character to a situation. Softer and lower levels of light emphasize informality and relaxation (as well as intimacy).

Proxemics and Haptics. Seating arrangements express the informal or formal character of situations. Work by Mehrabian (1981) and Sommer (1969) has shown that office furniture arrangements that create barriers and distance between interactants stress formality in a situation. Groupings that reduce distance and provide few or no barriers set up a more informal interaction style. This argues for not leaving office arrangements to chance or personal preference. If a professional's goal is to put clients at ease and develop rapport (in a therapeutic situation, for instance), furniture arrangements that create obstructions and distance make it all the more difficult to accomplish that goal.

As conversational distance increases, so does formality (Aiello & Cooper, 1972; Byrne, Baskett, & Hodges, 1971; Mehrabian, 1967; Sundstrom & Altman, 1976; Willis, 1966). Hall's distance categories are described in part according to the degree of formality of communication associated with each. Presumably, absence of touch is common in formal settings where distances tend to be greater, and frequency of touch coincides with more personal, informal communication at close distances.

Chronemics. Emphasis on punctuality marks the formality or informality of an occasion. It may not be a problem to arrive 30 minutes late for a pot-luck supper, but it definitely is one to arrive that late for a formal dinner party. More generally, adherence to schedules and a careful management of chronemic elements reflects formal situations, while a flexible and socially negotiated approach to chronemic elements reflects informality. A displaced point pattern of dealing with appointments is characteristic of the former; a diffused point pattern is characteristic of the latter.

Physical Appearance. As with privacy, physical appearance cues provide constants that help to define a situation in terms of culturally accepted levels of formality and informality. In our culture, phrases like "formal wear" and "black tie affair" denote occasions that require not only formal costumes but formal demeanor as well. Overdressing or underdressing for an occasion is a common social fear. If the dress requirements are unclear in advance, we usually inquire to be sure that our attire matches the formality of the situation.

Unfortunately, we do not always receive accurate advice. In self-presentational terms, we sometimes receive "inadequate dramaturgic direction." Recently, one of your authors and spouse decided to try a new restaurant. Calling ahead, we were assured that informal dress (jeans) was fine. However, upon arrival our waiter appeared dressed in a black tie and white dress shirt. As other well-dressed patrons began arriving, we were soon the most casually dressed people in the whole restaurant. Our embarrassment at being inappropriately dressed spoiled what should have been an enjoyable meal.

The Task–Social Dimension

A major feature that can distinguish one situation from another is whether it is task-related or social. Researchers in small group behavior, organizational behavior, and communication have found that the task-nontask dimension runs through virtually all interactions (Fisher, 1980; Goldhaber, 1983; Shaw, 1981). The features that characterize a task-oriented situation closely parallel those for a formal situation, whereas a socially oriented situation tends to be more informal.

Environment and Artifacts. Most contemporary adult life is spent in work settings. We might consider these settings to be task microenvironments that are designed to prompt task behavior (with greater or lesser efficiency). Such work microenvironments are a composite of diverse environmental elements that can indicate the type of task to be completed as well as the degree of task orientation required.

Lighting, color, temperature, and noise jointly set the scene for task behavior. Bright lights typify a task setting, dim lighting, a more social environment. Although there is no one color that people in our culture associate with task behavior, colors that provide moderate sensory stimulation, are easy on the eyes, and are nondistracting—greens, blues, earth tones—are most common in work settings. Imagine how nerve-racking it would be to work all day in a bright red cubicle! Moderate temperatures also correspond to task-oriented situations. Within the comfort range identified in Chapter 4 (68° to 80°F), cooler temperatures promote more of a work orientation. Noise operates in a similar fashion. White noise is commonly used to maintain a modest degree of sensory stimulation while masking distracting, irregular sound patterns. High levels of noise are avoided in environments requiring complex mental tasks. Loud music therefore becomes a cue (intentional or otherwise) that a situation is not devoted to task accomplishment. In some cases, such as the library, we have explicit rules to ensure that the environment is conducive to the task at hand. Such quiet environments in turn set expectations for the kinds of behavior that are appropriate.

The overall layout of a microenvironment and the artifacts in it give interactants very specific clues about the orientation to expect. Office environments, full of the implements of work (typewriters, computers, desks, workstations, etc.), give direct and obvious signals about the activities that occur there. Moreover, the layout of the workspace can clarify whether tasks are to be collaborative or independent. Common spaces in which workers can gather for task activity imply cooperative activities; layouts that isolate individuals, by contrast, point to individual effort. Unfortunately, the people responsible for the design of an environment are not always aware of its strong effect on interaction. Supervisors can find it difficult to get employees to work together cooperatively when the physical layout militates against such activity.

Proxemics. A study by Batchelor and Goethals (1972) found, not surprisingly, that closer interpersonal distances occur among people engaged in task interaction than those not working together. Small group research has likewise confirmed that the nature of the topic influences the direction of interaction patterns (Hare & Bales, 1963; Steinzor, 1950; Strodtbeck & Hook, 1961). In task discussions, people direct more comments to those seated across from them in a circle or at a table, whereas in social discussions, they are more likely to talk to the person seated next to them. The presence of a directive leader may also encourage more talking to those in adjacent seats.

Seating position in turn can affect group leadership in task-oriented groups. Not only do people who are of higher status or power gravitate toward seats that afford them access to the most other group members, but people who sit at the head of a table or opposite the most others, either by choice or assignment, tend to become more participative and dominant during ensuing discussions and to be perceived as leaders (Hare & Bales, 1963; Howells & Becker, 1962; Russo, 1967; Strodtbeck & Hook, 1961; Sommer, 1961; Ward, 1968). Thus leadership and "central" seating positions go hand in hand.

Seating arrangements can make a situation more social by encouraging interaction, or less social by discouraging it. We have noted that sociofugal arrangements tend to discourage interaction. Sommer (1969) found that state hospitals often arranged their lounges with chairs lining the walls so as to ease the work of custodians and orderlies. He found that by simply rearranging the chairs into sociopetal patterns, previously noncommunicative and depressed patients significantly increased their communication with others and concomitantly showed improvement in their mental health and ability to relate to others.

A two-part study was conducted to determine which seating arrangements are most conducive to participation in a classroom (Heston & Garner, 1972). In the first part, while the classroom was empty, all the chairs were piled in the center of the room. This forced entering students to create their own arrangement of chairs and to choose their own preferred distance from one another. It was assumed that they would place the seats in a pattern that was most comfortable and desirable for classroom interaction. The unexpected result was that students voluntarily placed themselves 17 inches apart, within the intimate zone. This was greater than the 13 inches found between seats in undisturbed classrooms but still closer than expected, revealing that people prefer proximity for situations involving interaction.

In the second part of the study, students were each given a floor grid and asked to draw on it the seating arrangement they considered most conducive to attention, comfort, learning, and participation. The preferred seating pattern was a circle or semicircle.

This preference seems to be based on two considerations: proximity and visual access to others. It is consistent with other research showing that as proximity and/or visual access increases, so does classroom participation (Sommer, 1969). For example, when a classroom has straight row seating, most participation comes from the front and center seats, creating a triangle of participation. These seats maximize visual contact between student and teacher. Similarly, the most active participants in a seminar seating arrangement are the people sitting opposite the teacher, and those sitting closest to the instructor may be shut out of a highly directed discussion. A laboratory seating arrangement (everyone seated around lab tables) produces the most total participation, probably because when people face so many others, they are more inclined to talk.

A final feature distinguishing task from social situations is territoriality, which is especially prominent in the workplace. Workers usually feel the need to identify an area as their own work space. Further, territories are often established and marked in terms of a given group's function. For example, at CBS headquarters in New York City, most upper-level managers have their offices on the 20th floor. Staffers are aware that this is the locus of decision making. When projects are proposed for broadcast, they have to be "cleared by the 20th floor" (Halberstam, 1979).

Chronemics. In a culture as obsessed with time as ours, it should come as no surprise that chronemic elements are significant definers of a task orientation. Preoccupation with the duration of tasks, punctuality, timing of events, deadlines, schedules, and the compartmentalization of time characterize a task-oriented situation. Contrast that with the more flexible approach to time in social situations. Although there may be a social agenda, punctuality is usually a minor issue, and there are no set schedules or deadlines to adhere to. Superimposing a task time orientation on a social situation can transform an enjoyable leisure activity like a hike into a chore, particularly when someone is bent on plotting out every minute's activities and insisting that everyone follow a schedule.

Physical Appearance. As with privacy and formality, uniforms and other occupational insignia may declare one's task role in an environment. In a large company, slight differences in style of clothing or personal artifacts may even distinguish members of one department from another. Salespeople may carry home valises large enough to hold sample merchandise, while supervisors carry thin attaché cases and upper managers carry nothing (the notion being that executives have complete freedom during their off-work hours). Engineers are stereotypically depicted as having a plastic sheath full of colored pens and pencils in their shirt pocket, something salespeople "wouldn't be caught dead wearing." Uniforms may also be useful in reducing ambiguity about role responsibilities. In a hospital, the doctors' and nurses' uniforms are distinct from one another and from those of lab technicians or orderlies. This enables patients and visitors as well as the staff themselves to know who is who. Consider how willing you would be to allow someone *not* dressed in a nurse's uniform to draw blood from your arm. Our guess is not very willing.

This use of uniforms to designate role or status is culture-specific. As noted previously, it is common in some Oriental businesses for the company president to wear the same uniform as an assembly line worker. This lack of role differentiation through clothing can cause consternation or embarrassment for Westerners, who are accustomed to relying on such cues to govern how they carry on international business dealings.

The Cooperative-Competitive Dimension

Embedded in a task situation is the degree to which a cooperative or competitive mode of behavior is expected. Deutsch (1973) has defined competition as a state of affairs where opposition in the goals of interdependent parties is such that the probability of goal attainment for one decreases as the probability for the other increases. Competing with coworkers for a promotion at work or competing with siblings for a parent's affection are examples. Cooperation, by contrast, involves mutual activity by both parties toward the attainment of a mutually beneficial goal.

Nonverbal elements play a role in the *perception* of a situation as cooperative or competitive. Sometimes individuals misperceive a situation, reading it as competitive when in fact it is cooperative, or vice versa. It is these perceptions, not actuality, that are relevant here.

Environment and Artifacts. Just as layout can determine whether a task is to be a joint or individual effort, so too can it determine whether it will be a cooperative or competitive endeavor. Highly compartmentalized work spaces tend to minimize cooperation, while open ones promote it. In fact, one of the main arguments for the use of open work environments is that they should foster more interaction and hence more cooperative spirit. The same principle applies to traditional versus open classrooms. The latter, by permitting students to work together in common areas and by physically facilitating group projects, reinforces the concept of collaborative effort.

Proxemics. At the most basic level, cooperative tasks require closer proximity than competitive or parallel (coaction) tasks. Thus closer interpersonal distances may signal a cooperative situation, farther distances, a competitive one. The designation of territories also implies competition, since territories are designed to create separate identities and to regulate access to scarce resources.

Seating arrangement also reveals the cooperative or competitive nature of task behavior. Several studies (Cook, 1970; Hasse, 1970; Mabry & Kaufman, 1973; Norum, Russo, & Sommer, 1967; Sommer, 1965) have shown that children, British and American university students, and other adults prefer side-by-side or cross-corner seating for cooperative tasks, opposite seating for competition, and catercorner seating for coaction. Sitting across from someone for competition is probably preferred because it allows one to watch the opponent while still being able to minimize surveillance of one's own work through body blocks.

We have now covered a variety of situational dimensions and have linked them to a number of nonverbal elements. It is useful to remind ourselves, however, that on a day-to-day basis, it is the totality of these elements that make the situation such a powerful determinant of behavior. It is also useful to remind ourselves that the relationships that have been outlined are likely to be quite different across cultures. As potent and complex as situational elements seem in our culture, other cultures go beyond ours in stressing them. Hall's (1959, 1981) notion of context sensitivity has particular importance for this point. High context cultures place strong emphasis on context and situation. Much information is embedded in the environment and ritualized behaviors, and interpretations of communication events depend on understanding the culture's contextual language. Consequently, such cultures are no doubt more attentive to the structuring of situations than low context cultures such as ours, which rely more on the content of the verbal messages that are exchanged to draw accurate interpretations. Even so, the context may play a crucial role in low context cultures in choosing among alternative interpretations of an event. To gain a clearer picture of how situational factors affect communication in daily interactions, "typical" or "standard" situations can be analyzed. Such case analysis can identify situational factors and gauge their combined strength.

APPLICATIONS

Situational Factors in Health Care

Various hospitals and mental health institutions may have different aims, but they share one situational goal: to provide patients with a therapeutic context that encourages regaining health. Do current health care contexts meet this goal? Do they actually help patients get well?

The answer seems to be no. Many experts are increasingly convinced that there is an important link between communication and one's state of health. To become well requires patients participating actively in the healing process. However, becoming a patient often means adopting a passive role and assuming others will "fix" the problem (Mechanic, 1972). Situational factors in health care facilities encourage this passive stance. Olsen (1978) suggests that the symbolic function of the health care environment often communicates to patients that they are ill and dependent and

Situational Factors in Health Care (*Continued*)

should behave in a passive manner, even though this is not in their best interest. Other researchers suggest that environmental factors in many health care facilities serve to dehumanize and deindividuate the patient (Leventhal, Nerenz, & Leventhal, 1982). Important to us are three aspects of dehumanization these authors cite: a sense of isolation, a sense of inability to communicate, and planlessness and loss of competency.

What environment and artifact elements contribute to patient dependency, inactivity, and dehumanization? Work by Sommer (1974b) provides some indications. His description of the "hard" architecture found in the design of mental institutions closely matches the conditions found in many health care institutions: long straight halls, cold tile, mostly white paint, chairs bolted to the floor in long rows, and small rectangular rooms. These conditions are better suited to a prison than a therapeutic context. Corridor arrangements of rooms along halls, sociofugal seating patterns in lounges, and the absence of areas for patients to congregate serve to lower social contact and isolate patients. The sterile atmosphere of health care facilities (lack of color, cool temperatures, few interesting artifacts) provides limited sensory stimulation, further reinforcing patient passivity. Moreover, patients lose social control over the environment. They cannot control who enters their space, nor do they have much ability to personalize their surroundings. This lack of environmental control can undermine a sense of well-being.

The technology and equipment that treatment sometimes involves can also contribute to a sense of helplessness and dehumanization. Patients may feel—as a result of radiation therapy, chemotherapy, or other invasive treatments—that they have lost the ability to care for themselves. They are likely to lose the motivation to communicate or may feel that they can no longer communicate competently. The effect on the process of healing is not positive—as is clearly affirmed in Norman Cousins's *Anatomy of an Illness* (1979), an anecdotal account of his struggle against these and other problems in health care settings. As the excerpt from his book reveals, only by taking an active role in his own healing—in this case, prescribing laughter therapy for himself and making arrangements to move to a hotel room—did he begin to feel that he would recover (something that did in fact occur and which he attributed to his gaining more control over the medical situation):

> There was, however, one negative side-effect of the laughter from the standpoint of the hospital. I was disturbing other patients. But that objection didn't last long, for the arrangements were now

Situational Factors in Health Care (*Continued*)

complete for me to move my act to a hotel room. One of the incidental advantages of the hotel room, I was delighted to find, was that it cost only about one-third as much as the hospital. The other benefits were incalculable. I would not be awakened for a bed bath or for meals or for medication or for a change of bed sheets or for tests or for examinations by hospital interns. The sense of serenity was delicious and would, I felt certain, contribute to a general improvement. (p. 40)

A recent review of research on hospital design and human behavior (Reizenstein, 1982) provides some surprising insights. First, there is surprisingly little empirical research on hospital design and behavior, despite the prompting of researchers like Sommer (1974b) and Goffman (1961a). Second, of the available literature, over half is not empirically based and is often the "show and tell" type that simply describes a new medical facility without evaluating design effectiveness. When recommendations are made about how to design health care facilities, they are often poorly substantiated. Third, user groups such as patients, visitors, and nonmedical staff have received far less research attention than the medical staff. Finally, those who make design decisions about health care facilities tend *not* to use the research that is available. The overall picture is rather disappointing. It confirms that health care environments, instead of being systematically designed to help patients take an active role in becoming healthy, increase patient passivity and dehumanization.

Chronemic elements in health care situations play much the same role. It is immediately obvious to patients that they have lost control over the scheduling of events. Patients control neither *who* enters their space nor *when*. Patients may be visited only during certain hours, must eat during certain times, take medication on a prescribed schedule, and undergo examination at times convenient for the medical staff. Admittedly, some aspects of this kind of scheduling have to do with large-scale institutional health care and are unavoidable. However, waking patients in the middle of the night for routine exams and tests is avoidable (see Cousins, 1979, for some vivid examples). All of these scheduling practices contribute to patients' sense of loss of control and planlessness.

Finally, physical appearance elements often reinforce the passive patient role. Patients are usually given hospital garb that may consist of a surgical gown or pajamas. Other clothes, including the patient's own sleepwear, are often prohibited. Since these clothes are not of the patient's choosing, the patient is deprived of yet

Situational Factors in Health Care (*Continued*)

another choice, and one more element of institutional control is imposed. In critical care situations, such practices are often necessary, but it is difficult to believe that in noncritical situations, clothing choice cannot be left to the patient.

You might begin to wonder at this point how anyone ever gets well in a hospital. Of course, people do get well in hospitals. But it is worth speculating whether more patients might get well and get well sooner if the nonverbal situational elements were different. Recent concern over the cost of medical care adds more fuel to the fire. If patients took less time to recover and more of them recovered quickly, it could significantly lower medical costs. Such considerations argue for more careful examination of how nonverbal situational elements structure interaction and behavior in health contexts and other institutional settings. Research that has begun to explore nonverbal communication in the medical context (Blanck, Buck, & Rosenthal, 1986; Buller & Buller, 1987; Burgoon, Pfau, Parrott, Birk, Coker, & Burgoon, 1987) should provide some partial answers.

Summary

Nonverbal patterns play a significant role in defining and structuring communicative situations. Situational definitions and constraints in turn have a strong effect on how we communicate and behave. Nonverbal situational features can affect communication by setting expectations for interaction, prompting the use of different social rules, and clarifying roles for interaction. As communicators, we sometimes have the ability to structure situations and therefore can influence the outcomes of interaction. At other times, we are passive respondents to situational factors. Among the most important continua along which situations are judged are *competitive-cooperative, task-social, dominant-equal,* and *impersonal/formal–personal/informal.* Most of the nonverbal elements that help to structure situations can be seen to do so by relating to these dimensions.

Elements from four nonverbal codes—environment and artifacts, proxemics, physical appearance, and chronemics—are especially important in structuring situational definitions and behavioral patterns. These code elements are most likely to play situational roles because they are relatively stable during and across encounters and therefore remain an unchanging frame of reference. As case analysis suggests, these code elements combine in an overall situational whole to provide strong influences on how interactants communicate.

Suggested Readings

Baum, A., & Singer, J. E. (1982). *Advances in environmental psychology. Vol. 4: Environment and health.* Hillsdale, NJ: Erlbaum.

Bossley, M. I. (1976). Privacy and crowding: A multidisciplinary analysis. *Man-Environment Systems, 6,* 8–19.

Burgoon, J. K. (1988). Spatial relations in small groups. In R. S. Cathcart & L. A. Samovar (Eds.), *Small group communication: A reader* (5th ed.) (pp. 351–366). Dubuque, IA: Brown.

Forgas, J. P. (1979). *Social episodes: The study of interaction routines.* London: Academic Press.

Furnham, A., & Argyle, M. (1981). *The psychology of social situations: Selected readings.* Elmsford, NY: Pergamon Press.

Goffman, E. (1959). *The presentation of self in everyday life.* Garden City, NY: Anchor Books/Doubleday.

Goffman, E. (1967). *Interaction ritual: Essays on face-to-face behavior.* Garden City, NY: Doubleday.

Korda, M. (1975). *Power! How to get it, how to use it.* New York: Ballantine.

Mehrabian, A. (1971). *Silent messages: Implicit communication of emotions and attitudes* (2nd ed.). Belmont, CA: Wadsworth.

Mehrabian, A. (1976). *Public places and private spaces: The psychology of work, play, and living environments.* New York: Basic Books.

Secord, P. (1982). *Explaining human behavior.* Beverly Hills, CA: Sage.

Sommer, R. (1974a). Studies of small group ecology. In R. S. Cathcart & L. A. Somovar (Eds.), *Small group communication: A reader* (2nd ed.) (pp. 283–293). Dubuque, IA: Brown.

CHAPTER 12

Managing Conversations

What can the body tell us? Plenty—if we observe how people actually move: whether they move together in synchrony or not, the kind of rhythm they are moving to, as well as the many tiny, unnoticeable events that make up any transaction.

Edward T. Hall (1981, p. 71)

Nature of Conversational Management

The term *conversational management* may seem strange and a little incongruous. After all, *management* seems to imply a deliberate attempt to control or affect something, and having a conversation with others may not seem to take on that quality very often. But throughout this chapter you will find that conversations are indeed managed in many ways. Participants use a wide variety of nonverbal behaviors to regulate many aspects of conversations. If the ability to use these cues were somehow taken away, it would be difficult, perhaps impossible, to have conversations at all.

What kinds of conversational phenomena do we regulate nonverbally? Among other things, we manage who speaks when (sometimes called turn taking), how we change topics, and how we enter and leave conversations. As we shall see, nonverbal cues that regulate have a profound effect on many aspects of the whole communication process.

First, we should take note of a few basics about the regulative function. One reason why it seems odd to think of conversations as managed is that we take much of the regulative process for granted as we talk. This makes conversations seem almost automatic and effortless, and in fact, much regulation is habitual and routine. We think about it only when something goes wrong and the conversational process breaks down, as when another conversational participant monopolizes the floor or when we make strategic choices in conversations.

Another basic characteristic of conversational regulation and management is that such processes are often rule-bound. That is, we follow a set of social rules, usually implicit ones, that tell us how to structure conversations. Rules theorists (e.g., Cushman & Whiting, 1972; Pearce, 1976) have suggested that we learn such rules in a variety of ways, including both modeling and explicit instruction, and that social rules affect a great deal of interpersonal behavior. Conversational regulation and management is one area of social behavior where rules are likely to apply. For example, here are some basic rules for turn taking:

> Only one speaker may speak at a time in a conversation.
> Interruptions by listeners are not allowed.
> Possession of the floor must change during conversations.
> Listeners must give cues indicating that they are paying attention to the speaker in a conversation.

It is important to remember that rules are *guidelines* for conversational behavior. As the old adage suggests, "rules are made to be broken," and we do break these rules during conversations with others. However, we do so at the risk of negative sanctions from other conversants.

Rule violations and sanctions do not occur often in conversations. Telling someone to pay attention to a conversation indicates that the conversational process is already in trouble, and such statements are typically a last resort. This reflects the fact that we prefer to regulate and manage conversations nonverbally. Another way to demonstrate this is to try the following thought experiment. What would interaction with others be like if you had to use verbal cues to manage who spoke when in a conversation? Dialogue might then sound something like this:

Joe: Yes, well that's very interesting. I've never thought of it that way. I'm finished—over to you, Sam.

Sam: The mind boggles, doesn't it? Who knows what possibilities exist! Back to you, Joe.

Joe: I guess it's true that we only use the smallest amount of our mental potential. To you again, Sam.

Sam: Truly remarkable! To think that we could be doing more with our brains. Take it again, Joe.

Joe: Indeed! Try once more, Sam. . . .

Whatever else might be said about regulating and managing conversations nonverbally, this example reveals how efficient nonverbal cues are.

A third basic characteristic of the regulative function is that conversational management is linked to other interpersonal functions, such as relational messages; that is, our structuring of conversations with others allows us not only to regulate the conversation but to accomplish other interpersonal functions as well. Wiemann (1985), for example, has summarized evidence that indicates that turn taking is very important in the definition of control and power in interpersonal relationships. We shall later consider research that links regulative behavior to a wide variety of interpersonal functions.

Finally, regulation and management behaviors are a fundamental part of one's skill and competence as a communicator. The ability to exchange the conversational floor smoothly, to shift topics without losing participants, and to initiate and terminate conversations skillfully are *interaction management skills* (Wiemann, 1977) that go a long way toward defining a person as a competent communicator. We tend to be most aware of these skills in their absence—in the person who ignores all efforts to terminate a telephone conversation or ends conversations abruptly. These individuals may simply lack skill and competence as communicators, but this behavior may lead to a number of other attributions about them. Thus effective conversational management has implications for the achievement of other desired communication outcomes.

Another proof of the importance of conversational regulation is the emotion we invest in it. Few situations are as infuriating as when someone consistently breaks conversational rules. Students complain about instructors they find difficult to follow because they can't tell when the teacher changes from one topic to another. Workers complain about a boss who interrupts their work, starts a conversation, and then leaves just as abruptly. Spouses complain about partners who fail to look at them during a conversation. Patients complain that they are not getting good medical care when doctors don't listen to them, spend little time talking to them, and end the doctor-patient dialogue too quickly. These are all examples that people have strong feelings about, and much of the problem in each involves regulation and management cues.

Conversations are managed on a number of levels, ranging from the microscopic to the macroscopic. Not all levels are likely to be involved in the communicative process; for example, some behaviors on the micro level are unlikely to affect communication in any socially significant way. Such microbehaviors are best considered *nonverbal behavior,* and they will be reviewed later in the chapter. We start with the first level of regulative behavior that clearly does have social significance, turn taking.

Turn Taking in Conversations: Regulating Who Speaks When

It has often been said that one characteristic of a skilled communicator is knowing when to say something and when not to. Yet most of us are able to engage in conversations without verbally tripping all over ourselves. How do we weave the fabric of conversation without becoming entangled in it? As we have already discovered, we do so primarily by nonverbal means.

Conversations and Turns

A conversation is a series of opportunities to speak and listen, an alternation of sound and silence. West and Zimmerman (1982) point out that conversations have variable turn order, turn size, and turn content peculiar to a given occasion and the participants involved. Who speaks first, about what, and for how long are not determined in advance but are negotiated in some way by the participants.

In the broadest sense, a turn in a conversation is simply an opportunity to speak. We all recognize such opportunities—somehow we know when it is our turn to speak and when it is not. Just how long is a turn? Researchers have estimated the average length of a conversational turn to be 6 seconds (Jaffe & Feldstein, 1970). But it is difficult to define a turn more precisely. Feldstein and Welkowitz (1978) note little agreement among researchers:

> Offhand, one would think it easy to know who in a conversation has the turn and who does not. It is, therefore, surprising to find so little agreement about not only what a turn is, but when it occurs and who has it. (p. 344)

The definitions of turn offered in the literature vary in the extent to which they rely on the start and end of speech on the one hand and semantic and gestural information on the other to mark where a turn begins and ends (Rosenfeld, 1978). One definition is based on the physical change of vocalization from one interactant to another: "A speaking turn begins when one interlocutor starts solo talking and ends when a different interlocutor starts solo talking" (Markel, 1975, p. 190). Similar vocalization-based definitions have been offered by other researchers (cf. Jaffe & Feldstein, 1970).

Other definitions use either some type of verbal content unit or gestural information to demarcate turns. Matarazzo and Wiens (1972) defined the turn as "the total duration of time it takes a speaker to emit all the words that he is contributing in that particular unit or exchange (as this would be judged by common social standards)" (p. 6). Thus this definition relies on some consensual notion of when a person has finished a verbal contribution to a particular exchange. Yngve (1970) also suggested that semantic content determines turns in conversations and in particular that the amount of information conveyed is relevant. Sacks, Schegloff, and Jefferson (1974) define the turn as a period of time during which one has the right or obligation to speak. Turns are constructed out of *unit types,* which can include words, phrases, clauses, or sentences. A speaker, on gaining the floor, can produce at least one of these unit types before losing the floor. Finally, Duncan and Fiske (1977) rely on a reading of intent based on gestural and vocalic information to determine where a turn occurs. "A speaker is a participant who claims the speaking turn. An auditor is a participant who does not claim the speaking turn at a given moment" (p. 177). Knowing when an interactant claims the speaking turn is based on the occurrence of "turn-requesting cues."

Thus knowing specifically where a turn begins and ends is not as simple as it might seem. The difficulty of definition stems in part from three other features of conversation. The first is *simultaneous speech.* Although the principle of conversation in this culture is that people speak one at a time, actual conversations are a little more sloppy than that. There are times in conversations when more than one person vocalizes, though we prefer to keep such periods short and brief. Simultaneous speech can occur in a variety of ways, including interruptions, listener responses, and simple mistakes or accidents. Feldstein and Welkowitz (1978) further distinguish two types of simultaneous speech: *noninterruptive simultaneous speech,* which begins and ends while the participant who has the floor continues to talk, and *interruptive simultaneous speech,* which begins while the person who has the floor is talking and ends after that person has stopped talking and the possession of the floor has changed.

The question then arises as to who has the floor during these periods of simultaneous vocalization. The answer, as you might guess, depends on the definition of *turn* that you adopt. For example, according to Markel's (1975) definition, the floor belongs to a conversant until another conversant starts *solo* talking. So, if Person A is talking and Person B interjects something in the midst of it, A still maintains possession of the floor and B's vocalization is simply considered simultaneous speech. Other definitions, however, would assign possession of the floor to both or neither of the participants during periods of simultaneous speech.

A second important feature of conversational interchange is the period of silence between turns, called a *switch pause* or *latency.* Vocalization-based definitions (Jaffe & Feldstein, 1970; Markel, 1975) assign these periods of silence to the person who has just stopped talking and include them in that person's turn duration. Sacks et al. (1974) consider these interspeaker pauses "transition-relevant places" (i.e., places in the conversation where the floor *could* be exchanged) and assign these periods of silence to neither participant. Figure 12.1 provides a running-time diagram of a conversational sequence, showing what a series of turns would look like using a vocalization-based definition of *turn.*

A third aspect of conversational interchange is that simultaneous with speaking turns there are *listening turns.* This term may be misleading because it often implies a passive role. To the contrary, listeners in conversations are quite active and communicative and often have important effects on speaker

FIGURE 12.1 Diagrammatic representation of a conversational sequence. The numbered line at the bottom represents time in 300-msec units. *V* stands for vocalization, *P* for pause, and *SP* for switching pause (the silence that frequently occurs immediately prior to a change in the speaking turn). The downward arrows mark the end of Speaker A's turns; the upward arrows, the end of Speaker B's. *ISS* and *NSS* stand for interruptive and noninterruptive simultaneous speech, respectively.

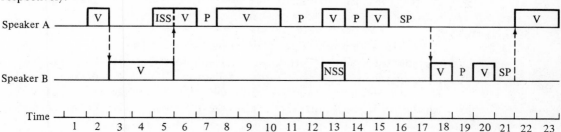

behavior. This point is often missed by researchers, partly because of the habit of focusing on an individual as the unit of analysis and not the multi-person unit. We will return later to consider the specific ways in which listeners communicate.

For our purposes, it is best to point out that all of the definitions of turn discussed so far have their advantages and disadvantages. Vocalization-based definitions have the advantage of operational clarity; that is, researchers and judges are in no doubt as to where a turn begins and ends. This also results in a high level of measurement reliability and precision, another advantage from a research point of view. These properties have worked to the advantage of Jaffe, Feldstein, and their associates, who have developed a computer-driven measuring system for tracking turns from audio tapes (the Automatic Voice Transaction Analyzer, or AVTA system; Cassotta, Feldstein, & Jaffe, 1964). However, these definitions do lead to a very literal demarcation of the conversational stream into turns. In some cases, turns can be quite short, less than a second, and can consist of statements like "Uh-huh" or even part of such an utterance if that turn overlaps with the previous turn. Such utterances may not seem like turns to the conversants or the investigators. Also, assigning the switch pause to the turn prior to it may not make sense to some analysts.

Definitions that use verbal and gestural criteria have the advantage of avoiding these short turn and switch pause problems. In addition, these definitions rely on a wider variety of cues to mark turn beginnings and endings, an advantage that takes into account the context of the conversation. However, the use of a greater number of cues also makes such definitions more complex and consequently more difficult to employ. Such definitions require more judgments and inferences by an observer, which raises the possibility for more error. Though most researchers using these definitions report good measurement reliability, their complexity makes them, at the least, more difficult. It may be particularly problematic to rely on a verbal unit for turn identification, as such units are often very difficult to identify in conversational interaction (try looking at a transcript of a conversation to prove this—transcripts often read in a very confused way). Finally, use of these definitions can sometimes result in the misidentification of turns where short turns by Person A are miscoded as simultaneous speech and folded into one long turn by Person B.

To summarize, the turn definition being used in any given piece of research can produce differences in the way turns are observed. Of greater interest to us as conversants are how turn exchanges are accomplished.

Turn Taking

Researchers generally agree that interactants use a set of nonverbal cues to regulate turn taking. The exchange of the floor from one conversant to the next is typically so smooth and swift that it is difficult to conceive otherwise. However, models concerned with these cues as turn-taking mechanisms do vary in the assumptions they make and the explanations they offer, and we shall consider these shortly. A description of turn taking can be conveniently divided into cues that speakers use and cues that listeners employ.

Speaker Cues. There are two basic classes of cues that speakers use to regulate turn taking in conversation: *turn-suppressing cues* and *turn-yielding cues.* Turn-suppressing cues are cues that a speaker uses to maintain possession of the floor. Duncan (1972) has identified five turn-suppressing cues: (a) an audible inhalation of breath by the speaker; (b) a continuation of gesture; (c) facing away, or diverting eye contact away from the listener; (d) a sustained intonation pattern, which lets the listener know that more vocalization is yet to come; and (e) *fillers,* also known as *vocalized pauses.* Examples of vocalized pauses are utterances like "hhmmm" and "uhhh." These vocalizations fill pauses in the speaking turn so that listeners will not use the silence as an opportunity to gain the floor. Knapp (1978) also suggests that speakers may increase the loudness of their voice or may lightly touch the listener to suppress the listener's attempt to take the floor. Other cues not identified by research may be used to maintain the floor, such as the "stop" hand gesture emblem.

Turn-yielding cues are cues that speakers use to give up the floor, in some cases to a particular interactant. Many turn-yielding cues are simply the opposite of turn-suppressing cues. Facing the listener and giving eye contact, using terminating gestures, and providing periods of silence by not filling pauses are examples of turn-yielding cues. Dropping intonation patterns also indicate to the listener that the speaker is about to give up the floor. Rising intonation patterns, when linked with a verbal question construction, also signal the end of a turn and implicitly indicate that a response is expected. Decreased loudness and slowed tempo may also be vocal turn-yielding cues. In conversations among three or more people, eye contact, gesturing, and head nodding in the direction of a given listener all serve to increase the probability of that person's being the next speaker.

Listener Cues. Listeners employ cues from three categories: *turn-requesting cues, backchannel cues,* and *turn-denying cues.* Turn-requesting cues are behaviors the listener uses to gain possession of the conversational floor. It is clear that listeners do not sit idly by, waiting for a chance to speak. Rather, they indicate their intention to speak by the display of this type of cue. Wiemann (1973) found that listeners use gaze directed at the speaker, head nods, and forward leans to gain access to the conversational floor. In a later study, Wiemann and Knapp (1975) identified the raised index finger and an inhalation of breath coupled with a straightened back as further turn-requesting cues.

Backchannel cues (Yngve, 1970) are behaviors the listener uses to communicate a variety of messages to the speaker without gaining access to the conversational floor. Also termed *listener responses* by other researchers (e.g., Dittmann, 1972a; Rosenfeld, 1978), such cues can communicate agreement and confirmation or disagreement and disconfirmation, involvement and interest or boredom and disinterest. Some backchannel cues can also be used to pace the speaker, as when a listener continuously nods at a fast pace to hurry the speaker up. Specific backchannel cues include smiling, frowning, head nodding and shaking, raised eyebrows, and short vocalizations ("uh-huh," "mm-hmm") and verbal statements ("yep," "right," "I see," "oh, good"). Again, note that these short verbal statements do not constitute turns, according to some researchers. If, however, a vocalization-based turn definition is being used, verbal statements by the listener would have to be simultaneous with speaker vocalization to be considered backchannel cues. Duncan (1974) has found that backchannel cues are distributed fairly evenly throughout the listening turn.

Backchannel or listener responses underscore the dynamic and simultaneous nature of face-to-face interaction. These cues allow a listener to communicate a variety of meanings without having to gain access to the conversational floor. Further, speakers *expect* listeners to display some level of these cues, particularly cues that fall into the involvement category. Speakers find it very disrupting if listeners fail to provide speakers with interest cues (such as smiling, lean toward the speaker, or gazing). Clearly, listener behavior can have potent effects on speaker behavior in a number of ways.

Finally, turn-denying cues provide a way for the listener to refuse a turn at the floor nonverbally. Although little studied, Knapp (1978) suggests that relaxed posture, silence, and staring away from the speaker are cues that qualify for this category.

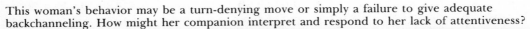

This woman's behavior may be a turn-denying move or simply a failure to give adequate backchanneling. How might her companion interpret and respond to her lack of attentiveness?

The effectiveness of both speaker and listener cues as regulators of turn exchange has been demonstrated in a number of studies. Duncan (1972) found that a smooth exchange of the floor occurred when a speaker displayed turn-yielding cues and that listeners were more likely to attempt to take the floor the more turn-yielding cues the speaker exhibited. In addition, when a speaker first displayed turn-yielding cues and then changed to a turn-suppressing cue, a single suppressing cue was effective. The use of suppressing cues essentially eliminated turn-taking attempts by the listener, regardless of how many turn-yielding cues accompanied them.

Turn-taking Models

In addition to investigations of such topics as turn-taking structure and strategy (Duncan & Fiske, 1985), explanatory models of turn taking are now emerging. Wiemann and his associates (Wiemann, 1985; Wilson, Wiemann, & Zimmerman, 1984) have identified three models of turn taking. The first

APPLICATIONS

Getting the Floor When You Want It

Some conversational management cues, such as nods, may be used for either turn-requesting or backchannel purposes. Such multi-use cues are often a source of confusion and lead to failure to gain a turn at talk. This may occur particularly often for women, as they employ nods more frequently than men as part of a socially facilitative style. As a result, women's use of nods as a turn-requesting cue is often taken as a backchannel response, and the request for a turn at talk is ignored.

How can both listeners and speakers distinguish between backchannel cues and turn-requesting cues? Two points might be helpful. First, other cues that occur with these multi-use cues may clarify their role. A nod, accompanied by other turn-requesting cues, will be interpreted as requesting a turn. Second, the point at which these cues occur may clarify their function. Backchannel cues can occur in a number of places during a turn, though they tend not to occur at the beginning. Turn-requesting cues are more likely to occur at turn junctures where the conversational floor could potentially be exchanged. Paying attention to the timing of multi-use cues as well as the other cues that are co-occurring should help clarify whether a cue is being used for backchannel or turn-requesting purposes. For women in the listening role, it may be especially important to be clear in the use of these cues. Using nods less frequently as a turn-requesting cue and employing other turn-requesting cues more should help you get the floor when you really want it.

model, termed the *signaling approach,* is best represented by Duncan's research program. This approach presumes that turns are exchanged by the display of turn-taking cues, as discussed. These cues constitute discrete and independent signals that are related to the exchange of turns by a set of rules or conventions that prescribe appropriate responses. Participants are thus bound by the rules associated with the signals. Wiemann (1985) points out that a *demand* characteristic is associated with these signal cues such that a participant who does not respond appropriately will be penalized for having broken a rule. For example, interruptions can be considered a violation of any number of turn-taking rules. As a result, the listener who has inappropriately tried to gain the floor by interrupting should suffer some sanction or penalty.

However, it is debatable whether participants who break such rules always suffer penalties. Wiemann (1985) suggests that they do not. For example, in some relationships, one partner continually interrupts the other partner but suffers no costs. The signaling approach offers no explanation for this inconsistency.

A second approach, identified with Sacks et al. (1974), is termed the *sequential production approach.* This approach assumes that turn taking must be managed sequentially by participants on a moment-to-moment basis. The model is less restrictive in terms of what is required of participants, and views conversation as a rather open and flexible process. Wiemann (1985) indicates that the approach has the following features:

1. Speech exchange occurs in which the order, length, and content of turns are free to vary.
2. The length of the conversation need not be fixed in advance.
3. The number of participants may vary.
4. In multiparty conversations, the relative distribution of turns is not specified in advance.
5. Talk can be continuous or discontinuous.
6. Typically, one party talks at a time.
7. Simultaneous talk is common, but its duration is usually brief.
8. Transitions from one turn to the next occur, for the most part, with little or no gap or overlap.
9. Explicit turn allocation techniques such as addressing a question or request to another party may, but need not, be used.
10. Turns may vary in their anticipated duration, for example, from one-word answers to lengthy stories.

While many of these features are common to all turn taking, this approach does point out that silences and simultaneous speech are an expected part of conversation (Points 5 and 7) rather than being viewed as breakdowns or rule violations.

Whereas the signaling approach emphasizes the role of the speaker in giving the floor to another interactant, the sequential production model places much of the responsibility with the listener. At the end of turn units, transition-relevant places occur. These transition-relevant places provide opportunities for listeners to acquire the floor, according to the following set of options:

1. The current speaker may, but need not, select another party to the conversation as the next speaker.
2. Should the current speaker not select the next, then another party to the conversation may, but again need not, select him- or herself as the next speaker. The first party to speak at such a point acquires the turn.
3. If no other party self-selects under the provisions of (2), then the current speaker may, but need not, continue.
4. In the event that the current speaker does not continue, the option to speak cycles back to the control of (2). (Wiemann, 1985, p. 92)

As these options, particularly Option 2, suggest, listeners can potentially wrest the floor from the speaker at the end of every unit type by treating the end of each unit type as a transition-relevant place. Clearly, though, this does not occur. If it did, conversation would be far more interruptive and would have much shorter turn durations and much quicker turn exchanges than in fact actually occur.

Wiemann and his associates (Wilson et al., 1984) have developed a third model of turn taking, termed the *resource model.* This approach incorporates elements of the previous two models and in doing so provides some advantages over them. Specifically, this model employs a modified signaling concept to clarify where transition-relevant places actually occur. The floor exchange options of the sequential production model are also retained to make clear what can possibly occur at transition-relevant places in conversation. As a result, responsibility for turn taking is mutually shared by all participants, and it becomes clearer when the floor can or should be exchanged. A final and important difference between this model and the other two is that turn-taking cues are viewed as resources available for interactants to use when needed. Instead of viewing these cues as signals, which must or should be responded to in a given way, turn-taking cues become a flexible means to an end—smooth and efficient turn taking. The model assumes that interactants have a broad repertoire of turn-taking cues, some of which may be as yet unidentified by research and some of which may be idiosyncratic. Further, the model assumes that no one turn-taking behavior always means precisely the same thing but rather that the meaning and function of turn-taking cues can vary across contexts and situations.

As you can see, this third model of turn taking does appear to provide some advantages in explaining how the floor is exchanged in conversation. At present, the model remains untested. Discussion, debate, and research will continue on the nature of conversational turn taking, but some conclusions can already be drawn at this point. First, what appears on the surface to be an effortless and rather easy feat, taking turns in conversations, is actually rather complex. As the models indicate, a number of factors have to be taken into account to explain how turns are exchanged. It is likely that more factors remain to be identified and there is much yet to understand about turn taking. Second, although we all have a general notion of what a turn is, defining a conversational turn is difficult. You are now aware of the variety of definitions. Third, conversations at the turn level are comprised not only of turns but also simultaneous speech, response latencies, turns that overlap, and listener responses. Conversations thus can have a rich and intricate weave. Finally, attempts to understand turn taking are becoming increasingly sophisticated. As we shall see shortly, models that link turn taking to other communicative functions may prove robust and valuable.

Topic Management and Exchange

On a broader level, conversations consist of a set of discussions on one or more topics. As with turn taking, we manage topics to some extent through the use of a series of nonverbal cues. Two units of analysis have been defined by researchers to describe the topic structure of conversations. *Episodes* are periods in a conversation when discussion is focused on a particular topic (Scheflen, 1974). Conversations may be made up of many episodes (that is, several topics) or only one. *Positions* are segments of interaction during which a person maintains a fairly consistent disposition toward the topic and other conversants (Scheflen, 1974). Thus positions have to do with the interactant's expressed attitude toward the topic at hand and other interactants. As interest in a given topic wanes or as attitudes about the topic or other interactants change, the position of an interactant changes.

Research has indicated that nonverbal cues are used to signal changes in both position and episode units in conversations. Nonverbal cues serve as *boundary markers* for position and episode units, marking when positions and episodes change in a conversation. Four classes of nonverbal cues function as boundary markers. *Proxemic shifts*—changes in leaning forward or backward and toward or away from other communicators—have been found to be reliable indicators of episode and position changes (Erickson, 1975). *Extrainteractional activities* are behaviors that are not directly part of the stream of communication, such as lighting a cigarette, reaching for a drink, rearranging personal articles (jacket, purse, etc.), or adjusting a cushion (Burgoon & Saine, 1978; Pittenger, Hockett, & Danehy, 1960). If they occurred at any place other than a segment boundary in conversation, these cues might be perceived as indicating low involvement and as inappropriate.

Silences also function to mark episode and position boundaries. Schegloff and Sacks (1973) have shown that silences serve as *topic closings* to indicate that participants are no longer interested in pursuing a given topic for discussion. Silences that occur at boundaries may also allow participants to relax physically and mentally before pursuing the next segment of interaction. Finally, Pittenger et al. (1960) found that certain *paralinguistic cues* mark the boundaries between episodes as well as positions. Sighs, gasps, clearing the throat, and other vocal sounds often mark boundaries. Researchers have suggested that such cues may facilitate changes in speaking style by releasing air from the lungs, relaxing the vocal cords, and thus allowing other vocal parameters such as loudness, pitch, and rate to change. Interactants can "start fresh" in a vocal sense with the next topic.

Research on topic changes has shown that interactants often move from one topic to the next in a rather flowing and effortless way (e.g., Sacks et al., 1974). Planalp and Tracy (1980) investigated perceptions of topic change strategies in a series of studies. They found that participants in the studies could reliably determine when a topic changed in a conversation on the basis of verbal information alone (conversational transcripts). Although these studies did not investigate the topic management role of nonverbal cues in particular, the results raise some interesting issues. If nonverbal cues are not necessary for conversational participants to know when topics change, as the study suggests, what might be the function of nonverbal boundary markers? One possibility is that nonverbal boundary markers provide further clarification that the topic is changing. Another possibility is that by reinforcing a topic change signal, nonverbal boundary markers bolster the perception of skill and competence in managing the conversation. One further possibility (see Woodall, 1984) is that by cuing that the topic is about to change, participants know that the relevant background knowledge required to comprehend the upcoming topic is changing and that they must be on their toes to discern what background knowledge will be pertinent.

Interactants sometimes switch topics without displaying nonverbal boundary markers. However, their absence may cause the other interactants to miss the topic change, to perceive the initiator of the topic change as an incompetent communicator, and to fail to comprehend much of the new topic initially (See Applications, p. 410). We will return to topic management and comprehension in Chapter 14.

There is still a great deal to be learned about how interactants keep on track in conversation. Beyond further work on nonverbal boundary markers, there may also be other nonverbal cues that function to keep interactants on a topic and allow them to extend the topic, return to a previous topic, or quickly refer to a topic in a conversation without really opening it up. Research on these possibilities may help us to understand the topic management process more fully.

Beginnings and Endings: Initiating and Terminating Interaction

The broadest (most macro) level of analysis for conversations focuses on how they begin and end. Initiating and terminating conversations are tasks that we sometimes perform effortlessly and at other times find difficult, uncomfortable, and problematic. As with the other levels of interaction management discussed so far, we prefer to manage this process mostly through nonverbal cues. Imagine having a conversation with a friend who, after a bit of discussion, said, "Well, that is the end of this conversation. I

APPLICATIONS

Staying on Track in Group Discussions

We have all suffered through lengthy group discussions that have wandered endlessly among what seemed to be irrelevant topics. This is an experience to be avoided if at all possible. But working in groups is a fact of life for most people. So how to avoid these experiences? If you are responsible for leading the group discussion, both verbal and nonverbal strategies can be helpful. First, organize the topics that you will lead the group through. Make the topics flow logically so that you and the other group members can follow.

Second, change topics in ways that are clear to the group members. Do so by making explicit or implicit reference to the topic just discussed and provide a bridge to the upcoming topic for the other conversants by making explicit reference to a topic covered earlier in the conversation or indicating to the conversants the nature of the upcoming topic (Planalp & Tracy, 1980). Otherwise, you run the risk of leaving your fellow conversants in the conversational dust. Third, when changing topics, make it clear via nonverbal cues that a topic change is about to occur. Use the boundary markers to signal shifts in topic. Although conversants can detect topic changes without these cues, the cues help them stay on track and preclude confusion. Finally, be sensitive to nonverbal cues that indicate that the group has exhausted a topic. Restlessness, inattentiveness as signaled by low eye contact, and fewer involvement cues (leaning away from the group, for example) indicate that it is time to move on to another topic.

As trainers of group facilitators point out, keeping a group on track is often the main part of the job (see Auvine, Densmore, Extrom, Poole, & Shanklin, 1978). Being sensitive to both verbal and nonverbal cues in topic management is an important part of the facilitation process. To ignore these cues is to run the risk of long, wandering, and ultimately boring meetings. Surely, that is a risk not worth running.

have run out of things to say to you. Good-bye." You would be bewildered by this behavior because the absence of nonverbal cues to signal termination would be very unusual indeed.

Initiation and termination cues are quite important for communicators. Starting a conversation in a smooth and skilled manner gets the rest of the conversation off on the right foot and facilitates effective communication between the interactants. Ending the conversation in a skilled and competent way makes subsequent interactions more likely. Finally, the fact that etiquette authors provide advice on how to start conversations "properly" suggests that people in our culture consider this particular level of conversational management to be important (this is not to say that people generally follow such advice). Let us now take a closer look at initiation and termination.

Initiating Interaction

Although most of us are not usually aware of it, interactants communicate several nonverbal cues before the first "hello" is said. These cues signal awareness of the presence of others and the willingness of people to become involved in conversation. Greeting cues tend to be habitually displayed, so much so that Goffman (1971) refers to them as an "access ritual."

Some researchers, primarily ethologists, have found similarities in some aspects of human and primate greetings that suggest an evolutionary and biological base for such behavior. For example, eye behavior patterns during greetings are similar for adults, infants, children, blind persons, and nonhuman primates (Pitcairn & Eibl-Eibesfeldt, 1976). The eyebrow flash, a quick raising of the eyebrows held for about one-sixth of a second before

Hanging Out Your Tongue As a Do-Not-Disturb Sign

While there are a variety of cues that indicate approachability and a willingness to interact, some indicate just the opposite—in effect saying, "Don't bother me now!" Recent research at the University of Western Australia identified the protruded tongue as a particularly effective cue for this message. Researchers had participants take a test, the last page of which was indecipherable. Participants had to get another copy of the test from a proctor in order to finish. The proctors had headphones on, kept their eyes closed and tried to appear absorbed, either with tongues showing or not. Participants took significantly longer to disturb proctors with their tongues showing than when they weren't.

To make sure that this wasn't just nervous test-taking behavior, the researchers set up another similar experiment, this time using a campus stall selling cacti manned by two salesclerks. The salesclerks read books and pretended to concentrate on their reading, one with the tongue showing and one not. As before, customers approaching the stall were more likely to disturb the salesclerk whose tongue was not showing. While hanging your tongue out may not be the most pleasant or hygienic way to avoid being disturbed, it does appear to be effective.

Source: Adapted from "Mind Openers" by P. McCarthy, January 1988, *Psychology Today, 22,* p. 16.

lowering, is part of greeting behavior among Europeans, Balinese, Papuans, Samoans, South American Indians, and Bushmen (Eibl-Eibesfeldt, 1972).

Kendon and Ferber (1973) noted some common stages that greetings progress through:

1. **Sighting, orientation, and initiation of the approach.** Eye contact and proximity are the nonverbal codes that play the most important role here.

2. **Distant salutation.** The "official ratification" that a greeting sequence has started occurs here. Smiling, waving, and verbal acknowledgment are likely to occur. Two head movements in particular were noted at this stage—the *head toss,* a somewhat rapid back-and-forth motion, and *head lowering,* followed by a slow rise.

3. **Head dip.** This behavior may indicate a shift in activities and/or psychological orientation. In this case, it could signal the change from a nongreeting phase to a greeting phase of behavior.

4. **Approach.** Increased gazing and occasional grooming behaviors were noted as the interactants moved toward each other.

5. **Final approach.** The interactants are within 10 feet of each other at this point in the sequence. Mutual gazing and smiling are the most frequent behaviors observed.

6. **Close salutation.** This is the final phase of greeting where the usual verbal salutations are exchanged. Direct body orientation and stance are assumed by the participants, and handshakes and embraces may occur if appropriate to the situation.

As Kendon and Ferber's stages suggest, a number of nonverbal codes, particularly kinesics, proxemics, and haptics, are involved in greeting sequences. Eye contact is especially important, as being able to see and visually acknowledge someone is an important precursor to interaction.

As similar as the structure and content of greetings are, there are also some systematic differences in the way interactants greet each other. Kendon and Ferber (1973) suggested that greetings between friends differ from those between mere acquaintances. A study by Krivonos and Knapp (1975) identified many of the behaviors observed by Kendon and Ferber. In addition, other emblematic hand gestures, such as the peace sign, thumbs up, and raised fist, were found to occur as part of greeting. However, Krivonos and Knapp failed to find consistent nonverbal differences in the way that acquainted and nonacquainted subjects greet each other.

In a study that followed up on this work, Riggio, Friedman, and DiMatteo (1981) examined the effects of gender, level of acquaintance, and personality factors on greetings. Role-played greetings were videotaped and were then rated by observers for the type of greeting and level of intimacy displayed. Greetings between role-played friends were judged more intimate than greetings between acquaintances. In particular, greetings that employed a higher level of touch (handshakes, hugs, taps on the shoulder or arm) appeared more frequently in role-played friends' interactions. Further, subjects who scored high on measures of nonverbal skills were judged more intimate overall in their greeting displays. The effects for gender were more difficult to interpret, however. Males were more likely to engage in handshakes than females (a finding consistent with previous research), more hugging occurred in opposite-sex pairs, same-sex pairs engaged in more high touch displays, and males tended to initiate greetings more than females. Interestingly, there were no differences in the observers' judgments of intimacy between these gender combinations, despite behavioral differences in the way males and females greeted each other. The researchers suggested that observers may have different perceptions of greetings according to the gender composition of the dyad, clearly an explanation worthy of further investigation. Although more research is needed on the factors that affect greetings, it rings true for most of us that we would greet someone we know well more warmly than someone we have just met. It also makes sense that more skilled communicators would be more expressive in their greeting displays.

In another study, Greenbaum and Rosenfeld (1980) observed the naturally occurring greetings of a sample of airline travelers and their greeters. These researchers were interested in the structure of greetings—the typical sequences of behaviors displayed—and any gender differences in the greetings they observed. They found that certain nonverbal cues occur early in the greeting—the handshake, mutual lip kiss, and face kiss. Hand-to-upper-body behavior occurs at the end of the greeting sequence. Gender differ-

What behaviors comprise this greeting ritual?

ences were also detected, with male-male dyads typically engaging in brief handshakes and female-female dyads and cross-sex dyads displaying longer physical contacts composed of mutual lip kisses, mutual face contacts, embraces, and hand-to-upper-body touches. This evidence suggests certain sequences of behavior in greeting. Similar to the Riggio et al. (1981) study, it also shows a greater degree of touch involved in greetings between females and cross-sex dyads than male-male dyads.

Other factors, such as status and power, may affect style of greeting. Unfortunately, no systematic evidence has yet been gathered in this area. Anecdotes and personal experience do suggest that greetings may vary with power and status. For example, the way you greet your superior at work is probably quite different from the way you greet a family member. In greeting superiors, cultural rules suggest that deference and respect be shown in the style of greeting. By contrast, intimacy and caring are the most likely messages to be expressed in greeting family members. Situational factors, such as a situation's formal or informal quality, are also likely to affect greeting style. The kinds of greetings observed in formal situations are likely restrained in their level of expressiveness, while greetings in informal situations are probably more effusive. In some extremely formal situations, such as greeting the Queen of England, for example, there are very specific rules about the nonverbal mode of greeting, including the use of curtseys and bows.

Terminating Interaction

You have probably found yourself involved in conversations that you wished you could terminate immediately but were unable to. Such situations are instructive in that they tell us several things about terminating conversations. First, terminating a conversation is not as simple as abruptly getting up and saying good-bye. Rather, ending a conversation is a process in and of itself, and although it is not absolutely necessary to end a conversation by going through a terminating sequence, it is clearly desirable, and most people do so most of the time. Second, as we shall see, the termination process is complex, with several goals being accomplished at once. Finally, the probability of future interaction is partly dependent on how well a current conversation is terminated.

In an early and now classic article on terminating interaction, Knapp, Hart, Friedrich, and Shulman (1973) explored both verbal and nonverbal correlates of leave-taking. These researchers devised an experimental situation in which subjects were asked to conduct an information-gathering interview in the shortest time possible. Subjects were further told that they would be paid for performing the interview, that the quicker they finished the interview, the more money they would make, and that under no circumstances should the interview go over 5 minutes. Subjects then conducted interviews with an interviewee who was actually a confederate instructed to prolong the encounter. The interviews were videotaped with the subjects' knowledge. Thus the experimental situation provided for an interaction during which subjects displayed extensive termination cues and were motivated to terminate the conversation as soon as possible.

Knapp et al. (1973) proposed three functions that are accomplished in terminating conversations. First, interactants signal *inaccessibility* by nonverbal and verbal cues, with a preference given to managing termination by nonverbal means. Usually one can tell that an interactant intends to leave a conversation before anything is said about leaving, due to nonverbal cues that indicate that the interactant is no longer available for conversation.

The second function identified by these researchers is the signaling of *supportiveness.* Typically, conversants seem to prefer to leave conversations on a positive note, indicating mutual support, points of agreement, satisfaction with the encounter, and positive anticipation of the next interaction in the future. Both verbal and nonverbal cues are used to reinforce and signal supportiveness to interactants. Other researchers (e.g., McLaughlin, 1984) claim that conversation at all stages may follow a "politeness maxim" that dictates that conversants ought not say anything offensive, vulgar, or rude and that conversational participants should be supportive.

Summarization is the third function accomplished during termination. It has been long suspected that we wish for psychological closure at the end of events, and it appears that conversants attempt to sum up the general themes and contents of conversation at the end. Summarizations may be detailed and specific, as when a group goes over decisions it has made. Summarizations may also be general and symbolic of the content covered, as when two interactants say to each other, "Boy, we sure had a good time," "Yes, we did. Let's do it again sometime."

Knapp et al. (1973) found that the coded verbal and nonverbal cues fit well within these functional categories. The specific nonverbal and verbal termination cues are ranked from most to least frequent in Table 12.1. All these cues, in one way or another, signal inaccessibility, supportiveness, or summarization. Clearly, there are other cues not observed by these researchers that also are used in terminating interaction. Glancing at one's watch is a common terminating cue. In the classroom setting, cues that class is coming to a close include a general shuffling of feet and movement of bodies in the chairs, the most symmetrical possible stacking of books in the absolute center of the desk, and longing looks at both the door and the classroom clock. Of course, skilled teachers know when to acknowledge these cues and when not to.

There have been only a few other investigations of conversational termination. Lockard, Allen, Schiele, and Wiemer (1978) found a number of cues associated with termination, including unequal weight stances, breaking eye contact, and hand gesturing. Summerfield and Lake (1977) observed differences between friends and strangers in leave-taking, with friends looking more at their partners and uttering more words when conversational endings were signaled by a buzzer in the experimental situation. In a more recent study, O'Leary and Gallois (1985) analyzed the final 10 turns of dyadic conversations and compared them to the middle turns in the

**TABLE 12.1 Leave-taking Behaviors in Order of
                Frequency**

Rank	Nonverbal Cues	Verbal Cues
1	Breaking eye contact	Reinforcement
2	Left positioning	Professional inquiry
3	Forward lean	Buffing
4	Nodding behavior	Appreciation
5	Major leg movements	Internal legitimizer
6	Smiling behavior	Tentative
7	Sweeping hand movements	External legitimizer
8	Explosive foot movements	Filling
9	Leveraging	Superlatives
10	Major trunk movements	Reference to other
11	Handshake	Personal inquiry
12	Explosive hand contact	Welfare concern
13	—	Continuance
14	—	Terminating

Source: From "The Rhetoric of Goodbye: Verbal and Nonverbal Correlates of
Human Leave-taking," by M. L. Knapp, R. P. Hart, G. W. Friedrich, & G. M.
Shulman, 1973, *Speech Monographs, 40,* 191.

conversations. A set of nonverbal cues was found to discriminate between
the end and the middle sections of the conversations studied. The researchers found a general increase in nonverbal activity in the end sections, with
increases in mutual smiling, leaning forward, and leveraging by the departing subjects in particular. O'Leary and Gallois also found that conversational closings were slightly different for friends than for strangers. For
friend dyads, mutual looking away and grooming by a departing subject
appeared more often, while for stranger dyads, head nodding by subjects
remaining after the conversation appeared more frequently. Other researchers (Albert & Kessler, 1978; Clark & French, 1981; Schegloff & Sacks,
1973) have examined conversational closings in phone conversations, but
have only investigated the verbal side of the sequences.

We have now covered a variety of work on conversations at different
levels of analysis. Regardless of whether we are concerned with turn taking
or termination, each level of analysis provides us with an interesting and
useful view of conversational management. Still, keep in mind that the
choice of unit and level of analysis is not trivial and ideally should be linked
to a researcher's theoretical point of view and research goals (see Lamb,
Suomi, & Stephenson, 1979, for a review of related issues).

Sequences and Patterns in Conversations

Some of the most intriguing and promising interaction research comes from
recent analyses of the patterns of nonverbal cues observed in conversations.

Researchers are now convinced that such patterns can be linked to a variety of communicative functions. Although research on conversational patterns has accumulated over the past two decades, only recently has there been an attempt to summarize the evidence (for general reviews, see Cappella, 1981, 1983, 1984; Patterson, 1973a, 1976, 1983). This work departs from much of the research we have reviewed in this text on three important points. First, this research looks at the dyad or group as the unit of analysis. As some researchers note (e.g., Millar & Rogers, 1976), research in communication and psychology has too often taken the individual as the unit of analysis and thus failed to observe and measure properties of interpersonal systems and relationships. Research on conversational patterns has avoided this problem by being explicitly interested in what interactants do together as a unit. Second, much of this research is interested in the sequential patterns and properties of communication behavior. We know little about sequences in interaction (Cappella, 1981), and this research attempts to shed some light on them. Third, much though not all of this research focuses on a variety of nonverbal cues across the channels and codes, giving a comprehensive view of the behavioral stream. The historical problem of focusing on a single behavior or code evident in much nonverbal research is thereby avoided.

Several patterns have been observed. One is *reciprocity,* whereby increases or decreases in a given behavior (or set of related behaviors) are met with concomitant, though not necessarily comparable, increases and decreases. For example, if Interactant A leans forward and smiles at Interactant B, and B leans forward and nods in response, a reciprocal pattern has occurred. As a special case of reciprocity, *matching,* occurs when B exhibits the identical behavior as A. For example, when A smiles and leans forward, and B smiles and leans forward as well, matching has occurred. Another possible pattern identified by Cappella is *compensation,* whereby increases or decreases in a given behavior (or set of behaviors) are met with decreases or increases in similar behavior. If A starts talking louder and gazing longer at B, and B responds by looking less and talking softer, a compensatory pattern has occurred. Over time, reciprocity and compensation can lead to *convergence* (increasing similarity in behaviors between A and B) and *divergence* (increasing difference between A and B), respectively, as noted in our earlier discussion of speech accommodation theory. Finally, *synchrony,* which entails the coordination of kinesic behaviors to the vocal-verbal stream, may occur on both microscopic and macroscopic levels.

Let us consider more microscopic patterns first. Probably the smallest micro unit yet employed by nonverbal researchers may be found in the work of W. S. Condon and his associates on synchrony (Condon, 1976; Condon & Ogston, 1966, 1967; Condon & Sander, 1974). These researchers employ high speed film and code body movements frame by frame. Since the film speed used here is usually 30 or 48 frames per second, the behavior is analyzed down to the .02-second level ($\frac{1}{48}$ sec; Condon, 1976). Onset, termination, and changes in direction of a variety of nonverbal behaviors are noted using this technique. At the same time, a phonetic transcription of the co-occurring language is made, and body movements are correlated with these subword sounds. Condon argues that "process units," places in the transcription where a number of nonverbal and verbal cues change simultaneously, emerge from the data. Figure 12.2 gives an example of this kind of microanalysis.

As can be seen, these are very small units of behavior to work with. Use of this technique requires special equipment and extensive amounts of time in coding for even small amounts of interaction. So far, this research has been primarily descriptive. Condon has provided evidence for two subtypes of synchrony: *self-synchrony,* where a speaker's body motion is organized with speech in process units, and *interactional synchrony,* where listeners move in sync with a speaker's speech. Some of this work has shown that neonates synchronize their movements to the mother's voice (Condon & Sander, 1974). Condon suggests that biological factors underlie these levels of synchronization and that synchrony may reflect neurophysiological processes, though there is no direct evidence to support this contention.

Although these patterns present some interesting speculative possibilities, the research on this kind of synchrony is inconclusive. McDowall

FIGURE 12.2 Interactional synchrony: The organization of change of the listener's behavior is entrained with the structure of the speaker's speech. The oscilloscopic display is presented directly above the microanalysis of the listener's behavior.

PRESSURE

Frame nos 3336	37	38	39	40	41	42	43	44	45	46	47	48	49	50
Phonetics	P	P	R e	E	S^v	S^v	S^v r	R	R	R^V	R^V			

LISTENER

Head	Us			Ds		Ls								
R. wrist	AB		Es		H			Fs						
R. thumb	Fs		(F, AD)f		Fs		Es		Ef					
R. index	F		Ff		Es		Ff							
R. finger			F		Es		Ff							
R. hip							F							
L. foot					Fs		Ff							

SPEAKER

Head	ORvs		OR.Us		D.Ls			Us		U				
R. el	E.Ps		E.P		Fs			H		Es				
R. wrist	Fs		F		Es			Evs		Fs				
R. fingers			Fs		Es									
L. hip	Rfs				ROs									

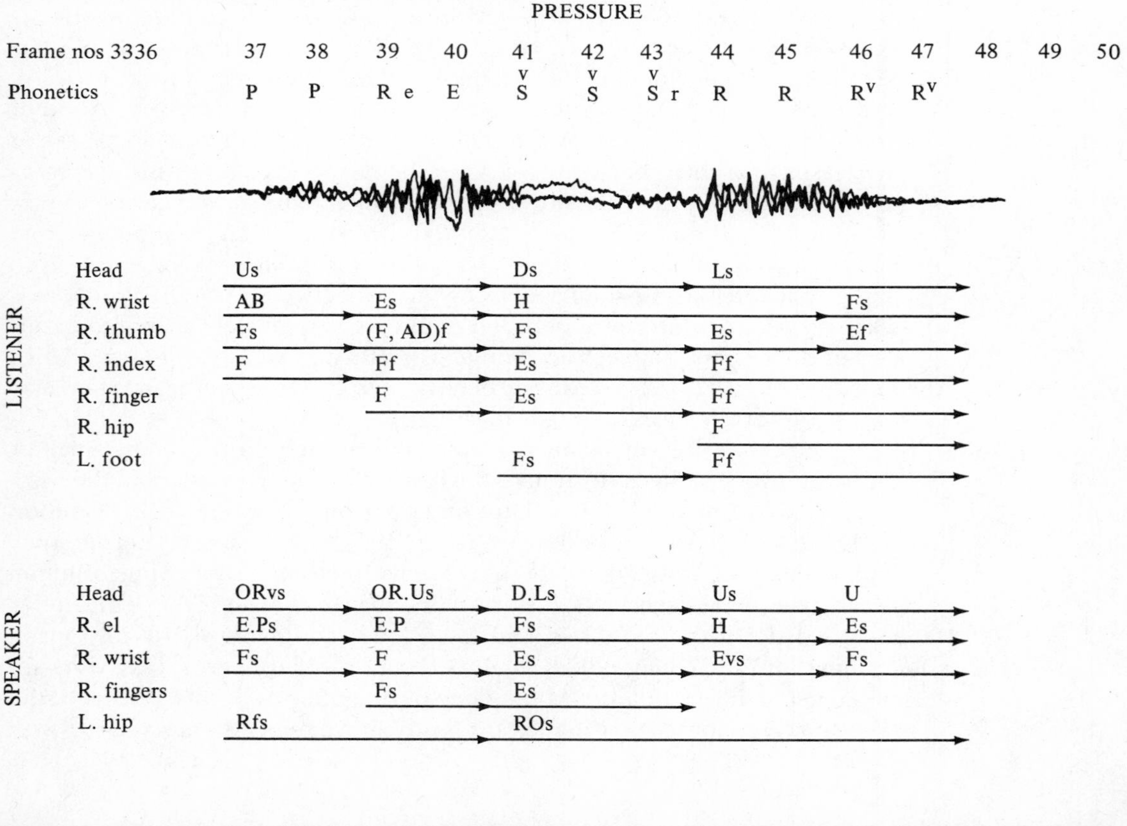

(1978a, 1978b) has made a number of strong criticisms of this research, the most serious of which is that no statistical control for baseline chance has been employed in the studies. In other words, some level of synchrony could occur by chance, and so far no systematic effort has been made to control for that. Cappella (1981) likewise points out that only five studies offer data on these types of synchrony in normal adult interactions and that

> the studies by Condon and Kendon, though claimed to offer support for the movement synchrony hypothesis, cannot be so strongly interpreted. They do offer anecdotal support, but the absence of an expected baseline against which to compare these observations raises questions about their coincidental nature. (Cappella, 1981, p. 119)

Despite some counterarguments raised by other researchers (e.g., Gatewood & Rosenwein, 1981), these criticisms are strong enough to raise some doubt about this kind of synchrony as it has been studied so far.

Research on more macroscopic types of synchrony is more encouraging. Here the attempt has been to assess synchrony by observing body postures and gestures that are matched or mirrored between interactants for some period of time (sometimes also called posture or gesture mirroring or congruence). As we indicated in Chapter 9, this type of synchrony has been linked mostly to rapport as a communication outcome (Charney, 1966; Hinchliffe, Hooper, Roberts, & Vaughan, 1975; LaFrance, 1979; LaFrance & Broadbent, 1976; Trout & Rosenfeld, 1980). In a recent study, LaFrance

An example of mirroring.

and Ickes (1981) investigated the effects of gender and gender typing (whether an interactant was traditional or androgynous in sex-role orientation) on posture mirroring. The results showed that in traditional gender-typed dyads, traditional female dyads showed significantly more posture mirroring than traditional male dyads. In androgynous dyads, however, the opposite was true: Androgynous male dyads showed significantly more posture mirroring than androgynous female dyads. Interestingly, then, gender-role orientation appears to have an effect on posture mirroring.

Matching and reciprocity also occur for a variety of vocal cues. Reciprocity patterns have been found for pausing, switch pauses, latency, vocal intensity, and various measures of verbal productivity such as utterance duration (Cappella & Planalp, 1981; Jaffe & Feldstein, 1970; Matarazzo & Wiens, 1972; Natale, 1975), dialect choice (Giles & Powesland, 1975), speech rate (Putman & Street, 1984; Webb, 1969, 1972), and amplitude (Meltzer, Morris, & Hayes, 1971; Natale, 1975). For in-depth reviews of this literature, see Cappella (1981, 1985) and Feldstein and Welkowitz (1978). In summing up this literature, Cappella (1985) concludes that "in over 33 studies representing some 40 separate subject pools, the overwhelming conclusion is that matching and reciprocity are the predominant forms of mutual influence" (p. 406). Cappella does note that a few studies have turned up evidence suggestive of compensatory patterns in vocal behavior, but further research must confirm such possibilities.

A third area where reciprocity is common is in a person's nonverbal intimacy in response to a partner's verbal intimacy. When one conversant increases self-disclosure or uses more immediate language, the partner may reciprocate with increased proximity and involvement as well as with increased verbal intimacy and immediacy (Firestone, 1977; Hale & Burgoon, 1984).

Finally, research on some nonverbal cues provides evidence for compensatory patterns. Probably the best known of the studies is the Argyle and Dean (1965) investigation of proxemic behavior and other related cues. The researchers posited the equilibrium theory of affiliation, which holds that once interactants have established a baseline of affiliative behaviors, they will adjust the frequency and duration of those behaviors to maintain the established baseline. For example, if a comfortable interaction pattern has been established between two interactants and one interactant starts to look more at the other interactant, the other interactant could be expected to decrease affiliative behavior by looking less, assuming less direct body orientation, and so on to restore the initial level of affiliation. In this particular study, Argyle and Dean varied proximity between interactants and observed the effects on eye contact. The results showed a compensatory response: As proximity increased by one interactant, eye contact of the other interactant decreased. Similar compensation patterns have been found in a wide variety of studies on the response to increased proximity. Reviews of this literature (Cappella, 1985; Hale & Burgoon, 1984; Harper, Wiens, & Matarazzo, 1978; Patterson, 1973a) suggest that increases in proximity cause partners to increase the distance from the interactant who is moving closer, to decrease eye gaze, to become less direct in orientation, and to decrease duration of vocalization. One exception to the general compensatory pattern is that interactants may reciprocate increased proximity and immediacy with shows of increased involvement, such as increased eye contact, nodding, and facial pleasantness while simultaneously compensating with an indirect body orientation (Hale & Burgoon, 1984). There are other exceptions (see Cappella, 1985; Firestone, 1977), but the most common pattern is a compensatory one.

Empirical work on eye contact indicates both compensatory patterns and reciprocal patterns. When the social situation is neutral or positive in affective tone, interactants reciprocate eye contact patterns. When the social situation is negative in affective tone, compensatory patterns are noted (see Cappella, 1985). For example, when you are having a pleasant conversation with friends of yours, you will likely match their eye contact patterns. However, when having a disagreement with your employer, you will likely look less if your boss is looking more.

Finally, there is considerable evidence that these patterns occur early in life. Infants and children of a variety of ages show clear regularity in the patterns of interactions with adults, primarily their caretakers (Bateson, 1975; Gewirtz & Boyd, 1976; Street, 1983). Some researchers, such as Bateson (1975), claim that these patterns are the precursors to adult turn taking. Infants and caretakers have been shown to have reciprocal patterns for vocalization length and voice pitch (Gewirtz & Boyd, 1976; Webster, Steinhardt, & Senter, 1972). Infants appear to use gaze as a way either to escape social interaction (compensatory pattern) or to increase social interaction (reciprocal pattern) (Als, Tronick, & Brazelton, 1979; Stern, 1971). Evidence for synchrony in overall level of involvement (a variety of behaviors indicating involvement) between infants and adults has been found by Als et al. (1979) and Brazelton, Tronick, Adamson, Als, and Wise (1975). These studies have shown that adults and infants cycle through periods of high and low involvement in interaction over time. For example, when adults are prompted to act unresponsively, infants increase their actions to obtain a response. As Cappella (1985) notes, the evidence on infant-adult patterns is remarkable and raises interesting questions about the interplay of innate, cognitive, and learning factors. The patterns of interaction and social competencies based on them that we employ as adults may be a function of both nature and nurture.

Continued investigation of conversational management patterns has practical as well as scientific implications. Such research may give us greater insight into long-term relationships, the role that communication patterns may play in keeping those relationships together, and what can be done when those relationships begin to come apart. Certainly, the divorce rate in our culture is an indication of how badly we need to understand such things. The research may also shed light on the nature of superior-subordinate relationships and the patterns that make those relationships functional and useful or dysfunctional. On an even more general level, such research could highlight the various conversational management skills and competencies that makes a good communicator or that would improve communication effectiveness. In other words, this research may affect many areas of everyday life.

Summary

Conversational behavior can be analyzed at several different levels. At each level, nonverbal cues play a vital role in the management process. At the turn level, a wide range of nonverbal cues facilitate the turn exchange process by allowing speakers to suppress or yield turns and listeners to request turns, deny turns, or give backchannel feedback. There are several models of the turn exchange process that have been proposed, the most promising of which is the resource model.

On the topic level, proxemic shifts, extrainteractional activities, silences, and paralinguistic cues are used to signal changes in topic in conversations. This is important not only in terms of conversants' ability to comprehend new topic information, but also in terms of the perceived communication skill of conversants.

On the conversation level, nonverbal cues are also instrumental in initiating and terminating interactions. Coupled with verbal behaviors, the nonverbal behaviors signal approachability during greetings and signal supportiveness and inaccessibility during departures.

Finally, recent work on patterns and sequences in conversations has uncovered reciprocal and compensatory patterns, various types of synchrony, and convergent and divergent patterns. Considerable evidence indicates that people match each other's postures and gestures, voice and speech patterns, and levels of involvement but may compensate for levels of proximity or immediacy that are uncomfortable. There is also some evidence that adults and infants synchronize their kinesic behaviors with their own verbal-vocal stream and that of other interactants. The patterns of convergence and divergence have long-term implications for successful human relationships.

Suggested Readings

Cappella, J. N. (1985). Controlling the floor in conversation. In A. W. Siegman & S. Feldstein (Eds.), *Multichannel integrations of nonverbal behavior* (pp. 69–104). Hillsdale, NJ: Erlbaum.

Duncan, S.D., Jr. (1975). Interaction units during speaking turns in dyadic, face-to-face conversations. In A. Kendon, R. M. Harris, & M. R. Key (Eds.), *Organization of behavior in face-to-face interaction* (pp. 199–213). The Hague: Mouton.

Jaffe, J., & Feldstein, S. (1970). *Rhythms of dialogue.* Orlando, FL: Academic Press.

Kendon, A. (1967). Some functions of gaze-direction in social interaction. *Acta Psychologica, 26,* 22–63.

Kennedy, C. W., & Camden, C. (1983). Interruptions and nonverbal gender differences. *Journal of Nonverbal Behavior, 8,* 91–108.

Knapp, M. L., Hart, R. P., Friedrich, G. W., & Schulman, G. M. (1973). The rhetoric of goodbye: Verbal and nonverbal correlates of human leave-taking. *Speech Monographs, 40,* 182–198.

Walker, M. B., & Trimboli, C. (1984). The role of nonverbal signals in coordinating speaking turns. *Journal of Language and Social Psychology, 3,* 257–272.

Wiemann, J. M. (1985). Power, status, and dominance: Interpersonal control and regulation in conversation. In R. L. Street, Jr., & J. N. Cappella (Eds.), *Sequence and pattern in communicative behaviour* (pp. 85–102). London: Edward Arnold.

CHAPTER 13

Social Influence
and Facilitation

> All of us, apparently, are constantly trying to influence
> the people around us by means of sounds and
> movements we are unconscious of making.
> Correspondingly, all of us make some unconscious use
> of the cues presented to us by the people around us.
>
> J. V. McConnell, L. Cutler, & B. McNeil

> You can persuade a man only insofar as you can talk his
> language by speech, gesture, tonality, order, image,
> idea, identifying your way with his.
>
> Kenneth Burke

In this chapter, we shall consider how nonverbal communication is employed to influence others. We have already discussed how nonverbal cues are used to shape impressions, create false beliefs, and structure and manage conversations. Now we shall explore how people actively select their nonverbal communication to modify what others think and do.

Social influence has interested students of human communication for millennia. Aristotle was one of the earliest to write about how humans influence one another. Our own century has witnessed great interest in social influence reflected in the large amount of time, effort, and resources devoted to its study (Insko, 1967; Miller & Burgoon, 1978; Roloff & Miller, 1980). A good deal of this interest has been stimulated by the often notorious success of current and past social influence attempts:

Item: During World War II, an unimpressive man of diminutive stature was able to move the German populace to commit atrocities so horrible that many Germans later denied knowledge of or responsibility for them. The man who wielded such enormous influence—Adolf Hitler.

Item: During the Korean and Vietnam wars, hard-nosed, well-trained military men who became prisoners of war were coerced into renouncing their country and espousing the philosophical tenets of a foreign government. These changes in behavior and attitude were not a charade put on for the benefit of their captors. Prisoners, once released, often retained the views acquired during brainwashing.

Item: Jim Jones, a self-proclaimed prophet of God, convinced a group of average Americans to follow him into the jungles of Guyana. There he controlled every aspect of their psychological, social, and physical lives until finally, under the threat of invasion by outsiders, he ordered them to commit mass suicide. They complied and died.

Item: In the past two decades, a number of religious cults have arisen in the United States. Followers of such leaders as the Reverend Sun Myung Moon and the Bhagwan Maharishi live in abject poverty while raising millions of dollars for their leaders through menial jobs. The psychological and social changes the cults bring are so striking that relatives of cult members have hired agents to kidnap and "deprogram" them.

In all these cases, certain psychological and physiological factors, as well as verbal strategies, enabled the leaders to garner great power and achieve mass conversions. But also playing a significant role were the nonverbal strategies and tactics that these manipulators used to advance and reinforce their control. It is to such nonverbal strategies and tactics that this chapter is devoted.

Nature of Social Influence

Definitions and Assumptions

Social influence is defined as one person's actions causing changes in another's thoughts and behaviors that would not have occurred in the absence of the actor's behaviors or maintaining the target's way of thinking and behaving in the face of influence attempts from another source. From a communication standpoint, we are most interested in the actor's communication behaviors and how those either change or reinforce a target's way of thinking and behaving.

This definition contains several important assumptions. First, social influence is motivated behavior. The actor desires something from the target that would not occur if the communication did not take place. These desires may be cast as motivations. Three are particularly important in the social influence process. *Instrumental objectives* are the specific changes or lack of changes desired by the communicator. *Interpersonal objectives* concern the establishment and maintenance of a particular interpersonal relationship.

Gestures, facial expressions, and posture are important elements in persuasive messages.

Identity objectives relate to the image projected by the influencer, such as credibility, dominance, expertise, and composure. These three motives are present in all social influence attempts, but each fluctuates in importance, at times competing, at other times complementing, and at still other times being irrelevant to one another. An influencer's nonverbal and verbal communication is a product of how he or she reconciles the three motives (Clark, 1984; Clark & Delia, 1979; O'Keefe & Delia, 1982).

Strategic Behavior and Strategy Selection

Another important assumption is that communication designed to influence is strategic: It is intentionally and purposely encoded (Edinger & Patterson, 1983; Patterson, 1983). The influencer (a) appraises the situation in which the influence attempt will occur, assessing important roles, norms, motives, and target characteristics, (b) develops a communication plan to achieve the desired outcome, (c) considers a diverse, differentiated repertoire of messages, (d) chooses a particular message and forgoes others, (e) monitors the success of this message, and (f) selects subsequent messages from the repertoire in response to the target's reactions and consistent with the situational appraisal and communication plan. Seibold, Cantrill, and Meyers (1985) have labeled this the "strategic choice model" of social influence.

One critical distinction in this process is between communication plans and communication messages. A communication plan represents the influencer's general *communication strategy* and is closely allied with motives (O'Keefe & Delia, 1982; Schenck-Hamlin, Wiseman, & Georgacarakos, 1982; Seibold et al., 1985). For instance, an actor may desire to secure a small loan from a friend (the instrumental motive). At the same time, he or she wants to maintain the friendship by not offending the partner (the interpersonal motive). The interaction between these two motives results in a communication strategy: to secure the loan while maintaining the friendship. With this strategy in mind, the influencer enacts a particular message or *communication tactic:* The influencer verbally requests the loan while encoding nonverbal cues signaling high affiliation and immediacy, such as eye contact, forward lean, and positive facial expressions.

Although social influence is a deliberate process, every move is not consciously premeditated or enacted. Communicators tend to be more cognizant of their general goals and strategies than their specific tactics for achieving them. Hence routinely enacted influence patterns may be intentional but occur at a low level of awareness.

Our approach to social influence also assumes that communicator and situational characteristics affect the selection and success of influence messages. The nonverbal expectancy violations theory, introduced in Chapter 7, illustrates how communicator reward frequently determines the success of nonverbal communication. The authority, dominance, status, and expertise of a source are likely to determine whether the target will comply with nonverbal influence messages, and the management of these images depends on the careful, deliberate display of nonverbal cues. Along with a source's image, the relationship between influencer and target can affect selection and consequences. Frequently, nonverbal cues during influence messages are designed to signal attraction, establish a relationship, or indicate the current nature of the relationship (e.g., touching someone when asking for his or her help). Co-occurring nonverbal and verbal appeals depend on the relationship for their impact.

Power Bases

One particularly important relationship characteristic is the power that the communicator wields over the target. *Power* is a relationally determined potential to influence another person that rests on the relevancy of a communicator's resources and actions to the target. As this relevancy increases, the likelihood of influence increases (Tedeschi & Bonoma, 1972). For instance, a manager has the ability to determine raises and promotions for her staff. This ability may make her more powerful and her messages more influential with staff members who value the raises and promotions. However, she may have a staff member who is soon to retire and is satisfied with remaining at his current pay and rank until retirement. Because the manager's ability to determine raises and promotions is no longer relevant to this staff member, her influence messages may be less successful.

French and Raven (1959) identified five bases of power dependent on the relationship between influencer and target. *Reward power* is the ability to provide rewards that the target finds attractive. *Coercive power* involves providing punishments that the target finds unattractive. *Expertise power* is based on the knowledge ascribed to the influencer relative to the amount of knowledge the target possesses and the amount of knowledge required in the situation. *Legitimate power* is conferred by an entity outside the relationship between the influencer and target, such as a school or corporation, and resides within prescribed roles like teacher, manager, president, and priest. *Referent power* derives from the target's attraction to the influencer and desire to be similar to the influencer. A common type of referent power is charisma.

To this point, we have focused on the communicator who is attempting social influence; however, keep in mind that social influence is a two-way process. The target also enters the influence situation with instrumental, interpersonal, and identity motivations that must be reconciled in the target's decision to change or maintain behavior in response to influence messages (O'Keefe & Delia, 1982). Forsyth (1987) points out that the outcome of a social influence attempt rests ultimately with the target, and sometimes the target's act of compliance or noncompliance is a social influence attempt in its own right.

Compresence

Although targets may show some natural resistance to influence attempts, there is reason to believe that a competing predisposition toward being influenced is also operative. Researchers have uncovered a phenomenon called *compresence,* which indicates that the mere presence of another individual in the environment is arousing and can alter our behavior (Borden, 1980; Cottrell, 1972; Geen, 1980; Sanders, 1981; Zajonc, 1965, 1980). We are highly attentive to the presence of others and perform differently on tasks when spectators, coactors, or audiences are present compared to when we are alone. Because the mere presence of another in our environment is a socially meaningful event (Horn, 1974; Zajonc, 1980), our heightened awareness and orienting toward others may predispose us to being receptive to stimuli from them and ultimately to being influenced by them. One reason for this attentiveness to other humans is that the social actions of another person are less regular, systematic, and predictable than the actions of physical stimuli. Thus some measure of alertness is required when another person is present, and this sensitivity prepares a communicator to respond to the other's actions. This alertness response may in fact have given rise to our social norm of attention. Ignoring another person in our vicinity is considered socially inappropriate and can cause that person to withdraw, speak less, and rate the ignoring source unfavorably (Geller, Goodstein, Silver, & Sternberg, 1974). The most important implication of this compresence phenomenon is that both actor and target are attuned to each other's presence, and this may open up the opportunity for mutual influence.

We will examine in detail the ways in which nonverbal cues are selected to achieve social influence. We will focus on nonverbal strategies and tactics used (a) to project an image of authority, power, and credibility, (b) to signal intimacy, (c) to manipulate attractiveness, (d) to evoke matching, modeling, and compensation, (e) to signal interpersonal expectations, (f) to violate nonverbal expectations so as to distract targets, and (g) to reinforce, reward, and punish another's behaviors.

Nonverbal Strategies and Tactics

Authority, Expertise, Dominance, and Status Appeals

Perhaps the most pervasive strategies for influencing the thoughts, behaviors, and communication of others are those that rely on establishing an image of authority, expertise, or power. As we discussed in Chapter 7, a major function of communication is to project an image that is favorable. Frequently, the self-presentation is not the end goal but is rather a means to the end of influencing others. Thus nonverbal patterns that foster a successful impression of power and credibility not only increase others' attraction, liking, and evaluations of us; they may also make others more receptive or susceptible to our influence. In analyzing how history's more notorious manipulators have come to power, one must give partial credit to their use of nonverbal messages of authority, dominance, power, or credibility. Let us examine some of the nonverbal strategies and tactics that doubtless contributed to their success.

Among the most immediate and potent cues are visible symbols of status and authority such as uniforms, personal artifacts, and environmental trappings. Their potency resides partly in serving as an ever-present status reminder during the course of an encounter and partly in the meanings we have come to associate with them.

Uniforms denote status and control of resources. They signal the ability to reward and bestow favors or to punish and take away valued commodities. Because the headwaiter in a restaurant controls whether we have a table by the window or by the kitchen, we become deferent and ingratiating. Because judges and police officers have the potential to levy severe penalties, we often become tense in their presence, acting as if we had just been caught with our hand in the cookie jar. Their clothing cues these responses, because we are conditioned to react to symbols of authority as clear markers of another's legitimate power and control.

Research demonstrates just how conditioned we are. In a landmark series of studies, Stanley Milgram explored how far people would go in obeying authority figures. His interest was prompted by trying to understand what mentality might lead people to commit the kinds of inhuman, heinous acts that the Germans committed under Hitler. Milgram (1963,

1974) devised an experiment in which one subject, assigned the role of teacher, was asked to administer increasing intensities of electrical shocks to another subject, given the role of learner, whenever the learner gave wrong answers. In actuality, the learner was a confederate who did not really receive any shocks. Amazingly, the majority (65%) of teacher subjects continued to deliver shocks far past the danger level as long as the uniformed experimenter told them to do so—despite sometimes hearing the learner groan and plead for the shocks to stop before eventually lapsing into silence and despite being told that the subject had a heart condition. Although Milgram was not directly testing the effects of clothing or artifactual symbols, it is clear that the white lab coat and the trappings of the Yale University research laboratory where the experiments took place contributed to the subjects' blind obedience to these outrageous requests and to their willingness to disavow responsibility for their actions.

More direct evidence of the role of uniforms comes from a series of clever field experiments by Bickman (1971a, 1974a, 1974b). He dressed male accomplices in civilian clothes (sport coat and tie), a milkman's uniform, or a nondescript guard's uniform (consisting of a jacket and pants similar to a policeman's but with a different badge and insignia and no gun). The accomplice then approached passersby on a Brooklyn street and made one of three requests to see if uniforms would affect people's compliance. The first asked people to pick up a small paper bag lying on the ground. If a person refused, the accomplice repeated the request and gave as justification that he had a bad back. In the second request, the accomplice pointed to a person standing by a parked car and said, "This fellow is overparked at the meter but doesn't have any change. Give him a dime!" If the subject didn't comply, the accomplice said he didn't have any change himself. In the third request, he told people standing at a bus stop that the Bus Stop—No Standing sign meant they couldn't stand there and had to move to the other side of the sign. If they refused to move, he told them it was a new law and the bus would not stop where they were standing. With all three requests, people were far more willing to comply when the request came from the uniformed guard than from the civilian or the milkman: 36% obeyed the guard, 20% obeyed the civilian, and 14% obeyed the milkman. In a later study that again asked pedestrians to give a dime for an expired parking meter, 83% obeyed the requester when dressed as a guard, while only 46% obeyed when he was dressed as a civilian or a milkman, regardless of whether or not the requester watched to see that the respondent obeyed.

In another set of experiments, Bickman (1971b, 1974a) explored whether the social status implied by one's attire and personal possessions would affect people's honesty in complying with a request. He went to airport and train terminals and dressed his three male and three female accomplices in high status clothing—suits and ties for men, dresses and a dress coat for women—or low status clothing—working clothes and a lunch pail for men, inexpensive, unkempt skirts and blouses for women. The accomplices first placed a dime in an obvious place in a phone booth, waited for the next user of the phone to exit, and then approached, saying, "Excuse me, I think I might have left a dime in this phone booth a few minutes ago. Did you find it?'' Regardless of the subject's age, race, sex, or status, far more people returned the money when the request came from a high status person (77% complied) than from a low status person (38% complied).

Follow-up research using questionnaires (Bickman, 1974a) showed that most people report that they would not be influenced by the status of a person's dress or the presence of a uniform when responding to a trivial request. That is, they claim they would not respond to illegitimate requests just because the person was wearing authoritative clothing.

These combined results reveal that despite what people claim they would do, most people are highly susceptible to influence when it is accompanied by clothing and artifactual symbols of authority and status. The potency of such nonverbal cues is especially apparent when compared with their absence. The striking contrast effect is evident in Alexander Solzhenitsyn's (1973) chilling account of the ruthless treatment given Russian prisoners en route to prison camps during the 1940s:

> "On your knees!" "Strip!" In these statutory orders of the convoy lay the basic power one could not argue with. After all, a naked person loses his self-assurance. He cannot straighten up proudly and speak as an equal to people who are still clothed. . . . Naked prisoners approach, carrying their possessions and the clothes they've taken off. A mass of armed soldiers surrounds them. It doesn't look as though they are going to be led to a prisoner transport but as though they are going to be shot immediately or put to death in a gas chamber—and in that mood a person ceases to concern himself with his possessions. The convoy does everything with intentional brusqueness, rudely, sharply, not speaking one word in an ordinary human voice. After all, the purpose is to terrify and dishearten. (p. 570)

The latter part of the Solzhenitsyn excerpt highlights another nonverbal tactic for conveying power and authority—the use of a harsh, dictatorial vocal tone. Although the "voice of authority" has not been studied directly, it appears that "confident" voices evoke more compliance from others. Recall from Chapter 7 that the confident voice has greater energy and loudness, faster tempo, fewer and shorter pauses, higher and more varied pitch, more expressiveness, and greater fluency, and is perceived as more businesslike, professional, and impersonal (Scherer, London, & Wolf, 1973). Such vocal patterns have proved to be persuasive in public and interpersonal contexts. Others appear under Applications, p. 432.

A number of other kinesic and proxemic behaviors identified as persuasive by Mehrabian and Williams (1969) are ones that are typically used by dominant or high status people and hence should qualify as authority, dominance, or status appeals. Speakers attempting to be persuasive (a) make more eye contact with their listeners, (b) gesture more, (c) use more affirmative nods, (d) are more facially expressive, (e) engage in fewer self-manipulations, and (f) lean backward less. Females also exhibit less head and trunk swiveling. The first five cues are the same ones exhibited by

APPLICATIONS

Persuading Others Through Vocal Cues

In a series of studies on the nonverbal cues speakers employ when attempting to be persuasive and the cues that audience members rate as persuasive, Mehrabian and Williams (1969) constructed a very detailed profile of persuasive nonverbal behaviors. In the first experiment, subjects gave a persuasive speech on one topic, a fairly neutral speech on a second topic, and a completely neutral speech on a third. Trained judges identified the nonverbal behaviors exhibited. Untrained subjects were then asked to rate how persuasive they found the messages to be. In the second experiment, subjects gave either a persuasive talk or an informative talk while being exposed to positive or negative audience feedback. In the final experiment, specific nonverbal cues were manipulated and observers again rated their persuasiveness. Out of these experiments came four vocal cues that are both encoded and decoded as persuasive: faster tempo, louder amplitude, more intonation, and greater fluency.

Other research comparing speeches delivered at slow, moderate, and fast speeds finds that faster speaking is rated as more knowledgeable and is typically more persuasive (Miller, Maruyama, Beaber, & Valone, 1976), although some studies show no effect (Gunderson & Hopper, 1976; Wheeless, 1971; Woodall & Burgoon, 1983). One possibility is that the relationship may be curvilinear such that moderately rapid tempo is most effective, while extremely slow or rapid tempo becomes counterproductive (Apple, Streeter, & Krauss, 1979; Bettinghaus & Cody, 1987). This would be consistent with the findings for credibility, discussed in Chapter 7. The interpretation given to the behavior may also make a difference. Buller and Aune (1988a) found that good decoders prefer a faster rate, see it as more immediate and intimate, and are more willing to comply with fast-paced requests. By contrast, poor decoders prefer the slower rate, see it as more intimate and immediate, and are more likely to comply with such a request. Because good decoders also speak faster themselves, whereas poor decoders speak slower, Buller and Aune concluded that a speech accommodation effect is at work—people prefer speech tempos most like their own and attribute more positive qualities to such rates.

Studies of legal presentations and job interviews confirm the beneficial effects of loudness and fluency. They reveal that louder, more fluent voices are more persuasive and earn more favorable employment decisions (Erickson, Lind, Johnson, & O'Barr, 1978; Hollandsworth, Kazelskis, Stevens, & Dressel, 1979). Research specifically on nonfluencies (sentence corrections, slips of the tongue, repetitions, vocalized pauses, and stutters) indicates that

Persuading Others Through Vocal Cues (*Continued*)

nonfluent speech results in lower ratings of a speaker's competence (McCroskey & Mehrley, 1969; Miller & Hewgill, 1964; Sereno & Hawkins, 1967) and that this reduction in credibility often but not always translates into being less persuasive. In public speaking studies, McCroskey and Mehrley (1969) and Birk, Pfau, and Burgoon (1988) found that nonfluent speakers produced less attitude change and were rated as less persuasive than a fluent speaker, but Giesen (1973) and Sereno and Hawkins (1967) failed to find any differences.

speakers who are perceived as persuasive, with the greater use of gaze being especially persuasive for females when speaking from a far distance. Speakers are also seen as more persuasive if they adopt closer distances to their audience, are moderately relaxed (with females being slightly more tense than males), and for male speakers, adopt an indirect body orientation. Finally, greater perceived persuasiveness is correlated with more dominance behaviors, a finding that reinforces the dominant or authoritative nature of these nonverbal patterns.

Birk et al. (1988) confirmed many of these findings in a study of student public speakers who were evaluated by their classmates on their performance and whose nonverbal behaviors were coded by trained judges. These researchers found that persuasiveness increases the more a speaker shows expressiveness and immediacy, that is, engages in more eye contact, exhibits more facial pleasantness, uses more illustrator gestures and fewer adaptor gestures, and engages in less backward lean.

In yet another series of studies, Maslow, Yoselson, and London (1971) and Timney and London (1973) found similar results when comparing confident to doubtful speaking styles. In the first experiment, the experimenters paid an actor to use a confident, neutral, or doubtful communication style while miming a prerecorded tape of a legal argument. Students viewing the presentation rated the confident style—which consisted of rhythmic, forceful gestures, continuous eye contact (with the camera), and a relaxed posture—as more persuasive than the doubtful style. The doubtful style included fidgeting with a piece of paper, twirling a pencil, bringing the hand to the mouth, pulling at the shirt collar, avoiding eye contact, and sitting in a tense, erect posture. In the second experiment, subjects played jurors and tried to persuade one another about the correct verdict. In this case, only eye contact distinguished successful from unsuccessful persuaders—those who actually were the more persuasive used more eye contact. The failure of other behaviors to make a difference across participants was probably due to the fact that everyone was trying to be persuasive.

Other research specifically on gaze further demonstrates that longer gazes and greater amount of gaze time promote more attitude change and improve the overall effectiveness of a persuasive presentation, if the position advocated is not opposed to the listener's views (Edinger & Patterson, 1983; Giesen, 1973; Scherer, 1978). Moreover, gaze has been shown to be a powerful influence on other people's willingness to help someone or to comply with a request.

The kinesic and proxemic cues that are associated with persuasion are summarized by Bettinghaus and Cody (1987), who conclude that

> there are a number of nonverbal behaviors that are *consistently* related to enhanced performance ratings in both public speaking and interview contexts: It is to the speaker's advantage to maintain eye contact, to nod, to smile, to illustrate, to avoid being too relaxed, and to refrain from using distracting adaptors. (p. 124)

These and the vocalic cues associated with persuasiveness are summarized in Table 13.1.

Finally, unidirectional (nonreciprocal) touch is a status and dominance cue that can be used to reinforce the influence of its user. As we shall see shortly, it is a very effective means of eliciting behavioral change from others.

Character, Sociability, Composure, and Dynamism Appeals

Akin to authority and competence appeals are persuasive messages related to the other four dimensions of credibility. It has been a long-standing assumption in communication that higher credibility leads to more attitude change and compliance. Psychologists likewise see credibility perceptions of nonverbal behaviors as an important mediator of social influence (Edinger & Patterson, 1983). Yet increased credibility does not guarantee that persuasion and compliance will follow. What conclusions can we draw?

One is that overall strong delivery, coupled with strong arguments, is effective in changing attitudes. If a speaker has a weak message to begin with, delivery will make no difference, but if the verbal part of a message is sound, a strong nonverbal presentation will produce more attitude change than a weak one. Moreover, if both visual and vocal delivery are weak, the effect is particularly detrimental. Good delivery also produces higher credibility ratings, providing some support for the linking of credibility and persuasion (see McCroskey, 1972; Rosnow & Robinson, 1967).

The question is, what constitutes good delivery? Much of it is what has been described as the confident speaking style—vocal variety, fluency, good use of gestures, and eye contact. However, depending on what vocal, kinesic, and proxemic cues are combined, it is possible to create several alternative "good" delivery styles. Experiments contrasting conversational with dynamic delivery style (Pearce & Brommel, 1972; Pearce & Conklin, 1971) discussed in Chapter 7 did just that. Recall that in the conversational speech version, the delivery was calm, slow, nonintense, consistent, deep-pitched, and soft. In the dynamic version, it was rapid, louder, higher pitched, and more varied. While the conversational style earned higher ratings of trustworthiness, honesty, sociability, likableness, and professionalism, the two

TABLE 13.1 Summary of Nonverbal Persuasive Behaviors

Cues Encoded As Persuasive	Cues Decoded As Persuasive	Cues Actually Achieving Persuasiveness	Cues Confirmed As Credible
Vocalics			
greater fluency	greater fluency	greater fluency[a]	yes
faster tempo	faster tempo	faster tempo[a]	yes
more variety/ intonation	more variety/ intonation	more variety/ intonation[a]	yes
louder/more intense	louder	louder[a]	yes
	greater vocal pleasantness		yes
		strong delivery greater gaze[b]	yes
Kinesics			
greater gaze	greater gaze (especially females)		yes
more nodding	more nodding	more nodding	
more facial activity	more facial pleasantness/ex-pressiveness		
less trunk swivel by females			
moderate relaxation	moderate relaxation		
		open body position	yes
more gesturing	more gesturing rhythmic gestures		
more self-adaptors[c]	fewer self- and object adaptors		
Proxemics and Haptics			
more immediacy	more immediacy/ affiliation	yes	
	closer distance/ distance violations[a]	closer and farther/distance violation[a]	yes
	indirect body orientation by males	indirect body orientation by males	
less backward lean			
		use of brief touch	

[a]Especially if speaker has high reward value.
[b]May backfire if speech is counterattitudinal.
[c]Only when audience is receptive.

styles by themselves did not differ in their effects on attitude change. Only when they were coupled with a high credibility introduction for the speaker did delivery make a difference: A highly credible speaker using a dynamic style was most persuasive, while a low credibility speaker using a dynamic style was least persuasive (Pearce & Brommel, 1972). These combined findings suggest that a conversational style may be more appealing and effective if we are held in moderate or low esteem by our audience. If we are held in high esteem, we are better off using a dynamic style.

Other vocal research also demonstrates the preferability of using a more dynamic, expressive (i.e., louder, faster, more varied) speaking style, as do the kinesic findings that more gesturing and facial animation contribute to greater persuasiveness. The experiment by Birk et al. (1988), one of the few to combine several vocal and kinesic behaviors in the same study and to test simultaneously their relationship to credibility and persuasion, confirms the link from kinesic expressiveness to credibility and perceived persuasiveness. Not only did greater expressiveness and immediacy increase persuasiveness, it also led to higher ratings on character, dynamism, and sociability. However, the study failed to find effects for tempo and loudness. Only vocal fluency and vocal pleasantness affected rated persuasiveness, and these voice qualities produced higher credibility ratings on composure and sociability (see Table 13.1).

Thus the verdict is out on how dynamic and forceful a speaker should be. It may depend on whether the speaker is held in high esteem by the audience. It may also be more effective to be kinesically dynamic than to be vocally forceful. Or it may be that a certain degree of animation and energy is desirable but being too assertive vocally and kinesically is not. Perhaps more important ultimately than dynamism is the overall fluency and coordination of the presentation. Greater fluency contributes to intended, perceived, and actual persuasiveness.

Creating an Intimate Relationship

Another major strategy for achieving influence is to use nonverbal messages to foster a more affiliative or intimate relationship and to draw on this as the basis for inducing changes in attitudes, behaviors, and communication patterns.

One of the difficulties in determining what behaviors serve the function of establishing intimacy is that many behaviors designated as immediacy and affiliation cues also have alternative meanings. For example, eye gaze may be interpreted as an affiliation or submission cue when used by and among women but as a threat or dominance cue when used by and among men (Burgoon, Coker, & Coker, 1986; Valentine & Ehrlichman, 1979). Hence many of the nonverbal behaviors discussed in this section may in fact gain their efficacy not because they are establishing intimacy, as we are inferring, but because they are expressing dominance, credibility, or all three. We have chosen to identify them as intimacy signals, first, because they are the cues most commonly cited as promoting intimacy and, second, because the subjects or the experimenters in many of these studies have given intimacy interpretations.

Billy Sunday, a famous evangelist in the first part of the twentieth century, relied on dynamic gestures, posture, and movement to make his messages more forceful. Many evangelists today continue this preaching style.

The primary behaviors that might serve as fostering intimacy and that have been studied for their ability to change attitudes and behaviors are the following immediacy and affiliation behaviors: gaze, proximity, touch, lean or orientation, posture, facial expressiveness (including nods and smiles), gestures, and vocal intonation. We consider each in turn.

Gaze. We have already noted that increased gaze is effective in increasing attitude change and perceived persuasiveness if the position one is advocating is agreeable to the subject. When the position advocated is counter to the audience's attitudes, use of too much gaze may backfire (Giesen, 1973). When gaze is coupled with other affiliative cues such as close proximity, forward lean, direct body orientation, and more gesturing, it not only promotes perceptions of persuasiveness, friendliness, and intimacy, but it also increases a job applicant's chances of being offered a job (Burgoon, Manusov, Mineo, & Hale, 1985; Forbes & Jackson, 1980; Imada & Hakel, 1977; LaCrosse, 1975; Washburn & Hakel, 1973).

One of the more interesting effects of prolonged gaze is on others' willingness to help. Several studies have explored whether staring at another person increases or decreases the likelihood of that person's offering assistance. In one experiment, a confederate carrying a cumbersome shopping bag dropped a stack of papers, apparently by accident. Regardless of whether the stare was straight or broken and accompanied by a smile or not, fewer passersby offered to help pick up the papers when they were stared at than when they were not. In a similar experiment, subjects working on a puzzle in the room with the researcher were more reluctant to help the researcher on a subsequent computer problem if he or she had stared at them (Horn, 1974).

Although these studies suggest that prolonged gaze may be an aversive behavior that is read as hostile or threatening, other research suggests that it may sometimes elicit approach. Ellsworth and Langer (1976) used the same bystander intervention technique, this time with a person in distress whose plight (a medical problem) and remedy were sometimes clear, sometimes not. When the nature of the problem and solution were clear, a stare increased the probability of a bystander's offering help. Gaze sometimes increases the probability that people will return dimes left in a phone booth (Kleinke, 1977). Making eye contact also increases helping when a falling confederate trips in front of a person rather than behind the person (Shotland & Johnson, 1978). Moreover, Kleinke (1980) found that staring produces greater compliance with a request than nonstaring when the request is legitimate. Kleinke sometimes coupled the gaze with touch to produce a high intimacy situation and found that males comply more with a high intimacy approach than with a low intimacy (no gaze or touch) approach. However, with an illegitimate request, low intimacy is the more successful approach. Kleinke surmises that gaze avoidance when making an illegitimate request may win sympathy from others by appearing tactful, embarrassed, or humble.

The gender of a potential helper also makes a difference. In female-female pairs, people offer more help in picking up dropped coins when eye contact is made, but in male-male pairs, they offer more help when there is no eye contact (Valentine & Ehrlichman, 1979). Also, eye contact with a brief hesitation increases willingness to help a female but decreases it for a male (Geller & Malia, 1981). Gaze may be a nonspecific activator whose interpretation and effects depend on the context (Ellsworth & Langer, 1976; Kleinke, 1977). Under some circumstances, prolonged gaze may serve as an affiliative cue in the form of a plea for help, while in other cases it may be seen as overly forward or aggressive behavior.

A final way in which gaze facilitates influence is in altering other people's communication behavior—again, with gender differences. Direct gaze by a partner causes women to make more intimate, self-disclosive statements but causes men to become less intimate, even though they think they have become more so. Conversely, gaze aversion reduces females' level of verbal intimacy and increases males' disclosiveness (Ellsworth & Ross, 1975).

Proximity and Touch. Like gaze, proximity and touch can have positive or negative consequences. In terms of persuading people, audiences pay more attention to a speaker who stands at intermediate distances but are more persuaded by the speech the farther away the speaker sits. At close and far distances, audiences focus more on the speaker's appearance (Albert & Dabbs, 1970); that is, they are distracted from the content of the speech. However, when it comes to persuading someone to hire you, we have already seen that close proximity is the best strategy, partly because it is among a set of behaviors conveying greater warmth and enthusiasm (Imada & Hakel, 1977).

Distancing and touch also affect helping behavior and compliance. In a series of four field experiments, Konečni, Libuser, Morton, and Ebbesen (1975) tested the effects of invading or not invading the personal space of pedestrians waiting at crosswalks on their willingness to return a lost object. They found not only that personal space violations prompt people to cross the intersection faster—an indication that a violation is arousing and/or threatening—but also that they reduce helping behavior, especially if the violation is prolonged and the lost object to be returned is of little value (e.g., a pencil as opposed to a set of keys). Greatest helping occurred at an intermediate distance (5 ft) and was considerably lower at very close and very far distances. Smith and Knowles (1979) pursued these findings in two additional field experiments using a modified version of the pedestrian violation format. In one version, the violator either had a plausible explanation for the violation (carrying an open sketch pad with a partially completed sketch of the intersection) or no apparent explanation for the proximity (the sketch pad being held closed at the side). A noninvading confederate who was the one in need of help was also present half the time. In the second experiment, subjects were asked to complete a questionnaire following the encounter. Results showed that when there is no apparent justification for the invasion, pedestrians cross the street faster, regard the invasion as inappropriate, and are less willing to return a dropped pen to either the invader or the noninvading bystander than when the invader has a reason for being close by or when no invasion occurs. These conditions, involving violations by strangers, conform to the nonverbal expectancy violations model, which predicts that violations by nonrewarding others produce more negative consequences than nonviolations.

Other studies in what could be considered high reward conditions present opposite results. Baron and Bell (1976), who originally set out to substantiate further that proximity reduces helping behavior, found instead that experimenters approaching diners in a cafeteria obtained greater willingness to help with a research project when the experimenters approached

Part of a minister's ability to influence stems from his interpersonal relationships with church members. Making physical contact helps establish those relationships.

them at a 1½-foot distance than a 3-foot distance. A follow-up study showed that closer distance communicates a greater need for help and greater friendliness, a conclusion consistent with our inference that gaze and proximity may appeal to basic interpersonal affiliation motives. A subsequent study by Baron (1978) further demonstrated, as Kleinke (1980) also found, that the close approach worked only when the request was legitimate; with a nonlegitimate request, a far distance was preferable.

In sum, close proximity may reduce persuasion, helping, and compliance when the communicator is nonrewarding, makes an illegitimate request, or distracts the receiver but may increase helping and compliance otherwise. Touch most often elicits helping and compliance.

Finally, the effects of proximity on communication behavior are mixed. Some research finds that subjects write more intimate disclosures for a surveyor standing 1 foot away rather than 2 feet away (Cozby, 1974). Other research finds that physical closeness has a dampening affect on the amount

APPLICATIONS

Touch and Helping Behavior

Touching typically increases helping and compliance. Kleinke (1977), in his study of people's willingness to return dimes, found that people returned them more often when they were touched briefly than when they were not. Patterson, Powell, and Lenihan (1986) also found that a light touch to the shoulder increased people's willingness to assist with scoring inventories, especially when the request was made by a female of a female. Willis and Hamm (1980) likewise found that a brief touch increased compliance, regardless of whether the request was easy to fulfill (sign a petition) or difficult (complete a questionnaire). Finally, Paulsell and Goldman (1984) discovered a slight sex difference: Males increased their helping behavior if touched, no matter where they were touched (shoulder, upper arm, lower arm, or hand); women were especially likely to increase assistance when touched on the lower or upper arm. Only one study (Stockwell & Dye, 1980) failed to find an effect for touch. Conclusion: Touching helps.

and nature of intimate verbal behavior (Dietch & House, 1975; Greenberg, 1976; Sundstrom, 1975). Intermediate distances may be best: Unacquainted dyads divulge more intimate information, descriptively and qualitatively, at 4 feet than at either 2 or 16 feet (Morton, 1974).

Body Lean, Body Orientation, and Posture. As we have seen, more forward lean and more direct body orientation, as part of a set of affiliative cues, are associated with greater persuasiveness (LaCrosse, 1975). Body posture may function in the same way. One study found that an open body position, in which limbs are turned outward from the trunk, engenders more attitude change, is evaluated more positively, and is seen as more active than a closed position (McGinley, LeFevre, & McGinley, 1975). However, when the target holds attitudes similar to those advocated by the communicator, a closed position may be preferable (McGinley, McGinley & Nicholas, 1978).

Another way in which body position influences others is in affecting their communication style. When an interviewer uses forward body lean, the interviewee displays expressive behaviors, speech patterns, and emotional reactions indicative of rapport (Bond & Shiraishi, 1974).

Facial, Gestural, and Vocal Expressiveness. As with other affiliative cues, more smiling, nodding, and gesturing are associated with greater persuasiveness and with greater success as a job applicant (Edinger & Patterson, 1983; Forbes & Jackson, 1980; LaCrosse, 1975; Maslow et al., 1971; Timney & London, 1973). Thus greater expressiveness and pleasantness seem to facilitate influence.

Attractiveness Appeals

Another relationship-enhancing strategy that may allow a communicator to gain influence is to maximize one's attractiveness to the target. Although physical attractiveness does not invariably override other message elements such as arguments or credibility (Chaiken, Eagly, Sejwacz, Gregory, & Christensen, 1978; Maddux & Rogers, 1980; Mills & Aronson, 1965), there is evidence that being physically attractive can help one's case.

Consider a few experiments that have confirmed this. In one set of experiments, a woman gives the same speech to two different audiences, altering only her appearance. For one audience, she is made to look unattractive with messy hair, oily skin, no makeup, a faint mustache, and loose, ill-fitting clothing. For the other audience, she has clean, neat hair, makeup, and fashionable clothing. When she makes clear her intent to persuade, the attractive speaker is somewhat more persuasive with her male audience than when she is unattractive or does not explicitly attempt to persuade (Mills & Aronson, 1965). In another type of study, a group of students deliver persuasive messages to passersby on campus, asking them to complete an attitude survey and sign a petition banning meat at lunch and dinner on campus. Canvassers independently judged more attractive have greater success in getting their petitions signed and also obtain more attitude agreement on the survey (Chaiken, 1979). A later version of this study finds that the persuasiveness of the communicator is complicated by the sex composition of the dyad (communicator and target) and anticipated future interactions. In a third variation, the same written speech, which is either supported by evidence or not, is attributed to an attractive male undergraduate or an unattractive but expert middle-aged professor. Whereas the professor is more persuasive when using evidence than when not, the attractive undergraduate is equally persuasive with the female audience with or without evidence, demonstrating that physical attractiveness alone is sufficient to gain influence and that other message variables such as arguments are primarily relevant when influence is based on expertise rather than attractiveness (Norman, 1976). Other studies using photographs of the supposed author of a persuasive message similarly have found that more attractive communicators obtain more opinion change (Horai, Naccari, & Fatoullah, 1974; Snyder & Rothbart, 1971). One study with children also shows that attractive children are more influential with their peers (Dion & Stein, 1978).

These sample experiments affirm that attractiveness can significantly affect people's susceptibility to influence. Why does it work? Bettinghaus and Cody (1987) offer this answer:

> While credibility causes attitude change primarily because of the apparent validity of the recommended position and the evidence presented, attitude change produced by an attractive source is caused, apparently, by our desire to identify with and be liked by good-looking persons. . . . Attractive sources influence us because of their attractiveness, not because of message content. That is, since we

Here is the same communicator made to look attractive and unattractive. Do you think you would be more influenced by the attractive or unattractive appearance?

identify with, and desire approval from, attractive sources, we respond to *them,* not the messages. (p. 95)

This concept of identification may help to explain some other seemingly contradictory findings regarding the effect of clothing and appearance on compliance. Numerous studies find that conventionally attired and well-groomed communicators are more successful in getting others to sign petitions, to accept political literature, to make change, or to pick them up when hitchhiking than if they are wearing unconventional or "hippie" attire such as bell-bottoms, bandannas, sandals, and shoulder-length hair (Bickman, 1971b; Crassweller, Gordon, & Tedford, 1972; Darley & Cooper, 1972; Keasy & Tomlinson-Keasy, 1973; MacNeil & Wilson, 1972; Raymond & Unger, 1972). For example, in one experiment, shoppers were less likely to accept a campaign leaflet from hippie-looking students, more likely to throw it in the trash if they did accept one, and more likely to regard the candidate as radical than when the campaigners were conventionally dressed. This led to the Clean for Gene movement in which college students campaigning for Senator Eugene McCarthy in the 1968 presidential primary dressed conventionally rather than in "hippie" attire (Darley & Cooper, 1972).

Yet other research finds that similarity of dress between actor and target is more persuasive. For example, Hensley (1981) found that a well-dressed solicitor gained more compliance at an airport but less compliance at a bus stop than a more casually dressed solicitor. The hypothesis is that people whose dress is more similar to their targets or is more conventional will receive more compliance and less aggression because of the reinforcing nature of similarity (Harris et al., 1983; Hensley, 1981). Thus if one identifies with a similarly dressed rather than a more formally dressed person, the similarly dressed communicator should be more influential.

Another factor is self-presentation. One study reports that people are less willing to seek help from an attractive as opposed to an unattractive source unless it is a female seeking help from an attractive male (Nadler, Shapira, & Ben-Itzhak, 1982). The researchers argue that people's concern with their self-presentation affects their behavior, and they are willing to appear needy only when they are anonymous, expect no future interaction, or recognize the helper's role as one of providing assistance. If concern about presenting oneself in the most favorable way affects willingness to seek help from attractive others, it may also affect willingness to comply with requests for help from attractive requesters. It is possible that the desire to win the approval of attractive others may lead to greater willingness to comply with their requests.

Another consideration is the juxtaposition of expectations set up by appearance and one's actual behavior. Cooper, Darley, and Henderson (1974) report that householders interviewed on a tax issue by hippie-looking students became more favorable toward the position they advocated and toward college students in general as compared to when they were interviewed by straight-looking students. The explanation offered is that appearance led them to expect to dislike the student and that listening to a disliked other created dissonance, causing them to change their attitude toward the other. An experiment by McPeek and Edwards (1975) similarly suggests that an unconventional appearance can sometimes produce positive results. They had a communicator dressed either as a seminarian or a hippie deliver a pro-marijuana or anti-marijuana speech. The long-haired, unconventional speaker was more persuasive than the conservative-looking seminarian when speaking against marijuana, no doubt because his appearance set up negative expectations that were positively violated by his atypical message. These findings indicate that more attractive or conventional appearance is not always the best strategy, particularly when appearance can be used strategically in setting up violations of expectations. We will return to the violations strategy shortly.

One additional consideration in how attractiveness facilitates influence is that attractive people may alter other elements of their communication style so that appearance alone does not account for their success. Singer

(1964) hypothesized that attractive women would earn better grades than less attractive women. He had male undergraduates rate photographs of 192 freshman women on physical attractiveness and then compared the ratings to the grades the women received. Consistent with his hypothesis, more attractive women received higher grades, but only if they were first-borns. Observations and interviews revealed that these women were more likely to talk to their male professors after class, make appointments with them, and sit in the front of the room—in other words, to be more manipulative. A follow-up study (Singer & Lamb, 1966) confirmed that firstborn women are more concerned with their appearance, more accurate in describing themselves, and more likely to distort their own measurements toward the ideal when they think no one will verify their answers. The petition-signing study by Chaiken (1979) found that the more attractive solicitors were judged as friendlier, talked somewhat faster, and were more fluent. Dion and Stein (1978) likewise found that attractive children were not only more successful than unattractive children in influencing their peers but that they also used different interaction styles. It is likely, therefore, that attractive communicators have an overall communication style that effuses confidence and charisma, which further reinforces the effect of their physical attractiveness. To understand fully the role of attractiveness must ultimately take into account the whole person—static appearance and attire cues, and more dynamic elements of demeanor.

Reciprocity, Compensation, and Modeling

In Chapters 9 and 12, we discussed the presence of relational patterns in nonverbal communication. Two prevalent patterns are reciprocity and compensation. Reciprocity occurs when one communicator exhibits behavior similar, though not necessarily identical, to that of the other communicator in the relationship. In contrast, compensation involves one communicator encoding a pattern of nonverbal cues that is opposite to the pattern exhibited by the relational partner. Communicators at times strategically rely on these patterns to influence the behavior of others (Edinger & Patterson, 1983).

Three recent experiments suggest that communicators choose to reciprocate or compensate expected nonverbal patterns from interaction partners in an effort to change the targets' undesirable nonverbal communication and to reward desirable nonverbal communication. Coutts, Schneider, and Montgomery (1980) manipulated expectations about an interaction partner by having her agree or disagree with the subject's opinions in an initial interaction. In a subsequent interaction, the partner either increased her immediacy (by increasing gaze and adopting a more direct body orientation) or did not change her level of immediacy. Subjects displayed a reciprocal immediacy pattern when the confederate initially disagreed with them, increasing their own immediacy when the confederate increased immediacy. Reciprocity, though, was not accompanied by favorable impressions of the confederate. Coutts et al. speculate that reciprocity may have been used as a reward for the unexpected increase in immediacy by the disagreeable partner or as a signal that her higher involvement was a more appropriate level of involvement.

Ickes, Patterson, Rajecki, and Tanford (1982) conducted two experiments in which prior to interacting with a partner, subjects were told to expect the partner to be either friendly or unfriendly (Experiment 1) and similar in personality and pleasant to talk with or dissimilar and unpleasant (Experiment 2). In the first experiment, communicators who expected a friendly interaction style displayed a reciprocal pattern by sitting closer and initiating communication more frequently. In contrast, communicators expecting an unfriendly style displayed a compensatory pattern of greater positive affect, immediacy, and nonverbal involvement. However, compensating communicators retained an unfavorable impression of the partner, suggesting that compensation was not indicative of liking or attraction but was designed to influence the partner's expected style of behavior. The second study provided similar results. Communicators who expected a dissimilar and unpleasant partner encoded a compensatory nonverbal pattern of greater involvement—greater facial pleasantness, gaze, and talking time and a more direct body orientation. Again, compensation was an attempt to influence the partner's behavior and not a result of liking or attraction, since compensating communicators rated the partner unfavorably.

Ickes et al. (1982) conclude that encoding compensatory patterns is a social influence tactic that relies on the assumption that others will reciprocate the compensatory nonverbal patterns:

> Compensation occurs when the perceiver (1) views the target's anticipated behavior as undesirable, but (2) believes that it is modifiable via the norm of reciprocity, and (3) is aware of and willing and able to display a contrasting pattern of behavior that, if reciprocated by the target, would render the target's behavior more desirable. (p. 163).

Thus reciprocity may be used to reward desired behaviors, whereas compensation may be used to induce the target to match the communicator's own behavior pattern.

A special case of reciprocity occurs when a communicator models or attempts to model the behavior of another communicator. Modeling is an important form of learning, especially among young children. A number of experiments have produced evidence that children and adults adopt behaviors they see modeled (Bandura, 1965, 1977). Children who watched an adult display aggressive behavior toward a doll later exhibited the same behavior in free play and were more violent than children who did not witness the model's behavior. In another study, Zimmerman and Brody (1975) showed that black and white children who observed a black child and a white child interacting on film adopted the interaction style they saw. When they observed the models interacting in a warm fashion, the children played closer together, faced each other more directly, and engaged in more eye contact than after the children observed the models interacting in a cold manner.

Modeling may also operate among older children and adults in novel situations and situations characterized by uncertainty. In such situations, communicators may look to the behavior of others for examples of appropriate behavior. For example, a new employee may observe and attempt to emulate the expressive behavior of a senior employee in a task situation. A new student may model the physical appearance behaviors of established students to conform to the norms of the university context. An unsuccessful suitor may model the nonverbal style of a more successful friend. Modeling is more likely to occur when either the model or the observer is reinforced for using the modeled behavior or when the model is highly regarded (Bandura, 1977; Tan, 1986). Hence favorable communicator image should increase the success of modeling, and unfavorable communicator image should decrease its success.

Modeling as a response also may manipulate behavior. Bates (1973) found that children who modeled the behavior of male college students attempting to teach basketball moves received more positive verbal and nonverbal responses than children instructed not to model the college students' behavior. Modeling, then, may be selected as a method of flattery and a way to obtain approval from others.

Signaling Expectations

A fourth relationally based social influence tactic is the use of nonverbal communication to signal interpersonal expectations. Communicators enter every interaction with expectancies about the partner's personality, attitudes, and behavior. These expectations shape the messages that are encoded and interpretation of the partner's messages. Expectations about strangers are based largely on stereotypes associated with the impressions we form about them. As stereotypes, they are oversimplified and overgeneralized (Snyder, Tanke, & Berscheid, 1977). When relationships develop, expectations become more elaborate and specific to the relational partner and continue to exert considerable influence on message selection and interpretation.

From a social influence perspective, an important result of holding expectations about another person is that expectations can cause a communicator to select verbal and nonverbal messages that covertly signal the expectations they hold. Moreover, behaviors that signal expectations often cause the target's behaviors to conform with the source's expectations. This form of influence has been labeled the *self-fulfilling prophecy* phenomenon (Merton, 1948; Rosenthal, 1981; Snyder et al., 1977; Word, Zana, & Cooper, 1974). An interesting characteristic of this form of influence is that the communicator is often not aware of doing it. Evidence for the effect of expectancies can be traced back to 1911 to the remarkable feats of Clever Hans, a horse that could spell, read, and solve mathematical problems simply by tapping out the answers with his hoof. A committee even certified that Hans received no clues from his questioners. However, a man named Pfungst was able to demonstrate that Hans was using minute head and eye movements from the questioners as cues. When a question was posed, the questioner looked at Hans's hoof, since that was where the answer would appear. When Hans approached the correct answer, the questioner would inadvertently move his head or eyes upward or simply flare his nostrils. This was all Hans needed to know to stop tapping (Pfungst, 1911). The scientific community did not recognize until the 1960s that the same thing was happening between people.

Robert Rosenthal (1976, 1985; Rosenthal & Jacobson, 1968) has conducted an extended analysis of the ways in which people signal expectations to others. He has been particularly interested in how teachers, clinicians, supervisors, and employers communicate performance expectations that influence the actual performance of students, clients, subordinates, and employees. He has also examined the ways in which experimenters signal expectations about the outcomes of their experiments to experimental subjects. His research has shown that nonverbal cues play an enormous role in signaling interpersonal expectations, often within the first 30 seconds of an interaction. At the macro level, relaxed, interested, enthusiastic, friendly, and dominant nonverbal presentations show greater expectancy effects (Rosenthal, 1976). At the micro level, kinesic cues related to leg movement and head cues are important for signaling expectations. Rosenthal (1976) has shown that experimenters frequently use smiling, head nodding, and facial expressions of happiness and interest to provide positive reinforcement to their subjects. Experimenters also negatively reinforce subjects by shaking the head, raising the eyebrows, looking surprised, looking disappointed, and tapping a pencil. Paralinguistic cues also signal expectations (Rosenthal, 1981). For instance, Duncan and Rosenthal (1968) conducted a person perception experiment in which subjects were given a series of photographs of people and asked to judge whether they were successful or unsuccessful. If an experimenter emphasized the success ratings using vocal and visual cues when instructing subjects, subjects rated people in the photographs as more successful. If, however, an experimenter emphasized the failure alternative, subjects rated the people in the photographs as less successful. Similar effects were found by Duncan, Rosenberg, and Finkelstein (1969) and Scherer, Rosenthal, and Koivumaki (1972); however, in the latter experiment, expectancy effects reversed following a second expectancy manipulation. Scherer et al. speculated that subjects may have recognized the vocal emphasis in the second manipulation as an attempt to manipulate them and became more resistant.

More recently, Sullins, Friedman, and Harris (1985) found that expressiveness and self-monitoring (the ability to monitor one's own behavior) moderate the communication of expectancies. In their experiment, teachers who were more expressive but low self-monitors were most likely to communicate performance expectations to their students. By contrast, teachers who were more expressive and high self-monitors were least likely to communicate performance expectations. It appears that high self-monitoring teachers controlled their nonverbal display to guard against communicating expectations to their students. In fact, these teachers actually may have

Signaling Expectancies in the Courtroom

[Covert cues] have a strong impact in key relationships such as those between judge and jury, physician and patient, or teacher and student.

Indeed, the tacit communication of expectations between one person and another are found, in many cases, to make all the difference between success or failure in various kinds of endeavors.

How a judge gives his instructions to a jury was perceived to double the likelihood that the jury would deliver a verdict of guilty or not guilty—even when on the surface the judge's demeanor seemed perfectly impartial. . . .

[A] judicial study, reported in . . . The Stanford Law Review is believed to be one of the first scientific tests of the courtroom lore that the judge's attitudes, even if never openly expressed, are often crucial to a trial's outcome. One striking finding concerned trials in which the judge knew that the defendant had a record of previous felonies, a fact that a jury, by law, is not allowed to know unless the defendant takes the stand. When the judges were aware of past felonies, the Stanford study found, their final instructions to juries were lacking in warmth, tolerance, patience and competence. . . .

"Judges can't come out and say 'This defendant is guilty,'" said Peter Blanck, who did the study. "But they may say it subtly, nonverbally—even if that message is inadvertent." . . .

[Blanck] said he believed that most of the biasing elements he found in his research were unintended. He sees his study as a first step in helping judges to neutralize their hidden messages, as well as, one day, providing lawyers with a new basis for challenging verdicts.

"If judges became sensitized to the problem, they could learn to be more impartial in their demeanor," Dr. Blanck said.

Source: From "Studies Point to Power of Nonverbal Signals" by D. Goleman, *New York Times*, April 8, 1986, pp. C1, C6.

overcompensated by being more positive with students they expected to perform poorly and slightly less positive with those they expected to perform well.

The influence of interpersonal expectations has also been investigated in social interactions. Mark Snyder (Snyder & Swann, 1978; Snyder et al., 1977) explains the self-fulfilling effect of social stereotypes as a process whereby stereotypes channel the communicator's behaviors in the interaction in ways that cause the target's behavior to confirm the stereotypes.

Snyder argues that expectations create predictions or hypotheses about the target's future behavior that communicators set out to test via their own verbal and nonverbal messages. Communicators' hypothesis-testing messages signal their expectations and must be dealt with by the target. Frequently, the target's method of dealing with the messages is to present behaviors that confirm the communicators' original expectations. Behavioral confirmation then leads the communicators to conclude that their initial expectations were correct. For example, say a person named Bob has a problem with his class schedule at State U. and must see the assistant registrar to clear it up. Recently, a friend, Sally, has interacted with the assistant registrar and tells Bob that the assistant registrar is aloof and did not seem concerned with her problem (in our terms, nonimmediate). Armed with these expectations, Bob enters the assistant registrar's office and adopts a very nonimmediate nonverbal pattern—indirect body orientation, backward lean, little smiling, and less eye contact. The assistant registrar responds to Bob's nonimmediate pattern by being nonimmediate and uninvolved in return. Bob leaves the interaction satisfied that Sally had been correct: The assistant registrar is an uncaring, unfeeling bureaucrat. Bob's fundamental error is his failure to recognize that the registrar's nonimmediacy cues were a response to his own nonverbal message, not a signal of the assistant registrar's indifference.

Snyder's research empirically demonstrates this process. He found that men who thought they were talking with attractive women in phone conversations were more sociable, sexually warm, interesting, independent, bold, outgoing, humorous, obvious, socially adept, attractive, confident, and animated than men who believed they were talking with less attractive women. Further, women in the high attractiveness condition were themselves more sociable, poised, humorous, and adept than women in the low attractiveness condition, regardless of their actual attractiveness (Snyder et al., 1977). In a second experiment, Snyder and Swann (1978) manipulated their subjects' expectations that the interaction partner would be hostile or nonhostile. Subjects who expected the partner to be hostile were more hostile themselves in the application of a noise weapon than subjects who expected the partner to be nonhostile. Moreover, subjects' hostility begot hostility by the partner, thereby confirming the subjects' expectations.

From a similar perspective, Word et al. (1974) reasoned that interracial attitudes and expectations would cause white interviewers to be less immediate with black interviewees, which would in turn produce less immediacy by black interviewees. As predicted, white interviewers were less immediate with black interviewees than white interviewees, and black interviewees were less immediate when a white interviewer was less immediate than when a white interviewer was more immediate. These data, however, should be viewed with caution, since these two findings were derived in separate experiments. That is, the reduction in black interviewees' immediacy was observed in response to experimental manipulation of interviewers' level of immediacy rather than the natural reduction in immediacy observed among interviewers interacting with black and white applicants.

Expectancy Violations and Distraction

As discussed in Chapter 7, a consideration in maximizing one's self-presentation is whether or not to conform to expectations. Just as nonverbal expectancy violations may sometimes increase the communicator's perceived attractiveness and credibility, they may also sometimes improve a communicator's chances of being persuasive, getting hired for a job, obtaining assistance, or altering someone else's communication style.

Recall that the nonverbal expectancy violations model holds that people develop expectations about the nonverbal behaviors of others; that violations of those expectations arouse and distract, shifting attention toward the communicator and relationship characteristics; and that the labeling of a violation as negative or positive depends on (a) the reward value of the communicator, (b) the direction and magnitude of the violation, and (c) the interpretation and evaluation given the violation act itself. Negative violations should hinder attitude change, compliance, helping behavior, and other forms of influence, while a positive violation should facilitate these kinds of communication outcomes.

In the first study to test the effect of distance violations on persuasion, Burgoon, Stacks, and Burch (1982) had three-person groups deliberate a murder trial. Subjects interacted with two confederates presenting opposite sides of the case. The confederates were either highly rewarding—both with a prestigious major, previous jury experience, interest in the task, well-groomed appearance and attractive—or nonrewarding—undeclared major, no previous experience, disinterest in the task, and physically unattractive. In each threesome, one confederate moved in very close or moved much farther away after the discussion had started, while the other confederate remained stationary. Results showed that subjects were more likely to accept the position advocated by the high reward discussants and to rate them as persuasive when they engaged in a violation, especially a far violation, than when they conformed to the originally established, normative distance. Violators were also more persuasive than equally rewarding nonviolators. In other words, a communicator was better off engaging in a violation, both compared to himself or herself when following the norm and to another equally rewarding person who conformed to distance expectations. By contrast, violations did not have much impact on actual message acceptance for low reward confederates, but such discussants were seen as less persuasive when they violated distance norms than when they conformed. They were also seen as less persuasive than nondeviating confederates. These results show that violations for a high reward person may gain ground absolutely and relative to other communicators present who do not violate. The converse is true for low reward communicators.

A second series of studies by Burgoon and Aho (1982) considered whether distance violations affect a salesperson's communication behavior and willingness to comply with a simple request (to use a telephone). Student experimenters approached salespeople and asked for help with a purchase or interviewed them about consumer behavior. When the experimenters were rewarding (e.g., interested in purchasing a big-ticket item, dressed more formally and attractively, or verbally indicated their expertise), salespeople were much more helpful and willing to comply with the phone request, showed greater interest in the experimenter, smiled more, talked more, and spent more time with the customer than when experimenters were nonrewarding (e.g., interested in a low priced purchase, dressed as if lower in status, or lacked expertise). Distance violations also induced salespeople to show more interest and talk louder with high reward experimenters. When the violator was low in reward value, salespeople talked less, spoke louder, and showed more tension as the experimenter moved farther away. Finally, distance violations produced evidence of arousal in the targets, who also appeared more distracted. These arousal and distraction effects were consistent with the predictions of the model.

Many of the earlier experiments that found distance adjustments to affect persuasion and helping behavior can also be interpreted as fitting a violations model. In the cases where the violator was a stranger or there was no apparent explanation for a violation, it can be assumed that such encounters qualified as nonrewarding. Hence one would predict, based on the theory, that distance violations such as invasions of personal space should produce less helping behavior or persuasion. Conversely, when the violation could be justified or seen as rewarding (e.g., by giving positive feedback or behaving enthusiastically), greater helpfulness and persuasiveness should have occurred. That is exactly what was found in the experiments by Baron (1978), Baron and Bell (1976), Imada and Hakel (1977), Konečni et al. (1975), and Smith and Knowles (1979).

Violations of proxemic expectations alone may be sufficient to improve persuasive success by increasing the arousal experienced by the target (Patterson, 1983). In a study by Buller (1987), confederates adopted either close, normative, or far distances when requesting that subjects sign a petition. Close distances produced the most compliance with the request, whereas compliance decreased in the normative and far conditions. This effect of close distances occurred even though the rewarding nature of the confederates was not manipulated. Buller concluded that violations of proxemic expectations that signal increased involvement arouse targets, who decide to comply with the request to reduce this arousal.

Three recent studies (Burgoon et al., 1986; Burgoon et al., 1985; Manusov, 1984) tested the effects of gaze violations on willingness to hire a job applicant. One experiment (Burgoon et al., 1985) found that nearly continuous or normal gaze produced the greatest likelihood of being endorsed for the job, while gaze aversion lowered one's prospects. The two other studies failed to find any effects on hiring likelihood. However, if the findings on attraction and credibility are considered, it appears that gaze aversion is a negative violation, regardless of who commits it, while high degrees of gaze may serve as a positive violation for some communicators. This conclusion is necessarily tentative until more research is completed.

Another nonverbal behavior tested within a violations framework is vocal patterns. Buller and Burgoon (1986) compared pleasant, normal, and hostile voices for their effects on compliance with a request for research participation. Although the reward level of the communicators was not effectively tested, the nonverbal sensitivity of the targets determined which voice produced the most and least compliance. Good decoders complied most with the pleasant voice and least with the hostile voice. This might be interpreted as the pleasant voice serving as a positive violation and the hostile voice as a negative violation. However, poor decoders did just the opposite, complying most with the hostile voice. Speculatively, the poor decoders may have found the positive voice overly friendly and a negative violation for them, while the hostile voice may have been more to their liking. However, the ratings of the voices themselves suggest that only the hostile voice qualified as a violation. Hence it is unclear at this stage whether vocal violations follow the model's predictions; however, the fact that vocal changes produced similar differences in targets' compliance in an earlier study by Hall (1980) implies that vocal violations may prove useful in social influence attempts.

Finally, the research on dress reveals that deviant dress can sometimes be successful in achieving influence *if* it is coupled with something else that serves as a positive violation. For example, if a nonconformist appearance sets up a negative expectation, a well-presented verbal message or an unexpected message position may serve as a positive violation, thereby enhancing persuasiveness. When there is no contrasting positive information, deviant dress most often produces less compliance and helping behavior than conformist dress.

In sum, although research on the effects of expectancy violations is just beginning, it reveals that popular advice to conform to norms may be poor advice. Under the right circumstances, violations may enhance influence. Moreover, violations may be important to the social influence process because they may determine on which messages targets focus their attention. Violations can shift a receiver's attention from the verbal message to communicator characteristics and to the relationship between communicator and target (Buller, 1986). Attention to the source or relationship increases the effect of appeals based on the source's image of authority, dominance, expertise, composure, and attractiveness and the nature and quality of the source-target relationship. Hence not only do nonverbal cues send messages about the communicator's image, the relationship between the communicator and target, and the communicator's positive and negative reactions to the target's behaviors, but nonverbal cues in one channel can also call attention to and increase the impact of messages in other nonverbal channels.

The importance of the instrumental task or topic of communication to the target may interfere with the ability of nonverbal cues to capture and control the target's attention. Stiff (1986) reported that when the topic of

454 Chapter 13 Social Influence and Facilitation

a persuasive speech is very salient, the target attends more closely to the central appeal, i.e., the verbal message, and devotes very little attention to what Stiff labels peripheral cues, which include nonverbal cues. Conversely, when the topic is not very important, the target's attention is free to focus on the peripheral cues. Thus an untested conclusion from Stiff's data is that changes in nonverbal behavior are more likely to draw the target's attention to the source's image and the relationship between source and target when the topic or instrumental task is unimportant than when they are very important to the target.

Use of Reinforcement, Reward, and Punishment

Nonverbal behaviors may be used quite effectively to shape others' learning, attitudes, and behavior. The basic strategies include use of positive or negative feedback designed to reinforce another's actions and the presentation of more negative cues, such as threat displays, that serve as punishment.

Positive and Negative Feedback. Positive and negative nonverbal feedback are forms of observable listener responses to another's behavior designed to maintain or change that behavior. Two forms of positive nonverbal feedback can be distinguished: positive and negative reinforcement. *Positive reinforcement* is the presentation of rewarding nonverbal cues after the desired behavior occurs. *Negative reinforcement* is providing some set of negative nonverbal cues that the target tries to escape or avoid through exhibiting the desired behavior. The key outcome of both types of reinforcement is the increase or maintenance of a particular behavior. Negative feedback, also called *punishment,* is the presentation of negative nonverbal cues following some behavior by the target with the goal of decreasing that behavior. When

APPLICATIONS

Shaping Behavior in the Classroom

Sara is attempting to explain to her fifth-grade classmates how Egyptians mummified their dead. As she begins her explanation, the teacher looks at her expectantly and nods frequently as Sara proceeds correctly. When Sara begins to make an error, the teacher cocks her head and narrows her eyes. Sara revises her statement, the teacher smiles and Sara continues. At the conclusion of Sara's presentation, the teacher gives another reassuring smile and praises Sara warmly for her informative talk. That night, Sara delightedly repeats without error her newfound knowledge to her parents.

This vignette illustrates the use of nonverbal cues to achieve influence. The teacher's kinesic cues served as positive and negative feedback, which shaped Sara's behavior and ultimately reinforced her learning of the material.

applying feedback, communicators must choose between positive and negative feedback. Educators argue that positive feedback is preferable to negative feedback, because positive feedback both rewards the target and informs the target about the appropriate, desired behavior. Negative feedback simply punishes undesirable behavior but does not inform about appropriate, desired behavior. Moreover, many people have difficulty managing negative feedback effectively and at the same time fail to realize how often they communicate negative feedback to others who behave undesirably.

It has generally been assumed that smiles, nods, forward leaning, frequent gaze, touching, approving vocal cues, and the like serve as positive feedback. Frowns, scowls, knitted brows, reduced eye contact, neutral and negative facial expressions, angry or cold vocal tones, and silence serve as negative reinforcement if they function to increase a desired behavior and punishment if they function to extinguish or reduce undesired behavior.

Evidence supports the beneficial effects of positive feedback. When male and female interviewers display head nodding and smiling, alone or in combination, interviewers increase the number of feeling and self-reference statements they make (Hackney, 1974). When teachers use nonverbal approval cues (smiling and touch), students increase their attention in class (Kazdin & Klock, 1973). Researchers also report that positive nonverbal patterns increase children's play activity (Jacunska-Iwinska, 1975), self-disclosure, and ratings of a source's attractiveness (Woolfolk & Woolfolk, 1974). Positive nonverbal feedback—increased smiling, eye contact, positive facial expressions, and positive vocalic cues—from a counselor increases clients' interest in trying to make changes to solve their problems (Bourget, 1977). In turn, when clients use increased eye contact, forward lean, nodding, gesturing, and verbal reinforcers in response to counselors' feeling statements, counselors make more such statements (Lee, Hallberg, Hassard, & Haase, 1979).

Positive feedback does not always work in expected ways. Experiments by Banks (1974), Isenberg and Bass (1974), and Furbay (1965) failed to show reinforcing effects for eye contact, nodding, smiling, forward lean, increased proximity, and vocal expression of agreement ("mm-hmm") on subjects' speech production, intelligence test scores, learning, and persuasion. However, these findings should not be taken as evidence that positive nonverbal feedback does not function as a reinforcer. The specific combination of nonverbal cues and their relationship to the verbal message are important determinants of the reinforcing effect of positive feedback on a target's behavior. Stewart and Patterson (1973) found that thematic responses by subjects increased most when eye contact was coupled with greater distance. Greene (1977) found that closer proximity increased compliance with a counselor's recommendations only when coupled with accepting verbal feedback. When coupled with neutral feedback, increased proximity reduced compliance. This latter combination may have transmitted an inconsistent or mixed message, whereas the combination of proximity and accepting verbal feedback was a more consistent and powerful reinforcing message.

In much of the research just reported, the effect of positive feedback was compared to no feedback or negative feedback. Thus these experiments, which show increased behavior following positive feedback, also provide evidence of decreased behavior following negative or less positive feedback. Taken together, the research indicates that the most effective positive nonverbal reinforcement cues are eye contact, smiling, and nodding, and changes in proximity are important to the extent that they complement co-occurring verbal and nonverbal feedback (Edinger & Patterson, 1983).

Not only do communicators attempt to change other people's behavior through reinforcement cues, but they also often seek to obtain reinforcing behaviors from others. Rosenfeld (1966a, 1966b) investigated people's approval-seeking behavior. He reports that when asked to seek approval from a target, people increased their smiling, nodding, gesturing, and utterance duration. They also reduced the display of adaptors but increased the number of speech disturbances. Further, targets interacting with approval-seeking communicators provided them with more positive feedback, particularly in the form of more smiling. Approval-seeking may involve two processes discussed earlier. First, many approval-seeking cues can also be used as positive nonverbal feedback cues, so when used to seek approval, they may signal interpersonal expectations that are fulfilled by the target's subsequent positive feedback. In addition, approval-seeking strategies may rely on the norm of reciprocity. Targets may be predisposed to reciprocate the positive cues displayed by approval-seeking communicators.

Threat Cues. Threat cues are another evaluative nonverbal message. However, rather than being designed exclusively to punish the target's behavior, threat cues are often encoded to inhibit future behavior and to cause the target to leave the environment. The ability of threat cues to influence a target's behavior lies in their arousing, aversive nature. This is evident in the way people respond to threat displays. A very common response is flight. Drawing on Hediger's (1950) critical flight distance theory, Ginsburg, Pollman, Wauson, and Hope (1977) believe that if the environment allows flight as an adaptive response, one may flee when threatened or display submissive behaviors such as lowering the head, avoiding eye contact, or increasing conversational distance that dissipate the threat. If flight is not an option, either due to physical or social constraints, aggressive responses, such as a reciprocal threat display or actual physical aggression, may be more adaptive. Ginsburg et al. showed that children in a small, physically constrained playground were more aggressive toward each other than children in a larger, less constrained playground. Similar findings were reported over 50 years ago by Jersild and Markey (1935) and Murphy (1937). The upshot of all this is that threat cues arouse targets. In coping with the aversive arousal, targets choose the most adaptive response, either some form of flight or a reciprocal display of aggression.

Alexander Solzhenitsyn's (1973) chilling description of how Russian prisoners were treated en route to prison camps during the 1940s, exerpted earlier in this chapter, demonstrates some of the ruthless, effective ways in which nonverbal threat cues have been used to elicit desired behavior. The brusque movements and loud, threatening voices are very familiar to us as the stock repertoire of film dictators, military men, and gangsters. Of course, these methods are not just media fantasies. They exist in real life, and they need not be blatant to work. A slight innuendo in a voice can make a child stop whining or an assembly line worker buy an unwanted lottery ticket from his supervisor. Battered wives have reported that they knew when their husbands intended to beat them by their tone of voice.

As noted in our discussion of intimacy cues, the eyes are powerful threat cues. The infamous Rasputin was alleged to have gained his great command over men and women through his penetrating, almost hypnotic stare. Charles Manson's eyes were the subject of much comment and apprehension during his trial; even his lawyer, Vincent Bugliosi, said that he found something frightening in Manson's steady gaze. If a stranger has ever held eye contact with you too long, you know how uncomfortable and disconcerting that can be.

Several investigations confirm that prolonged staring is aversive and interpreted as threatening (Edinger & Patterson, 1983; Ellsworth & Carlsmith, 1973; Ellsworth, Carlsmith, & Henson, 1972; Geller & Malia, 1981; Patterson, 1983). Cross-species comparisons show staring to be a frequent component of threat displays in primates. Staring is often observed immediately preceding an attack or as a substitute for it. In humans, staring may take on special significance because it is a very salient interpersonal stimulus that demands a response. Staring is less threatening if the appropriate response is readily apparent. When situational or relational cues do not indicate the appropriate response, staring is more threatening, evokes more tension in the target, and increases the target's motivations to escape the situation. Flight, which removes the aversive staring stimulus, then becomes negatively reinforced (Ellsworth & Carlsmith, 1973; Ellsworth et al., 1972).

Several laboratory and field experiments provide support for the threat message in staring. Kidd (1975) found that staring reduced a target's aggressiveness. Ellsworth and Carlsmith (1973) reported that when a confederate stared at an angered subject, the subject reduced the level of electric shock supposedly being delivered to the confederate. An earlier field experiment by Ellsworth et al. (1972) showed that when a confederate stared at a driver who was waiting at a stoplight, the driver drove much faster across the intersection after the light changed to green.

For staring to be an effective threat cue, it is necessary that it be unwavering. That is, constant staring at another person can engender anxiety and escape. However, if the stare vacillates, its impact is severely curtailed (Ellsworth & Carlsmith, 1973; Geller & Malia, 1981; Schlenker, 1980). A vacillating stare may signal uncertainty or weakness by the communicator. Targets then may feel that they possess the ability to resist or punish the communicator. In Ellsworth and Carlsmith's experiment, vacillating stares increased the severity of shocks supposedly delivered by subjects to the staring confederate. Geller and Malia found that a brief hesitation in staring

Sticking out one's tongue is a threat display more often used by children than adults.

reduced the assistance given to male confederates. Staring may be a more relevant threat cue for males, so vacillation did more harm to male than female confederates in this study (see also our earlier discussion of the 1979 experiment by Valentine and Ehrlichman).

Kinesic cues are also used in threat displays. In Chapters 3 and 12, we noted that one use of tongue showing is as a threat cue, particularly when one wants to be left alone or wants others to keep their distance (Horn, 1973). The same behavior appears among apes and monkeys. Certain emblems, particularly those with negative or obscene meanings (e.g., "the finger") and those that connote power (e.g., a clenched fist), are frequently used as threat displays. Forceful gestures are also included in many threat displays, as are hostile, negative facial expressions. It should not be surprising that staring is a dominant component in a facial expression of anger.

Finally, physical appearance cues can be threatening. Physical size, both muscle mass and height, can be used to threaten others. The cliché "I wouldn't want to meet that guy in a dark alley" attests to the threatening nature of some physical appearance cues.

Summary

This chapter has examined the multifaceted role of nonverbal communication in achieving social influence. It began with the assumption that communicators strategically select their nonverbal messages to influence others. One set of nonverbal messages is designed to project an image of authority, power, and credibility. A second set of nonverbal messages relies on establishing an intimate relationship between the communicator and the target. Communicators use nonverbal cues to signal affiliation, liking, and immediacy. Often physical appearance cues are manipulated to influence the communicator's attractiveness on the assumption that beauty persuades. In interpersonal relationships, communicators also employ patterns of nonverbal behavior that reciprocate, model, or compensate the nonverbal pattern employed by the target in order to change the target's behavior. Interpersonal expectations about the target's behavior are important in the social influence process, because communicators can subtly and unknowingly signal these expectations to targets, who may fulfill them. Further, communicators can violate nonverbal expectations to improve persuasiveness and compliance or to distract attention to favorable communicator characteristics. A final group consists of nonverbal messages that signal positive and negative evaluations to targets to maintain, change, or inhibit behavior. This group of messages includes positive and negative nonverbal feedback and nonverbal threat cues.

Suggested Readings

Bickman, L. (1974, April). Social roles and uniforms: Clothes make the person. *Psychology Today, 7,* 48–51.

Buller, D. B., & Aune, R. K. (1988). The effects of vocalics and nonverbal sensitivity on compliance: A speech accommodation theory explanation. *Human Communication Research, 14,* 301–332.

Burgoon, J. K. (1983). Nonverbal violations of expectations. In J. M. Wiemann & R. P. Harrison (Eds.), *Nonverbal interaction* (pp. 77–111). Beverly Hills, CA: Sage.

Edinger, J. A., & Patterson, M. L. (1983). Nonverbal involvement and social control. *Psychological Bulletin, 93,* 30–56.

Harris, M. J., & Rosenthal, R. (1985). Mediation of interpersonal expectancy effects: 31 meta-analyses. *Psychological Bulletin, 97,* 363–386.

Rosenthal, R. (1985). Nonverbal cues in the mediation of interpersonal expectancy effects. In A. W. Siegman & S. Feldstein (Eds.), *Multichannel integrations of nonverbal behavior* (pp. 105–128). Hillsdale, NJ: Erlbaum.

Wiemann, J. M. (1985). Power, status, and dominance: Interpersonal control and regulation in conversation. In R. L. Street, Jr., & J. N. Cappella (Eds.), *Sequence and pattern in communicative behavior* (pp. 85–102). London: Edward Arnold.

CHAPTER 14

Message Production, Processing, and Comprehension

> The communicator's problem . . . is not to get stimuli across, or even to package his stimuli so they can be understood and absorbed. Rather, he must deeply understand the kinds of information and experiences stored in his audience, the patterning of this information, and the interactive resonance process whereby stimuli evoke this stored information.
>
> Tony Schwartz (1974, p. 25)

> To understand a man, you must know his memories.
>
> Old Chinese proverb

The ability of people to understand one another is at the very heart of communication. Until recently, many scholars thought that nonverbal cues had little to do with human understanding and thinking processes, that they were more relevant to the affective or emotional side of human behavior. Now, however, research is beginning to show that nonverbal cues are involved in a variety of processes that lead to understanding. These processes, which focus on how information embedded in messages is processed, can be divided into (a) production or encoding and (b) comprehension or decoding.

Human information processing is best viewed as concerned with how humans acquire, store, retrieve, and use information (see Anderson, 1980; Craig, 1978; Reed, 1982; also see Roloff & Berger, 1982, for work relevant to communication). Often, information processing models describe a series of processing stages or sequences such as attention, short-term memory storage, conceptual knowledge activation, inference making, long-term memory storage, and long-term memory retrieval. Regardless of the particular model, it is clear that, in one way or another, people do "process" information and that both verbal and nonverbal information are processed in some way. How, then, do nonverbal cues affect the production and comprehension of the overall communication message? Do they play a supportive role for verbal processing? Are they sometimes the focus of message production and comprehension efforts? These questions, and others, are the central concerns of this chapter.

Our earliest understandings of nonverbal communication forecast some roles for nonverbal cues in cognitive processing. For example, the verbal-nonverbal relationships discussed in Chapter 5 indicate the kinds of roles that are possible. The *substitution* relationship suggests that nonverbal cues may be processed (that is, understood) on their own, in the absence of language. The *complementation* relationship suggests that nonverbal cues are necessary for some utterances to be understood. In such cases, we can say that nonverbal cues disambiguate the concurrent language. Nonverbal cues may repeat the verbal message, providing helpful *redundancy*. Finally, some authors (Ellis, 1982; Markel, 1975) have noted that most nonverbal cues occur simultaneously with language. Markel in fact has suggested using the term *coverbal* instead of nonverbal because of this. The close structural relationship between many nonverbal cues and verbal behavior makes it likely that nonverbal cues share functional relationships with their companionate language and that they are processed concurrently with verbal information. In this chapter, we will show that nonverbal cues are a rich source of information for a variety of cognitive processes.

Nonverbal Cues Associated with Message Production

The way that humans construct utterances in communication situations is remarkable, yet it is often taken for granted. The quickness with which we can produce novel utterances, the amount of information embedded in utterances, and the depth and clarity that utterances can have for other communicators are all qualities that distinguish humans as a species very concerned with communication.

Nonverbal cues are involved in message production in three ways. First, nonverbal cues provide the structural frame for utterances—that is, they mark the units in which utterances are produced. Second, nonverbal cues facilitate language encoding by helping the speaker activate and recall words, thoughts, images, and ideas that become part of the utterance. Third, some nonverbal cues are indicators of difficulty in encoding and constructing utterances.

The Phonemic Clause: Language Encoding Unit

One characteristic of conversational utterances is that they occur in "chunks." *Phonemic clauses* constitute the chunks of speech that make up the overall stream of spontaneous conversational verbalization. Conversational speech is not made up of sentences and paragraphs like written language. But there are discernible units in speech, the turn (discussed in Chapter 12) being one. Within turns, there are noticeable segments of speech, and these segments are for the most part phonemic clauses. Boomer (1978, pp. 246–247) gives the following example to illustrate phonemic clauses. Imagine hearing someone say the following:

The man who called me yesterday just telephoned again.

How do you hear this phrase being uttered in your mind? Research on phonemic clauses suggests that you hear this in two chunks:

The man who called me yesterday / just telephoned again.

The slash indicates where most people are likely to put a break point in the phrase, separating it into two chunks, or phonemic clauses (Boomer, 1965; Boomer & Dittmann, 1962).

Boomer (1978) indicates that three vocal cues identify a phonemic clause: *pitch, rhythm,* and *loudness.* The pitch contour or intonation pattern accompanying our sample phrase should have a characteristic pattern, with the pitch being relatively level over *The man who called me,* abruptly rising over the *yes* in *yesterday,* and gliding back down over *-terday.* A similar though not identical pattern should be found over *just telephoned again.* A change in the rhythm of the utterance typically coincides with the pitch change just described. Specifically, *The man who called me* and *just telephoned a-* parts of the phrases should be heard with relatively even rhythm. *Yesterday* and *-gain* should be heard as slightly longer and stretched out, the same points where the pitch changes occur. Finally, Boomer indicates that the *yes-* and *-gain* parts of the utterance should be slightly louder than the rest of the segment. The simultaneous changes in pitch, rhythm, and loudness produce what is called *primary stress* and mark the whole phrase into two segments. In phonemic clauses, primary stress occurs at or near the end of the clause. Pitch, rhythm, and loudness fall off and assume previous levels, a feature called a *terminal juncture.* A phonemic clause, then, is defined by one primary stress and a terminal juncture.

Thus spoken language is segmented into noticeable units, but instead of those units being sentences marked by grammatical rules, the units are rhythmic and marked by vocal properties. Research supports the importance of the phonemic clause as a production unit for speakers and a decoding unit for listeners. One study (Dittmann & Llewellyn, 1967) linked the phonemic clause to *listeners'* reactions. Listener responses such as nods and brief interjections like "um-hmm"—what we referred to earlier as backchannel responses—were found to occur primarily at the end of phonemic clauses, immediately after terminal junctures. This suggests that listeners recognize phonemic clause units and coordinate their responses to the units so that they don't "step on" the speaker's lines. Dittmann (1972a) has found similar patterns for other kinesic cues. Boomer (1978) reports evidence that phonemic clause units may be found in a number of languages, including Russian, French, and Dutch. These units provide the frame for conversational utterances and as such play an important role in language production.

Nonverbal Cues That Aid Utterance Production

Some nonverbal cues facilitate the encoding of language, "priming the pump," so to speak. Have you noticed that people talking on the telephone continue to use facial expressions and hand gestures, even though their listeners can't see them? Kinesic expressiveness is such a natural part of the encoding process that even when it serves no benefit to the listener, it helps us get our thoughts out smoothly. Rhythmic illustrator gestures that are synchronized to the vocal-verbal stream and self-touching or other adaptor behavior may be especially useful in this respect (Ekman & Friesen, 1972; Freedman, 1972; Harrigan, 1985).

Other types of illustrator gestures may be as essential to the meaning we are trying to convey as the words themselves. Researchers (Freedman & Steingart, 1975; Kendon, 1980, 1983; McNeill & Levy, 1982) have found that hand movements coincide with or even precede language construction. People use significantly more illustrator gestures when they are giving complex directions or making fine verbal discriminations (Baxter, Winters, & Hammer, 1968; Cohen, 1977). Moreover, gestural forms tend to convey the

Even when we can't be seen, we use gestures to facilitate our own encoding.

semantic meaning of a complete situation as well as correspond to the verb forms associated with the action. This suggests a very close link between what is going on mentally and the combined nonverbal-verbal expression that is subsequently produced. Our thoughts give rise to words and actions simultaneously. The process also appears to work in reverse. Instructions to produce certain types of gestures affect verbal output (Wolff & Gutstein, 1972). For example, if speakers are induced to use a circular gesture, they will tend to produce stories with circular objects (e.g., the moon), circular verbal action (e.g., rolling), and larger circular themes. And if speakers are prevented from using gestures at all, they pause more and resort to more extensive verbal descriptions (Graham & Heywood, 1975).

Of course, we also adapt to the auditor and situation. Cohen (1977; Cohen & Harrison, 1973) found that people attempting to give directions to a location used more hand illustrators in a face-to-face situation than over an intercom or when speaking to a tape recorder. This demonstrates that communicators are cognizant of their listeners' needs and abilities when trying to fashion their messages.

To recap, gestures do appear to aid the process of language construction (a) by providing the encoder with a mode in which to express content (a mode that may be more efficient for certain kinds of information, such as spatial or visual information), and (b) by facilitating the activation of words, concepts, ideas, and images that can be used in utterance construction. Cognitive theories that posit dual coding of mental representation (employing a semantic code and an imagistic code) and use semantic activation concepts to explain utterance production are quite compatible with these possibilities (Collins & Loftus, 1975; Paivio, 1971; for examples of how these models can be applied to nonverbal and verbal communication, see Kendon, 1983, and Motley, Camden, & Baars, 1981).

Nonverbal Cues That Indicate Encoding Difficulty and Complexity

A potent signal of encoding effort and difficulty is pausing. Research shows that longer pausing reflects cognitive planning involved in speech production (Goldman-Eisler, 1961a, 1961b, 1968; Siegman, 1976; Siegman & Pope, 1965). Hesitation pauses occur more frequently at places in utterances where it is difficult to anticipate the next word. More difficult tasks, which require a greater degree of cognitive planning for the encoding of utterances, also result in longer pausing. Longer pausing is associated with a vague probe by an interviewer (for example, "Tell me about your family") and shorter pausing, with specific probes ("What kind of work do you do?"). This evidence links pausing, and the duration of pausing, to different kinds of cognitive planning, including word choice, the difficulty and complexity of encoding speech, and the ambiguity associated with encoding speech. Other evidence indicates that cognitive planning is associated with a variety of pausing phenomena, including silent pauses, filled pauses, and speech disruptions (verbal repetition, incomplete sentences, omission of words, tongue slips, and stutters) (Siegman, 1978).

It is likely that there are other nonverbal cues associated with language encoding that we have yet to discover. For example, one cue currently under investigation is the encoder's eye position. Although some research has suggested that eye position may indicate something about an encoder's mode of thought, the available evidence is contradictory (Spain, 1985) and requires further study.

Nonverbal Cues Associated with Message Reception

Message processing has been and continues to be a major subject of study for communication, psychology, and other social science disciplines. Most previous efforts to explain message processing have focused on language and its features. Now, however, it is evident that nonverbal as well as verbal cues must be taken into account. Moreover, the theoretical models used to explain message processing have shifted over the past two decades from an emphasis on operant and classical conditioning principles to information processing principles, which provide a more elaborate view of comprehension than previous conceptions.

The term *comprehension* may be an overly simplistic misnomer. Comprehension is not a process in and of itself but a series of stages through which information is processed in order to gain an understanding of a message. We shall first examine the properties of each stage and then consider the nonverbal cues associated with them.

Attention

Traditionally, this is the first stage in most information processing models. Beyond the importance of understanding attention for its own sake, attention has an impact on subsequent stages of processing. You cannot understand something unless you have attended to it. Although there are several views of attention, most researchers agree on a number of its attributes (Reed, 1982). First, *attention is selective.* When humans attend, they take in some part of the total possible stimulus field and screen out the rest. The implication for nonverbal cues is that some nonverbal cues are likely to be included in the focus of attention, while others are not. Those that are focal may be determined by several factors, including the observational goals of the communicator, situational factors, and the nature of the cues themselves. Nonverbal cues that meet the definitional criteria outlined in Chapter 1 are especially likely to receive attention.

Second, *attention requires mental concentration.* One well-known illustration of how concentration is involved with attention is the cocktail party situation (see Cherry, 1964). At such a party, it takes serious concentration to focus on a conversation with the host in the midst of a crowded room. If you wish to eavesdrop on another conversation nearby, concentration is required to do this as well, especially if you are still talking to the host. Such concentration inevitably entails paying attention to both verbal and nonverbal cues.

Third, *attention is a limited-capacity stage.* That is, there is some upper limit to the mental effort humans can use to attend to the world. At some point, when attention is divided by different kinds of tasks and stimuli, humans become less efficient. For example, suppose you are trying to listen carefully to a speech given by another person while at the same time being intrigued by the speaker's striking clothes and physical attractiveness. You are likely to pay poor attention to what is being said. Although there must be some upper limit on how much nonverbal and verbal information a communicator can take in, just what that upper limit is has yet to be established. In a now classic work, Miller (1956) identified one limit to attention and short-term memory capacity: Humans can process roughly seven bits of information, plus or minus two bits, at a time. However, Miller and other researchers identified strategies that humans can use to exceed the $7 + 2$ limit: *chunking,* or combining units of information into larger units, and *rehearsal,* repeating information and keeping it active in short-term memory. Some of the rhythmic properties of nonverbal cues may aid in chunking or rehearsing, thus expanding the capacity of attention and short-term memory. Research by Newtson and his colleagues (Newtson, 1973; Newtson & Engquist, 1976; Newtson, Engquist, & Bois, 1977) has suggested that features of nonverbal behavior are used to segment the stream of interaction into perceptual chunks.

Finally, there are two distinctions that tell us something about the variability of attention. *Attention can be either automatic or effortful in nature.* Automatic processing occurs when attending requires very little effort or capacity, as when dressing or eating, because the activity is habitual and routine. Effortful processing occurs when attention requires much or most of one's mental capacity, as learning to utter a phrase in a new language. Whether nonverbal cues as a whole are attended to in an automatic or effortful way is difficult to say. It is plausible that most are attended to automatically when a person communicates with a familiar other because one is accustomed to their nonverbal displays. However, behavior from an unfamiliar other, as in an employment interview situation, may prompt effortful processing in order to form a distinct impression of the job applicant. Similarly, deviant or unexpected behavior may prompt more focused attention (Burgoon & Hale, 1988).

The second distinction concerned with the variability of attention suggests that *attention can occur in either a bottom-up or a top-down fashion.* Bottom-up processing occurs when features of the stimulus field determine where attention is focused. Thus when some features of the stimulus field catch our eye, bottom-up processing may be said to occur. Some research (e.g., Nisbett & Ross, 1980) suggests that vivid and novel stimuli attract attention. Nonverbal cues that are vivid or novel, such as hand gestures that point at objects or rhythmically reinforce phrases, may promote a bottom-up attention mode. Stacks and Burgoon (1981) have proposed that extremes in physical attractiveness and extreme conversational distances distract attention from what is being said and draw it to the speaker.

Top-down processing occurs when units of knowledge (that is, what we already know) determine the focus of attention. We pay more attention to a familiar other compared to a stranger, for example. Nonverbal cues may be involved with a top-down attention mode in at least two ways. First, they may help to activate semantic concepts that are then used to guide attention. For example, presume that one communicator tells another about a recent fishing trip and uses a hand gesture to indicate the size of the one that got away. Use of such a gesture may prompt the listener to recall a variety of details about similar fishing trips (not to mention the stories told about them) and may affect what the listener pays attention to subsequently. Second, nonverbal cues may be the focus of a top-down attention mode as a result of a communicator's observational goal. A communicator may be suspicious of deceit on the part of another communicator and as a result pay a great deal of attention to nonverbal cues for leakage, or an observer forming an impression of another may scrutinize a communicator's nonverbal behavior.

Many of these features of attention have yet to be investigated empirically by nonverbal researchers, in part because some of these distinctions are relatively recent. However, the research that we shall discuss suggests that nonverbal cues do facilitate attention levels.

Vocal Cues and Attention. Vocal variety and speech rate are two vocalic variables that have been linked to increased attention levels. Usually increased attention is inferred from evidence that nonverbal behaviors lead to increased comprehension. For example, vocal variety, which includes variations in pitch, tempo, intensity, and tonal quality, has been shown to result in increased comprehension (Beighley, 1952, 1954; Glasgow, 1952; Woolbert, 1920). The explanation for these effects is that variations in these vocal parameters serve to increase the listener's attentiveness, and as a result, comprehension is facilitated. Further, listeners have reported that they prefer the more varied pitch presentation (Diehl, White, & Satz, 1961).

A key vocal behavior thought to increase attention is tempo. Research on the speed of vocalization has established that the normal rate of speech ranges from roughly 125 to 195 words per minute (wpm). Investigators have found that, contrary to what might be expected, listeners can comprehend verbal messages presented at faster tempos than the normal rate. Researchers have used a variety of techniques to speed up the rate of presentation of recorded speech artificially. One technique, called the *speed-changing method,* increases the rate of speech by reproducing a message at a higher playback speed. However, when this is done, vocal pitch is also raised, which results in an unwanted confounding effect (voices begin to sound like Alvin the chipmunk). Another technique, termed the *sampling method,* accelerates speech by removing most periods of silence from tape-recorded speech (Foulke & Sticht, 1969). This method increases speech rate without increasing vocal pitch and is currently accomplished by computerized devices that sample the verbal stream for periods of silence to eliminate. Most researchers now agree that the sampling method is the best technique for compressing speech.

These compression techniques have allowed researchers to investigate the effects of accelerated speech on attention and comprehension. Early research showed that speech could be speeded up significantly without serious loss of comprehension until it reached around 325 wpm (Orr, 1968). For example, one study (Fairbanks, Guttman, & Miron, 1957) found that at 282 wpm (close to double the normal rate of speaking), listener comprehension was 90% of what it was at normal rates of presentation; at 353 wpm, comprehension dropped to 50%. More recent research (e.g., Duker, 1974; LaBarbera & MacLachlan, 1978; MacLachlan, 1981; MacLachlan & LaBarbera, 1979; MacLachlan & Siegel, 1980) has shown that accelerated speech not only does not jeopardize comprehension but may actually aid it. For example, radio commercials that are speeded up by 25% are 50% better remembered and also better liked (LaBarbera & MacLachlan, 1979). Psychology students who heard either a compressed or normal speed version of a "60 Minutes" segment had much higher recall two days later if they heard the compressed speech version (MacLachlan & Siegel, 1980). Commercials produced for industry yield higher recall and motivation when they have a 10–15% speed-up, which is almost imperceptible, and the preferred rate of speech is about 30% faster than normal (200 wpm) (MacLachlan, 1981).

A plausible explanation for these findings is that faster-paced speaking requires more effort from listeners. They must attend more carefully and exert more effort to keep up with what the speaker is saying. At the same time, moderately accelerated speech does not exceed the listener's information capacity, yet prevents attention from wandering, which might make such presentations more enjoyable. The net result is that a faster pace may be the most desirable if comprehension and attention are the goal.

Of course, time-compression techniques can be used successfully in mass media contexts but not in interpersonal ones. The application of rapid speech to interpersonal settings may be limited by several factors. First, some people may be unable to vocalize as fast or faster than 200 wpm. Second, verbal variables such as the complexity of the information being presented may interact with tempo, making a rapid rate less effective with difficult verbal material. Finally, listeners' interest and motivation in paying attention can affect whether a faster rate facilitates attention. Speaking faster may aid attention when you are talking to a friend about a topic of mutual interest but may harm it when talking to a stranger on a boring topic. Nevertheless, a moderately quickened pace usually should increase attention, comprehension, and receiver pleasure.

Environmental Cues and Attention. Environmental features have the potential to stimulate the senses, making it easier to comprehend and retain information or to distract. Noble (cited in Proshansky, Ittleson, & Rivlin, 1970) explains:

> Normal consciousness, perception and thought can be maintained
> only in a constantly changing environment; when there is no change
> a state of "sensory deprivation" occurs. Experiment has shown that a
> homogeneous and unvarying environment produces boredom, rest-

lessness, lack of concentration and reduction in intelligence. . . . Office blocks in which each floor has the same layout, color, materials and climate are just asking for trouble. . . . The sort of variation that we often demand instinctively on aesthetic grounds has a sound physiological and psychological basis. A change in environment stimulates our built-in devices to perceive and respond rapidly to significant events and efficiency is thereby increased. (p. 464)

One environment where paying attention is especially crucial is the classroom. Yet many classrooms are poorly designed and may actually be distracting. The windowless classroom, an innovation intended to reduce the distractions from outdoors (and to reduce heating costs), has failed to improve learning and has resulted in less pleasant student moods (Karmel, 1965). Open classroom designs, also intended to aid learning, have likewise harmed attention by not providing enough privacy for groups of students and by allowing too much noise to occur in the environment (Rivlin & Rothenberg, 1976). It has been argued that learning environments should tend toward simplicity, as too many stimuli can prove distracting (see Fisher, Bell, & Baum, 1984). One study has confirmed that greater learning occurs in less complex settings (Porteous, 1972). Ideally, one would like to strike a balance between environments that are too complex and distracting and environments that are so simple and bland as to be boring. It is possible that the type of learning (rote versus experiential versus semantic-based) and the complexity of the material to be learned may determine the level of attention and environmental stimulation needed.

Finally, color and intensity of lighting may affect attention and comprehension. German experimenters found that placing children in brightly colored playrooms increased their IQ by 12 points, while those placed in white, black, or brown rooms lost 14 IQ points (cited in Silden, 1973). Presumably, the environment affected their general level of alertness and mental quickness. In another investigation (Sadesky, 1974), subjects received the highest scores on a multiple-choice test after interacting in a room with either low intensity red lighting or medium intensity blue lighting. Test scores were lowest when high intensity white light was used. If an attention effect was at work in this study, high intensity white light might be distracting. Such an effect seems plausible, as there are many reflective surfaces (white paper, floor tile) off which white light may bounce, creating distraction in typical classrooms. This does give pause to think about how most classrooms are lit.

Other environmental elements such as obstructions to view or inefficient climate control doubtless affect student attention.

Kinesic and Haptic Nonverbal Cues and Attention. Smiles and touch from teachers have been found to increase student attentiveness in the classroom (Kazdin & Klock, 1973). Emphatic hand gestures that accompany the verbal stream and underscore high information segments should also promote attention. A varied overall nonverbal style may operate much like vocal variety, enhancing a decoder's attention because the nonverbal part of the

Windowless classrooms, like this one, can impede student attention and comprehension.

message is intrinsically more interesting. Finally, some work has suggested that nonverbal cues may refocus a communicator's attention by shifting it away from the verbal portion of the message and toward the nonverbal part (see Woodall & Burgoon, 1981). In a review of this research, Buller (1986) has concluded that some nonverbal cues, particularly nonverbal violations of expectations, shift the communicator's attention away from verbal message components and toward nonverbal source characteristics. Two in particular that may draw attention away from the verbal message are physical attractiveness and distance changes (Stacks & Burgoon, 1981).

One qualification should be made about much of the research just cited. As you may have noticed, *comprehension* is often used as a measure of attention. The attention stage of information processing is quite difficult to assess directly. Strictly speaking, this presents us with a somewhat confounded situation. Some researchers have argued that since various factors can affect attention and comprehension, using comprehension as a criterion to measure attention can be potentially misleading. Other options do exist. For example, reaction time techniques, whereby researchers measure the time it takes for a decoder to identify some target stimulus, can be used as a more direct way to assess attention. However, comprehension does indicate *something* about what was attended to and can be used—carefully—as a rough guide.

To sum up, nonverbal communication is often the first mode of communication to occur between interactants. By dint of this fact alone, nonverbal cues are put in a position to affect and direct attention. It is increasingly clear that nonverbal communication and the attention stage of information processing are related in many ways.

Comprehension: Memory, Understanding, and Nonverbal Cues

Ortony (1978) has argued that two fundamental and important cognitive capacities make up an adequate model of human cognition: the capacity to understand and the capacity to remember. Although Ortony points out that one can understand and retrieve the same set of information, the processes involved in understanding information are different from those involved in recalling it. This distinction between understanding and memory is a break from previous work that either lumped such capacities together or treated them as one and the same (for a discussion of research that ignores the understanding-memory distinction, see Folger & Woodall, 1982, or Woodall, Davis, & Sahin, 1983). In addition, this distinction reinforces the fact that these two capacities are often independent of each other in our day-to-day experience; that is, we often understand something but later cannot remember it, and we may also remember something that we did not understand very well.

In addition to clarifying the nature of comprehension, this distinction provides a useful basis for understanding how nonverbal cues are processed in communicative settings. We may now ask how and what nonverbal cues affect the understanding of a message and the later recall of it.

Understanding and Associated Nonverbal Cues. Space is inadequate to cover all the models that have been offered to explain how understanding occurs (for a review see Anderson, 1980, or Reed, 1982). Ortony's (1978) view of understanding incorporates a number of important principles and is useful for our purposes. Ortony uses semantic network models of long-term memory (e.g., Collins & Loftus, 1975) to explain the understanding process. These models conceive of human long-term memory as a network of associated nodes that represent the storehouse of knowledge that a person holds. Each node in the network could be a concept or proposition, and the nodes are connected by different types of relationships. For example, the node "professor" would be linked to the node "professional" by a class relationship, allowing the proposition "a professor is a professional" to be generated. "Professor" could be linked to other nodes, such as "hardworking," "intelligent," "insightful," and "underpaid."

Although the formal and structural characteristics of semantic networks are still debatable, for our purposes we need to know how such networks allow understanding to occur. Understanding, according to Ortony (1978), occurs as information stored in a semantic network is used to make inferences about information just received (verbal and nonverbal cues that make up a message). The input information activates some relevant set of concepts in memory: "The process of comprehension involves activating concepts related to those of the input and the context and engaging in inferences based primarily on those concepts" (p. 59). Hewes and Planalp (1982) point out that both *integration* and *inference making* are components of the understanding process. Integration is the process of combining new data with prior knowledge; inference making refers to deductions based on existing and newly integrated information. In slightly more simple terms, we understand because what we already know is related to the message and allows us to make inferences.

Many factors determine the nature of understanding. First, understanding rests partly on how far activation "spreads" in the network, or how many concepts are activated at input. Two factors affect spread of activation: (a) contextual information and (b) depth of processing. Contextual information—cues that surround and accompany language—can enhance the number of concepts activated when new information (a message) is encountered. As you might observe, nonverbal cues fit the description of contextual information quite well. Depth of processing simply has to do with the degree of semantic involvement during the processing of a message (Craik & Lockhart, 1972). Greater levels of semantic involvement entail the activation of more concepts in a semantic network (for a more extensive discussion, see Folger & Woodall, 1982).

Two important points can be drawn from this characterization of understanding. First, *understanding is not an all-or-nothing process.* As the semantic network and activation spread models would suggest, understanding occurs to a greater or lesser extent and to a greater or lesser depth. Second *nonverbal cues can affect understanding by providing contextual information that prompts greater spread of activation of concepts, greater integration of input information, more inference-making, and thus deeper processing.*

Some nonverbal cues such as hand gestures have semantic features that provide a basis for spread of activation and integration. Freedman (1972) describes two categories of gestures. *Speech primacy gestures,* which include any gesture that has no clear representational or semantic properties, occur as an "overflow from the emphatic aspects of speech" (p. 158) and are tied to the rhythm of speech. *Motor primacy gestures* include gestures that are representational and carry some semantic information and relationship to concurrent language. Similar classifications have been offered by Ekman and Friesen (1969b, *illustrators* versus *emblems*) and McNeill and Levy (1982, *iconic gestures* versus *beats*). All these classifications distinguish between gestures that have semantic content and those that do not.

Motor primacy gestures have the potential to result in greater activation and integration because they offer some form of semantic representation. Further, they may do so in a way not embodied in language; that is, they provide semantic information in a visual mode. Stimuli that are visual may be more concrete and vivid (Paivio, 1971) and have the potential to affect strongly both integration and inference making (Nisbett & Ross, 1980). Support for hand gestures affecting processing in this way has been found in two studies. In one investigation (Woodall & Folger, 1981), a series of random sentences was paired with either an emphasizing gesture or a semantically related gesture. Participants in the study viewed a videotape in which an actor spoke the sentences and performed one gesture or the other. Later, participants were shown the videotape with the gestures (without sound) and asked to recall the accompanying sentence. Recall of the sentences was significantly higher when the utterances were accompanied by semantically related gestures. Here, higher levels of recall are a likely indication of greater concept activation, integration, and inference making. Similarly, Rogers (1978) has shown that the presence of a number of visual cues, including nods, eye movements, lip and facial movements, and hand gestures, significantly improves comprehension of concurrent verbal information. Other nonverbal cues could be processed in a similar manner. For example, some environmental cues may have semantic features that prompt greater concept activation, integration, and inference making.

Nonverbal cues such as speech primacy gestures that do not have semantic features can also be employed in a way that prompts deeper and more involved information processing. In some cases, a communicator may turn to nonverbal cues to provide further information that can help in understanding a verbal message. Folger and Woodall (1982) have indicated that at least three ambiguous encoding situations fit this description. First, in any case where an utterance could have more than one meaning (e.g., metaphors, double entendres, ironic statements), nonverbal cues lacking semantic features could be relied on to clarify and disambiguate the communicator's intended meaning. In such cases, these cues highlight that the message is not to be taken at face value.

Second, when some form of incongruity exists between language and nonverbal cues, nonverbal cues that lack semantic features may be used to make sense of the incongruity. When a communicator is sarcastic through incongruity, is joking, or acts deceptively, the accompanying nonverbal cues may be used by other communicators to activate concepts and make inferences that allow an understanding of the incongruous message.

Finally, an ambiguous situation occurs when nonverbal cues are out of sync with the verbal stream. How often this occurs is difficult to say, given what we know about synchrony at the present time. One study (Woodall & Burgoon, 1981) found that dissynchronous cues strongly distracted participants and resulted in low levels of verbal comprehension. However, a listener may also spend a great deal of time and cognitive effort in making inferences about why the nonverbal cues are out of sync. Dissynchronous cues could be interpreted as indications of nervousness, deceit, or physical disorder. In such cases, then, the dissynchronous nonverbal cues become the focus of attention instead of the verbal utterance. Regardless of whether the understanding is accurate or not, nonverbal cues strongly determine concept activation, inference making, and understanding in these cases.

So far, we have concentrated on how nonverbal cues might affect semantic understanding (that is, the direct semantic meaning of a communication message). Another part to understanding is derived from social information. Social cognition theorists (e.g., Hastie & Carlston, 1980) point out that humans have a social memory domain that includes social concepts (stereotypes and implicit personality traits) and information about social events, processes, and persons (whether social information is a separate information domain or part of an overall semantic network has not been determined). In any communicative situation, inferences about what is said as well as who said it can be made and can determine the nature of one's overall understanding. As we noted in Chapter 7, the formation of impressions of others rests heavily on nonverbal cues. From an information processing point of view, impression formation relies on inference making that uses both message information and social information stored in social memory. Burgoon (1980) indicated three general types of social judgments that rely on nonverbal cues: (a) sociological and personality judgments, (b) judgments of credibility and attraction, and (c) judgments of veracity and deception. In these cases, nonverbal cues trigger inferences about others and determine the concepts activated in social memory. Social understanding—a grasp of who the other communicators are, why they act as they do, and what their intentions and motivations are—is based on information processing principles.

Does our social understanding of people affect our semantic understanding of their messages? One investigation (McMahan, 1976) suggests a limited yes as an answer. In this study, participants viewed one of four different videotapes in which nonverbal cues displayed either dominance or submissiveness consistent with or in contrast to dominant or submissive verbal statements. After viewing a tape, participants were asked to give written impressions of the speaker and to recall the message. McMahan coded the references to either verbal or nonverbal information in these accounts, and participants responded on a number of other measures as well. The results indicated that impressions of the speaker were dominated by references to nonverbal cues, while reconstruction of the verbal message was dominated by references to verbal information. Moreover, in the inconsistent conditions, participants rated the intent of the speakers as less sincere than the sincerity of their statements. According to McMahan, the result "lends support to the theory that perceivers discriminate between statement and intention, and they attribute intentions to the person which are used to reinterpret the verbal message when the incongruent verbal and nonverbal cues are received" (p. 202). At least in incongruent message conditions (what we referred to earlier as an ambiguous encoding condition), inferences about the person may affect inferences about the semantic meaning of the message.

To sum up, nonverbal cues affect the understanding stage of information processing by having an impact on concept activation, integration of message information with what is already stored, and inference making. Nonverbal cues may have these effects by either providing a context that offers semantic features or features that can clarify ambiguous encoding situations, by providing social information that can be used to reinterpret the verbal message, and by affecting the topic management process.

Memory and Associated Nonverbal Cues. Equally important to an account of nonverbal cues and their relationship to information processing is how such cues affect what we remember. According to Ortony (1978), memory

APPLICATIONS

Tracking Topics in Conversations

Because nonverbal regulative cues are used to manage the content of what is talked about, they may affect our understanding of dialogue. This is clearest when the topic regulation process breaks down and affects understanding in a negative way. For example, if a communicator does not use nonverbal cues in clear and skillful ways to mark a change in topic, other communicators are likely to lose track of what is being talked about. In information processing terms, losing track of the conversational topic could have several implications. First, concept activation, integration of message information, and inference making are likely to suffer because the communicator is no longer sure of the overall theme of information being discussed. A second possibility is that misunderstandings develop because one communicator assumes that Topic A is being discussed and the other, Topic B. This is most likely to occur when a subtle shift has occurred to a closely related topic and when a topic change is implicitly signaled but not explicitly noted by the person changing topics.

The importance of topic shifting in a clear and comprehensible way has probably occurred to you before, although you may not have recognized the issue as such. More than likely, you have found yourself lost in a conversation, unsure of what the other person is talking about. This can be an uncomfortable situation, to say the least. Do you stop the other person to clarify the topic? This could be embarrassing, as an admission of inattention. Open criticism of the other person for having lost you in the conversation is rude and can be construed as an accusation of incompetence as a communicator. Clearly, the skillful use of nonverbal cues to demarcate topic shifts is important for keeping interactants on track in their understanding of each other and also promotes positive perceptions of a communicator's skill.

"involves the retrieval, recognition and in some cases even the regeneration of representations of knowledge" (p. 57). Memory, then, has to do with the storage and retrieval of information. There are at least three areas of concern to explore here. First, what can be said about the storage and retrieval of nonverbal cues themselves? Are nonverbal cues of various types an important part of one's memory? Second, do nonverbal cues aid in the storage and retrieval of other information about the communication interaction? Third, what role do nonverbal cues play in one's memory of other people, often called person memory?

With a little reflection, you probably realize that nonverbal cues themselves are often an important part of our memory. The clearest example of this is facial recognition. A number of studies have supported what most of us have no doubt experienced personally—that it is easier for people (at least in our culture) to recognize a person's face than it is to recall the person's name (see Watkins, Ho, & Tulving, 1976). This is primarily applicable to people that one is only somewhat acquainted with (for example, the students in a class with you).

The ability to decode, store, and retrieve facial features develops early in humans. At 6 months, infants are able to discriminate familiar faces from unfamiliar faces, and stranger anxiety emerges as a result. Although facial recognition may have a number of functional bases, its early appearance means that it can be considered from an ethological point of view. An infant's ability to discriminate parent from stranger could have had survival value at some point in human history. Thus, as noted in Chapter 2, the ability to recognize faces may have an innate basis.

Two things should be noted about the information processing that underlies facial recognition, as well as memory for other nonverbal cues. First, the ability to recognize a face suggests something about how nonverbal information is coded in memory. Of the many possible views on the coding of information in memory, the one that makes the most sense for our purposes is the *dual-coding position* (see Paivio, 1971, for a full discussion of coding theories). This position holds that information can be coded in two ways for storage: via a semantic code (as in a semantic network) or via an imagistic code that stores information pictorially (or perhaps both). Facial recognition probably uses an imagistic code, the features of a familiar face being stored as an image; it seems implausible that they could be stored only semantically. It is thus likely that other nonverbal cues are stored imagistically as well.

The second important issue has to do with the term *recognition*. In the information processing literature, *recognition* has a specified meaning, different and distinct from *recall*. Both recognition and recall are ways of retrieving information from storage. However, recognition occurs when the information to be remembered is presented and the person must determine whether he or she remembers (recognizes) it. Recall occurs when retrieval of information is made through some association other than the information to be remembered. So, for example, if you were asked the open-ended question, "Who was the president after Franklin Delano Roosevelt?" and you were able to answer, "Truman," the answer would be based on a recall retrieval process. If you were asked the multiple-choice question, "Which of the following was president after Franklin Delano Roosevelt: Kennedy, Johnson, Harding, or Truman?" and you said, "Truman," the answer would be based on a recognition retrieval process. Memory for nonverbal cues may employ either retrieval strategy. In the case of face recognition, a recognition retrieval process is used; in other cases to be discussed shortly, a recall retrieval process is used.

Other kinesic cues are also likely to be recognizable and stored in memory. For example, emblematic gestures such as the A-OK sign and the

Conversational Amnesia: Didn't I Talk to You Yesterday?

People often claim that they remember who they have conversed with during the recent past. How accurate is that claim? Not very accurate, according to studies by Russell Bernard, an anthropologist at the University of Florida. Russell has conducted a number of studies where he surveyed, at random intervals, a variety of people about the conversations they were having at that moment (members of a consulting firm, a university office, and a fraternity, have been used in these studies). A week later, Bernard would again ask these individuals to look at lists of people in their organization and indicate how often they had spoken with each. Results showed that the respondents remembered talking to individuals that they had in fact never spoken to, denied speaking with individuals to whom they had spoken, and that respondents were accurate about the amount of contact they had with others less than 50% of the time.

On the face of it, these results aren't very encouraging for one's ability to recall conversations. However, they do fit with the research we have been discussing. First, it seems to be the case that we are better at recalling some nonverbal visual features of conversation, primarily other interactants' faces, than their names. So, it is not surprising that interactants would have difficulty recalling who they had spoken to a week prior. Second, it may very well be the case that the difficulty in recall is due to the inability of respondents to retrieve information, and not due to forgetting the information. Information processing principles that govern the storage and retrieval of conversational event information suggest that some kind of contextual cue is necessary for retrieval. Simply asking the respondents who they had spoken to may not have given them enough context to retrieve the names of the other interactants. Although what individuals can recall from conversations is still being studied, Bernard's studies do indicate that we should treat such recalled information with care and some skepticism.

Source: Adapted from "Crosstalk," by C. T. Cory, 1983, *Psychology Today,* February 17, (2), p. 22.

peace sign are immediately recognized by most members of our culture. We recognize these gestures not only because the meaning associated with them is well understood but also because we know what the gestures look like. This suggests that the shape of the gestures is stored in visual memory and the associated meaning is stored in semantic memory. When an emblematic gesture is recognized, the information stored in both imagistic and semantic domains is used to help make the discrimination.

It is likely that cues from other nonverbal codes are processed in much the same way. Researchers in environmental psychology (Fisher et al., 1984) have pointed out that rather elaborate cognitive "maps" of environments are stored as part of memory. Such map information allows a person to recognize familiar and known environments and discriminate them from unfamiliar environments. In addition to allowing humans to adapt and function in a given environment, such maps may also provide procedural information (in the form of scripts) and situational information that affects how communication proceeds between interactants. Similarly, when the territorial dimension of the proxemic code is considered, determining that an area is territory partly rests on the ability to recognize as familiar certain environmental and proxemic features. The recognition retrieval process is more than likely used to make such discriminations. Finally, unique vocal characteristics may be part of recognition memory. Clearly, we have all come to recognize certain voices as familiar. The ability to know what a person's voice sounds like suggests that we have features of that voice stored in memory and can recognize the voice if we hear it.

Nonverbal cues are related to memory processing in a second way: Some nonverbal cues are decoded and stored as context for other features of communication events, primarily verbal behavior. As stored context, nonverbal cues may be used to help recall features of the communication event at a later point. Thus nonverbal cues may help one to remember what another person said. To support this claim, we need to refer to research concerned with episodic memory (memory for episodes and events). Tulving and his colleagues have explored how we store and recall information for events. For example, presume that you and a friend are at a social gathering, discussing the music being played on the stereo. You are unfamiliar with the group's music, and your friend casually mentions the name of the group (the Alan Parsons Project). Later, you try to recall the name of the band because you want to purchase one of their records. How do you recall such information? Tulving's research suggests that the most likely way to recall such incidentally learned information (that is, information not purposely learned) is first to try to think of the context in which you encountered the information to be remembered. In this case, you could try to recall what the party was like, who was there, what your friend was wearing, what else he or she said, what the music sounded like. Thinking of this contextual information should help you to recall the name of the group.

Why does context information help to recall the to-be-remembered information and what information processing principles underlie this kind of retrieval? Tulving and Thomson (1973) approached these questions using a list-learning paradigm, whereby a subject in a study learns a list of paired words. Subjects are given a list of word pairs in which input words (the first word of each pair) are paired with target words to be remembered (the second word of each pair). *Cold* might serve as the input for the target word *ground, sun* for *day,* and so on. Note that these word pairs have weak semantic links, not strong ones. After learning the list of word pairs, subjects are given another list of single words (target words and others) and asked to circle words they recognize as target words. In the Tulving and Thomson study, subjects recognized only about 24% of the target words from the list. Subsequently, subjects were given a cued recall test where the input words were given and subjects were asked to recall the associated target words. Surprisingly, subjects recalled 63% of the target words under these conditions. Subjects, then, were able to recall words that they did not recognize, even though when asked to recognize a word, an exact copy of the to-be-remembered word was right in front of them. Subsequent studies (see Watkins & Tulving, 1975) varied research design conditions and still obtained similar results, termed "recall without recognition" or "recognition failure."

How is it possible that a person can recall information that he or she is unable to recognize? Tulving formulated the *encoding specificity principle* (note that the term *encoding* here stands for the taking in and storing of information by a communicator): Contextual cues can provide access to information stored in memory if and only if both context and target information have been stored as part of the specific memory trace of an event. In other words, contextual cues can help one recall information if the context and target are stored together at the time of input. In the case of the word pairs, the input word provided the context for the target word and later aided in the recall of the target word. Watkins, Ho, and Tulving (1976) have shown similar effects with pairs of pictures of unfamiliar faces and with descriptive phrases paired with pictures of faces. On a broader social level, other cues may play a contextual role for event information. As suggested earlier, remembering what someone said to you at a party can be facilitated by first recalling a variety of contextual cues that might be linked to the utterance you are trying to recall.

Most research on the encoding specificity principle has used the rather narrow list-learning paradigm, and questions remain about whether the principle can be extended beyond such experimental conditions that are not representative of everyday social situations (Anderson, 1980, p. 212). However, it seems likely that a variety of nonverbal cues could play a contextual role for accompanying language. Several investigations have tested this possibility. In one experiment (Woodall & Folger, 1981), a modified and broadened version of the list-learning paradigm was used to determine if different types of hand gestures could act as context for concurrent utterances. This study attempted to determine (a) if evidence for recognition failure that would support encoding specificity could be found and (b) whether different kinds of hand gestures would have a different impact on recall.

Participants saw a series of short videotaped segments, each containing a short verbal utterance (for example, "We just seem to go around and around in circles") and an accompanying gesture. There were two hand gesture conditions in the study: an emphasizing condition, in which an emphasizing gesture accompanied the verbal utterance, and an emblematic condition, in which a gesture that was semantically linked to the utterance was included in the segment (for example, a gesture of drawing circles in the air accompanying the "around in circles" phrase). After viewing the videotaped segments, participants were given a recognition test for the verbal utterances. Contextually cued recall was then tested by playing the videotaped segments back to the participants without the sound.

Results showed that recognition failure did occur. By using hand gestures that accompanied the utterances, participants were able to recall utterances that they were previously unable to recognize. This occurred in both gesture conditions, indicating that nonverbal cues can play a contextual role for accompanying language as the encoding specificity principle would suggest.

The results also indicated much higher cued recall for emblematic than for emphasizing gestures (see Figure 14.1). Since the emblematic cues have more semantic features, they provide a more elaborate and richer context for the verbal utterances. This results in deeper processing of both context and target information, a more elaborate form of storage, and better retrieval after storage. Riseborough (1981) reports somewhat similar results for iconographic and kinetographic gestures and single words. These gestures, which depict shape, size, and movement of objects (and thus have semantic features), showed a facilitating effect on recall of single words when paired with those words. These results are also consistent with an episodic view of memory.

Two further investigations (Woodall & Folger, 1985) extended these patterns to natural conversations and explored whether nonverbal cues be used over longer periods of time as effective retrieval cues. To simulate conversational conditions, the researchers developed a script for a conversation between two interactants (actually actors). Actors learned the script and were then videotaped under one of three gesture conditions: (a) a no-gesture condition, in which the actors used no gestures during dialogue; (b) an emphasizing-gesture condition, in which only emphasizing gestures were used during dialogue; and (c) an emblematic-gesture condition, in which only emblematic gestures were used during dialogue. After viewing

FIGURE 14.1 These gestures might accompany the statement "The discussion kept going around in circles." The emblematic gesture (a) aids recall of the accompanying phrase more than the emphasizing gesture (b).

(a)   (b)

one of the three versions of the videotaped conversation, a series of video-only gesture-utterance segments, edited from the videotaped conversation, was shown to the participants, who were to use the gestures to help recall the utterances in the segments. Strong differences in cued recall were obtained across gesture types: participants recalled 5% of the utterances in the no-cues condition, 11% in the emphasizing-cues condition, and 34% in the emblematic-cues condition, thus providing support for application of the encoding specificity principle to more naturalistic social contexts. Riseborough (1981) likewise found that iconographic and kinetographic gestures enhanced recall when embedded in a short conversational text.

The second investigation (Woodall & Folger, 1985) examined the durability of these nonverbal behaviors as retrieval cues over a greater period of time. Cued recall tests were given immediately and then repeated a week later. Although recall should be less after a week's interval, the differences in recall across the type of cue should persist if these cues still provide access to the concurrent utterances. The results conformed to these expectations: participants were able to recall 37% of the utterances in the emblematic condition after a week, whereas 7% of the utterances were recalled in both no-cues and emphasizing-cues conditions after a week's time. This suggests that nonverbal cues with semantic features can act as effective retrieval cues even after some passage of time. Although conversants are generally poor at recalling conversational content (Stafford & Daly, 1984), nonverbal cues may enhance that recall.

Other nonverbal behaviors such as facial and head cues may possibly act as retrieval cues for concurrent language as well. Although such cues are likely to have fewer semantic features than hand gestures, they may still provide access and retrieval. Vocalic cues also may play a contextual role (Geiselman & Bellezza, 1976, 1977; Geiselman & Crawley, 1983). In one set of studies, Geiselman and his colleagues found that subjects could identify which of two speakers had spoken a given sentence from a list of sentences about 70% of the time. This occurred even when subjects were not told to remember who said what—that is, they stored and recalled characteristics of the speaker's voice incidentally. The researchers explained these findings by way of a voice connotation hypothesis, which states that a speaker's voice is sometimes remembered because the connotation of the voice influences the perceived meaning of what is said. Thus vocal cues can provide an important context for utterances, possibly resulting in deeper processing of utterances and better retrieval later.

The third way in which nonverbal cues may be related to memory has to do with memory for people. Person memory (see Hastie, Ostrom, Ebbesen, Wyer, Hamilton, & Carlston, 1980) is concerned with how humans store and retrieve information about others. A large part of what was earlier termed social information is concerned with what one knows and remembers about other people. Although there is little direct evidence to show that nonverbal cues are linked to this aspect of memory (primarily because person memory is a relatively new topic of study), there is reason to believe that nonverbal cues may be instrumental.

Memory, Aging, and Vocal Cues

Although we all rely on vocal cues to clarify the meaning of the messages that we receive and process, recent evidence indicates that older people rely on vocal cues for information processing more than younger individuals do. A recent study by Stine and Wingfield compared older adults and college graduates in the ability to recall tape-recorded messages. A variety of messages were used, including actual sentences, strings of nonsense words, sentences read with normal intonation, others without, and sentences read at both normal and speeded up rates.

Large differences in recall between elderly and college age participants occurred when sentences were read without intonation, particularly at high speed. Under these conditions, elderly participants recalled only half the words correctly, while college students made very few mistakes. The authors explained the findings by suggesting that, with age, people lose mental speed in processing information. In order to compensate, elderly individuals tune into and rely more on vocal intonation, emphasis, and timing in order to clarify what others say to them. Interestingly, as we grow older, vocal cues take on extra added importance for our understanding of messages.

Source: Adapted from "Mind Openers," by S. Chollar, May 1988, *Psychology Today,* *22,* p. 10.

First, as we discovered in Chapter 7, a wide variety of nonverbal cues affect the impressions we form of others. Another way to view impressions is to conceptualize them as person memory. Nonverbal cues often contribute to impressions by being linked to a social stereotype or a set of implicit personality traits (an example being the color of a person's hair indicating something about his or her personality). Thus nonverbal cues may be linked to person memory by facilitating impressions that make use of stereotypes. Such memories of people are most likely formed during early acquaintanceship stages in relationships where stereotypes are most likely to be employed.

Second, nonverbal cues may prompt recollection of very idiosyncratic and unique qualities of individuals. Trager (1958) suggested that vocal characterizers impart information about the person through vocal properties. Such information, if central to the impression of a particular individual, could be a telling and important part of one's memory of that individual. For example, no one who was listening will ever forget the sound of Edward R. Murrow's voice on the radio as he broadcast from London's rooftops during the blitzkrieg, opening each broadcast with the familiar "This . . . is

London." Similarly, small nonverbal mannerisms that were earlier termed adaptive and manipulative behaviors sometimes become part of person memory for a particular individual. Many people (in our culture) instantly recognize a certain adjustment of the tie as belonging to Rodney Dangerfield and the adjustment of shirt cuffs as a Johnny Carson gesture. It is likely that you have made similar cue identifications with many of your friends and instructors.

APPLICATIONS

Nonverbal Cues in the Classroom

Another way to approach nonverbal cues that affect comprehension and learning is to study a context where communication and information processing are the main focus of activity—the classroom. The literature indicates that nonverbal cues can affect learning in the classroom in three main ways (for reviews, see Andersen, 1986, and Smith, 1979). First, a teacher's nonverbal immediacy behaviors can affect students' attitudes and feelings toward a subject area (Andersen, 1979). More eye contact, smiling, vocal expressiveness, physical proximity, appropriate touching, leaning toward a person, gesturing, overall body movements, and relaxation (Andersen, 1979, 1986) communicate liking and positive affect toward students and the educational experience. Students respond to teacher immediacy behaviors by developing positive attitudes toward the content area being taught, by becoming more likely to take courses in the content area in the future (Andersen, 1979; Andersen, Norton, & Nussbaum, 1981; Kearney, Plax, & Wendt-Wasco, 1985; McDowell, McDowell, & Hyerdahl, 1980; Plax, Kearney, McCroskey, & Richmond, 1986), and, according to students' own perceptions, by actually learning more (Gorham, 1988; Richmond, Gorham, & McCroskey, 1986). Studies of Eskimo and Caucasian children found that a warmer teaching style—smiling, close distances, touch, and direct body orientation—increased learning for both groups of children (Kleinfeld, 1973, 1974).

If you reflect on your own educational experience, these findings are not surprising. One of the factors that probably influenced you to continue taking courses in a certain area is an instructor who was very positive, enthusiastic, and approachable. The relationship between instructor immediacy and positive student attitude also suggests that the opposite can happen: Instructors who do not display immediacy cues may turn students off to a given area of content, resulting in students' having negative attitudes toward the content and being less likely to continue study in that area.

Nonverbal Cues in the Classroom (*Continued*)

Another way in which nonverbal cues may facilitate comprehension has to do with their regulative function (Andersen, 1986). As we noted earlier, regulation cues serve to keep conversants on track and can therefore enhance comprehension. Similar to informal conversation, these cues regulate who speaks when, for how long, and on what topic, although in the classroom, the regulation process is a bit more formalized. Skillful use of regulative cues by an instructor can apportion floor time fairly among students, prompt some students to speak and limit others, keep student comments on the topic, and provide a better overall flow for class

Do the nonverbal cues displayed by the instructor in these two photos affect student learning?

Nonverbal Cues in the Classroom (*Continued*)

discussion. The upshot of these regulative effects is to make the material being discussed in class more comprehensible for students.

Finally, instructor power and status cues can enhance a productive and supportive classroom climate (Andersen, 1986; Plax, Kearney, McCroskey, & Richmond, 1986; Richmond, McCroskey, Kearney, & Plax, 1985). Since we often like people of high status and power, who are in a position to reward us, nonverbal cues that send power and status messages can increase liking for an instructor among students. Greater liking can in turn enhance student motivation and cognitive learning. As Andersen points out, nonverbal power and status messages may be especially effective because they can be nonoffensive ways of indicating power and status. However, an instructor's verbal behavior, in both style and content, must be congruent with nonverbal power and status messages; over time, students pick up on inconsistent or unconvincing signals.

One final point must be reemphasized. At the beginning of this chapter, we pointed out that understanding and the other information processing stages are a fundamental part of a basic aim of communication—to know. But how many times have you left important situations *not knowing?* Whether it be an interaction with a doctor, a lawyer, an educator, or a financial adviser, the consequences of not understanding in these situations are usually negative. This chapter could be relevant to these situations. Application of what is being discovered about information processing and nonverbal behavior could help to achieve knowledge and understanding where little existed before. And that is what communication is about.

Summary

Human information processing can be said to occur in a series of stages that involve both message production and message decoding. Nonverbal cues of various types play roles in all these stages. For message production, a number of nonverbal cues are associated with complexity and difficulty in message encoding. Nonverbal cues also provide the frame for verbal utterances by supplying vocal cues that define phonemic clauses.

Message decoding also involves a number of information processing stages. Nonverbal cues have been shown to affect the attention a communicator pays to a message. A rapid tempo, for example, may enhance comprehension by increasing a listener's attentiveness. Other cues may serve as distractors. Understanding of a message likewise can be affected by concomitant nonverbal cues. Nonverbal behaviors that have close ties to the accompanying language, through either semantic links or rhythmic and proximity links, appear to be most efficient in prompting retrieval of event information. When nonverbal cues provide the context for verbal behavior in communication situations, they can aid retrieval of message information at a later point. Nonverbal cues responsible for impression formation may also facilitate person memory. Finally, we reviewed the nonverbal cues that occur in the classroom. Immediacy and power or status cues have strong potential to affect comprehension and learning.

Suggested Readings

Andersen, J. F. (1986). Instructor nonverbal communication: Listening to our silent messages. In J. M. Civikly (Ed.), *Communicating in college classrooms: New directions for teaching and learning* (pp. 41–49). San Francisco: Jossey-Bass.

Anderson, J. R. (1980). *Cognitive psychology and its implications.* New York: Freeman.

Boomer, D. S. (1978). The phonemic clause: Speech unit in human communication. In A. W. Siegman & S. Feldstein (Eds.), *Nonverbal behavior and communication* (pp. 245–262). Hillsdale, NJ: Erlbaum.

Craig, R. T. (1978). Cognitive science: A new approach to cognition, language, and communication. *Quarterly Journal of Speech, 64,* 439–467.

Craik, F. I. M., & Lockhart, R. S. (1972). Levels of processing: A framework for memory research. *Journal of Verbal Learning and Verbal Behavior, 11,* 671–684.

Folger, J. P., & Woodall, W. G. (1982). Nonverbal cues as linguistic context: An information processing view. In M. Burgoon (Ed.), *Communication Yearbook 6* (pp. 63–91). Beverly Hills, CA: Sage.

Hastie, R., Ostrom, T. R., Ebbesen, E. B., Wyer, R. S., Hamilton, D. L., & Carlston, D. E. (1980). *Person memory: The cognitive basis of social perception.* Hillsdale, NJ: Erlbaum.

Hewes, D. E., & Planalp, S. (1982). "There is nothing as useful as a good theory . . .": The influence of social knowledge on interpersonal communication. In C. Berger & M. Roloff (Eds.), *Social cognition and communication* (pp. 107–150). Beverly Hills, CA: Sage.

Kendon, A. (1983). Gesture and speech: How they interact. In J. M. Wiemann & R. P. Harrison (Eds.), *Nonverbal interaction* (pp. 13–45). Beverly Hills, CA: Sage.

Woodall, W. G., & Folger, J. P. (1985). Nonverbal cue context and episodic memory: On the availability and endurance of nonverbal behaviors as retrieval cues. *Communication Monographs, 52,* 319–333.

REFERENCES

Abelson, R. P., & Sermat, V. (1962). Multidimensional scaling of facial expressions. *Journal of Experimental Psychology, 63,* 546–554.

Abrahamson, M. (1966). *Interpersonal accommodation.* New York: Van Nostrand.

Acking, C. A., & Kuller, R. (1972). The perception of an interior as a function of its colour. *Ergonomics, 15,* 645–654.

Acton, W. I. (1970). Speech intelligibility in a background noise and noise-induced hearing loss. *Ergonomics; 13,* 546–554.

Addington, D. W. (1968). The relationship of selected vocal characteristics to personality perception. *Speech Monographs, 35,* 492–503.

Addington, D. W. (1971). The effect of vocal variations on ratings of source credibility. *Speech Monographs, 38,* 242–247.

Ahmed, S. M. S. (1980). Reactions to crowding in different settings. *Psychological Reports, 46,* 1279–1284.

Aiello, J. R., & Aiello, T. D. (1974). The development of personal space: Proxemic behavior of children 6 through 16. *Human Ecology, 2,* 177–189.

Aiello, J. R., & Cooper, R. E. (1972). Use of personal space as a function of social affect. *Proceedings of the 80th Annual Convention of the American Psychological Association, 7* (1), 207–208.

Aiello, J. R., DeRisi, D. T., Epstein, Y. M., & Karlin, R. A. (1977). Crowding and the role of interpersonal distance preference. *Sociometry, 40,* 271–282.

Aiello, J. R., Epstein, Y. M., & Karlin, R. A. (1975). Effects of crowding on electrodermal activity. *Sociological Symposium, 14,* 43–57.

Aiello, J. R., & Jones, S. E. (1971). Field study of the proxemic behavior of young school children in three subcultural groups. *Journal of Personality and Social Psychology, 19,* 351–356.

Aiken, L. R. (1963). The relationship of dress to selected measures of personality in undergraduate women. *Journal of Social Psychology, 59,* 119–128.

Albert, S., & Dabbs, J. M., Jr. (1970). Physical distance and persuasion. *Journal of Personality and Social Psychology, 15,* 265–270.

Albert, S., & Kessler, S. (1978). Ending social encounters. *Journal of Experimental Social Psychology, 14,* 541–553.

Alexander, I. E., & Babad, E. Y. (1981). Returning the smile of the stranger: Within-culture and cross-cultural comparisons of Israeli and American children. *Genetic Psychology Monographs, 103,* 31–77.

Allen, V. L., & Atkinson, M. L. (1978). Encoding of nonverbal behavior by high-achieving and low-achieving children. *Journal of Educational Psychology, 70,* 298–305.

Allport, F. H. (1924). *Social psychology.* Boston: Houghton Mifflin.

Allport, G. W., & Cantril, H. (1934). Judging personality from voice. *Journal of Social Psychology, 5,* 37–54.

Allport, G. W., & Vernon, P. E. (1937). *Studies in expressive movement.* New York: Hafner.

Als, H., Tronick, E., & Brazelton, T. B. (1979). Analysis of face-to-face interaction in infant-adult dyads. In M. E. Lamb, S. J. Suomi, & G. R. Stephenson (Eds.), *Social interaction analysis* (pp. 33–76). Madison: University of Wisconsin Press.

Altman, I. (1971). Ecological aspects of interpersonal functioning. In A. H. Esser (Ed.), *Behavior and environment: The use of space by animals and men* (pp. 291–306). New York: Plenum.

Altman, I. (1975). *The environment and social behavior.* Monterey, CA: Brooks/Cole.

Altman, I., & Chemers, M. M. (1980). *Culture and environment.* Monterey, CA: Brooks/Cole.

Altman, I., & Haythorn, W. W. (1967). The ecology of isolated groups. *Behavioral Science, 12,* 169–182.

Altman, I., Nelson, P. A., & Lett, E. E. (1972). The ecology of home environments. *Man-Environment Systems, 2,* 189–191.

Altman, I., Taylor, D. A., & Wheeler, L. (1971). Ecological aspects of group behavior in social isolation. *Journal of Applied Social Psychology, 1,* 76–100.

Altman, I., & Vinsel, A. M. (1977). Personal space: An analysis of E. T. Hall's proxemics framework. In I. Altman & J. F. Wohlwill (Eds.), *Human behavior and environment: Advances in theory and research* (Vol. 2, pp. 181–259). New York: Plenum.

Amabile, T. M., & Kabat, L. G. (1982). When self-descriptions contradict behavior: Actions do speak louder than words. *Social Cognition, 1,* 311–335.

Andersen, J. F. (1979). The relationship between teacher immediacy and teaching effectiveness. In B. Ruben (Ed.), *Communication Yearbook 3.* New Brunswick, NJ: Transaction.

Andersen, J. F. (1986). Instructor nonverbal communication: Listening to our silent messages. In J. M. Civikly (Ed.), *Communicating in college classrooms: New directions for teaching and learning* (pp. 41–49). San Francisco: Jossey-Bass.

Andersen, J. F., Andersen, P. A., & Jensen, A. D. (1979). The measurement of nonverbal immediacy. *Journal of Applied Communication Research, 7,* 153–180.

Andersen, J. F., Andersen, P. A., & Landgraf, J. (1985, May). *The development of nonverbal communication competence in childhood.* Paper presented at the annual meeting of the International Communication Association, Honolulu.

Andersen, J. F., Norton, R. W., & Nussbaum, J. F. (1981). Three investigations exploring relationships between perceived teacher communication behaviors and student learning. *Communication Education, 30,* 377–392.

Andersen, P. A. (1985). Nonverbal immediacy in interpersonal communication. In A. W. Siegman & S. Feldstein (Eds.), *Multichannel integrations of nonverbal behavior* (pp. 1–36). Hillsdale, NJ: Erlbaum.

Andersen, P. A., & Andersen, J. F. (1984). The exchange of nonverbal intimacy: A critical review of dyadic models. *Journal of Nonverbal Behavior, 8,* 327–349.

Andersen, P. A., Andersen, J. F., Wendt, N. J., & Murphy, M. A. (1981, May). *The development of nonverbal communication behavior in school children, grades K-12.* Paper presented at the annual meeting of the International Communication Association, Minneapolis.

Andersen, P. A., Garrison, J. P., & Andersen, J. F. (1979). Implications of a neurophysiological approach for the study of nonverbal communication. *Human Communication Research, 6,* 72–89.

Andersen, P. A., Jensen, T. A., & King, L. B. (1972). *The effects of homophilous hair and dress styles on credibility and comprehension.* Paper presented at the annual meeting of the International Communication Association, Atlanta.

Andersen, P. A., & Liebowitz, K. (1978). The development and nature of the construct touch avoidance. *Environmental Psychology and Nonverbal Behavior, 3,* 89–106.

Andersen, P. A., & Sull, K. K. (1985). Out of touch, out of reach: Tactile predispositions as predictors of interpersonal distance. *Western Journal of Speech Communication, 49,* 57–72.

Anderson, J. R. (1980). *Cognitive psychology and its implications.* New York: Freeman.

Anderson, N. H., & Jacobson, A. (1965). Effect of stimulus inconsistency and discounting instructions in personality impression formation. *Journal of Personality and Social Psychology, 2,* 531–539.

Andrew, R. J. (1972). The information potentially available in mammal displays. In R. A. Hinde (Ed.), *Nonverbal communication* (pp. 179–204). Cambridge: Cambridge University Press.

Anttila, R. (1972). *An introduction to historical and comparative linguistics.* New York: Macmillan.

Apple, W. (1979). *Perceiving emotion in others: Integration of verbal, nonverbal and contextual cues.* Unpublished doctoral dissertation, Columbia University.

Apple, W., & Hecht, K. (1982).

Speaking emotionally: The relation between verbal and vocal communication of affect. *Journal of Personality and Social Psychology, 42,* 864–875.

Apple, W., Streeter, L. A., & Krauss, R. M. (1979). Effects of pitch and speech rate on personal attributions. *Journal of Personality and Social Psychology, 37,* 715–727.

Archer, D., & Akert, R. M. (1977). Words and everything else: Verbal and nonverbal cues in social interpretation. *Journal of Personality and Social Psychology, 35,* 443–449.

Ardrey, R. (1966). *The territorial imperative.* New York: Atheneum.

Ardrey, R. (1970). *African genesis.* New York: Dell.

Argyle, M. (1969). *Social interaction.* New York: Atherton.

Argyle, M. (1972a). Non-verbal communication in human social interaction. In R. A. Hinde (Ed.), *Nonverbal communication* (pp. 243–268). Cambridge: Cambridge University Press.

Argyle, M. (1972b). *The psychology of interpersonal behaviour* (2nd ed.). Baltimore: Penguin.

Argyle, M. (1975). *Bodily communication.* London: Methuen.

Argyle, M. (1979). Sequences in social behaviour as a function of the situation. In G. P. Ginsburg (Ed.), *Emerging strategies in social psychological research* (pp. 11–37). New York: Wiley.

Argyle, M., Alkema, F., & Gilmour, R. (1971). The communication of friendly and hostile attitudes by verbal and nonverbal signals. *European Journal of Social Psychology, 1,* 385–402.

Argyle, M., & Cook, M. (1976). *Gaze and mutual gaze.* Cambridge: Cambridge University Press.

Argyle, M., & Dean, J. (1965). Eye contact, distance, and affiliation. *Sociometry, 28,* 289–304.

Argyle, M., & Kendon, A. (1967). The experimental analysis of social performance. In L. Berkowitz (Ed.), *Advances in experimental social psychology* (pp. 55–91). New York: Academic Press.

Argyle, M., Lalljee, M., & Cook, M. (1968). The effects of visibility on interaction in a dyad. *Human Relations, 21,* 3–17.

Argyle, M., Salter, V., Nicholson, H., Williams, M., & Burgess, P. (1970). The communication of inferior and superior attitudes by verbal and nonverbal signals. *British Journal of Social and Clinical Psychology, 9,* 221–231.

Aries, E. J. (1982). Verbal and nonverbal behavior in single-sex and mixed-sex groups: Are traditional

sex-roles changing? *Psychological Reports, 51,* 127–134.

Aronovitch, C. D. (1976). The voice of personality: Stereotyped judgments and their relation to voice quality and sex of speaker. *Journal of Personality and Social Psychology, 33,* 255–270.

Aronson, E., & Linder, D. (1965). Gain and loss of esteem as determinants of interpersonal attractiveness. *Journal of Experimental Social Psychology, 1,* 156–171.

Auvine, B., Densmore, B., Extrom, M., Poole, S., & Shanklin, M. (1978). *A manual for group facilitators.* Madison, WI: Center for Conflict Resolution.

Axelrod, J. (1980). *The effect of sex-role attitude, status and sex of the addressee on the nonverbal communication of women.* Unpublished doctoral dissertation, New York University.

Baglan, T., & Nelson, D. J. (1982). A comparison of the effects of sex and status on the perceived appropriateness of nonverbal behaviors. *Women's Studies in Communication, 5,* 29–38.

Bakker, C. B., & Bakker-Rabdau, M. K. (1985). *No trespassing! Explorations in human territoriality.* San Francisco: Chandler & Sharp.

Bandura, A. (1965). Influence of models' reinforcement contingencies on the acquisition of imitative responses. *Journal of Personality and Social Psychology, 1,* 589–595.

Bandura, A. (1977). *Social learning theory.* Englewood Cliffs, NJ: Prentice-Hall.

Banks, D. L. (1974). A comparative study of the reinforcing potential of verbal and nonverbal cues in a verbal conditioning paradigm. (Doctoral dissertation, University of Massachusetts). *Dissertation Abstracts International, 35,* 2671A. (University Microfilms No. 74–25,819).

Barak, A., Patkin, J., & Dell, D. M. (1982). Effects of certain counselor behaviors on perceived expertness and attractiveness. *Journal of Counseling Psychology, 29,* 261–267.

Barner-Barry, C. (1980). The structure of young children's authority relationships. In D. R. Omark, F. F. Strayer, & D. G. Freedman (Eds.), *Dominance relations* (pp. 177–190). New York: Garland.

Barnlund, D. C. (1975). Communicative styles in two cultures: Japan and the United States. In A. Kendon, R. M. Harris, & M. R. Key (Eds.), *Organization of behavior in face-to-face interaction* (pp. 427–456). The Hague: Mouton.

Baron, R. A. (1978). Invasions of per-

References

sonal space and helping: Mediating effects of invader's apparent need. *Journal of Experimental Social Psychology, 14,* 304–312.

Baron, R. A., & Bell, P. A. (1976). Physical distance and helping: Some unexpected benefits of "crowding in" on others. *Journal of Applied Social Psychology, 6,* 95–104.

Barroso, F., Freedman, N., Grand, S., & Van Meel, J. (1978). Evocation of two types of hand movements in information processing. *Journal of Experimental Psychology, 4,* 321–329.

Bar-Tal, D., & Saxe, L. (1976). Perceptions of similarly and dissimilarly attractive couples and individuals. *Journal of Personality and Social Psychology, 33,* 772–781.

Baskett, G. D., & Freedle, R. O. (1974). Aspects of language pragmatics and the social perception of lying. *Journal of Psycholinguistic Research, 3,* 117–131.

Bass, B. M., & Klubeck, S. (1952). Effects of seating arrangement on leaderless group discussions. *Journal of Abnormal and Social Psychology, 47,* 724–727.

Batchelor, J. P., & Goethals, G. R. (1972). Spatial arrangements in freely formed groups. *Sociometry, 35,* 270–279.

Bates, J. E. (1973). *The effects of a child's imitation versus nonimitation on adults' verbal and nonverbal positivity.* Unpublished doctoral dissertation, University of California, Los Angeles.

Bateson, G. (1935). Culture contact and schismogenesis. *Man, 35,* 178–183.

Bateson, G. (1958). *Naven* (2nd ed.). Stanford, CA: Stanford University Press.

Bateson, M. C. (1975). Mother-infant exchanges: The epigenesis of conversational interaction. *Annals of the New York Academy of Sciences, 263,* 101–113.

Bauchner, J. E. (1978). *Accuracy in detecting deception as a function of level of relationship and communication history.* Unpublished doctoral dissertation, Michigan State University.

Bauer, E. A. (1973). Personal space: A study of blacks and whites. *Sociometry, 36,* 402–408.

Baum, A., & Greenberg, C. I. (1975). Waiting for a crowd: The behavioral and perceptual effects of anticipated crowding. *Journal of Personality and Social Psychology, 32,* 671–679.

Baum, A., Harpin, R. E., & Valins, S. (1975). The role of group phenomena in the experience of crowding. *Environment and Behavior, 7,* 185–198.

Baum, A., Riess, M., & O'Hara, J.

(1974). Architectural variants of reaction to spatial invasion. *Environment and Behavior, 6,* 91–100.

Baum, A., & Singer, J. E. (1982). *Advances in environmental psychology, Vol. 4: Environment and health.* Hillsdale, NJ: Erlbaum.

Bavelas, J. B., Black, A., Chovil, N., Lemery, C. R., & Mullett, J. (1988). Form and function in motor mimicry: Topographic evidence that the primary function is communicative. *Human Communication Research, 14,* 275–300.

Bavelas, J. B., Black, A., Lemery, C. R., & Mullett, J. (1986). "I *show* how you feel": Motor mimicry as a communicative act. *Journal of Personality and Social Psychology, 50,* 322–329.

Baxter, J. C. (1970). Interpersonal spacing in natural settings. *Sociometry, 33,* 444–456.

Baxter, J. C., & Deanovitch, B. F. (1970). Anxiety effects of inappropriate crowding. *Journal of Consulting and Clinical Psychology, 35,* 174–178.

Baxter, J. C., Winters, E. P., & Hammer, R. E. (1968). Gestural behavior during a brief interview as a function of cognitive variables. *Journal of Personality and Social Psychology, 8,* 303–307.

Baxter, L., & Ward, J. (1975, December). Cited in "Newsline." *Psychology Today,* 28.

Bayes, M. A. (1970). *An investigation of the behavioral cues of interpersonal warmth.* Unpublished doctoral dissertation, University of Miami.

Bayes, M. A. (1972). Behavioral cues of interpersonal warmth. *Journal of Consulting and Clinical Psychology, 39,* 333–339.

Becker, F. D. (1973). Study of spatial markers. *Journal of Personality and Social Psychology, 26,* 439–445.

Beebe, S. A. (1980). Effects of eye contact, posture and vocal inflection upon credibility and comprehension. *Australian SCAN: Journal of Human Communication, 7–8,* 57–70.

Beekman, S. (1975). *Sex differences in nonverbal behavior.* Paper presented at the annual meeting of the American Psychological Association, Chicago.

Beier, E. G. (1974). Nonverbal communication: How we send emotional messages. *Psychology Today, 8(5),* 52–59.

Beier, E. G., & Sternberg, D. P. (1977). Subtle cues between newlyweds. *Journal of Communication, 27(3),* 92–97.

Beighley, K. C. (1952). An experimental study of the effect of four speech variables on listener comprehension. *Speech Monographs, 19,* 249–258.

Beighley, K. C. (1954). An experimen-

tal study of three speech variables on listener comprehension. *Speech Monographs, 21,* 248–253.

Bell, P. A., & Barnard, W. A. (1984). Effects of heat, noise, and sex of subject on a projective measure of personal space permeability. *Perceptual and Motor Skills, 59,* 422.

Bem, S. L. (1974). The measurement of psychological androgyny. *Journal of Consulting and Clinical Psychology, 42,* 155–162.

Berger, C. R. (1977). The covering law perspective as a theoretical basis for the study of human communication. *Communication Quarterly, 25,* 7–18.

Berger, C. R. (1979). Beyond initial interaction: Uncertainty, understanding, and the development of interpersonal relationships. In H. Giles & R. St. Clair (Eds.), *Language and social psychology* (pp. 122–144). Oxford: Blackwell.

Berger, C. R., & Bradac, J. J. (1982). *Language and social knowledge: Uncertainty in interpersonal relations.* London: Arnold.

Berger, C. R., & Calabrese, R. J. (1975). Some explorations in initial interaction and beyond: Toward a developmental theory of interpersonal communication. *Human Communication Research, 1,* 99–112.

Berman, H. J., Shulman, A. D., & Marwit, S. J. (1976). Comparison of multidimensional decoding of affect from audio, video, and audio-video recordings. *Sociometry, 39,* 83–89.

Berman, P. W., & Smith, V. L. (1984). Gender and situational differences in children's smiles, touch, and proxemics. *Sex Roles, 10,* 347–356.

Berscheid, E., Dion, K. K., Walster, E. H., & Walster, G. W. (1971). Physical attractiveness and dating choice: Tests of the matching hypothesis. *Journal of Experimental Social Psychology, 7,* 173–189.

Berscheid, E., & Walster, E. H. (1969, 1978). *Interpersonal attraction* (2nd ed.). Reading, MA: Addison-Wesley.

Berscheid, E. & Walster, E. H. (1972, September). Beauty and the best. *Psychology Today, 5,* 42–46, 74.

Berscheid, E., & Walster, E. H. (1974). Physical attractiveness. In L. Berkowitz (Ed.), *Advances in experimental social psychology* (Vol. 7, pp. 158–215). New York: Academic Press.

Berscheid, E., Walster, E. H., & Bohrnstedt, G. (1973, November). Body image: The happy American body. *Psychology Today, 7,* pp. 119–131.

Bettinghaus, E. P., & Cody, M. J. (1987). *Persuasive communication.* New York: Holt, Rinehart and Winston.

Bickman, L. (1971a). Effect of different uniforms on obedience in field situations. *Proceedings of the 79th Annual American Psychological Association Convention,* 359–360.

Bickman, L. (1971b). The effect of social status on the honesty of others. *Journal of Social Psychology, 85,* 87–92.

Bickman, L. (1974a). The social power of a uniform. *Journal of Applied Social Psychology, 4,* 47–61.

Bickman, L. (1974b). Social roles and uniforms: Clothes make the person. *Psychology Today, 7(11),* 48–51.

Birdwhistell, R. (1955). Background to kinesics. *ETC., 13,* 10–18.

Birdwhistell, R. (1970). *Kinesics and context: Essays on body motion communication.* Philadelphia: University of Pennsylvania Press.

Birk, T., Pfau, M., & Burgoon, J. K. (1988). *The pattern of influence: The relationship between nonverbal behaviors, source credibility and persuasion.* Manuscript submitted for publication.

Birren, F. (1950). *Color psychology and color therapy.* New York: McGraw-Hill.

Birren, F. (1952). Emotional significance of color preference. *American Journal of Occupational Therapy, 6,* 61–65, 72, 88.

Blake, R., Rhead, C. C., Wedge, B., & Mouton, J. S. (1956). Housing architecture and social interaction. *Sociometry, 19,* 133–139.

Blanck, P. D., Buck, R., & Rosenthal, R. (Eds.) (1986). *Nonverbal communication in the clinical context.* University Park, PA: The Pennsylvania State University Press.

Blanck, P. D., Rosenthal, R., & Vannicelli, M. (1986). Talking to and about patients: The therapist's tone of voice. In P. D. Blanck, R. Buck, & R. Rosenthal (Eds.), *Nonverbal communication in the clinical context* (pp. 99–143). University Park, PA: The Pennsylvania State University Press.

Blonston, G. (1985, July/August). The translator. *Science,* 79–85.

Bloom, L. J., Weigel, R. G., & Trautt, G. M. (1977). Therapeugenic factors in psychotherapy: Effects of office decor and subject-therapist sex pairing on perception of credibility. *Journal of Consulting and Clinical Psychology, 45(5),* 867–873.

Boderman, A., Freed, D. W., & Kinnucan, M. T. (1972). "Touch me, like me": Testing an encounter group assumption. *Journal of Applied Behavioral Science, 8,* 527–533.

Boggs, D. H., & Simon, J. R. (1968). Differential effect of noise on tasks of varying complexity. *Journal of Applied Psychology, 52,* 148–153.

Boice, R., & Monti, P. M. (1982). Specification of nonverbal cues for clinical assessment. *Journal of Nonverbal Behavior, 7,* 79–94.

Bok, S. (1978). *Lying: Moral choice in public and private life.* New York: Pantheon Books.

Bok, S. (1982). *Secrets: On the ethics of concealment and revelation.* New York: Pantheon Books.

Bond, M. H., & Komai, H. (1976). Targets of gazing and eye contact during interviews: Effects on Japanese nonverbal behavior. *Journal of Personality and Social Psychology, 34,* 1276–1284.

Bond, M. H., & Shiraishi, D. (1974). The effect of interviewer's body lean and status on the nonverbal behavior of interviewees. *Japanese Journal of Experimental Social Psychology, 13,* 11–21.

Boomer, D. S. (1965). Hesitation and grammatical encoding. *Language and Speech, 8,* 148–158.

Boomer, D. S. (1978). The phonemic clause: Speech unit in human communication. In A. W. Siegman & S. Feldstein (Eds.), *Nonverbal behavior and communication* (pp. 245–262). Hillsdale, NJ: Erlbaum.

Boomer, D. S., & Dittmann, A. T. (1962). Hesitation pauses and juncture pauses in speech. *Language and Speech, 5,* 215–220.

Borden, R. J. (1980). Audience influence. In P. B. Paulus (Ed.), *Psychology of group influence* (pp. 99–131). Hillsdale, NJ: Erlbaum.

Bossley, M. I. (1976). Privacy and crowding: A multidisciplinary analysis. *Man-Environment Systems, 6,* 8–19.

Boucher, J. D., & Ekman, P. (1975). Facial areas and emotional information. *Journal of Communication, 25(2),* 21–29.

Boulding, K. E. (1968). Am I a man or a mouse—or both? In M. F. A. Montagu (Ed.), *Man and aggression* (pp. 83–90). London: Oxford University Press.

Bourget, L. G. C. (1977). Delight and information specificity as elements of positive interpersonal feedback (Doctoral dissertation, Boston University). *Dissertation Abstracts International, 38,* 1946B–1947B. (University Microfilms No. 77–21,580).

Brady, A. T., & Walker, M. B. (1978). Interpersonal distance as a function of situationally induced anxiety. *British Journal of Social and Clinical Psychology, 17,* 127–133.

Brandt, D. R. (1980). A systematic approach to the measurement of dominance in human face-to-face interaction. *Communication Quarterly, 28,* 31–43.

Brandt, D. R., Miller, G. R., & Hocking, J. E. (1980a). Effects of self-monitoring and familiarity on deception detection. *Communication Quarterly, 28,* 3–10.

Brandt, D. R., Miller, G. R., & Hocking, J. E. (1980b). The truth-deception attribution: Effects of familiarity on the ability of observers to detect deception. *Human Communication Research, 6,* 99–110.

Brandt, D. R., Miller, G. R., & Hocking, J. E. (1982). Familiarity and lie detection: A replication and extension. *Western Journal of Speech Communication, 46,* 276–290.

Brannigan, C. R., & Humphries, D. A. (1972). Human non-verbal behavior: A means of communication. In N. G. Blurton Jones (Ed.), *Ethological studies of child behavior* (pp. 37–64). London: Cambridge University Press.

Brault, G. J. (1962). Kinesics and the classroom: Some typical French gestures. *French Review, 36,* 374–382.

Brazelton, T. B., Tronick, E., Adamson, L., Als, H., & Wise, S. (1975). Early mother-infant reciprocity. In M. A. Hofer (Ed.), *Parent-infant interaction, Ciba Foundation Symposium 33* (pp. 137–168). Amsterdam: Elsevier.

Breed, G., & Ricci, J. S. (1973). "Touch me, like me": Artifact? *Proceedings of the 81st Annual Convention of the American Psychological Association, 8,* 153–154.

Brend, R. M. (1975). Male-female intonation patterns in American English. In B. Thorne & N. Henley (Eds.), *Language and sex: Difference and dominance* (pp. 84–87). Cambridge, MA: Newbury House.

Brislin, R. W., & Lewis, S. A. (1968). Dating and physical attractiveness: Replication. *Psychological Reports, 22,* 976.

Broch, H. (1964). *The sleepwalkers: A triology.* New York: Pantheon Books.

Brodey, W. M. (1969). Information exchange in the time domain. In W. Gray, F. J. Diehl, & N. D. Rizzo (Eds.), *General systems theory and psychiatry* (pp. 220–243). Boston: Little, Brown.

Brody, E. B. (1963). Color and identity conflict in young boys. *Psychiatry, 26,* 188–201.

Broekmann, N. C., & Moller, A. T. (1973). Preferred seating position and distance in various situations. *Journal of Counseling Psychology, 20,* 504–508.

Brooks, A. D. (1975). *Responses to three American dialects.* Paper presented at the AILA Congress, Stuttgart, West Germany.

Brown, B. L. (1980). Effects of speech rate on personality attributions and competency evaluations. In H.

Giles, W. P. Robinson, & P. M. Smith (Eds.), *Language: Social psychological perspectives* (pp. 293–300). Oxford: Pergamon.

Brown, B. L., Strong, W. J., & Rencher, A. C. (1973). Perceptions of personality from speech: Effects of manipulations of acoustic parameters. *Journal of the Acoustical Society of America, 54,* 29–35.

Brown, B. L., Strong, W. J., & Rencher, A. C. (1974). Fifty-four voices from two: The effects of simultaneous manipulations of rate, mean fundamental frequency and variance of fundamental frequency on ratings of personality from speech. *Journal of the Acoustical Society of America, 55* (2), 313–318.

Brown, B. L., Strong, W. J., & Rencher, A. C. (1975). Acoustic determinants of perceptions of personality from speech. *International Journal of the Sociology of Language, 6,* 11–32.

Bruneau, T. J. (1973). Communicative silences: Forms and functions. *Journal of Communication, 23,* 17–46.

Bruneau, T. J. (1979). The time dimension in intercultural communication. In D. Nimmo (Ed.), *Communication yearbook 3* (pp. 169–181). New Brunswick, NJ: Transaction.

Bruneau, T. J. (1980). Chronemics and the verbal-nonverbal interface. In M. R. Key (Ed.), *The relationship of verbal and nonverbal communication* (pp. 101–118). New York: Mouton.

Brunetti, F. A. (1972). Noise, distraction, and privacy in conventional and open school environments. In W. J. Mitchell (Ed.), *Environmental design: Research and practice* (Vol. 1, pp. 12.2.1–12.2.6). Los Angeles: University of California Press.

Buck, J. (1968). The effects of Negro and White dialectical variations upon attitudes of college students. *Speech Monographs, 35,* 181–186.

Buck, R. (1975). Nonverbal communication of affect in children. *Journal of Personality and Social Psychology, 31,* 644–653.

Buck, R. (1977). Nonverbal communication of affect in preschool children: Relationships with personality and skin conductance. *Journal of Personality and Social Psychology, 35,* 225–236.

Buck, R. (1979a). Individual differences in nonverbal sending accuracy and electrodermal responding: The externalizing-internalizing dimension. In R. Rosenthal (Ed.), *Skill in nonverbal communication: Individual differences* (pp. 140–170). Cambridge, MA: Oelgeschlager, Gunn & Hain.

Buck, R. (1979b). Measuring individual differences in the nonverbal communication of affect: The slide-viewing paradigm. *Human Communication Research, 6,* 47–57.

Buck, R. (1980). Nonverbal behavior and the theory of emotion: The facial feedback hypothesis. *Journal of Personality and Social Psychology, 38,* 811–824.

Buck, R. (1981). The evolution and development of emotion expression and communication. In S. S. Brehm, S. M. Kassin, & F. X. Gibbons (Eds.), *Developmental social psychology* (pp. 127–151). New York: Oxford University Press.

Buck, R. (1982, February). *A theory of spontaneous and symbolic expression: Implications for facial lateralization.* Paper presented at the annual meeting of the International Neuropsychological Society, Pittsburgh.

Buck, R. (1984). *The communication of emotion.* New York: Guilford Press.

Buck, R., Miller, R. E., & Caul, W. F. (1974). Sex, personality and physiological variables in the communication of emotion via facial expression. *Journal of Personality and Social Psychology, 30,* 587–596.

Buck, R., Savin, V. J., Miller, R. E., & Caul, W. F. (1972). Nonverbal communication of affect in humans. *Journal of Personality and Social Psychology, 23,* 362–371.

Bugental, D. E. (1974). Interpretations of naturally occurring discrepancies between words and intonation: Modes of inconsistency resolution. *Journal of Personality and Social Psychology, 30,* 125–133.

Bugental, D. E., Henker, B., & Whalen, C. K. (1976). Attributional antecedents of verbal and vocal assertiveness. *Journal of Personality and Social Psychology, 34,* 405–411.

Bugental, D. E., Kaswan, J. W., & Love, L. R. (1970). Perceptions of contradictory meanings conveyed by verbal and nonverbal channels. *Journal of Personality and Social Psychology, 16,* 647–655.

Bugental, D. E., Kaswan, J. W., Love, L. R., & Fox, M. N. (1970). Child versus adult perception of evaluative messages in verbal, vocal, and visual channels. *Developmental Psychology, 2,* 367–375.

Bugental, D. E., Love, L. R. & Gianetto, R. M. (1971). Perfidious feminine faces. *Journal of Personality and Social Psychology, 17,* 314–318.

Bugental, D. E., Love, L. R., Kaswan, J. W., & April, C. (1971). Verbal-nonverbal conflict in parental messages to normal and disturbed children. *Journal of Abnormal Psychology, 77,* 6–10.

Buller, D. B. (1983). *Deception detection and the passive receiver: Are we assuming too little?* Paper presented at the annual meeting of the Eastern Communication Association, Ocean City, MD.

Buller, D. B. (1986). Distraction during persuasive communication: A meta-analytic review. *Communication Monographs, 53,* 91–114.

Buller, D. B. (1987). Communication apprehension and reactions to proxemic violations. *Journal of Nonverbal Behavior, 11,* 13–25.

Buller, D. B., & Aune R. K. (1988a). The effects of vocalics and nonverbal sensitivity on compliance: A speech accommodation theory explanation. *Human Communication Research, 14,* 301–332.

Buller, D. B., & Aune, R. K. (1988b). Nonverbal cues to deception among intimates, friends, and strangers. *Journal of Nonverbal Behavior, 11.*

Buller, D. B., & Burgoon, J. K. (1986). The effects of vocalics and nonverbal sensitivity on compliance: A replication and extension. *Human Communication Research, 13,* 126–144.

Buller, D. B., & Burgoon, J. K. (in press). Deception. In J. A. Daly & J. M. Wiemann (Eds.), *Communicating strategically: Strategies in interpersonal communication.* Hillsdale, NJ: Erlbaum.

Buller, M. K., & Buller, D. B. (1987). Physicians' communication style and patient satisfaction. *Journal of Health and Social Behavior, 28,* 375–388.

Burgess, J. W. (1983). Developmental trends in proxemic spacing behavior between surrounding companions and strangers in casual groups. *Journal of Nonverbal Behavior, 7,* 158–169.

Burgoon, J. K. (1978a). Attributes of the newscaster's voice as predictors of his credibility. *Journalism Quarterly, 55,* 276–281, 300.

Burgoon, J. K. (1978b). A communication model of personal space violations: Explication and an initial test. *Human Communication Research, 4,* 129–142.

Burgoon, J. K. (1980). Nonverbal communication in the 1970s: An overview. In D. Nimmo (Ed.), *Communication yearbook 4* (pp. 179–197). New Brunswick, NJ: Transaction.

Burgoon, J. K. (1982). Privacy and communication. In M. Burgoon (Ed.), *Communication yearbook 6* (pp. 206–249). Beverly Hills, CA: Sage.

Burgoon, J. K. (1983). Nonverbal violations of expectations. In J. M. Wiemann & R. P. Harrison (Eds.), *Nonverbal interaction* (pp. 77–111). Beverly Hills, CA: Sage.

Burgoon, J. K. (1985a). Nonverbal

References

signals. In M. L. Knapp & G. R. Miller (Eds.), *Handbook of interpersonal communication* (pp. 344–390). Beverly Hills, CA: Sage.

Burgoon, J. K. (1985b). The relationship of verbal and nonverbal codes. In B. Dervin & M. J. Voight (Eds.), *Progress in communication sciences* (Vol. 6, pp. 263–298). Norwood, NJ: Ablex.

Burgoon, J. K. (1986, February). *Expectancy violations: Theory, research and critique*. Paper presented at the annual meeting of the Western Speech Communication Association, Tucson, AZ.

Burgoon, J. K. (1988). Spatial relationships in small groups. In K. S. Cathcart & L. A. Samovar (Eds.), *Small group communication: A reader* (5th ed., pp. 351–366). Dubuque: Wm. C. Brown.

Burgoon, J. K., & Aho, L. (1982). Three field experiments on the effects of violations of conversational distance. *Communication Monographs, 49,* 71–88.

Burgoon, J. K., Buller, D. B., Hale, J. L., & deTurck, M. A. (1984). Relational messages associated with nonverbal behaviors. *Human Communication Research, 10,* 351–378.

Burgoon, J. K., & Coker, D. A. (1987, May). *Nonverbal expectancy violations and conversational involvement*. Paper presented at the annual meeting of the International Communication Association, New Orleans.

Burgoon, J. K., Coker, D. A., & Coker, R. A. (1986). Communicative effects of gaze behavior: A test of two contrasting explanations. *Human Communication Research, 12,* 495–524.

Burgoon, J. K., & Hale, J. L. (1984). The fundamental topoi of relational communication. *Communication Monographs, 51,* 193–214.

Burgoon, J. K., & Hale, J. L. (1987a, May). *Nonverbal expectancy violations: Model elaboration and application to immediacy behaviors*. Paper presented at the annual meeting of the International Communication Association, Montreal.

Burgoon, J. K., & Hale, J. L. (1987b). Validation and measurement of the fundamental themes of relational communication. *Communication Monographs, 54,* 19–41.

Burgoon, J. K., & Hale, J. L. (1988). Nonverbal expectancy violations: Model elaboration and application to immediacy behaviors. *Communication Monographs, 55,* 58–79.

Burgoon, J. K., & Jones, S. B. (1976). Toward a theory of personal space expectations and their violations. *Human Communication Research, 2,* 131–146.

Burgoon, J. K., & Koper, R. J. (1984). Nonverbal and relational communication associated with reticence. *Human Communication Research, 10,* 601–626.

Burgoon, J. K., Manusov, V., Mineo, P., & Hale, J. L. (1985). Effects of eye gaze on hiring credibility, attraction, and relational message interpretation. *Journal of Nonverbal Behavior, 9,* 133–146.

Burgoon, J. K., Parrott, R., Le Poire, B., Kelley, D., Walther, J., & Perry, D. (1988, May). *Privacy and communication: Maintaining and restoring privacy through communication*. Paper presented at the annual meeting of the International Communication Association, New Orleans.

Burgoon, J. K., Pfau, M., Parrott, R., Birk, T., Coker, R., & Burgoon, M. (1987). Relational communication, satisfaction, compliance-gaining strategies, and compliance in communication between physicians and patients. *Communication Monographs, 54,* 307–324.

Burgoon, J. K., & Saine, T. J. (1978). *The unspoken dialogue: An introduction to nonverbal communication*. Boston: Houghton-Mifflin.

Burgoon, J. K., Stacks, D. W., & Burch, S. A. (1982). The role of interpersonal rewards and violations of distancing expectations in achieving influence in small groups. *Communication, Journal of the Communication Association of the Pacific, 11,* 114–128.

Burgoon, J. K., Stacks, D. W., & Woodall, W. G. (1979). A communicative model of violations of distancing expectations. *Western Journal of Speech Communication, 43,* 153–167.

Burley, T. D. (1972). *An investigation of the roles of imagery, kinesthetic cues and attention in tactile nonverbal communication*. Unpublished doctoral dissertation, University of Tennessee.

Burns, J. (1972). Development and implementation of an environmental evaluation and redesign process for a high school science department. In W. J. Mitchell (Ed.), *Environmental design: Research and practice* (Vol. 1, pp. 12.3.1–12.3.9). Los Angeles, University of California Press.

Burns, K. L., & Beier, E. G. (1973). Significance of vocal and visual channels in the decoding of emotional meaning. *Journal of Communication, 23,* 118–130.

Burris, P. A. (1982, November). *An interactionist view of small group leadership: Studies of influence relationships and leadership perception*. Paper presented at the annual convention of the Speech Communication Association, Louisville, KY.

Bush, L. E., II (1973). Individual differences in multidimensional scaling of adjectives denoting feelings. *Journal of Personality and Social Psychology, 25,* 50–57.

Byers, P., & Byers, H. (1972). Nonverbal communication and the education of children. In C. B. Cazden, V. P. John, & D. Hymes (Eds.), *Functions of language in the classroom* (pp. 3–31). New York: Teachers College Press.

Byrne, D. (1961). The influence of propinquity and opportunities for interaction on classroom relationships. *Human Relations, 14,* 63–70.

Byrne, D., Baskett, G. D., & Hodges, L. (1971). Behavioral indicators of interpersonal attraction. *Journal of Applied Social Psychology, 1,* 137–149.

Byrne, D., Ervin, C. R., & Lamberth, J. (1970). Continuity between the experimental study of attraction and real-life computer dating. *Journal of Personality and Social Psychology, 16,* 157–165.

Byrne, D., London, O., & Reeves, K. (1968). The effects of physical attractiveness, sex, and attitude similarity on interpersonal attraction. *Journal of Personality, 36,* 259–272.

Cahnman, W. J. (1968). The stigma of obesity. *Sociological Quarterly, 9,* 283–299.

Calhoun, J. B. (1962). Population density and social pathology. *Scientific American, 206,* 139–148.

Calhoun, J. B. (1966). The role of space in animal sociology. *Journal of Social Issues, 22,* 46–58.

Calhoun, J. B. (1970). Space and the strategy of life. *Ekistics, 29,* 425–437.

Camden, C., Motley, M. T., & Wilson, A. (1984). White lies in interpersonal communication: A taxonomy and preliminary investigation of social motivations. *Western Journal of Speech Communication, 48,* 309–325.

Campbell, J. (1982). *Grammatical man.* New York: Simon & Schuster.

Camras, L. A. (1977). Facial expressions used by children in a conflict situation. *Child Development, 48,* 1431–1435.

Camras, L. A. (1980a). Animal threat displays and children's facial expressions: A comparison. In D. R. Omar, F. F. Strayer, & D. G. Freedman (Eds.), *Dominance relations: An ethological view of human conflict and social interaction* (pp. 124–127). New York: Garland STPM.

Camras, L. A. (1980b). Children's understanding of facial expressions used during conflict encounters. *Child Development, 51,* 879–885.

Camras, L. A. (1982). Ethological approaches to nonverbal communication. In R. S. Feldman (Ed.), *Development of nonverbal behavior in children* (pp. 3–28). New York: Springer-Verlag.

Camras, L. A. (1984). Children's verbal and nonverbal communication in a conflict situation. *Ethology and Sociobiology, 5,* 257–268.

Cappella, J. N. (1981). Mutual influence in expressive behavior: Adult-adult and infant-adult dyadic interaction. *Psychological Bulletin, 89,* 101–132.

Cappella, J. N. (1983). Conversational involvement: Approaching and avoiding others. In J. M. Wiemann & R. P. Harrison (Eds.), *Nonverbal interaction* (pp. 113–148). Beverly Hills, CA: Sage.

Cappella, J. N. (1984). The relevance of microstructure of interaction to relationship change. *Journal of Social and Personal Relationships, 1,* 239–264.

Cappella, J. N. (1985). The management of conversations. In M. L. Knapp & G. R. Miller (Eds.), *Handbook of interpersonal communication* (pp. 393–438). Beverly Hills, CA: Sage.

Cappella, J. N., & Greene, J. O. (1982). A discrepancy-arousal explanation of mutual influence in expressive behavior for adult-adult and infant-adult dyadic interaction. *Communication Monographs, 49,* 89–114.

Cappella, J. N., & Greene, J. O. (1984). The effects of distance and individual differences in arousability on nonverbal involvement: A test of discrepancy-arousal theory. *Journal of Nonverbal Behavior, 8,* 259–286.

Cappella, J. N., & Planalp, S. (1981). Talk and silence sequences in informal conversations III: Interspeaker influence. *Human Communication Research, 7,* 117–132.

Carroll, J. M. (1975). *Confidential information sources: Public and private.* Los Angeles: Security World.

Cassotta, L., Feldstein, S., & Jaffe, J. (1964). AVTA: A device for automatic vocal transaction analysis. *Journal of Experimental Analysis of Behavior, 7,* 99–104.

Cathcart, D., & Cathcart, R. (1976). The Japanese social experience and concept of groups. In L. A. Samovar & R. E. Porter (Eds.), *Intercultural communication: A reader* (2nd ed., pp. 58–66). Belmont, CA: Wadsworth.

Chaiken, S. (1979). Communicator physical attractiveness and persuasion. *Journal of Personality and Social Psychology, 37,* 1387–1397.

Chaiken, S., Eagly, A. H., Sejwacz, D., Gregory, W. L., & Christensen, D. (1978). Communicator physical attractiveness as a determinant of opinion change. *JSAS Catalog of Selected Documents in Psychology, 8,* (Ms. No. 1639).

Chaikin, A. L., Derlega, V. J., & Miller, S. J. (1976). Effects of room environment on self-disclosure in a counseling analogue. *Journal of Counseling Psychology, 23,* 479–481.

Chaikin, A. L., Sigler, E., & Derlega, V. J. (1974). Nonverbal mediators of teacher expectancy effects. *Journal of Personality and Social Psychology, 30,* 144–149.

Chance, M. R. A. (1967). Attention structures as the basis of primate rank orders. *Man, 2,* 503–518.

Chapin, F. S. (1951). Some housing factors related to mental hygiene. *Journal of Social Issues, 7,* 164–171.

Chapman, A. J. (1975). Eye contact, physical proximity and laughter: A re-examination of the equilibrium model of social intimacy. *Social Behavior and Personality, 3,* 143–155.

Charlesworth, W. R., & Kreutzer, M. A. (1973). Facial expressions of infants and children. In P. Ekman (Ed.), *Darwin and facial expression* (pp. 91–168). New York: Academic Press.

Charney, E. J. (1966). Psychosomatic manifestation of rapport in psychotherapy. *Psychosomatic Medicine, 28,* 305–315.

Cherry, C. (1957, 1964). *On human communication.* Cambridge, MA: MIT Press.

Christian, J. J., Flyer, V., & Davis, D. E. (1961). Phenomena associated with population density. *Proceedings of the National Academy of Sciences, 47 (4),* 428–449.

Christie, R., & Geis, F. L. (1970). *Studies in Machiavellianism.* New York: Academic Press.

Claiborn, C. D. (1979). Counselor verbal intervention, nonverbal behavior, and social power. *Journal of Counseling Psychology, 26,* 378–383.

Clark, H. H., & French, J. W. (1981). Telephone goodbyes. *Language in society, 10,* 1–19.

Clark, M. S., Milberg, S., & Erber, R. (1984). Effects of arousal on judgments of others' emotions. *Journal of Personality and Social Psychology, 46,* 551–560.

Clark, R. A. (1984). *Persuasive messages.* New York: Harper & Row.

Clark, R. A., & Delia, J. G. (1979). Topoi and rhetorical competence. *Quarterly Journal of Speech, 65,* 187–206.

Cliff, N., & Young, F. W. (1968). On the relation between unidimensional judgments and multidimensional scaling. *Organizational Behavior and Human Performance, 3,* 269–285.

Clifford, M. M., & Walster, E. H. (1973). The effect of physical attractiveness on teacher expectation. *Sociology of Education, 46,* 248–258.

Clore, G. L., Wiggins, N. H., & Itkin, S. (1975a). Gain and loss in attraction: Attributions from nonverbal behavior. *Journal of Personality and Social Psychology, 31,* 706–712.

Clore, G. L., Wiggins, N. H., & Itkin, S. (1975b). Judging attraction from nonverbal behavior: The gain phenomenon. *Journal of Consulting and Clinical Psychology, 43,* 491–497.

Cloudsley-Thompson, J. L. (1981). Time sense of animals. In J. T. Fraser, *The voices of time* (2nd ed., 296–311). Amherst: University of Massachusetts Press.

Cochran, C. D., Hale, W. D., & Hissam, C. P. (1984). Personal space requirements in indoor versus outdoor locations. *Journal of Psychology, 117,* 121–123.

Cody, M. J., & McLaughlin, M. L. (1985). The situation as a construct in interpersonal communication research. In M. L. Knapp & G. R. Miller (Eds.), *Handbook of interpersonal communication* (pp. 263–312). Beverly Hills, CA: Sage.

Cohen, A., & Starkweather, J. (1961). Vocal cues to the identification of language. *American Journal of Psychology, 74,* 90–93.

Cohen, A. A. (1977). The communicative functions of hand illustrators. *Journal of Communication, 27,* 54–63.

Cohen, A. A., & Harrison, R. P. (1973). Intentionality in the use of hand illustrators in face-to-face communication situations. *Journal of Personality and Social Psychology, 28,* 276–279.

Cohen, S., & Weinstein, N. (1981). Nonauditory effects of noise on behavior and health. *Journal of Social Issues, 37,* 36–70.

Coker, D. A., & Burgoon, J. K. (1986). The nature of conversational involvement and nonverbal encoding patterns. *Human Communication Research, 13,* 463–494.

Collett, P. (1971). On training Englishmen in the non-verbal behavior of Arabs: An experiment in intercultural communication. *International Journal of Psychology, 6,* 209–215.

Collins, A. M., & Loftus, E. F. (1975). A spreading-activation theory of semantic processing. *Psychological Review, 82,* 407–428.

Collins, B. E., & Guetzkow, H. (1964). *A social psychology of group processes.* New York: Wiley.

Comadena, M. E. (1982). Accuracy in

detecting deception: Intimate and friendship relationships. In M. Burgoon (Ed.), *Communication Yearbook 6* (pp. 446–472). Beverly Hills, CA: Sage.

Compton, N. H. (1962). Personal attributes of color and design preferences in clothing fabrics. *Journal of Psychology, 54,* 191–195.

Condon, J. C., & Kurata, K. (1974). *In search of what's Japanese about Japan.* Tokyo, Japan: Shufunotomo Co. Ltd.

Condon, J. C., & Yousef, F. (1975). *An introduction to intercultural communication.* Indianapolis: Bobbs-Merrill.

Condon, W. S. (1976). An analysis of behavior organization. *Sign Language Studies, 13,* 285–318.

Condon, W. S., & Ogston, W. D. (1966). Sound film analysis of normal and pathological behavior patterns. *Journal of Nervous and Mental Disease, 143,* 338–347.

Condon, W. S., & Ogston, W. D. (1967). A segmentation of behavior. *Journal of Psychiatric Research, 5,* 221–235.

Condon, W. S., & Sander, L. W. (1974). Synchrony demonstrated between movement of the neonate and adult speech. *Child Development, 45,* 456–462.

Cook, M. (1970). Experiments on orientation and proxemics. *Human Relations, 23,* 61–76.

Cook, M. (1979). *Perceiving others: The psychology of interpersonal perception.* London: Methuen.

Coombs, R. H., & Kenkel, W. F. (1966). Sex differences in dating aspirations and satisfaction with computer-selected partners. *Journal of Marriage and the Family, 28,* 62–66.

Cooper, C. L., & Bowles, D. (1973). Physical encounter and self-disclosure. *Psychological Reports, 33,* 451–454.

Cooper, J., Darley, J. M., & Henderson, J. E. (1974). On the effectiveness of deviant- and conventional-appearing communicators: A field experiment. *Journal of Personality and Social Psychology, 29,* 752–757.

Copeland, J. B., Shapiro, D., Williams, E., & Matsumoto, N. (1987, February). How to win over a Japanese boss. *Newsweek, 109,* 46–48.

Cortes, J. B., & Gatti, F. M. (1965). Physique and self-description of temperament. *Journal of Consulting Psychology, 29,* 432–439.

Cortes, J. B., & Gatti, F. M. (1970, October). Physique and propensity. *Psychology Today, 4,* pp. 32–34, 42–44.

Costanzo, F. S., Markel, N. N., & Costanzo, R. R. (1969). Voice quality profile and perceived emotion.

Journal of Counseling Psychology, 16, 267–270.

Cottrell, N. B. (1972). Social facilitation. In C. G. McClintock (Ed.), *Experimental social psychology* (pp. 185–236). New York: Holt, Rinehart and Winston.

Cousins, N. (1979). *Anatomy of an illness as perceived by the patient: Reflecting on healing and regeneration.* New York: Norton.

Coutts, L. M., & Schneider, F. W. (1976). Affiliative conflict theory: An investigation of the intimacy equilibrium and compensation hypothesis. *Journal of Personality and Social Psychology, 34,* 1135–1142.

Coutts, L. M., Schneider, F. W., & Montgomery, S. (1980). An investigation of the arousal model of interpersonal intimacy. *Journal of Experimental Social Psychology, 16,* 545–561.

Cozby, P. C. (1974). *Some recent research on self-disclosure processes.* Paper presented at the annual meeting of the American Psychological Association, New Orleans.

Craig, R. T. (1978). Cognitive science: A new approach to cognition, language, and communication. *Quarterly Journal of Speech, 64,* 439–467.

Craik, F. I. M., & Lockhart, R. S. (1972). Levels of processing: A framework for memory research. *Journal of Verbal Learning and Verbal Behavior, 11,* 671–684.

Crassweller, P., Gordon, M. A., & Tedford, W. H., Jr. (1972). An experimental investigation of hitchhiking. *Journal of Psychology, 82,* 43–47.

Crawford, C. C., & Michael, W. (1927). An experiment in judging intelligence by the voice. *Journal of Educational Psychology, 18,* 107–114.

Cronkhite, G. (1986). On the focus, scope, and coherence of the study of human symbolic activity. *Quarterly Journal of Speech, 72,* 231–246.

Crown, C. L. (1980). Impression formation and the chronography of dyadic interactions. In M. Davis (Ed.), *Interaction rhythms: Periodicity in communicative behavior* (pp. 225–248). New York: Human Sciences Press.

Crystal, D. (1969). *Prosodic systems and intonation in English.* Cambridge: Cambridge University Press.

Cuceloglu, D. M. (1970). Perception of facial expressions in three different cultures. *Ergonomics, 13,* 93–100.

Cuceloglu, D. M. (1972). Facial code in affective communication. In D. C. Speer (Ed.), *Nonverbal communication* (pp. 395–407). Beverly Hills, CA: Sage.

Cupchik, G. C. (1973). Expression and impression: The decoding of nonverbal affect. *Dissertation Abstracts International, 33,* 5536B.

Cupchik, G. C., & Poulos, C. X. (1984). Judgments of emotional intensity in self and others: The effects of stimulus context, sex, and expressivity. *Journal of Personality and Social Psychology, 46,* 431–439.

Cushman, D., & Whiting, G. C. (1972). An approach to communication theory: Toward consensus on rules. *Journal of Communication, 22,* 217–238.

Dabbs, J. M., Evans, M. S., Hopper, C. H., & Purvis, J. A. (1980). Self-monitors in conversation: What do they monitor? *Journal of Personality and Social Psychology, 39,* 278–284.

Daley, J. P. (1973). *The effects of crowding and comfort on interaction behavior and membership satisfaction in small groups.* Paper presented at the annual meeting of the International Communication Association, Montreal.

Daly, E. M., Lancee, W. J., & Polivy, J. (1983). A conical model for the taxonomy of emotional experience. *Journal of Personality and Social Psychology, 45,* 443–457.

Daly, J. A., Hogg, E., Sacks, D., Smith, M., & Zimring, L. (1983). Sex and relationship affect social self-grooming. *Journal of Nonverbal Behavior, 7,* 183–189.

d'Angeljan, A., & Tucker, G. R. (1973). Sociolinguistic correlates of speech style in Quebec. In R. Shuy & R. Fasold (Eds.), *Language attitudes: Current trends and prospects* (pp. 1–27). Washington, DC: Georgetown University Press.

Danziger, K. (1976). *Interpersonal communication.* Oxford: Pergamon.

Darley, J. M., & Cooper, J. (1972). The "Clean for Gene" phenomenon: The effect of students' appearance on political campaigning. *Journal of Applied Social Psychology, 2,* 24–33.

Darwin, C. (1965). *The expression of the emotions in man and animals.* Chicago: University of Chicago Press. (Originally published 1872.)

Davidson, L. G. (1950). Some current folk gestures and sign languages. *American Speech, 25,* 3–9.

Davis, D. E. (1971). Physiological effects of continued crowding. In A. H. Esser (Ed.), *Behavior and environment* (pp. 133–147). New York: Plenum.

Davis, R. C. (1961). Physiological responses as a means of evaluating information. In A. D. Biderman & H. Zimmer (Eds.), *The manipulation of human behavior* (pp. 142–168). New York: Wiley.

References

Davitz, J. R. (1964). *The communication of emotional meaning.* New York: McGraw-Hill.

Davitz, J. R., & Davitz, L. J. (1959). The communication of feelings by content-free speech. *Journal of Communication, 9,* 6–13.

D'Augelli, A. R. (1974). Nonverbal behavior of helpers in initial helping interactions. *Journal of Counseling Psychology, 21,* 360–363.

Dean, L. M., Willis, F. N., & Hewitt, J. (1975). Initial interaction distance among individuals equal and unequal in military rank. *Journal of Personality and Social Psychology, 32,* 294–299.

Dean, L. M., Willis, F. N., & Rinck, C. M. (1978). *Patterns of interpersonal touch in the elderly.* Paper presented at the annual meeting of the Western Psychological Association, San Francisco.

Delia, J. G. (1972). Dialects and the effects of stereotypes on interpersonal attraction and cognitive processes in impression formation. *Quarterly Journal of Speech, 58,* 285–297.

DePaulo, B. M. (1981). Success at detecting deception: Liability or skill? *Annals of the New York Academy of Sciences, 364,* 245–255.

DePaulo, B. M., Jordan, A., Irvine, A., & Laser, P. S. (1982). Age changes in the detection of deception. *Child Development, 53,* 701–709.

DePaulo, B. M., Kenny, D. A., Hoover, C. W., Webb, W., & Oliver, P. V. (1987). Accuracy of person perception: Do people know what kinds of impressions they convey? *Journal of Personality and Social Psychology, 52,* 303–315.

DePaulo, B. M., Lassiter, G. D., & Stone, J. I. (1982). Attentional determinants of success at detecting deception and truth. *Personality and Social Psychology Bulletin, 8,* 273–279.

DePaulo, B. M., & Rosenthal, R. (1979a). Ambivalence, discrepancy, and deception in nonverbal communication. In R. Rosenthal (Ed.), *Skill in nonverbal communication: Individual differences* (pp. 204–248). Cambridge, MA: Oelgeschlager, Gunn & Hain.

DePaulo, B. M., & Rosenthal, R. (1979b). Telling lies. *Journal of Personality and Social Psychology, 37,* 1713–1722.

DePaulo, B. M., Rosenthal, R., Eisenstat, R. A., Rogers, P. L., & Finkelstein, S. (1978). Decoding discrepant nonverbal cues. *Journal of Personality and Social Psychology, 36,* 313–323.

DePaulo, B. M., Rosenthal, R., Finkelstein, S., & Eisenstat, R. A. (1979).

The developmental priority of the evaluative dimension in perceptions of nonverbal cues. *Environmental Psychology and Nonverbal Behavior, 3,* 164–171.

DePaulo, B. M., Rosenthal, R., Green, C. R., & Rosenkrantz, J. (1982). Diagnosing deceptive and mixed messages from verbal and nonverbal cues. *Journal of Experimental Social Psychology, 18,* 433–446.

DePaulo, B. M., Stone, J. I., & Lassiter, G. D. (1985a). Deceiving and detecting deceit. In B. R. Schlenker (Ed.), *The self and social life* (pp. 323–370). New York: McGraw-Hill.

DePaulo, B. M., Stone, J. I., & Lassiter, G. D. (1985b). Telling ingratiating lies: Effects of target sex and target attractiveness on verbal and nonverbal deceptive success. *Journal of Personality and Social Psychology, 48,* 1191–1203.

DePaulo, B. M., Zuckerman, M., & Rosenthal, R. (1980a). Detecting deception: Modality effects. In L. Wheeler (Ed.), *Review of personality and social psychology* (Vol. 1, pp. 125–162). Beverly Hills, CA: Sage.

DePaulo, B. M., Zuckerman, M., & Rosenthal, R. (1980b). The deceptions of everyday life. *Journal of Communication, 30,* 216–218.

Derlega, V. J., & Chaikin, A. L. (1977). Privacy and self-disclosure in social relationships. *Journal of Social Issues, 33,* 102–122.

Desor, J. A. (1972). Toward a psychological theory of crowding. *Journal of Personality and Social Psychology, 21,* 79–83.

Despert, J. L. (1941). Emotional aspects of speech and language development. *International Journal of Psychiatry and Neurology, 105,* 193–222.

deTurck, M. A., & Miller, G. R. (1985). Deception and arousal: Isolating the behavioral correlates of deception. *Human Communication Research, 12,* 181–202.

Deutsch, M. (1973). *The resolution of conflict: Constructive and destructive processes.* New Haven, CT: Yale University Press.

Deutsch, M., & Collins, M. (1951). *Interracial housing: A psychological evaluation of a social experiment.* Minneapolis: University of Minnesota Press.

Dew, D., & Jensen, P. J. (1977). *Phonetic processing: The dynamics of speech.* Columbus, OH: Merrill.

Diehl, C. F., White, R. C., & Satz, P. H. (1961). Pitch change and comprehension. *Speech Monographs, 28,* 65–68.

Dietch, J., & House, J. (1975). Affiliative conflict and individual differences in self-disclosure. *Representa-*

tive Research in Social Psychology, 6, 69–75.

Dillard, J. L. (1972). *Black English.* New York: Random House.

DiMatteo, M. R., Prince, L. M., & Hays, R. (1986). Nonverbal communication in the medical context: The physician-patient relationship. In P. D. Blanck, R. Buck, & R. Rosenthal (Eds.), *Nonverbal communication in the clinical context* (pp. 74–98). University Park, PA: The Pennsylvania State University Press.

Dion, K. K. (1972). Physical attractiveness and evaluations of children's transgressions. *Journal of Personality and Social Psychology, 24,* 207–213.

Dion, K. K., Berschied, E., & Walster, E. (1972). What is beautiful is good. *Journal of Personality and Social Psychology, 24,* 285–290.

Dion, K. K., & Stein, S. (1978). Physical attractiveness and interpersonal influence. *Journal of Experimental and Social Psychology, 14,* 97–108.

Dittmann, A. T. (1972a). The body movement-speech rhythm relationship as a cue to speech encoding. In A. W. Siegman & B. Pope (Eds.), *Studies in dyadic communication* (pp. 135–151). New York: Pergamon.

Dittmann, A. T. (1972b). *Interpersonal messages of emotion.* New York: Springer.

Dittmann, A. T. (1978). The role of body movement in communication. In A. W. Siegman & S. Feldstein (Eds.), *Nonverbal behavior and communication* (pp. 69–95). Hillsdale, NJ: Erlbaum.

Dittmann, A. T., & Llewellyn, L. G. (1967). The phonemic clause as a unit of speech decoding. *Journal of Personality and Social Psychology, 6,* 341–349.

Doob, L. W. (1971). *Patterning of time.* New Haven, CT: Yale University Press.

Dosey, M. A., & Meisels, M. (1969). Personal space and self-protection. *Journal of Personality and Social Psychology, 11,* 93–97.

Douty, H. I. (1963). Influence of clothing on perception of persons. *Journal of Home Economics, 55,* 197–202.

Dovidio, J. F., & Ellyson, S. L. (1982). Decoding visual dominance behavior: Attributions of power based on the relative percentages of looking while speaking and looking while listening. *Social Psychology Quarterly, 45,* 106–113.

Dovidio, J. F., & Ellyson, S. L. (1985). Patterns of visual dominance behavior in humans. In S. L. Ellyson & J. F. Dovidio (Eds.), *Power, dominance, and nonverbal behavior* (pp. 129–150). New York: Springer-Verlag.

Dubos, R. (1965). *Man adapting*. New Haven, CT: Yale University Press.

Duker, S. (1974). *Time compressed speech: An anthology and bibliography* (Vol. 3). Metuchen, NJ: Scarecrow Press.

Duncan, S. D., Jr. (1972). Some signals and rules for taking speaking turns in conversations. *Journal of Personality and Social Psychology, 23*, 283–292.

Duncan, S. D., Jr. (1974). On the structure of speaker-auditor interaction during speaking turns. *Language in Society, 2*, 161–180.

Duncan, S. D., Jr. (1975). Interaction units during speaking turns in dyadic, face-to-face conversations. In A. Kendon, R. Harris, & M. R. Key (Eds.), *The organization of behavior in face-to-face interaction* (pp. 199–213). The Hague: Mouton.

Duncan, S. D., Jr., & Fiske, D. W. (1977). *Face-to-face interaction: Research, methods, and theory*. Hillsdale, NJ: Erlbaum.

Duncan, S. D., Jr., & Fiske, D. W. (1985). *Interaction structure and strategy*. Cambridge: Cambridge University Press.

Duncan, S. D., Jr., Rosenberg, M. J., & Finkelstein, J. (1969). The paralanguage of experimenter bias. *Sociometry, 32*, 207–219.

Duncan, S. D., Jr., & Rosenthal, R. (1968). Vocal emphasis in experimenters' instruction reading as unintended determinant of subjects' responses. *Language and Speech, 11*, 20–26.

Eakins, B. W., & Eakins, R. G. (1978). *Sex differences in human communication*. Boston: Houghton Mifflin.

Edelmann, R. J., & Hampson, S. E. (1981a). Embarrassment in dyadic interaction. *Social Behavior and Personality, 9*, 171–177.

Edelmann, R. J., & Hampson, S. E. (1981b). The recognition of embarrassment. *Personality and Social Psychology Bulletin, 7*, 109–116.

Edinger, J. A., & Patterson, M. L. (1983). Nonverbal involvement and social control. *Psychological Bulletin, 93*, 30–56.

Edney, J. J. (1972). Property, possession and permanence: A field study in human territoriality. *Journal of Applied Social Psychology, 3*, 275–282.

Edney, J. J. (1976). Human territories: Comment on functional properties. *Environment and Behavior, 8*, 31–47.

Edney, J. J., & Buda, M. A. (1976). Distinguishing territoriality and privacy: Two studies. *Human Ecology, 4*, 283–296.

Edney, J. J., & Jordan-Edney, N. L. (1974). Territorial spacing on a beach. *Sociometry, 37*, 92–103.

Educational Facilities Laboratories (1965). *Profiles of significant schools: Schools without walls*. New York: Author.

Edwards, D. J. A. (1981). The role of touch in interpersonal relations: Implications for psychotherapy. *South African Journal of Psychology, 11*, 29–37.

Edwards, D. J. A. (1984). The experience of interpersonal touch during a personal growth program: A factor analytic approach. *Human Relations, 37*, 769–780.

Efran, J. S. (1968). Looking for approval: Effects on visual behavior of approbation from persons differing in importance. *Journal of Personality and Social Psychology, 10*, 21–25.

Efran, M. G. (1974). The effect of physical appearance on the judgment of guilt, interpersonal attraction and severity of recommended punishment in a simulated jury task. *Journal of Experimental Research in Personality, 8*, 45–54.

Efron, D. (1972). *Gesture, race and culture*. The Hague: Mouton.

Eibl-Eibesfeldt, I. (1971). *Love and hate: The natural history of behavioral patterns* (G. Strachan, Trans.). New York: Holt, Rinehart & Winston.

Eibl-Eibesfeldt, I. (1972, 1979). Similarities and differences between cultures in expressive movements. In R. A. Hinde (Ed.), *Nonverbal communication* (pp. 297–314). Cambridge: Cambridge University Press. Reprinted in S. Weitz (Ed.), *Nonverbal communication* (2nd ed., pp. 37–48). New York: Oxford University Press.

Eibl-Eibesfeldt, I. (1973). The expressive behavior of the deaf-and-blind born. In M. von Cranach & I. Vine (Eds.), *Social communication and movement* (pp. 163–194). New York: Academic Press.

Eibl-Eibesfeldt, I. (1975). *Ethology: The biology of behavior*. New York: Holt, Rinehart and Winston.

Eisenberg, A. M., & Smith, R. R., Jr. (1971). *Nonverbal communication*. Indianapolis: Bobbs-Merrill.

Ekman, P. (1971). Universal and cultural differences in facial expressions of emotion. In J. K. Cole (Ed.), *Nebraska symposium on motivation* (pp. 207–283). Lincoln, NE: University of Nebraska Press.

Ekman, P. (1973). Cross-cultural studies of facial expression. In P. Ekman (Ed.), *Darwin and facial expression: A century of research in review* (pp. 169–222). New York: Academic Press.

Ekman, P. (1975, September). The universal smile: Face muscles talk every language. *Psychology Today, 9*, pp. 35–39.

Ekman, P. (1976). Movements with precise meanings. *Journal of Communication, 26*, 14–26.

Ekman, P. (1978). Facial expression. In A. W. Siegman & S. Feldstein (Eds.), *Nonverbal behavior and communication* (pp. 97–116). Hillsdale, NJ: Erlbaum.

Ekman, P. (1980). Asymmetry in facial expression. *Science, 209*, 833–834.

Ekman, P., & Friesen, W. V. (1967). Head and body cues in the judgment of emotion: A reformulation. *Perceptual and Motor Skills, 24*, 711–724.

Ekman, P., & Friesen, W. V. (1969a). Nonverbal leakage and clues to deception. *Psychiatry, 32*, 88–106.

Ekman, P., & Friesen, W. V. (1969b). The repertoire of nonverbal behavior: Categories, origins, usage, and coding. *Semiotica, 1*, 49–98.

Ekman, P., & Friesen, W. V. (1972). Hand movements. *Journal of Communication, 22*, 353–374.

Ekman, P., & Friesen, W. V. (1974). Detecting deception from the body or face. *Journal of Personality and Social Psychology, 29*, 288–298.

Ekman, P., & Friesen, W. V. (1975). *Unmasking the face*. Englewood Cliffs, NJ: Prentice-Hall.

Ekman, P., & Friesen, W. V. (1976). Measuring facial movement. *Environmental Psychology and Nonverbal Behavior, 1*, 56–75.

Ekman, P., & Friesen, W. V. (1978). *Investigator's guide to the Facial Action Coding System, part II*. Palo Alto, CA: Consulting Psychologists Press.

Ekman, P., & Friesen, W. V. (1982). Felt, false and miserable smiles. *Journal of Nonverbal Behavior, 6*, 238–252.

Ekman, P., Friesen, W. V., & Ancoli, S. (1980). Facial signs of emotional experience. *Journal of Personality and Social Psychology, 39*, 1125–1134.

Ekman, P., Friesen, W. V., & Ellsworth, P. (1972). *Emotion in the human face*. New York: Pergamon.

Ekman, P., Friesen, W. V., O'Sullivan, M., & Scherer, K. R. (1980). Relative importance of face, body and speech in judgments of personality and affect. *Journal of Personality and Social Psychology, 38*, 270–277.

Ekman, P., Friesen, W. V., & Scherer, K. R. (1976). Body movement and voice pitch in deceptive interaction. *Semiotica, 16*, 23–27.

Ekman, P., Friesen, W. V., & Tomkins, S. S. (1971). Facial affect scoring technique: A first validity study. *Journal of Communication, 3*, 37–58.

Ekman, P., Levinson, R. W., & Friesen, W. V. (1983). Autonomic nervous system activity distinguishes among emotions. *Science, 221,* 1208–1210.

Ekman, P., & Oster, H. (1979). Facial expression of emotion. *Annual Review of Psychology, 30,* 527–554.

Ekman, P., Roper, G., & Hager, J. C. (1980). Deliberate facial movement. *Child Development, 1,* 886–891.

Ekman, P., Sorenson, E. R., & Friesen, W. V. (1969). Pan-cultural elements in facial displays of emotion. *Science, 164,* 86–88.

Elliot, G. C. (1979). Some effects of deception and level of self-monitoring on planning and reacting to a self-presentation. *Journal of Personality and Social Psychology, 37,* 1282–1292.

Ellis, D. G. (1982). Language and speech communication. In M. Burgoon (Ed.), *Communication yearbook 6* (pp. 34–62). Beverly Hills, CA: Sage.

Ellis, D. S. (1967). Speech and social status in America. *Social Forces, 45,* 431–451.

Ellsworth, P. C., & Carlsmith, J. M. (1973). Eye contact and gaze aversion in an aggressive encounter. *Journal of Personality and Social Psychology, 28,* 280–292.

Ellsworth, P. C., Carlsmith, J. M., & Henson, A. (1972). The stare as a stimulus to flight in human subjects: A series of field experiments. *Journal of Personality and Social Psychology, 21,* 302–311.

Ellsworth, P. C., & Langer, E. J. (1976). Staring and approach: An interpretation of the stare as a nonspecific activator. *Journal of Personality and Social Psychology, 33,* 117–122.

Ellsworth, P. C., & Ludwig, L. M. (1972). Visual behavior in social interactions. *Journal of Communication, 22,* 375–403.

Ellsworth, P. C., & Ross, L. (1975). Intimacy in response to direct gaze. *Journal of Experimental Social Psychology, 11,* 592–613.

Ellyson, S. L., & Dovidio, J. F. (1985). Power, dominance, and nonverbal behavior: Basic concepts and issues. In S. L. Ellyson & J. F. Dovidio (Eds.), *Power, dominance, and nonverbal behavior* (pp. 1–27). New York: Springer-Verlag.

Ellyson, S. L., Dovidio, J. F., & Corson, R. L. (1981). Visual behavior differences in females as a function of self-perceived expertise. *Journal of Nonverbal Behavior, 5,* 164–171.

Ellyson, S. L., Dovidio, J. F., Corson, R. L., & Vinicur, D. L. (1980). Visual behavior in female dyads: Situational and personality factors. *Social Psychology Quarterly, 43,* 328–336.

Elman, D., Schulte, D. C., & Bukoff, A. (1977). Effects of facial expression and stare duration on walking speed: Two field experiments. *Environmental Psychology and Nonverbal Behavior, 2,* 93–99.

Elzinga, R. H. (1975). Nonverbal communication: Body accessibility among the Japanese. *Psychologia, 18,* 205–211.

Emde, R. N. (1984). Levels of meaning for infant emotions: A biosocial view. In K. R. Scherer & P. Ekman (Eds.), *Approaches to emotion* (pp. 77–107). Hillsdale, NJ: Erlbaum.

Engebretson, D., & Fullman, D. (1972). Cross-cultural differences in territoriality: Interaction distances of Native Japanese, Hawaii Japanese, and American Caucasians. In L. A. Samovar & R. E. Porter (Eds.), *Intercultural communication: A reader* (pp. 220–226). Belmont, CA: Wadsworth.

Epstein, A., & Ulrich, J. H. (1966). The effect of high- and low-pass filtering on the judged vocal quality of male and female speakers. *Quarterly Journal of Speech, 52,* 267–272.

Epstein, C. F. (1986). Symbolic segregation: Similarities and differences in the language and non-verbal communication of women and men. *Sociological Forum, 1,* 27–49.

Epstein, Y. M., & Karlin, R. A. (1975). Effects of acute experimental crowding. *Journal of Applied Social Psychology, 5,* 34–53.

Epstein, Y. M., Woolfolk, R. L., & Lehrer, P. M. (1981). Physiological, cognitive, and nonverbal responses to repeated exposure to crowding. *Journal of Applied Social Psychology, 11,* 1–13.

Erickson, B., Lind, E. A., Johnson, B. C., & O'Barr, W. M. (1978). Speech style and impression formation in a court setting: The effects of "powerful" and "powerless" speech. *Journal of Experimental Social Psychology, 14,* 266–279.

Erickson, F. (1975). One function of proxemic shifts in face-to-face interaction. In A. Kendon, R. Harris, & M. Key (Eds.), *Organization of behavior in face-to-face interaction* (pp. 175–187). The Hague: Mouton.

Erickson, F. (1979). Talking down: Some cultural sources of miscommunication in interracial interviews. In A. Wolfgang (Ed.), *Nonverbal behavior: Applications and cultural implications* (pp. 99–126). New York: Academic Press.

Erickson, F., & Shultz, J. (1982). *The counselor as gatekeeper: Social interaction in interviews.* New York: Academic Press.

Eschenbrenner, A. J., Jr. (1971). Effects of intermittent noise on the performance of a complex psychomotor task. *Human Factors, 13,* 59–63.

Esser, A. H. (1971). Social pollution. *Social Education, 35(1),* 10–18.

Esser, A. H. (1972). A biosocial perspective on crowding. In J. F. Wohlwill & D. H. Carson (Eds.), *Environment and the social sciences: Perspectives and applications* (pp. 15–28). Washington, DC: American Psychological Association.

Evans, G. W., & Eichelman, W. (1976). Preliminary models of conceptual linkages among proxemic variables. *Environment and Behavior, 9,* 87–116.

Evans, G. W., & Howard, R. B. (1973). Personal space. *Psychological Bulletin, 80,* 334–344.

Evans, G. W., & Lovell, B. (1979). Design modification in an open-plan school. *Journal of Educational Psychology, 71,* 41–49.

Exline, R. V. (1963). Explorations in the process of person perception: Visual interaction in relation to competition, sex, and the need for affiliation. *Journal of Personality, 31,* 1–20.

Exline, R. V. (1972). Visual interaction: The glances of power and preference. In J. D. Cole (Ed.), *Nebraska symposium on motivation* (Vol. 19, pp. 163–206). Lincoln: University of Nebraska Press.

Exline, R. V. (1985). Multichannel transmission of nonverbal behavior and the perception of powerful men: The presidential debates of 1976. In S. L. Ellyson, & J. F. Dovidio (Eds.), *Power, dominance, and nonverbal behavior* (pp. 183–206). New York: Springer-Verlag.

Exline, R. V., Ellyson, S. L., & Long, B. (1975). Visual behavior as an aspect of power role relationships. In P. Pliner, L. Krames, & T. Alloway (Eds.), *Nonverbal communication of aggression* (pp. 21–52). New York: Plenum.

Exline, R. V., & Fehr, B. J. (1978). Applications of semiosis to the study of visual interaction. In A. W. Siegman & S. Feldstein (Eds.), *Nonverbal behavior and communication* (pp. 117–158). Hillsdale, NJ: Erlbaum.

Exline, R. V., Gray, D., & Schuette, D. (1965). Visual behavior in a dyad as affected by interview content and sex of respondent. *Journal of Personality and Social Psychology, 1,* 201–209.

Exline, R. V., Thibaut, J., Hickey, C., & Gumpert, P. (1970). Visual interaction in relation to Machiavellianism and an unethical act. In P. Christie & F. Geis (Eds.), *Studies in Machiavellianism* (pp. 53–75). New York: Academic Press.

Exline, R. V., & Winters, L. C. (1965).

Affective relations and mutual glances in dyads. In S. S. Tomkins & C. E. Izard (Eds.), *Affect, cognition, and personality* (pp. 319–350). New York: Springer-Verlag.

Fairbanks, G., Guttman, N., & Miron, M. (1957). Effects of time compression upon the comprehension of connected speech. *Journal of Speech and Hearing Disorders, 22,* 10–19.

Fay, P. J., & Middleton, W. G. (1940). Judgment of intelligence from the voice as transmitted over a public address system. *Sociometry, 3,* 186–191.

Feinman, J. A., & Feldman, R. S. (1982). Decoding children's expressions of affect. *Child Development, 53,* 710–716.

Feldman, R. S. (1976). Nonverbal disclosure of teacher deception and interpersonal affect. *Journal of Educational Psychology, 68,* 807–816.

Feldman, R. S., Devin-Sheehan, L., & Allen, V. L. (1978). Nonverbal cues as indicators of verbal dissembling. *American Educational Research Journal, 15,* 217–231.

Feldman, R. S., Jenkins, L., & Popoola, O. (1979). Detection of deception in adults and children via facial expressions. *Child Development, 50,* 350–355.

Feldman, R. S., & White, J. B. (1980). Detecting deception in children. *Journal of Communication, 30,* 121–139.

Feldstein, S., & Welkowitz, J. (1978). A chronography of conversation: In defense of an objective approach. In A. W. Siegman & S. Feldstein (Eds.), *Nonverbal behavior and communication* (pp. 329–378). Hillsdale, NJ: Erlbaum.

Felipe, N. J., & Sommer, R. (1966). Invasions of personal space. *Social Problems, 14,* 206–214.

Festinger, L. (1951). Architecture and group membership. *Journal of Social Issues, 7,* 152–163.

Festinger, L., Schachter, S., & Back, K. (1950). *Social pressures in informal groups: A study of human factors in housing.* New York: Harper & Row.

Firestone, I. J. (1977). Reconciling verbal and nonverbal models of dyadic communication. *Environmental Psychology and Nonverbal Behavior, 2,* 30–43.

Fisher, B. A. (1978). *Perspectives on human communication.* New York: Macmillan.

Fisher, B. A. (1980). *Small group decision making* (2nd ed.). New York: McGraw-Hill.

Fisher, J. D., Bell, P. A., & Baum, A. (1984). *Environmental psychology*

(2nd ed.). New York: Holt, Rinehart and Winston.

Fisher, J. D., & Byrne, D. (1975). Too close for comfort: Sex differences in response to invasions of personal space. *Journal of Personality and Social Psychology, 32,* 15–21.

Fisher, J. D., Rytting, M., & Heslin, R. (1976). Hands touching hands: Affective and evaluative effects of an interpersonal touch. *Sociometry, 39,* 416–421.

Folger, J. P., & Woodall, W. G. (1982). Nonverbal cues as linguistic context: An information processing view. In M. Burgoon (Ed.), *Communication Yearbook 6* (pp. 63–91). Beverly Hills, CA: Sage.

Forbes, R. J., & Jackson, P. R. (1980). Non-verbal behaviour and the outcome of selection interviews. *Journal of Occupational Psychology, 53,* 65–72.

Forgas, J. P. (1976). The perception of social episodes: Categorical and dimensional representations in two different social milieus. *Journal of Personality and Social Psychology, 33,* 199–209.

Forgas, J. P. (1978). The effects of behavioural and cultural expectation cues on the perception of social episodes. *European Journal of Social Psychology, 8,* 203–213.

Forgas, J. P. (1979). *Social episodes: The study of interaction routines.* London: Academic Press.

Forston, R. F., & Larson, C. U. (1968). The dynamics of space: An experimental study in proxemic behavior among Latin Americans and North Americans. *Journal of Communication, 18,* 109–116.

Forsyth, D. R. (1987). *Social psychology.* Monterey, CA: Brooks/Cole.

Forsyth, G. A., Kushner, R. I., & Forsyth, P. D. (1981). Human facial expression judgment in a conversational context. *Journal of Nonverbal Behavior, 6,* 115–130.

Fortenberry, J. H., Maclean, J., Morris, P., & O'Connell, M. (1978). Mode of dress as a perceptual cue to deference. *Journal of Social Psychology, 104,* pp. 139–140.

Foulke, E., & Sticht, T. G. (1969). Review of research on the intelligibility and comprehension of accelerated speech. *Psychological Bulletin, 72,* 50–62.

Fraenkel, D. L. (1983). The relationship of empathy in movement to synchrony, echoing, and empathy in verbal interactions. *American Journal of Dance Therapy, 6,* 31–48.

Fraiberg, S. (1971). Intervention in infancy: A program for blind infants. *Journal of the American Academy of Child Psychiatry, 10,* 381–405.

Frank, L. K. (1957). Tactile communi-

cation. *Genetic Psychology Monographs, 56,* 204–255.

Frank, L. K. (1971). Tactile communication. In H. A. Bosmajian (Ed.), *The rhetoric of nonverbal communication* (pp. 34–56). Glenview, IL: Scott, Foresman.

Frank, L. K. (1972). Cultural patterning of tactile experiences. In L. A. Samovar & R. E. Porter (Eds.), *Intercultural communication: A reader* (pp. 200–204). Belmont, CA: Wadsworth.

Freedman, D. G. (1969, October). The survival value of the beard. *Psychology Today, 3,* pp. 36–39.

Freedman, J. L. (1975). *Crowding and behavior.* San Francisco: Freeman.

Freedman, J. L., Levy, A. S., Buchanan, R. W., & Price, J. (1972). Crowding and human aggressiveness. *Journal of Experimental Social Psychology, 8,* 528–548.

Freedman, N. (1972). The analysis of movement behavior during the clinical interview. In A. Siegman & B. Pope (Eds.), *Studies in dyadic communication* (pp. 153–175). New York: Pergamon.

Freedman, N., & Steingart, I. (1975). Kinesic internalization and language construction. *Psychoanalysis & Contemporary Science, 4,* 355–403.

French, J. R. P., Jr., & Raven, B. (1959). The bases of social power. In D. Cartwright (Ed.), *Studies in social power* (pp. 150–167). Ann Arbor, MI: Institute for Social Research.

French, P., & von Raffler-Engel, W. (1973). The kinesics of bilingualism. Unpublished manuscript, Vanderbilt University. Cited in LaFrance, M. & Mayo, C. (1978). *Moving bodies.* Monterey, CA: Brooks/Cole.

Fretz, B. R., Corn, R., Tuemmler, J. M., & Bellet, W. (1979). Counselor nonverbal behaviors and client evaluations. *Journal of Counseling Psychology, 26,* 304–311.

Friedman, H. S. (1978). The relative strength of verbal versus nonverbal cues. *Personality and Social Psychology Bulletin, 4(1),* 147–150.

Friedman, H. S. (1979a). The concept of skill in nonverbal communication: Implications for understanding social interaction. In R. Rosenthal (Ed.), *Skill in nonverbal communication: Individual differences* (pp. 2–27). Cambridge, MA: Oelgeschlager, Gunn & Hain, Publishers.

Friedman, H. S. (1979b). The interactive effects of facial expressions of emotion and verbal messages on perceptions of affective meaning. *Journal of Experimental Social Psychology, 15,* 453–469.

Friedman, H. S. (1979c). Nonverbal communication between patients and medical practitioners. *Journal of Social Issues, 35,* 82–99.

Friesen, W. V. (1972). *Cultural differences in facial expressions in a social situation: An experimental test of the concept of display rules.* Unpublished dissertation, University of California, San Francisco.

Friesen, W. V., Ekman, P., & Wallbott, H. (1979). Measuring hand movements. *Journal of Nonverbal Behavior, 4,* 97–112.

Frieze, I., & Ramsey, S. (1976). Nonverbal maintenance of traditional sex roles. *Journal of Social Issues, 32,* 133–141.

Fromme, D. K., & Beam, D. C. (1974). Dominance and sex differences in nonverbal responses to differential eye contact. *Journal of Research in Personality, 8,* 76–87.

Fugita, S. S. (1974). Effects of anxiety and approval on visual interaction. *Journal of Personality and Social Psychology, 29,* 586–592.

Fugita, S. S., Wexley, K. N., & Hillery, J. M. (1974). Black-white differences in nonverbal behavior in an interview setting. *Journal of Applied Social Psychology, 4,* 343–350.

Fujimoto, E. K. (1971). *The comparative power of verbal and nonverbal symbols.* Unpublished doctoral dissertation, Ohio State University.

Fujita, B. N., Harper, R. G., & Wiens, A. N. (1980). Encoding-decoding of nonverbal emotional messages: Sex differences in spontaneous and enacted expressions. *Journal of Nonverbal Behavior, 4,* 131–145.

Fulcher, J. S. (1942). "Voluntary" facial expression in blind and seeing children. *Archives of Psychology, 38,* No. 272.

Furbay, A. L. (1965). The influence of scattered versus compact seating on audience response. *Speech Monographs, 32,* 144–148.

Furnham, A., & Argyle, M. (1981). *The psychology of social situations: Selected readings.* New York: Pergamon.

Gales, A., Spratt, G., Chapman, A. J., & Smallbone, A. (1975). EEG correlates of eye contact and interpersonal distance. *Biological Psychology, 3,* 237–245.

Gallois, C., & Markel, N. M. (1975). Turn taking: Social personality and conversational style. *Journal of Personality and Social Psychology, 31,* 1134–1140.

Garfinkel, H. (1964). Studies of the routine grounds of everyday activities. *Social Problems, 11,* 225–250.

Garner, P. H. (1972). *The effects of invasion of personal space on interpersonal communication.* Unpublished thesis, Illinois State University.

Garratt, G. A., Baxter, J. C., & Rozelle, R. M. (1981). Training university police in black-American nonverbal behaviors: An application to police-community relations. *Journal of Social Psychology, 113,* 217–229.

Gatewood, J. B., & Rosenwein, R. (1981). Interactional synchrony: Genuine or spurious? A critique of recent research. *Journal of Nonverbal Behavior, 6,* 12–29.

Geen, R. G. (1980). The effects of being observed on performance. In P. B. Paulus (Ed.), *Psychology of group influence* (pp. 62–97). Hillsdale, NJ: Erlbaum.

Geis, F. L., & Moon, T. H. (1981). Machiavellianism and deception. *Journal of Personality and Social Psychology, 41,* 766–775.

Geiselman, R. E., & Bellezza, F. S. (1976). Long term memory for speaker's voice and source location. *Memory and Cognition, 4,* 483–489.

Geiselman, R. E., & Bellezza, F. S. (1977). Incidental retention of speaker's voice. *Memory and Cognition, 5,* 658–665.

Geiselman, R. E., & Crawley, J. M. (1983). Incidental processing of speaker characteristics: Voice as connotative information. *Journal of Verbal Learning and Verbal Behavior, 22,* 15–23.

Geldhard, F. A. (1960). Some neglected possibilities of communication. *Science, 131,* 1583–1587.

Geller, D. M., Goodstein, L., Silver, M., & Sternberg, W. C. (1974). On being ignored: The effects of the violation of implicit rules of social interaction. *Sociometry, 37,* 541–556.

Geller, D. M., & Malia, G. P. (1981). The effects of noise on helping behavior reconsidered. *Basic and Applied Social Psychology, 2,* 11–25.

Gewirtz, J. L., & Boyd, E. F. (1976). Mother-infant interaction and its study. In H. W. Reese (Ed.), *Advances in child development and behavior* (Vol. 11, pp. 141–163). New York: Academic Press.

Gibbons, K., & Gwynn, T. K. (1975). A new theory of fashion change: A test of some predictions. *British Journal of Social and Clinical Psychology, 14,* 1–9.

Giesen, J. M. (1973). *Effects of eye contact, attitude agreement, and presentation mode on impressions and persuasion.* Unpublished doctoral dissertation, Kent State University.

Giesen, M., & McClaren, H. A. (1976). Discussion, distance and sex: Changes in impressions and attraction during small group interaction. *Sociometry, 39,* 60–70.

Gifford, R., Ng, C. F., & Wilkinson, M. (1985). Nonverbal cues in the employment interview: Links between applicant qualities and interviewer judgments. *Journal of Applied Psychology, 70,* 729–736.

Gilbert, G. S., Kirkland, K. D., & Rappoport, L. (1977). Nonverbal assessment of interpersonal affect. *Journal of Personality Assessment, 41,* 43–48.

Giles, H. (1973a). Accent mobility: A model and some data. *Anthropological Linguistics, 15,* 87–105.

Giles, H. (1973b). Communicative effectiveness as a function of accented speech. *Speech Monographs, 40,* 330–331.

Giles, H. (1977). Social psychology and applied linguistics: Towards an integrative approach. *ILT: Review of Applied Linguistics, 33,* 27–40.

Giles, H. (1979). Ethnicity markers in speech. In K. R. Scherer & H. Giles (Eds.), *Social markers in speech* (pp. 251–290). Cambridge: Cambridge University Press.

Giles, H. (1980). Accommodation theory: Some new directions. In S. de Silva (Ed.), *Aspects of linguistic behavior* (pp. 105–136). York: University of York Press.

Giles, H., Bourhis, R. Y., & Taylor, D. M. (1977). Towards a theory of language in ethnic group relations. In H. Giles (Ed.), *Language, ethnicity, and intergroup relations* (pp. 307–348). London: Academic Press.

Giles, H., Brown, B. L., & Thakerar, J. N. (1981). *The effects of speech rate, accent, and context on the attribution of a speaker's personality characteristics.* Unpublished manuscript, University of Bristol.

Giles, H., & Powesland, P. F. (1975). *Speech style and social evaluation.* London: Academic Press.

Giles, H., & Smith, P. M. (1979). Accommodation theory: Optimal levels of convergence. In H. Giles & R. St. Clair (Eds.), *Language and social psychology* (pp. 45–65). Baltimore: University Park.

Giles, H., & Street, R. L., Jr. (1985). Communicator characteristics and behavior. In M. L. Knapp & G. R. Miller (Eds.), *Handbook of interpersonal communication* (pp. 205–261). Beverly Hills, CA: Sage.

Gillespie, D. L. (1978). *The effects of status differentiation on selected nonverbal behaviors at settled distances.* Unpublished doctoral dissertation, University of California, Berkeley.

Ginsburg, H. J., Pollman, V. A., Wauson, M. S., & Hope, M. L. (1977). Variation of aggressive interaction among male elementary school children as a function of changes in spatial density. *Environmental Psy-*

chology and Nonverbal Behavior, 2, 67–75.

Gitter, A. G., Black, H., & Fishman, J. E. (1975). Effect of race, sex, nonverbal communication and verbal communication on perception of leadership. *Sociology and Social Research, 60,* 46–57.

Givens, D. B. (1978). The nonverbal basis of attraction: Flirtation, courtship, and seduction. *Psychiatry, 41,* 346–359.

Givens, D. B. (1983). *Love signals.* New York: Crown.

Glasgow, G. M. (1952). A semantic index of vocal pitch. *Speech Monographs, 19,* 64–68.

Glass, D. C., & Singer, J. E. (1972). Behavioral after effects of unpredictable and uncontrollable aversive events. *American Scientist, 80,* 457–465.

Glass, D. C., Singer, J. E., & Friedman, L. N. (1969). Psychic cost of adaptation to an environmental stressor. *Journal of Personality and Social Psychology, 12,* 200–210.

Goffman, E. (1959). *The presentation of self in everyday life.* Garden City, NY: Anchor Books/Doubleday.

Goffman, E. (1961a). *Asylums: Essays on the social situation of mental patients and other inmates.* Garden City, NY: Anchor Books/Doubleday.

Goffman, E. (1961b). *Encounters: Two studies in the sociology of interaction.* Indianapolis: Bobbs-Merrill.

Goffman, E. (1963). *Behavior in public places.* New York: The Free Press.

Goffman, E. (1967). *Interaction ritual: Essays on face-to-face behavior.* Garden City, NY: Anchor Books/Doubleday.

Goffman, E. (1969). *Strategic interaction.* Philadelphia: University of Pennsylvania Press.

Goffman, E. (1971). *Relations in public: Microstudies of the public order.* New York: Basic Books.

Goffman, E. (1974). *Frame analysis.* New York: Harper & Row.

Goldberg, G. N., Kiesler, C. A., & Collins, B. E. (1969). Visual behavior and face-to-face distance during interaction. *Sociometry, 32,* 43–53.

Goldberg, K. Y., & Bajcsy, R. (1984). Active touch and robot perception. *Cognition and Brain Theory, 7,* 199–214.

Goldberg, M. L. (1980). *Effects of shifts in listeners' looking behavior upon speakers' verbal and nonverbal immediacy behavior: A test of affiliative conflict and intimacy-arousal models.* Unpublished doctoral dissertation, University of Miami.

Goldberg, S., & Lewis, M. (1969). Play behavior in the year-old infant: Early sex differences. *Child Development, 40,* 21–31.

Goldberg, S., & Rosenthal, R. (1986). Self-touching behavior in the job interview: Antecedents and consequences. *Journal of Nonverbal Behavior, 10,* 65–80.

Goldhaber, G. M. (1983). *Organizational communication* (3rd ed.). Dubuque, IA: Brown.

Goldman-Eisler, F. (1961a). A comparative study of two hesitation phenomena. *Language and Speech, 4,* 18–26.

Goldman-Eisler, F. (1961b). Hesitation and information in speech. In C. Cherry (Ed.), *Information theory.* London: Butterworths.

Goldman-Eisler, F. (1968). *Psycholinguistics: Experiments in spontaneous speech.* New York: Academic Press.

Goleman, D. (1986, April 8). Studies point to power of nonverbal signals. *The New York Times,* pp. C1, C6.

Gonzales, A., & Zimbardo, P. G. (1985, March). Time in perspective. *Psychology Today,* pp. 21–26.

Gonzales, G. E. (1982). *Nonverbal behavior and person perception in dyads of varied sex and ethnicity.* Unpublished doctoral dissertation, University of California, Santa Cruz.

Goodenough, F. L. (1932). Expression of the emotions in a blind-deaf child. *Journal of Abnormal and Social Psychology, 27,* 328–333.

Gorer, G. (1968). Ardrey on human nature: Animals, nations, imperatives. In M. F. A. Montagu (Ed.), *Man and aggression* (pp. 74–82). London: Oxford University Press.

Gorham, J. (1988). The relationship between verbal teacher immediacy behaviors and student learning. *Communication Education, 37,* 40–53.

Gottlieb, A. (1980). Touching and being touched. *Mademoiselle, 88,* 80–81, 167, 174.

Graham, J. A., & Heywood, S. (1975). The effects of elimination of hand gestures and of verbal codability on speech performance. *European Journal of Social Psychology, 5,* 189–195.

Greenbaum, P. E., & Rosenfeld, H. M. (1980). Varieties of touching in greetings: Sequential structure and sex-related differences. *Journal of Nonverbal Behavior, 5,* 13–25.

Greenberg, C. I. (1976). *Intimacy overload, intrusion, and behavior restriction: An interpersonal distance-equilibrium approach to the stressful experience of crowding.* Unpublished doctoral dissertation, Wayne State University.

Greenberg, C. I., & Firestone, I. J. (1977). Compensatory responses to crowding: Effects of personal space intrusion and privacy reduction. *Journal of Personality and Social Psychology, 35,* 637–644.

Greenberg, E. (1979). *The effects of dominance on sex differences in nonverbal behavior in mixed-sex dyads.* Unpublished dissertation, New School for Social Research.

Greene, L. R. (1977). Effects of verbal evaluative feedback and interpersonal distance on behavioral compliance. *Journal of Counseling Psychology, 24,* 10–14.

Griffitt, W. (1970). Environmental effects on interpersonal affective behavior: Ambient effective temperature and attraction. *Journal of Personality and Social Psychology, 15,* 240–244.

Griffitt, W., & Veitch, R. (1971). Hot and crowded: Influence of population density and temperature on interpersonal affective behavior. *Journal of Personality and Social Psychology, 17,* 92–98.

Guardo, C. J. (1969). Personal space in children. *Child Development, 40,* 143–151.

Guardo, C. J., & Meisels, M. (1971). Factor structure of children's personal space schemata. *Child Development, 42,* 1307–1312.

Guerin, D. V. (1967). Implications of the communication process for school plant design. *Audiovisual Instruction, 12,* 815–817.

Gump, P. V., & Good, L. R. (1976). Environments operating in open space and traditionally designed schools. *Journal of Architectural Research, 5,* 20–26.

Gunderson, D. F., & Hopper, R. (1976). Relationship between speech delivery and speech effectiveness. *Communication Monographs, 43,* 158–165.

Gurel, L. M., Wilbur, J. C., & Gurel, L. (1972). Personality correlates of adolescent clothing styles. *Journal of Home Economics, 64,* 42–47.

Gutsell, L. M., & Andersen, J. F. (1980). *Perceptual and behavioral responses to smiling.* Paper presented at the annual meeting of the International Communication Association, Acapulco, Mexico.

Haase, R. F. (1970). The relationship of sex and instructional set to the regulation of interpersonal interaction distance in a counseling analogue. *Journal of Counseling Psychology, 17,* 233–236.

Haase, R. F., & Dimattia, D. (1976). Spatial environments and verbal conditioning in a quasi-counseling interview. *Journal of Counseling Psychology, 23,* 414–421.

Haase, R. F., & Tepper, D. T., Jr. (1972). Nonverbal components of empathetic communication. *Journal of Counseling Psychology, 19,* 417–424.

Hackney, H. (1974). Facial gestures and subject expression of feelings. *Journal of Counseling Psychology, 21,* 173–178.

Hai, D. M., Khairullah, Z. Y., & Coulmas, N. (1982). Sex and the single armrest: Use of personal space during air travel. *Psychological Reports, 51,* 743–749.

Halberstam, D. (1979). *The powers that be.* New York: Dell.

Halberstam, D. (1986). *The reckoning.* New York: Morrow.

Hale, J. L., & Burgoon, J. K. (1984). Models of reactions to changes in nonverbal immediacy. *Journal of Nonverbal Behavior, 8,* 287–314.

Hall, E. T. (1959, 1973). *The silent language.* Garden City, NY: Anchor Books/Doubleday.

Hall, E. T. (1963). A system for the notation of proxemic behavior. *American Anthropologist, 65,* 1003–1026.

Hall, E. T. (1966). *The hidden dimension* (2nd ed.). Garden City, NY: Anchor Books/Doubleday.

Hall, E. T. (1974). *Handbook for proxemic research.* Washington, DC: Society for the Anthropology of Visual Communication.

Hall, E. T. (1981). *Beyond culture.* Garden City, NJ: Anchor Books/Doubleday.

Hall, E. T., & Whyte, W. F. (1966). Intercultural communication: A guide to men of action. In A. G. Smith (Ed.), *Communication and culture* (pp. 567–575). New York: Holt, Rinehart & Winston.

Hall, J. A. (1979). Gender, gender roles, and nonverbal communication skills. In R. Rosenthal (Ed.), *Skill in nonverbal communication: Individual differences* (pp. 32–67). Cambridge, MA: Oelgeschlager, Gunn & Hain.

Hall, J. A. (1980). Voice tone and persuasion. *Journal of Personality and Social Psychology, 38,* 924–934.

Hall, J. A., & Halberstadt, A. G. (1986). Smiling and gazing. In J. S. Hyde & M. Linn (Eds.), *The psychology of gender: Advances through meta-analysis* (pp. 136–158). Baltimore: Johns Hopkins University Press.

Hall, J. A., Roter, D. L., & Rand, C. S. (1981). Communication of affect between patient and physician. *Journal of Health and Social Behavior, 22,* 18–30.

Hamilton, M. L. (1973). Imitative behavior and expressive ability in facial expression of emotion. *Developmental Psychology, 8,* 138.

Hamner, K. C. (1981). Experimental evidence for the biological clock. In J. T. Fraser (Ed.), *The voices of time* (2nd ed., pp. 281–295). Amherst,

MA: University of Massachusetts Press.

Hare, A., & Bales, R. F. (1963). Seating position and small group interaction. *Sociometry, 26,* 480–486.

Harlow, H. F. (1958). The nature of love. *American Psychologist, 13,* 673–685.

Harlow, H. F. (1959). Love in monkeys. *Scientific American, 200,* 68–74.

Harlow, H. F., & Harlow, M. K. (1962). The effect of rearing conditions on behavior. *Bulletin of the Meninger Clinic, 26,* 213–224.

Harlow, H. F., Harlow, M. K., & Hansen, E. W. (1963). The maternal affectional system of rhesus monkeys. In H. L. Rheingold (Ed.), *Maternal behaviors in mammals* (pp. 254–281). New York: Wiley.

Harlow, H. F., & Zimmerman, R. R. (1958). The development of affectional responses in infant monkeys. *Proceedings, American Philosophical Society, 102,* 501–509.

Harms, L. S. (1961). Listener judgments of status cues in speech. *Quarterly Journal of Speech, 47,* 164–168.

Harper, L., & Sanders, K. M. (1975). Preschool children's use of space: Sex differences in outdoor play. *Developmental Psychology, 11,* 119.

Harper, R. G. (1985). Power, dominance, and nonverbal behavior: An overview. In S. L. Ellyson & J. F. Dovidio (Eds.), *Power, dominance, and nonverbal behavior* (pp. 29–48). New York: Springer-Verlag.

Harper, R. G., Wiens, A. N., & Matarazzo, J. D. (1978). *Nonverbal communication: The state of the art.* New York: Wiley.

Harper, R. G., Wiens, A. N., & Matarazzo, J. D. (1979). The relationship between encoding and decoding of visual nonverbal emotional cues. *Semiotica, 28,* 171–192.

Harre, H., & Secord, P. F. (1972). *The explanation of social behavior.* Oxford: Blackwells.

Harrigan, J. A. (1985). Self-touching as an indicator of underlying affect and language processes. *Social Science and Medicine, 20,* 1161–1168.

Harrigan, J. A., Kues, J. R., & Weber, J. G. (1986). Impressions of hand movements: Self-touching and gestures. *Perceptual and Motor Skills, 63,* 503–516.

Harrigan, J. A., Oxman, T. E., & Rosenthal, R. (1985). Rapport expressed through nonverbal behavior. *Journal of Nonverbal Behavior, 9,* 95–110.

Harrigan, J. A., & Rosenthal, R. (1983). Physicians' head and body positions as determinants of perceived rapport. *Journal of Applied Social Psychology, 13,* 496–509.

Harrigan, J. A., & Rosenthal, R.

(1986). Nonverbal aspects of empathy and rapport in physician-patient interaction. In P. D. Blanck, R. Buck, & R. Rosenthal (Eds.), *Nonverbal communication in the clinical context* (pp. 36–73). University Park, PA: The Pennsylvania State University Press.

Harrigan, J. A., Weber, J. G., & Kues, J. R. (1986). Attributions of self-touching performed in spontaneous and posed modes. *Journal of Social and Clinical Psychology, 4,* 433–446.

Harris, M. J. & Rosenthal, R. (1985). Mediation of interpersonal expectancy effects: 31 meta-analyses. *Psychological Bulletin, 97,* 363–386.

Harris, M. B., James, J., Chavez, J., Fuller, M. L., Kent, S., Massanari, C., Moore, C., & Walsh, F. (1983). Clothing: Communication, compliance, and choice. *Journal of Applied Social Psychology, 13,* 88–97.

Harris, M. B., Ramsey, S., Sims, D., & Stevenson, M. (1974). Effects of uniforms on perceptions of pictures of athletes. *Perceptual and Motor Skills, 39,* 59–62.

Harris, R. M., & Rubenstein, D. (1975). Paralanguage, communication, and cognition. In A. Kendon, R. M. Harris, & M. R. Key (Eds.), *Organization of behavior in face-to-face interaction* (pp. 251–276). Chicago: Aldine.

Harrison, R. P. (1974). *Beyond words: An introduction to nonverbal communication.* Englewood Cliffs, NJ: Prentice-Hall.

Hartley, L. R., & Adams, R. G. (1974). Effect of noise on the Stroop test. *Journal of Experimental Psychology, 102,* 62–66.

Hartnett, J. J., Bailey, K. G., & Gibson, F. W., Jr. (1970). Personal space as influenced by sex and type of movement. *Journal of Psychology, 76,* 139–144.

Hastie, R., & Carlston, D. E. (1980). Theoretical issues in person memory. In R. Hastie, T. R. Ostrom, E. B. Ebbesen, R. S. Wyer, D. L. Hamilton, & D. E. Carlston (Eds.), *Person memory: The cognitive basis of social perception* (pp. 1–53). Hillsdale, NJ: Erlbaum.

Hastie, R., Ostrom, T. R., Ebbesen, E. B., Wyer, R. S., Hamilton, D. L., & Carlston, D. E. (1980). *Person memory: The cognitive basis of social perception.* Hillsdale, NJ: Erlbaum.

Haviland, J. M. (1977). Sex-related pragmatics in infants' nonverbal communication. *Journal of Communication, 27(2),* 80–84.

Haviland, S. E., & Clark, H. H. (1974). What's new? Acquiring new information as a process in comprehension. *Journal of Verbal Learning and Verbal Behavior, 13,* 512–521.

References

Hayduk, L. A. (1978). Personal space: An evaluative and orienting overview. *Psychological Bulletin, 85,* 117–134.

Hayes, D. P., & Meltzer, L. (1972). Interpersonal judgments based on talkativeness: I. Fact or artifact. *Sociometry, 35,* 538–561.

Hearn, G. (1957). Leadership and the spatial factor in small groups. *Journal of Abnormal and Social Psychology, 54,* 269–272.

Heckel, R. V. (1973). Leadership and voluntary seating choice. *Psychological Reports, 32,* 141–142.

Hediger, H. P. (1950). *Wild animals in captivity.* London: Butterworths.

Hediger, H. P. (1961). The evolution of territorial behavior. In S. L. Washburn (Ed.), *Social life of early man* (pp. 34–57). Chicago: Aldine.

Hegstrom, T. G. (1979). Message impact: What percentage is nonverbal? *Western Journal of Speech Communication, 43,* 134–142.

Heinberg, P. (1964). *Voice training for speaking and reading aloud.* New York: Ronald Press.

Heller, J. G., Groff, B. D., & Solomon, S. H. (1977). Toward an understanding of crowding: The role of physical attraction. *Journal of Personality and Social Psychology, 35,* 183–190.

Helson, H. (1964). *Adaptation-level theory.* New York: Harper & Row.

Hemsley, G. D. (1977). *Experimental studies in the behavioral indicants of deception.* Unpublished doctoral dissertation, University of Toronto.

Hemsley, G. D., & Doob, A. T. (1978). The effect of looking behavior on perceptions of a communicator's credibility. *Journal of Applied Social Psychology, 8,* 136–144.

Hendershot, J., & Hess, A. K. (1982). *Detecting deception: The effects of training and socialization levels on verbal and nonverbal cue utilization and detection accuracy.* Unpublished manuscript, Auburn University.

Henley, N. M. (1973). Status and sex: Some touching observations. *Bulletin of the Psychonomic Society, 2,* 91–93.

Henley, N. M. (1977). *Body politics: Power, sex, and nonverbal communication.* Englewood Cliffs, NJ: Prentice-Hall.

Henley, N. M., & Freeman, J. (1975). The sexual politics of interpersonal behavior. In J. Freeman (Ed.), *Women: A feminist perspective* (pp. 391–401). Palo Alto, CA: Mayfield.

Henley, N. M., & Harmon, S. (1985). The nonverbal semantics of power and gender: A perceptual study. In S. L. Ellyson & J. F. Dovidio (Eds.), *Power, dominance, and nonverbal behavior* (pp. 151–164). New York: Springer-Verlag.

Hensley, W. E. (1981). The effects of attire, location, and sex on aiding behavior: A similarity explanation. *Journal of Nonverbal Behavior, 6,* 3–11.

Heslin, R. (1974, May). *Steps toward a taxonomy of touching.* Paper presented at the annual convention of the Midwestern Psychological Association, Chicago.

Heslin, R. (1978). *Responses to touching as an index of sex-role norms and attitudes.* Paper presented at the American Psychological Association Symposium, Toronto.

Heslin, R., & Alper, T. (1983). Touch: A bonding gesture. In J. M. Wiemann & R. P. Harrison (Eds.), *Nonverbal interaction* (pp. 47–75). Beverly Hills, CA: Sage.

Heslin, R., & Boss, D. (1980). Nonverbal intimacy in airport arrival and departure. *Personality and Social Psychology Bulletin, 6,* 248–252.

Heslin, R., Nguyen, T. D., & Nguyen, M. L. (1983). Meaning of touch: The case of touch from a stranger or same sex person. *Journal of Nonverbal Behavior, 7,* 17–157.

Hess, E. H. (1975). The role of pupil size in communication. *Scientific American, 233,* 110–119.

Hess, E. H., & Polt, J. M. (1960). Pupil size as related to interest value of visual stimuli. *Science, 132,* 349–350.

Heston, J. K., & Garner, P. (1972, April). *A study of personal space and desk arrangement in the learning environment.* Paper presented at the annual meeting of the International Communication Association, Atlanta.

Hewes, D. E., & Planalp, S. (1982). "There is nothing as useful as a good theory . . .": The influence of social knowledge on interpersonal communication. In C. Berger & M. Roloff (Eds.), *Social cognition and communication* (pp. 107–150). Beverly Hills, CA: Sage.

Hewes, G. W. (1957). The anthropology of posture. *Scientific American, 196,* 123–132.

Hickson, M. L., III, & Stacks, D. W. (1985). *NVC: Nonverbal communication studies and applications.* Dubuque, IA: Brown.

Higginbotham, D. J., & Yoder, D. E. (1982). Communication within natural conversational interaction: Implications for severe communicatively impaired persons. *Topics in Language Disorders, 2,* 1–19.

Hill, S. D., & Smith, J. M. (1984). Neonatal responsiveness as a function of maternal contact and obstetrical drugs. *Perceptual and Motor Skills, 58,* 859–866.

Hillison, J. (1983). Communicating

humanism nonverbally. *Journal of Humanistic Education and Development, 22,* 25–29.

Hilpert, F. P., Kramer, C., & Clark, R. A. (1975). Participants' perceptions of self and partner in mixed-sex dyads. *Central States Speech Journal, 26,* 52–56.

Hinchliffe, M. K., Hooper, D., Roberts, F. J., & Vaughan, P. W. (1975). A study of interaction between depressed patients and their spouses. *British Journal of Psychiatry, 126,* 164–172.

Ho, R., & Mitchell, S. (1982). Students' nonverbal reaction to tutors' warm/cold nonverbal behavior. *Journal of Social Psychology, 118,* 121–131.

Hockett, C. F. (1960). The origin of speech. *Scientific American, 203,* 86–96.

Hocking, J. E., Bauchner, J., Kaminski, E. P., & Miller, G. R. (1979). Detecting deceptive communication from verbal, visual, and paralinguistic cues. *Human Communication Research, 6,* 33–46.

Hocking, J. E., & Leathers, D. G. (1980). Nonverbal indicators of deception: A new theoretical perspective. *Communication Monographs, 47,* 119–131.

Hocking, J. E., Miller, G. R., & Fontes, N. E. (1978). Videotape in the courtroom. *Trial, 14,* 52–55.

Hoffman, S. A. (1988, February). The doctor as dramatist. *Newsweek,* p. 10.

Holahan, C. J. (1982). *Environmental psychology.* New York: Random House.

Hollandsworth, J. G., Jr., Kazelskis, R., Stevens, J., & Dressel, M. E. (1979). Relative contributions of verbal, articulative, and nonverbal communication to employment decisions in the job interview setting. *Personnel Psychology, 32,* 359–367.

Hollien, H., Dew, D., & Philips, P. (1971). Phonational frequency ranges of adults. *Journal of Speech and Hearing Research, 14,* 755–760.

Honkavaara, S. (1961). The psychology of expression: Dimensions in human perception. *British Journal of Psychology Monograph Supplements, 32,* 1–96.

Hooker, D. (1952). *The prenatal origin of behavior.* Lawrence: University of Kansas Press.

Horai, J., Naccari, N., & Fatoullah, E. (1974). The effects of expertise and physical attractiveness upon opinion agreement and liking. *Sociometry, 37,* 601–606.

Horn, P. (1973, June). Newsline. *Psychology Today, 7,* p. 92.

Horn, P. (1974, April). Newsline. *Psychology Today, 7,* p. 27.

Horn, J. (1975, January). Newsline. *Psychology Today, 8,* p. 28.

Horner, T. M. (1983). On the formation of personal space and self-boundary structures in early human development: The case of infant stranger reactivity. *Developmental Review, 3,* 148–177.

Hornstein, M. G. (1967). Accuracy of emotional communication and interpersonal compatibility. *Journal of Personality, 35,* 20–30.

Horowitz, M. J., Duff, D. F., & Stratton, L. O. (1964). Body-buffer zones. *Archives of General Psychiatry, 11,* 651–656.

Howells, L. T., & Becker, S. W. (1962). Seating arrangement and leadership emergence. *Journal of Abnormal and Social Psychology, 64,* 148–150.

Hutt, C., & Vaizey, M. J. (1967). Differential effects of group density on social behavior. *Nature, 209,* 1371–1372.

Huxley, A. (1954). *The doors of perception.* New York: Harper & Row.

Ickes, W., & Barnes, R. (1977). The role of sex and self-monitoring in unstructured dyadic interactions. *Journal of Personality and Social Psychology, 35,* 315–330.

Ickes, W., Patterson, M. L., Rajecki, D. W., & Tanford, S. (1982). Behavioral and cognitive consequences of reciprocal versus compensatory responses to preinteraction expectancies. *Social Cognition, 1,* 160–190.

Ickes, W., Schermer, B., & Steeno, J. (1979). Sex and sex-role influences in same-sex dyads. *Social Psychology Quarterly, 42,* 373–385.

Iliffe, A. H. (1960). A study of preferences in feminine beauty. *British Journal of Psychology, 51,* 267–273.

Imada, A. S., & Hakel, M. D. (1977). Influence of nonverbal communication and rater proximity on impressions and decisions in simulated employment interviews. *Journal of Applied Psychology, 62,* 295–300.

Insko, C. A. (1967). *Theories of attitude change.* Englewood Cliffs, NJ: Prentice-Hall.

Institute for Environmental Education. (1978). *User participation and requirements in planning Navajo school facilities in New Mexico* (Monograph #2). Albuquerque: University of New Mexico.

Isenberg, S. J., & Bass, B. A. (1974). Effects of verbal and nonverbal reinforcement on the WAIS performance of normal adults. *Journal of Consulting and Clinical Psychology, 42,* 467.

Ishii, S. (1973). Characteristics of Japanese nonverbal communicative behavior. *Communication, Journal of the Communication Association of the Pacific, 2,* 3.

Ittelson, W. H. (Ed.) (1973). *Environment and cognition.* New York: Seminar Press.

Ittelson, W. H., Proshansky, H. M., Rivlin, L. G., & Winkel, G. H. (1974). *An introduction to environmental psychology.* New York: Holt, Rinehart, and Winston.

Izard, C. E. (1971). *The face of emotion.* Englewood Cliffs, NJ: Prentice-Hall.

Izard, C. E. (1972). *Patterns of emotion: A new analysis of anxiety and depression.* New York: Academic Press.

Izard, C. E. (1977). *Human emotions.* New York: Plenum.

Izard, C. E. (1978). Emotions as motivations: An evolutionary-developmental perspective. In R. A. Dienstbier (Ed.), *Nebraska symposium on motivation* (Vol. 25, pp. 163–200). Lincoln: University of Nebraska Press.

Izard, C. E. (1979). Facial expression, emotion and motivation. In A. Wolfgang (Ed.), *Nonverbal behavior: Applications and cultural implications* (pp. 31–49). New York: Academic Press.

Izard, C. E. (1981). Differential emotions theory and the facial feedback hypothesis of emotion activation: Comments on Tourangeau and Ellsworth's "The role of facial response in the experience of emotion." *Journal of Personality and Social Psychology, 40,* 350–354.

Jacobson, M. B. (1981). Effects of victim's and defendant's physical attractiveness on subjects' judgments in a rape case. *Sex Roles, 7,* 247–255.

Jacunska-Iwinska, M. (1975). An experimental modification of the young child's level of activity. *Polish Psychological Bulletin, 6,* 27–35.

Jaffe, J., & Feldstein, S. (1970). *Rhythms of dialogue.* New York: Academic Press.

Jakobson, R. (1972). Motor signs for "yes" and "no." *Language in Society, 1,* 91–96.

James, P. B. (1969). *Children's interpretations of multi-channel communications conveying verbal and nonverbal meanings.* Unpublished dissertation, Ohio State University.

James, W. (1890). *The principles of psychology.* New York: Dover.

Janisse, M. P., & Peavler, W. S. (1974, February). Pupillary research today: Emotion in the eye. *Psychology Today, 7,* 60–73.

Janzen, S. A. (1984). *Empathic nurse's nonverbal communication.* Unpublished doctoral dissertation, University of Illinois, Chicago.

Jensen, J. V. (1985). Perspective on nonverbal intercultural communication. In L. A. Samovar & R. E. Porter (Eds.), *Intercultural communication: A reader* (3rd ed., pp. 256–272). Belmont, CA: Wadsworth.

Jerison, H. J. (1959). Effects of noise on human performance. *Journal of Applied Psychology, 43,* 96–101.

Jersild, A. T., & Markey, F. V. (1935). Conflicts between preschool children. *Child Development Monographs, 21,* ix–181.

Johnson, D. W., McCarty, K., & Allen, T. (1976). Congruent and contradictory verbal and nonverbal communications of cooperativeness and competitiveness in negotiations. *Communication Research, 3,* 275–291.

Johnson, H. G., Ekman, P., & Friesen, W. V. (1975). Communicative body movement: American emblems. *Semiotica, 15,* 335–353.

Johnson, J. D. (1987). Development of the communication and physical environment scale. *Central States Speech Journal, 38,* 35–43.

Johnson, K. R. (1972). Black kinesics: Some non-verbal communication patterns in the black culture. In L. A. Samovar & R. E. Porter (Eds.), *Intercultural communication: A reader* (2nd ed., pp. 181–189). Belmont, CA: Wadsworth.

Johnson, R. N. (1972). *Aggression in man and animals.* Philadelphia: Saunders.

Johnston, D. (1981). The pink jail. *Corrections Magazine,* June, 28–32.

Jones, E. E. (1964). *Ingratiation.* New York: Appleton-Century-Crofts.

Jones, E. E. (1979). The rocky road from acts to dispositions. *American Psychologist, 34,* 107–117.

Jones, E. E., & Harris, V. A. (1967). The attribution of attitudes. *Journal of Experimental Social Psychology, 3,* 1–24.

Jones, E. E., & Nisbett, R. E. (1972). The actor and the observer: Divergent perceptions of the causes of behavior. In E. E. Jones, D. E. Kanouse, H. H. Kelley, R. E. Nisbett, S. Valins, & B. Weiner (Eds.), *Attribution: Perceiving the causes of behavior* (pp. 79–94). Morristown, NJ: General Learning Press.

Jones, S. E. (1971). A comparative proxemics analysis of dyadic interaction in selected subcultures of New York City. *Journal of Social Psychology, 84,* 35–44.

Jones, S. E. (1984). *An exploratory study of sex differences in tactile communication.* Paper presented at the annual meeting of the Speech Communication Association, Chicago.

Jones, S. E. (1985). *A study of the validity of Jourard's tactile body-accessibility questionnaire.* Paper presented at the annual meeting of the Speech Communication Association, Denver.

Jones, S. E. (1986). Sex differences in touch communication. *Western Journal of Speech Communication, 50,* 227–241.

Jones, S. E., & Aiello, J. R. (1973). Proxemic behavior of black and white first-, third-, and fifth-grade children. *Journal of Personality and Social Psychology, 25,* 21–27.

Jones, S. E., & Yarbrough, A. E. (1985). A naturalistic study of the meanings of touch. *Communication Monographs, 52,* 19–56.

Jorgenson, D. O. (1975). Field study of the relationship between status discrepancy and proxemic behavior. *Journal of Social Psychology, 97,* 173–179.

Jourard, S. M. (1966a). An exploratory study of body accessibility. *British Journal of Social and Clinical Psychology, 5,* 221–231.

Jourard, S. M. (1966b). Some psychological aspects of privacy. *Law and Contemporary Problems, 31,* 307–318.

Jourard, S. M., (1971). *The transparent self.* New York: Van Nostrand Reinhold.

Jourard, S. M., & Friedman, R. (1970). Experimenter-subject "distance" and self-disclosure. *Journal of Personality and Social Psychology, 15,* 278–282.

Jourard, S. M., & Secord, P. F. (1955). Body-cathexis and personality. *British Journal of Psychology, 46,* 130–138.

Jurich, A. P., & Jurich, J. A. (1974). Correlations among nonverbal expressions of anxiety. *Psychological Reports, 34,* 199–204.

Karmel, L. J. (1965). Effects of windowless classroom environment on high school students. *Perceptual and Motor Skills, 20,* 277–278.

Katz, A. M., & Katz, V. T. (1983). Introduction to nonverbal communication. In A. M. Katz & V. T. Katz (Eds.), *Foundations of nonverbal communication: Readings, exercises and commentary* (pp. xv–xvii). Carbondale, IL: Southern Illinois Press.

Katz, D. (1937). *Animals and men.* White Plains, NY: Longman.

Kauffman, L. E. (1971). Tacesics, the study of touch: A model for proxemic analysis. *Semiotica, 4,* 149–161.

Kazdin, A. E., & Klock, J. (1973). The effect of nonverbal teacher approval on student attentive behavior. *Journal of Applied Behavior Analysis, 6,* 643–654.

Kearney, P., Plax, T. G., & Wendt-

Wasco, N. J. (1985). Teacher immediacy for affective learning in divergent college classes. *Communication Quarterly, 33,* 61–74.

Keasy, C. B., & Tomlinson-Keasy, C. (1973). Petition signing in a naturalistic setting. *Journal of Social Psychology, 89,* 313–314.

Keating, C. F. (1985). Human dominance signals: The primate in us. In S. L. Ellyson & J. F. Dovidio (Eds.), *Power, dominance, and nonverbal behavior* (pp. 89–108). New York: Springer-Verlag.

Keeley-Dyreson, M. P., Bailey, W., & Burgoon, J. K. (1988, May). *The effect of stress on decoding of kinesic and vocalic channels.* Paper presented at the annual meeting of the International Communication Association, New Orleans.

Keiser, G., & Altman, I. (1976). Relationship of nonverbal behavior to the social penetration process. *Human Communication Research, 2,* 147–161.

Kelley, J. (1969, May). *Dress as non-verbal communication.* Paper presented at the annual conference of the American Association for Public Opinion Research.

Kelvin, P. (1973). A social-psychological examination of privacy. *British Journal of Social and Clinical Psychology, 12,* 248–261.

Kendon, A. (1967). Some functions of gaze-direction in social interaction. *Acta Psychologica, 26,* 22–63.

Kendon, A. (1975). Some functions of the face in a kissing round. *Semiotica, 15,* 299–334.

Kendon, A. (1978). Looking in conversation and the regulation of turns at talk: A comment on the papers of G. Beattie and D. R. Rutter et al. *British Journal of Social and Clinical Psychology, 17,* 23–24.

Kendon, A. (1980). Gesticulation and speech: Two aspects of the process of utterance. In M. R. Key (Ed.), *The relationship of verbal and nonverbal communication* (pp. 207–227). The Hague: Mouton.

Kendon, A. (1983). Gesture and speech: How they interact. In J. M. Wiemann & R. P. Harrison (Eds.), *Nonverbal interaction* (pp. 13–45). Beverly Hills, CA: Sage.

Kendon, A., & Ferber, A. (1973). A description of some human greetings. In R. P. M. Michael & J. H. Crook (Eds.), *Comparative ecology and behavior of primates* (pp. 591–668). New York: Academic Press.

Kennedy, C. W., & Camden, C. (1981). Gender differences in interruption behavior: A dominance perspective. *International Journal of Women's Studies, 4,* 18–25.

Kennedy, C. W., & Camden, C.

(1983). Interruptions and nonverbal gender differences. *Journal of Nonverbal Behavior, 8,* 91–108.

Kennedy, R. (1943). Premarital residential propinquity. *American Journal of Sociology, 48,* 580–584.

Key, M. R. (Ed.). (1980). *The relationship of verbal and nonverbal communication.* The Hague: Mouton.

Kidd, R. F. (1975). Pupil size, eye contact, and instrumental aggression. *Perceptual and Motor Skills, 41,* 538.

Kimble, C. E., Forte, R. A., & Yoshikawa, J. C. (1981). Nonverbal concomitants of enacted emotional intensity and positivity: Visual and vocal behavior. *Journal of Personality, 49,* 271–283.

King, M. G. (1966). Interpersonal relations in preschool children and average approach distance. *Journal of Genetic Psychology, 109,* 109–116.

Kintsch, W. (1974). *The representation of meaning in memory.* Hillsdale, NJ: Erlbaum.

Kira, A. (1966). *The bathroom: Criteria for design.* New York: Center for Housing and Environmental Studies, Cornell University.

Kira, A. (1970). Privacy and the bathroom. In H. M. Proshansky, W. H. Ittleson, & L. G. Rivlin (Eds.), *Environmental psychology: Man and his physical setting* (pp. 269–275). New York: Holt, Rinehart & Winston.

Kleck, R. E. (1969). Physical stigma and task oriented interaction. *Human Relations, 22,* 53–60.

Kleck, R. E., & Nuessle, W. (1968). Congruence between the indicative and communicative functions of eye-contact in interpersonal relations. *British Journal of Social and Clinical Psychology, 7,* 241–246.

Kleinfeld, J. S. (1973). Effects of nonverbally communicated personal warmth on intelligence test performance of Indian and Eskimo adolescents. *Journal of Social Psychology, 91,* 149–150.

Kleinfeld, J. S. (1974). Effects of nonverbal warmth on learning of Eskimo and white children. *Journal of Social Psychology, 92,* 3–90.

Kleinke, C. L. (1977). Compliance to requests made by gazing and touching experimenters in field settings. *Journal of Experimental Social Psychology, 13,* 218–223.

Kleinke, C. L. (1980). Interaction between gaze and legitimacy of request on compliance in a field setting. *Journal of Nonverbal Behavior, 5,* 3–12.

Kleinke, C. L., Lenga, M. R., Tully, T. B., Meeker, F. B., & Staneski, R. A. (1976). *Effect of talking rate on first impressions of opposite-sex and same-sex interactions.* Paper presented at the annual meeting of the Western Psychological Association, Los Angeles.

Kleinke, C. L., Meeker, F. B., & LaFong, C. (1974). Effects of gaze, touch, and use of name on evaluation of "engaged" couples. *Journal of Research in Personality, 7,* 368–373.

Knapp, M. L. (1972). *Nonverbal communication in human interaction.* New York: Holt, Rinehart and Winston.

Knapp, M. L. (1978). *Nonverbal communication in human interaction* (2nd ed.). New York: Holt, Rinehart and Winston.

Knapp, M. L. (1983a). Dyadic relationship development. In J. M. Wiemann & R. P. Harrison (Eds.), *Nonverbal interaction* (pp. 179–207). Beverly Hills CA: Sage.

Knapp, M. L. (1983b). *The study of nonverbal behavior vis-a-vis human communication theory.* Paper presented at the 2nd International Conference on Nonverbal Behavior, Toronto.

Knapp, M. L. (1984). *Interpersonal communication and human relationships.* Boston: Allyn & Bacon.

Knapp, M. L., & Comadena, M. E. (1979). Telling it like it isn't: A review of theory and research on deceptive communications. *Human Communication Research, 5,* 270–285.

Knapp, M. L., Hart, R. P., & Dennis, H. S. (1974). An exploration of deception as a communication construct. *Human Communication Research, 1,* 15–29.

Knapp, M. L., Hart, R. P., Freidrich, G. W., & Shulman, G. M. (1973). The rhetoric of goodbye: Verbal and nonverbal correlates of human leave-taking. *Speech Monographs, 40,* 182–198.

Knapp, M. L., Wiemann, J. M., & Daly, J. A. (1978). Nonverbal communication: Issues and appraisal. *Human Communication Research, 4,* 271–280.

Knower, F. H. (1945). Studies in the symbolism of voice and action, V: The use of behavioral and tonal symbols as tests of speaking achievement. *Journal of Applied Psychology, 29,* 229–235.

Knowles, E. S. (1972). Boundaries around social space: Dyadic responses to an invader. *Environment and Behavior, 4,* 437–445.

Knowles, E. S. (1973). Boundaries around group interaction: The effect of group size and member status on boundary permeability. *Journal of Personality and Social Psychology, 26,* 327–331.

Knowles, E. S. (1980). An affiliative conflict theory of personal and group spatial behavior. In P. B. Paulus (Ed.), *Psychology of group influence* (pp. 133–188). Hillsdale, NJ: Erlbaum.

Knudsen, H. R., & Muzekari, L. H.

(1983). The effects of verbal statements of context on facial expressions of emotion. *Journal of Nonverbal Behavior, 7,* 202–212.

Konečni, V. J., Libuser, L., Morton, H., & Ebbesen, E. B. (1975). Effects of a violation of personal space on escape and helping responses. *Journal of Experimental Social Psychology, 11,* 288–299.

Korda, M. (1975). *Power! How to get it, how to use it.* New York: Ballantine.

Kowal, S., O'Connel, D. C., & Sabin, E. J. (1975). Development of temporal patterning and vocal hesitations in spontaneous narratives. *Journal of Psycholinguistic Research, 4,* 195–207.

Krauss, R. M., Apple, W., Morency, N., Wenzel, C., & Winton, W. (1981). Verbal, vocal, and visible factors in judgments of another's affect. *Journal of Personality and Social Psychology, 40,* 312–319.

Krauss, R. M., Geller, V., & Olson, C. (1976, September). *Modalities and cues in the detection of deception.* Paper presented at the annual meeting of the American Psychological Association, Washington, DC.

Kraut, R. E. (1978). Verbal and nonverbal cues in the perception of lying. *Journal of Personality and Social Psychology, 36,* 380–391.

Kraut, R. E. (1980). Humans as lie detectors: Some second thoughts. *Journal of Communication, 30(4),* 209–216.

Kraut, R. E., & Poe, D. (1980). On the line: The deception judgements of customs inspectors and laymen. *Journal of Personality and Social Psychology, 39,* 784–798.

Kraut, R. E., Thompson, A., & Lewis, S. H. (1980). *Listener responsiveness, deception, and semantic structure in conversation.* Unpublished manuscript, Cornell University.

Krivonos, P. D., & Knapp, M. L. (1975). Initiating communication: What do you say when you say hello? *Central States Speech Journal, 26,* 115–125.

Krout, M. H. (1935). Autistic gestures: An experimental study in symbolic movement. *Psychological Monographs, 46,* 1–119.

Krout, M. H. (1942). *Introduction to social psychology.* New York: Harper & Row.

Krout, M. H. (1954a). An experimental attempt to determine the significance of unconscious manual symbolic movements. *Journal of General Psychology, 51,* 93–120.

Krout, M. H. (1954b). An experimental attempt to produce unconscious manual symbolic movements. *Journal of General Psychology, 51,* 121–152.

Krout, M. H. (1971). Symbolism. In H. A. Bosmajian (Ed.), *The rhetoric of nonverbal communication* (pp. 15–33). Glenview, IL: Scott, Foresman.

Kunihiro, M. (1976). The Japanese language and intercultural communication. *Japan Interpreter, 10,* 267–283.

LaBarbera, P., & MacLachlan, J. (1979). Time compressed speech in radio advertising. *Journal of Marketing, 43,* 30–36.

LaBarre, W. (1947). The cultural basis of emotions and gestures. *Journal of Personality, 16,* 49–68.

LaBarre, W. (1972). Paralinguistics, kinesics, and cultural anthropology. In L. A. Samovar & R. E. Porter (Eds.), *Intercultural communication: A reader* (2nd ed., pp. 172–180). Belmont, CA: Wadsworth.

LaCrosse, M. B. (1975). Nonverbal behavior and perceived counselor attractiveness and persuasiveness. *Journal of Counseling Psychology, 22,* 563–566.

LaFrance, M. (1979). Nonverbal synchrony and rapport: Analysis by the cross-lag panel technique. *Social Psychology Quarterly, 42,* 66–70.

LaFrance, M. (1985a). Postural mirroring and intergroup relations. *Personality and Social Psychology Bulletin, 11,* 207–217.

LaFrance, M. (1985b). The school of hard knocks: Nonverbal sexism in the classroom. *Theory into Practice, 24,* 40–44.

LaFrance, M., & Broadbent, M. (1976). Group rapport: Posture sharing as a nonverbal indicator. *Group and Organizational Studies, 1,* 328–333.

LaFrance, M., & Ickes, W. (1981). Postural mirroring and interactional involvement: Sex and sex-typing effects. *Journal of Nonverbal Behavior, 5,* 139–154.

LaFrance, M., & Mayo, C. (1976). Racial differences in gaze behavior during conversations: Two systematic observational studies. *Journal of Personality and Social Psychology, 33,* 547–552.

LaFrance, M., & Mayo, C. (1978a). Cultural aspects of nonverbal communication. *International Journal of Intercultural Relations, 2,* 71–89.

LaFrance, M., & Mayo, C. (1978b). *Moving bodies.* Monterey, CA: Brooks/Cole.

LaFrance, M., & Mayo, C. (1979). A review of nonverbal behaviors of women and men. *Western Journal of Speech Communication, 43,* 96–107.

Laird, J. D. (1974). Self-attribution of emotion: The effects of expressive behavior on the quality of emotional experience. *Journal of Personality and Social Psychology, 29,* 475–486.

Lakoff, R. (1973). Language and woman's place. *Language in Society, 2,* 45–79.

Lamb, M. E., Suomi, S. J., & Stephenson, G. R. (1979). *Social interaction analysis: Methodological issues.* Madison: University of Wisconsin Press.

Lamb, T. A. (1981). Nonverbal and paraverbal control in dyads and triads: Sex or power differences? *Social Psychology Quarterly, 44,* 49–53.

Lambert, W. E., Hodgson, R. C., Gardner, R. C., & Fillenbaum, S. (1960). Evaluational reactions to spoken languages. *Journal of Abnormal and Social Psychology, 60,* 44–51.

Langer, E. J., & Imber, L. (1980). Role of mindlessness in the perception of deviance. *Journal of Personality and Social Psychology, 39,* 360–367.

Langer, E. J., & Saegert, S. (1977). Crowding and cognitive control. *Journal of Personality and Social Psychology, 35,* 175–182.

Lanzetta, J. T., Cartwright-Smith, J., & Kleck, R. E. (1976). Effects of nonverbal dissimulation on emotional experience and autonomic arousal. *Journal of Personality and Social Psychology, 33,* 354–370.

Lass, N. L., & Davis, M. (1976). An investigation of speaker height and weight identification. *Journal of the Acoustical Society of America, 60,* 700–707.

Laver, R. H. (1981). *Temporal man.* New York: Praeger.

Lavrakas, P. J. (1975). Female preferences for male physiques. *Journal of Research in Personality, 9,* 324–333.

Lay, C. H., & Burron, B. F. (1968). Perception of the personality of the hesitant speaker. *Perceptual and Motor Skills, 26,* 951–956.

Leach, E. (1968). Don't say "boo" to a goose. In M. F. A. Montagu (Ed.), *Man and aggression* (pp. 65–73). London: Oxford University Press.

Leach, E. (1972). The influence of cultural context on non-verbal communication in man. In R. A. Hinde (Ed.), *Non-verbal communication* (pp. 315–344). Cambridge: Cambridge University Press.

Leakey, R. E., & Lewin, R. (1978). *People of the lake: Mankind and its beginnings.* Garden City, NY: Anchor Books/Doubleday.

Leary, T. (1957). *Interpersonal diagnosis of personality.* New York: Ronald Press.

Leathers, D. G. (1976). *Nonverbal communication systems.* Boston: Allyn & Bacon.

Leathers, D. G. (1979). The impact of multichannel message inconsist-

ency on verbal and nonverbal decoding behaviors. *Communication Monographs, 46,* 88–100.

LeCompte, W. F., & Rosenfeld, H. M. (1971). Effects of minimal eye contact in the instruction period on impressions of the experimenter. *Journal of Experimental Social Psychology, 7,* 211–220.

Lee, D. Y., Hallberg, E. T., Hassard, J. H., & Haase, R. F. (1979). Client verbal and nonverbal reinforcement of counselor behavior: Its impact on interviewing behavior and postinterview evaluation. *Journal of Counseling Psychology, 26,* 204–209.

Leffler, A., Gillespie, D. L., & Conaty, J. C. (1982). The effects of status differentiation on nonverbal behavior. *Social Psychology Quarterly, 45,* 153–161.

Leibman, M. (1970). The effects of sex and race norms on personal space. *Environment and Behavior, 2,* 208–248.

Leighton, A. H., & Leighton, D. C. (1944). *The Navaho door: An introduction to Navaho life.* Cambridge, MA: Harvard University Press.

Leventhal, H., Nerenz, D. R., & Leventhal, E. (1982). Feelings of threat and private views of illness: Factors in dehumanization in the medical care system. In A. Baum & J. E. Singer (Eds.), *Advances in environmental psychology: Environment and health* (Vol. 4, pp. 85–114). Hillsdale, NJ: Erlbaum.

Levin, H., Silverman, I., & Ford, B. L. (1967). Hesitations in children's speech during explanation and description. *Journal of Verbal Learning and Verbal Behavior, 6,* 560–564.

Levine, M. H. (1972). *The effects of age, sex, and task on visual behavior during dyadic interaction.* Unpublished doctoral dissertation, Columbia University.

Levine, R., & Wolff, E. (1985, March). Social time: The heartbeat of culture. *Psychology Today,* pp. 28–35.

Levy, P. (1964). The ability to express and perceive vocal communication of feeling. In J. R. Davitz (Ed.), *Communication of emotional meaning* (pp. 43–56). New York: McGraw-Hill.

Lewin, K. (1935). *A dynamic theory of personality.* New York: McGraw-Hill.

Lewinski, R. H. (1938). An investigation of individual responses to chromatic illumination. *Journal of Psychology, 6,* 6.

Lewis, M. (1972). Parents and children: Sex-role development. *School Review, 80,* 229–240.

Lewis, M., & Goldberg, S. (1969). Perceptual-cognitive development in infancy: A generalized expectancy model as a function of the mother-

infant interaction. *Merrill-Palmer Quarterly, 15,* 81–100.

Leyhausen, P. (1971). Dominance and territoriality as complemented in mammalian social structure. In A. H. Esser (Ed.), *Behavior and environment* (pp. 22–33). New York: Plenum.

Libby, W. L., Jr. (1970). Eye contact and direction of looking as stable individual differences. *Journal of Experimental Research in Personality, 4,* 303–312.

Lieberman, P. (1967). *Intonation, perception, and language.* Cambridge, MA: MIT Press.

Lindskold, S., & Walters, P. S. (1983). Categories for acceptability of lies. *Journal of Social Psychology, 120,* 129–136.

Lipman, A. (1970). Territoriality: A useful architectural concept? *Royal Institute of British Architects Journal, 77,* 68–70.

Lippa, R. (1976). Expressive control and the leakage of dispositional introversion-extraversion during role-played teaching. *Journal of Personality, 44,* 541–559.

Lippard, P. V. (1988). "Ask me no questions, I'll tell you no lies": Situational exigencies for interpersonal deception. *Western Journal of Speech Communication, 52,* 91–103.

Liska, J. (1986). Symbols: The missing link? In J. G. Else & P. Lee (Eds.), *Proceedings of the Tenth Congress of the International Primatological Society: Vol. 3. Primate ontogeny, cognition, and social behavior.* Cambridge: Cambridge University Press.

Little, K. B. (1968). Cultural variations in social schemata. *Journal of Personality and Social Psychology, 10,* 1–7.

Littlepage, G. E., & Pineault, M. A. (1979). Detection of deceptive factual statements from the body and the face. *Personality and Social Psychology Bulletin, 5,* 325–328.

Lochman, J. E., & Allen, G. (1981). Nonverbal communication of couples in conflict. *Journal of Research in Personality, 15,* 253–269.

Lockard, J. S., Allen, D. J., Schiele, B. J., & Wiemer, M. J. (1978). Human postural signals: Stance, weight-shifts and social distance as intention movements to depart. *Animal Behaviour, 26,* 219–224.

Lomranz, J., & Shapira, A. (1974). Communicative patterns of self-disclosure and touching behavior. *Journal of Psychology, 88,* 223–227.

Lomranz, J., Shapira, A., Choresh, N., & Gilat, Y. (1975). Children's personal space as a function of age and sex. *Developmental Psychology, 11,* 541–545.

Loo, C. (1972). The effects of spatial

density on the social behavior of children. *Journal of Applied Social Psychology, 4,* 172–181.

Loo, C., & Smetana, J. (1978). The effects of crowding on the behavior and perception of 10-year-old boys. *Environmental Psychology and Nonverbal Behavior, 2,* 226–249.

Lott, D. F., & Sommer, R. (1967). Seating arrangements and status. *Journal of Personality and Social Psychology, 7,* 90–94.

Lüscher, M. (1971). *The Lüscher color test* (I. Scott, Trans.). New York: Washington Square Press Pocket Books.

Lyman, S. M., & Scott, M. B. (1967). Territoriality: A neglected sociological dimension. *Social Problems, 15,* 236–249.

Lyons, J. (1972). Human language. In R. A. Hinde (Ed.), *Non-verbal communication* (pp. 49–85). Cambridge: Cambridge University Press.

Mabry, E. A., & Kaufman, S. (1973, April). *The influence of sex and attraction on seating positions in dyads.* Paper presented at the annual meeting of the International Communication Association, Montreal.

Mach, R. S. (1972). *Postural carriage and congruency as nonverbal indicators of status differentials and interpersonal attraction.* Unpublished doctoral dissertation, University of Colorado.

Mackey, W. C. (1976). Parameters of the smile as a social signal. *Journal of Genetic Psychology, 129,* 125–130.

MacLachlan, J. (1979, November). What people really think of fast talkers. *Psychology Today, 13,* 113–117.

MacLachlan, J. (1981, April). *New Developments in time compression.* Paper presented at the annual meeting of the American Psychological Association, Pittsburgh.

MacLachlan, J., & LaBarbera, P. (1978). Time-compressed TV commercials. *Journal of Advertising Research, 18,* 11–15.

MacLachlan, J., & Siegel, M. H. (1980). Reducing the cost of TV commercials by use of time compressions. *Journal of Marketing Research, 17,* 52–57.

MacNeil, L., & Wilson, B. (1972). *Effects of clothing and hair length on petition-signing behavior.* Unpublished manuscript, Illinois State University.

Maddux, J. E., & Rogers, R. W. (1980). Effects of source expertness, physical attractiveness, and supporting arguments on persuasion: A case of brains over beauty. *Journal of Personality and Social Psychology, 39,* 235–244.

Magnusson, D. (1971). An analysis of situational dimensions. *Perceptual and Motor Skills, 32,* 851–867.

Magnusson, D. (1978). *On the psychological situation.* Stockholm: University of Stockholm Reports.

Maier, N. R. F., & Thurber, J. A. (1968). Accuracy of judgments of deception when an interview is watched, heard, and read. *Personnel Psychology, 21,* 23–30.

Maier, R. A., & Ernest, R. C. (1978). Sex differences in the perception of touching. *Perceptual and Motor Skills, 46,* 577–578.

Maines, D. R. (1977). Tactile relationships in the subway as affected by racial, sexual, and crowded seating situations. *Environmental Psychology and Nonverbal Behavior, 2,* 100–108.

Maisonneuve, J., Palmade, G., & Fourment, C. (1952). Selective choices and propinquity. *Sociometry, 15,* 135–140.

Major, B. (1981). Gender patterns in touching behavior. In C. Mayo & N. M. Henley (Eds.), *Gender and nonverbal behavior* (pp. 15–37). New York: Springer-Verlag.

Major, B., & Heslin, R. (1982). Perceptions of cross-sex and same-sex nonreciprocal touch: It is better to give than to receive. *Journal of Nonverbal Behavior, 6,* 148–162.

Major, B., & Williams, L. (1980). *Frequency of touch by sex and race: A replication of some touching observations.* Unpublished manuscript, State University of New York, Buffalo.

Malandro, L. A., & Barker, L. (1983). *Nonverbal communication.* Reading, MA: Addison-Wesley.

Mallory, E., & Miller V. (1958). A possible basis for the association of voice characteristics and personality traits. *Speech Monographs, 25,* 255.

Mann, J. M. (1959). The effect of interracial contact on sociometric choices and perceptions. *Journal of Social Psychology, 50,* 143–152.

Mansfield, E. (1973). Empathy: Concept and identified psychiatric nursing behavior. *Nursing Research, 22,* 525–530.

Manusov, V. L. (1984). *Nonverbal violations of expectations theory: A test of gaze behavior.* Unpublished thesis, Michigan State University.

Markel, N. N. (1969). Relationship between voice-quality and MMPI profiles in psychiatric patients. *Journal of Abnormal Psychology, 74,* 61–66.

Markel, N. N. (1975). Coverbal behavior associated with conversational turns. In A. Kendon, R. Harris, & M. R. Key (Eds.), *Organization of behavior in face-to-face interaction*

(pp. 189–197). The Hague: Mouton.

Markel, N. N., Long, J. F., & Saine, T. J. (1976). Sex effects in conversational interaction: Another look at male dominance. *Human Communication Research, 2,* 356–364.

Markel, N. N., Phillis, J. A., Vargas, R., & Howard, K. (1972). Personality traits associated with voice types. *Journal of Psycholinguistic Research, 1,* 249–255.

Markel, N. N., Prebor, L. D., & Brandt, J. F. (1972). Biosocial factors in dyadic communication: Sex and speaking intensity. *Journal of Personality and Social Psychology, 23,* 11–13.

Marks, L. E. (1975, June). Synesthesia: The lucky people with mixed-up senses. *Psychology Today 9,* 48–52.

Marshall, N. J. (1972). Privacy and environment. *Human Ecology, 1,* 93–110.

Martin, J. G. (1964). Racial ethnocentrism and judgment of beauty. *Journal of Social Psychology, 63,* 59–63.

Maslow, C., Yoselson, K., & London, H. (1971). Persuasiveness of confidence expressed via language and body language. *British Journal of Social and Clinical Psychology, 10,* 234–240.

Massie, H. N. (1978). Blind ratings of mother-infant interaction in home movies of prepsychotic and normal infants. *American Journal of Psychiatry, 135,* 1371–1374.

Matarazzo, J. D., & Wiens, A. N. (1972). *The Interview: Research on its anatomy and structure.* Chicago: Aldine.

Matarazzo, J. D., Wiens, A. N., Jackson, R. H., & Manaugh, T. S. (1970). Interviewee speech behavior under conditions of endogenously-present and exogenously-induced motivational states. *Journal of Clinical Psychology, 26,* 141–148.

Matarazzo, J. D., Wiens, A. N., & Saslow, G. (1965). Studies in interviewer speech behavior. In L. Krasner & L. P. Ullmann (Eds.), *Research in behavior modification: New developments and implications* (pp. 179–210). New York: Holt, Rinehart and Winston.

Matthews, R. W., Paulus, P. B., & Baron, R. A. (1979). Physical aggression after being crowded. *Journal of Nonverbal Behavior, 4,* 5–17.

Mattingly, I. M. (1966). Speaker variation and vocal tract size. *Journal of the Acoustical Society of America, 39,* 1219.

Mayo, C., & LaFrance, M. (1978). On the acquisition of nonverbal communication: A review. *Merrill Palmer Quarterly, 24,* 213–228.

References

McAdams, D. P., Jackson, R. J., & Kirshnit, C. (1984). Looking, laughing, and smiling in dyads as a function of intimacy motivation and reciprocity. *Journal of Personality, 52,* 261–273.

McBride, G. (1971). Theories of animal spacing: The role of flight, fight and social distance. In A. H. Esser (Ed.), *Behavior and environment* (pp. 53–68). New York: Plenum.

McBride, G. (1975). Interactions and the control of behavior. In A. Kendon, R. M. Harris, & M. R. Key (Eds.), *Organization of behavior in face-to-face interaction* (pp. 415–425). The Hague: Mouton.

McBride, G., King, M. G., & James, J. W. (1965). Social proximity effects on galvanic skin responses in adult humans. *Journal of Psychology, 61,* 153–157.

McCain, G., Cox, V. C., & Paulus, P. B. (1976). The relationship between illness complaints and degree of crowding in a prison environment. *Environment and Behavior, 8,* 283–290.

McCallum, R., Rusbult, C. E., Hong, G. K., Walden, T. A., & Schopler, J. (1979). Effects of resource availability and importance of behavior on the experience of crowding. *Journal of Personality and Social Psychology, 37,* 1304–1313.

McCarthy, P. (1988, January). Mind openers. *Psychology Today,* p. 16.

McCauley, C., Coleman, G., & DeFusco, P. (1978). Commuters' eye contact with strangers in city and suburban train stations: Evidence of short-term adaptation to interpersonal overload in the city. *Environmental Psychology and Nonverbal Behavior, 2,* 215–225.

McClintock, C. C., & Hunt, R. G. (1975). Nonverbal indicators of affect and deception in an interview setting. *Journal of Applied Social Psychology, 5,* 54–67.

McConnell, J. V., Cutler, L., & McNeil, B. (1958). Subliminal stimulation: An overview. *American Psychologist, 13,* 235.

McConnell-Ginet, S. (1974). *Intonation in a man's world.* Paper presented at the annual meeting of the American Anthropological Association, Mexico City.

McCormick, E. J. (1976). *Human factors in engineering and design.* New York: McGraw-Hill.

McCornack, S. A., & Parks, M. R. (1985). Deception detection and relationship development: The other side of trust. In M. L. McLaughlin (Ed.), *Communication Yearbook 9* (pp. 377–389). Beverly Hills CA: Sage.

McCroskey, J. C. (1972). *An introduction to rhetorical communication.* Englewood Cliffs, NJ: Prentice-Hall.

McCroskey, J. C., & Mehrley, R. S. (1969). The effects of disorganization and nonfluency on attitude change and source credibility. *Speech Monographs, 36,* 13–21.

McDowall, J. J. (1978a). Interactional synchrony: A reappraisal. *Journal of Personality and Social Psychology, 36,* 963–975.

McDowall, J. J. (1978b). Microanalysis of filmed movement: The reliability of boundary detection by observers. *Environmental Psychology and Nonverbal Behavior, 3,* 77–88.

McDowell, E. E., McDowell, C. E., & Hyerdahl, J. (1980). *A multivariate study of teacher immediacy, effectiveness and student attentiveness at the junior high and senior high levels.* Paper presented at the annual meeting of the Speech Communication Association, New York.

McDowell, K. V. (1973). Accommodations of verbal and nonverbal behaviors as a function of the manipulation of interaction distance and eye contact. *Proceedings of the 81st Annual Convention of the American Psychological Association, 8,* 207–208.

McGinley, H., Blau, G., & Takai, M. (1984). Attraction effects of smiling and body position: A cultural comparison. *Perceptual and Motor Skills, 58,* 915–922.

McGinley, H., LeFevre, R., & McGinley, P. (1975). The influence of a communicator's body position on opinion change in others. *Journal of Personality and Social Psychology, 31,* 686–690.

McGinley, H., McGinley, P., & Nicholas, K. (1978). Smiling, body position, and interpersonal attraction. *Bulletin of the Psychonomic Society, 12,* 21–24.

McGlone, R. E. (1966). Vocal pitch characteristics of children aged one to two years. *Speech Monographs, 33,* 178–181.

McGlone, R. E., & Hollien, H. (1963). Vocal pitch characteristics of aged women. *Journal of Speech and Hearing Research, 6,* 164–170.

McHarg, I. (1963). Man and his environment. In L. J. Dahl (Ed.), *The urban condition* (pp. 57–58). New York: Basic Books.

McLaughlin, M. L. (1984). *Conversation: How talk is organized.* Beverly Hills, CA: Sage.

McLuhan, M., & Fiore, Q. (1967). *The medium is the massage.* New York: Random House.

McMahan, E. M. (1976). Nonverbal communication as a function of attribution in impression formation. *Communication Monographs, 43,* 287–294.

McMullan, G. R. (1974). *The relative contribution of selected nonverbal behaviors to the communication of empathy in a counseling interview.* Unpublished doctoral dissertation, West Virginia University.

McNeill, D. (1970). *The acquisition of language: The study of developmental psycholinguistics.* New York: Harper & Row.

McNeill, D. (1979). *The conceptual basis of language.* Hillsdale, NJ: Erlbaum.

McNeill, D., & Levy, E. (1982). Conceptual representations in language activity and gesture. In R. J. Jarvella & W. Klein (Eds.), *Speech, place, and action: Studies in deixis and related topics* (pp. 271–295). Chichester, England: John Wiley.

McPeek, R. W., & Edwards, J. D. (1975). Expectancy disconfirmation and attitude change. *Journal of Social Psychology, 96,* 193–208.

Mead, M. (1975). Review of *Darwin and facial expression: A century of research in review by P. Ekman. Journal of Communication, 25,(1),* 209–213.

Mechanic, D. (1972). Social psychologic factors affecting the presentation of bodily complaints. *New England Journal of Medicine, 286,* 1132–1139.

Meditch, A. (1975). The development of sex-specific speech patterns in young children. *Anthropological Linguistics, 17,* 421–433.

Meerloo, J. A. M. (1955). Archaic behavior and the communicative act. *Psychiatric Quarterly, 29,* 60–73.

Meerloo, J. A. M. (1970). *Along the fourth dimension.* New York: Harper & Row.

Mehrabian, A. (1967). Orientation behaviors and nonverbal attitude communication. *Journal of Communication, 17,* 324–332.

Mehrabian, A. (1968a, September). Communication without words. *Psychology Today, 2,* 52–55.

Mehrabian, A. (1968b). Inference of attitude from the posture, orientation, and distance of a communicator. *Journal of Consulting and Clinical Psychology, 32,* 296–308.

Mehrabian, A. (1968c). Relationship of attitude to seated posture, orientation, and distance. *Journal of Personality and Social Psychology, 10,* 26–30.

Mehrabian, A. (1969). Significance of posture and position in the communication of attitude and status relationships. *Psychological Bulletin, 71,* 359–372.

Mehrabian, A. (1970a). A semantic space for nonverbal behavior. *Journal of Consulting and Clinical Psychology, 35,* 248–257.

Mehrabian, A. (1970b). When are feelings communicated inconsistently? *Journal of Experimental Research in Personality, 4,* 198–212.

Mehrabian, A. (1971a). Nonverbal betrayal of feelings. *Journal of Experimental Research in Personality, 5,* 64–73.

Mehrabian, A. (1971b). Verbal and nonverbal interaction of strangers in a waiting situation. *Journal of Experimental Research in Personality, 5,* 127–138.

Mehrabian, A. (1972). *Nonverbal communication.* Chicago: Aldine-Atherton.

Mehrabian, A. (1976). *Public places and private spaces: The psychology of work, play, and living environments.* New York: Basic Books.

Mehrabian, A. (1981). *Silent messages: Implicit communication of emotions and attitudes* (2nd ed.). Belmont, CA: Wadsworth.

Mehrabian, A., & Diamond, S. G. (1971). Seating arrangement and conversation. *Sociometry, 34,* 281–289.

Mehrabian, A., & Ferris, S. R. (1967). Inference of attitudes from nonverbal communication in two channels. *Journal of Consulting Psychology, 31,* 248–252.

Mehrabian, A., & Friar, J. T. (1969). Encoding of attitude by a seated communicator via posture and position cues. *Journal of Consulting and Clinical Psychology, 33,* 330–336.

Mehrabian, A., & Ksionzky, S. (1970). Models for affiliative and conformity behavior. *Psychological Bulletin, 74,* 110–126.

Mehrabian, A., & Ksionzky, S. (1972). Categories of social behavior. *Comparative Group Studies, 3,* 425–436.

Mehrabian, A., & Russell, J. A. (1974). *An approach to environmental psychology.* Cambridge, MA: MIT Press.

Mehrabian, A., & Wiener, M. (1967). Decoding of inconsistent communications. *Journal of Personality and Social Psychology, 6,* 108–114.

Mehrabian, A., & Williams, M. (1969). Nonverbal concomitants of perceived and intended persuasiveness. *Journal of Personality and Social Psychology, 13,* 37–58.

Meisels, M., & Guardo, C. J. (1969). Development of personal space schemata. *Child Development, 40,* 1167–1178.

Meltzer, L., Morris, W. N., & Hayes, D. P. (1971). Interruption outcomes and vocal amplitude: Explorations in social psychophysics. *Journal of Personality and Social Psychology, 18,* 392–402.

Menyuk, P. (1971). *The acquisition and development of language.* Englewood Cliffs, NJ: Prentice-Hall.

Menyuk, P. (1972). *The development of speech.* New York: Bobbs-Merrill.

Merton, R. K. (1948). The self-fulfilling prophecy. *Antioch Review, 8,* 193–210.

Metts, S., & Chronis, H. (1986, May). *An exploratory investigation of relational deception.* Paper presented at the annual meeting of the International Communication Association, Chicago.

Metts, S., & Hippensteele, S. (1988). *Characteristics of deception in close relationships.* Paper presented at the annual meeting of the Western Speech Communication Association, San Diego.

Michael, G., & Willis, F. N., Jr. (1969). The development of gestures in three subcultural groups. *Journal of Social Psychology, 79,* 35–41.

Michener, J. A. (1980). *The covenant.* New York: Fawcett Crest.

Milgram, S. (1963). Behavioral study of obedience. *Journal of Abnormal and Social Psychology, 67,* 371–378.

Milgram, S. (1970). The experience of living in cities. *Science, 167,* 1461–1468.

Milgram, S. (1974). *Obedience to authority: An experimental view.* New York: Harper & Row.

Millar, F. E., & Rogers, L. E. (1976). A relational approach to interpersonal communication. In G. R. Miller (Ed.), *Explorations in interpersonal communication* (pp. 87–104). Beverly Hills, CA: Sage.

Miller, A. (1970). Role of physical attractiveness in impression formation. *Psychonomic Science, 19,* 241–243.

Miller, G. A. (1956). The magical number seven, plus or minus two: Some limits on our capacity for processing information. *Psychological Review, 63,* 81–97.

Miller, G. R., Bauchner, J. E., Hocking, J. E., Fontes, N. E., Kaminski, E. P., & Brandt, D. R. (1981). ". . . and nothing but the truth": How well can observers detect deceptive testimony? In B. D. Sales (Ed.), *Perspectives in law and psychology. Volume 3. The jury, judicial, and trial process.* New York: Plenum.

Miller, G. R., & Burgoon, J. K. (1982). Factors affecting witness credibility. In N. L. Kerr & R. M. Bray (Eds.), *The psychology of the courtroom* (pp. 169–194). New York: Academic Press.

Miller, G. R., & Burgoon, M. (1978). Persuasion research: Review and commentary. In B. Rubin (Ed.), *Communication yearbook 2* (pp. 29–47). New Brunswick, NJ: Transaction.

Miller, G. R., & Hewgill, M. A. (1964). The effect of variations in nonfluency on audience ratings of source

credibility. *Quarterly Journal of Speech, 50,* 36–44.

Miller, G. R., & Steinberg, M. (1975). *Between people.* Chicago: Science Research Associates.

Miller, N., Maruyama, G., Beaber, R. J., & Valone, K. (1976). Speed of speech and persuasion. *Journal of Personality and Social Psychology, 34,* 615–624.

Miller, R. A. (1982). *Japan's modern myth: The language and beyond.* Tokyo: Weatherhill.

Mills, J., & Aronson, E. (1965). Opinion change as a function of the communicator's attractiveness and desire to influence. *Journal of Personality and Social Psychology, 1,* 73–77.

Mischel, W. (1968). *Personality and assessment.* New York: Wiley.

Mischel, W. (1979). On the interface of cognition and personality: Beyond the person-situation debate. *American Psychologist, 34,* 740–754.

Mitchell, G. (1975). What monkeys tell us about human violence. *The Futurist, 9,* 75–80.

Mitchell, G., & Maple, T. L. (1985). Dominance in nonhuman primates. In S. L. Ellyson & J. F. Dovidio (Eds.), *Power, dominance, and nonverbal behavior* (pp. 49–66). New York: Springer-Verlag.

Mobbs, N. A. (1969). Eye contact and introversion-extroversion. Cited in A. Kendon & M. Cook, The consistency of gaze patterns in social interaction. *British Journal of Psychology, 60,* 481–494.

Modigliani, A. (1971). Embarrassment, facework, and eye contact: Testing a theory of embarrassment. *Journal of Personality and Social Psychology, 17,* 15–24.

Moe, J. D. (1972). Listener judgments of status cues in speech: A replication and extension. *Speech Monographs, 39,* 144–147.

Molloy, J. T. (1975). *Dress for success.* New York: Warner Books.

Molloy, J. T. (1977). *The woman's dress for success book.* Chicago: Follett.

Montagu, A. (1971). *Touching: The human significance of the skin.* New York: Columbia University Press.

Montagu, A. (1978). *Touching: The human significance of the skin* (2nd ed.). New York: Harper & Row.

Montagu, M. F. A. (1968). The new litany of "innate depravity," or original sin revisited. In M. F. A. Montagu (Ed.), *Man and aggression* (pp. 3–17). New York: Oxford University Press.

Moore, H. T., & Gilliland, A. R. (1921). The measurement of aggressiveness. *Journal of Applied Psychology, 5,* 97–118.

Moore, W. E. (1939). Personality traits and voice quality deficiencies.

Journal of Speech and Hearing Disorders, 4, 33–36.

Morency, N. L., & Krauss, R. M. (1982). Children's nonverbal encoding and decoding of affect. In R. S. Feldman (Ed.), *Development of nonverbal behavior in children* (pp. 181–199). New York: Springer-Verlag.

Morley, I. E., & Stephenson, G. M. (1969). Interpersonal and interparty exchange: A laboratory simulation of an industrial negotiation at the plant level. *British Journal of Psychology, 60,* 543–545.

Morris, D. (1967). *The naked ape.* New York: McGraw-Hill.

Morris, D. (1971). *Intimate behavior.* New York: Random House.

Morris, D. (1977). *Manwatching: A field guide to human behavior.* New York: Abrams.

Morris, D. (1985). *Bodywatching.* New York: Crown.

Morris, D., Collett, P., Marsh, P., & O'Shaughnessy, M. (1979). *Gestures.* New York: Stein & Day.

Morsbach, H. (1973). Aspects of nonverbal communication in Japan. *Journal of Nervous and Mental Disease, 157,* 262–277.

Morton, T. L. (1974). *The effects of acquaintance and distance on intimacy and reciprocity.* Unpublished master's thesis, University of Utah.

Mosby, K. D. (1978). *An analysis of actual and ideal touching behavior as reported on a modified version of the body accessibility questionnaire.* Unpublished doctoral dissertation, Virginia Commonwealth University.

Motley, M. T. (1974). Acoustic correlates of lies. *Western Speech, 38,* 81–87.

Motley, M. T., Camden, C. T., & Baars, B. J. (1981). Toward verifying the assumptions of laboratory-induced slips of the tongue: The output-error and editing issues. *Human Communication Research, 8,* 3–15.

Moyer, D. M. (1975). The development of children's ability to recognize and express facially posed emotion. *Dissertation Abstracts International, 35,* 5622.

Mulac, A., Hanley, T. D., & Prigge, D. Y. (1974). Effects of phonological speech foreignness upon three dimensions of attitude of selected American speakers. *Quarterly Journal of Speech, 60,* 411–420.

Mulac, A., Studley, L. B., Wiemann, J. W., & Bradac, J. J. (1987). Male/female gaze in same-sex and mixed-sex dyads: Gender-linked differences and mutual influence. *Human Communication Research, 13,* 323–344.

Murphy, L. B. (1937). *Social behavior and child personality.* New York: Columbia University Press.

Murray, D. C. (1971). Talk, silence and anxiety. *Psychological Bulletin, 75,* 244–260.

Murray, R. P., & McGinley, H. (1972). Looking as a measure of attraction. *Journal of Applied Social Psychology, 2,* 267–274.

Mysak, E. D. (1959). Pitch and duration characteristics of older males. *Journal of Speech and Hearing Research, 2,* 46–54.

Nadler, A., Shapira, R., & Ben-Itzhak, S. (1982). Good looks may help: Effects of helper's physical attractiveness and sex of helper on males' and females' help-seeking behavior. *Journal of Personality and Social Psychology, 42,* 90–99.

Natale, M. (1975). Convergence of mean vocal intensity in dyadic communication as a function of social desirability. *Journal of Personality and Social Psychology, 32,* 790–804.

Natale, M., Entin, E., & Jaffe, J. (1979). Vocal interruptions in dyadic communication as a function of speech and social anxiety. *Journal of Personality and Social Psychology, 37,* 865–878.

Navarre, D. (1982). Posture sharing in dyadic interaction. *American Journal of Dance Therapy, 5,* 28–42.

Nerbonne, G. P. (1967). *The identification of speaker characteristics on the basis of aural cues.* Unpublished doctoral dissertation, Michigan State University.

Nesbitt, P. D., & Steven, G. (1974). Personal space and stimulus intensity at a southern California amusement park. *Sociometry, 37,* 105–115.

Neufeld, R. W. J. (1975). A multidimensional scaling analysis of schizophrenics' and normals' perceptions of verbal similarity. *Journal of Abnormal Psychology, 84,* 498–507.

Neufeld, R. W. J. (1976). Simultaneous processing of multiple stimulus dimensions among paranoid and nonparanoid schizophrenics. *Multivariate Behavioral Research, 11,* 425–441.

Newman, H. M. (1982). The sounds of silence in communicative encounters. *Communication Quarterly, 30,* 142–149.

Newman, O. (1972). *Defensible space: Crime prevention through urban design.* New York: Collier.

Newtson, D. A. (1973). Attribution and the unit of perception of ongoing behavior. *Journal of Personality and Social Psychology, 28,* 28–38.

Newtson, D. A., & Engquist, G. (1976). The perceptual organization of ongoing behavior. *Journal of Experimental Social Psychology, 12,* 436–450.

Newtson, D. A., Engquist, G., & Bois, J. (1977). The objective basis of behavior units. *Journal of Personality and Social Psychology, 35,* 847–862.

Nguyen, M. L., Heslin, R., & Nguyen, T. D. (1976). The meaning of touch: Sex and marital status differences. *Representative Research in Social Psychology, 7,* 13–18.

Nguyen, T., Heslin, R., & Nguyen, M. L. (1975). The meaning of touch: Sex differences. *Journal of Communication, 25(3),* 92–103.

Nisbett, R., & Ross, L. (1980). *Human inference: Strategies and shortcomings of social judgment.* Englewood Cliffs, NJ: Prentice-Hall.

Noesjirwan, J. (1978). A laboratory study of proxemic patterns of Indonesians and Australians. *British Journal of Social and Clinical Psychology, 17,* 333–334.

Nolan, M. J. (1975). The relationship between verbal and nonverbal communication. In G. J. Hanneman & W. J. McEwen (Eds.), *Communication and behavior* (pp. 98–118). Reading, MA: Addison-Wesley.

Noller, P. (1980a). Gaze in married couples. *Journal of Nonverbal Behavior, 5,* 115–129.

Noller, P. (1980b). Misunderstandings in marital communication: A study of couples' nonverbal communication. *Journal of Personality and Social Psychology, 39,* 1135–1148.

Noller, P. (1985). Video primacy—a further look. *Journal of Nonverbal Behavior, 9,* 28–47.

Norman, R. (1976). When what is said is important: A comparison of expert and attractive sources. *Journal of Experimental Social Psychology, 12,* 294–300.

Norum, G. A., Russo, N. J., & Sommer, R. (1967). Seating patterns and group tasks. *Psychology in the Schools, 4,* 276–280.

Norwood, P. E. (1979). *The effects of personality, sex and race variables on touching behavior.* Unpublished doctoral dissertation, Virginia Commonwealth University.

Odom, R. D., & Lemond, C. M. (1972). Developmental differences in the perception and production of facial expressions. *Child Development, 43,* 359–369.

O'Hair, H. D., Cody, M. J., & McLaughlin, M. L. (1981). Prepared lies, spontaneous lies, Machiavellianism, and nonverbal communication. *Human Communication Research, 7,* 325–340.

O'Keefe, B. J., & Delia, J. G. (1982). Impression formation and message production. In M. E. Roloff & C. R. Berger (Eds.), *Social cognition and communication* (pp. 33–72). Beverly Hills, CA: Sage.

O'Leary, M. J., & Gallois, C. (1985). The last ten turns: Behavior and sequencing in friends' and strangers' conversational findings. *Journal of Nonverbal Behavior, 9,* 8–27.

Olsen, R. (1978). *The effect of the hospital environment.* Unpublished doctoral dissertation, City University of New York.

Oregon Project Dayshoot Photographs (1984). *One average day.* U.S.A.: Western Imprints Press of the Oregon Historical Society.

Orr, D. B. (1968). Time compressed speech—a perspective. *Journal of Communication, 18,* 288–292.

Ortony, A. (1978). Remembering, understanding, and representation. *Cognitive Science, 2,* 53–69.

Osmond, H. (1957). Function as the basis of psychiatric ward design. *Mental Hospitals, 8,* 23–32.

Oster, H., & Ekman, P. (1978). Facial behavior in child development. In W. A. Collins (Ed.), *Minnesota symposia on child psychology* (pp. 231–276). Hillsdale, NJ: Erlbaum.

Packwood, W. T. (1974). Loudness as a variable in persuasion. *Journal of Counseling Psychology, 21,* 1–2.

Paivio, A. (1971). *Imagery and verbal processes.* New York: Holt, Rinehart and Winston.

Parke, R. D., & Sawin, D. B. (1979). Children's privacy in the home: Developmental, ecological, and child-rearing determinants. *Environment and Behavior, 11,* 87–104.

Parks, R., & Burgess, E. (1924). *Introduction to the science of sociology.* Chicago: University of Chicago Press.

Parrott, R., & Le Poire, B. (1988, February). *The pediatrician's voice: Impact on the pediatrician-parent relationship.* Paper presented at the annual meeting of the Western Speech Communication Association, San Diego.

Pastalan, L. A. (1970). Privacy as an expression of human territoriality. In L. A. Pastalan & D. H. Carson (Eds.), *Spatial behavior of older people* (pp. 88–101). Ann Arbor: University of Michigan Press.

Patterson, A. H. (1978). Territorial behavior and fear of crime in the elderly. *Environmental Psychology and Nonverbal Behavior, 2,* 131–144.

Patterson, M. L. (1973a). Compensation in nonverbal immediacy behaviors: A review. *Sociometry, 36,* 237–252.

Patterson, M. L. (1973b). Stability of nonverbal immediacy behaviors.

Journal of Experimental Social Psychology, 9, 97–109.

Patterson, M. L. (1976). An arousal model of interpersonal intimacy. *Psychological Review, 83,* 235–245.

Patterson, M. L. (1977). Interpersonal distance, affect, and equilibrium theory. *Journal of Social Psychology, 101,* 205–214.

Patterson, M. L. (1983). *Nonverbal behavior: A functional perspective.* New York: Springer-Verlag.

Patterson, M. L. (1985). Social influences and nonverbal exchange. In S. L. Ellyson & J. F. Dovidio (Eds.), *Power, dominance, and nonverbal behavior* (pp. 207–217). New York: Springer-Verlag.

Patterson, M. L., Jordan, A., Hogan, M. B., & Frerker, D. (1981). Effects of nonverbal intimacy on arousal and behavioral adjustment. *Journal of Nonverbal Behavior, 5,* 184–198.

Patterson, M. L., Mullens, S., & Romano, J. (1971). Compensatory reactions to spatial intrusion. *Sociometry, 34,* 114–121.

Patterson, M. L., Powell, J. L., & Lenihan, M. G. (1986). Touch, compliance and interpersonal affect. *Journal of Nonverbal Behavior, 10,* 41–50.

Patterson, M. L., & Schaeffer, R. E. (1977). Effects of size and sex composition on interaction distance, participation, and satisfaction in small groups. *Small Group Behavior, 8,* 433–442.

Patterson, M. L., & Sechrest, L. B. (1970). Interpersonal distance and impression formation. *Journal of Personality, 38,* 161–166.

Paulsell, S., & Goldman, M. (1984). The effect of touching different body areas on prosocial behavior. *Journal of Social Psychology, 122,* 269–273.

Paulus, P. B., Annis, A. B., Seta, J. J., Schkade, J. K., & Matthews, R. W. (1976). Density does affect task performance. *Journal of Personality and Social Psychology, 34,* 248–253.

Pear, T. H. (1931). *Voice and personality.* London: Chapman and Hall.

Pearce, W. B. (1971). The effect of vocal cues on credibility and attitude change. *Western Speech, 35,* 176–184.

Pearce, W. B. (1976). The coordinated management of meaning: A rules-based theory of interpersonal communication. In G. R. Miller (Ed.), *Explorations in interpersonal communication* (pp. 17–36). Beverly Hills, CA: Sage.

Pearce, W. B., & Brommel, B. J. (1972). Vocalic communication in persuasion. *Quarterly Journal of Speech, 58,* 298–306.

Pearce, W. B., & Conklin, F. (1971). Nonverbal vocalic communication

and perception of a speaker. *Speech Monographs, 38,* 235–241.

Pedersen, D. M. (1973). Developmental trends in personal space. *Journal of Psychology, 83,* 3–9.

Pei, M. (1965). *The story of language* (2nd ed.). Philadelphia: Lippincott.

Pellegrini, R. J. (1973). The virtue of hairiness. *Psychology Today, 6,* 14.

Pellegrini, R. J., & Empey, J. (1970). Interpersonal spatial orientation in dyads. *Journal of Psychology, 76,* 67–70.

Pellegrini, R. J., Schauss, A. G., & Miller, M. E. (1978). Room color and aggression in a criminal detention holding cell: A test of the "tranquilizing pink" hypothesis. *Journal of Orthomolecular Psychiatry, 10,* 174–181.

Pendleton, K. L., & Snyder, S. S. (1982). Young children's perceptions of nonverbally expressed "preference": The effects of nonverbal cue, viewer age, and sex of viewer. *Journal of Nonverbal Behavior, 6,* 220–237.

Perdue, V. P., & Connor, J. M. (1978). Patterns of touching between preschool children and male and female teachers. *Child Development, 49,* 1258–1262.

Perlmutter, K. B., Paddock, J. R., & Duke, M. P. (1985). The role of verbal, vocal, and nonverbal cues in the communication of evoking message styles. *Journal of Research in Personality, 19,* 31–43.

Peterson, K., & Curran, J. C. (1976). Trait attribution as a function of hair length and correlates of subjects' preferences for hair style. *Journal of Psychology, 93,* 331–339.

Peterson, P. (1976). An investigation of sex differences in regard to nonverbal body gestures. In B. Eakins, G. Eakins, & B. Lieb-Brilhard (Eds.), *Siscom '75: Women's (and men's) communication* (pp. 20–27). Falls Church, VA: Speech Communication Association.

Pfungst, O. (1911). *Clever Hans (the horse of Mr. von Osten): A contribution to experimental, animal, and human psychology.* New York: Holt, Rinehart and Winston.

Philpott, J. S. (1983). *The relative contribution to meaning of verbal and nonverbal channels of communication: A meta-analysis.* Unpublished master's thesis, University of Nebraska.

Piaget, J. (1965). *The moral judgment of the child.* New York: The Free Press.

Piaget, J. (1981). Time perception in children. In J. T. Fraser, *The voices of time* (2nd ed., pp. 202–216). Amherst: University of Massachusetts Press.

Pinaire-Reed, J. A. (1979). Interpersonal attraction: Fashionability and perceived similarity. *Perceptual and Motor Skills, 48,* 571–576.

Pisano, M. D., Wall, S. M., & Foster, A. (1986). Perceptions of nonreciprocal touch in romantic relationships. *Journal of Nonverbal Behavior, 10,* 29–40.

Pitcairn, T. K., & Eibl-Eibesfeldt, I. (1976). Concerning the evolution of nonverbal communication in man. In M. E. Hahn & E. C. Simmel (Eds.), *Communicative behavior and evolution* (pp. 81–113). New York: Academic Press.

Pittenger, R. E., Hockett, C. F., & Danehy, J. J. (1960). *The first five minutes.* Ithaca, NY: Martineau.

Planalp, S., & Tracy, K. (1980). Not to change the topic but . . .: A cognitive approach to the management of conversation. In D. Nimmo (Ed.), *Communication Yearbook 4* (pp. 237–258). New Brunswick, NJ: Transaction.

Plax, T. G., Kearney, P., McCroskey, J. C., & Richmond, V. P. (1986). Power in the classroom VI: Verbal control strategies, nonverbal immediacy, and affective learning. *Communication Education, 35,* 43–55.

Plazewski, J. G., & Allen, V. L. (1985). The effect of verbal content on children's encoding of paralinguistic affect. *Journal of Nonverbal Behavior, 9,* 147–159.

Plutchik, R. (1962). *The emotions: Facts, theories, and a new model.* New York: Random House.

Plutchik, R. (1980). *Emotion: A psychoevolutionary synthesis.* New York: Harper & Row.

Poling, T. H. (1978). Sex differences, dominance, and physical attractiveness in the use of nonverbal emblems. *Psychological Reports, 43,* 1087–1092.

Porteous, C. W. (1972). *Learning as a function of molar environmental complexity.* Unpublished master's thesis, University of Victoria, British Columbia.

Porter, R. H., Matochik, J. A., & Makin, J. W. (1983). The role of familiarity in the development of social preferences in spiny mice. *Behavioural Processes, 9,* 241–254.

Posner, M. I., Nissen, M. J., & Klein, R. M. (1976). Visual dominance: An information-processing account of its origins and significance. *Psychological Review, 83,* 157–171.

Poyatos, F. (1983). *New perspectives in nonverbal communication.* New York: Pergamon.

Poyatos, F. (1984). Linguistic fluency and verbal-nonverbal cultural fluency. In A. Wolfgang (Ed.), *Nonverbal behavior: Perspectives, applications, intercultural insights* (pp. 431–459). Lewiston, NY: C. J. Hogrefe.

Prescott, J. W. (1975). Body pleasure and the origins of violence. *Futurist, 9,* 64–74.

Priest, R. F., & Sawyer, J. (1967). Proximity and peership: Bases of balance in interpersonal attraction. *American Journal of Sociology, 72,* 633–649.

Proshansky, H. M., & Altman, I. (1979). Overview of the field. In W. P. White (Ed.), *Resources in environment and behavior* (pp. 3–36). Washington, D.C.: American Psychological Association.

Proshansky, H. M., Ittelson, W. H., & Rivlin, L. G. (1970). Freedom of choice and behavior in a physical setting. In H. M. Proshansky, W. H. Ittelson, & L. G. Rivlin (Eds.), *Environmental psychology: Man and his physical setting* (pp. 173–183). New York: Holt, Rinehart and Winston.

Prosser, M. H. (1978). *The cultural dialogue: An introduction to intercultural communication.* Boston: Houghton Mifflin Co.

Public Broadcasting System [Broadcast] (1984). Signs and signals: The discovery of animal behavior. *Nature,* January 22, 1984.

Putman, W. B., & Street, R. L. (1984). The conception and perception of noncontent speech performance: Implications for speech-accommodation theory. *International Journal of the Sociology of Language, 46,* 97–114.

Quattrone, G. A. (1982). Overattribution and unit formation: When behavior engulfs the person. *Journal of Personality and Social Psychology, 42,* 593–607.

Ramsey, S. J. (1976). Prison codes. *Journal of Communication, 26,* 39–45.

Ramsey, S. J. (1981). The kinesics of feminity in Japanese women. *Language Sciences, 3,* 104–123.

Ramsey, S. J. (1983, May). *Double vision: Nonverbal Behavior East and West.* Paper presented at the Second International Conference on Nonverbal Behavior, Toronto.

Ramsey, S. J., & Birk, J. (1983). Training North Americans for interaction with Japanese: Considerations of language and communication style. In R. Brislin & D. Landis (Eds.), *The handbook of intercultural training, Vol. III: Area studies in intercultural training* (pp. 227–259). New York: Pergamon Press.

Rapoport, A. (1982). *The meaning of the built environment: A nonverbal communication approach.* Beverly Hills, CA: Sage.

Ray, G. B. (1986). Vocally cued personality prototypes: An implicit personality theory. *Communication Monographs, 53,* 266–276.

Raymond, B. J., & Unger, R. K. (1972). The apparel oft proclaims the man: Cooperation with deviant and conventional youths. *Journal of Social Psychology, 87,* 75–82.

Reade, M. N., & Smouse, A. D. (1980). Effect of inconsistent verbal-nonverbal communication and counselor response mode on client estimate of counselor regard and effectiveness. *Journal of Counseling Psychology, 27,* 546–553.

Reece, M. M., & Whitman, R. N. (1961). Warmth and expressive movements. *Psychological Reports, 8,* 76.

Reece, M. M., & Whitman, R. N. (1962). Expressive movements, warmth, and verbal reinforcement. *Journal of Abnormal and Social Psychology, 64,* 234–236.

Reed, C. (1981). *The impact of consistent-inconsistent combinations of visual and verbal cues on communication of empathy and genuineness in the therapeutic situation.* Unpublished doctoral dissertation, Texas Tech University.

Reed, S. K. (1982). *Cognition: Theory and applications.* Monterey, CA: Brooks/Cole.

Reilly, S. S., & Muzekari, L. H. (1979). Responses of normal and disturbed adults and children to mixed messages. *Journal of Abnormal Psychology, 88,* 203–208.

Reinert, J. (1971). What your sense of time tells you. *Science Digest, 69,* 8–12.

Reiss, M., & Rosenfeld, P. (1980). Seating preferences as nonverbal communication: A self-presentational analysis. *Journal of Applied Communications Research, 8,* 22–30.

Reizenstein, J. E. (1982). Hospital design and human behavior: A review of the recent literature. In A. Baum & J. E. Singer (Eds.), *Advances in environmental psychology: Environment and health* (Vol. 4, pp. 137–169). Hillsdale, NJ: Erlbaum.

Restak, R. M. (1979). *The brain: The last frontier.* Garden City, NY: Anchor Books/Doubleday.

Richmond, V. P., Gorham, J. S., & McCroskey, J. C. (1986). The relationships between selected immediacy behavior and cognitive learning. In M. McLaughlin (Ed.), *Communication Yearbook 10* (pp. 574–590). Beverly Hills CA: Sage.

Richmond, V. P., McCroskey, J. C., Kearney, P., & Plax, T. (1985, November). *Power in the classroom VII: Linking behavior alteration techniques to cognitive learning.* Paper presented at the annual meeting of the Speech Communication Association, Denver.

References

Richmond, V. P., McCroskey, J. C., & Payne, S. K. (1987). *Nonverbal behavior in interpersonal relations.* Englewood Cliffs, NJ: Prentice-Hall.

Riggio, R. E., & Friedman, H. S. (1983). Individual differences and cues to deception. *Journal of Personality and Social Psychology, 45,* 899–915.

Riggio, R. E., & Friedman, H. S. (1986). Impression formation: The role of expressive behavior. *Journal of Personality and Social Psychology, 50,* 421–427.

Riggio, R. E., Friedman, H. S., & DiMatteo, M. R. (1981). Nonverbal greetings: Effects of the situation and personality. *Personality and Social Psychology Bulletin, 7,* 682–689.

Riggio, R. E., Tucker, J., & Widaman, K. F. (1987). Verbal and nonverbal cues as mediators of deception ability. *Journal of Nonverbal Behavior, 11,* 126–145.

Riseborough, M. G. (1981). Physiographic gestures as decoding facilitators: Three experiments exploring a neglected facet of communication. *Journal of Nonverbal Behavior, 5,* 172–183.

Rivlin, L. G., & Rothenberg, M. (1976). The use of space in open classrooms. In H. M. Proshansky, W. H. Ittelson, & L. G. Rivlin (Eds.), *Environmental psychology: People and their physical settings* (2nd ed.) (pp. 479–490). New York: Holt, Rinehart and Winston.

Roberts, M. (1987, June). No language but a cry. *Psychology Today, 21,* 57–58.

Robson, K. S. (1967). The role of eye-to-eye contact in maternal-infant attachment. *Journal of Child Psychology and Psychiatry, 8,* 13–25.

Rodin, J., Solomon, S. K., & Metcalf, J. (1978). Role of control in mediating perceptions of density. *Journal of Personality and Social Psychology, 36,* 988–999.

Roedell, W. C., & Slaby, R. G. (1977). The role of distal and proximal interaction in infant social preference formation. *Developmental Psychology, 13,* 266–273.

Rogers, W. T. (1978). The contribution of kinesic illustrators toward the comprehension of verbal behavior within utterances. *Human Communication Research, 5,* 54–62.

Rohles, F. H. (1967, June). Environmental psychology: A bucket of worms. *Psychology Today, 1,* 55–63.

Rohles, F. H. (1971). Thermal sensations of sedentary man in moderate temperatures. *Human Factors, 13,* 553–560.

Roll, S. A., Crowley, M. A., & Rappl, L. E. (1985). Client perceptions of counselors' nonverbal behavior: A reevaluation. *Counselor Education and Supervision, 24,* 234–243.

Roloff, M. E., & Berger, C. R. (1982). Social cognition and communication: An introduction. In M. E. Roloff & C. R. Berger (Eds.), *Social cognition and communication* (pp. 9–32). Beverly Hills CA: Sage.

Roloff, M. E., & Miller, G. R. (1980). *Persuasion: New directions in theory and research.* Beverly Hills, CA: Sage.

Rom, A. (1979). *Comparison of nonverbal and verbal communicative skills of language impaired and normal speaking children.* Unpublished dissertation, Wayne State University.

Romano, J. M., & Bellack, A. S. (1980). Social validation of a component model of assertive behavior. *Journal of Consulting and Clinical Psychology, 48,* 473–490.

Roos, P. D. (1968). Jurisdiction: An ecological concept. *Human Relations, 21,* 75–84.

Rosa, E., & Mazur, A. (1979). Incipient status in small groups. *Social Forces, 58,* 18–37.

Rosekrans, R. L. (1955). Do gestures speak louder than words? *Collier's, 135,* 56–57.

Roseman, I. (1984). Cognitive determinants of emotions: A structural theory. In P. Shaver (Ed.), *Review of personality and social psychology: Vol. 5. Emotions, relationships, and health* (pp. 11–36). Beverly Hills CA: Sage.

Rosencranz, M. L. (1962). Clothing symbolism. *Journal of Home Economics, 54,* 18–22.

Rosencranz, M. L. (1965). Sociological and psychological approaches to clothing research. *Journal of Home Economics, 57,* 26–29.

Rosenfeld, H. M. (1965). Effect of approval-seeking induction on interpersonal proximity. *Psychological Reports, 17,* 120–122.

Rosenfeld, H. M. (1966a). Approval-seeking and approval-inducing functions of verbal and nonverbal responses in the dyad. *Journal of Personality and Social Psychology, 4,* 597–605.

Rosenfeld, H. M. (1966b). Instrumental affiliative functions of facial and gestural expressions. *Journal of Personality and Social Psychology, 4,* 65–72.

Rosenfeld, H. M. (1978). Conversational control functions of nonverbal behavior. In A. W. Siegman & S. Feldstein (Eds.), *Nonverbal behavior and communication* (pp. 291–328). Hillsdale, NJ: Erlbaum.

Rosenfeld, L. B., & Civikly, J. M. (1976). *With words unspoken: The nonverbal experience.* New York: Holt, Rinehart and Winston.

Rosenfeld, L. B., Kartus, S., & Ray, C. (1976). Body accessibility revisited. *Journal of Communication, 26(3),* 27–30.

Rosenfeld, L. B., & Plax, T. G. (1977). Clothing as communication. *Journal of Communication, 27,* 24–31.

Rosenthal, R. (1976). *Experimenter effects in behavioral research* (enlarged ed.). New York: Irvington.

Rosenthal, R. (1981). Pavlov's mice, Pfungst's horse, and Pygmalion's PONS: Some models for the study of interpersonal expectancy effects. In T. A. Sebeok & R. Rosenthal (Eds.), *The Clever Hans phenomenon: Communication with horses, whales, apes, and people* (pp. 182–198). New York: Annals of the New York Academy of Sciences.

Rosenthal, R. (1985). Nonverbal cues in the mediation of interpersonal expectancy effects. In R. L. Street, Jr., & J. N. Cappella (Eds.), *Sequence and pattern in communicative behavior* (pp. 85–102). London: Edward Arnold.

Rosenthal, R., & DePaulo, B. M. (1979a). Expectancies, discrepancies, and courtesies in nonverbal communication. *Western Journal of Speech Communication, 43,* 76–95.

Rosenthal, R., & DePaulo, B. M. (1979b). Sex differences in accommodation in nonverbal communication. In R. Rosenthal (Ed.), *Skill in nonverbal communication: Individual differences* (pp. 68–103). Cambridge, MA: Oelgeschlager, Gunn & Hain.

Rosenthal, R., Hall, J. A., DiMatteo, M. R., Rogers, P. L., & Archer, D. (1979). *Sensitivity to nonverbal communication: The PONS test.* Baltimore: Johns Hopkins University Press.

Rosenthal, R., & Jacobson, L. (1968). *Pygmalion in the classroom: Teacher expectation and pupils' intellectual development.* New York: Holt, Rinehart and Winston.

Rosnow, R. L., & Robinson, E. J. (1967). *Experiments in persuasion.* New York: Academic Press.

Royal, D. C., & Hays, W. L. (1959). Empirical dimensions of emotional behavior. *Acta Psychologica, 15,* 419.

Rubin, M. E. Y. (1977). *Differences between distressed and nondistressed couples in verbal and nonverbal communication codes.* Unpublished doctoral dissertation, Indiana University.

Rubin, Z. (1970). Measurement of romantic love. *Journal of Personality and Social Psychology, 16,* 265–273.

Ruesch, J., & Kees, W. (1956). *Nonverbal communication: Notes on the visual perception of human relations.* Berkeley: University of California Press.

Ruesch, J., & Kees, W. (1970). Function and meaning in the physical environment. In H. M. Proshansky, W. H. Ittelson, & L. G. Rivlin (Eds.), *Environmental psychology: Man and his physical setting* (pp. 141–153). New York: Holt, Rinehart and Winston.

Russell, J. A. (1978). Evidence of convergent validity on the dimensions of affect. *Journal of Personality and Social Psychology, 36,* 1152–1168.

Russell, J. A. (1980). A circumplex model of affect. *Journal of Personality and Social Psychology, 39,* 1161–1178.

Russell, J. A. (1983). Pancultural aspects of the human conceptual organization of emotions. *Journal of Personality and Social Psychology, 45,* 1281–1288.

Russell, J. A., & Bullock, M. (1985). Multidimensional scaling of emotional facial expressions: Similarity from preschoolers to adults. *Journal of Personality and Social Psychology, 48,* 1290–1298.

Russell, J. A., & Steiger, J. H. (1982). The structure in persons' implicit taxonomy of emotions. *Journal of Research in Personality, 16,* 447–469.

Russo, N. F. (1967). Connotation of seating arrangement. *Cornell Journal of Social Relations, 2,* 37–44.

Russo, N. F. (1975). Eye contact, interpersonal distance, and the equilibrium theory. *Journal of Personality and Social Psychology, 31,* 497–502.

Rutter, D. R., Pennington, D. C., Dewey, M. E., & Swain, J. (1984). Eye contact as a chance product of individual looking: Implications for the intimacy model of Argyle and Dean. *Journal of Nonverbal Behavior, 8,* 250–258.

Rutter, D. R., & Stephenson, G. M. (1979). The functions of looking: Effects of friendship on gaze. *British Journal of Social and Clinical Psychology, 18,* 203–205.

Rutter, D. R., Stephenson, G. M., Ayling, K., & White, P. A. (1978). The timing of looks in dyadic conversation. *British Journal of Social and Clinical Psychology, 17,* 17–21.

Ryan, E. B. (1979). Why do low-prestige language varieties persist? In H. Giles & R. N. St. Clair (Eds.), *Language and social psychology* (pp. 145–157). Oxford: Basil Blackwell.

Saarni, C. (1979). Children's understanding of display rules for expressive behavior. *Developmental Psychology, 15,* 424–429.

Saarni, C. (1982). Social and affective functions of nonverbal behavior: Developmental concerns. In R. S. Feldman (Ed.), *Development of nonverbal behavior in children* (pp. 123–147). New York: Springer-Verlag.

Sabatelli, R. M., Buck, R., & Dreyer, A. (1980). Communication via facial cues in intimate dyads. *Personality and Social Psychology Bulletin, 6,* 242–247.

Sachs, J., Lieberman, P., & Erickson, D. (1973). Anatomical and cultural determinants of male and female speech. In R. W. Shuy & R. W. Fasold (Eds.), *Language attitudes: Current trends and prospects* (pp. 74–84). Washington, DC: Georgetown University Press.

Sackeim, H. A., Gur, R. C., & Saucy, M. C. (1978). Emotions are expressed more intensely on the left side of the face. *Science, 202,* 434–435.

Sacks, H., Schegloff, E., & Jefferson, G. (1974). A simplest systematics for the organization of turn-taking for conversation. *Language, 50,* 696–735.

Sacks, O. W. (1985). *The man who mistook his wife for a hat and other clinical tales.* New York: Summit Books.

Sadesky, G. A. (1974). *The effects of lighting color and intensity on small group communication.* Paper presented at the annual convention of the International Communication Association, New Orleans.

Sainsbury, P. (1955). Gestural movement during psychiatric interview. *Psychosomatic Medicine, 17,* 458–469.

Saitz, R. L., & Cervenka, E. J. (1972). *Handbook of gestures: Colombia and the United States.* The Hague: Mouton.

Samovar, L. A., & Porter, R. E. (1985). *Intercultural communication: A reader* (2nd ed.). Belmont, CA: Wadsworth.

Sanders, G. S. (1981). Driven by distraction: An integrative review of social facilitation theory and research. *Journal of Experimental Social Psychology, 17,* 227–251.

Sanders, M., Gustanski, J., & Lawton, M. (1974). Effect of ambient illumination on noise level of groups. *Journal of Applied Psychology, 59,* 527–528.

Sandhu, D. S. (1984). *The effects of mirroring vs. non-mirroring of clients' nonverbal behaviors on empathy, trustworthiness, and positive interaction in cross-cultural counseling dyads.* Unpublished doctoral dissertation, Mississippi State University.

Sapir, E. (1928). The unconscious patterning of behavior in society. In E. S. Dummer (Ed.), *The unconscious* (pp. 114–142). New York: Knopf.

Schachter, S., & Singer, J. E. (1962). Cognitive, social, and physiological determinants of emotional state. *Psychological Review, 69,* 379–399.

Schaefer, E. S., & Plutchik, R. (1966). Interrelationships of emotions, traits, and diagnostic constructs. *Psychological Reports, 18,* 399–419.

Schaeffer, G. H., & Patterson, M. L. (1980). Intimacy, arousal, and small group crowding. *Journal of Personality and Social Psychology, 38,* 283–290.

Schank, R. C., & Abelson, R. P. (1977). *Scripts, plans, goals, and understanding: An inquiry into human knowledge structures.* Hillsdale, NJ: Erlbaum.

Scheflen, A. E. (1964). The significance of posture in communication systems. *Psychiatry, 27,* 316–331.

Scheflen, A. E. (1965). Quasi-courtship behavior in psychotherapy. *Psychiatry, 28,* 245–257.

Scheflen, A. E. (1967). On the structuring of human communication. *American Behavioral Scientist, 10,* 8–12.

Scheflen, A. E. (1971). Living space in an urban ghetto. *Family Process, 10,* 429–450.

Scheflen, A. E. (1974). *How behavior means.* Garden City, NY: Anchor Books/Doubleday.

Scheflen, A. E., & Scheflen, A. (1972). *Body language and the social order: Communication as behavior control.* Englewood Cliffs, NJ: Prentice-Hall.

Schegloff, E., & Sacks, H. (1973). Opening up closings. *Semiotica, 8,* 289–327.

Schenck-Hamlin, W. J., Wiseman, R. L., & Georgacarakos, G. N. (1982). A model of properties of compliance-gaining strategies. *Communication Quarterly, 30,* 92–100.

Scherer, K. R. (1979a). Acoustic concomitants of emotional dimensions: Judging affect from synthesized tone sequences. In S. Weitz (Ed.), *Nonverbal communication* (2nd ed., pp. 249–253). New York: Oxford University Press.

Scherer, K. R. (1979b). Personality markers in speech. In K. R. Scherer & H. Giles (Eds.), *Social markers in speech* (pp. 147–209). Cambridge: Cambridge University Press.

Scherer, K. R. (1979c). Voice and speech correlates of perceived social influence in simulated juries. In H. Giles & R. St. Clair (Eds.), *Language and social psychology* (pp. 88–120). Oxford: Basil Blackwell.

Scherer, K. R. (1982a). Emotion as process: Function, origin and regulation. *Social Science Information, 21,* 555–570.

Scherer, K. R. (1982b). Methods of research on vocal communication: Paradigms and parameters. In K. R. Scherer & P. Ekman (Eds.), *Handbook of methods in nonverbal behavior research* (pp. 136–198). Cambridge: Cambridge University Press.

Scherer, K. R., London, H., & Wolf, J. J. (1973). The voice of confidence: Paralinguistic cues and audience evaluation. *Journal of Research in Personality, 7,* 31–44.

References

Scherer, K. R., & Oshinsky, J. S. (1977). Cue utilization in emotion attribution from auditory stimuli. *Motivation and Emotion, 1,* 331–346.

Scherer, K. R., Rosenthal, R., & Koivumaki, J. (1972). Mediating interpersonal expectancies via vocal cues: Differential speech intensity as a means of social influence. *European Journal of Social Psychology, 2,* 163–176.

Scherer, K. R., Scherer, U., Hall, J. A., & Rosenthal, R. (1977). Differential attribution of personality based on multi-channel presentation of verbal and nonverbal cues. *Psychological Research, 39,* 221–247.

Scherer, S. E. (1974). Proxemic behavior of primary school children as a function of their socioeconomic class and subculture. *Journal of Personality and Social Psychology, 29,* 800–805.

Scherer, S. E. (1978). The influence of linguistic style, interpersonal distance and gaze on attitude acquisition (Doctoral dissertation, University of Toronto). *Dissertation Abstracts International, 38,* 4479B.

Schlenker, B. R. (1980). *Impression management.* Monterey, CA: Brooks/Cole.

Schlosberg, H. (1952). The description of facial expressions in terms of two dimensions. *Journal of Experimental Psychology, 44,* 229–237.

Schlosberg, H. (1954). Three dimensions of emotion. *Psychological Review, 61,* 81–88.

Schneirla, T. C. (1965). Aspects of stimulation and organization in approach/withdrawal processes underlying vertebrate behavior development. *Advances in the Study of Behavior, 1,* 1–74.

Schneirla, T. C. (1968). Instinct and aggression. In M. F. A. Montagu (Ed.), *Man and aggression* (pp. 59–64). New York: Oxford University Press.

Schulz, R., & Barefoot, J. (1974). Nonverbal responses and affiliative conflict theory. *British Journal of Social and Clinical Psychology, 13,* 237–243.

Schutz, W. C. (1958). *FIRO: A three dimensional theory of interpersonal behavior.* New York: Holt, Rinehart and Winston.

Schwartz, B. (1968). The social psychology of privacy. *American Journal of Sociology, 73,* 741–752.

Schwartz, B., Tesser, A., & Powell, E. (1982). Dominance cues in nonverbal behavior. *Social Psychology Quarterly, 45,* 114–120.

Schwartz, M. F., & Rine, H. E. (1968). Identification of speaker sex from isolated whispered vowels. *Journal of the Acoustical Society of America, 44,* 1736–1737.

Schwartz, T. (1974). *The responsive chord.* Garden City, NY: Anchor Books/Doubleday.

Schweitzer, D. A. (1970). The effect of presentation on source evaluation. *Quarterly Journal of Speech, 56,* 33–39.

Seay, T. A., & Altekruse, M. K. (1979). Verbal and nonverbal behavior in judgments of facilitative conditions. *Journal of Counseling Psychology, 26,* 108–119.

Sechrest, L. (1969). Nonreactive assessment of attitudes. In E. P. Willems & H. L. Raush (Eds.), *Naturalistic viewpoints in psychological research* (pp. 147–161). New York: Holt, Rinehart and Winston.

Seibold, D. R., Cantrill, J. G., & Meyers, R. A. (1985). Communication and interpersonal influence. In M. L. Knapp & G. R. Miller (Eds.), *Handbook of interpersonal communication* (pp. 551–611). Beverly Hills, CA: Sage.

Selye, H. (1956). *The stress of life.* New York: McGraw-Hill.

Sereno, K. K., & Hawkins, G. J. (1967). The effects of variations in speakers' nonfluency upon audience ratings of attitude toward the speech topic and speakers' credibility. *Speech Monographs, 34,* 58–64.

Seta, J. J., Paulus, P. B., & Schkade, J. K. (1976). Effects of group size and proximity under cooperative and competitive conditions. *Journal of Personality and Social Psychology, 34,* 47–53.

Shaffer, D. R., & Sadowski, C. (1975). [An investigation of territorial invasion in a barroom environment.] This table is mine: Respect for marked barroom tables as a function of gender of spatial marker and desirability of locale. *Sociometry, 38,* 408–419.

Shapiro, J. G. (1968). Responsivity to facial and linguistic cues. *Journal of Communication, 18,* 11–17.

Shaw, M. E. (1981). *Group dynamics: The psychology of small group behavior* (3rd ed.). New York: McGraw-Hill.

Shennum, W. A., & Bugental, D. B. (1982). The development of control over affective expression in nonverbal behavior. In R. S. Feldman (Ed.), *Development of nonverbal behavior in children* (pp. 101–122). New York: Springer-Verlag.

Shepard, R. N. (1962). The analysis of proximities: Multidimensional scaling with an unknown distance function. *Psychometrika, 27,* 125–140, 219–246.

Sheppard, W. C., & Lane, H. L. (1968). Development of the prosodic features of infant vocalizing. *Journal of Speech and Hearing Research, 11,* 94–108.

Shively, C. (1985). The evolution of dominance hierarchies in nonhuman primate society. In S. L. Ellyson & J. F. Dovidio (Eds.), *Power, dominance, and nonverbal behavior* (pp. 67–88). New York: Springer-Verlag.

Shotland, R. L., & Johnson, M. P. (1978). Bystander behavior and kinesics: The interaction between the helper and victim. *Environmental Psychology and Nonverbal Behavior, 2,* 181–190.

Shuter, R. (1976). Proxemics and tactility in Latin America. *Journal of Communication, 26,* 46–52.

Shuter, R. (1977). A field study of nonverbal communication in Germany, Italy, and the United States. *Communication Monographs, 44,* 298–305.

Shuter, R. (1979). A study of nonverbal communication among Jews and Protestants. *Journal of Social Psychology, 109,* 31–41.

Shuter, R. (September 2, 1984). The new rules of global competition. *New York Times,* F1.

Siegman, A. W. (1976). *The effects of cognition on hesitation phenomena in speech.* Paper presented at the Interdisciplinary Conference on Perspectives on Language, University of Louisville, KY.

Siegman, A. W. (1978). The telltale voice: Nonverbal messages of verbal communication. In A. W. Siegman & S. Feldstein (Eds.), *Nonverbal behavior and communication* (pp. 183–243). Hillsdale, NJ: Erlbaum.

Siegman, A. W. (1979). The voice of attraction: Vocal correlates of interpersonal attraction in the interview. In A. W. Siegman & S. Feldstein (Eds.), *Of speech and time* (pp. 89–114). Hillsdale, NJ: Erlbaum.

Siegman, A. W. (1985). Expressive correlates of affective states and traits. In A. W. Siegman & S. Feldstein (Eds.), *Multichannel integrations of nonverbal behavior* (pp. 37–68). Hillsdale, NJ: Erlbaum.

Siegman, A. W., & Pope, B. (1965). Effects of question specificity and anxiety producing messages on verbal fluency in the initial interview. *Journal of Personality and Social Psychology, 4,* 188–192.

Siegman, A. W., & Reynolds, M. (1982). Interviewer-interviewee nonverbal communications: An interactional approach. In M. A. Davis (Ed.), *Interaction rhythms: Periodicity in communication behavior* (pp. 249–278). New York: Human Sciences Press.

Sigelman, C. K., & Davis, P. J. (1978). Making good impressions in job interviews: Verbal and nonverbal predictors. *Education and*

Training of the Mentally Retarded, 13, 71–77.

Silden, I. (1973, December). Psychological effects of office planning. *Mainliner,* pp. 30–34.

Sillars, A. L., Coletti, S. F., Parry, D., & Rogers, M. A. (1982). Coding verbal conflict tactics: Nonverbal and perceptual correlates of the "avoidance-distributive-integrative" distinction. *Human Communication Research, 9,* 83–95.

Silveira, J. (1972). Thoughts on the politics of touch. *Women's Press, 1,* 13.

Simmel, G. (1950). Secrecy and group communication. In K. H. Wolff (Ed. and Trans.), *The sociology of George Simmel* (pp. 330–375). Glencoe, IL: Free Press.

Simonds, J. O. (1961). *Landscape architecture.* New York: McGraw-Hill.

Singer, J. E. (1964). The use of manipulative strategies: Machiavellianism and attractiveness. *Sociometry, 27,* 128–151.

Singer, J. E., & Lamb, P. F. (1966). Social concern, body size, and birth order. *Journal of Social Psychology, 68,* 143–151.

Slane, S., & Leak, G. (1978). Effects of self-perceived nonverbal immediacy behaviors on interpersonal attraction. *Journal of Psychology, 98,* 241–248.

Smith, A. (1983). Nonverbal communication among black female dyads: An assessment of intimacy, gender, and race. *Journal of Social Issues, 39(3),* 55–67.

Smith, B. L., Brown, B. L., Strong, W. J., & Rencher, A. C. (1975). Effects of speech rate on personality perception. *Language and Speech, 18,* 145–152.

Smith, C. A., & Ellsworth, P. C. (1985). Patterns of cognitive appraisal in emotion. *Journal of Personality and Social Psychology, 48,* 813–838.

Smith, D. E., Willis, F. N., & Gier, J. A. (1980). Success and interpersonal touch in a competitive setting. *Journal of Nonverbal Behavior, 5,* 26–34.

Smith, H. A. (1979). Nonverbal communication in teaching. *Review of Educational Research, 49,* 631–672.

Smith, M. J., Reinheimer, R. E., & Gabbard-Alley, A. (1981). Crowding, task performance, and communicative interaction in youth and old age. *Human Communication Research, 7,* 259–272.

Smith, R. J., & Knowles, E. S. (1979). Affective and cognitive mediators of reactions to spatial invasions. *Journal of Experimental Social Psychology, 15,* 437–452.

Smith, S., & Haythorn, W. W. (1972). The effects of compatability, crowding, group size, and leadership seniority on stress, anxiety, hostility, and annoyance in isolated groups. *Journal of Personality and Social Psychology, 22,* 67–69.

Smith, W. J. (1974). Displays and messages in intraspecific communication. In S. Weitz (Ed.), *Nonverbal communication: Readings with commentary* (pp. 331–340). New York: Oxford University Press.

Smith, W. J., Chase, J., & Lieblich, A. K. (1974). Tongue-showing: A facial display of humans and other primate species. *Semiotica, 11,* 201–246.

Smith-Hanen, S. S. (1977). Effects of nonverbal behaviors on judged levels of counselor warmth and empathy. *Journal of Counseling Psychology, 24,* 87–91.

Smutkupt, S., & Barna, L. (1976). Impact of nonverbal communication in an intercultural setting: Thailand. In F. Casmir (Ed.), *International and intercultural communication annual* (Vol. 3, pp. 130–138). Falls Church, VA: Speech Communication Association.

Snyder, M. (1974). Self-monitoring of expressive behavior. *Journal of Personality and Social Psychology, 30,* 526–537.

Snyder, M. (1979). Self-monitoring processes. In L. Berkowitz (Ed.), *Advances in experimental social psychology* (Vol. 12, pp. 85–128). New York: Academic Press.

Snyder, M., & Rothbart, M. (1971). Communicator attractiveness and opinion change. *Canadian Journal of Behavioral Science, 3,* 377–387.

Snyder, M., & Swann, W. B., Jr. (1978). Behavioral confirmation in social interaction: From social perception to social reality. *Journal of Experimental Social Psychology, 14,* 148–162.

Snyder, M., Tanke, E. D., & Berscheid, E. (1977). Social perception and interpersonal behavior: On the self-fulfilling nature of social stereotypes. *Journal of Personality and Social Psychology, 35,* 656–666.

Snyder, R. A., & Sutker, L. W. (1977). The measurement of the construct of dominance and its relationship to nonverbal behavior. *Journal of Psychology, 97,* 227–230.

Sobelman, S. A. (1973). *The effects of verbal and nonverbal components on the judged level of counselor warmth.* Unpublished doctoral dissertation, The American University.

Solomon, D., & Yeager, J. (1969a). Determinants of boys' perceptions of verbal reinforcers. *Developmental Psychology, 1,* 637–645.

Solomon, D., & Yeager, J. (1969b). Effects of content and intonation on perceptions of verbal reinforcers. *Perceptual and Motor Skills, 28,* 319–327.

Solzhenitsyn, A. (1973). *The Gulag archipelago.* New York: Harper & Row.

Sommer, R. (1959). Studies in personal space. *Sociometry, 22,* 247–260.

Sommer, R. (1962). The distance for comfortable conversation: A further study. *Sociometry, 25,* 111–116.

Sommer, R. (1965). Further studies in small group ecology. *Sociometry, 28,* 337–348.

Sommer, R. (1966). Man's proximate environment. *Journal of Social Issues, 22,* 59–70.

Sommer, R. (1968). Intimacy ratings in five countries. *International Journal of Psychology, 3,* 109–114.

Sommer, R. (1969). *Personal space: The behavioral basis of design.* Englewood Cliffs, NJ: Prentice-Hall.

Sommer, R. (1970). The ecology of privacy. In H. M. Proshansky, W. H. Ittelson, & L. G. Rivlin (Eds.), *Environmental psychology: Man and his physical setting* (pp. 256–266). New York: Holt, Rinehart and Winston.

Sommer, R. (1971). Spatial parameters in naturalistic research. In A. H. Esser (Ed.), *Behavior and environment: The use of space in animals* (pp. 281–290). New York: Plenum.

Sommer, R. (1974a). Studies of small group ecology. In R. S. Cathcart & L. A. Samovar (Eds.), *Small group communication: A reader* (pp. 283–293). Dubuque, IA: Brown.

Sommer, R. (1974b). *Tight spaces: Hard architecture and how to humanize it.* Englewood Cliffs, NJ: Prentice-Hall.

Sommer, R., & Becker, F. D. (1969). Territorial defense and the good neighbor. *Journal of Personality and Social Psychology, 11,* 85–92.

Sommers, S. (1984). Reported emotions and conventions of emotionality among college students. *Journal of Personality and Social Psychology, 46,* 207–215.

Sorrentino, R. M., & Boutillier, R. G. (1975). The effect of quantity and quality of verbal interaction on ratings of leadership ability. *Journal of Experimental Research in Personality, 11,* 403–411.

Soskin, W. F., & John, V. P. (1963). The study of spontaneous talk. In R. G. Barker (Ed.), *The stream of behavior* (pp. 228–287). Englewood Cliffs, NJ: Prentice-Hall.

Spain, C. (1985). *Reflective eye positions as indicators of cognitive information processing within an English and Spanish speaking sample.* Unpublished master's thesis, University of New Mexico.

References

Spiegel, J. P., & Machotka, P. (1974). *Messages of the body.* New York: Free Press.

Spignesi, A., & Shor, R. E. (1981). The judgment of emotion from facial expressions, contexts and their combination. *Journal of General Psychology, 104,* 41–58.

Springer, S. P., & Deutsch, G. (1981). *Left brain, right brain.* New York: Freeman.

Stacks, D. W. (1982, May). *Hemispheric and evolutionary use: A re-examination of verbal and nonverbal communication and the brain.* Paper presented at the annual meeting of the Eastern Communication Association, Hartford.

Stacks, D. W., & Burgoon, J. K. (1981). The role of nonverbal behaviors as distractors in resistance to persuasion in interpersonal contexts. *Central States Speech Journal, 32,* 61–73.

Stafford, L., & Daly, J. A. (1984). Conversational memory: The effects of recall mode and memory expectancies on remembrances of natural conversations. *Human Communication Research, 10,* 379–402.

Stang, D. J. (1973). Effect of interaction rate on ratings of leadership and liking. *Journal of Personality and Social Psychology, 27,* 405–408.

Starkweather, J. A. (1964). Variations in vocal behavior. In D. M. Rioch & E. A. Weinstein (Eds.), *Disorders of communication* (pp. 424–449). Baltimore: Waverly Press.

Stea, D. (1965, Autumn). Territoriality, the interior aspect: Space, territory, and human movements. *Landscape,* pp. 13–17.

Stea, D. (1970). Space, territory and human movements. In H. M. Proshansky, W. H. Ittelson, & L. G. Rivlin (Eds.), *Environmental psychology: Man and his physical setting* (pp. 37–42). New York: Holt, Rinehart and Winston.

Stechler, G., & Latz, E. (1966). Some observations on attention and arousal in the human infant. *Journal of the American Academy of Child Psychology, 5,* 517–525.

Steinzor, B. (1950). The spatial factor in face-to-face discussion groups. *Journal of Abnormal and Social Psychology, 45,* 552–555.

Stephan, F. F. (1952). The relative rate of communication between members of small groups. *American Sociological Review, 17,* 482–486.

Stephenson, G. M., Ayling, K., & Rutter, D. R. (1976). The role of visual communication in social exchange. *British Journal of Social and Clinical Psychology, 15,* 113–120.

Stern, D. N. (1971). A micro analysis of mother-infant interaction. *Journal of the American Academy of Child Psychiatry, 10,* 501–517.

Stern, D. N. (1980). *The first relationship: Mother and infant.* Cambridge, MA: Harvard University Press.

Stewart, D. J., & Patterson, M. L. (1973). Eliciting effects of verbal and nonverbal cues on projective test responses. *Journal of Consulting and Clinical Psychology, 41,* 74–77.

Stewart, M. A., & Ryan, E. B. (1982). Attitudes toward younger and older adult speakers: Effects of varying speech rates. *Journal of Language and Social Psychology, 1,* 91–110.

Stier, D. S., & Hall, J. A. (1984). Gender differences in touch: An empirical and theoretical review. *Journal of Personality and Social Psychology, 47,* 440–459.

Stiff, J. B. (1986). Cognitive processing of persuasive message cues: A meta-analytic review of the effects of supporting information on attitudes. *Communication Monographs, 53,* 75–89.

Stiff, J. B., & Miller, G. R. (1986). "Come to think of it . . .": Interrogative probes, deceptive communication, and deception detection. *Human Communication Research, 12,* 339–358.

Stockwell, S. R., & Dye, A. (1980). Effects of counselor touch on counseling outcomes. *Journal of Counseling Psychology, 27,* 443–446.

Stokols, D. (1972). A social-psychological model of human crowding phenomena. *Journal of the American Institute of Planners, 38,* 72–84.

Stokols, D. (1976). The experience of crowding in primary and secondary environments. *Environment and Behavior, 8,* 49–85.

Stokols, D., Rall, M., Pinner, B., & Schopler, J. (1973). Physical, social, and personal determinants of the perception of crowding. *Environment and Behavior, 5,* 87–117.

Street, R. L., Jr. (1982). Evaluation of noncontent speech accommodation. *Language and Communication, 2,* 13–31.

Street, R. L., Jr. (1983). Noncontent speech convergence in adult-child interactions. In R. N. Bostrom (Ed.), *Communication Yearbook 7* (pp. 369–395). Beverly Hills, CA: Sage.

Street, R. L., Jr. (1984). Speech convergence and speech evaluation in fact-finding interviews. *Human Communication Research, 11,* 139–169.

Street, R. L., Jr., & Brady, R. M. (1982). Speech rate acceptance ranges as a factor of evaluative domain, listener speech rate, and communication context. *Communication Monographs, 49,* 290–308.

Street, R. L., Jr., Brady, R. M., & Put-man, W. B. (1983). The influence of speech rate stereotypes and rate similarity on listeners' evaluations of speakers. *Journal of Language and Social Psychology, 2,* 37–56.

Street, R. L., Jr., & Giles, H. (1982). Speech accommodation theory: A social cognitive approach to language and speech behavior. In M. Roloff & C. Berger (Eds.), *Social cognition and communication* (pp. 193–226). Beverly Hills, CA: Sage.

Street, R. L., Jr., & Hopper, R. (1982). A model of speech style evaluation. In E. B. Ryan & H. Giles (Eds.), *Attitudes towards language variation: Social and applied contexts* (pp. 175–188). London: Arnold.

Streeter, L. A., Krauss, R. M., Geller, V., Olson, C., & Apple, W. (1977). Pitch changes during attempted deception. *Journal of Personality and Social Psychology, 35,* 345–350.

Strodtbeck, F. L. (1951). Husband-wife interaction over revealed differences. *American Sociological Review, 16,* 468–473.

Strodtbeck, F. L., & Hook, L. H. (1961). The social dimensions of a twelve-man jury table. *Sociometry, 24,* 397–415.

Strodtbeck, F. L., & Mann, R. D. (1956). Sex role differentiation in jury deliberations. *Sociometry, 19,* 3–11.

Strongman, K. T., & Champness, B. G. (1968). Dominance hierarchies and conflict in eye contact. *Acta Psychologica, 28,* 376–386.

Sullins, E. S., Friedman, H. S., & Harris, M. J. (1985). Individual differences in expressive style as a mediator of expectancy communication. *Journal of Nonverbal Behavior, 9,* 229–238.

Summerfield, A. B., & Lake J. A. (1977). Non-verbal and verbal behaviors associated with parting. *British Journal of Psychology, 68,* 133–136.

Summerhayes, D. L., & Suchner, R. W. (1978). Power implications of touch in male-female relationships. *Sex-roles, 4,* 103–110.

Sundstrom, E. (1975). An experimental study of crowding: Effects of room size, intrusion, and goal blocking on nonverbal behavior, self-disclosure, and self-reported stress. *Journal of Personality and Social Psychology, 32,* 645–654.

Sundstrom, E. (1978). A test of equilibrium theory: Effects of topic intimacy and proximity on verbal and nonverbal behavior in pairs of friends and strangers. *Environmental Psychology and Nonverbal Behavior, 3,* 3–16.

Sundstrom, E., & Altman, I. (1976). Interpersonal relationships and personal space: Research review and theoretical model. *Human Ecology, 4,* 47–67.

Sundstrom, E., & Sundstrom, M. G. (1977). Personal space invasions: What happens when the invader asks permission? *Environmental Psychology and Nonverbal Behavior, 2,* 76–82.

Sunnafrank, M. (1986). Predicted outcome value during initial interactions: A reformulation of uncertainty reduction theory. *Human Communication Research, 13,* 3–33.

Sussman, N. M., & Rosenfeld, H. M. (1982). Influence of culture, language, and sex on conversational distance. *Journal of Personality and Social Psychology, 42,* 66–74.

Sybers, R., & Roach, M. E. (1962). Clothing and human behavior. *Journal of Home Economics, 54,* 184–187.

Sykes, R. E. (1983). Initial interaction between strangers and acquaintances: A multivariate analysis of factors affecting choice of communication partners. *Human Communication Research, 10,* 27–53.

Talese, G. (1969). *The kingdom and the power.* New York: World Publishing.

Tan, A. S. (1986). Social learning of aggression from television. In J. Bryant & D. Zillman (Eds.), *Perspectives on media effects* (pp. 41–55). Hillsdale, NJ: Erlbaum.

Taylor, L. C., & Compton, N. H. (1968). Personality correlates of dress conformity. *Journal of Home Economics, 60,* 653–656.

Tedeschi, J. T. (Ed.). (1981). *Impression management theory and social psychological research.* New York: Academic Press.

Tedeschi, J. T., & Bonoma, T. V. (1972). Power and influence: An introduction. In J. T. Tedeschi (Ed.), *The social influence processes* (pp. 1–49). Chicago: Aldine.

Tedeschi, J. T., & Norman, N. (1985). Social power, self-presentation, and the self. In B. R. Schlenker (Ed.), *The self and social life* (pp. 293–322). New York: McGraw-Hill.

Tedeschi, J. T., & Reiss, M. (1981). Identities, the phenomenal self, and laboratory research. In J. T. Tedeschi (Ed.), *Impression management theory and social psychological research* (pp. 3–22). New York: Academic Press.

Tepper, D. T., Jr. (1972). *The communication of counselor empathy, respect and genuineness through verbal and nonverbal channels.* Unpublished dissertation, University of Massachusetts.

Tepper, D. T., Jr., & Haase, R. F. (1978). Verbal and nonverbal communication of facilitative condi-

tions. *Journal of Counseling Psychology, 25,* 35–44.

Thakerar, J. N., & Giles, H. (1981). They are—so they spoke: Noncontent speech stereotypes. *Language and Communication, 1,* 255–261.

Thakerar, J. N., Giles, H., & Cheshire, J. (1982). Psychological and linguistic parameters of speech accommodation theory. In C. Fraser & K. R. Scherer (Eds.), *Advances in the social psychology of language* (pp. 205–255). Cambridge: Cambridge University Press.

Thalhofer, N. N. (1980). Violation of a spacing norm in high social density. *Journal of Applied Social Psychology, 10,* 175–183.

Thayer, S. (1969). The effect of interpersonal looking duration on dominance judgments. *Journal of Social Psychology, 79,* 285–286.

Thayer, S. (1986). Touch: Frontier of intimacy. In S. Thayer (Ed.), The psychology of touch (A special issue of the *Journal of Nonverbal Behavior*), *10,* 7–11.

Thayer, S. (1988, March). Close encounters. *Psychology Today,* pp. 31–36.

Thayer, S., & Schiff, W. (1974). Observer judgment of social interaction: Eye contact and relationship inferences. *Journal of Personality and Social Psychology, 30,* 110–114.

Theologus, G. C., Wheaton, G. R., & Fleishman, E. A. (1974). Effects of intermittent, moderate intensity noise stress on human performance. *Journal of Applied Psychology, 59,* 539–547.

Thompson, D. F., & Meltzer, L. (1964). Communication of emotional intent by facial expression. *Journal of Abnormal and Social Psychology, 68,* 129–135.

Thorpe, W. H. (1972). The comparison of vocal communication in animals and man. In R. A. Hinde (Ed.), *Non-verbal communication* (pp. 27–48). Cambridge: Cambridge University Press.

Thrasher, F. M. (1927). *The gang.* Cited in Abrahamson, M. [1966]. *Interpersonal accommodation.* Princeton, NJ: D. Van Nostrand.

Timney, B., & London, H. (1973). Body language concomitants of persuasiveness and persuasibility in dyadic interaction. *International Journal of Group Tensions, 3,* 48–67.

Tomkins, S. S. (1962). *Affect, imagery, consciousness: Vol. 1. The positive affects.* New York: Springer-Verlag.

Tomkins, S. S. (1963). *Affect, imagery, consciousness: Vol. 2. The negative affects.* New York: Springer-Verlag.

Tomkins, S. S. (1981). The role of facial response in the experience of emotion: A reply to Tourangeau

and Ellsworth. *Journal of Personality and Social Psychology, 40,* 355–357.

Toomb, J. K., & Divers, L. T. (1972, April). *The relationship of somatotype to source credibility.* Paper presented at the annual convention of the International Communication Association, Atlanta.

Toomb, J. K., Quiggins, J. G., Moore, D. L., MacNeil, L. B., & Liddell, C. M. (1972, April). *The effects of regional dialects on initial source credibility.* Paper presented at the annual convention of the International Communication Association, Atlanta.

Toris, C., & DePaulo, B. M. (1985). Effects of actual deception and suspiciousness of deception on interpersonal perceptions. *Journal of Personality and Social Psychology, 47,* 1063–1073.

Tourangeau, R., & Ellsworth, P. C. (1979). The role of facial response in the experience of emotion. *Journal of Personality and Social Psychology, 37,* 1519–1531.

Trager, G. L. (1958). Paralanguage: A first approximation. *Studies in Linguistics, 13,* 1–12.

Trager, G. L. (1961). The typology of paralanguage. *Anthropological Linguistics, 3,* 17–21.

Trevarthen, C. (1984). Emotions in infancy: Regulators of contact and relationships with persons. In K. R. Scherer & P. Ekman (Eds.), *Approaches to emotion* (pp. 129–157). Hillsdale, NJ: Erlbaum.

Trout, D. L., & Rosenfeld, H. M. (1980). The effect of postural lean and body congruence on the judgment of psychotherapeutic rapport. *Journal of Nonverbal Behavior, 4,* 176–190.

Tulving, E., & Thomson, D. M. (1973). Encoding specificity and retrieval processes in episodic memory. *Psychological Review, 80,* 359–380.

Tulving, E., & Watkins, M. (1975). Structure of memory traces. *Psychological Review, 82,* 261–275.

Turner, R. E., Edgley, C., & Olmstead, G. (1975). Information control in conversations: Honesty is not always the best policy. *Kansas Journal of Speech, 11,* 69–89.

Valentine, M. E., & Ehrlichman, H. (1979). Interpersonal gaze and helping behavior. *Journal of Social Psychology, 107,* 193–198.

Valins, S., & Baum, A. (1973). Residential group size, social interactions and crowding. *Environment and Behavior, 5,* 421–439.

Vande Creek, L., & Watkins, J. T. (1972). Responses to incongruent verbal and nonverbal emotional cues. *Journal of Communication, 22,* 311–316.

van Hooff, J. A. R. A. M. (1972). A comparative approach to the phylogeny of laughter and smiling. In R. A. Hinde (Ed.), *Non-verbal communication* (pp. 209–238). Cambridge: Cambridge University Press.

Vaught, L. A. (1902). *Vaught's practical character reader.* Chicago: Vaught-Rocine.

Vickroy, S. C., Fisher, C. D., & Shaw, J. B. (1982). Effects of temperature, clothing, and task complexity on task performance and satisfaction. *Journal of Applied Psychology, 67,* 97–102.

Vine, I. (1975). Territoriality and the spatial regulation of interaction. In A. Kendon, R. M. Harris, & M. R. Key (Eds.), *Organization of behavior in face-to-face interaction* (pp. 357–387). The Hague: Mouton.

Vinsel, A., Brown, B. B., Altman, I., & Foss, C. (1980). Privacy regulation, territorial displays, and effectiveness of individual functioning. *Journal of Personality and Social Psychology, 39,* 1104–1115.

von Cranach, M., & Ellgring, J. H. (1973). Problems in the recognition of gaze direction. In M. von Cranach & I. Vine (Eds.), *Social communication and movement* (pp. 419–443). New York: Academic Press.

Wagner, H. L., MacDonald, C. J., & Manstead, A. S. R. (1986). Communication of individual emotions by spontaneous facial expressions. *Journal of Personality and Social Psychology, 50,* 737–743.

Wahlers, K. J. (1976). *An investigation of the effects of selected inconsistent verbal/nonverbal messages on channel preference.* Unpublished doctoral dissertation, Florida State University.

Waid, W. M., & Orne, M. T. (1981). Cognitive, social, and personality processes in the physiological detection of deception. In L. Berkowitz (Ed.), *Advances in experimental social psychology* (Vol. 14, pp. 61–106). New York: Academic Press.

Waitzkin, H. (1984). Doctor-patient communication: Clinical implications of social scientific research. *Journal of the American Medical Association, 252,* 2441–2446.

Walden, T. A., Nelson, P. A., & Smith, D. E. (1981). Crowding, privacy, and coping. *Environment and Behavior, 13,* 205–224.

Waldron, J. (1975). Judgment of likedislike from facial expression and body posture. *Perceptual and Motor Skills, 41,* 799–804.

Walker, M. B., & Trimboli, C. (1984). The role of nonverbal signals in coordinating speaking turns. *Journal of Language and Social Psychology, 3,* 257–272.

Walker, R. N. (1963). Body build and behavior in young children; II. Body build and parents' ratings. *Child Development, 34,* 1–23.

Walster, E., Aronson, V., Abrahams, D., & Rottman, L. (1966). Importance of physical attractiveness in dating behavior. *Journal of Personality and Social Psychology, 4,* 508–516.

Ward, C. D. (1968). Seating arrangement and leadership emergence in small discussion groups. *Journal of Social Psychology, 74,* 83–90.

Warren, C., & Laslett, B. (1977). Privacy and secrecy—conceptual comparison. *Journal of Social Issues, 33,* 43–51.

Washburn, P. V., & Hakel, M. D. (1973). Visual cues and verbal content as influences on impressions formed after simulated employment interviews. *Journal of Applied Psychology, 58,* 137–141.

Wass, H. (1973). Pupil evaluation of teacher messages in three channels of communication. *Florida Journal of Educational Research, 15,* 46–52.

Watkins, M. J., Ho, E., & Tulving, E. (1976). Context effects in recognition memory for faces. *Journal of Verbal Learning and Verbal Behavior, 15,* 505–517.

Watkins, M. J., & Tulving, E. (1975). Episodic memory: When recognition fails. *Journal of Experimental Psychology: General, 104,* 5–29.

Watson, O. M. (1970). *Proxemic behavior: A cross-cultural study.* The Hague: Mouton.

Watson, O. M., & Graves, T. D. (1966). Quantitative research in proxemic behavior. *American Anthropologist, 68,* 971–985.

Watson, W. H. (1975). The meanings of touch: Geriatric nursing. *Journal of Communication, 25,* 104–112.

Watzlawick, P., Beavin, J. H., & Jackson, D. D. (1967). *Pragmatics of human communication: A study of interactional patterns, pathologies, and paradoxes.* New York: W. W. Norton.

Webb, J. T. (1969). Subject speech rates as a function of interviewer behavior. *Language and Speech, 12,* 54–67.

Webb, J. T. (1972). Interview synchrony: An investigation of two speech rate measures. In A. W. Siegman & B. Pope (Eds.), *Studies in dyadic communication* (pp. 115–133). New York: Pergamon.

Webb, S. D. (1978). Privacy and psychosomatic stress: An empirical analysis. *Social Behavior and Personality, 6,* 227–234.

Webster, R. L., Steinhardt, M. H., & Senter, M. G. (1972). Changes in infants' vocalizations as a function of differential acoustic stimulation. *Developmental Psychology, 7,* 39–43.

Wegner, D. M., & Vallacher, R. R. (1977). *Implicit psychology: An introduction to social cognition.* New York: Oxford University Press.

Weisfeld, G. E., & Linkey, H. E. (1985). Dominance displays as indicators of a social success motive. In S. L. Ellyson & J. F. Dovidio (Eds.), *Power, dominance, and nonverbal behavior* (pp. 109–128). New York: Springer-Verlag.

Weitz, S. (1976). Sex differences in nonverbal communication. *Sex Roles, 2,* 175–184.

Welkowitz, J., & Feldstein, S. (1969). Dyadic interactions and induced differences in perceived similarity. *Proceedings of the 78th Annual Convention of the American Psychological Association, 5,* 387–388.

Welkowitz, J., & Kuc, M. (1973). Interrelationships among warmth, genuineness, empathy, and temporal speech patterns in interpersonal interaction. *Journal of Consulting and Clinical Psychology, 41,* 472–473.

Werner, C. M., & Haggard, L. M. (1985). Temporal qualities of interpersonal relationships. In M. L. Knapp & G. R. Miller (Eds.), *Handbook of interpersonal communication* (pp. 59–99). Beverly Hills, CA: Sage.

West, C. (1979). Against our will: Male interruptions of females in cross-sex conversation. *Annals of the New York Academy of Sciences, 327,* 81–97.

West, C., & Zimmerman, D. H. (1977). Women's place in everyday talk: Reflections on parent-child interaction. *Social Problems, 24,* 521–529.

West, C., & Zimmerman, D. H. (1982). Conversational analysis. In K. R. Scherer & P. Ekman (Eds.), *Handbook of methods in nonverbal behavior research* (pp. 506–541). Cambridge: Cambridge University Press.

Westin, A. (1967). *Privacy and freedom.* New York: Atheneum.

Wexner, L. B. (1954). The degree to which colors (hues) are associated with mood-tones. *Journal of Applied Psychology, 38,* 432–435.

Wheeless, L. R. (1971). Some effects of time-compressed speech on persuasion. *Journal of Broadcasting, 15,* 415–420.

Whitcher, S. J., & Fisher, J. D. (1979). Multidimensional reaction to therapeutic touch in a hospital setting. *Journal of Personality and Social Psychology, 37,* 87–96.

References

Whitehurst, T. C., & Derlega, V. J. (1985). Influence of touch and preferences for control on visual behavior and subjective responses. In S. L. Ellyson & J. F. Dovidio (Eds.), *Power, dominance, and nonverbal behavior* (pp. 165–182). New York: Springer-Verlag.

Whiting, B., & Edwards, C. (1973). A cross-cultural analysis of sex differences in the behavior of children aged three through 11. *Journal of Social Psychology, 91,* 171–188.

Whyte, W. F. (1943). *Street corner society: The structure of an Italian slum.* Chicago: University of Chicago Press.

Wiemann, J. M. (1973). *An exploratory study of turn-taking in conversations: Verbal and nonverbal behavior.* Unpublished master's thesis, Purdue University.

Wiemann, J. M. (1974). *An experimental study of visual attention in dyads: The effects of four gaze conditions on evaluations by applicants in employment interviews.* Paper presented at the annual convention of the Speech Communication Association, Chicago.

Wiemann, J. M. (1977). Explication and test of a model of communicative competence. *Human Communication Research, 3,* 195–213.

Wiemann, J. M. (1985). Power, status and dominance: Interpersonal control and regulation in conversation. In R. L. Street & J. N. Cappella (Eds.), *Sequence and pattern in communicative behavior* (pp. 85–102). London: Arnold.

Wiemann, J. M., & Knapp, M. L. (1975). Turn-taking in conversations. *Journal of Communication, 25,* 75–92.

Wiener, M., Devoe, S., Rubinow, S., & Geller, J. (1972). Nonverbal behavior and nonverbal communication. *Psychological Review, 79,* 185–214.

Wiener, M., & Mehrabian, A. (1968). *Language within language: Immediacy, a channel in verbal communication.* Englewood Cliffs, NJ: Prentice-Hall.

Wiggers, M. (1982). Judgments of facial expressions of emotion predicted from facial behavior. *Journal of Nonverbal Behavior, 7,* 101–116.

Wilkinson, R. (1969). Some factors influencing the effect of environmental stressors upon performance. *Psychological Bulletin, 72,* 260–272.

Williams, S. J., & Willis, F. N. (1978). Interpersonal touch among preschool children at play. *Psychological Record, 28,* 501–508.

Willis, F. N. (1966). Initial speaking distance as a function of the speakers' relationship. *Psychonomic Science, 5,* 221–222.

Willis, F. N., & Hamm, H. K. (1980). The use of interpersonal touch in securing compliance. *Journal of Nonverbal Behavior, 5,* 49–55.

Willis, F. N., & Hoffman, G. E. (1975). Development of tactile patterns in relation to age, sex, and race. *Developmental Psychology, 11,* 866.

Willis, F. N., & Reeves, D. L. (1976). Touch interactions in junior high students in relation to sex and race. *Developmental Psychology, 12,* 91–92.

Willis, F. N., Reeves, D. L., & Buchanan, D. R. (1976). Interpersonal touch in high school relative to sex and race. *Perceptual and Motor Skills, 43,* 843–847.

Willis, F. N., Rinck, C. M., & Dean, L. M. (1978). Interpersonal touch among adults in cafeteria lines. *Perceptual and Motor Skills, 47,* 1147–1152.

Wilson, G. D. (1966). Arousal properties of red versus green. *Perceptual and Motor Skills, 23,* 947–949.

Wilson, P. R. (1968). Perceptual distortion of height as a function of ascribed academic status. *Journal of Social Psychology, 74,* 97–102.

Wilson, T., Wiemann, J. M., & Zimmerman, D. H. (1984). Models of turn taking in conversational interaction. *Journal of Language and Social Psychology, 3(3),* 159–183.

Winton, W. M. (1986). The role of facial response in self-reports of emotion: A critique of Laird. *Journal of Personality and Social Psychology, 50,* 808–812.

Wish, M. (1979). Dimensions of dyadic communication. In S. Weitz (Ed.), *Nonverbal communication: Readings with commentary* (2nd ed., pp. 371–378). New York: Oxford University Press.

Wish, M., Deutsch, M., & Kaplan, S. J. (1976). Perceived dimensions of interpersonal relations. *Journal of Personality and Social Psychology, 33,* 409–420.

Wolfe, M., & Laufer, R. (1974). The concept of privacy in childhood and adolescence. In S. T. Margulis (Ed.), *Privacy* (pp. 29–54). Stony Brook, NY: Environmental Design Research Association.

Wolff, P., & Gutstein, J. (1972). Effects of induced motor gestures on vocal output. *Journal of Communication, 22,* 277–288.

Wolk, R., & Henley, A. (1970). *The right to lie.* New York: Wyden.

Wood, B. S. (1981). *Children and communication: Verbal and nonverbal language development* (2nd ed.). Englewood Cliffs, NJ: Prentice-Hall.

Wood, M. H. (1985). Learning disabilities and human sexuality. *Academic Therapy, 20,* 543–547.

Woodall, W. G. (1984, May). *Attitude and comprehension processes: Some unexamined and re-examined relations.* Paper presented at the annual meeting of the International Communication Association, San Francisco, CA.

Woodall, W. G., & Burgoon, J. K. (1981). The effects of nonverbal synchrony on message comprehension and persuasiveness. *Journal of Nonverbal Behavior, 5,* 207–223.

Woodall, W. G., & Burgoon, J. K. (1983). Talking fast and changing attitudes: A critique and clarification. *Journal of Nonverbal Behavior, 8,* 126–142.

Woodall, W. G., Burgoon, J. K., & Markel, N. N. (1980). The effects of facial-head cue combinations on interpersonal evaluations. *Communication Quarterly, 28(3),* 47–55.

Woodall, W. G., Davis, D. K., & Sahin, H. (1983). From the boob tube to the black box: Television news comprehension from an information processing perspective. *Journal of Broadcasting, 27,* 1–23.

Woodall, W. G., & Folger, J. P. (1981). Encoding specificity and nonverbal cue context: An expansion of episodic memory research. *Communication Monographs, 48,* 39–53.

Woodall, W. G., & Folger, J. P. (1985). Nonverbal cue context and episodic memory: On the availability and endurance of nonverbal behaviors as retrieval cues. *Communication Monographs, 52,* 319–333.

Woodhead, M. M. (1964). Searching of a visual display in intermittent noise. *Journal of Sound and Vibration, 1,* 157–161.

Woodhead, M. M. (1966). An effect of noise on the distribution of attention. *Journal of Applied Psychology, 50,* 296–299.

Woolbert, C. (1920). The effects of various models of public reading. *Journal of Applied Psychology, 4,* 162–185.

Woolfolk, R. L., & Woolfolk, A. E. (1974). Effects of teacher verbal and nonverbal behaviors on student perceptions and attitudes. *American Educational Research Journal, 11,* 297–303.

Worchel, S., & Teddlie, C. (1976). The experience of crowding: A two-factor theory. *Journal of Personality and Social Psychology, 34,* 30–40.

Worchel, S., & Yohai, S. M. L. (1979). The role of attribution in the experience of crowding. *Journal of Experimental Social Psychology, 15,* 91–104.

Word, C. O., Zanna, M. P., & Cooper, J. (1974). The nonverbal mediation of self-fulfilling prophecies in interracial interaction. *Journal of Experimental Social Psychology, 10,* 109–120.

References

Wylie, L., & Stafford, R. (1977). *Beaux gestes: A guide to French body talk.* Cambridge, MA: Undergraduate Press.

Yerkes, R. M., & Dodson, J. D. (1908). The relation of strength of stimulus to rapidity of habit-formation. *Journal of Comparative and Neurological Psychology, 18,* 459–482.

Yngve, V. H. (1970). On getting a word in edgewise. In M. A. Campbell, et al. (Eds.), *Papers from the sixth regional meeting, Chicago Linguistics Society.* Chicago: University of Chicago Press.

Zabel, R. (1979). Recognition of emotions in facial expressions by emotionally disturbed and nondisturbed children. *Psychology in the Schools, 16,* 119–126.

Zahn, G. L. (1973). Cognitive integration of verbal and vocal information in spoken sentences. *Journal of Experimental Social Psychology, 9,* 320–334.

Zaidel, S. F., & Mehrabian, A. (1969). The ability to communicate and infer positive and negative attitudes facially and vocally. *Journal of Experimental Research in Personality, 3,* 233–241.

Zajonc, R. B. (1965). Social facilitation. *Science, 149,* 269–274.

Zajonc, R. B. (1980). Compresence. In P. B. Paulus (Ed.), *Psychology of group influence* (pp. 35–60). Hillsdale, NJ: Erlbaum.

Zeilik, M. (1985a). A reassessment of the fajada butte solar marker. *Archaeoastronomy, 9,* 69–85.

Zeilik, M. (1985b). Sun shrines and sun symbols in the U.S. southwest. *Archaeoastronomy, 9,* 86–96.

Zimmerman, B. J., & Brody, G. H. (1975). Race and modelling influences on the interpersonal play patterns of boys. *Journal of Educational Psychology, 67,* 591–598.

Zimmerman, D. H., & West, C. (1975). Sex roles, interruptions and silences in conversation. In B. Thorne & N. Henley (Eds.), *Language and sex: Difference and dominance* (pp. 105–129). Cambridge, MA: Newbury House.

Zuckerman, M., Amidon, M. D., Bishop, S. E., & Pomerantz, S. D. (1982). Face and tone of voice in the communication of deception. *Journal of Personality and Social Psychology, 43,* 347–357.

Zuckerman, M., DeFrank, R. S., Hall, J. A., Larrance, D. T., & Rosenthal, R. (1979). Facial and vocal cues of deception and honesty. *Journal of Experimental Social Psychology, 15,* 378–396.

Zuckerman, M., DePaulo, B. M., & Rosenthal, R. (1981). Verbal and nonverbal communication of deception. In L. Berkowitz (Ed.), *Advances in experimental social psychology* (Vol.14, pp. 1–59). New York: Academic Press.

Zuckerman, M., & Driver, R. E. (1985). Telling lies: Verbal and nonverbal correlates of deception. In A. W. Siegman & S. Feldstein (Eds.), *Multichannel integrations of nonverbal behavior* (pp. 129–148). Hillsdale, NJ: Erlbaum.

Zuckerman, M., Driver, R. E., & Koestner, R. (1982). Discrepancy as a cue to actual and perceived deception. *Journal of Nonverbal Behavior, 7,* 95–100.

Zuckerman, M., Fischer, S. A., Osmun, R. W., Winkler, B. A., & Wolfson, L. R. (1987). Anchoring in lie detection revisited. *Journal of Nonverbal Behavior, 11,* 4–12.

Zuckerman, M., Hall, J. A., DeFrank, R. S., & Rosenthal, R. (1976). Encoding and decoding of spontaneous and posed facial expressions. *Journal of Personality and Social Psychology, 34,* 966–977.

Zuckerman, M., Koestner, R., Colella, M. J., & Alton, A. O. (1984). Anchoring in the detection of deception and leakage. *Journal of Personality and Social Psychology, 47,* 301–311.

Zuckerman, M., Koestner, R., & Driver, R. E. (1981). Beliefs about cues associated with deception. *Journal of Nonverbal Behavior, 6,* 105–114.

Zuckerman, M., Larrance, D. T., Hall, J. A., DeFrank, R. S., & Rosenthal, R. (1979). Posed and spontaneous communication of emotion via facial and vocal cues. *Journal of Personality, 47,* 712–733.

Zuckerman, M., Larrance, D. T., Spiegel, N. H., & Klorman, R. (1981). Controlling nonverbal displays: Facial expressions and tone of voice. *Journal of Experimental Social Psychology, 17,* 506–524.

Zuckerman, M., Lipets, M. S., Koivumaki, J. H., & Rosenthal, R. (1975). Encoding and decoding nonverbal cues of emotion. *Journal of Personality and Social Psychology, 32,* 1068–1076.

Zuckerman, M., Spiegel, N. H., DePaulo, B. M., & Rosenthal, R. (1982). Nonverbal strategies for decoding deception. *Journal of Nonverbal Behavior, 6,* 171–187.

CREDITS

Text, Tables, and Boxes (listed by page number)

3 Poem: Copyright © 1985 by The New York Times Company. Reprinted by permission.   **5** Box: Copyright 1981 Time Inc. All rights reserved. Reprinted by permission from TIME.   **37** Box: From *The Gospel According to Zen* (pp. 3–4) by R. Sohl and A. Carr, Eds., 1970, New York: New American Library. (Originally published in *Zen Flesh, Zen Bones* by P. Reps, 1957, Tokyo: Tuttle.)   **53** Box: Reprinted from *Lansing State Journal,* February 17, 1981, p. A3.   **54** Box: Ann Landers, Los Angeles Times Syndicate and *Lansing State Journal,* May 12, 1981, p. D2.   **78** Box: Helen Colton, June 1983, *Cosmopolitan,* pp. 140–142.   **86** Box: Joyce Walker-Tyson, May 31, 1981, *Detroit Free Press,* pp. 1B, 4B.   **106** Table 3.2: From *Body Politics: Power, Sex, and Nonverbal Communication* (p. 105) by N. Henley, 1977, Englewood Cliffs, NJ: Prentice-Hall.   **109** Box: Copyright 1985, USA TODAY. Reprinted with permission.   **111–116** Table 3.3: From "A Naturalistic Study of the Meanings of Touch," by S. E. Jones & A. E. Yarbrough, 1985, *Communication Monographs, 52,* pp. 28–35. Reprinted by permission.   **130** Table 4.1: From *The Unspoken Dialogue: An Introduction to Nonverbal Communication* (p. 110) by J. K. Burgoon and T. Saine, 1978, Boston: Houghton Mifflin. Used with permission.   **143–144** Table 4.2: Reprinted with permission from *Psychology Today* magazine. Copyright © 1985 (PT Partners, L.P.).   **159** Poem: From *The Blue Scar and Other Poems* (p. 54) by A. Grilikhes, 1988, New York: Folder Editions. Reprinted with permission.   **216** Table 6.4: From *The Unspoken Dialogue: An Introduction to Nonverbal Communication* (p. 163) by J. K. Burgoon and T. Saine, 1978, Boston: Houghton Mifflin. Used with permission.   **223** Box: The Associated Press.   **241–242** Applications Box: Excerpted from "The Doctor As Dramatist," by S. A. Hoffman, *Newsweek,* February 1, 1988. Reprinted with permission.   **243** Table 7.3: From "Social Power, Self-Presentation, and the Self," by J. T. Tedeschi and N. Norman, in *The Self and Social Life* (pp. 293–322), edited by B. R. Schlenker, 1985, Orlando, Florida: Academic Press, Inc. Copyright 1985 by Academic Press, Inc. Reprinted with the permission of Academic Press.   **253** Box: Copyright 1988, USA TODAY. Excerpted with permission.   **280** Box: Reprinted with permission from *Psychology Today* magazine. Copyright © 1981 (PT Partners, L.P.).   **303** Table 9.2: From *Body Politics* (p. 181) by Nancy M. Henley, 1977, Englewood Cliffs, NJ: Prentice-Hall.   **305** Quotation: Copyright © 1984 by The New York Times Company. Reprinted by permission.   **305** Box: Copyright 1981 Time Inc. All rights reserved. Reprinted by permission from TIME.   **316** Box: From "Miss Manners," by J. Martin, *The Knoxville News-Sentinal,* March 16, 1986.   **340** Box: The Associated Press.   **342** Table 10.2: From *Affect, Imagery, Consciousness,* Vol. 1: *The Positive Affects* and Vol. 2: *The Negative Affects* by S. S. Tomkins, 1962–1963, New York: Springer-Verlag; "Universal and Cultural Differences in Facial Expressions of Emotions," by P. Ekman in J. K. Cole (Ed.), 1971, *Nebraska Symposium on Motivation,* Vol. 19 (pp. 207–283), Lincoln: University of Nebraska Press; *Human Emotions* by C. E. Izard, 1977, New York: Plenum. Reprinted with permission of the publisher.   **355** Table 10.4: Adapted from "Cue Utilization in Emotion Attribution from Auditory Stimuli," by K. R. Scherer and J. S. Oshinsky, 1977, *Motivation and Emotion, 1* (4), p. 340.   **362** Table 10.6: Adapted from "The Communication of Feelings by Content-free Speech," by J. R. Davitz and L. J. Davitz, 1959, *Journal of Communication, 9,* 6–13. Reprinted with permission of International Communication Association.   **378** Quotation: From J. Edney, "Human Territories: Comment on Functional Properties," *Environment and Behavior, 8* (1976), pp. 31–47. Copyright © 1976 by Human Sciences Press. Reprinted by permission of Sage Publications, Inc.   **382** Box: From "Prison Codes," by S. J. Ramsey, 1976, *Journal of Communication,* pp. 39, 43–44.   **411** Box: Reprinted with permission from *Psychology Today* magazine. Copyright © 1988 (PT Partners L. P.).   **416** Table 12.1: From "The Rhetoric of Goodbye: Verbal and Nonverbal Correlates of Human Leave-taking," by M. L. Knapp, R. P. Hart, G. W. Friedrich, & G. M. Shulman, 1973, *Speech Monographs, 40,* 191. Reprinted with permission.   **449** Box: Copyright © 1986 by The New York Times Company. Reprinted by permission.   **478** Box: Reprinted with permission from *Psychology Today* magazine. Copyright © 1983 (PT Partners, L.P.).   **483** Box: Reprinted with permission from *Psychology Today* magazine. Copyright © 1988 (PT Partners, L.P.).

Text Illustrations/Art (listed by page number)

8 From "A Comparative Approach to the Phylogeny of Laughter and Smiling" by J. A. R. A. M. von Hooff, in *Non-verbal Communication* (p. 237), edited by R. A. Hinde, 1972, Cambridge, England: Cambridge University Press. Copyright 1972 by Cambridge University Press. Reprinted with the permission of Cambridge University Press. **27** From "Similarities and Differences Between Cultures in Expressive Movements" by I. Eibl-Eibesfeldt, in *Non-verbal Communication* (p. 302), edited by R. A. Hinde, 1972, Cambridge, England: Cambridge University Press. Copyright 1972 by Cambridge University Press. Reprinted with the permission of Cambridge University Press. **41** From "The Anthropology of Posture" by G. W. Hewes. Copyright © 1957 by Scientific American, Inc. All rights reserved. **43** Redrawn from Ray L. Birdwhistell, *Kinesics and Context: Essays on Body Motion Communication* (Philadelphia: University of Pennsylvania Press, 1970). **49** Drawing by Priscilla Barrett from *Manwatching* by Desmond Morris, first published in Great Britain by Jonathan Cape Ltd., London; planned and produced by Equinox (Oxford) Ltd. in cooperation with Jonathan Cape Ltd., 1977. **59** Drawing by Richard Geiger from *Manwatching* by Desmond Morris, first published in Great Britain by Jonathan Cape Ltd., London; planned and produced by Equinox (Oxford) Ltd. in cooperation with Jonathan Cape Ltd., 1977. **99** Reproduced by permission of the American Anthropological Association. Not for further reproduction. Based on E. T. Hall, "A System for the Notation of Proxemic Behavior," *American Anthropologist* 65:5, 1963. **108** From *Responses to Touching as an Index of Sex Role Norms and Attitudes* by R. Heslin, Washington, D.C.: American Psychological Association. Copyright 1978 by the American Psychological Association. Reprinted by permission of the author. **148** "Hagar the Horrible" cartoon reprinted with special permission of King Features Syndicate, Inc. **163** From "A Comparative Approach to the Phylogeny of Laughter and Smiling" by J. A. R. A. M. von Hooff, in *Non-verbal Communication* (p. 233), edited by R. A. Hinde, 1972, Cambridge, England: Cambridge University Press. Copyright 1972 by Cambridge University Press. Reprinted with the permission of Cambridge University Press. **188** From a drawing by Larry Ratzkin in *Gestures*, by D. Morris, P. Collett, P. Marsh, and M. O'Shaughnessy, 1979, London: Jonathan Cape Ltd. Copyright 1979 by Jonathan Cape Ltd. Reprinted by permission. **191** From "The Kinesics of Femininity in Japanese Women," by S. J. Ramsey, 1981, *Language Sciences, 3,* pp. 108–110. Reprinted by permission. **208** From "An Exploratory Study of Body-Accessibility" by S. M. Jourard, 1966, *British Journal of Social and Clinical Psychology, 5,* p. 223. Copyright 1966 by the British Psychological Society. Reprinted by permission. **308** From "Patterns of Visual Dominance Behavior in Humans," by J. F. Dovidio and S. L. Ellyson, in *Power, Dominance, and Nonverbal Behavior* (pp. 135–139), edited by J. F. Dovidio and S. L. Ellyson, 1985, New York: Springer Verlag, Inc. Copyright 1985 by Springer Verlag, Inc. Reprinted with permission of Springer Verlag. **327** From *How Behavior Means* by A. E. Scheflen, 1974, New York: Science Publishers, Inc. Copyright 1974 by Science Publishers, Inc. Reprinted by permission. **343** From "A Circumplex Model of Affect" by J. A. Russell, 1980, *Journal of Personality and Social Psychology, 39,* pp. 1161–1178. Copyright 1980 by the American Psychological Association. Reprinted by permission of the author. **344** From "A Conical Model for the Taxonomy of Emotional Experience" by E. M. Daly, W. J. Lancee, and J. Polivy, 1983, *Journal of Personality and Social Psychology, 45,* pp. 443–457. Copyright 1983 by the American Psychological Association. Reprinted by permission of the authors. **346** From "Universal and Cultural Differences in Facial Expressions of Emotion" by P. Ekman, in *Nebraska Symposium on Motivation* (pp. 207–283), edited by J. K. Cole, 1971, Lincoln, Nebraska: University of Nebraska Press. Copyright 1971 by the University of Nebraska Press. Reprinted by permission of the author. **350** DENNIS THE MENACE® cartoon used by permission of Hank Ketcham and © by North America Syndicate. **357** "Hagar the Horrible" cartoon reprinted with special permission of King Features Syndicate, Inc. **372–373** From *Landscape Architecture: A Manual of Site Planning and Design* (pp. 137–139) by J. O. Simonds, 1961, New York: F. W. Dodge Corporation. Copyright 1961 by F. W. Dodge Corporation. Reprinted with the permission of McGraw-Hill Book Company. **381** From "Spatial Relationships in Groups" by J. K. Burgoon, in *Small Group Communication* (pp. 351–366), edited by R. Cathcart and L. Samovar, 1988, Dubuque, Iowa: William C. Brown. Copyright 1988 by William C. Brown. Reprinted with permission of the publisher and the author. **386** From *Landscape Architecture: A Manual of Site Planning and Design* (p. 142) by J. O. Simonds, 1961, New York: F. W. Dodge Corporation. Copyright 1961 by F. W. Dodge Corporation. Reprinted with the permission of McGraw-Hill Book Company. **401** Adapted from *Rhythms of Dialogue* (p. 20) by J. Jaffe and S. Feldstein, 1970, Orlando, Florida: Academic Press, Inc. Copyright 1970 by Academic Press, Inc. Reprinted with the permission of Academic Press. **418** From "An Analysis of Behavioral Organization" by W. S. Condon, 1986, *Sign Language Studies, 13,* pp. 285–318, Copyright 1986 by Linstok Press. Reprinted by permission.

NAME INDEX

527

SUBJECT INDEX